Open Learning as a Means of Advancing Social Justice

Cases in Post-School Education and Training in South Africa

Edited by
Tabisa Mayisela
Shanali C. Govender
Cheryl Ann Hodgkinson-Williams

Published in 2022 by African Minds
4 Eccleston Place, Somerset West, 7130, Cape Town, South Africa
info@africanminds.org.za
www.africanminds.org.za

ISBN (paper): 978-1-928502-42-5
eBook edition: 978-1-928502-43-2
ePub edition: 978-1-928502-44-9

Copies of this book are available for free download at:
www.africanminds.org.za

ORDERS:
African Minds
Email: info@africanminds.org.za

To order printed books from outside Africa, please contact:
African Books Collective
PO Box 721, Oxford OX1 9EN, UK
Email: orders@africanbookscollective.com

Disclaimer This publication was produced with the financial support of the European Union. Its contents are the responsibility of the COOL research team and do not necessarily reflect the views of the European Union.

 Department of Higher Education & Training, 2022

 Co-funded by the European Union

How to cite this book
Mayisela, T., Govender, S. C., & Hodgkinson-Williams, C. A. (Eds.). (2022). *Open learning as a means of advancing social justice: Cases in post-school education and training in South Africa*. African Minds. DOI: 10.47622/9781928502425

Contents

Acknowledgements — v
Acronyms and abbreviations — vii

Introducing open learning as a means towards social justice in post-school education and training
Tabisa Mayisela, Shanali C. Govender & Cheryl Ann Hodgkinson-Williams — 1

PART 1: FOCUS ON ACCESS

1 Recognition of prior learning as a form of open learning in post-school education and training in South Africa: A social justice perspective
Susan Gredley & Cheryl Ann Hodgkinson-Williams — 16

2 Opening learning to students in a South African university through innovative institutional fundraising initiatives: A social justice view
Susan Gredley & Janice McMillan — 44

3 Using a social justice lens to explore the possibilities and limitations of flexible learning provision in a South African TVET college
Gertrude van Wyk, Cheng-Wen Huang & Cheryl Ann Hodgkinson-Williams — 70

PART 2: FOCUS ON PEDAGOGY

4 Blended learning as a means of opening up learning at Northlink TVET College in South Africa: A social justice perspective
Mukhtar Raban & Tabisa Mayisela — 86

5 Online learning at the Durban University of Technology during the COVID-19 pandemic: Insights on openness and parity of participation
Sinethemba Zungu & Sukaina Walji — 106

6 Exploring the possibilities and constraints of online assessment to advance open learning in a South African TVET college: A social justice perspective
Cheng-Wen Huang & Tabisa Mayisela — 131

PART 3: FOCUS ON SUPPORT FOR SUCCESS

7 Exploring how student support services address economic, cultural and political injustices: Insights from Elangeni TVET College, South Africa
Sinethemba Zungu & Cheryl Ann Hodgkinson-Williams ... 152

8 Staff insights on opening up learning to students with disabilities at Motheo TVET College, South Africa: A social justice perspective
Gertrude van Wyk & Cheryl Ann Hodgkinson-Williams ... 178

9 Insights on OER adoption models to inform ways of opening up learning materials to address economic, cultural and political injustices in South African education
Anelisa Dabula, Glenda Cox & Cheryl Ann Hodgkinson-Williams ... 199

10 Advancing social justice through small grants for the development of open educational resources at the University of Cape Town and the Cape Peninsula University of Technology
Mahlatse Maake-Malatji & Glenda Cox ... 217

PART 4: FOCUS ON INSTITUTIONAL VISION

11 "Understanding the TVET game": A case study on maximising available opportunities for open educational practices within the broader TVET field
Sara Black ... 241

12 Enabling open learning and participatory parity through increased e-learning: The case of leadership at Gert Sibande TVET College, South Africa
Mukhtar Raban & Tabisa Mayisela ... 269

13 Access, quality and success: Working towards social justice through open initiatives at the University of the Free State
Thasmai Dhurumraj & Shanali C. Govender ... 291

PART 5: FOCUS ON NATIONAL ASPIRATIONS

14 "Who do you think they are?" Troubling how mental conceptions of TVET lecturers shape lecturer support interventions: The case of the Lecturer Support System in South Africa
Sara Black ... 314

15 Opening up TVET lecturer professional learning and development through work integrated learning in South Africa: A social justice perspective
Shanali C. Govender & Thasmai Dhurumraj ... 338

16 The potential for microcredentials as a form of open learning to contribute to a social justice agenda in South African higher education
Barbara Jones ... 374

About the authors and the COOL team ... 391

Acknowledgements

We would like to express our deepest gratitude to the following people for all the support that they have provided to the Cases on Open Learning (COOL) project.

DHET: Trudi van Wyk for commissioning the research project and Mike Adendorff, Randall Faulmann and Gerda Venter for managing it.

UCT: Laura Czerniewicz, Sukaina Walji and Stephen Marquard for managerial guidance and support, Cindy Gilbert for administrative support, and Sanjin Muftic for curation advice.

COOL researchers (alphabetical, by surname): Sara Black, Anelisa Dabula, Thasmai Dhurumraj, Susan Gredley, Cheng-Wen Huang, Barbara Jones, Mahlatse Maake-Malatji, Mukhtar Raban, Gertrude van Wyk and Sinethemba Zungu for enthusiastic participation in such an amazing research journey.

COOL mentors: Cheryl Hodgkinson-Williams, Tabisa Mayisela, Shanali Govender and Glenda Cox for the endless hours of mentoring, editing and proofing-reading.

COOL advisors: Laura Czerniewicz, Janice McMillan and Sukaina Walji for insightful guidance and support for the researchers in scoping and design of their studies.

COOL support: Ntobeko Mbuyisa and Tess Cartmill for meticulous project management support, and Thomas King for curation support.

COOL publishing manager and booklet editor: Henry Trotter for conducting the scoping research for the case studies, for superb management of the entire publishing process and for compiling and editing the text of the 16 accompanying case study booklets.

Chapter editors: Barbara Jones, Bianca Masuku and Michelle Willmers for the careful editing of chapters 1 and 3, 8, and 9 respectively.

Chapter reviewers (alphabetical, by surname): Maggie Albro, Jo Badenhorst, Patricia Chikune, Desire Chiwandire, Pam Christie, Andrew Deacon, Kerry de Hart, Rob Farrow, Cheryl Foxcroft, Johanna Funk, Daniela Gachago, James Glapa-Grossklag, Cookie Govender, Pauline Hanesworth, Henri Jacobs, Jens Jungblut, Joshua Kim, Bruce Kloot, Anthea Jacobs, David Jeffery, James Keevy, Marcia Lyner-Cleophas, Mpine Makoe, Lunga Mantashe, Jan McArthur, Sioux McKenna, Jolanda Morkel, Seamus Needham, Beverley Oliver, Jako Olivier, Nicola Pallitt, Joy Papier, Shikha Raturi, Patti Silbert, Clive Smith, Lily Todorinova, Nompilo Tshuma and Martin Weller for their critical engagement with the chapters and generous comments.

Open access publisher: François van Schalkwyk and African Minds for shepherding the publication of the 16 booklets and the chapters in this edited volume.

Acronyms and abbreviations

ACET	Adult and Community Education and Training
ACT	Advanced Certificate in Teaching
ADC	Alternative Digital Credential
AP	Admission Point
APEL	Assessment of Prior Experiential Learning
AUNEGe	Association des Universités pour l'Enseignement Numérique en Economie et Gestion (Association of Universities for Digital Education in Economics and Management)
BC	British Columbia
BCIT	British Columbia Institute of Technology
B Ed	Bachelor of Education
BL	Blended Learning
BORD	Bologna Open Recognition Declaration
CAT	Credit Accumulation and Transfer
CD	Compact Disk
CELT	Centre for Excellence in Learning and Teaching
CEO	Chief Executive Officer
CET	Community Education and Training
CFO	Chief Financial Officer
CHE	Council on Higher Education
CHED	Centre for Higher Education Development
CIET	Centre for Innovative Educational Technology
CILT	Centre for Innovation in Learning and Teaching
COOL	Cases on Open Learning
CoP	Communities of Practice
COVID-19	Coronavirus Disease of 2019
CPD	Continuous Professional Development
CPUT	Cape Peninsula University of Technology
CTOED	Cape Town Open Education Declaration
DBE	Department of Basic Education
DHET	Department of Higher Education and Training
DIT	Durban Institute of Technology

DLC	Digital Learning Committee
DLL	Division for Lifelong Learning
DoE	Department of Education
DoL	Department of Labour
DOT4D	Digital Open Textbooks for Development
DRU	Disability Rights Unit
DSD	Department of Social Development
DSU	Disability Support Unit
DUT	Durban University of Technology
ECCHOE	European Credit Clearing House for Opening Up Education
ECD	Early Childhood Development
EDCI	Europass Digital Credentials Infrastructure
ELMA	Education Leadership Management and Administration
EMS	Economic and Management Sciences
EQF	European Qualifications Framework
ERT	Emergency Remote Teaching
ESQR	European Society for Quality Research
ETDP SETA	Education and Training Development Practices Sector Education and Training Authority
ETU	Education and Training Unit
EU	European Union
FBC	False Bay College
FET	Further Education and Training
FYSE	First-Year Student Experience
GCIS	Government Communication Information System
GET	General Education and Training
GIZ	Gesellschaft für Internationale Zusammenarbeit (Corporation for International Cooperation)
GSC	Gert Sibande TVET College
HC	Higher Certificate
HE	Higher Education
HEI	Higher Education Institution (i.e. university or university of technology)
HEQSF	Higher Education Qualifications Sub-Framework
HoD	Head of Department
HR	Human Resources
HRD	Human Resource Development
HSS	Human and Social Sciences
IBM	International Business Machines
IBP	Internet Broadcast Project
ICASS	Internal Continuous Assessment
ICT	Information and Communication Technologies
ICTISE	ICT Innovation in School Education
ICTS	Information and Communication Technology Systems
IDRC	International Development Research Centre
ILC	Inclusive Learning Centre

IP	Intellectual Property
IQ	Intelligence Quotient
IQMS	Integrated Quality Management System
ISFAP	Ikusasa Student Financial Aid Programme
ISP	Internet Service Provider
IT	Information Technology
ITE	Initial Teacher Education
IVTE	Initial Vocational Teacher Education
JAWS	Job Access With Speech
JISC	Joint Information Systems Committee
KPI	Key Performance Indicator
KPU	Kwantlen Polytechnic University
KZN	KwaZulu-Natal
L&T	Learning and Teaching
LMS	Learning Management System
LO	Life Orientation
LSS	Lecturer Support System
LTSM	Learning and Teaching Support Materials
MBChB	Bachelor of Medicine and Surgery
MC	Monitoring Committee
MERLOT	Multimedia Educational Resource for Learning and Online Teaching
merSETA	Manufacturing, Engineering and Related Services Sector Education and Training Authority
MIT	Massachusetts Institute of Technology
MoA	Memoranda of Agreement
MOOC	Massive Open Online Course
MoU	Memoranda of Understanding
MRTEQ	Minimum Requirements for Teacher Education Qualifications
MS	Microsoft (e.g., MS Teams)
MTA	Microsoft Technology Associate
MTSF	Medium Term Strategic Framework
MTT	Ministerial Task Team
NAS	Natural and Agricultural Sciences
NATED	National Technical Education (vestigial programmes and curricula from pre-2007)
NC(V)	National Certificate (Vocational)
NEED	Need for Education and Elevation (Programme)
NGO	Non-Governmental Organisation
NOLA	National Open Learning Agency
NOLS	National Open Learning System
NQF	National Qualifications Framework
NSC	National Senior Certificate
NSFAS	National Student Financial Aid Scheme
NWU	North-West University
NZQA	New Zealand Qualifications Authority

NZQF	New Zealand Qualifications Framework
OBI	Open Badges Infrastructure
ODL	Open and Distance Learning
OE	Open Education
OECD	Organisation for Economic Co-operation and Development
OEI	Open Education Initiative
OEP	Open Educational Practices
OER	Open Educational Resources
OERu	OER University
OL	Open Learning
OLC	Open Learning Centre
OLPF	Open Learning Policy Framework
OLU	Open Learning Unit
OU	Open University
P2PU	Peer–2–Peer University
PDS	Previously Disadvantaged Students
PhD	Doctor of Philosophy
PLA	Prior Learning Assessment
PLP	Pre-Vocational Learning Programme
PSET	Post-School Education and Training
PWD	Persons With Disabilities
QA	Quality Assurance
QC	Quality Council
QCTO	Quality Council for Trades and Occupations
R	Rands
REAP	Rural Education Access Programme
RICA	Regulation of Interception of Communications and Provision of Communication-Related Information Act
ROER4D	Research on Open Educational Resources for Development
RPL	Recognition of Prior Learning
RSA	Republic of South Africa
SA	South Africa
SABC	South African Broadcasting Corporation
SADC	Southern African Development Community
SAIVCET	South African Institute for Vocational, Education and Training
SALDRU	Southern Africa Labour and Development Research Unit
SANReN	South African National Research Network
SAQA	South African Qualifications Authority
SASCO	South African Students Congress
SASL	South African Sign Language
SETA	Sector Education and Training Authority
SITA	State Information Technology Agency
SLO	Student Liaison Officer
SNE	Special Needs Education

SRC	Student Representatives Council
SSACI	Swiss South Africa Cooperation Initiative
SSS	Student Support Services
STEM	Science, Technology, Engineering and Mathematics
SWD	Students With Disabilities
TEL	Technology-Enhanced Learning
TESSA	Teacher Education in Sub-Saharan Africa
TLDCIP	Teaching and Learning Development Capacity Improvement Programme
TNC	Tshwane North TVET College
TVET	Technical and Vocational Education and Training
TVETMIS	TVET Management Information System
UAP	University Access Programme
ÜBZO	Überbetriebliches Bildungszentrum in Ostbayern (Inter-Company Training Center in Eastern Bavaria)
UCDG	University Capacity Development Grant
UCT	University of Cape Town
UDL	Universal Design for Learning
UFS	University of the Free State
UK	United Kingdom
UNESCO	United Nations Educational, Scientific and Cultural Organization
UNEVOC	UNESCO's International Centre for Technical and Vocational Education and Training
UNISA	University of South Africa
UoT	University of Technology
UP	University of Pretoria
US / USA	United States of America
USAF	Universities South Africa
UWC	University of Western Cape
VC	Vice-Chancellor
VEOP	Vocational Educator Orientation Programme
VNFIL	Validation of Non-Formal and Informal Learning
W&RSETA	Wholesale and Retail Sector Education and Training Authority
WBE	Workplace-Based Experience
WCED	Western Cape Education Department
WGDEOL	Working Group on Distance Education and Open Learning
WIL	Work Integrated Learning
Wits	University of the Witwatersrand
WPBL	Workplace-Based Learning
ZTC	Zero Textbook Cost

Introducing open learning as a means towards social justice in post-school education and training

Tabisa Mayisela, Shanali C. Govender & Cheryl Ann Hodgkinson-Williams

Introduction

Worldwide, there has been a long-standing need for economically affordable, culturally inclusive and politically representative education. This has been foregrounded globally in the United Nations Sustainable Development Goal 4 that calls for "inclusive and quality education for all" (United Nations, 2015)[1]. The COVID-19 pandemic[2] has exposed and exacerbated multiple axes of disparity, foregrounding the entanglement of inequalities along intersectional axes of class, gender, race, language and place[3], and affirming that neoliberal policies have failed to deliver on their promise of improved access to opportunity and/or quality of life for the majority of people.

The South African education system has not escaped these conditions. Extensive education inequities remain massive challenges for the post-apartheid South African dispensation 28 years after the official demise of apartheid. In the South African *White Paper for Post-School Education and Training*, the Department of Higher Education and Training (DHET) envisions "a transformed post-school system" that is hoped to "improve the economic, social and cultural life of its people … to bring about social justice, to overcome the legacy of our colonial and apartheid past, and to overcome inequity and injustice whatever its origins" (DHET, 2013, p. 75). Policymakers are tasked to govern extremely diverse Post School Education and Training (PSET) institutions under their remit, while seeking to offer 'access, quality and success' (DHET, 2017) to eligible school leavers. But what *constitutes* 'access', 'quality' and 'success', along with *how* to pursue these goals, requires more discussion.

Against this backdrop, DHET has identified seven barriers students face when wanting to learn in PSET, including:

---

[1] https://www.un.org/sustainabledevelopment/

[2] https://www.undp.org/content/undp/en/home/news-centre/news/2020/COVID19_Human_development_on_course_to_decline_for_the_first_time_since_1990.html

[3] https://www.worldbenchmarkingalliance.org/black-lives-matter-wba-and-the-sdgs-blog-series/

1. geographic isolation from campuses or learning centres within reasonable proximity;
2. lack of reliable access to digital infrastructure, adequate bandwidth, the internet and ICT[4];
3. inability to take time off from work or family obligations for structured learning;
4. discrimination [by institutions] on the basis of physical disability, gender, age, social class or race;
5. a lack of qualifications considered necessary as requirements for admission to particular programmes;
6. financial constraints and an inability to meet the cost of studies; and
7. past experience of content-based, transmission-type pedagogy and assessment that restrict accessibility, alienate the learner or contribute to a loss of confidence. (DHET, 2017, p. 367)

In response to these barriers, DHET proposed the notion of 'open learning' as a framework to inform existing and future PSET policies. The vision for this approach is expressed primarily in the draft *Open Learning Policy Framework* (OLPF) (DHET, 2017), as discussed below.

While the draft OLPF received responses from various quarters of the PSET sector (e.g., Goodier, 2017; USAF, 2017), at the time of publication, it had yet to be interrogated or promulgated by Parliament. Also, initial training was offered to TVET lecturers and administrators over the course of 2019, reaching 200 staff and focusing on advocacy and capacity-building[5]. During consultations for feedback on the draft, amongst various PSET institutions and stakeholders, questions arose about how 'open learning' as a concept is understood, mediated, taken up or resisted within the sector (M. Adendorff, personal communication, October 2019).

This uncertainty prompted DHET to commission research by members of the University of Cape Town's Centre for Innovation in Learning and Teaching (CILT) on the understanding of 'open learning' principles amongst actors in the PSET sector (including managers, lecturers and students), along with any evidence of open learning in PSET institutions' practices. The CILT research project, Cases on Open Learning (COOL) was mandated with: (1) building the capacity of young researchers (of which at least 60% are Black, Coloured or Indian South African) who were to conduct 16 case studies on open learning initiatives in an African context; and (2) sharing each of the case studies produced as a chapter in an openly licensed edited volume (*this* book), and as an abridged booklet in the Cases on Open Learning Knowledge Collection.

Since "open learning … is driven by a concern for social justice" (DHET, 2017, p. 412), the COOL project investigation focused on the relation between open learning and social justice, both as it is understood and enacted. How open learning might enhance social justice (as defined by Fraser [2005, 2009]) — if at all — is of interest, and forms the central axis of the research presented in this volume. Findings from the research suggest potential ways in which institutional open learning practices could help address economic inequalities, socio-cultural marginalisation and political misrepresentation, as well as uncover challenges and barriers to transformative social justice aspirations at various levels of the PSET sector.

---

[4] Information and Communications Technology

[5] DHET. (2019). The Bulletin: Bumper 2019 Year End Edition October – December 2019. Internal publication by email from M Adendorff. Mr Adendorff is the former DHET Project Manager: Open Learning for Lecturer Development.

The chapter begins by describing the South African PSET landscape, then provides a description of open learning and the cluster of principles that inform it to present "an ideal or goal rather than an absolute, all-or-nothing imperative" (DHET, 2017, p. 373). Having addressed DHET's open learning agenda, the chapter then outlines Fraser's (2005, 2009) social justice theory and how it is used in this volume to interrogate the notion of open learning. Finally, the chapter closes with a brief synopsis of the case studies that constitute this volume.

The South African PSET landscape, past and present

DHET currently oversees the diverse PSET sector which comprises "all education and training provision for those who have completed school, those who did not complete their schooling, and those who never attended school" (DHET, 2014, p. xi). Figure 1 attempts to capture the broad church of PSET in South Africa.

The South African PSET sector currently consists of three types of institutions: 26 public universities (including traditional universities, comprehensive universities and universities of technology [UoTs]), 50 Technical and Vocational Education and Training (TVET) colleges, and Community Education and Training (CET) colleges[6].

Participation in the PSET sector occurs at a number of entry points. Learners who are successful in the General Education and Training (GET: Grades 1-9) phase either enrol for Further Education and Training (FET: Grades 10–12) or TVET qualifications. Of learners who complete the FET phase, approximately 36% attain sufficient grades to apply for a bachelor degree at university level[7]. The other 64% might qualify for access to a UoT or TVET qualification, or might not be eligible for any form of PSET enrolment. Enrolment in TVET colleges reached 673 490 in 2019 (DHET, 2021), which was a 2.5% (16 357) increase on 2018. Although the National Development Plan (NDP) indicates that headcount enrolment in TVET colleges should reach 2.5 million by 2030, the rate of enrolment has varied between 2010 and 2019 (DHET, 2021). Meanwhile 1 283 890 students were enrolled at public and private Higher Education Institutions (HEIs) in 2019, with the majority of enrolments in public institutions (1 074 912). While the NDP seeks to enrol 1.6 million students in public HEIs by 2030, completion rates at public universities remain alarmingly low, averaging in 2017 at 20.3% (Essop, 2020).

The PSET sector also includes other more specialised structures such as the Sector Education and Training Authorities (SETAs), the National Skills Fund (NSF) and the National Student Financial Aid Scheme (NSFAS). Additionally there are regulatory bodies responsible for qualifications and quality assurance in the post-school system, namely the South African Qualifications Authority (SAQA), and three quality councils: the Council on Higher Education (CHE), Umalusi, and Quality Council for Trades and Occupations (QCTO). These different structures in the system are at various stages of development and maturity, with some remaining essentially unchanged for decades, while others are relatively new organisations, and some are planned structures, such as the South African Institution for Vocational and Continuing Education and Training (SAIVCET).

---

[6] The cases in this volume do not address the CET institutions charged with assisting those who are perhaps the most educationally marginalised, i.e., those who have not even completed the GET phase of education. Nonetheless, as part of the PSET sector, they significantly broaden the remit of DHET.

[7] https://www.sabcnews.com/the-class-of-2021-has-performed-exceptionally-well-motshekga/

4 CASES ON OPEN LEARNING

Figure 1: An overview of the South African PSET landscape

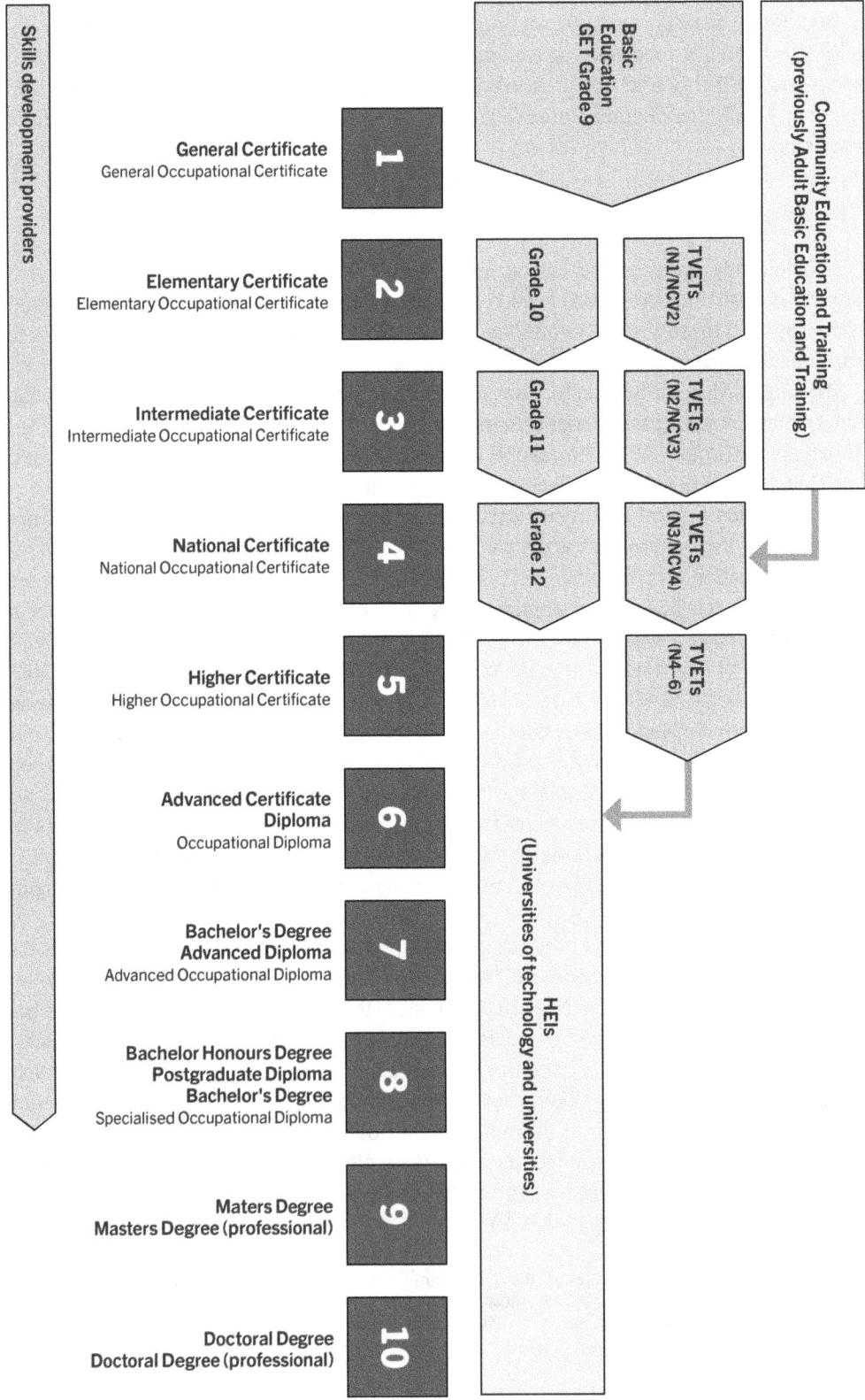

The focus of the case studies in this volume are South Africa's public universities and TVET colleges. What follows describes historical and contemporary issues that affect these institutions specifically.

Historical and contemporary factors shaping universities and TVET colleges in South Africa

Historically, South African TVET colleges and universities have followed differentiated development pathways, being managed by different government entities and targeted at different demographics and regions. The higher education landscape, consisting of universities and 'Polytechnique' universities (locally known as 'technikons'), was significantly restructured between 2003 and 2007, when the historically fractured and racially differentiated sector was overhauled into a more unified system through a series of 'mergers' intended to break the "structural embrace" (Hall, 2015; cf. Badat & Sayed, 2014) of the apartheid-era. Thirty-six institutions were merged into 23 universities and universities of technology, affecting more than 62% of the higher education population (Hall, 2015). On the vocational side, 150 public technical colleges administered by provincial authorities and/or Bantustan[8] administrations prior to 1994 were merged into 50 Further Education and Training (FET) colleges in the period 1994-1998 (Jansen, 2004) spread over 364 campuses (Wyngaard & Kapp, 2004, p. 187), and later renamed as Technical and Vocational Education and Training (TVET) colleges.

The outcomes of these mergers have remained contentious (see, e.g., Baloyi & Naidoo, 2016; Hall, 2015; Jansen, 2003; Mfusi, 2004; SASCO, 2009 for a sample of differing perspectives). In both types of institutions, the lingering effects of such restructuring is of interest when studying open learning principles and whether organisational arrangements support said principles. But in addition to these mergers, reconfigurations also occurred later at the administrative level. In 2009, the Department of Education was divided into the Department of Basic Education (in charge of public schools from Grades R-12) and the Department of Higher Education and Training (in charge of universities and certain training functions taken over from the Department of Labour) (Kgobe & Baatjes, 2014). In 2014, TVET colleges were also transferred from the remit of provincial education departments to the national DHET in Pretoria, thus centralising this sector across provinces (DHET, 2013, p. 12). As a result of these changes, previously separate post-school systems now sit awkwardly in relation to each other and face discernible differences in social justice challenges.

The institutions examined in this volume exist within these histories of educational privilege and disadvantage. Some, such as the University of Cape Town, enjoy historical and contemporary advantages economically and spatially. Others, including TVET college campuses established in rural areas formerly governed by Bantustan administrations under apartheid (e.g., some of the more remote campuses of Elangeni and Motheo Colleges), suffer plural forms of *disadvantage*, including historical under-development (especially regarding infrastructure), widely spaced campuses creating spatial barriers to institutional cohesion

---

[8] The term 'Bantustan' was used as a pejorative to mock the apartheid government's 'separate but equal' system of balkanising Black land ownership and residence into ten homeland territories that effectively made up only 13% of the total of South Africa's land area. To indicate derision and resistance, these euphemistically named 'homelands' were termed 'Bantustans' by many who resisted the apartheid regime.

and synchronicity, as well as attracting and enrolling students of vulnerable socio-economic status.

Further, PSET institutions receive and amplify inequities from the basic education sector, and many of the ideals outlined in the OLPF such as recognition of prior learning (RPL) or student support are exacerbated by – yet indispensable to ameliorating – the prior education inequities that students bring to their post-school endeavours.

Key policies informing the PSET landscape

Most chapters in this book draw explicitly on the *Open Learning Policy Framework* (OLPF) for PSET (DHET, 2017), and the *White paper for post school education and training* (DHET, 2013a). The White Paper aspires to "a transformed post-school system" that seeks to "improve the economic, social and cultural life of its people ... to bring about social justice, to overcome the legacy of our colonial and apartheid past, and to overcome inequity and injustice whatever its origins" (DHET, 2013a, p. 75).

In addition, various chapters draw on the *Policy on Professional Qualifications for Lecturers in TVET* (DHET, 2013b), *Policies on the Recognition of Prior Learning, Credit Accumulation and Transfer, and Assessment in Higher Education* (CHE, 2016), *Recognition of Prior Learning (RPL) Policy Coordination Policy* (DHET, 2016), *Department of Higher Education and Training's Position on Online Programme and Course Offerings* (DHET, 2017), *Strategic Policy Framework on Disability for the PSET system* (DHET, 2018), and the *TVET Colleges' 2020 Student Support Services Annual Plan* (DHET, 2020). While detailed policy analysis and critical policy study are not possible here, the chapters in this volume understand policy as a contingent, interpreted and political tool of the state, with differentiated reach, varied authority and often riddled with contradictions.

Open learning

What is construed as 'open', 'opening' or 'openness' in an educational context is specific to the international and national economic, socio-cultural and political fabric of society at a particular point in time. Broadly speaking, openness in educational contexts has historically exhibited two main trajectories: (1) *open learning* which focuses on the removal of barriers to learning in the formal context (Caliskan, 2012); and (2) *open education* which endeavours to provide access to education in informal and nonformal settings through open educational resources (OER) and open educational practices (OEP) (Conole & Brown, 2018). DHET's notion of open learning is a rather complex amalgam of the older concept of open learning and the newer concept of open education.

The notion of open learning originated from the United Kingdom's Open University's (OU) conception of 'open' in the 1970s which was interpreted as prospective students not being subject to special "*entry requirements* [but] only exit standards" (Gourley & Lane, 2009, p. 57, emphasis added), thereby opening up learning to those who would not normally have been allowed access to traditional universities. Initially this type of open learning was conducted at a distance, first as paper-based correspondence courses, but later through online learning. Open learning in the OU context has sought to reduce barriers to entry, enable flexible learning in terms of time and place, provide learning support, construct learning programmes in the expectation that learners can succeed and maintain strict quality assurance of materials and systems.

The open education movement (Conole & Brown, 2018) has in the past 20 years actively encouraged the opening up of education for all, which has been partly realised through the creation, adaptation and re-use of free and legally shareable open educational resources (d'Antoni, 2007), open textbooks (Feldstein et al., 2012), and Massive Open Online Courses (MOOCs) (Rambe & Moeti, 2017) which are all inherently underpinned by OEP (Cronin & MacLaren, 2018).

Similarly to institutions such as the OU, DHET operates within the ambit of formal education and holds that:

> Open learning ... is driven by a concern for social justice and therefore motivated by the need for redress, equity in access to opportunity, flexibility and choice, and by an equal concern for quality and real success in learning. (2017, p. 412)

The Open Learning Policy Framework

The OLPF works with a definition of 'open learning' from the *PSET White Paper* (DHET, 2014), which itself draws on the original *White Paper for Education and Training* (DoE, 1995) that was outlined by the government of national unity at the dawn of South African democracy. The definition of 'open learning' offered in the OLPF emphasises that it an 'approach' that seeks to remove barriers to 'access' and 'success' for students across the sector:

> an approach which combines principles of learner centredness, lifelong learning, flexibility of learning provision, the removal of barriers to access learning, the recognition for credit of prior learning experience, the provision of learner support, the construction of learning programmes in the expectation that the learner can succeed, and the maintenance of rigorous quality assurance over the design of learning materials and support systems. (DHET, 2017, p. 363)

The OLPF includes terms that warrant scrutiny: terms like 'access', 'quality', 'support' and 'success' that are far from self-evident and may take on different meanings for different actors and contexts. In particular, 'success' is premised on 'access and quality', and 'quality'[9] is then folded into 'meaningful access'; that is, the idea of 'access' is where the OLPF's theory of change is grounded. The definition of open learning in the OLPF points to a composite of ideals that might be categorised as quality standards or 'good pedagogy' (e.g., learner centredness, believing that students can succeed, student support, etc.), open and distance learning (ODL) (flexibilization, online and e-learning), assessment practices such as RPL and micro-credentials, and the use of OER as a cost-saving strategy (DHET, 2017).

As reflected in the chapters in this volume, there are broadly speaking three groups of 'open' in connection to *student learning*: (1) entry to those who would, under usual circumstances, not be admitted to a formal educational institution (e.g., recognition of prior

---

[9] Biesta has argued elsewhere (2015) that the term 'quality' is a classic floating signifier in education policy, signalling everything to everyone, and hence nothing to anyone.

learning); (2) free or low cost of tuition and materials (e.g., OER and open textbooks); and (3) the inclusion of students' voices in the materials. With regard to *educators*, the concept of 'open' pertains to: (1) free access to OER, open access (OA) journal articles, open data and free images; (2) the legal re-use and adaptation of OER; (3) the legal re-distribution of OER, OA journals and lecture notes/presentations using free images and/or open data.

Additionally, the OLPF appropriates strategies from the open education movement and indicates that OER be used wherever possible and be curated on DHET's nascent National Open Learning System (NOLS). The OLPF also indicates that recognition for credit of prior learning experience should be provided for those successfully completing MOOCs or other certified online courses.

In order to make visible the ways in which open learning principles may or may not be understood, accepted or implemented in the PSET sector in South Africa, we have drawn upon the social justice theory of political philosopher Nancy Fraser.

Fraser's theory of social justice

Fraser understands social justice as participation in society as peers, what she refers to as 'parity of participation' (Fraser, 2005, p. 73). She conceives of 'participatory parity' both as an *outcome* where "all the relevant social actors ... participate as peers in social life" and a *process* in which procedural standards are followed "in fair and open processes of deliberation" (Fraser, 2005, p. 87). According to Fraser, both outcomes and processes can be socially unjust in three ways, which she terms: (1) economic maldistribution; (2) cultural misrecognition; and (3) political misrepresentation. It is, however, critical to note that economic inequalities, cultural inequities and political misrepresentations, while analytically distinct, are in practice enmeshed and, hence, always co-present and simultaneously in play. The analytical distinction assists in anticipating the tensions between different claims-making strategies and apprehending the overlaps as well as the gaps that would need to be addressed in practice (Fraser & Naples, 2004).

Economic maldistribution, redistribution and restructuring

With respect to economic injustice or *maldistribution*, Fraser explains that "people can be impeded from full participation by economic structures that deny them the resources they need in order to interact with others as peers" (2005, p. 73). Here the key financial inequality is that of the "class structure of society" (Fraser, 2005, p. 74) and the "economic disadvantage" (Fraser, 1995, p. 69) or "economic subordination" (1995, p. 73) that it engenders.

Connecting this to open learning principles, this implies that students in the PSET sector in South Africa may be impeded from full participation by, for example, the lack of access to geographically convenient campuses, unaffordable travelling costs, unaffordable registration fees, unaffordable tuition fees, expensive accommodation rentals, expensive textbooks, and in TVET colleges, insufficient workplace placement positions to complete their qualifications in time. During the COVID-19 pandemic, students shouldered additional economic burdens such as the expense of internet enabled devices and high data costs. These types of hurdles, following Fraser, indicate "distributive injustice or maldistribution" (2005, p. 73) and need to be addressed through economic redistribution or economic restructuring.

Fraser refers to economic *redistribution* as an "affirmative" change, where actions taken to address inequitable processes or outcomes provide ameliorative adjustments and advance "*re*-formation rather than *radical* (getting to the *root* of what matters) transformation" (Zipin, 2017, p. 68; italics in the original). Examples of open learning as an affirmative response, or what Hodgkinson-Williams and Trotter prefer to call an "ameliorative intervention" (2018, p. 207), would include, for example, the availability of affordable full-time or part-time, in-person and/or online tuition, the use of free OER (e.g., open textbooks) and flexible submission sites and times for assessments.

Whereas economic *restructuring*, which is a "transformative" response, would directly address the "*root* of what matters" (Zipin, 2017, p. 68, italics in original), such as through fully state-funded PSET, supported by commerce and industry and state-sponsored open textbooks which could be customised by staff and students to better suit local settings. These types of transformative remedies would therefore directly aim at "correcting inequitable outcomes precisely by restructuring the underlying generative frameworks" (Fraser, 1997, as cited in Nilsson, 2008, p. 33) and encourage procedures that support the deliberation of the curriculum by those most affected, namely the staff, students and even local industry.

Cultural misrecognition, recognition and re-acculturation

In relation to cultural injustice, or '*misrecognition*', Fraser points out that "people can also be prevented from interacting in terms of [participatory] parity by institutionalised hierarchies of cultural value that deny them the requisite standing" (2005, p. 73). Cultural inequities include all forms of discrimination that priviledge some and disrepect, stigmatize and/or diminish others along, for example, gender, race, language, ability, nationality, religious and/or ethnic lines.

In terms of open learning, this means that PSET students may be deprived of participatory parity due to challenges faced by groups historically marginalised under colonial and then apartheid rule, the scars of which remain today in challenges faced by formally racially segregated PSET institutions. This manifests particularly with respect to the prevalence of Western-oriented epistemic perspectives and educational resources such as textbooks which ignore local knowledge and alienate or estrange students (Hodgkinson-Williams & Trotter, 2018). Moreover the language of teaching and learning, which is predominantly English, may unwittingly disadvantage other South African languages even while it provides possible access to potential international prospects. Likewise, students with disabilities continue to face hurdles in participating on an equal footing in the PSET sector.

Counteracting cultural inequality or misrecognition with ameliorative modifications or symbolic change would, for example, assist in valuing local knowledge and languages, as well as esteeming various cultural perspectives and interpretations. This type of ameliorative cultural *recognition* would, for example, involve students having educational materials translated into the language of their choice and for those with disabilities, not only having these mediated through various assistive technologies, but having administrative and academic support offered in sign language and experiencing the educational environment as welcoming and non judgemental.

As Luckett and Shay suggest, a "transformative approach would involve dismantling the power relations, social hierarchies and cultural hegemonies that currently underpin the canons, the assumed norms and values of inherited curricula and setting up processes to reimagine more inclusive ways of participating in curriculum and pedagogic practices" (2017, p. 3). A fully transformative approach would involve what Hodgkinson-Williams and Trotter (2018) refer to as *"re-acculturation"* which is seen as a process of automatic inclusion of marginalised groups and resolutely acknowledging and valuing other cultural perspectives (e.g., epistemic, ethnic, religious) and mainstreaming of a disability-friendly culture.

Political misrepresentation, reframing

In terms of political inequality, or *"misrepresentation"*, Fraser explains that this "tells us who is included in, and who is excluded from, the circle of those entitled to a just distribution and reciprocal recognition" (2005, p. 75). Fraser distinguishes two levels of misrepresentation: (1) decision-making and (2) boundary setting.

The *decision-making aspect* is an issue when the "political decision rules wrongly deny some of the included the chance to participate fully, as peers" (Fraser, 2005, p. 76) and is what Fraser calls *"ordinary-political misrepresentation"* (Fraser, 2005, p. 76, italics in original). With respect to open learning principles in the PSET sector, denying student and staff input into economic matters (e.g., infrastructural and/or equipment requirements, financial arrangements for bursaries), cultural matters (e.g., curricula, institutional norms) and political matters (e.g., institutional governance, national policy) can be seen as ordinary-political misrepresentation.

The *boundary-setting aspect* is a "matter of social belonging" where the primary "injustice arises when the community's boundaries are drawn in such a way as to wrongly exclude some people from the chance to participate at all in its authorised contests over justice" (Fraser, 2005, p. 76). For example, in order for OER to be legally shared optimally, alternatives to the existing fully copyrighted laws need to operate at an international level, not only at a national one.

Entanglement of economic, cultural and political dimensions

Although analytically distinct and not reducible to one another, in reality these economic, cultural and political dimensions are intertwined or 'imbricated' (Fraser & Naples, 2004) with one another. Issues of economic class are entangled with one or more cultural differences including, but not limited to race, gender, sexuality, nationality, ethnicity, language, religion, epistemic perspectives and identity, as well as with historical and current power and privilege. Understanding the root challenges to open learning analytically can assist in planning for or understanding the variable uptake of open learning.

Cases on open learning

The COOL research team at CILT invited 10 young South Africa researchers (with 70% comprising DHET's target group) to research one or two case studies for the project. They were supported and mentored during the research and writing process by seven CILT academics. Significant focus was placed on researcher development activities in which the researchers were able to engage extensively with the academics and their peers. COOL conducted nearly 70 60- and 90-minute long research related webinars, hosted a researcher reading group, provided six 3-hour slots for group writing and support (where researchers were invited to write their chapters and have intermittent discussions with a group of mentors), and four 90-minute engagements to help researchers prepare presentations on their work for the 2021 DHET Research Colloquium on "Open learning: Flexible and Blended Learning in Post-School Education and Training".[10]

The 16 studies produced from the research are published both as booklets and as the chapters in this book. The book is structured according to five parts, each focusing on a different theme: Access, Pedagogy, Support for Success, Institutional Vision, and National Aspirations.

The first section, *Focus on Access*, comprises three cases supporting access to learning, through examining RPL, embracing alternative forms of student financial support, and enabling flexible learning opportunities. Barriers to accessing PSET education are often related to entry requirements and financial obstacles. Chapter 1, drawing on research undertaken with national experts as well as engagement with national RPL policies, asserts that while RPL policy at a national level is robust, inadequate national and institutional funding for the implementation of RPL, and the inherent complexity of RPL for access and/or credit, result in weak implementation at institutional level. Chapter 2 discusses a cluster of activities undertaken at the University of the Western Cape, including an annual alumni phonathon, a staff pledge campaign, corporate fundraising events, and the #NoStudentWillBeLeftBehind campaign, designed to respond, at an institutional level, to help financially precarious students and remediate barriers to access. Access to learning can often be improved through strengthening flexibility, as Goldfields TVET College demonstrates in Chapter 3, allowing students who have failed a course to repeat it via a flexible learning approach so that they can continue with their studies (though without NSFAS funding support).

The second section, *Focus on Pedagogy*, shares three chapters that describe digitally innovative approaches to pedagogy – examining an instance of blended learning, one of online learning, and another of online assessment. Chapter 4 draws on the experiences of Northlink TVET College in Cape Town to examine how an inclusive approach to blended learning can be understood through a social justice lens through considering stakeholder experiences before and during the pandemic. Turning next to the experiences of the Durban University of Technology (DUT), Chapter 5 explores how the COVID-19 pandemic accelerated DUT's engagement with online learning, discovering how economic inequalities and cultural inequities require the attention of national and institutional players respectively. Online assessment remains a substantial challenge for institutions. Chapter 6 investigates this through the experiences of students and staff from the Open Learning Unit at Tshwane North TVET College in relation to continuous online assessment. This chapter points strongly to the need for policy changes at a national level that currently hamper the opportunity for TVET colleges to make use of different modalities of assessment.

The third section, *Focus on Support for Success*, discusses four different interventions that respond to barriers to student success in four different institutions. Through exploring the experiences of a centralised Student Support Service unit at Elangeni TVET College, Chapter 7 highlights the need to take a multi-organisational social justice approach to supporting

---

[10] https://www.dhetresearchcolloquium.co.za/

students, along various stages of the student journey. Similarly, Chapter 8, which looks at the work of Motheo TVET College in addressing the needs of students with disabilities (SWDs), recognises that educational institutions remain only one of many government entities, including municipalities and health services, which must adopt social justice approaches to create conducive learning conditions for SWDs. Chapters 9 and 10 consider the potential of OER adoption models and OER small grants, respectively, to respond to economic, cultural and political instances of injustice. Chapter 9, after examining a number of OER adoption models available online, recommends a coordinated, aggregate model, locating a range of responsibilities at national and institutional levels to optimise DHET's developing National Open Learning System (NOLS). Chapter 10 focuses on the impact of the provision of OER small grants, through an examination of two programmes at two Western Cape universities, noting that even relatively modest funding acts as an incentive for the creation, adaption and adoption of OER, and in so doing, results in the production of locally relevant, free and legally shareable resources.

The fourth section, *Focus on Institutional Vision*, offers three chapters which consider how three specific institutions respond to economic, cultural and political inequities through adopting a range of open learning interventions. Each institution is located at the confluence of particular contemporary factors and is simultaneously rooted in and shaped by particular historical trajectories. For example, the management practices of False Bay College, the focus of Chapter 11, viewed through a Bourdieusian lens, emerge as historically and contextually specific, and by no means a 'silver bullet' solution to leadership challenges experienced at other colleges and in the broader PSET landscape. Similarly, Chapter 12's exploration of the influence of leadership on the early adoption of e-learning at Gert Sibande TVET College suggests that visionary and socially just leadership practices contribute to increasing e-learning implementation. Chapter 13 explores instances of openness at the University of the Free State (UFS) through tracing the history of five long-term initiatives that individually and collectively work towards enacting the institution's vision of creating more enabling conditions for transformative shifts towards opening up education.

The final section of this book, *Focus on National Aspirations*, offers three cases that function at a national level to address issues of staff development and the structures that enable innovative approaches to credentialing. Chapters 14 and 15 examine specific interventions, supporting teaching staff in the TVET context. Chapter 14 explores the design and development over time of the Lecturer Support System (LSS) and what the findings suggest for how staff are imagined in professional developmental endeavours. Chapter 15 turns its attention to work integrated learning as a mechanism for strengthening lecturers' professional identities and, in so doing, to improve teaching and learning. Chapter 16, our final case, investigates work done on microcredentialing, both internationally and at the North-West University, demonstrating that this practice can address systemic inequities through recognising alternative accreditation mechanisms.

Acknowledgements

Special thanks to Sara Black for her critical engagement with the chapter and for her constructive recommendations. Thanks are also due to the Centre for Innovation in Learning and Teaching at the University of Cape Town, which hosted the COOL project, and the South African Department of Higher Education and Training for funding it.

References

Badat, S., & Sayed, Y. (2014). Post-1994 South African education: The challenge of social justice. *The Annals of the American Academy of Political and Social Science*, 652(1), 127–148.

Baloyi, M. C., & Naidoo, G. (2016). Higher education mergers in South Africa: A means towards an end.African *Journal of Public Affairs*, 9 (3) 19–29. https://repository.up.ac.za/bitstream/handle/2263/58225/Baloyi_Higher_2016.pdf?sequence=1

Biesta, G. J. J. (2015). Education, measurement and the professions: Reclaiming a space for democratic professionality in education. *Educational Philosophy and Theory*, 49(4), 315–330. https://doi.org/10.1080/00131857.2015.1048665

Caliskan, H. (2012). Open learning. In N. M. Seel (Ed.), *Encyclopaedia of the sciences of learning* (pp. 2516–2518). Springer US. https://doi.org/10.1007/978-1-4419-1428-6_52

CHE (Council for Higher Education). (2016). Policies on the recognition of prior learning, credit accumulation and transfer, and assessment in higher education. https://www.che.ac.za/sites/default/files/RPL-CAT%20Assessment%20Policy%20Document.pdf

Conole, G., & Brown, M. (2018). Reflecting on the impact of the open education movement. *Journal of Learning for Development*, 5(3), 187–203.

Cronin, C., & MacLaren, I. (2018). Conceptualising OEP: A review of theoretical and empirical literature in open educational practices. *Open Praxis*, 10(2), 127-143. https://search.informit.org/doi/pdf/10.3316/informit.559671315718016

D'Antoni, S. (2007). Open educational resources and open content for higher education. RUSC. *Universities and Knowledge Society Journal*, 4(1). https://rusc.uoc.edu/rusc/ca/index.php/rusc/article/download/v4n1-dantoni/292-1209-1-PB.pdf

DHET (Department of Higher Education and Training). (2013a). White paper for post-school education and training: Building an expanded, effective and integrated post-school system. *Government Gazette*, 37229. https://www.gov.za/documents/white-paper-post-school-education-and-training-building-expanded-effective-and-integrated

DHET. (2013b). Policy on professional qualifications for lecturers in technical and vocational education and training. *Government Gazette*, 36554. https://www.dhet.gov.za/Gazette/Policy%20on%20professional%20qualifications%20for%20lecturers%20in%20technical%20and%20vocational%20education%20and%20training.pdf

DHET. (2014). Qualification profile of lecturers employed in public technical and vocational education and training colleges in South Africa in 2014. https://www.dhet.gov.za/Teacher%20Education%20Reports/DHET%20%20Qualification%20Profile%20of%20Lecturers%20Employed%20in%20Public%20Technical%20and%20Vocational%20Education%20and%20Training%202014.pdf

DHET. (2017). Call for comment on the Open Learning Policy Framework for Post-School Education and Training. *Government Gazette*, 335(40772). http://pmg-assets.s3-website-eu-west-1.amazonaws.com/170407openlearningframework-postschooleduc.pdf

DHET. (2018). Strategic policy framework on disability for the post-school education and training system. https://www.dhet.gov.za/SiteAssets/Gazettes/Approved%20Strategic%20Disability%20Policy%20Framework%20Layout220518.pdf

DHET. (2020). Technical and vocational education and training colleges' 2020 Student Support Services Annual Plan. https://www.dhet.gov.za/SiteAssets/Technical%20and%20Vocational%20 Education%20and%20Training%20Colleges%202020%20Student%20Support%20Services%20 Annual%20Plan.pdf

DHET. (2021). Post-school education and training monitor: Macro-indicator trends. Government Printer. https://www.dhet.gov.za/Planning%20Monitoring%20and%20Evaluation%20Coordination/Post-School%20Education%20and%20Training%20Monitor%20-%20Macro-Indicator%20Trends%20-%20March%202021.pdf

DoE (Department of Education). (1995). White paper on education and training. https://www.education.gov.za/Portals/0/Documents/Legislation/White%20paper/White%20paper%20on%20Education%20and%20Training%201995.pdf?ver=2008-03-05-111656-000

Essop, A. (2020). The changing size and shape of the higher education system in South Africa, 2005–2017. University of Johannesburg. https://heltasa.org.za/wp-content/uploads/2020/08/Size-and-Shape-of-the-HE-System-2005-2017.pdf

Feldstein, A. P., Martin, M., Hudson, A., Warren, K., Hilton III, J., & Wiley, D. (2012). Open textbooks and increased student access and outcomes. *European Journal of Open, Distance and E-Learning*. https://scholars.fhsu.edu/cgi/viewcontent.cgi?article=1003&context=learning_tech_facpubs

Fraser, N. (1995). From redistribution to recognition? Dilemmas of justice in a 'postsocialist' age. *New Left Review*, 1/212, 68–93. https://newleftreview.org/issues/i212/articles/nancy-fraser-from-redistribution-to-recognition-dilemmas-of-justice-in-a-post-socialist-age

Fraser, N. (2005). Reframing justice in a globalizing world. *New Left Review*, 36, 69–88. https://newleftreview.org/II/36/nancy-fraser-reframing-justice-in-a-globalizing-world

Fraser, N. (2009). *Scales of justice: Reimagining political space in a globalizing world*. Columbia University Press.

Fraser, N., & Naples, N. A. (2004). To interpret the world and to change it: An interview with Nancy Fraser. *Signs: Journal of Women in Culture and Society*, 29(4), 1103–1124. https://www.journals.uchicago.edu/doi/epdf/10.1086/382631

Goodier, S. (2017). A look at the open learning policy framework for post-school education and training in South Africa. ROER4D. https://roer4d.org/3091

Gourley, B., & Lane, A. (2009). Re-invigorating openness at The Open University: The role of open educational resources. *Open Learning: The Journal of Open, Distance and e-Learning*, 24(1), 57–65.

Hall, M. (2015). Institutional culture of mergers and alliances in South Africa. In A. Curaj, L. Georghiou, J. Cassingena Harper & E. Egron-Polak (Eds.), *Mergers and alliances in higher education: International practice and emerging opportunities* (pp. 145–173). Springer Nature.

Hodgkinson-Williams, C. A., & Trotter, H. (2018). A social justice framework for understanding open educational resources and practices in the Global South. *Journal of Learning for Development*, 5(3), 204–224. https://files.eric.ed.gov/fulltext/EJ1197462.pdf

Jansen, J. (2003). The state of higher education in South Africa: From massification to mergers. In J. Daniel, A. Habib & R. Southhall (Eds.), *State of the nation: South Africa 2003–2004* (pp. 290–311). HSRC Press.

Jansen, J. (2004). Changes and continuities in South Africa's higher education system, 1994 to 2004. In L. Chisholm (Ed.), *Changing class: Education and social change in post-apartheid South Africa* (pp. 293–314). HSRC Press.

Kgobe, P., & Baatjes, I. (2014). White Paper on post school education and training: Some new policy directions. *Post-School Education Journal*, 1(1), 2–4. https://www.uj.ac.za/wp-content/uploads/2021/11/post-school-education-review-1.pdf

Mfusi, M. X. (2004). The effects of higher education mergers on the resultant curricula of the combined institutions: Perspectives on higher education. *South African Journal of Higher Education*, 18(1), 98–110. https://journals.co.za/doi/pdf/10.10520/EJC37051

Nilsson, M. (2008). Rethinking redistribution. *New Proposals: Journal of Marxism and Interdisciplinary Inquiry*, 2(1), 31–44. https://ojs.library.ubc.ca/index.php/newproposals/article/view/119/235

Rambe, P., & Moeti, M. (2017). Disrupting and democratising higher education provision or entrenching academic elitism: Towards a model of MOOCs adoption at African universities. *Educational Technology Research and Development*, 65(3), 631–651. https://link.springer.com/article/10.1007/s11423-016-9500-3

SASCO (South African Students Congress). (2009). Beyond the big bang mergers: A critical review of the higher education mergers in South Africa. 16th National Congress Discussion Document: Education Transformation. https://kipdf.com/beyond-the-big-bang-mergers-a-critical-review-of-the-higher-education-mergers-in_5ac38ae31723dd2f96f74abd.html

United Nations. (2015). Sustainable Development Agenda. https://www.un.org/sustainabledevelopment/development-agenda/

USAF (Universities South Africa). (2017). Comment on the Draft Policy Framework on Open Learning and Distance Education. http://www.usaf.ac.za/wp-content/uploads/2017/08/2017_USAF-Commentary_ODL-Policy-Framework_12-May-2017.pdf

Wyngaard, A., & Kapp, C. (2004). Rethinking and reimagining mergers in further and higher education: A human perspective. *South African Journal of Higher Education*, 18(1), 185–201. https://journals.co.za/doi/pdf/10.10520/EJC37045

Zipin, L. (2017). Pursuing a problematic-based curriculum approach for the sake of social justice. *Journal of Education (University of KwaZulu-Natal)*, 69, 67–92. http://www.scielo.org.za/scielo.php?script=sci_arttext&pid=S2520-98682017000200004

HOW TO CITE THIS CHAPTER

Mayisela, T., Govender, S. C., & Hodgkinson-Williams, C. A. (2022). Introducing open learning as a means towards social justice in post school education and training. In T. Mayisela, S. C. Govender & C. A. Hodgkinson-Williams (Eds.), *Open learning as a means of advancing social justice: Cases in post-school education and training in South Africa* (pp. 1–15). African Minds. doi: 10.47622/9781928502425_0

This work is licensed under a Creative Commons Attribution 4.0 International (CC BY 4.0) licence.

1

Recognition of prior learning as a form of open learning in post-school education and training in South Africa

A social justice perspective

Susan Gredley & Cheryl Ann Hodgkinson-Williams

SUMMARY Recognition of Prior Learning (RPL) in its earliest forms, both globally and locally, was driven by agendas of social inclusion and redress, but has been compromised by rapid globalisation, increasingly market-driven neoliberal agendas, and the rise of the knowledge economy. One of the ambitions of the draft *Open Learning Policy Framework* (OLPF) for Post-School Education and Training (PSET) in South Africa is to open up learning to students via RPL, especially via credit for online learning. This qualitative case study sought to explore current RPL practices, and ways in which they have opened up access to PSET institutions, in order to explore the benefits and challenges of RPL as envisaged in the OLPF. Given the OLPF's ambition to address social justice in South Africa, Nancy Fraser's (2005) notion of parity of participation is used to explore the extent to which current forms of RPL including RPL for credit can address the underlying economic, cultural and political injustices faced by aspirant PSET students. In-depth interviews with two experts in the field of RPL in South Africa were undertaken to ascertain in what ways students without formal qualifications are given opportunities to access, progress through and succeed in post-school education through formal RPL processes. The experts' views are instructive for the implementation of the OLPF's concept of 'open learning'. They indicate that the existing RPL policy at national level is quite robust, but weakly implemented at public institutions mainly due to inadequate national and institutional funding, but also because it is a complex knowledge-mediating process that cannot be reduced to simple tests or assessments of knowledge equivalence. The ambition of recognition for credit of prior learning experience, as envisaged by the OLPF, is likely to succumb to the same epistemic and financial stumbling blocks unless sound national mechanisms and support systems are established for RPL practices and processes each step of the way.

Keywords: recognition of prior learning, experiential learning, optimal inclusion, open learning, social justice

Introduction and context

One of the ambitions of the draft *Open Learning Policy Framework for Post-School Education and Training* (DHET, 2017) is to open up learning to aspirant students via recognition of prior learning (RPL). RPL is defined in South African national policy as "the principles and processes through which the prior knowledge and skills of a person are made visible, mediated and assessed, for the purposes of alternative access and admission, recognition and certification, or further learning and development" (SAQA, 2019, p. 3). RPL is conceptualised and implemented differently in different contexts[1], but broadly encompasses a range of approaches for recognising experiential, non-formal and informal learning gained through self-study, activism, work-based and volunteering experiences, parenting and so on (Andersson et al., 2013; Cooper & Ralphs, 2016).

RPL in its earliest forms, both globally and locally, was driven by agendas of social inclusion and redress; it sought to promote study and employment opportunities for under-represented groups by acknowledging knowledge and skills gained in spaces outside formal education (Ralphs, 2016). However, this focus on personal development to promote social progress and social justice was soon eroded by rapid globalisation, increasingly market-driven neoliberal agendas, and the rise of the knowledge economy (Andersson et al., 2013). RPL became increasingly positioned by governments and policymakers less as a personal and social good and more as an economic necessity to build workers' knowledge and skills, strengthen business and bolster a country's global standing (Andersson et al., 2013; Cooper & Ralphs, 2016; Ralphs, 2012).

South Africa has not escaped these global pressures and tensions. Nevertheless, RPL in the country has retained a strong social justice orientation and it remains an important vehicle for redressing past injustices through promoting access to formal qualifications. As such, it features prominently in the Department of Higher Education and Training's (DHET) 2017 draft OLPF as one of the approaches which can help to "transform teaching, learning and access to education and training in quite radical ways" (p. 373). As part of the process of revising this draft policy, DHET commissioned research to better understand current RPL practices, their role in opening up access to the post-school education and training (PSET) sector, and in particular the benefits and challenges that RPL for credit might entail. This chapter reports on this research which explored RPL through expert interviews to ascertain ways in which students without formal qualifications are given opportunities to access, progress through and succeed in post-school education, and attendant challenges and barriers.

RPL in the South African context has a long and at times contested history. This chapter starts with a brief review of RPL models and practices followed by an outline of RPL in the South African context: policies, challenges to implementation, and the seminal knowledge debate. This is followed by a closer look at RPL in the OLPF and then an explication of

---

[1] RPL in the South African context is related to international strategies such as Prior Learning Assessment (PLA) in the USA, Assessment of Prior Experiential Learning (APEL) in the UK, and the Validation of Non-formal and Informal Learning (VNFIL) in the European context.

the study's conceptual framework. Given the OLPF's ambition to address social justice, Nancy Fraser's (2003, 2005, 2008) notion of parity of participation was used to explore and evaluate RPL and the extent to which it, as envisaged by the OLPF, can address the underlying economic, cultural and political injustices faced by aspirant PSET students. A key outcome of this case study was thus to understand not just what RPL as a form of OL *is* but how it could better enable economic equity, cultural recognition and political participation in South Africa.

A brief overview of RPL models and practices

South African RPL practitioners, drawing on local and global scholarship, have categorised RPL in various ways. Using Harris' four models (1999, 2000; Cooper, 2016) and Breier's (2005) three perspectives (technical/market, liberal/humanist and critical/radical), four broad models of RPL can be distinguished each with their own purpose and methodologies (Table 1).

Table 1: Four broad models of RPL

Procrustean RPL » Technical » Market	"technicist and instrumentalist in orientation, matching prior learning to prescribed outcomes or standards" (Cooper, 2016, p. 27), often referred to as a narrow form of credit exchange. It has also been critiqued for colluding with credentialism and market-driven commodifications of informal learning.
Learning and development RPL » Liberal » Humanist	"influenced by liberal and humanist discourses, helps to orient and induct candidates into standard ways of expressing knowledge and skill" (Cooper, 2016, p. 27). Critiqued by Elana Michelson for "privileging individualised and rationalist ways of knowing over contextualised and collective practices" (Cooper, 2016, pp. 27–28).
Radical RPL » Critical	transformative in orientation; RPL viewed as "a means to recognise and assign value to 'subjugated' knowledges and to challenge dominant forms of knowing" (Cooper, 2016, p. 27).
Trojan horse RPL » Critical » Realistic » Optimally inclusive	aims for "a realistic set of educational goals fully cognizant of their grounding social conditions", is "non-sentimentalized", and "optimally socially inclusive" (Harris, 2013, np). Seeks to bring different knowledges into critical dialogue to bring about "greater equality between different forms of knowledge" (Cooper, 2016, p. 27); "allow diverse and some divergent knowledge to be recognised", "challenge what counts as knowledge" and "contribute to broad social advancement" (Harris, 2000, p. 79).

These purposes are translated into three 'generic forms of practice' which have been widely acknowledged by researchers in the field, namely (1) RPL for credit; (2) for access; and (3) in-curriculum RPL (Breier, 2003; Harris, 2000).

RPL for credit

RPL for credit is the most well established and widely used form of assessment. It can be understood in two ways: (1) as the process where "experiential learning can be certified in the credit bearing currency of national standards or qualifications" (Ralphs, 2012, p. 84); and (2) as assigning credit values to knowledge produced and acquired outside of the academy or to a pre-existing standard[2] (Ralphs, 2012, p. 85). Represented as a form of "credit exchange" in the discourse of human capital theory (Harris, 2000; Osman, 2003; Ralphs, 2012), it is most often associated with certifying practical and craft-based skills acquired through self-study or 'on the job' learning. It is also known as "RPL for advanced standing" (Ralphs, 2012, p. 84), in other words "joining studies mid-way" (Bolton et al., 2020, p. 57), when used in the context of formal qualifications in higher education.

Certifying experiential learning

Experiential learning is "technically not certifiable" (Ralphs, 2012, p. 85) and aspirant candidates have to recontextualise their informal learning so as to make their knowledge comparable for the purposes of assessment and certification. In terms of practice, credit for experiential learning is student-focused and centres upon the "process of extracting and evidencing the knowledge and skills acquired from experience, and the process of judging whether the evidence matches the specifications of the standard or qualification" (Ralphs, 2012, p. 84). By implication the RPL process is time-consuming – and therefore costly – both for the would-be student and the assessor. With respect to experiential learning, Ralphs (personal communication, July 25, 2021) cautions that neither the NQF nor the academy is able to capture and document all knowledge and skills available to a society but that does not mean it has no (credit) value.

Credit values of knowledge produced and acquired elsewhere

With regard to credit value, Ralphs (personal communication, July 25, 2021) emphasises that even though knowledge and skills produced and/or acquired outside of the academy do not correspond exactly with the standards of existing qualifications, these can nevertheless be considered as creditworthy, subject to a credible set of assessment criteria. The concept 'credit value' most accurately approximates the understanding of RPL in the OLPF where RPL is suggested as a possible mechanism for those seeking accreditation of experience or self-study undertaken through completing Massive Open Online Courses (MOOCs) or other in-person or online courses (cf. DHET, 2017, p. 382).

The accreditation of non-formal study involves an educational institution, employer or organisation recognising competences already assessed and certified (e.g., badges or micro-credential) by another public or private education provider. This credit-exchange form of RPL accredits the course and would thus be applicable to any student who has completed the course successfully, providing that the academics involved have undertaken a thorough review of the course content and assessment criteria. It is worth drawing the distinction between these non-formal courses that have been formally assessed and those non-formal courses that do not offer assessment. The latter include short courses offered as part of continuing professional development (CPD) programmes, workplace-based training programmes, and MOOCs that are designed and delivered for many different purposes, and frequently do not include any formal assessment.

---

[2] See Clause 4.2.9 of CHE (2016, p. 9) Policies on Recognition of Prior Learning, Credit Accumulation and Transfer, and Assessment in higher education.

RPL for access

RPL for access are arrangements by formal education providers of "alternative route[s] of entry for those who do not meet the prerequisites for admission to a specific programme or course" (Ralphs, 2012, p. 86). This form of RPL is primarily formative, for example, through a portfolio development course which is reflective and developmental. The focus is "on the intrinsic development of meta-cognitive and reflective capabilities required for success in further and higher education" (Ralphs, 2012, p. 87). Rather than focusing on assessed performance measured against a set of standards, it is more "prospective" and aligned with the student's "potential to succeed" (Ralphs, 2012, p. 86).

In-curriculum RPL

In-curriculum RPL is, as the term suggests, located within an academic curriculum which then includes "opportunities for the recognition *and* assessment of prior work-based learning as part of the course" (Ralphs, 2012, p. 87, emphasis in original; DHET, 2013). This equates to Breier's (2005, p. 51) "rpl", i.e. "the recognition of learning in post-entry pedagogy" as opposed to pre-entry RPL for access.

RPL in the South African context: Policy and practice

The history of RPL in South Africa has been well documented (see Bolton et al., 2016; Breier, 2005; Cooper, 1998; Cooper & Ralphs, 2016; Kistan, 2002; Michelson, 2004; Ralphs, 2012). Whilst it has been influenced by global economistic discourses, local RPL policies were conceptualised and implemented in the early post-apartheid democratic era and took on particular salience as an effort to redress severe historical injustices. Explicitly driven by political and social justice agendas, RPL aimed to ensure that mature learners, and especially those disadvantaged through apartheid's repressive policies, could gain access to further education in the absence of formal prerequisite qualifications, and/or receive recognition of skills and experience gained through work and life experience (Botha, 2009; Ralphs, 2012). In this way it also hoped to address the skills backlog in South Africa (Botha, 2009). Saidi reiterates the purposes of RPL in South African HE as being about:

> (1) [promotion of] alternative access and admission to higher education learning programmes for those who do not have formal prerequisites; (2) recognition of knowledge and skills acquired through learning that does not lead to a formal qualification; (3) certification as having fulfilled the equivalence of the requirements for a particular formal qualification; (4) promotion of lifelong learning on the understanding that any knowledge and skill acquired will be recognised. (2017, p. 4)

RPL policy landscape in South Africa

Over the twenty-plus years since enshrining of the right to basic and further education in the South African Constitution[3] there have been a range of RPL policy-related documents (Table 2).

Table 2: Policies related to RPL

Year	Policy-related document	Description
1998	*Skills Development Act 97*[4]	Section 26D(2)(c) & (d) recognise RPL as route towards access to a trade test (Saidi, 2017).
2002	*Recognition of Prior Learning Policy*	The South African Qualifications Authority (SAQA) published the first RPL policy based on the provisions of the SAQA Act 58 of 1995.
2004	Criteria and Guidelines for the Implementation of the Recognition of Prior Learning[5]	SAQA published criteria and guidelines for RPL in 2004.
2008	*National Qualifications Framework Act 67* amended by *Higher Education Laws Amendment Acts 2010*[6]	Section 13(1)(h)(iii) of the NQF Act mandates SAQA to develop overarching policy and criteria for RPL. Section 27(h)(ii) mandates the CHE, as the Quality Council for higher education, to develop and implement policy and criteria for RPL in higher education, taking into account the RPL policy and criteria developed by SAQA.
2013	*National Policy for the Implementation of RPL*[7]	SAQA published following the repeal of the SAQA Act by the NQF Act 27 of 2008. Developed with support from the SAQA RPL Reference Group, which includes staff representatives from the Quality Councils. Opportunity provided for public comment.
2013	*White Paper for Post-school Education and Training*[8]	DHET published and identified RPL as key to redressing past injustices and recognising competence gained through practical workplace learning & experience. The WP for PSET "lamented the lack of common understanding of, & approach to RPL across the PSET" (Saidi, 2017, p. 8).
2013	Final report incorporating a proposal for the national implementation strategy[9]	DHET report by the Ministerial Task Team (MTT) on a national strategy for RPL. The report explored the complexities of RPL in South Africa and why it "has not begun to fulfil its potential or early promise" (p. 1).

---

[3] With respect to the, Section 29 states that: "Everyone has the right — (a) to a basic education, including adult basic education; and (b) to further education, which the state, through reasonable measures, must make progressively available and accessible." (Constitution of the Republic of South Africa, Act 108 of 1996, 12)
[4] https://www.gov.za/sites/default/files/gcis_document/201409/a97-98.pdf
[5] https://www.saqa.org.za/docs/guide/2004/rpl.pdf
[6] https://www.saqa.org.za/docs/legislation/2010/act67.pdf
[7] https://www.saqa.org.za/docs/pol/2013/natpol_irpl.pdf
[8] https://www.gov.za/sites/default/files/gcis_document/201409/37229gon11.pdf
[9] https://www.dhet.gov.za/Reports%20Doc%20Library/Report%20of%20the%20Ministerial%20task%20team%20on%20a%20National%20strategy%20for%20the%20Recognition%20of%20Prior%20Learning(RPL).pdf

2014	*Policy for Credit Accumulation and Transfer within the National Qualifications Framework*[10]	SAQA published the Policy for Credit Accumulation and Transfer (CAT) to provide for the implementation of CAT within the context of the National Qualifications Framework (NQF) Act 67 of 2008.
2016	*RPL Coordination Policy* (No 381, Government Gazette No 39876, 31 March 2016)	DHET published this policy to "provide a strong enabling policy environment for the further development & implementation of RPL across the PSET" (Saidi, 2017, p. 8).
2016	*Policies on the Recognition of Prior Learning, and Credit Accumulation and Transfer, and Assessment in Higher Education*[11]	CHE published these policies to "provide guidelines for the higher education sector with regard to the development of institutional RPL, CAT and Assessment policies in the context of the national policies developed by SAQA and within the framework of the HEQSF" (CHE, 2016, p. 5).
2017	*DRAFT Open Learning Policy Framework for Post-School Education and Training*[12]	DHET published this draft for public comment in March 2017. RPL for credit is seen as one of the principles of open learning (cf. DHET, 2017, p. 377).
2019	*Amended National Policy and Criteria for the Implementation of RPL*[13]	SAQA's amended policy for implementing RPL aimed to further embed "RPL in the national education and training agenda, and ensure clarity and consistency regarding the contexts, roles and responsibilities of all RPL role-players in the country" (p. 3). One of its key intentions is to "facilitate change in the lives of RPL candidates, including workers and learners of all ages (both employed and unemployed), and other marginalised groups" (p. 3).

RPL's explicit social justice intent has been long enshrined in policy, for example SAQA says that RPL in South Africa has,

> unlike similar initiatives in other countries, a very specific agenda ... to support *transformation* of the education and training system of the country [through] an approach ... that explicitly *addresses the visible and invisible barriers* to learning and assessment. (2002, p. 11; emphasis in original)

However, despite concerted efforts to create useful and coherent RPL policy over more than two decades, and despite extensive research, there have been a range of ongoing challenges in conceptualising and implementing RPL in PSET institutions, including academic challenges, institutional constraints and learner needs (Kizito, 2006), among others (see Botha, 2009; DHET, 2013; Kistan, 2002). Realising that not enough was being done to support the development, coordination, implementation, funding, monitoring and evaluation of RPL across the PSET system, DHET's 2016 *RPL Coordination Policy* sought to provide "a strong enabling policy environment" (p. 7). It allocates roles for DHET, SAQA and the Quality Councils (QC). The establishment of a "funding mechanism for RPL implementation" (DHET, 2016, p. 7) was one of DHET's core responsibilities. However, lamentably, according to Ralphs

---

[10] https://www.saqa.org.za/sites/default/files/2019-11/National%20Policy%20for%20CAT.pdf
[11] https://www.policysa.com/images/CHE%20Policies_201608.pdf
[12] https://static.pmg.org.za/170407openlearningframework-postschooleduc.pdf
[13] https://www.saqa.org.za/sites/default/files/2020-09/National-Policy-and-Criteria-for-the-Implementation-of-RPL-Amended-in-March-2019.pdf

(personal communication, July 25, 2021), DHET has not yet been able to act adequately on these responsibilities and the lack of a funding mechanism which means that there is no incentive for public universities and colleges in the PSET system to undertake RPL.

In 2017, DHET published the draft OLPF for PSET for public comment, yet to be approved by the Minister. According to the OLPF, the coordination policy offers "a clear statement and indicator that supports and recognises the need to open access to education for students, and acknowledges that RPL is an important component of addressing this need" (DHET, 2017, p. 382). The OLPF is discussed below.

Challenges to practice

Initially, RPL was welcomed and actively embraced by higher educational institutions in SA but, echoing global concerns and challenges, it has proved complex to implement, time and labour intensive, and more costly than originally envisaged, all of which "eroded the initial enthusiasm" (Botha, 2009, p. 165). Michelson describes RPL in South Africa as having had a "disappointing history", noting multiple issues including:

> a discrepancy between policies on paper and the realities of implementing them; the development of an ornate but dysfunctional bureaucratic labyrinth; and a lack of funding mechanisms. (2014, p. 214)

Stubborn problems remain and implementation is uneven. Persistent challenges include resistance from senior academics in public HEIs who see it as diluting quality; inadequate institutional administrative and technical support; costly and time-consuming assessment and validation processes; the overall costs associated with RPL which mean that some institutions, especially private HEIs, charge prohibitive fees to recoup costs (Ralphs, 2016; Saidi, 2017); policies which subtly reflect notions that prior and unstructured knowledge and learning is inferior (Mantashe & Nkonki, 2019), and gaps "between the intentions of RPL and the way in which it plays out in practice" (Botha, 2019, p. 96).

Whilst the majority of higher education institutions (HEIs) offer some version of RPL, private institutions show more interest than public institutions (perhaps because the former can charge for RPL services[14]), and both utilise RPL more for generic programmes than specialised professional qualifications (Saidi, 2017). Perhaps the most obdurate challenge is that RPL remains:

> a completely unfunded mandate at public universities and colleges despite the rash of government policies promoting RPL and 'articulation' practices, and acknowledgment of the need for adequate resources to ensure quality, affordability, and the professionalisation of practitioners. (Ralphs et al., 2020, p. 26)

As Bolton et al. (2020, p. 72) explain, "funding is awarded to HEIs for students only if they complete 50% or more of a programme at the institution. Moreover, no additional funding is provided for RPL – institutions are expected to resource RPL from the funds that they already

---

[14] Public Service Sector Education and Training http://pseta.org.za/wp-content/uploads/2017/10/Implementation-of-recognition-of-prior-learning-in-Public-Se2.compressed.pdf

have" (Bolton et al., 2020, p. 72). However, the need for RPL – as one way of enhancing opportunities for parity of participation in the formal PSET sector – remains strong in a country plagued by growing inequalities and extreme poverty.

The knowledge debate and RPL as specialised pedagogy

A salient and "distinctively South African theme" (DHET, 2013, p. 23) in RPL over the past twenty or so years has been the debate around the nature of knowledge and contestations around the relationship between formal, academic, disciplinary, curricular knowledge on the one hand, and prior and experiential knowledges on the other (e.g., Breier, 2005; Harris, 2004; Michelson, 2004; Morrow, 2007, 2010; Muller, 2014; Osman, 2003; Young, 2005). The five-year SAQA / University of the Western Cape research project – an important point in the theorising of RPL in the South African context – took these knowledge debates as a starting point (Cooper & Ralphs, 2016).

Based on four very different case studies, the researchers, on the one hand, contested the notion of knowledge binaries arguing that "we need to remain alert to the politics of knowledge and the unequal power relations that lead to the privileging of some sources of epistemological authority over others" (Cooper, 2016, p. 26). They also, on the other hand, understood knowledge as differentiated: "Where and how knowledge is acquired or constructed really does matter and cannot be assumed as insignificant in the assessment and certification thereof" (Cooper, 2016, p. 26).

Moreover, they saw that navigating between different forms of knowledge does not happen automatically, nor through reflection alone; rather, it is a complex process that requires a deliberate pedagogy. Hence, they posited that specialised pedagogies are needed to support RPL as a process of mediation and navigation between different forms of knowledge and sites of practice:

> RPL is seldom reducible to a technical formula for measuring equivalence and allocating common currency (credits); it is itself *a distinctive pedagogical practice*, an encoded practice with distinctive purposes and rules that provides the cognitive and therapeutic tools for navigating learning and assessment practices in and across the different contexts in the system. These include the tools for understanding the social and epistemological determinants of what knowledge and forms of learning are to be recognized, and … acquired and represented in different contexts. (Ralphs, 2012, p. 13; emphasis added)

Thus, they argued, RPL practices will take different forms in different institutional and disciplinary settings, and RPL as specialised pedagogy "provides tools for navigating access to new learning opportunities across diverse contexts" (Cooper & Harris, 2013, p. 2). Understandings of RPL as a form of specialised pedagogy have fed into policy and been explored in recent research (Brenner et al., 2021; DALS, 2019), and have important repercussions for RPL and OL.

RPL and OL: Mapping the intersections

Open learning, discussed in more length in the Introduction of this volume, is defined in the OLPF as:

an *approach* which combines the principles of learner-centeredness, *lifelong learning*, flexibility of learning provision, the removal of barriers to access learning, *the recognition for credit of prior learning experience*, the provision of learner support, the construction of learning programmes in the expectation that learners can succeed, and the maintenance of rigorous quality assurance over the design of learning materials and support systems. (DHET, 2017, p. 363, emphasis added)

OL is thus positioned as a principle-based concept and an "ideal or goal rather than an absolute, all-or-nothing imperative" (DHET, 2017, p. 373). It is embedded in the PSET system, has "the capacity to transform teaching, learning and access to education and training in quite radical ways, whatever mode is used" (DHET, 2017, p. 373) and "enables many people to take advantage of cost-effective and meaningful, quality education and training opportunities throughout their lives" (DHET, 2017, p. 371). DHET's role is to "strive to make this possible through acknowledging the diversity of learning contexts of learners in SA; reducing barriers to learning; sharing expertise, knowledge, and resources; and increasing access to diverse learning opportunities" (DHET, 2017, p. 371).

Recognising prior, informal and experiential learning has a significant presence in the OLPF and features strongly across the eight OL principles, in particular:

"i. learners are provided with *opportunities and capacity for lifelong learning*"; "ii. learning processes *build on [learners'] experience*"; "v. *prior learning and experience is recognised* wherever possible," and "vi. *arrangements for credit transfer and articulation* between qualifications facilitate further learning". (DHET, 2017, p. 371, emphasis added)

The OLPF acknowledges that RPL itself is not a new process, however the principles and approaches of OL have generated renewed interest and urgency in RPL. For example, new learning opportunities such as MOOCs offer alternative ways of acknowledging learning and allowing admission to – or advanced standing in – academic programmes "through the assessment of prior learning, or learning by means other than conventional courses" (DHET, 2017, p. 377). Whilst the OLPF does not go into detail about the ways in which RPL should be implemented, or the role that OL can play in this respect, it is similarly focused on conceptions, strategies and institutional practices to support access and the provision of more inclusive education for students.

Social justice as participatory parity implicit in RPL

The institutional and systemic understandings of RPL and open learning outlined above, have an implicit social justice intent. One theorist who has written extensively on social justice issues is political philosopher Nancy Fraser. Fraser conceives of social justice as "parity of participation" (2005, p. 73), as both an outcome where "all the relevant social actors … participate as peers in social life" and a process in which procedural standards are followed "in fair and open processes of deliberation" (Fraser, 2005, p. 87). However, both these outcomes and processes can be undermined in three ways, which Fraser terms: (1) economic maldistribution; (2) cultural misrecognition; and (3) political misrepresentation or misframing.

Economic maldistribution

With respect to economic injustice or maldistribution, Fraser explains that "people can be impeded from full participation by economic structures that deny them the resources they need in order to interact with others as peers" (2005, p. 73). Maldistribution means that RPL applicants may be impeded from full participation by factors such as historical and current lack of access to quality schooling and higher education, the challenges of having to take on full- or part-time work, and having to care for family which impacts on finances and time available for studies. These barriers, which affect historically disadvantaged South Africans most acutely, indicate "distributive injustice or maldistribution" (Fraser, 2005, p. 73) and need to be addressed through economic redistribution or economic restructuring.

Cultural misrecognition

In relation to cultural inequality or misrecognition, Fraser points out that "people can also be prevented from interacting on terms of [participatory] parity by institutionalized hierarchies of cultural value that deny them the requisite standing" (2005, p. 73). Fraser (2003, 2005) views misrecognition as occurring when societal claims about supposedly fundamental, intrinsic differences between different groups of people, along the lines of cultural attributes such as gender, sexuality, ethnicity, race, language, dis/ability, age, etc., are used to justify the oppression and marginalisation of particular groups, placing some in positions of privilege whilst restricting others' lives.

RPL candidates and students may be deprived of recognitional participatory parity if the institutional patterns of cultural values explicitly or implicitly constitute them and their forms of knowledge as non-standard, deficient or inferior in some way which could relate to race, ethnicity, gender, age and "cultures of knowledge" (Cooper et al., 2016, p. 197), amongst others. A key consideration in the South African context is the prevalence of Western-oriented epistemic perspectives and educational resources which may be culturally inappropriate or alienating (Mbembe, 2015). Moreover, the language of teaching and learning is predominantly English as are marketing, administration and registration documents and student support services, including RPL services, which disadvantages speakers of other South African languages.

Political misrepresentation and misframing

In terms of political inequality, which takes the form of misrepresentation and misframing, Fraser (2005, p. 75) explains that this "tells us who is included in, and who excluded from, the circle of those entitled to a just distribution and reciprocal recognition". The political dimension thus "furnishes the stage on which struggles over distribution and recognition" play out and "tells us not only *who* can make claims for redistribution and recognition, but also *how* such claims are to be mooted and adjudicated" (Fraser, 2005, p. 75, emphasis added). Whilst misrepresentation signifies a lack of voice in political decision-making, and is therefore a serious injustice, Fraser (2005, p. 77) argues that misframing is the most severe form of injustice and "a kind of 'political death'" as one is excluded from claims for justice in all three dimensions, economic, cultural and political.

In relation to RPL, political questions can be asked about who decides on — and how decisions are made — in relation to aspects such as the source and framing of knowledge and skills acquired outside of formal education, and related assessment methods and criteria; the provision of information and advising services to RPL applicants in their languages of choice; the selection, training and quality assurance of RPL practitioners and assessors who understand the paradox of misrepresentation and misframing within the complex transformations taking place in curriculum and qualification design (including textbooks, online resources, study guides, etc.) in South Africa, and so on. These questions take on particular salience for many South African students whose prior and experiential learning has been forged in the struggle for sustainable livelihoods in contexts and conditions far removed from those associated with formal education and related labour markets.

Affirmative and transformative approaches

For each dimension, Fraser distinguishes between affirmative and transformative approaches for dealing with issues of injustice. She views affirmative approaches as ameliorative (Bozalek & Carolissen, 2012; Hodgkinson-Williams & Trotter, 2018). While they may correct inequities created by social arrangements (e.g., pedagogies), they do not disturb the underlying social structures that generate group inequities (e.g., entrenched Western knowledges) (Fraser, 2005). This approach may have the "perverse effect of promoting [group] differentiation" (Fraser, 2008, p. 33). Transformative approaches, on the other hand, acknowledge the legitimacy of other social structures and seek to blur differences (e.g., between different knowledge systems and their underlying epistemological assumptions), and therefore address the underlying root causes or generative framework (Fraser, 2008). From a social justice perspective, it is important, as Ralphs (2012, p. 76) suggests, to heed the caution of RPL scholars such as Michelson and Harris who argue "that RPL is not by definition a radical or transformative practice and cannot be easily separated from conservative conventions that are set up to monitor compliance with national standards and registered qualifications". In other words, RPL can even be a regressive practice if it upholds an unjust status quo.

Methodology

This small-scale qualitative study (Maxwell, 2009) was one of 16 commissioned by DHET to provide insights into OL practices to inform the OLPF. In order to explore RPL as a form of OL, the study initially sought to investigate RPL practices at one South African HEI which had a long and rich history in this field. However, well into the research process we were forced to rethink the focus as the original site identified refused research permission, and it shifted from a case study approach to data generation through in-depth interviews with experts (Bogner et al., 2009). Further challenges arose as ethical clearance took much longer than expected and data collection coincided with the arrival of the COVID-19 pandemic in 2020, and subsequent strict lockdowns, which made accessing participants challenging. Ultimately, to gain insight into the national RPL context, two RPL experts were interviewed. Whilst a small sample, these experts provided rich data from their wealth of experience in the field of RPL. Both are recently retired from academia, but have been involved as lecturers and adult educators in formal education, and activists in social movements and workers' organisations for decades. As activists, practitioners and scholars they have made significant contributions to RPL in the South African context through practice, research and policy development. Both are currently involved in a number of different RPL-related projects at a range of institutions and organisations including a private non-profit university, a Quality Council and a public university of technology.

Interviews were conducted via Zoom, transcribed by the researcher and a transcription company, and analysed inductively (using qualitative thematic analysis) and deductively in MSExcel. The study was also informed by national RPL policy frameworks and local research to date. Full ethical clearance was obtained from UCT's Centre for Higher Education Development (CHED) Research Ethics Committee and informed consent obtained from interviewees. Verbatim quotations from the interviewees have been used in the analysis and discussion, and pseudonyms (Intv1 and Intv2) applied. To enhance anonymity, we have referred to s/he or her/his with respect to the interviewees.

Findings and discussion

RPL in South Africa: Debates and complexities

Interviewees noted the long history of RPL in South Africa, "going back to at least WWII" (Intv1) and that it has a long – though not in every case – social justice orientation. In describing the particular challenges and complexities around conceptualising and implementing RPL in the post-apartheid era, the interviewees emphasised the importance of early debates around the nature of knowledge. As Intv2 said, these debates are key to "understanding where RPL is at in South Africa at the moment" in that:

> it was never totally appropriated by a very strong corporate or business technical orientation, but it was never fully either accepted by a ... more conventional academic culture and community.

The interviewees themselves grappled with these debates. Intv1 acknowledged that whilst drawn to more radical critiques (e.g., Michelson, 1996a, 1996b, 2004) s/he and colleagues were "influenced by the opposing argument" which is that "there are important [knowledge] boundaries that have to be crossed" (Intv1). However, s/he also understood knowledge gained outside the academy as having its own value and worth:

> people who have been active in civil society, active citizens, having to engage with policy or fight out various battles on school boards, or, in the trade unions having to engage with the economy and so on, that it exposes them to particular kinds of knowledge ... at the heart of it is an exposure to a particular kind of critical questioning and critical thinking. (Intv1)

Intv1 emphasised that this kind of active engagement means "what they're bringing is often of equal worth to what they will learn in the academy". RPL can therefore be a "disruptive principle", "offer another way of knowing and understanding", and "if one is going to take RPL seriously, then you may well have students ... bringing with them a kind of knowledge base which is critical and which is different [to academic knowledge]" (Intv2). Intv2 pointed out that this "disruptive principle" should work both ways. Inasmuch as academic knowledges should be open to being troubled and disrupted, prior and experiential knowledges should also be open to interrogation in the current context of proliferating 'fake news', conspiracy theories and so on (see Michelson, 2020, 2021). Thus, as Intv2 put it, RPL also needs to function:

> as a space for recognising what [candidates] *don't* know.... if when we enter into a space of dialogue and I hold up a mirror to you ... and the mirror I'm holding up is another knowledge source, am I enabling you to see not only what you *do* know, but also what you *don't* know? How do academic concepts and knowledge and principles ... challenge what you already know?

As the above begins to make evident, both interviewees argued that RPL is a complex process which takes different forms depending on a range of factors. Economically certain forms of RPL take more time (e.g., e-portfolio development) and therefore have a higher cost of engagement on the part of both the aspiring student and the RPL practitioner. Culturally, the experiential knowledge and skills being presented by the RPL candidate need to be interpreted by the RPL practitioner and both may not fully understand how this prior experience maps onto disciplinary norms. Politically, the power dynamics can be complicated as the candidate's voice might hold little power and the RPL practitioner may have, at the same time, both the power and limited knowledge of RPL so the student may not receive a fair hearing. Complexities such as these highlight the importance of an expansive understanding of RPL as a form of pedagogy which offers opportunities for mediating between different kinds of knowledge, and critiquing knowledge wherever it is generated. This understanding of RPL means that whilst versions of RPL such as for credit and tests for access do have a role to play, they cannot alone capture the range and complexity of prior knowledges as "there's a whole lot of knowledge that cannot be substantially captured in ... the form of a unit standard or a standards-based qualification system and qualifications framework" (Intv2).

The OLPF in its current form tends to focus on RPL for access to PSET through awarding credits, which does a disservice to this broader and more expansive understanding of RPL as a pedagogical device. Understood as a pedagogy, RPL can (1) promote access through assisting candidates in crossing knowledge boundaries; (2) promote reflection on different knowledges by the RPL practitioner; and (3) promote access and success for all students through being drawn on "in-curriculum" by academics (Breire, 2005; Ralphs, 2012), i.e., integrated into formal teaching spaces, "allowing it to do some *work* in there, and the work ... is to offer another way of knowing and understanding" (Intv2).

Challenges and barriers to RPL in the PSET sector

Interviewees noted a number of challenges and barriers to the success of RPL in the PSET sector. Three of particular concern are highlighted here: (1) challenges around institutional RPL policy development and implementation; (2) resourcing challenges; and (3) quality assurance. These are issues previously raised by Joe Samuels (then CEO of SAQA) who noted that "large scale implementation of RPL in South Africa is hampered by a number of barriers relating to the delivery, quality assurance and resourcing of RPL" (SAQA, 2019, p. 3).

Institutional policy development and implementation

Both interviewees were concerned by the lack of actual implementation of over two decades of RPL-related policy and initiatives: "a lot of the policies do lip service to the importance of RPL but it's low down on DHET's priorities" (Intv1). They noted that whilst some institutions have good policies, and there are pockets of good practice, more can be done as progressive policy does not necessarily translate into progressive practice. Referring to one public HEI, Intv1 argued that:

> [University X's] RPL policy remains one of the most progressive RPL policies of a higher education institution in the country, except that it's hardly ever been implemented. So you've got this beautiful policy, but very little implementation. ... It's been very weakly supported over the last few years.

On the other hand, Intv2 foregrounded some of the changes that have taken place. For example, s/he argued that implementation in HEIs was given a boost after the CHE published its first RPL policy in 2016. Further, the recent report on flexible learning pathways (Bolton, et al., 2020) provides evidence of slow but growing implementation of RPL at HEIs in SA, albeit more so in private providers than public institutions.

Considered from the cultural and political dimensions, a further important aspect of implementation is the training of RPL candidates and professional development of RPL practitioners. On the one hand, aspirant students need training in how to prepare well-formulated and substantiated claims for RPL, whatever form it takes. On the other hand, RPL practitioners (e.g., RPL specialists and academics) should receive professional development and support in how to thoroughly and efficiently undertake RPL processes, which often involve complex knowledge claims.

Resourcing challenges

Both interviewees emphasised that policy alone is not enough, and that more resources are needed for RPL implementation and monitoring at PSET institutions. As Intv2 put it, the lack of sufficient resources "is the key to a limited expansion of RPL programmes and services at publicly funded Colleges and HEIs in South Africa". S/he argued further that:

> if you don't have the resources for this work, if you don't have dedicated personnel for this work, then it is not going to be done ... certainly not on any kind of scale. It'll always just be ... an afterthought. And probably will be done badly. (Intv2)

The lack of sufficient resources came through as perhaps the most severe barrier to implementing RPL. Interviewees noted that recent research (e.g., CHE, 2017; Cooper & Ralphs, 2016; SAQA, 2020) and their own practice has shown them that academics are, somewhat surprisingly given resource constraints, generally quite open and supportive of RPL practices, and that whilst there is some political resistance, "it's actually probably quite small, and I think it's even smaller or weaker as time has gone on" (Intv1). Viewed through the lens of participatory parity, culturally and politically RPL has good and even growing support (e.g., Bolton et al., 2020), but implementation and expansion of RPL within and beyond institutions is hampered by ongoing resource-related economic constraints.

The interviewees asserted that although a specialised and niche offering, RPL is a valuable and necessary part of an inclusive open learning system and must be prioritised; this means providing adequate resources, because, as Intv1 put it:

> to do justice to people's prior knowledge, experiential knowledge, it's really quite time consuming ... people are so overstretched at the best of times that ... it doesn't get done, just because people don't have the time or the resources.

Thus, s/he argued, DHET needs to allocate more funding for RPL, and s/he was hopeful that including RPL in the OLPF might facilitate this:

> we've repeatedly said ... that DHET has to actually allocate [a] budget to do this work and until it does it's unlikely to be taken up in any widespread way. And maybe nesting it within an open learning frame would possibly ... allow it to get some resources that it can't get on its own. (Intv1)

Here Intv1 raises a potential economic opportunity of conceiving of RPL as a form of OL as her/his perception is that there may be an earmarked funding stream for OL initiatives where there are not directly for RPL practices. However, given the OLPF's ambition of "cost-effectiveness of provision" (DHET, 2017, p. 391), it is worth raising a caution: including RPL in OL is not likely to lead to lower costs. In fact, as Intv2 emphasised, more funding is needed, not less, "to support the development and provision of quality RPL programmes and services, particularly in public institutions." S/he argued this is "absolutely ... bottom line" as "relying on fees, or relying on the generosity of the executive that happens to be in office at the time, is just too fragile" (Invt2).

Monitoring, evaluation and quality assurance

Related to resourcing is quality assurance (QA) which was seen as another significant issue by both interviewees. QA features heavily in the OLPF (DHET, 2017), including as one of the principles in the definition ("the maintenance of rigorous quality assurance over the design of learning materials and support systems" [p. 371]) and as part of the purpose (i.e., to steer "the PSET system towards increasing access and quality ... through appropriate monitoring, evaluation and quality assurance" [p. 368]).

The interviewees contended that QA is an ongoing challenge and that rigorous QA procedures and processes need to be implemented and monitored by the QCs and PSET institutions. Intv1 noted that QA can be tricky to measure in the short term as:

> ultimately the quality assurance of RPL ... and maybe open learning in general ... can only be established ... at the *end* of a person's studies. So, if you've let them in, you won't know really whether it was the right thing to do until they graduate ... The RPL process is crucial at the beginning, but the test of its validity is actually at the end of that person's immediate studies. (Intv1)

However, Intv2 disputed this, arguing that many variables, not necessarily RPL-related, will impact an RPL student's progress through their studies. Instead, one approach s/he had used was to benchmark the progress of RPL students in their first semester exams against those of the young students who came straight from school and gained admission on the basis of their matric results. Overall though, both agreed that QA needs more government funding: "if government were funding it, if there was a way to find... funding, almost certainly what would come with it would be a proper quality assurance" (Intv2).

Finally, an important challenge with monitoring and evaluating RPL is that the current RPL data are combined with CAT and other alternative pathways and so, whilst "it is clear that considerable RPL is taking place in public HEIs", it is impossible to monitor RPL uptake at a national level (Bolton et al., 2020, p. 75).

As the above has shown, whilst the economic, cultural and political challenges and barriers to RPL in the PSET sector are varied, more funding is seen as key to addressing these issues, whether they are related to institutional policy development and implementation, training and development, RPL implementation and expansion, or monitoring, evaluation and QA. This raises questions about the OLPF's focus on cost-efficiency through economies of scale. Although the OLPF (DHET, 2017, p. 374) acknowledges that OL may mean "considerably higher levels of initial expenditure than more traditional approaches," it also envisages that expenditure "may diminish over time as economies of scale" (DHET, 2017, p. 374) come into effect. However, as the interviewees noted time and again, RPL does not scale easily; economic support is central to the success of RPL, and additional and ongoing funding, not less, is needed to implement RPL.

RPL and 'optimal inclusion'

Optimal inclusion is an important concept in thinking about RPL as a form of open learning. The term was first used by Harris (2000, 2013) with reference to the 'Trojan Horse' form of RPL described above (see Table 1) and later extended by Cooper and Ralphs (2016) to all forms of RPL. The interviewees in this study described optimal inclusion as both "a principle as well as an ideal" (Intv2) which acknowledges "that inclusion is not easy" (Intv1) and that RPL processes are complex for candidates and staff alike. In thinking about promoting access, optimal inclusion recognises that candidates may have "unconventional knowledge" and "unconventional ways of speaking, learning and engaging" (Intv2) and may therefore need "a special kind of support" (Intv1) to help them cross the boundaries from informal learning to formal academic spaces; to help them to:

> interpret, to reinterpret their knowledge in another context, understand who they're speaking to, appreciate what it is that they bring in that will be recognised and be seen as significant or not. (Intv1)

Optimal inclusion is also an acknowledgement that in many cases candidates need to be redirected to alternative career or study paths. As Intv2 said, RPL can be "a very, very powerful programme for redirecting" candidates unlikely to succeed at university or college, whose knowledge, skills and aspirations are not an optimal fit and might be better suited to alternative educational spaces or career paths. For example, based on her/his experience running an established undergraduate RPL programme, s/he noted that only about 10% of applicants who expressed interest in the programme were successful, and that "the vast majority of people didn't get in" after going through the information and advising services offered. S/he explained that the link between access and success is central to the notion of optimal inclusion and that a large part of her/his team's role was redirecting people who applied "on the basis of a dream or hope or a wish but who didn't necessarily have the literacies or didn't have the prior formal foundations for their knowledge to be able to succeed" (Intv2).

Given this need to counsel and redirect candidates, the interviewees underscored that as much as RPL should open access, at the same time it must do so for people who have a reasonable chance of succeeding. That is, RPL needs to be "inclusionary, but on the basis of some kind of clear understanding that this person is likely to succeed. And that requires quite careful investigation" (Intv1). The phrase, "careful investigation" alerts one to the cultural and political dimensions of whose knowledge is being valorised and against what standard. Therefore, as Intv2 argued, RPL cannot be understood or practiced as a "mass-based system" relying on tests and credit for access. S/he added that most adults wanting formal qualifications will go through "more conventional pathways" (Intv2) and RPL as a niche offering is:

> just one of the important vehicles or tools in helping to ensure that our systems, institutions and learning pathways remain open and inclusive of those who have not followed the conventional routes to a qualification, [thereby contributing to] building an inclusive education and training system. (Intv2)

Additionally, many other spaces and processes need to be 'optimised' to assist candidates with translating culturally acquired knowledge from one context to another; optimal inclusion therefore includes:

> optimising the curriculum spaces, the alternative access routes, optimising the knowledge and learning of the learner ... In my mind [there is] absolutely no doubt that ... building a more optimally inclusive programme is about building all the programmes and services, not just the assessment practices that are limited. (Intv2)

RPL as 'optimal inclusion' complicates any simple notion of opening "access to education and training opportunities for *all*" (DHET, 2017, p. 367, emphasis added) and is better understood as a strategy, as described elsewhere in the OLPF, to "give learners a fair chance of success" (DHET, 2017, p. 386) or to offer them a "reasonable chance of success" (DHET, 2017, p. 380). It also requires vigilance on the part of the RPL practitioner to ensure that the RPL candidate has had a fair hearing.

Viewed through the lens of participatory parity, optimally inclusive RPL offers the potential for fostering recognition and redistribution and representation / reframing. Culturally, optimal inclusion seeks to avoid the injustice of misrecognition through emphasising that access should be provided appropriately, to candidates who have the ability to succeed, who are able to participate on a par with their peers in HE. It also acknowledges that candidates' diverse prior knowledges may not be easily transferable between contexts, and therefore advocates RPL as a pedagogical practice aimed at supporting students and academics in navigating differences between and across knowledge boundaries. Economically, and pedagogically, optimal inclusion acknowledges that RPL is aligned with the provision of holistic services including career counselling and advice around study options, both within an institution and in the PSET system as a whole, which requires skilled and experienced staff. Politically, optimal inclusion does not stop once students are accepted into the institution via an RPL process. Academic staff may be challenged to reframe curricula to include and engage with other knowledge systems and acknowledge their contribution (an issue widely discussed and debated, particularly since the 2015/2016 #Fallist[15] protests, by scholars and students seeking to 'decolonise the curriculum'). Students too may need to work at engaging with, integrating – and challenging – their prior knowledge in relation to other knowledge systems as well as a range of pedagogies.

Recommendations: What is needed for successful and socially just RPL in South Africa?

The interviewees made a number of recommendations for RPL as part of an OL system, grouped into five sections below: first, an understanding that RPL is not "one size fits all" (Intv1) and needs will vary across different contexts; second, that candidates and students need a range of support services; third, that academic staff and RPL practitioners need training and support; fourth, that tracking, monitoring and further research is needed; and fifth, that funding is needed to support all of this.

RPL is not 'one size fits all'

The interviewees emphasised that RPL is "not one size fits all" (Intv1), and that different institutions and programmes will require different RPL interventions. When conceptualising and designing RPL initiatives, therefore, a range of factors need to be considered, including the institutional context; disciplinary and course requirements; candidates' contexts of prior learning, to get "a firm grip on who would be the constituency from which they would draw" (Intv1); the tools candidates will need in traversing knowledge terrains; and the tools needed by academics and lecturers "to engage with these forms of knowledge" (Intv2). Given these complexities, RPL practitioners need resources – dedicated funding and time – to go into specific sites and map what RPL looks like in those sites as "we can't actually talk about specialised experiential knowledge in general terms, we've got to actually go into specific sites and map it, map what it looks like" (Intv1).

RPL, they argued, as an OL practice, should therefore be approached holistically and viewed as a process rather than event:

> it really is a process, and we've defined it very strongly as a process. And in that sense ... I think in many ways it does meet a lot of those principles that you see written into the approach around open learning. (Intv2)

---

[15] The #Fallist movement encompasses #FeesMustFall, #RhodesMustFall, #OpenStellenbosch and other student protests against classism, racism, hetero/sexism, patriarchy, ableism, language injustices, and other forms of oppression and prejudice, and advocates for free and decolonised education for all (Chinguno et al., 2018; Langa, 2017).

As Intv2 said, the OL principles do speak to the idea of RPL (and other OL practices) as a process. However, in also emphasising cost-efficiency and RPL for credit, the OLPF may contradict this more expansive understanding of RPL. RPL for credit is often understood in a technicist and instrumentalist (i.e. Procrustean) way as a form of credit exchange. This would not promote cultural and political parity. A more expansive understanding of RPL (i.e. Radical and Trojan horse) as part of pedagogical processes and practices would be more consistent with Fraser's transformative approach to participatory parity, i.e., offering RPL candidates equal opportunities to participate as peers with those with formal educational qualifications.

Candidate and student support

The interviewees argued that RPL as OL should offer candidates a range of supportive and developmental services before, during and after the RPL process. First, when considering and on applying for RPL, candidates should be offered career, study and other information and advisory services. These could be provided through a regional or national office and would cover, for example, RPL options, what a return to formal education entails, provide information about educational institutions and the wider PSET sector, and advise on the varied education and training opportunities in different PSET institutions. As Intv1 pointed out, to simply "open learning and then [expect] people must find their way now through a much bigger, more complex terrain" is a big ask and unjust. The interviewees noted that the recent DHET Draft *National Policy on Students and Community Support Services for Community Education and Training Colleges* (DHET, 2020) provides a good example of a government policy taking education, employment and career guidance seriously' for people entering formal education.

During the RPL process, candidates need support and scaffolding in connecting and translating everyday, informal and experiential knowledges to academic knowledge; in other words, an approach that recognises RPL as a form of pedagogy. The OLPF, in its "learner-centred orientation" (Intv2), must therefore "[hold] the knowledge question very seriously" (Intv2) which places "a limit on … open learning … as open access." Intv2 emphasised that RPL reduced to tests and assessments without supportive interventions is "a blunt instrument", "a joke" and "a very dangerous thing":

> All that you're going to have, is you are going to be taking people's money to write that exam. And we are going to have to charge them. It is going to be a mass failure mechanism. … It's nothing more, in my view, than establishing … deficits and taking money. It's a money-making activity. And it would be appalling.

Finally, for those accepted via RPL, "the question of what comes after the access is really important" (Intv1). A range of factors need to be considered including academic support, the in- or exclusive nature of institutional cultures, and psycho-social support services. These kinds of support services are in fact necessary for all students to be able to participate as equals with their peers, not just those considered 'non traditional' (February, 2017). Additionally, a truly open learning system should value and draw on students' prior and experiential knowledges "to actually recognise their knowledge as part of the curriculum ... so that it's not just about what [students] lack, it's about what they're bringing" (Intv1).

As Intv1 said, these are "big issue[s] for open learning ... what are all the other things that it brings in with it?" Again, this applies to all students, not just those coming in via RPL.

The forms of candidate and student support recommended by the interviewees offer a number of suggestions for promoting participatory parity. First, in terms of prior advisory services, a formal regional or national advisory service would boost cultural parity and further, it would do this for all RPL candidates, not just those who manage to access a supportive lecturer or administrator. In other words, rather than offering individualised and affirmative interventions, this could offer transformative recognition, or re-acculturation (Hodgkinson-Williams & Trotter, 2018), addressing the root causes of injustice that unfairly exclude some people from formal qualifications through changing the way the system works. An advisory service, though, will require initial and ongoing investment of resources, although the ongoing need for resources may decrease over time.

Staff / practitioner support and development

Another important consideration for successful RPL is the role and experience of RPL practitioners and specialists. Interviewees reiterated the argument in Cooper and Ralphs (2016) that RPL requires an 'artistry of practice' which involves a 'complex choreography', terminology which alludes to:

> the dance between people's experience and ... formal bodies of knowledge that they're going to have to engage with once they're in the academy [and] knowing how to move between those two. And all of that together making up quite a specialised kind of pedagogy ... intimately familiar with your learner's background but also intimately familiar with what they're going into. (Intv1)

Because of this, "there's no way you could really prescribe how to do RPL", each RPL practitioner "need[s] to learn it, learn how to do it in practice and that it might well have to be adapted to different groupings that they work with" (Intv1). RPL therefore requires skill, time, experience (which, as Intv2 noted, often includes 'real world' work experience, social activism, and/or formal teaching experience), and an understanding of the epistemological complexities and challenges involved. This would apply to all forms of RPL, including RPL for credit, as whatever the means of assessment, academic knowledge and prior knowledges need be held in relation with one another, and students need opportunities to engage with — and/or disrupt — both.

Finally, RPL should provide a dedicated career pathway for academics. It should be considered a valuable "specialisation within the broader and administrative systems of the institutions" (Intv2) and supported through more offerings of customised and context-appropriate training and development. This would promote practitioners' professional credibility in their institutions:

> Because unless [the RPL practitioner/specialist has] that level of understanding about the way in which knowledge is constructed and crafted into curriculum, you don't even get in the door with the academics and it will be perceived to be a second-rate option. (Intv2)

Again, this highlights the need for sufficient resources to be channelled to RPL as well as emphasising that RPL needs to be recognised as a valuable and necessary part of the academic project.

Tracking, monitoring and research

The interviewees also mentioned that institutions need to do more tracking and monitoring of RPL candidates, and that they should — but often do not — have good record keeping systems. Intv1 said that as a first step, "all it needs is a tick box" for RPL candidates when applying to an institution. In her/his experience, this is an easy but neglected step in tracking and tracing RPL students:

> [University X] has had an unpredictable history of recording who's come in via RPL ... technically, you should be able to go in and see who came in via RPL, how many years did they take to finish, did they finish, and how does that compare with the norm. ... But to get that to work you've got to have proper record keeping, and because [many] institutions have not put the resources into developing their record systems, we can't easily do that work.

Linked to this, Intv2 strongly recommended that current RPL research be extended and saw value in exploring and mapping RPL as an OL practice:

> so that we can follow, and we can map out ... how effective is [RPL] in opening up, in creating that kind of flexibility, both within the curriculum as well as with the questions of access and removing barriers. Which are critical to the discourse of open learning as well.

As Intv1 said that "our sense is that, if anything, RPL students have done better than other students partly because it's been a very rigorous process of letting them in".

As the above demonstrates, tracking and monitoring can start with a simple tick-box on an application form. However, a more thorough integration of RPL records and reports into effective data management systems, training staff in using these systems, etc., is likely to be resource-intensive in terms of time and money. Research can also be resource-intensive, but, as part of an OL system in which there is perhaps an RPL department with dedicated academic staff, research would be incorporated into day-to-day RPL processes. Another way of keeping costs low and potentially boosting participatory parity amongst students is to integrate research into courses. For example, senior undergraduate and postgraduate students could be recruited as part of their studies to contribute to RPL research, which might be based on their own life experiences (see e.g., Gredley, 2020; Ngabaza et al., 2015, 2018; Shefer et al., 2020) thereby potentially boosting cultural and representational parity in HEIs for these students.

Funding

Finally, and as the above recommendations make clear, the interviewees see funding as crucial – and perhaps the most important, overarching consideration – in supporting and promoting RPL. They hoped that by linking RPL to OL it may gain these much-needed resources:

> the issue of resources is really essential. ... I made the point that ... maybe RPL on its own is not going to win that battle, but maybe by linking RPL to some kind of broader project-, and that's why I think the open learning one is an exciting one, it could address that. (Intv1)

For RPL to access more resources, Intv2 argued, publicly funded colleges and universities will require more support from government, from the QCs, but especially from DHET: "the driver and then funder of most of this".

Conclusion

As the findings and discussion above show, RPL as a form of OL has enormous potential to offer more socially just educational practices, if sufficient national and institutional funding is provided for proper implementation. Economically, from a student's perspective RPL can build on and optimise previous investment in hard-won experience, self-study and fee-based courses by allowing students to apply for access or for credit. Apart from the time taken to prepare a portfolio as part of a workshop programme, or complete RPL for credit documentation, the actual cost to the student is relatively low. However, from the national and institutional perspective, RPL needs on-going funding for the development of institutional RPL policies, the training of RPL candidates, professional development of RPL specialists, assessment of portfolios or evaluation of prior informal courses, curation of RPL data, reporting of data at a national level, monitoring, evaluation and overall quality assurance. In addition, RPL is not easily scalable as it is so person-specific, but cost efficiencies could be gained by refining the implementation workflow.

Culturally, from a student's perspective, RPL can offer opportunities for recognising and possibly accrediting different knowledge traditions or perspectives, and offer access to formal education for those not from the traditional cohort of students. Depending on the extent to which students' diverse knowledges are recognised and valorised, RPL may take some strides towards a more transformative approach. However, this is dependent on the extent to which RPL is undertaken as an approach seeking 'optimal inclusion', i.e., one which responsibly and appropriately promotes access for candidates on the one hand (e.g., recognising candidates' knowledges or redirecting them to alternate career paths when necessary), as well as considering ways in which lecturers incorporate and engage with different knowledge systems and inclusive pedagogies in-curriculum. Specialised RPL can make a significant difference in the lives of mature learners, but in order to do so it needs to be thought of as much more than simply a system of testing or credit for access.

From a political perspective, RPL raises a number of questions about who the standard-setters are and what standards RPL candidates are being measured against. It calls for a level of openness, transparency and responsiveness from the national bodies and education institutions, including sound mechanisms for awarding credit for courses assessed and accredited from other national *and* international institutions or organisations.

One of the advantages in considering RPL as a form of OL is that, as a long-established approach, attitudes towards RPL are already relatively open; in other words, it has cultural recognition, by government, in some institutional spaces, and amongst a growing number of academics. What this also means, though, is that giving RPL a label of "OL" will not on its own make it more successful. In fact, RPL policies (see Table 2) are already well formulated and appear to be strong. In other words, RPL does not need additional policy making; what it needs, as interviewees repeatedly argued, is more, dedicated resources, including dedicated practitioners at institutions and a commitment from government bodies to make this work. Future implementation and research activities in this regard could include better support for RPL candidates before entry and during their studies (e.g., candidates may need help in accessing and using digital technologies), and improved identification, reporting and tracking of RPL candidates not just on entry, but on-course and upon exit.

Acknowledgements

Many thanks to the two RPL experts who shared their time and expertise regarding RPL in South Africa. Special thanks are due to reviewers Lunga Mantashe and Dr Anthea Jacobs for their thoughtful, incisive feedback on the chapter, Associate Professor Janice McMillan for additional mentoring support, Barbara Jones for constructive engagement, and Dr Tabisa Mayisela for guiding the entire COOL project. Thanks are also due to the Centre for Innovation in Learning and Teaching at the University of Cape Town, which hosted the COOL project, and the South African Department of Higher Education and Training for funding it.

References

Andersson, P., Fejes, A., & Sandberg, F. (2013). Introducing research on recognition of prior learning. *International Journal of Lifelong Education*, 32(4), 405–411.

Bogner, A., Littig, B., & Menz, W. (2009). Introduction: Expert interviews – an introduction to a new methodological debate. In A. Bogner, B. Littig & W. Menz (Eds.), *Interviewing experts* (pp. 1–13). Palgrave Macmillan.

Bolton, H., Matsau, L., & Blom, R. (2020). *Report for the IIEP-UNESCO Research "SDG4: Planning for flexible learning pathways in higher education."* South African Qualifications Authority (SAQA). https://www.saqa.org.za/sites/default/files/2020-12/Flexible-Learning-Pathways-in-SA-2020-12.pdf

Bolton, H., Samuels, J., Mofokeng, T., Akindolani, O., & Shapiro, Y. (2016). *Lifelong learning at the centre: The National Recognition of Prior Learning (RPL) system in South Africa*. South African Qualifications Authority (SAQA). http://www.saqa.org.za/docs/papers/2017/Lifelong%20Learning%20at%20the%20Centre%20%20the%20National%20Recognition%20of%20Prior%20Learning%20(RPL)%20system%20in%20South%20Africa.pdf

Botha, N. (2009). Some current curriculum issues in South African higher education. In E. Bitzer (Ed.), *Higher education in South Africa: A scholarly look behind the scenes* (pp. 155–182). African Sun Media.

Bozalek, V. (2017). Participatory parity and emerging technologies. In M. Walker & M. Wilson-Strydom (Eds.), *Socially just pedagogies, capabilities and quality in higher education: Global perspectives* (pp. 89–107). Palgrave Macmillan.

Bozalek, V., & Carolissen, R. (2012). The potential of critical feminist citizenship frameworks for citizenship and social justice in higher education. *Perspectives in Education*, 30(4), 9–18.

Breier, M. (2005). A disciplinary-specific approach to the recognition of prior informal experience in adult pedagogy: 'rpl' as opposed to 'RPL'. *Studies in Continuing Education.* https://www.tandfonline.com/doi/abs/10.1080/01580370500056448

Brenner, A., Goodman, S., Meadows, A., & Cooper, L. (2021). From prior learning assessment to specialised pedagogy: Facilitating student transition through RPL assessment and selection. *Studies in Continuing Education*, 1–16. https://doi.org/10.1080/0158037x.2021.1874333

CHE (Council on Higher Education). (2016). *Policies on recognition of prior learning, credit accumulation and transfer, and assessment in higher education.* Council on Higher Education.

Chinguno, C., Kgoroba, M., Mashibini, S., Masilela, B. N., Maubane, B., Moyo, N., Mthombeni, A., & Ndlovu, H. (Eds.). (2018). *Rioting and writing: Diaries of Wits Fallists.* Society, Work and Development Institute (SWOP) Institute, University of the Witwatersrand. https://www.swop.org.za/single-post/2018/07/04/FeesMustFall-Book-Rioting-and-Writing-now-Available-for-Free-Download

Cooper, L. (1998). From 'rolling mass action" to 'RPL': the changing discourse of experience and learning in the South African labour movement. *Studies in Continuing Education*, 20(2), 143–157. https://doi.org/10.1080/0158037980200203

Cooper, L. (2016). Conceptual starting points. In L. Cooper & A. Ralphs (Eds.), *RPL as specialised pedagogy: Crossing the lines* (pp. 23–30). HSRC Press. http://saqa.org.za/docs/webcontent/2018/RPL_as_Specialised_Pedagogy_-_Full_Book.pdf

Cooper, L., & Harris, J. (2013). Recognition of prior learning: exploring the 'knowledge question'. *International Journal of Lifelong Education*, 32(4), 447–463. https://doi.org/10.1080/02601370.2013.778072

Cooper, L., & Ralphs, A. (Eds.). (2016). *RPL as specialised pedagogy: Crossing the lines.* HSRC Press. https://www.hsrcpress.ac.za/books/rpl-as-specialised-pedagogy

Cooper, L., Ralphs, A., & Harris, J. (2017). Recognition of prior learning: The tensions between its inclusive intentions and constraints on its implementation. *Studies in Continuing Education*, 39(2), 197–213. https://doi.org/10.1080/0158037X.2016.1273893

DALS (Department of Applied Legal Studies). (2019). Recognition of prior learning for community-based paralegals. Cape Peninsula University of Technology. http://digitalknowledge.cput.ac.za/handle/11189/7231

DHET (Department of Higher Education and Training). (2013). White paper for post-school education and training: Building an expanded, effective and integrated post-school system. *Government Gazette*, 37229. https://www.gov.za/documents/white-paper-post-school-education-and-training-building-expanded-effective-and-integrated

DHET. (2016). Recognition of prior learning (RPL) coordination policy. *Government Gazette*, 609. http://www.dhet.gov.za/System%20Planning%20and%20Monitoring%20Policies/Recognition%20of%20Prio%20Learning%20RPL%20coordination%20Policy.pdf

DHET. (2017). Call for comments on the open learning policy framework for post-school education and training. *Government Gazette*, 40772. http://pmg-assets.s3-website-eu-west-1.amazonaws.com/170407openlearningframework-postschooleduc.pdf

DHET. (2018). Statistics on post-school education and training in South Africa: 2016. http://www.dhet.gov.za/Research%20Coordination%20Monitoring%20and%20Evaluation/6_DHET%20Stats%20Report_04%20April%202018.pdf

DHET. (2020). Draft national policy on students and community support services for Community Education and Training Colleges. https://www.dhet.gov.za/GETCA%20Draft%20Curriculum%20Statements/draft%20national%20policy%20students%20and%20community%20support%20services%20for%20cet%20colleges%20for%20public%20comments.pdf

February, C. (2016). Re-imagining 'nontraditional' student constructs in higher education: A case study of one South African university [Doctoral dissertation, University of the Western Cape].

Fraser, N. (2005). Reframing justice in a globalizing world. *New Left Review*, 36, 69–88. https://newleftreview.org/II/36/nancy-fraser-reframing-justice-in-a-globalizing-world

Fraser, N. (2008). From redistribution to recognition? Dilemmas of justice in a 'post-socialist' age. In K. Olson (Ed.), *Adding insult to injury: Nancy Fraser debates her critics* (pp. 11–41). Verso.

Fraser, N., & Honneth, A. (2003). *Redistribution or recognition? A political-philosophical exchange*. Verso.

Gredley, S. (2020). "When it rains [our house] rains too": Exploring South African students' narratives of maldistribution. In V. Bozalek, D. Hölscher & M. Zembylas (Eds.), *Nancy Fraser and participatory parity: Reframing social justice in South African higher education* (pp. 94–110). Routledge.

Harris, J. (1999). Ways of seeing the Recognition of Prior Learning (RPL): What contribution can such practices make to social inclusion? *Studies in the Education of Adults*, 31(2), 124–139.

Harris, J. (2000). *RPL: Power Pedagogy and Possibility: Conceptual and implementation guides*. The Human Sciences Research Council (HSRC). https://www.hsrcpress.ac.za/books/rpl-power-pedagogy-and-possibility

Harris, J. A. (2013). Ways of Seeing the Recognition of Prior Learning (RPL): What Contribution Can Such Practices Make to Social Inclusion? *PLA Inside Out: An International Journal on Theory, Research and Practice in Prior Learning Assessment*, 2(1). https://www.plaio.org/index.php/home/article/view/56

Hodgkinson-Williams, C. A., & Trotter, H. (2018). A social justice framework for understanding Open Educational Resources and Practices in the Global South. *Journal of Learning for Development*, 5(3). https://jl4d.org/index.php/ejl4d/article/view/312

Jacobs, A. H. M. (2018). Values, institutional culture and recognition of prior learning. *South African Journal of Higher Education*, 32(4), 96–108.

Kistan, C. (2002). Recognition of prior learning: a challenge to higher education. *South African Journal of Higher Education*, 16(1), 169–173.

Kizito, R. (2006). The future is not so bleak: Challenges with recognition of prior learning (RPL) systems and processes at Unisa. *Progressio*, 28(1–2), 127–139. https://uir.unisa.ac.za/bitstream/handle/10500/5039/RPL.pdf

Langa, M. (Ed.). (2017). *#Hashtag: An analysis of the #FeesMustFall movement at South African universities*. Centre for the Study of Violence and Reconciliation. http://www.csvr.org.za/pdf/An-analysis-of-the-FeesMustFall-Movement-at-South-African-universities.pdf

Mantashe, L. X., & Nkonki, V. (2019). Recognition of prior learning: A critique of Council on Higher Education policy provisions. *Critical Studies in Teaching and Learning (CriSTaL)*, 7(2), 34–51.

Maxwell, J. A. (2009). Designing a qualitative study. In L. Bickman & D. J. Rog (Eds.), *The Sage Handbook of applied social research methods* (pp. 214–253). Sage.

Michelson, E. (1996a). 'Auctoritee' and 'experience': Feminist epistemology and the assessment of experiential learning. *Feminist Studies: FS*, 22(3), 627–655. www.jstor.org/stable/3178133

Michelson, E. (1996b). Usual suspects: Experience, reflection and the (en) gendering of knowledge. *International Journal of Lifelong Education*, 15(6), 438–454. https://doi.org/10.1080/0260137960150604

Michelson, E. (1997). Multicultural approaches to portfolio development. *New Directions for Adult and Continuing Education*, 1997(75), 41–53. https://doi.org/10.1002/ace.7504

Michelson, E. (2004). On trust, desire and the sacred: A response to Johann Muller's "Reclaiming Knowledge." *Journal of Education*, 32, 7–30.

Michelson, E. (2014). Epistemic injustice and the struggle for recognition: Human Dignity and the recognition of prior learning. In S. Vally & E. Motala (Eds.), *Education, economy & society* (pp. 213–229). Unisa Press.

Michelson, E. (2020). Truthiness, alternative facts, and experiential learning. *New Directions for Adult and Continuing Education*, 165, 103–114. https://doi.org/10.1002/ace.20371

Michelson, E. (2021). Last thoughts on 'The Ethical Knower: Rethinking Our Pedagogy in the Age of Trump'. *Adult Education Quarterly*, 71(1), 90–97. https://doi.org/10.1177/0741713620968075

Morrow, W. (2007). *Learning to teach in South Africa*. HSRC Press. https://www.hsrcpress.ac.za/books/learning-to-teach-in-south-africa

Morrow, W. (2010). *Bounds of democracy: Epistemological access in higher education*. HSRC Press.

Muller, J. (2014). Every picture tells a story: Epistemological access and knowledge. *Education as Change*, 18(2), 255–269. https://doi.org/10.1080/16823206.2014.932256

Ngabaza, S., Bojarczuk, E., Masuku, M. P., & Roelfse, R. (2015). Empowering young people in advocacy for transformation: A photovoice exploration of safe and unsafe spaces on a university campus. *African Safety Promotion: A Journal of Injury and Violence Prevention*, 13(1), 30–48.

Ngabaza, S., Shefer, T., & Clowes, L. (2018). Students' narratives on gender and sexuality in the project of social justice and belonging in higher education. *South African Journal of Higher*, 32(3), 139–153.

Osman, R. (2003). The recognition of prior learning (RPL): An emergent field of enquiry in South Africa [Doctoral dissertation, University of the Witwatersrand]. http://wiredspace.wits.ac.za/handle/10539/23937

Ralphs, A. (2012). Exploring RPL: Assessment Device and/or Specialised Pedagogical Practice? *Journal of Education*, 53, 75–96.

Ralphs, A. (2016). Overview. In L. Cooper & A. Ralphs (Eds.), *RPL as specialised pedagogy: Crossing the lines* (pp. 1–22.). HSRC Press. http://saqa.org.za/docs/webcontent/2018/RPL_as_Specialised_Pedagogy_-_Full_Book.pdf

Ralphs, A., Prinsloo, N., & Mcube, R. (2020). The history, artistry and challenges of recognition of prior learning (RPL) for access to undergraduate study at a South African university. *The South African Qualifications Authority Bulletin*, 19(1), 23-55. https://www.saqa.org.za/news/saqa-bulletin-volume-19-number-1-march-2020?language_content_entity=en

Saidi, A. (2017). Implementation of Recognition of Prior Learning (RPL) in Higher Education. 19th Public Sector Trainers' Forum (PSTF) Conference Breakaway Session 3.1. 16 October. https://www.thensg.gov.za/wp-content/uploads/2016/10/Implementation-of-RPL-in-Higher-Education-Dr-Amani-Saidi-1.pptx

SAQA (South African Qualifications Authority). (2002). The recognition of prior learning in the context of the South African National Qualifications Framework. https://www.saqa.org.za/docs/pol/2002/rpl_sanqf.pdf

SAQA. (2019). National policy and criteria for the implementation of recognition of prior learning. SAQA. http://www.saqa.org.za/docs/pol/2019/National%20Policy%20and%20Criteria%20for%20the%20Implementation%20of%20RPL%20(Amended%20in%20March%202019).pdf

SAQA. (2020). *The South African Qualifications Authority Bulletin*, 19(1). https://www.saqa.org.za/news/saqa-bulletin-volume-19-number-1-march-2020?language_content_entity=en

Shefer, T., Clowes, L., & Ngabaza, S. (2020). Student experience A participatory parity lens on social (in)justice in higher education. In V. Bozalek, D. Hölscher, & M. Zembylas (Eds.), *Nancy Fraser and participatory parity: Reframing social justice in South African higher education* (pp. 63–76). Routledge.

Young, M. (2005). The knowledge question and the future of education in South Africa: A reply to Michelson's "On trust, desire and the sacred": A response to Johan Muller's "Reclaiming Knowledge". *Journal of Education*, 36(1), 7–18. https://journals.co.za/doi/pdf/10.10520/AJA0259479X_137.

HOW TO CITE THIS CHAPTER

Gredley, S., & Hodgkinson-Williams, C. A. (2022). Recognition of prior learning as a form of open learning in post-school education and training in South Africa: A social justice perspective. In T. Mayisela, S. C. Govender & C. A. Hodgkinson-Williams (Eds.), *Open learning as a means of advancing social justice: Cases in post-school education and training in South Africa* (pp. 16–43). African Minds. doi: 10.47622/9781928502425_1

This work is licensed under a Creative Commons Attribution 4.0 International (CC BY 4.0) licence.

2

Opening learning to students in a South African university through innovative institutional fundraising initiatives
A social justice view

Susan Gredley & Janice McMillan

SUMMARY One of the ambitions of the draft *Open Learning Policy Framework* (OLPF) is to open up learning to students burdened by financial constraints and an inability to meet the full costs of their studies. This case study sought to better understand ways in which the University of the Western Cape (UWC) opened up learning through the provision of funding for financially precarious students. The study focused on UWC's 'Access to Success' campaign which has comprised various fundraising activities including an annual phonathon, a staff pledge campaign, corporate fundraising events, and the #NoStudentWillBeLeftBehind campaign. A qualitative methodological approach was adopted, employing in-depth interviews with key stakeholders to ascertain and explore the ways in which the institution has provided opportunities for access to poor and financially precarious students. Given the OLPF's ambition to foster social justice, Nancy Fraser's (2008, 2010) framework of participatory parity was used as a lens for evaluating whether and to what extent social justice was promoted within and across three dimensions: economic, cultural and political. Findings demonstrate that a range of factors are important in considering funding for students including knowledge of institutional history, culture and context, knowledge of students' contextual challenges and needs, and the importance of supportive leadership. Through the lens of participatory parity, the study shows that UWC has had some success in opening learning to students through funding. In the economic dimension, fundraising efforts have facilitated access through supplementing fees and study expenses, providing nutrition programmes, and sourcing donations of essential goods such as toiletries. Culturally, the phonathon offered students opportunities for recognition through valuing them as important contributors to the academic project, and Access to Success projects fostered community across diverse groups on campus. Politically, the phonathon fostered representation, allowing students to contribute to debates and issues, and highlighted the importance of institutional leadership. Overall, whilst Access to Success provided important and necessary interventions, these tended to be short term and ameliorative rather than transformative measures for students and the university itself. For much needed deep and systemic change, significantly more and sustained government funding is needed.

Keywords: student funding, fundraising, open learning, social justice, university

Introduction

Legacies of colonialism and apartheid continue to plague South Africa (SA) nearly three decades into democracy. Despite early and ongoing efforts to reverse inequalities, the country is beset by endemic poverty and enduring inequalities[1], further exacerbated by the COVID-19 pandemic and associated lockdowns. As one of the world's most unequal nations (Odusola et al., 2017) over half its citizens, particularly 'black'[2] women and children, those living in rural areas, and those without formal education, live below the poverty line and struggle to access basic services and material resources necessary to flourish (DHET, 2019a; Stats SA, 2017).

Education is widely regarded as a key driver for lifting people out of poverty and enabling longer, healthier and more socially engaged lives. Recent reports posit the strong relationship between education status and poverty, arguing that the more educated one is, the more benefits will accrue both to individuals and their families as well as communities and broader society (Odusola et al., 2017; World Bank, 2018, 2019). Similarly, the SA government argues that the higher the qualification, the greater the "potential to eradicate poverty and minimise the impact of ... poverty, unemployment and inequality" (DHET, 2019a; Stats SA, 2017).

However, as the recent #Fallist[3] student movements vividly highlighted, the SA higher education (HE) system remains untransformed on many levels (CHE, 2016a, 2016b). Students entering HE continue to do so from positions of extreme inequality. Higher education institutions (HEIs) themselves remain vulnerable, especially those historically disadvantaged, with intensified pressure from government on HEIs to increase enrolment (DHET, 2019a) even as expenditure on HE remains low in global terms (CHE, 2016a). In addition, the intersections of the market and higher education cannot be ignored. A range of scholars (CHE, 2016a; Le Grange, 2020; Mbembe, 2016; Valley & Motala, 2014) argue that universities are increasingly structured by market-driven neoliberal agendas and positioned as vehicles for promoting knowledge and skills for economic growth, an approach which disregards inherent structural barriers.

As one response to these multifaceted complexities and challenges, the Department of Higher Education and Training's (DHET) draft *Open Learning Policy Framework* (OLPF) aims

---

[1] https://www.news.uct.ac.za/article/-2021-05-21-inequality-in-south-africa-is-a-ticking-timebomb

[2] Despite widespread criticism of the ongoing use of Apartheid-era racial markers they persist partly as they are seen as necessary for remedying past injustices. Whilst acknowledged as social constructs, they continue to have a profound impact on the lives, experiences, and opportunities of 'black' (broadly speaking), poor and marginalised South Africans.

[3] The #Fallist movement encompasses #FeesMustFall, #RhodesMustFall, and other student protests against classism, racism, hetero/sexism, patriarchy, ableism and other forms of oppression and prejudice, and which advocate for free and decolonised education for all (Chinguno et al., 2018; Langa, 2017).

to support post-school education and training (PSET) institutions in "widening access to affordable, quality learning opportunities" (DHET, 2017, p. 366), and addressing financial barriers, for example through reviewing National Student Financial Aid Scheme (NSFAS) funding "to facilitate the appropriate support of learners" (DHET, 2017, p. 411).

This 'Access to Success' case study is one of 16 commissioned by DHET to explore various ways for opening learning. Through a small-scale qualitative approach, the study explores the funding of continuing students as one way of opening learning at the University of the Western Cape (UWC), a contact teaching university. Over and above NSFAS funding, UWC has embarked on a fundraising campaign – Access to Success[4] – to help fund financially precarious students. This study primarily focused on one aspect of this campaign, an innovative phonathon in which student callers reached out to alumni. Given the OLPF's ambition to reduce inequities and foster social justice, Nancy Fraser's (2008, 2010) concept of 'parity of participation' was used to explore and evaluate the phonathon and the extent to which it addressed underlying economic, cultural and political injustices faced by students. The study found that the phonathon had an impact and benefits beyond fundraising but raises concerns around the funding of HEIs and the impact that one institution can have in a resource constrained context such as SA.

Open learning and funding in SA HE

Promoting HE access and success post-1994

Post-1994, the SA government enshrined the right of access to further education in the Constitution[5], with the promise that it would be made "progressively available and accessible" (DoE, 1997) to all. A bold vision, aims and objectives for the transformation and democratisation of HE were presented in the 1997 *White Paper, A Programme for the Transformation of Higher Education*. The White Paper had a clear social justice intent, emphasising equity in terms of "fair opportunities both to *enter* higher education programmes and to *succeed* in them" and noting that "[f]inancial need should not be an insuperable barrier to access and success" in HE (DoE, 1997, np, emphasis added).

Subsequent government efforts have reiterated these core dual priorities of promoting access to and success within HE for marginalised and disadvantaged students. The 2013 *White Paper for Post-School Education and Training* emphasised that universities have a crucial role to play in tackling national problems of poverty, unemployment and inequality; to do so, DHET argued, the PSET system needs to "substantially expand access" (DHET, 2013, p. 7). Further, these students continue to enter post-school studies from positions of extreme inequality including poor schooling, which often results in a lack of 'academic preparedness', as well as insufficient financial and other material resources to fund their studies and daily living requirements (CHE, 2010, 2016a; DHET, 2019a; Gredley, 2020; Khan, 2020; Swartz et al., 2018). Thus, despite the participation rates of black, coloured and Indian students increasing significantly over the past decade (DHET 2019a, 2019b), black students remain underrepresented in HE compared to their white peers, and student

---

[4] https://accesstosuccess.uwc.ac.za/access-to-success/

[5] With respect to the, Section 29 states that: "Everyone has the right – (a) to a basic education, including adult basic education; and (b) to further education, which the state, through reasonable measures, must make progressively available and accessible." (Constitution of the Republic of South Africa, Act 108 of 1996, p. 12)

success is still "sharply skewed by race and prior education" (CHE, 2016a, p. 7; Cooper, 2015).

Additionally, whilst government recognises that funding for institutions and students remains "much lower than desirable or needed" (CHE, 2016a, p. 7), gross domestic product (GDP) expenditure on HE remains low in global terms (CHE, 2016a; DHET, 2013, 2019a, 2019b), government funding continues to fall in real terms, and tuition fees as well as other expenses – notably student accommodation and living expenses – continue to rise (Ayuk & Koma, 2018; DHET, 2019a; Wangenge-Ouma & Carpentier, 2018). As a result, tuition fees, third stream income and corporate sponsorships have become a necessary and increasingly important source of funds for public universities to support, inter alia, research and students in need (Ayuk & Koma, 2018; CHE, 2016a; DHET, 2018).

Challenges and complexities of funding constraints

It has long been recognised that black students face particular socio-economic challenges with recent research highlighting the depth, range and complexity of resource constraints on students in SA HEIs (Case et al., 2018; Clowes et al., 2017; Gredley, 2020; Khan, 2020; Swartz et al., 2018). Financial pressures have a significant impact on student access and progress through their studies. Many students who come from families with no financial flexibility, are frequently in financial crisis (Case et al., 2018), and must fund their studies through a range of avenues including bursaries and loans, family resources, and part or full-time work (Case et al., 2018; Gredley, 2020; Swartz et al., 2018).

Whilst students at historically black and disadvantaged universities have been protesting for decades against inequalities in HE, and especially against unaffordable fees (Case et al., 2018; Davids & Waghid, 2016; Langa, 2017; Mathebula & Calitz, 2018), the #Fallist protests highlighted complexities around access such as:

> who has what kind of access (secure or provisional); for how long (weeks, a term, a semester or the whole year); under what conditions (upfront payments, high matric grades); to what kinds of institutions of higher learning (well- or under-resourced) – and how these factors intersect to compromise access in the same way that annual increases in funds payable for registration, tuition fees and living expenses do. (Mathebula & Calitz, 2018, p. 178)

In the wake of the protests, there has been much debate around the possibilities and viability of free tertiary education. Some argue that free HE is both feasible and necessary (Motala et al., 2016, 2018) whilst others posit HE as more of a private than public good and as such see income-contingent loans or a combination of loans and grants as more sustainable solutions to the student funding crisis (Ayuk & Koma, 2019; Burger, 2016; Hull, 2016; see also World Bank, 2019).

Scholars have also cautioned that financial aid is not a 'silver bullet'. Funding is just one necessary pillar of support (Case et al., 2018, p. 130) and may inadvertently increase the risk of academic exclusion as poor students send money home to ameliorate family poverty rather than using it to support their studies (Mngomezulu et al., 2017). The COVID-19 pandemic and associated lockdowns have added another layer of complexity to student precarity, with poor students struggling to access devices and/or connectivity and having to work in unconducive home study environments (Czerniewicz et al., 2020; Gredley, 2020; Landa et al., 2021; Le Grange, 2020).

Current funding initiatives and opportunities

The key governmental mechanism for funding students from poor and low-income households is the National Student Financial Aid Scheme (NSFAS) which is mandated to promote more equitable access to public TVET colleges and universities. However, it has been in a state of administrative and financial turmoil for many years and is unable to fully address the needs of all students (CHE, 2016a; DHET, 2020). NSFAS funds have been disbursed inefficiently, unfairly or not at all which takes a toll on students and their families, and many are excluded from the system or put themselves and their families under great financial stress (Devdiscourse, 2021; Macupe, 2021; Sikhakhane, 2021; Stats SA, 2019). Even those with NSFAS funding may struggle; managing finances takes time and energy, and there is a low likelihood of a safety net being in place for financial crises (Case et al., 2018). In addition, there are few options for students in the so-called 'missing middle' – students 'too rich' to qualify for NSFAS funding but too poor to pay for their studies – as highlighted by the #Fallist protests (Devdiscourse, 2021; Matika, 2016; Sikhakhane, 2021). Unsurprisingly, given these challenges, student debt continues to escalate (Naidu, 2021; SA News, 2021).

Alternatives to NSFAS include loans, bursaries and crowdfunding. Banks and private financial institutions (e.g., Fundi[6]) offer student loans. Private and non-profit institutions offer bursaries which may include 'wrap around' support, e.g., skills development, academic and career counselling services, work experience, etc., although these tend to be limited in their reach. For example, the Ikusasa Student Financial Aid Programme[7] (ISFAP) funds poor and 'missing middle' students pursuing 'high-priority occupations' such as actuaries, accountants, doctors and engineers. The Rural Education Access Programme[8] (REAP) focuses on students from specific geographic areas taking specific courses at selected institutions, and the Allan Gray Orbis Foundation[9] targets students with "an entrepreneurial attitude and a belief in the future of their country". Finally, some students turn to crowdfunding platforms such as Feenix[10] which connects students with sponsors, or more informal means such as BackaBuddy[11] or GoFundMe[12], flagged as a potentially "dehumanising" approach by a student who explained it as "literally begging strangers to help you out" (Staff Reporter, 2017).

A recent World Bank report (2019) posits that fundraising by SA HEIs has not been a major priority area until recently, partly due to limited resources throughout the economy and partly as philanthropy is not culturally entrenched. This report also suggests that "international experience shows that even in resource-constrained countries, universities can find a few rich companies and individuals – locally and among members of the Diaspora – who can be persuaded to make financial contributions to universities" (World Bank, 2019,

---

[6] https://www.fundi.co.za/
[7] https://www.isfap.co.za/about-us/
[8] http://www.reap.org.za/index.html
[9] https://www.allangrayorbis.org/
[10] https://feenix.org/
[11] https://www.backabuddy.co.za/
[12] https://www.gofundme.com/

p. 53). Recent local reports offer an alternative to the above view arguing that SA philanthropy is fairly developed, multifaceted and growing, though acknowledging systemic issues such as the "excesses of power, corruption, and broader governance challenges" (IPASA, 2019; Murisa & Murat-Prater, 2020, p. 9).

Open learning to widen access and success in HE

Given the global and local complexities and challenges outlined above, it is unsurprising that funding features prominently in the draft *Open Learning Policy Framework*. Open learning is broadly conceived by DHET (2017, p. 363) as an approach for promoting access to and success within post-school studies. It aims to remove barriers to access caused by a range of challenges, many of which are directly and indirectly related to socio-economic issues facing students and their families, including:

> geographic distance from educational campuses, timetable scheduling that is incompatible with people's working lives or family responsibilities, unaffordable fees, alienating pedagogic practices, lack of access to technology, lack of physical educational infrastructure, and discrimination on the basis of gender, age, race, ethnicity, social class, language or disability. (DHET, 2017, p. 373)

The OLPF recognises that a core obligation of DHET "is to increase access to educational opportunities for those who experience ... financial constraints and an inability to meet the cost of studies" (DHET, 2017, p. 367). DHET also acknowledges that funding is one support strategy amongst others, and that to best support student success, it must be substantial and holistic:

> Wherever necessary, student funding must go beyond a simple provision to cover student fees. It should also cover reasonable living costs and other study-related expenses. These amounts must develop in line with inflation and recognise the relevance of funding to academic success. In this way, student funding, though not a sufficient condition for academic success in itself, may progressively support greater levels of academic success. (DHET, 2013, p. 37)

Whilst stressing that financial obstacles should not be a barrier to HE, the OLPF does not go into detail about how students facing poverty and financial precarity could obtain additional financial assistance for their studies and other related costs over and above NSFAS funding. This study therefore sought to explore current institutional funding initiatives in SA HE which offer supplements to NSFAS and other government funding. Before outlining the study's methodology, and introducing the research site, we discuss the conceptual framework used in this study and across the Cases on Open Learning (COOL) project, that of participatory parity (Fraser, 2008, 2010).

Participatory parity and opening learning through funding

Open learning as conceptualised in the OLPF has a clear social justice intent; it is "motivated by the need for redress, equity in access to opportunity, flexibility and choice, and by an equal concern for quality and real success in learning" (DHET, 2017, p. 44). To explore the extent to and ways in which open learning practices promote social justice, this case study and the COOL project more broadly drew on Nancy Fraser's (2008, 2010; Fraser & Honneth, 2003) conception of social justice as *parity of participation*. Fraser's comprehensive and pragmatic approach to theorising social justice has been central to contemporary debates over what constitutes a just society and has deeply influenced conceptualisations of and dialogues around social justice (Blackmore, 2017; Bozalek & Carolissen, 2012; Moura, 2016).

Participatory parity encompasses three dimensions of justice: the economic and issues of (mal)distribution, the cultural and issues of (mis)recognition and the political and issues of (mis)representation and (mis)framing. Importantly, Fraser conceives of participatory parity as both an *outcome* where "all the relevant social actors ... participate as peers in social life" (Fraser, 2010, p. 28) and a *process* in which procedural standards are followed "in fair and open processes of deliberation" (Fraser, 2010, p. 29). She also emphasises that whilst useful to separate the three dimensions for analytic purposes, in real world situations they are interimbricated and dialectically reinforce one another (Fraser, 2008).

Economic dimension

With respect to economic injustice or *maldistribution*, Fraser explains that "people can be impeded from full participation by economic structures that deny them the resources they need in order to interact with others as peers" (2010, p. 16). In this dimension, participatory parity can be prevented or constrained by injustices including economic marginalisation, exploitation and deprivation (Fraser, 2008; Fraser & Honneth, 2003). In higher education, students may be impeded from economic parity by a range of factors including high transport costs to access geographically distant campuses; challenges in securing sufficient, affordable and nutritious food; high tuition fees; unaffordable textbooks and data; lack of access to mobile devices; having to perform unpaid, time-consuming care duties; having to take on part- or full-time work to support themselves and their families; insufficient workplace placement positions to complete their qualifications, and so on. These barriers, which affect poor and financially precarious students most acutely, indicate "distributive injustice or maldistribution" (2010, p. 16) and need to be addressed through redistribution or restructuring.

Cultural dimension

Fraser (2010, p. 16) points out that "people can also be prevented from interacting on terms of parity by institutionalized hierarchies of cultural value that deny them the requisite standing". The cultural dimension is concerned with ways in which society assigns attributes to particular social groups and how these attributes are interpreted and either valued or devalued, or in Fraser's terminology, *recognised* or *misrecognised*. Fraser's (Fraser & Honneth, 2003) view is that misrecognition occurs when societal claims about supposedly fundamental or intrinsic differences between different groups of people along the lines of cultural attributes such as gender, sexuality, ethnicity, race, language, dis/ability and so on are used to justify the oppression and marginalisation of particular social groups, putting some in positions of privilege whilst restricting others' lives. Students may be deprived of recognitional parity if the institutional patterns of cultural values explicitly or implicitly constitute them as deficient, inferior or other, for example in the implicit expectation that the average student is young, able-bodied, cisgender, middle class and unencumbered by family and domestic responsibilities (Bozalek, 2017).

Importantly for Fraser (2008; Fraser & Honneth, 2003) misrecognition relates to the relative standing of social actors and their ability to participate on a par with their peers in social life. She refers to this as the *status model* of recognition. In this model, recognition requires that individual group members can interact as full partners in social groups, and misrecognition comes about when institutionalised relations and hierarchies of cultural values subordinate some over others. Importantly, misrecognition in this view is not simply to be "thought ill of, looked down upon or devalued in others' attitudes, beliefs or representations. It is rather to be denied the status of a full partner in social interactions with one's peers" (Fraser, 2000, p. 13).

In emphasising social status over the identity model of recognition, Fraser (Fraser & Honneth, 2003) makes clear that she is interested in institutional rather than psychological ways of devaluation or misrecognition. The status model approach thus situates misrecognition within the larger frame of modern, complex capitalist societies in which both culture and economy contribute to social ordering and subordination as "the status order and the economic structure interpenetrate and reinforce each other" (Fraser, 2000, p. 118). Therefore, misrecognition cannot be overcome by a politics of recognition alone: "A politics of redistribution is also necessary" (Fraser, 2000, p. 118).

Political dimension

Fraser's (2008, 2010) third political dimension was developed in the context of rapid globalisation and resulting in destabilisation of national borders as the primary unit of justice. It is concerned with issues of representation and political voice. Fraser describes two levels of political injustice, *misrepresentation* and *misframing*. Together, Fraser (2010, p. 17) explains, these highlight "who is included in, and who is excluded from, the circle of those entitled to a just distribution and reciprocal recognition". At the first-order level, "representation has the straightforward sense of political voice and democratic accountability" (Fraser, 2010, p. 147), and *misrepresentation* denies people "the chance to participate fully, as peers" (Fraser 2010, p. 19) with those already included within a bounded frame or given political community. Students lack representational parity when denied a political voice and the ability to influence decisions which affect them. For example, insufficient funding for studies and daily life may impede a student's ability to participate fully in student life on campus through student organisations, activism, voting, etc.

Fraser (2010) also argues for a second-order level of representation which relates to boundary-setting; the related injustice is *misframing*. To be misframed is to be situated outside the bounds of justice and thus to be excluded from consideration for first-order claims against maldistribution, misrecognition and misrepresentation. As such, misframing has far-reaching effects; those excluded cannot make claims for justice, resulting in "a kind of political death", and those who suffer misframing "become non-persons with respect to justice" (Fraser, 2010, p. 20). In HE, current and aspirant students face misframing through a range of issues such as exclusionary fees, lacking funds for study-related and everyday resources, barriers such as geographical distance / rurality and refugee or immigrant status, language barriers, and so on. Bozalek and Boughey (2020) discuss misframing at the level of the whole SA HE system. They argue that there is a major form of injustice still at work which separates and oppresses historically black universities and continues to privilege advantaged institutions within the system.

Affirmative and transformative remedies for injustice

For each dimension, Fraser (2008, 2010) distinguishes between affirmative and transformative approaches for dealing with issues of injustice. She views affirmative approaches as ameliorative (Bozalek & Carolissen, 2012); while they may correct inequities created by social arrangements, they do not disturb the underlying social structures that generate these inequities. They may also have the "perverse effect of promoting [group] differentiation" (Fraser, 2008, p. 33), for example, affirmative action policies along the lines of gender, race, class, etc., can generate backlash against the people they seek to support. Transformative approaches, on the other hand, do address underlying root causes of injustice, and seek to blur rather than reify differences and boundaries, for example making "entitlements universal so that vulnerable groups of people are not regarded as citizens who are a burden to society, supplicants, or as benefiting from special treatment" (Bozalek & Carolissen, 2012, p. 15).

Methodology

This study sought to explore and evaluate the ways in which funding contributed to parity of participation of poor and financially precarious students at UWC through surfacing institutional initiatives which aimed to open up learning. The study focused on UWC's Access to Success programme (detailed below) which was chosen by DHET as worth investigating for its innovative fundraising methods. The study was led by the first author, a research fellow with the COOL project and PhD candidate at UWC.

The study took a small-scale qualitative approach through in-depth interviews with key stakeholders (Maxwell, 2009). Data collection coincided with the arrival of the COVID-19 pandemic in SA in 2020. This resulted in strict lockdowns closing UWC's campus for the duration of the project, and a sudden and challenging shift to remote and online learning for students and staff. For these reasons accessing participants was challenging, especially students but also staff. Ultimately four staff members were interviewed, three of whom were current and former senior managers (Intv1, Intv2 and Intv4) in UWC's Alumni and Donor Relations offices, based within the Department of Institutional Advancement, with the other being Faculty based (Intv3).

Given the lockdown, interviews were conducted via Zoom which offered affordances but also raised challenges (Archibald et al., 2019). Whilst in some ways online interviews benefitted the interview process (e.g., flexibility around timings, location and proximity given the lockdown), there were also challenges (e.g., insufficient bandwidth for quality video connections). Interviews held in person and on campus may have yielded different results through offering more opportunities for meeting stakeholders, developing rapport, accessing documents, and viewing fundraising efforts 'in action'.

Interviews were conducted and transcribed by the first author and a transcription company. Data was analysed inductively using qualitative thematic analysis (Maxwell, 2009) and deductively, using Fraser's three dimensions of justice, with the use of *MS Excel*.

The study also draws on Annual Donor Reports from 2014-2019 as well as institutional documents available online. Full ethical clearance was obtained from the University of Cape Town's Centre for Higher Education Development (CHED) Research Ethics Committee and UWC's Office of the Registrar, and consent was obtained from each of the individuals interviewed. Pseudonyms have been used to maintain confidentiality.

This case study is limited in some ways as there were relatively few interviews and the focus was one particular institutional context. These limitations need to be borne in mind if extrapolating from the study. However, the study highlights issues, complexities and enablers of student funding and institutional fundraising which can be more broadly applied. Following Maxwell (2009, p. 47) the generalisability of this study is "based not on explicit sampling of some defined population to which the results can be extended, but on the development of a theory that can be extended to other cases". In this case, the ways in which funding and fundraising – as open learning practices – enable and constrain socially just practices in each of the three dimensions (the economic, cultural and political) could be used to develop a more in-depth conceptual framework for use in similar HE contexts.

Institutional context and 'Access to Success'

UWC is one of four public universities located in greater Cape Town. It was established in 1960 as a college for 'coloured' students, the only of its kind nationally[13]. Within a decade it had become an important space for anti-apartheid activism and in the 1980s declared itself a non-racial institution, "the intellectual home of the democratic left" (Jacobs, 2012), and committed itself to developing poor and marginalised communities (Lalu & Murray, 2012).

Scholarship since the 1990s has shown the ongoing effects of multi-layered and complex economic and cultural legacies of apartheid on the institution and its students (Clowes et al., 2017; Cooper, 2015; Gredley, 2020; Helen Suzman Foundation, 1996; Khan, 2020; Leibowitz et al., 2012). The university remains located in "an urban wasteland surrounded by underdeveloped industrial land as well as very poor, densely populated communities" (UWC, 2015, p. 3). Whilst UWC does have some affluent students, the majority come from poor and working-class backgrounds; most are first generation students, and many, therefore, require a range of academic and other support services (UWC, 2015, 2018). Due to the shortage of on campus accommodation most students live off campus in what is at times precarious, crowded and poorly resourced accommodation, and travelling to campus is often arduous and unsafe (Gredley, 2020; Hames, 2007; Khan, 2020; UWC, 2018).

UWC today takes pride in its anti-apartheid struggle history[14], ongoing commitment to supporting and developing local communities (Badat, 2013; Lalu & Murray, 2012) and role as an anchor institution[15]. It positions itself as personifying hope and resilience, locally and globally engaged and connected, and committed to community engagement and partnership (UWC, 2018). Key to this positioning is UWC's asserted commitment to assist disadvantaged students gain access to HE and succeed in their studies (UWC, 2016, 2018). UWC is therefore one of the most affordable universities in SA (UWC, 2017). Nevertheless, around 80% of students would not be able to pursue their studies without financial assistance (UWC,

---

[13] https://www.uwc.ac.za/Pages/History.aspx
[14] https://www.uwc.ac.za/about/mission-vision-and-history/mission
[15] https://www.iop2025.uwc.ac.za/anchorinstitution

2018). Most students have NSFAS funding or fall within the so-called 'missing middle' and struggle to access sufficient funding for their studies and daily living expenses (UWC, 2019).

Out of this particular history and context, UWC's Access to Success[16] campaign was born. Collaboratively conceptualised by Institutional Advancement and the Students' Representative Council (SRC) and supported by Executive Management, Access to Success launched in 2016, coinciding with #Fallist student protests against long standing injustices in HE (Langa, 2017). Access to Success encompasses a range of initiatives including the SRC-driven 'Ikamva Lethu – Our Future Fund' campaign, the Jakes Gerwel Education, Development and Endowment Fund, an alumni phonathon, and a staff pledge campaign which aspires to draw on UWC's "culture steeped in social activism" and foster a sense of community and ownership amongst staff to help "uplift academically deserving UWC students"[17]. The Access to Success campaign has involved advocacy partnerships with the South African Broadcasting Corporation (SABC), collaborations with diverse local and national radio stations, and social media campaigns. These initiatives aimed to draw on local community support and highlight:

> the importance of a collective solution-finding effort through which the UWC community, alumni, corporate South Africa and friends of UWC collaborate towards finding sustainable funding solutions for students in need.[18,19]

Funds raised through the phonathon and other Access to Success campaigns have primarily been used to support "academically deserving" (Intv1) students needing small amounts of money to graduate; as the current alumni manager explained, "It wasn't like R50,000 or R30,000; it was R2300, R837, R5000". Donations in kind were also welcomed, and at times these were substantial. Intv4, for example, remembered an alum arriving on campus and "loading off thousands and thousands of rands' worth of sanitary towels and toiletries", and Intv2 described a large corporate sponsor agreeing to be the first funder of the UWC Nutrition Project which "provides food for 500 students on a monthly basis, when they're on campus [and] during the lockdown now we've been providing food for students who couldn't get home".

As noted, this study focuses primarily on the UWC alumni phonathon, an annual month-long fundraising campaign in which a team of student callers phoned alumni to raise funds for academically deserving students who could not pay the full costs of their education.[20,21] The alumni phonathon first took place in 2016 and ran each year until 2019 after which it was suspended due to the COVID-19 lockdown. Also, under the Access to Success

---

[16] https://accesstosuccess.uwc.ac.za/access-to-success/
[17] https://accesstosuccess.uwc.ac.za/uwc-staff-campaign/
[18] https://www.uwc.ac.za/news-and-announcements/news/uwc-alumni-phonathon-934
[19] https://www.uwc.ac.za/news-and-announcements/news/access-to-success-campaign-a-success-928
[20] https://www.uwc.ac.za/news-and-announcements/news/uwc-alumni-phonathon-934
[21] In 2015/2016, despite interruptions due to student protests, iKamva Lethu, the phonathon and the staff pledge campaign raised approximately R3,7 million in pledges and donations and about 100 "academically deserving students" received financial assistance to assist them with completing their studies (UWC Annual Report, 2016). In 2018 the phonathon together with staff contributions raised more than R400 000 which was dispersed to 52 "academically deserving financially needy students". In 2019 over 200 final year students were assisted with small amounts of funding to enable them to clear debt in order to graduate.

banner is an on-campus nutrition programme[22,23] as well as collaborations with a range of institutional support services. In 2020, the alumni phonathon was replaced with the #NoStudentWillBeLeftBehind[24] campaign that raised funds for laptops and connectivity for students learning remotely.

Findings

Three key themes emerged through the data: the launch of the phonathon and how it came to "serve a bigger purpose" (Intv4); unexpected outcomes; and institutional challenges and enablers of fundraising endeavours. Each theme is considered through Fraser's three dimensions to explore whether and how these fundraising interventions contributed to participatory parity and open learning.

The phonathon: Serving 'a bigger purpose'

The phonathon was conceived by staff who recognised UWC's particular history and context and students' often challenging circumstances and were committed to finding ways of promoting access. Intv4, for example, argued that she wanted to position UWC "as a university that provides that access, particularly because of our history, our historical legacy". The interviewees were well aware of the complexities and ramifications of poverty and the ways it impacted on students and their families, as the following quote shows:

> We found that even students who received full cost bursaries, who lived on campus, were taking their food or money and sending it back home because of the very extreme conditions under which the family unit was continuing to live. So they felt ... guilty having hot water and formal housing, a meal to eat every day. But then at home, they know that the folks are struggling just to fend from day to day, so they would send home their meal money, their food money, and then try and support the folks at home with it. (Intv2)

Interviewees were also aware of the cultural challenges facing many UWC students such as the impact of being first generation and the "culture shock" on having to adapt to tertiary studies and "fend for themselves":

> It takes quite a while for students to adapt to the culture and climate of a university set-up. They are now living in a very different space, if they're living on campus they now have to fend for themselves. They have to adapt to huge classes and the technologies and the dynamics of a very metropolitan student population. And all of this does hit students with a bit of culture shock, and you could see that transferred to their grades. (Intv2)

---

[22] https://www.uwc.ac.za/news-and-announcements/news/uwc-and-tiger-brands-launch-food-security-programme-834

[23] https://www.uwc.ac.za/news-and-announcements/news/food-security-on-uwc-campus-gets-a-boost-from-students-168

[24] https://www.backabuddy.co.za/champion/project/nswblb; https://www.uwc.ac.za/news-and-announcements/announcements/urgent-notice-to-uwc-students-uwc-to-make-laptops-available-for-students-in-need

Since the phonathon was launched in 2016 in response to these multifaceted challenges, and coincided with the #Fallist protests in which students were challenging HE's lack of economic, cultural and political openness, Intv4 called the timing "opportune". She argued that the protests were more than "a fight with government" and more than "a challenge to institutions to reform our financial sustainability models"; they were a call to all "constituencies and stakeholders" to better support students. The phonathon was therefore deliberately conceptualised as one which went beyond fundraising, to "serve a bigger purpose", to "nurture the sense of responsibility and collectiveness" for "our children", a purpose which was entangled with UWC's "unique history":

> Because UWC's history is so unique, that purpose was almost inculcated into the mission of what we were trying to achieve ... we wanted to get the message across that this is a collective responsibility. (Intv4)

Headed by the alumni relations manager and a small support team, the phonathon was a significant undertaking. A cohort of 50 students was recruited and trained and for one month would gather in the evenings and weekends to call alumni. Their aims were to engage in "warm conversations", update the institution's alumni database, and deliberately, "the 'ask' would be the very last thing they do" (Intv4). A training manual was developed and students were provided with debriefing sessions, "where we could share some of the important lessons in that call" (Intv4). A software programme was created "with every requirement that we wanted to see come out of this telethon", including a database which allowed students to see details of an alum's time at UWC, including their discipline, whether they had stayed in residential accommodation or not and when they had graduated, "because the more detail we had about the alum, the easier it was to have the conversation" (Intv4). A space was set up with computers and big screens, and incentives and rewards were offered; as Intv4 put it: "It was a hype. We were all young and in jeans, and hyping students up and speaking their language. We would get celebrities in to come and inspire them."

As the above demonstrates, fundraising staff were cognisant of students' historical and contemporary economic and cultural challenges, and the ways in which these were imbricated, and reinforced each. Through mobilising UWC's particular history and context, the team sought to foster a sense of community and shared responsibility amongst alumni and students. Further, the team saw students as an important part of the UWC collective, and thus part of the solution. As such, students were positioned as central role players in the phonathon, as ambassadors for their peers and the university. Further, the phonathon aimed to inculcate in them "a sense of responsibility ... generating and inspiring a collective to take responsibility for our students and their future" (Intv4). The phonathon from the start thus sought to do more than raise funds. As Intv4 put it:

> It was not only about the money, it was about creating a platform that inspires students to take ownership of their own cause ... to generate the sense of pride in their alma mater, and speaking to people that have gone and walked those corridors already. (Intv4)

Viewed through the lens of participatory parity, in addition to efforts to mitigate maldistribution through fundraising, the team sought to promote recognition through "inspir[ing] students to take ownership of their own cause" (Intv4) and representation through offering students a platform and voice to engage with stakeholders across and beyond campus. This more expansive approach to fundraising seems to offer important considerations for others seeking to open learning and foster social justice with and for students.

Over time, the complexity of students' socio-economic and cultural challenges and the desire to support not just access but success led to the growing realisation that "finances were only one aspect of ensuring successful students" and that "a segment of students needed holistic support" (Intv2). Efforts were therefore made to collaborate with colleagues in academic and counselling support services. Intv2 referred to these as the "three pillars of wrap-around support" to help students succeed in their studies. Further, interviewees recognised that supporting student success required a range of interventions such as peer mentoring, job shadowing, work integrated learning and volunteering opportunities. One interviewee argued that the university has a moral obligation to connect students with industry "because success cannot end at the podium when you receive your degree and we all clap hands and tomorrow you're still in bed, you don't have a job" (Intv3). This interviewee lamented the lack of will from some quarters of the university to support students beyond their academics, to thrive "in all spheres, becoming that holistic person that we want them to be" (Intv3).

Interviewees thus recognised that opening learning, i.e., supporting access and success, requires creating conditions that foster just economic parity but cultural and political parity too. This holistic approach echoes DHET's (2017, p. 371) understanding of open learning, e.g., as being about "sharing expertise, knowledge, and resources" and "increasing access to diverse opportunities", as well as open learning principles, e.g., fostering "success through learner support, contextually appropriate resources and sound pedagogical practices".

Unexpected outcomes

Whilst the phonathon was in many ways a deliberate endeavour which provided practical training and ongoing support (e.g., through debriefing sessions), there were a number of unanticipated outcomes. One of these was related to the timing of the launch. In 2016 students were making calls "in a very volatile climate [and] there were various perceptions about students from our very own alumni, around the protests" (Intv4). The phonathon offered students a platform to engage with alumni around the protests, and students who found themselves interrogated about "the burning of campus"[25] (Intv4) had an opportunity to "change the narrative of how alumni viewed the institution" (Intv4), to:

> set the record straight and to say that this is a very important issue, this is why we are fighting for access to education, because we are struggling, we are hungry [in our] residences. But at the same time, it's not all of us that are burning this institution. In actual fact, this campaign is about trying to find other solutions, and we are calling on your support to help us. (Intv4)

Because the phonathon allowed this space for dialogue and debate, some students and alumni forged bonds that led to ongoing relationships and associations:

---

[25] https://www.iol.co.za/news/students-arrested-after-uwc-rampage-1944121

> We would find that students would be on the call for a long time because people started to reminisce about their days, tell us about which residence, what sports they did, the friendships they have made ... And there's one case in particular I remember, when one law student phoned one of our alumni who happened to be a judge, and he was so intrigued and so pleased by the call and the level of confidence with which the student spoke and articulated himself, that he offered to mentor the student. (Intv4)

The phonathon thus opened learning for students in a range of ways. Through the training, debriefing and engagements with staff and alumni, students developed communication and relationship building skills, gained valuable 'real world' work experience, were offered opportunities to engage around difficult issues, and forged unexpected relationships with supportive alumni. Students were thus offered opportunities which fostered cultural and political parity through allowing them to interact and engage with alumni on a more equal footing. Further, although it is beyond the scope of this paper to explore this in any depth, the phonathon in effect offered a co-curricular pedagogical space in which students learned not only practical skills but also qualities and dispositions that could stand them in good stead in their studies and beyond (Barnett, 2009; Carolissen, 2014). Whilst some of the outcomes were planned, the results exceeded expectations. As such, Intv4 said, she now intentionally and "very strategically" considers the potential of campaigns to have benefits beyond fundraising.

A second unexpected outcome was the extent to which the phonathon and other Access to Success campaigns would affect people, encouraging alumni, lecturers, cleaners and students themselves to donate what they could to support students in need. Intv4 remembered an alum pledging R50 a month, explaining that:

> I [the alum] really don't have any money, I don't have any spare cash, I'm not rich, I'm trying to stay afloat too. But what I will do is still commit R50 a month because ... I understand what it is like to stay in res and go hungry. (Intv4)

Intv4 saw this desire to contribute replicated across campus:

> money came from staff, because staff could see first-hand, I mean, lecturers could sit in classes and see and understand what the struggles were. Cleaners were giving us money because they supported their children. (Intv4)

When the phonathon was postponed in 2020 due to COVID-19, and all fundraising teams were called on to support the #NoStudentWillBeLeftBehind campaign, small amounts were again donated from a range of vulnerable constituencies including students themselves. Intv2, for example, related a moment which stood out for him:

> I received a message [from] one of the students who took a screenshot of his bank balance after he had made a R40 donation ... and he had four cents left in his bank account. And he said, as a student I'm convinced that this project is going to make a difference to me and my fellow students and I'm willing to give R40. (Intv2)

These small amounts had enormous symbolic value for the fundraising team:

> It wasn't that we were getting hundreds of thousands of money. We were generating R50 a month, which was in the bigger scheme of things, and comparatively speaking to other institutions, is really nothing .... But the amount of pride and the value that that R50 was given with, and generosity, for me that was the most valuable thing. (Intv4)

As Intv4 went on to say:

> I think of that as a metaphor, as a symbol for really just completely shifting the needle and overcoming adversity and the sense of resilience UWC as an institution has, but also we as the people have. (Intv4)

As these quotes show, Access to Success initiatives fostered pride, camaraderie, community and a sense of belonging amongst diverse constituencies. Further, the fundraising efforts elicited small contributions from unlikely sources, including cleaners on campus and students themselves, i.e., those with direct experience of financial precarity. Campaigns such as the phonathon and staff giving drive therefore contributed to participatory parity for donors and recipients in a range of ways. Economically, recipients were assisted through funds raised. Culturally and politically, spaces were created which allowed a range of role-players to be included and valued as contributors to student access and success. However, it is clear that whilst important and necessary outcomes, these are affirmative interventions which cannot transform underlying economic, cultural and political inequities. It is particularly problematic that inadequate government funding means that the poorest should need to contribute to funding students. It is also troublesome that many of the contributors would be South Africa taxpayers and thus already contributing to government coffers. The focus in the OLPF (DHET, 2017) on cost efficient strategies should therefore be questioned as successful open learning efforts like Access to Success are already operating in extremely financially constrained contexts, now further exacerbated by the global pandemic.

Institutional fundraising: Challenges and enablers of success

As the above findings begin to make clear, fundraising at an institution like UWC faces particular constraints and challenges. Students and their families are often financially precarious, alumni tend not to be wealthy nor able to donate substantial amounts, and there is not an entrenched culture of donating to one's alma mater. As Intv 1 explained, "under the apartheid regime [alumni associations] were considered illegal" and thus UWC's fundraising efforts are new compared to historically white institutions where alumni associations are decades old.

In the face of these constraints and challenges, interviewees described several factors that enabled success in the phonathon and other fundraising initiatives. Two salient points are discussed here: an understanding of institutional context and supporting fundraising teams through skilled leadership.

Understanding institutional context

A key enabler was interviewees' deep understanding of the institution's particular history and context. Interviewees, most of them alumni themselves, were acutely aware of the challenges and constraints facing UWC students; they were also aware of the value of a university degree, for students and their families. Intv4 for example described education as "the liberator for us ... if you come from a disadvantaged community ... it means so much for us, coming from where we come from". This, she said, informed her work to find ways of creating:

> more opportunities for young people to access, so that they could not liberate [only] themselves, but also their families, and that's been kind of a personal mantra of my own. (Intv4)

Further, interviewees had a sense of UWC's "unique" history and saw it as engendering resilience, a shared sense of struggle against adversity, a willingness to "pay it forward" and "band together" in tackling common goals, and unafraid of "punching above our weight" (Intv2). Intv1 for example described the value of a shared sense of resilience and struggle, which he saw as "deeply rooted in UWC's ethos":

> You know, though UWC alumni or staff may not necessarily always see eye to eye on a variety of issues, but when there is a common threat or a common goal everybody there drops their issues, they band together as a community and network and they tackle the common 'foe', for the lack of a better word, and that I think gives us a good stepping point for our fundraising initiative. (Intv1)

Like Intv1, Intv4 saw UWC's history and context as fostering resilience and a desire to 'give back'. As she explained:

> there's an element of resilience in our struggle. How we come back matters. Every time we get up matters. Every time we pay it forward for somebody else, matters. (Intv4)

Both Intv4's and Intv1's comments demonstrate a perceived sense of a shared struggle, of collectively resisting and overcoming adversity, of collaborating on common goals. They saw these cultural and political considerations as important enablers of fundraising endeavours in often challenging socio-economic circumstances.

Supportive leadership

The second noteworthy enabler was leadership. The swift conceptualisation and launch of the #NoStudentWillBeLeftBehind campaign in 2020 was attributed in part due to the intervention of the acting Vice Chancellor "really push[ing] the campaign" (Intv2). Similarly, the success of the phonathon was attributed to a departmental head who had vision, trusted her team, fostered creativity, allowed risk-taking and innovation, championed their efforts, and facilitated access to funding. As Intv4 said, "leadership enables innovation":

> you need to have dynamic leadership that ... gives people the space to be creative and to support them. ... I had the support with whatever I came up with, there was a trust that it will be done and it will be done well. And then even if there's failures or lessons to be learned, she would still support me unconditionally. ... When you are head of the

department ... you support the plan and you facilitate funds, you facilitate access, you champion the plan. (Intv4)

Intv4 particularly valued this kind of leadership, which supports and facilitates innovation, in an organisation like a university in which "cultures are so set and resistant to change". Considered through the lens of participatory parity, the value and necessity of this style of leadership demonstrates the importance of the cultural and political dimensions in what may seem a purely economic endeavour.

Closely connected to the above was the fundraising teams themselves: UWC's alumni relations team is small compared to others in historically white and privileged universities. This means that each staff member must be a "jack of all trades" (Intv1), which may have allowed the team to be more flexible, adaptable, responsive, etc. Intv4 argued that leaders need to choose fundraising teams with care – "the right people in the right jobs to turn the wheels, to make things run". She further recommended ongoing specialised coaching support for fundraisers because training, whilst important, was on its own insufficient; as she said: "so many people go for training and still nothing happens". Supporting fundraising teams through coaching may have a positive knock-on effect for financially precarious students and the institution itself, and again draws attention to ways in which the economic dimension is entangled with the cultural and political dimensions. However, interventions like coaching are likely to be costly and thus challenging to introduce in an already resource constrained environment.

Discussion: Possibilities for and challenges in promoting open learning through funding initiatives

The research findings highlighted a range of institutional funding and fundraising efforts to open learning to financially precarious students, and associated constraints and challenges. The discussion that follows uses the framework of participatory parity to explore and evaluate these efforts, and the extent to which they promote justice in affirmative and transformative ways.

Economic dimension

Considering the economic dimension, UWC, a 'historically disadvantaged' institution, still largely caters to working-class and financially insecure students. UWC's fundraising aims to support students who are academically deserving and in financial need, and additional efforts are made to open up learning through nutrition programmes, donations of toiletries, mentoring support, funds raised through the phonathon and more recently laptops and data through the #NoStudentWillBeLeftBehind campaign. Whilst some students will require just one intervention, for example funding that allows them to graduate, others will require ongoing interventions for fees, food, toiletries and so on. Furthermore, interviewees recognised that students require holistic support systems including academic and counselling support, peer mentoring, job shadowing, work integrated learning and volunteering opportunities. This multifaceted approach is advocated by the OLPF which suggests four elements of student support: academic, counselling, administrative and technology (DHET, 2017). However, the extent to which an holistic approach will translate into employment opportunities for students

— a key focus of the OLPF — is debatable given the desperate state of youth unemployment in SA (Allais, 2020; Buchanan et al., 2020; Stats SA, 2021).

Current interventions by UWC, including deliberately low fees, are thus important but largely affirmative. They ameliorate financial hardship and, hopefully, allow students to remain at university. However, there is always a risk that if any of these forms of support fail, students may be forced to drop out or take up potentially harmful practices such as sex work to support their studies (Khan, 2019). Further, as tuition and other fees continue to rise, poor students will be excluded from HE and they and their families will sink further into debt, thus fuelling further increases in educational and wage inequities (Garritzman, 2016). As Garritzman (2016) points out, finding solutions to these spiralling inequalities is important politically, socially and at the level of macro-economics.

A more transformative approach might question and disrupt criteria such as "academically deserving" as a requisite for funding, recognising that the academic progress of poor and working-class students is impacted by a current and historical lack of access to resources such as quality basic schooling and insufficient funds for study-related expenses and daily living. There is evidence of potentially more transformative interventions, e.g., funding and mentorship may boost future employment opportunities which may change a student's life in the longer term, and thus possibly the lives of their families too. However, this is by no means certain given current youth unemployment statistics. Finally, requiring financial support from the poorest and most vulnerable is unjust when the government is mandated to fund HEIs. In sum, it is clear that universities and other PSET institutions cannot alone bring about the deep structural changes needed to overcome economic injustices rooted in SA society.

Cultural dimension

Culturally, the phonathon opened learning for student callers, and contributed to cultural justice in that students were recognised — i.e., included, valued and respected — as partners in the UWC community, as peers who could contribute to sustaining and improving the community's well-being. Through this recognition they were offered opportunities to learn and grow skills and values through 'real world' experience. These are useful and necessary interventions, offering potential for promoting success within and beyond a student's university career. They might thus be transformative for a student, especially in the longer term. However, these efforts tend to be small-scale and offered to few; to be truly transformative all university students would have access to such learning and development opportunities. This would be challenging for any one institution to do, particularly those with fewer and constrained resources, but government investments in such initiatives could pay dividends in multiple ways.

An additional cultural benefit of the fundraising campaigns was their ability to foster a sense of community and shared responsibility amongst diverse groups of people so that lecturers, students, cleaners and alumni felt they had a role to play in student access and success. This was done in part through drawing on shared histories of struggle and resilience, and through facilitating less hierarchical, more egalitarian and community-oriented interventions such as the phonathon. This kind of approach provides useful considerations for other open learning initiatives. However, institutional history and context does need to be considered; this particular approach emanates from and is embedded within a particular HEI and would not be neatly transferable to other institutions and other contexts.

Finally, it is worth noting that whilst resilience — i.e., the capacity of individuals and organisations to 'absorb shocks' and 'bounce back' — is often lauded, for example impoverished students' resilience, agency and resourcefulness (McLean, 2018), it is also troubled in relation to vulnerable people as it is "not a pro-poor concept [and] poverty reduction cannot simply be substituted by resilience building" (Béné et al., 2012, p. 3). Fraser would agree with Béné et al. (2012) as her status model approach eschews psychologised aspects of misrecognition, seeks to overturn structural subordination, and emphasises the imbrication of recognition with redistribution.

Political dimension

In the political dimension, students' abilities to participate as equals was boosted in some ways. For example, through fronting the phonathon they were given a unique platform to engage with alumni around volatile issues of the day, and an opportunity to inform and shape narratives around student protests. At a broader political level, however, UWC as an institution remains unable to participate on a par with its 'historically advantaged' peers. As Bozalek and Boughey (2020, p. 55) explain, historically black and disadvantaged institutions suffer double inequities of a "paucity of resources" and students' unpreparedness for university. The result, they argue, is the misframing of differentially positioned students and institutions. If inequities in the HE system were recognised, "it would be clear that both students and staff at these differently placed universities would require different sorts and amounts of resources" (Bozalek & Boughey, 2020, p. 56).

Other political considerations are leadership and teamwork. The success of the phonathon was attributed in part due to dynamic, supportive leaders who trusted their teams and facilitated access to resources. The OLPF (DHET, 2017) states that DHET's role is to provide strategic leadership, but the policy tends to favour the language of managerialism, administrative efficiency, and measurement and evaluation over dynamic, flexible and responsive leadership for citizenship and social change (CHE, 2016a; Komives et al., 2016; Swartz et al., 2018). DHET and universities would therefore benefit from approaching leadership intentionally, exploring what kinds of leadership — amongst many possibilities (Hallinger, 2018) — will promote open learning.

Affirmative vs transformative interventions

This case study has shown that HEIs can successfully contribute to opening learning through fundraising. UWC's phonathon provides an example of an endeavour that contributed to promoting economic, cultural and political participatory parity for students. However, whilst an innovative and exciting campaign and full of potential for opening learning in various ways, the Access to Success interventions described here tend to offer what Fraser terms affirmative justice. That is, whilst providing valuable and even necessary remedies for injustice, they tend to be ameliorative, limited in scale and offering short term or stopgap relief to some students, e.g., nutrition programmes and giving small amounts of funding to select students to help them graduate. As Fraser (2008, p. 34) argues, affirmative interventions may promote redistribution, recognition and representation, but these will be "surface reallocations of existing good to existing groups", will support group differentiation and thus can generate misrecognition, and cannot significantly transform an unjust status quo. Perhaps an institution like UWC could find more avenues for raising funds and supporting students economically, culturally and politically, but ultimately effecting deep systemic social change is beyond the remit and capacity of any one institution. That ultimate responsibility and power lies with the national government.

There is evidence of potentially more transformative justice, i.e., longer term and deeper restructuring, which might disrupt the root causes of injustice. For example, the phonathon offered students opportunities to learn new skills, be part of and contribute to the broader UWC community, form mentoring relationships with prominent alumni, and so on, which may have had ongoing economic, cultural and political repercussions for themselves and their families. However, truly transformative justice would mean that all students would have access to similar initiatives, or, taken even further, there would be no need for interventions like nutrition programmes, and financially precarious students' study related expenses would be fully covered. These again are measures which require national government intervention. Overall, as Fraser would argue, current initiatives are affirmative; they may ameliorate hardship in the short term but do not offer long term solutions for maldistribution. Further, these affirmative measures may increase systemic economic inequities in the longer term (see Garritzmann, 2016).

Conclusion and recommendations

This study, whilst small scale, offers several insights for other PSET institutions and government stakeholders. First, it shows that a range of factors impact funding and fundraising initiatives to open learning in HE. These include an awareness of the institution's history, context and organisational culture, how these can be drawn on to support fundraising endeavours, and the challenges that they might raise. The four universities in greater Cape Town for example have very different histories and cultures though are geographically close to one another.

Another core consideration is students, and by extension their families. Questions should be asked – by government and institutions – around the kinds and depth of support students require, ranging from funding for fees, food, transport, mobile devices, textbooks and so on, to academic and counselling support services. Whilst an institution might be able to step in and provide some of these kinds of support, as UWC has done, ultimately the socio-economic challenges in SA require interventions well beyond what any one institution can deliver.

Finally, the fundraisers themselves played a key role. Access to Success fundraisers demonstrated passion, creativity, innovation, responsiveness and resilience, and they benefited from less hierarchical leadership which fostered creativity and innovation and facilitated access to resources. It is noteworthy (and worth exploring further) that this took place within the kind of institution and sector known for more hierarchical, individualist and increasingly managerialist leadership. Despite the fundraising teams' efforts and successes, the context in which they are fundraising is, like many in SA HE, significantly constrained by the inability of its alumni – and other community members – to 'give back' through large and sustainable philanthropic donations. Further, despite supportive and passionate leadership, UWC's fundraising teams are small. Whilst this may boost their responsiveness and flexibility, it also means fewer heads, hearts and hands available for fundraising endeavours.

Given the complexities of the HE sector's and SA students' resource constraints, and the challenges in fundraising particularly for historically disadvantaged HEIs, the OLFP's emphasis on promoting access and success through providing "cost-effective ... quality education" (DHET, 2017, p. 371) is important. However, the OLPF also emphasises cost efficiency through economies of scale and keeping operational and ongoing costs low. The policy anticipates that this may mean "higher levels of initial expenditure" but hopes that "this expenditure may diminish over time" (DHET, 2017, p. 374). What this case study shows though is that significant and sustained funding is needed for both institutions and students from national government and in particular DHET – tasked with managing and funding the PSET sector – as any funds raised through a phonathon are the 'cherry on top' and insufficient to truly open up learning.

Acknowledgements

Many thanks to the staff involved with the University of the Western Cape's Access to Success Programme whose contributions made this case study possible. Special thanks are due to reviewers Professor Sioux McKenna and Dr Jens Jungblut for their thoughtful, incisive feedback on the chapter, Emeritus Associate Professor Cheryl Ann Hodgkinson-Williams for additional writing support, and Dr Tabisa Mayisela for writing support and guiding the entire COOL project. Thanks are also due to the Centre for Innovation in Learning and Teaching at the University of Cape Town, which hosted the COOL project, and the South African Department of Higher Education and Training for funding it.

References

Allais, S. (2020). Skills for industrialisation in sub-Saharan African countries: why is systemic reform of technical and vocational systems so persistently unsuccessful? *Journal of Vocational Education & Training*. https://www.tandfonline.com/doi/abs/10.1080/13636820.2020.1782455

Archibald, M. M., Ambagtsheer, R. C., Casey, M. G., & Lawless, M. (2019). Using Zoom videoconferencing for qualitative data collection: Perceptions and experiences of researchers and participants. *International Journal of Qualitative Methods*, 18, 1–8. https://doi.org/10.1177/1609406919874596

Ayuk, P. T., & Koma, S. B. (2018). The elusive quest for a functional higher education funding mechanism for South Africa: a time to walk the talk. Presented at The 3rd Annual International Conference on Public Administration and Development Alternatives, 28–39. http://ulspace.ul.ac.za/bitstream/handle/10386/2433/ayuk_elusive_2018.pdf?sequence=1

Badat, S. (2013). Jakes Gerwel (1946-2012): Humble intellectual, scholar and leader. *South African Journal of Science*, 109(1–2), 1–2.

Barnett, R. (2009). Knowing and becoming in the higher education curriculum. *Studies in Higher Education*, 34(4), 429–440. https://doi.org/10.1080/03075070902771978

Béné, C., Wood, R. G., Newsham, A., & Davies, M. (2012). Resilience: New utopia or new tyranny? Reflection about the potentials and limits of the concept of resilience in relation to vulnerability reduction programmes. *IDS Working Papers*, 2012(405), 1–61. https://onlinelibrary.wiley.com/doi/10.1111/j.2040-0209.2012.00405.x

Blackmore, J. (2016). *Educational leadership and Nancy Fraser*. Routledge.

Bozalek, V. (2017). Participatory parity and emerging technologies. In M. Walker & M. Wilson-Strydom (Eds.), *Socially just pedagogies, capabilities and quality in higher education: Global perspectives* (pp. 89–107). Palgrave Macmillan. https://doi.org/10.1057/978-1-137-55786-5_5

Bozalek, V., & Boughey, C. (2020). (Mis)framing higher education in South Africa. In V. Bozalek, D. Hölscher, & M. Zembylas (Eds.), *Nancy Fraser and participatory parity: Reframing social justice in South African higher education* (pp. 47–59). Routledge.

Bozalek, V., & Carolissen, R. (2012). The potential of critical feminist citizenship frameworks for citizenship and social justice in higher education. *Perspectives in Education, 30*(4), 9–18. https://www.ingentaconnect.com/content/sabinet/persed/2012/00000030/00000004/art00003

Buchanan, J., Allais, S., Anderson, M., Calvo, R. A., & Peter, S. (2020). *The futures of work: What education can and can't do*. HSRC Press. http://www.hsrc.ac.za/uploads/pageContent/1044864/2020.09.21.UNESCO%20Education%20and%20Work.pdf

Burger, P. (2016). Between the devil and the deep blue sea? The financing of higher education. Econ3X3. http://www.econ3x3.org/article/between-devil-and-deep-blue-sea-financing-higher-education

Carolissen, R. (2014). A critical feminist approach to social inclusion and citizenship in the context of the co-curriculum. *Journal of Student Affairs in Africa, 2*(1), 83–88.

Case, J. M., Marshall, D., McKenna, S., & Mogashana, D. (2018). *Going to University: The influence of higher education on the lives of young South Africans*. African Minds. https://www.africanminds.co.za/going-to-university-the-influence-of-higher-education-on-the-lives-of-young-south-africans/

CHE (Council on Higher Education). (2010). Access and throughput in South African higher education: Three case studies. *Higher Education Monitor, 9*. https://www.che.ac.za/sites/default/files/publications/Higher_Education_Monitor_9.pdf

CHE. (2016a). *South African higher education reviewed: Two decades of democracy*. CHE.

CHE (Ed.). (2016b). *Student funding – Kagisano number 10*. Council on Higher Education. https://www.ru.ac.za/media/rhodesuniversity/content/equityampinstitutionalculture/documents/Kagisano_Number_10_-_Student_Funding_2016_-_electronic.pdf

Chinguno, C., Kgoroba, M., Mashibini, S., Masilela, B. N., Maubane, B., et al. (Eds.). (2018). *Rioting and writing: Diaries of Wits Fallists*. SWOP Institute, University of the Witwatersrand. https://www.swop.org.za/single-post/2018/07/04/FeesMustFall-Book-Rioting-and-Writing-now-Available-for-Free-Download

Clowes, L., Shefer, T., & Ngabaza, S. (2017). Participating unequally: Student experiences at UWC. *Education as Change, 21*(2), 86–108. https://doi.org/10.17159/1947-9417/2017/2029

Cooper, D. (2015). Social justice and South African university student enrolment data by 'race', 1998–2012: From 'skewed revolution' to 'stalled revolution'. *Higher Education Quarterly, 69*(3), 237–262. https://onlinelibrary-wiley-com.ezproxy.uwc.ac.za/doi/abs/10.1111/hequ.12074

Czerniewicz, L., Agherdien, N., Badenhorst, J., Belluigi, D., Chambers, et. al. (2020). A wake-up call: Equity, inequality and COVID-19 emergency remote teaching and learning. *Postdigital Science and Education, 2*(3), 946–967. https://doi.org/10.1007/s42438-020-00187-4

Davids, N., & Waghid, Y. (2016). Higher education as a pedagogical site for citizenship education. *Education, citizenship and social justice, 11*(1), 34–43. https://doi.org/10.1177/1746197915626079

Devdiscourse. (2021, 25 June). University chancellors urged to find solutions for missing middle. Devdiscourse: Discourse on Development. https://www.devdiscourse.com/article/education/1627032-university-chancellors-urged-to-find-solutions-for-missing-middle

DHET (Department of Higher Education and Training). (2013). White paper for post-school education and training: Building an expanded, effective and integrated post-school system. *Government Gazette*, 37229. https://www.gov.za/documents/white-paper-post-school-education-and-training-building-expanded-effective-and-integrated

DHET. (2017). Call for comments on the open learning policy framework for post-school education and training. *Government Gazette* 40772(335). http://pmg-assets.s3-website-eu-west-1.amazonaws.com/170407openlearningframework-postschooleduc.pdf

DHET. (2018). Statistics on post-school education and training in South Africa: 2016. DHET. http://www.dhet.gov.za/Research%20Coordination%20Monitoring%20and%20Evaluation/6_DHET%20Stats%20Report_04%20April%202018.pdf

DHET. (2019a). Annual performance plan 2019/20. DHET. https://www.dhet.gov.za/SiteAssets/Media%20Release%20and%20Statements%202019/DHET%202019_20%20Annual%20Performance%20Plan.pdf

DHET. (2019b). *Post-school education and training monitor: Macro-indicator trends (March 2019)*. DHET. https://www.dhet.gov.za/SiteAssets/Post-School%20Education%20and%20Training%20Monitor%20Report_March%202019.pdf.

DHET. (2020). *Strategic plan 2020–2025*. DHET. https://www.dhet.gov.za/SiteAssets/DHET%20Strategic%20Plan%202020.pdf.

DoE (Department of Education). (1997). *A programme for the transformation of higher education*. General Notice 1196. Education White Paper 3. Pretoria. July. https://www.gov.za/documents/programme-transformation-higher-education-education-white-paper-3-0#.

Fraser, N. (2000). Rethinking recognition. *New Left Review*, 3. https://newleftreview.org/II/3/nancy-fraser-rethinking-recognition

Fraser, N. (2008). From redistribution to recognition? Dilemmas of justice in a 'post-socialist' age. In K. Olson (Ed.), *Adding insult to injury: Nancy Fraser debates her critics* (pp. 11–41). Verso.

Fraser, N. (2010). *Scales of justice: Reimagining political space in a globalizing world*. Polity.

Fraser, N., & Honneth, A. (2003). *Redistribution or recognition? A political-philosophical exchange*. Verso.

Garritzmann, J. L. (2016). *The political economy of higher education finance: The politics of tuition fees and subsidies in OECD countries, 1945–2015*. Springer.

Gredley, S. (2020). "When it rains [our house] rains too." In V. Bozalek, D. Hölscher & M. Zembylas (Eds.), *Nancy Fraser and participatory parity* (1st ed., pp. 94–110). Routledge. https://doi.org/10.4324/9780429055355-7

Hallinger, P. (2018). Surfacing a hidden literature: A systematic review of research on educational leadership and management in Africa. *Educational Management Administration & Leadership*, 46(3), 362–384. https://doi.org/10.1177/1741143217694895

Hames, M. (2007). Sexual Identity and transformation at a South African university. *Social Dynamics*, 33(1), 52–77.

Helen Suzman Foundation. (1996). *Talking sense about university transformation*. http://hsf.org.za/resource-centre/focus/issue-5-fourth-quarter-1996/talking-sense-about-university-transformation.

Hull, G. (2016). Reconciling efficiency, access, fairness and equality: The case for income-contingent student loans with universal eligibility. In CHE (Eds.), *Student funding – Kagisano number 10* (pp. 187–213). Council on Higher Education (CHE). https://www.ru.ac.za/media/rhodesuniversity/content/equityampinstitutionalculture/documents/Kagisano_Number_10_-_Student_Funding_2016_-_electronic.pdf

IPASA (Independent Philanthropy Association South Africa). (2019). *Annual review of South African philanthropy*. IPASA. https://www.omt.org.za/wp-content/uploads/2020/07/IPASA-Review-Issue-1-2019.pdf

Jacobs, S. (2012, October 23). Jakes Gerwel and 'the intellectual home of the left'. *Africa is a Country*. https://africasacountry.com/2012/10/the-intellectual-home-of-the-democratic-left

Khan, F. (2019). *Social justice and participatory parity: Students' experiences of university residence life at a historically disadvantaged institution in South Africa*. https://etd.uwc.ac.za/handle/11394/7024.

Khan, F. (2020). Addressing economic constraints impeding the achievement of Fraser's notion of participatory parity in student learning: A study at a historically disadvantaged institution. In V. Bozalek, D. Hölscher, & M. Zembylas (Eds.), *Nancy Fraser and participatory parity: Reframing social justice in South African higher education* (pp. 111–127). Routledge. https://doi.org/10.4324/9780429055355

Komives, S. R., Wagner, W., & Associates (Eds.). (2016). *Leadership for a better world: Understanding the social change model of leadership development*. Jossey-Bass.

Lalu, P., & Murray, N. (Eds.). (2012). *Becoming UWC: Reflections, pathways and unmaking apartheid's legacy*. Centre for Humanities Research, UWC.

Landa, N., Zhou, S., & Marongwe, N. (2021). Education in emergencies: Lessons from COVID-19 in South Africa. *International Review of Education*, 67(1), 167–183. https://doi.org/10.1007/s11159-021-09903-z

Langa, M. (Ed.). (2017). *#Hashtag: An analysis of the #FeesMustFall movement at South African universities*. Centre for the Study of Violence and Reconciliation. http://www.csvr.org.za/pdf/An-analysis-of-the-FeesMustFall-Movement-at-South-African-universities.pdf

Le Grange, L. (2020). Could the COVID-19 pandemic accelerate the uberfication of the university? *South African Journal of Higher Education*, 34(4), 1–10. https://doi.org/10.20853/34-4-4071.

Leibowitz, B., Swartz, L., Bozalek, V., Carolissen, R., Nicholls, L., & Rohleder, P. (Eds.). (2012). *Community, self, and identity: Educating South African university students for citizenship*. HSRC Press.

Macupe, B. (2021, March 6). "It is so hard being a black and broke": How access to NSFAS funding involves privilege, luck. *Mail & Guardian*. https://mg.co.za/education/2021-03-06-it-is-so-hard-being-a-black-and-broke-how-access-to-nsfas-funding-involves-privilege-luck/

Mathebula, M., & Calitz, T. (2018). FeesMustFall: A media analysis of students' voices on access to universities in South Africa. In P. Ashwin & J. Case (Eds.), *Higher education pathways: South African undergraduate education and the public good* (pp. 177–191). African Minds.

Matika, S. (2016, June 14). Five SRC campaigns raising funds for the missing middle. *The Daily Vox*. https://www.thedailyvox.co.za/wits-ukzn-nmmu-ufs-uwc-5-src-campaigns-raising-funds-for-the-missing-middle/

Maxwell, J. A. (2009). Designing a qualitative study. In L. Bickman & D. J. Rog (Eds.), *The Sage handbook of applied social research methods* (pp. 214–253). Sage.

Mbembe, J. A. (2016). Decolonizing the university: New directions. *Arts and Humanities in Higher Education*, 15(1), 29–45. https://doi.org/10.1177/1474022215618513

McLean, M. (2018). How higher education research using the capability approach illuminates possibilities for the transformation of individuals and society in South Africa. In P. Ashwin & J. M. Case (Eds.), *Higher education pathways: South African undergraduate education and the public good* (pp. 112–124). African Minds. http://www.africanminds.co.za/wp-content/uploads/2018/11/HIgher_Education_Pathways_9781928331902.pdf

Mngomezulu, S., Dhunpath, R., & Munro, N. (2017). Does financial assistance undermine academic success? Experiences of 'at risk' students in a South African university. *Journal of Education*, 68, 131–148. https://doi.org/10.17159/2520-9868/i68a05

Motala, E., Naidoo, L.A., Hlatshwayo, M., Maharajh, R., Vally, S., & Marawu, Z. (2016). Free education is possible if South Africa moves beyond smoke and mirrors. *The Conversation*. http://theconversation.com/free-education-is-possible-if-south-africa-moves-beyond-smoke-and-mirrors-65805

Motala, E., Vally, S., & Maharajh, R. (2018). Education, the state and class inequality: The case for free higher education in South Africa. In G. Khadiagala, S. Mosoetsa, D. Pillay, et al. (Eds.), *New South African Review 6: The crisis of inequality* (pp.167–182). Wits University Press.

Moura, J. S. (2016). Charting shifts and moving forward in abnormal times: An interview with Nancy Fraser. *International Journal for Moral Philosophy*, 15(1), 1–13.

Murisa, T., & Murat-Prater, K. (2020). Global philanthropy tracker: South Africa. *Scholarworks*. https://scholarworks.iupui.edu/handle/1805/26132

Naidu, E. (2021). Escalating student debt deepens universities' funding crisis. *University World News Africa Edition*. https://www.universityworldnews.com/post.php?story=20210318090703152

Odusola, A., Cornia, G. A., Bhorat, H., & Conceição, P. (Eds.). (2017). *Income inequality trends in sub-Saharan Africa: Divergence, determinants and consequences*. United Nations Development Programme (UNDP). https://en.unesco.org/inclusivepolicylab/sites/default/files/publication/document/2019/7/Overview-Income%20inequality%20Trends%20SSA-EN-web.pdf

SA News. (2021). We don't have money to clear all student debt, says Nzimande. *BusinessTech*. https://businesstech.co.za/news/government/475812/we-dont-have-money-to-clear-all-student-debt-says-nzimande/

Sikhakhane, N. (2021). Losing Yoyo: The consequences of late NSFAS funding. *New Frame*. https://www.newframe.com/losing-yoyo-the-consequences-of-late-nsfas-funding/

Staff Reporter. (2017). Wanelisa Xaba on using crowdfunding to pay fees: "I got a lot of shaming from people." *Mail & Guardian*. https://mg.co.za/article/2017-05-03-wanelisa-xaba-on-using-crowdfunding-to-pay-fees-i-got-a-lot-of-shaming-from-people/

Stats SA (Statistics South Africa). (2017). *Poverty trends in South Africa: An examination of absolute poverty between 2006 and 2015*. Statistics South Africa.

Stats SA. (2019). Education series volume V: Higher education and skills in South Africa, 2017 (Report 92-01-05). Statistics South Africa. http://www.statssa.gov.za/publications/Report-92-01-05/Report-92-01-052017.pdf

Stats SA. (2021). Youth still find it difficult to secure jobs in South Africa. Statistics South Africa. http://www.statssa.gov.za/?p=14415

Swartz, S., Mahali, A., Moletsane, R., Arogundade, E., Khalema, N. E., Cooper, A., & Groenewald, C. (2018). *Studying while black: Race, education and emancipation in South African universities.* HSRC Press.

UWC (University of the Western Cape). (2015). UWC 2014 annual report. UWC.

UWC. (2016). Institutional operating plan 2016–2020. UWC. https://ikamva.uwc.ac.za/content/whitepaper.pdf

UWC. (2018). 2017 Annual donor report. UWC.

UWC. (2019). UWC 2018 annual report. UWC.

Vally, S., & Motala, E. (Eds.). (2014). *Education, economy & society.* Unisa Press.

Wangenge-Ouma, G., & Carpentier, V. (2018). Subsidy, tuition fees and the challenge of financing higher education in South Africa. In P. Ashwin & J. M. Case (Eds.), *Higher education pathways: South African undergraduate education and the public good* (pp. 27–43). African Minds. http://www.africanminds.co.za/wp-content/uploads/2018/11/HIgher_Education_Pathways_9781928331902.pdf

World Bank. (2018). *World development report 2018: Learning to realize education's promise.* World Bank. https://www.worldbank.org/en/publication/wdr2018

World Bank. (2019). South African economic updates: Tertiary education must rise. World Bank. https://documents1.worldbank.org/curated/en/173091547659025030/pdf/South-Africa-Economic-Update-Enrollments-in-Tertiary-Education-Must-Rise.pdf

HOW TO CITE THIS CHAPTER

Gredley, S., & McMillan, J. (2022). Opening learning to students in a South African university through innovative institutional fundraising initiatives: A social justice view. In T. Mayisela, S. C. Govender & C. A. Hodgkinson-Williams (Eds.), *Open learning as a means of advancing social justice: Cases in post-school education and training in South Africa* (pp. 44–69). African Minds. doi: 10.47622/9781928502425_2

This work is licensed under a Creative Commons Attribution 4.0 International (CC BY 4.0) licence.

3

Using a social justice lens to explore the possibilities and limitations of flexible learning provision in a South African TVET college

Gertrude van Wyk, Cheng-Wen Huang & Cheryl Ann Hodgkinson-Williams

SUMMARY In its preamble, the Department of Higher Education and Training's (DHET) strategic plan for 2015 to 2020 identified ways to expand access to education and training. However, in South Africa, Technical and Vocational Education and Training (TVET) colleges' enrolment growth is inhibited by inadequate physical infrastructure and a shortage of additional and relevant human resources (DHET, 2018). The draft *Open Learning Policy Framework for the Post-School Education and Training* (2017) recommends that the principle of flexibility be applied to increase student access and support their success. This exploratory case study focuses on possibilities and limitations of flexible learning provision at a selected TVET college in the Free State province. It adopts Nancy Fraser's (1995, 2005) theory of social justice, which emphasizes parity of participation with respect to economic, cultural and political dimensions, to discuss ways in which flexible learning is socially just. COVID-19 lockdowns severely curtailed this study to virtual interviews with two institutional managers only, as students were not readily available. The transcripts were subsequently coded along Fraser's three dimensions of social justice. The study demonstrates that flexible learning provision responded to the economic dimensions of transport poverty by providing access to curriculum content via online platforms, radio broadcasts and hardcopy materials deposited for collection at selected physical destinations. In relation to cultural parity, it reveals that the college provides a pedagogically responsive intervention programme as a second opportunity for students to succeed. Politically, the study indicates that assessment practices at the college are exclusionary due to national assessment policies that constrain flexibility. This chapter contributes towards understanding the practices and policies that influence flexible learning provision as an aspirational form of open learning as well as the complex ways in which social injustices are entangled in the South African PSET sector.

Keywords: flexible learning, second-chance students, open learning, social justice, TVET

Introduction

In 2017, the Department of Higher Education and Training (DHET) published the *Open Learning Policy Framework for Post-School Education and Training* for public comment. The policy framework was conceived with the aim of addressing the 2013 *White Paper for Post-School Education*'s mandate to increase student access and improve their success. Within the framework, 'open learning' is introduced as comprising several principles to promote access and success in the post-school education and training (PSET) sector. Underpinning the open learning concept is an innate concern for social justice. In DHET's (2017) words, open learning "is driven by a concern for social justice and therefore motivated by the need for redress, equity in access to opportunity, flexibility and choice, and by an equal concern for quality and real success in learning" (p. 412). In 2019, DHET's Open Learning Directorate sought to understand how PSET institutions are understanding and enacting open learning principles and consequently commissioned the Cases on Open Learning (COOL) research project.

The COOL project comprises 16 cases focused on strategies in which various technical and vocational education and training (TVET) colleges and universities are enacting open learning or not. The focus of this chapter is on flexible learning as one of the key open learning principles. Using the case of Goldfields TVET College, this chapter illustrates how flexible learning is employed to support success by providing students an alternative route to complete selected courses that are impeding graduation. Drawing on Nancy Fraser's (1995, 2005) theory of social justice, the chapter explores how the intervention at Goldfields TVET College enables or inhibits parity of participation from an economic, cultural and political perspective.

Open learning to widen access and success

First introduced in the 1995 *White Paper on Education and Training*, the concept of open learning was reiterated in the 2013 *White Paper for Post-School Education* and consolidated in the draft *Open Learning Policy Framework for Post-School Education and Training* that was released for comment in 2017. According to DHET (2017), the purpose and explicit goal of the policy framework is to "introduce open learning practices as one practical way of addressing crucial issues of widening access to affordable, quality learning opportunit[ies]" (p. 366). The policy framework is explicitly motivated by a concern for social justice and the need for redress in South African PSET.

The two key fundamentals grounding the open learning concept are access and success. As written in the policy framework:

> The policy framework steers the sector towards making increasing use of cost-effective modalities conducive to open learning, in the interests of increased *access* (translating into increased enrolments) and increased *success* (translating into improved throughput, success rates and employability), without sacrificing learning quality. (DHET, 2017, p. 386)

Access is interpreted as increased enrolment. In relation to the TVET sector, in particular, the 2013 White Paper mandated an expansion of 2.5 million headcount enrolments by 2030. In a statistics report released in 2021, DHET reported an enrolment of 673 490 in 2019. This reflects a 2.5% increase when compared with 2018 (657 133), but a decrease when compared to 2017 (703 705). The number is thus still some way off the 2013 *White Paper* target of 2.5 million by 2030. To assist in the process of increasing enrolment, the Open Learning Policy Framework (OLPF) outlines the need to remove barriers to access and provide flexibility of provision.

Success is specifically interpreted as improved throughput rate and employability. DHET defines throughput rate as "the rate at which a cohort successfully completes a qualification within the stipulated timeframe for that qualification" (Khuluvhe & Mathibe, 2021, p. 3). The throughput rate for all students in South Africa who enrolled in 2016 for NCV Level 2 and who completed NCV Level 4 in 2018 is reported at 9.2%. As Khuluvhe and Mathibe (2021) note, this figure is significantly off the target of 75% as set by the National Development Plan for 2030. To assist in the process of improving success, the OLPF highlights the need for quality of provision.

With access and success established as two guiding tenets of open learning, open learning is defined as:

> An educational approach which combines the principles of learner-centredness, lifelong learning, *flexibility of learning provision*, the *removal of barriers to access learning*, the recognition for credit of prior learning experience, the provision of learner support, the *construction of learning programmes in the expectation that learners can succeed*, and the maintenance of rigorous quality assurance over the design of learning materials and support systems. (DHET, 2017, p. 363, emphasis added)

The principle of flexibility is described as "allowing learners to increasingly determine where, when, what and how they learn, as well as the pace at which they will learn" (DHET, 2017, p. 371). In the case of Goldfields TVET College, flexibility of learning provision manifests in the form of when and how second-chance students are taught. These are students who have failed the mainstream programme but are given an opportunity to retake the course through a second-chance intervention programme. Second-chance students are taught at a slightly adjusted pace, but they cover the same curriculum content and adhere to the same assessment protocols as the students undertaking a course for the first time. Pedagogical interventions by the college to support remote teaching and learning during the COVID-19 pandemic further showcase the possibilities of flexible learning provision to support the concept of 'where, when, and how' students can learn, but also accentuates the tensions around the set assessment times.

Understanding flexible learning

In a draft report mapping flexible learning and teaching at the University of Western Cape, the Division for Lifelong Learning (DLL) (2014) offers a comprehensive review of the concept of flexible learning both in relation to South African policies and international literature. In relation to national policies in South Africa, the DLL observes that flexible learning is often described in relation to online, distance and blended learning. Moreover, there tends to be a distinction made between full-time and part-time provisions. The DLL (2014) posits that "perpetuat[ing] the dichotomy of 'full-time' and 'part-time' provision" impoverishes the call for open learning (p. 17). Jones and Walters (2015) argue that, in fact, "the notion of a 'traditional' student is no longer valid" (p. 63) and that instead the 'non-traditional' student has become the norm. As Jones and Walters explain:

> The majority of *all* students either work in the formal or informal sector; care for the old or the young; are parents and/or surrogate parents to siblings; live and learn with disability or chronic illness; are returning or interrupting students; and live and learn in informal or informal housing environments. (2015, p. 63)

In relation to international literature, the DLL (2014) observes that there is no uniform understanding of the concept; instead, flexibility is conceived as a "wide range of responses to different situations, to different needs, underpinned by different discourses" (p. 65).

Within neoliberal discourses, for instance, the DLL (2014) observes that flexibility is used to describe "multi-skilled, flexible workers", that is, "flexible citizens" who can survive in the fast-paced knowledge economy (p. 18). Within managerialist discourses around the massification of higher education, flexibility is described in relation to "cost-effective means of taking education to scale"; and within economic discourses, that focus on the efficiency of higher education following diminished state funding, flexibility is discussed in relation to reducing costs to the academic institution (DLL, 2014, p. 18). The social justice discourse that is of relevance to this study, and aligns with the concept of open learning, is that which relates to lifelong learning and the democratisation of higher education. This discourse "emphasises learner-centeredness, enhancing equity and access, and alternative admission pathways, with second-and even third-chance opportunities for mature learners" (DLL, 2014, pp. 18-19). According to the DLL (2014), flexible learning in this context:

> takes on multiple forms to accommodate the different challenges that people face at different stages of their lives. It is seen as enabling lifelong learning and increasing and widening participation – both increasing actual numbers as well as diversity of participation – in higher education. (p. 19)

The notion of 'second-and even third-chance' resonates with how flexibility is employed in this case study, where Goldfields TVET College has developed a pedagogic intervention programme to help students who have failed the full-time programme, a second opportunity at passing a course.

Exploring enabling national policies and institutional practices in South Africa, Bolton et al. (2020) broadly described flexible learning as comprising:

> aspects which supported learners, such as using RPL [Recognition of Prior Learning] and CAT [Credit Accumulation and Transfer] processes for access or advanced standing, flexible hours, part-time studies, the opportunity to 'stop in and stop out' of studies, repeat lessons, blended learning, extended programmes, flexible teaching and learning methods, using technology in teaching and learning, flexible administration systems, flexible modes of assessment, flexible mind-sets in organisational leadership, and others. (p. 107)

Bolton et al. (2020) observe that although there was no commonly understood definition for flexible learning pathways, the interviewees in their study were in general more acquainted with the terms "articulation" and "articulated learning-and-work pathway" (p. 107). Furthermore, they discern at least three ways which flexible learning pathways can take: systemic, specific and individual. Systemic learning pathways involve "'joined-up' qualifications and/or part-qualifications, professional designations, and other elements that are part of the official system"; specific learning pathways involve "arrangements such as RPL, CAT, Memoranda of Understanding (MoU), Memoranda of Agreement (MoA) and others that support systemic articulation"; and individual learning pathways entail "flexible responsive systems that enable students to navigate and transition across barriers that they encounter" (Bolton et al., 2020, p. 11).

While there is no common understanding of flexible learning, Jones and Walters (2015) note that there is a general consensus that flexible learning is concerned about when, where, how and at what pace learning occurs. In this sense, flexible learning is about providing the learner the power to choose. According to the UK's Higher Education Academy (2015), "Flexible learning requires a balance of power between institutions and students and seeks to find ways in which choice can be provided that is economically viable and appropriately manageable for institutions and students alike" (p. 1).

To foreground what flexible learning means in practice for institutions, the DLL (2014) makes use of the term 'flexible learning and teaching provision'. This is defined as

> an inclusive, student-centred approach that promotes flexibility in admissions criteria, curriculum design, teaching and learning modes and assessment, with appropriate support systems and services, for the purpose of developing graduate attributes throughout the learning process so that students can make a positive difference in the world (DLL, 2014, p. 7).

This definition highlights flexibility in relation to (1) admission criteria; (2) curriculum design; (3) teaching and learning modes and assessments; and (4) support system and services. Identifying these as parameters for flexible learning and teaching provision, these components have been used as a framework to reflect on flexible learning within a blended part-time Baccalaureus Technologiae (BTech) Architectural Technology programme aimed at mature students (Morkel & Cronjé, 2019). For DHET's open learning agenda, the strength of this definition is that it highlights specifically where flexibility needs to be applied to increase access and improve success.

Theoretical framework: Social justice

This study draws on Nancy Fraser's (1995, 2005) social justice framework to understand how flexible learning can enable or inhibit social justice. The framework has been used to explore the adoption of open educational resources (Hodgkinson-Williams & Trotter, 2018) and development of open textbooks (Cox et al., 2020) from a social justice perspective.

According to Fraser (2005), social justice involves 'parity of participation' which "requires social arrangements that permit all to participate as peers in social life" (p. 73). Fraser identifies three dimensions that can affect parity of participation, namely, the economic, the cultural and the political. While recognising that the three dimensions are "imbricated with one another" in reality, Fraser (1995, p. 70) separates the three dimensions for analytical purposes. Moreover, Fraser (1995) distinguishes between affirmative and transformative responses to addressing economic, cultural and political injustices. Affirmative responses, or what Hodgkinson-Williams and Trotter (2018) refer to as "ameliorative" responses, involves "correcting inequitable outcomes of social arrangements without disturbing the underlying framework that generates them", while transformative responses involve "correcting inequitable outcomes precisely by restructuring the underlying framework" (p. 82).

With respect to the economic dimension, Fraser (2005) proposes that economic maldistribution can arise when people are "impeded from full participation by economic structures that deny them resources they need in order to interact with others as peers" (p. 73). In relation to flexible learning, economic maldistribution can manifest as a result of what can be described as 'time poverty'. That is, where individuals are denied the opportunity to interact with others as peers because of time constraints. Working individuals, for instance, may be denied the opportunity to gain a better qualification or upskill because of rigid educational programmes that prevent working individuals from working and studying at the same time. An ameliorative response may be offering affordable part-time courses to suit students' home and working commitments. A transformative response would be "fundamental shift in thinking about learning and teaching in higher education" (Jones & Walters, 2015, p. 77) and in the way that it is financed (cf. Bolton et al., 2020). Another form of economic maldistributed is 'transport poverty'. In the case of this study, transport poverty – where individuals are denied the opportunity to interact with others as peers because of transport constraints – is a barrier that can have consequences for personal safety as well.

In relation to the cultural dimension, Fraser (2005) posits that cultural misrecognition can bar people "from interacting on terms of parity by institutionalised hierarchies of cultural value that deny them the requisite standing" (p. 73). For example, in the case with TVET colleges, English is the mandated language of instruction. Students who struggle with fluency in English thus can be disadvantaged in successfully engaging with the TVET curriculum because of the language barrier. More fundamentally the content with which students are engaging is likely, at this point in South Africa's history, to be from a Western perspective and unlikely to take much local indigenous knowledge into account. An ameliorative response, for example, would be to provide some options for the language of teaching and learning, whereas a transformative response would allow for students' choice of any national language.

Cultural misrecognition can also manifest in pedagogical approaches. That is, where the cultural norms of tuition deny students participation. Didactic pedagogies, for instance, are potentially exclusionary in that these approaches to teaching and learning promote absorption of information and rote learning rather than active engagement with learning. Social constructivist pedagogies (Vygotsky, 1978), on the other hand, can be argued to be more inclusive in that they allow students to interrogate and construct their own knowledge. The findings in this chapter indicate that the pedagogical approach adopted in the second-chance intervention programme may have been key to the success of students within the programme.

In the political dimension, Fraser (2005) advances the idea that misrepresentation "wrongly deny some of the included the chance to participate fully as peers" and more troublesome misframing that can arise when the political decision rules are drawn in such a way that "wrongly exclude some people from the chance to participate at all" (Fraser, 2005, p. 76). For instance, when an educational policy is drawn up without consulting those whom the policy affects, this can be considered as an injustice arising from political misrepresentation. An ameliorative response, for instance, would be to consult with students about course scheduling, assessment submission times, etc., whereas a transformative response would involve them in the deliberation of the practices that affect them (e.g., curriculum and assessment methods).

The case study

The site of study is Goldfields TVET College which is situated in the mining town, Welkom, in Matjhabeng Local Municipality of the Free State Province. The majority of the students at the college come from poor socio-economic backgrounds, some from informal settlements. The tuition fees at the college, however, are high and unaffordable for most students. For this reason, the college has made it a policy that all prospective students are required to apply for National Student Financial Aid Scheme (NSFAS) funding prior to admission at the college.

Flexible learning at this college is illustrated through two programmes that cater for two different kinds of students. The one programme is a second-chance intervention programme that is aimed at providing provision for students who are prohibited from proceeding to the next level, as a result of failing more than two or three subjects within a programme or course of study. In the second programme, flexible learning is provided as a means for working students to improve their skills or qualification. With respect to the second-change intervention programme, the college did not have sufficient physical space to meet the demand of the re-intake of second-chance students as part of the usual on-campus classes. As a way to meet the needs of these second-chance students, additional, but less frequent, sessions of a shorter duration were arranged in the late afternoons (17:00–19:00) to accommodate the working students who would then complete the outstanding work on their own at home.

Unfortunately, these second-chance students no longer qualify for NSFAS funding and thus must fund their own studies. The cost in 2020 was an average of R3 500 per subject, much higher than the full-time student fee, and students are limited to a maximum of two subjects per semester (6 months).

Method

The site of study was purposely chosen by DHET at the start of the project because the college was perceived as applying flexible learning innovatively. Fieldwork for the study was conducted in 2020, but due to lockdown regulations following the COVID-19 pandemic, the scale of the study was reduced from including staff and students to staff only. For this case, one manager and one senior manager were interviewed remotely through Zoom. DHET had provided the COOL team with an initial contact and the manager and the senior manager were recommended through the applications made to conduct the research at the site. The semi-structured interview questions centred around understanding how flexibility of learning provision was being applied at the college and the extent to which the practice enables or inhibits social justice. After the interviews were transcribed, the transcripts were returned to the participants for member checking. The data was then analysed and coded deductively in MSExcel along Fraser's three dimensions of social justice.

A key limitation of the study is that, due to the pandemic, students were not interviewed. This has limitations in terms of understanding how students perceive the flexible learning and teaching provisions at the institution and whether there may be tensions or contradictions between what the institution perceives as flexible learning and students' needs and desires.

Findings

Flexibility as a means to support success

Within the second-chance intervention programme, flexibility is employed as an intervention to assist students, who have failed subjects within the full-time programme, to retake the failed subjects through the programme. Flexibility of learning provision, in this way, supports the concept of success through aiding students' completion.

The intervention programme for this group of students consists of one-to-two-hour contact sessions that are held once a week. Due to infrastructure limitations, sessions are held in the late afternoons and early evenings (17:00-19:00) when the full-time programme students are not making use of campus facilities. This is also a time that accommodates the working students.

At the inception of the intervention programme in June 2018, eleven subjects were made available for students to repeat. The subjects were chosen because of their status as poor performance subjects. The pass rate in the first cycle was approximately 60%. In the second cycle of the intervention programme in 2019, it was reported that ten of the eleven subjects had a 100% pass rate. The manager, recounting this, described being 'quite surprised' by the success rate.

> So I was also quite surprised because those were traditionally learners that actually failed the subjects in the past, and I'm very sure that if those learners were just put back in the mix, I'm not sure if some of them even would have passed in the normal methods of teaching that we use. (Manager)

The list of subjects offered in the intervention programme in 2020 increased to include information processing, computer practice, public relations, labour relations, personnel management, sales management, marketing communication, education didactic practical and training, personnel training, marketing management, day care personnel development, child health, education, day care communication, education psychology, day care management, communication, office practice, financial accounting and entrepreneurship.

The pedagogical strategy adopted in the limited one-hour weekly contact sessions per subject, involves facilitation more than direct teaching. Students are given the opportunity to pose questions on what was done the previous week and work for the next week is then assigned.

> Like I said, a very shortened one-hour session a week is a face-to-face interaction, but the lecturers quickly learned how to do with that one hour because you can't teach in one hour, you actually basically need to facilitate and you need to say to them, listen, this is what, you know, they can ask questions on what they had to do the previous week and you basically give them work for the next week. (Manager)

In this sense, learning mostly happened outside the classroom, within the students' own space, according to their own pace and during times convenient to them. The classroom space was mainly used to monitor progress, clarify concepts and plan for self-study. WhatsApp groups were created for communication between sessions.

When asked about what factors might have contributed to the success of the intervention programme, the manager suggested that student commitment played a key role since they have limited time with the lecturer and that these students must fund themselves because DHET will no longer fund their studies. In the manager's words:

> Commitment from learners, as they have to work very hard most of their time alone, they realize that due to limited time with a lecturer, they will not be spoon fed thus if they do not work on their own, they will fail. Furthermore 99% of these students repeat the subject and they have to pay unfunded rates, which is very high, they cannot afford to keep failing and paying for themselves. (Manager)

The manager clarified the intricacies of the second-chance system that highlights the importance of the examination grades and financial implications.

> If a student gets between 35% and 39% during the first attempt, the college can register a student for examination only. This student will not sit in during normal class and only write the exam or the supplementary exam during the next exam cycle. The fee for [the] exam only is R183 per subject. If a student gets below 35% he must fully repeat the subject and also attend more than 80% of the class in order to write exams. In this case the [second-chance] students will have to pay the full fee. (Manager)

In another programme at the college, flexibility of learning provision is employed as a strategy to help working students upskill. In this sense, it offers them an opportunity to study during their discretionary time while employed.

The limitations of assessment timing in optimising flexible learning

A constraint of the intervention programme described above is that the assessment policy, which all TVET colleges must follow, has not been adjusted to reflect the concept of flexible learning. The manager described the assessment practice as being 'very rigid' as assessment in the intervention programme follows exactly the same practice and timeline as the full-time programme. In other words, the students in the intervention programme are required to complete the same assessments as students in the ordinary programme.

> The Department of Higher Education and Training is encouraging us to go the route of open learning, but when it comes to assessment, the structures are very rigid. Because our approach to open learning is still fitting within the courses that the Department is presenting, we have to stick to the number of assessments because learners must have ICASS [Internal Continuous Assessment] marks to write the final examination. (Manager)

The manager hinted that this is seemingly unfair as students within the intervention programme have fewer contact hours compared to the full-time students in the ordinary programme.

> So even if … the learners are basically studying from home and they're just coming in for a very short time during the week, those learners still have to write all the tasks, the tests and

> the assignments, like any other learner that's on a full-time basis. The Department doesn't give us due to say, because these learners only have a few hours contact, they can write less assignments or do less tasks. (Manager)

Also, the intervention programme students must make themselves available to write exams at the same time as the full-time students, thereby not optimising the flexible learning imperative of allowing students to "determine where, when, what and how they learn, as well as the pace at which they will learn" (DHET, 2017, p. 371).

> We had to arrange it in such a way that those learners, although they're studying mostly from home, when the full-time students are writing a particular assessment, they had to come in and write it with them, because we cannot draw up different papers all the time, for various reasons, also to try and maintain the standard. (Manager)

In this way, the assessment practice is at odds with the principles that underpin flexible learning provision.

Flexibility as a means to overcome transport poverty and threats to personal safety

The case of Goldfields TVET College points towards the possibility of flexibility as a means of overcoming transport poverty and threats to personal safety. The senior manager described the availability, the cost and safety of transport as being barriers to learning, explaining that a lack of adequate transport not only affects attendance, but also students' safety, as gender-based violence is reportedly a persistent problem in the town in which the college is situated.

> I think I've mentioned that we are serving students from informal settlements. Students don't have transport. They're using lifts to come to the college, which we are discouraging that because so many things happening, especially for our lady students. It affects us also because they are late. When it's raining, the attendance is poor. (Senior manager)

Flexible use of technology as a means of addressing the lack of in-person contact

The possibility of using technology to support flexible learning provision to overcome the lack of in-person contact is showcased through descriptions of emergency remote teaching (ERT) strategies adopted by the institution during lockdown regulations following the COVID-19 pandemic. For instance, in one ERT strategy, the senior manager described how the college's zero-rated website was utilised in combination with the messaging platform, WhatsApp, to deliver content.

> We opened a portal on our college website, which we zero-rated, so the challenge of our learners obviously is data. Eventually it started to work very well because what we realized was, in WhatsApp, you can send messages which doesn't take a lot of data, then you can direct the learners to the website and tell them 'listen, there's a voice note for you on what you need to do today for 10 minutes and the learners can, free of charge, listen to the

voicemail. So I think the two — initially we separated them — but, after a while the two actually started to work very well together. (Manager)

Flexible use of radio broadcasts and other media to support the lack of in-person contact

Another creative strategy employed during ERT was the college's partnership with a local radio station to broadcast live sessions and then follow up via other media for queries from students. While the main language of the radio station was Sesotho, the lessons were broadcast in English.

> We partnered with a local radio station. We've got two radio stations, but there is one which covers a bigger area in terms of radius, so we partnered with that and we were giving a few lessons through the radio. Lecturers were there live, offering those lessons, and then thereafter they'll make follow ups through WhatsApp and other means. (Senior manager)

Delivery of paper-based materials to central locations

During ERT, for students who did not have the means to access the online content, paper-based learning materials were delivered to central locations, such as post offices and police stations, where students could collect them at times convenient to them.

> Learners even came to us saying that they don't have phones or they don't have any means. Then we also put the notes on whatever we had ... We tried to leave them in central places like post offices and police stations and learners picked them up. (Manager)

These strategies point towards the possibilities for creatively using multiple delivery platforms and media to extend learning beyond face-to-face provision.

Retrieval system of used textbooks unsuccessful as a means to alleviate material costs

The COVID-19 context has also prompted considerations for use of teaching materials other than textbooks. Prior to the pandemic, the college primarily relied on textbooks as the prime teaching materials. The institution pays for the textbooks and the senior manager described these as being costly. As a result, the college proposed, and attempted, to implement a retrieval system, which entailed students returning their used textbooks in exchange for some economic gain. However, the system failed to work as students were not keen to return their textbooks for several reasons, including the need to consult the previous year's textbooks given the continuation of their courses.

Fully copyrighted materials a barrier to flexible learning

During the COVID-19 pandemic, with full copyright licences attached to textbooks hindering the sharing of textbook content online, lecturers were prompted to search for alternative materials online including open access articles available via Google Scholar and other openly licenced educational materials.

> One of the questions is copyright, obviously, because it came up during the lockdown. You can't just upload a publisher's book ... So I think that was one of the things that limited us from using the textbooks that we bought if I can put it that way. There's a lot of online material that is open source that's available in different programs. I think a lot of lectures realized this when they started compiling lessons at home. When they started using Google Scholar ... they saw there were online materials that you can use. (Manager)

This points towards the possibilities of open educational resources and open access articles, which are free and openly licenced as a way to overcoming the legal constraints of fully copyrighted materials and economic barriers associated with their purchase.

Discussion

Flexible learning as culturally affirmative, but economically maldistributive for students

The case of Goldfields TVET College demonstrates how flexible learning provision may be used as a means to address cultural injustices stemming from the traditional education model by providing students a second opportunity to succeed through the intervention programme. Yet, this chance to succeed a second time around comes at a cost. No longer qualifying for NSFAS funding, these students must repeat the subjects at their own cost. In this way, although the flexible learning provision opens up the opportunity to succeed given another chance, it also places constraints on who may be at liberty to pay for this second chance. In this sense, success comes with an economic cost and, arguably, furthers the divide between those who can afford education and those who cannot. It thus furthers economic maldistribution as education and, by implication, job opportunities, are still strongly tied to economics. The intervention, as such, can be described as 'affirmative', as while it provides students a second chance at success, this is only for some students (those who can afford the additional cost) and not all students. Moreover, it does not address the root causes of the failure rate in the first instance.

The high failure rate in the mainstream programme suggests that a more appropriate intervention may be for the college to interrogate the reasons for the failure. A possible reason for failure in the mainstream programme may well be the didactic model of teaching in which teachers are positioned as disseminators of knowledge and students are receivers of knowledge. The success within the intervention programme suggests that the 'flipped classroom' model, where students engage with the learning tasks within their own time, and classroom time is left for interrogating, discussing and dealing with questions, seems to be producing engaged students who are able to take more control of their learning. This pedagogical approach appears to be more inclusive, as it allows students to construct their own knowledge and learning, with teachers acting more as facilitators in this process. In this way, the opportunity to succeed in the intervention programme can be described as 'culturally transformative' as it affords students the opportunity to engage with a different pedagogical model rather than a mere second chance at success.

Flexible learning as economically affirmative for students and the TVET college

The college's response during the COVID-19 pandemic to supporting ERT points towards the possibilities of flexible learning provision to address some economic injustices. At the individual level, the flexible approach to providing content delivery, from online platforms, to radio broadcasts, to dropping off materials at physical destinations, point towards the possibilities of flexibility of provision to circumvent transport poverty. The implications can be significant as the case study reveals that transport poverty is not only a barrier to class attendance (and performance by implication), but, importantly, it can have grave consequences in relation to personal safety. It is important to note that while the findings indicate that flexible modes of delivery may be a means to addressing the issue of transport poverty and threats to personal safety, other costs can be generated in the process such as costs related to data and electricity consumption. In relation to data costs, zero-rating the college's website during the ERT period has proved to be effective in overcome this barrier. This suggests that, in alleviating economic injustice, flexible modes of provision are not enough, but interventions must be in place to support access to and success in the mode of provision.

At the institutional level, the move away from textbooks to the use of open educational resources during the pandemic points towards the possibility of freeing the college from having to carry the financial burden of providing students with textbooks. However, there were obviously costs that the college had to bear in relation to printing materials and transport costs to deliver these to central points as well as the invisible costs of lecturers locating and selecting open access journal articles and open educational resources.

Flexible learning as culturally affirmative, but politically exclusionary

The case of Goldfields TVET College suggests that the ideals of open learning and the notion of flexible learning provision can be undermined when the assessment policy does not correspond accordingly. Arguably, by requiring students in the intervention programme to write assessments at the same time as the full-time students, this is likely to constrain the pace of their learning and their readiness to be assessed. In other words, while students may pace themselves in their own time, they are still obliged to work within a particular time frame, because of the fixed assessment deadlines. Flexibility, in this sense, is only an ameliorative means of overcoming time, pace and place (issues that problematises the traditional education approach) as opposed to a transformative response, where students are given the decision-making power of the time, pace and place of their learning and assessment.

Flexible learning as politically constrained for students, lecturers and the institution

Furthermore, the interview with the manager suggests an injustice arising from political misrepresentation of the policies that govern TVET colleges as those who are directly affected by the policies (lecturers and students) are not given a voice in the design of policies or practices. In this case, it would appear that the assessment policy is constraining the support that institutional management feels it can provide in fully realising the open learning vision as set out in the OLPF.

Conclusion

This chapter examined how flexible learning manifests as a principle within DHET's (2017) OLPF and investigated how the principle is being applied in the case of Goldfields TVET College. Fraser's theory of social justice has been drawn on as a conceptual framework to understand how the flexible interventions can enable or inhibit social justice. The findings indicate that the college's intervention programme addresses cultural justice by providing students a second opportunity at success. Economically, however, given that NSFAS funding does not provide support for repeating students, the intervention is only accessible to those who can afford the fees. This is an example of 'imbrication' (Fraser, 2004, p. 1115), where dimensions of social justice are intricately entangled. In essence, the intervention is an affirmative response as flexible learning, as a form of open learning, still functions within a system in which education is firmly tied to personal finances.

Beyond the intervention programme, the college has shown, through its flexible approach to disseminating content during the ERT period instigated by the COVID-19 pandemic, that diverse modes of provision can assist in addressing transport poverty. The chapter has highlighted the significant consequences of transport poverty — affecting not only quality of learning, but, importantly, personal safety.

Paradoxically, the findings suggest that although diverse modes of provision can assist in overcoming one form of poverty, they can also heighten poverty in other ways, depending one's ability to access the provision. Data costs, for instance, can be an obstacle for learners in accessing online modes of provision. The chapter thus proposes that, along with diverse modes of provision, interventions that support access to modes of provision must also be in place to fully realise the potential of flexible learning. In relation to teaching resources, the findings indicate that the financial burden which TVET colleges have to carry in supplying students with textbooks can be mitigated through the use of open educational resources.

Lastly, from a political perspective, the chapter has highlighted the need for assessment policies to be recalibrated to reflect the principle of flexible learning. It has been argued that there is political misrepresentation in the current policy practice in which those who are directly affected by the policies are not given a 'voice' in policy deliberations, or the agency to make changes that suit the specific context.

Acknowledgements

Many thanks to Butch Duvenage and Francis Mahlangu at Goldfields TVET College, whose inputs made the case study possible. Special thanks are due to reviewers Jolanda Morkel and Dr Daniela Gachago for their thoughtful, incisive feedback on the chapter, Barbara Jones for constructive engagement, and Dr Tabisa Mayisela for guiding the entire COOL project. Thanks are also due to the Centre for Innovation in Learning and Teaching at the University of Cape Town, which hosted the COOL project, and the South African Department of Higher Education and Training for funding it.

References

Bolton, H., Matsau, L., & Blom, R. (2020). Flexible learning pathways: The National Qualifications Framework backbone. Report for the IIEP-UNESCO Research – SDG4: Planning for flexible learning pathways in higher education. IIEP-UNESCO. https://www.saqa.org.za/sites/default/files/2020-12/Flexible-Learning-Pathways-in-SA-2020-12.pdf

Cox, G., Masuku, B., & Willmers, M. (2020). Open textbooks and social justice: Open educational practices to address economic, cultural and political injustice at the University of Cape Town. *Journal of Interactive Media in Education,* 1(2), 1–10. https://open.uct.ac.za/handle/11427/31887

DHET (Department of Higher Education and Training). (2013). White paper for post-school education and training: Building an expanded, effective and integrated post-school system. *Government Gazette*, 37229. https://www.gov.za/documents/white-paper-post-school-education-and-training-building-expanded-effective-and-integrated

DHET. (2017). Open learning policy framework for post-school education and training. *Government Gazette.* http://pmg-assets.s3-website-eu-west-1.amazonaws.com/170407openlearningframework-postschooleduc.pdf

DHET. (2018). Committee report on higher education and training 2018/19 budget. https://pmg.org.za/committee-meeting/26339/

DHET. (2021). Statistics on post-school education and training in South African 2019. https://cdn.lgseta.co.za/resources/research_and_reports/Statistics%20on%20Post-School%20Education%20and%20Training%20in%20South%20Africa,%202019.pdf

DLL (Division for Lifelong Learning). (2014). Draft report: Mapping of flexible learning and teaching at University of Western Cape (UWC).

DoE (Department of Education). (1995). White paper on education and training. https://www.education.gov.za/Portals/0/Documents/Legislation/White%20paper/White%20paper%20on%20Education%20and%20Training%201995.pdf?ver=2008-03-05-111656-000

Fraser, N. (1995). From redistribution to recognition? Dilemmas of justice in a 'postsocialist' age. *New Left Review*, 1/212, 68–93. https://newleftreview.org/issues/i212/articles/nancy-fraser-from-redistribution-to-recognition-dilemmas-of-justice-in-a-post-socialist-age

Fraser, N. (2005). Reframing justice in a globalizing world. *New Left Review,* 36, 69–88.

Fraser, N., & Naples, N. A. (2004). To interpret the world and to change it: An interview with Nancy Fraser. *Signs: Journal of Women in Culture and Society*, 29(4), 1103–1124. https://www.journals.uchicago.edu/doi/full/10.1086/382631

HEA (Higher Education Academy). (2015). *Framework for flexible learning in higher education.* Higher Education Academy.

Hodgkinson-Williams, C. A., & Trotter, H. (2018). A social justice framework for understanding open educational resources and practices in the global south. *Journal of Learning for Development*, 5(3), 204–224.

Jones, B., & Walters, S. (2015). Flexible learning and teaching: looking beyond the binary of full-time/part-time provision in South African higher education. *Critical Studies in Teaching and Learning*, 3(1), 61–84.

Khuluvhe, M., & Mathibe, R. (2021). Fact Sheet: Throughput rate for TVET College Students (National Certificate Vocational for the period 2016 to 2018). DHET.

Morkel, J., & Cronjé, J. (2019). Flexible learning provision for architecture in South Africa: Lessons learnt from an industry-university collaboration. In E. N. Ivala & C. L. Scott (Eds.), *Faculty perspectives on vocational training in South Africa* (pp. 19–33). Routledge.

NPC (National Planning Commission). (2013). *National development plan vision 2030.* http://policyresearch.limpopo.gov.za/bitstream/handle/123456789/941/NDP%20Vision%202030.pdf?s

Vygotsky, L. S. (1978). *Mind in society.* Harvard University Press.

HOW TO CITE THIS CHAPTER

Van Wyk, G., Huang, C.-W., & Hodgkinson-Williams, C. A. (2022). Using a social justice lens to explore the possibilities and limitations of flexible learning provision in a South African TVET college. In T. Mayisela, S. C. Govender & C. A. Hodgkinson-Williams (Eds.), *Open learning as a means of advancing social justice: Cases in post-school education and training in South Africa* (pp. 70–85). African Minds. doi: 10.47622/9781928502425_3

This work is licensed under a Creative Commons Attribution 4.0 International (CC BY 4.0) licence.

4

Blended learning as a means of opening up learning at Northlink TVET College in South Africa

A social justice perspective

Mukhtar Raban & Tabisa Mayisela

SUMMARY Blended learning has become a critical element in the ensemble of learning and teaching approaches in post-school education and training (PSET) as a means to provide flexible and pedagogically inclusive education. With the Department of Higher Education and Training (DHET) in South Africa calling for increased open learning initiatives, many Technical and Vocational Education and Training (TVET) colleges are responding through ICT-mediated adaptations of their learning and teaching approaches, such as blended learning. Northlink TVET College in Cape Town, the top performer in South Africa in the 2018 final National Certificate Vocational (NCV) examination results and well-known for its blended learning initiatives, was chosen to showcase its flexible and inclusive pedagogical approaches. This case study employed a qualitative approach that used in-depth interviews and a focus group with the college's Education and Training Unit manager, two lecturers, and six students to explore the blended learning initiative and practices at the college. This was to interrogate the ways in which the blended learning initiatives were informed by open learning principles, and the extent to which this mode of learning provision at the college can be deemed to be, using Fraser's (2005) critical theory for analysis, socially just. Findings indicate that explicit accommodations in the pedagogical design and implementation of blended learning were made by the college to ameliorate certain financial and political injustices often experienced by students and staff. However, significant strides are yet to be taken to address certain cultural injustices. This study holds the potential to inspire teaching and learning practices and blended learning provision at the college and other PSET institutions, in realisation of the open learning agenda. Recommendations for both the college and DHET have been made.

Keywords: blended learning, emergency remote teaching, open learning, social justice, TVET

Introduction

Technological advancements in most areas of society have changed the ways in which knowledge is shared and disseminated, and how communication and relationship-building take place (Allen & Seaman, 2014). These societal shifts have had an indelible influence on the educational landscape, arguably the most pervasive of these is the proliferation of online and blended learning (BL) initiatives in educational institutions (Domingue, 2016). With educational institutions facing an array of challenges, including the need to increase numbers of students accessing quality education, the high cost of full-time education and diminishing faculty resources due to large student numbers, online learning and BL are being explored as possible solutions to these strains in the sector (Godlewska et al., 2019). Similarly, the COVID-19 pandemic resulted in most higher education institutions (HEIs) globally shifting to some form of online or ICT-mediated, emergency remote teaching (ERT) (Marinoni et al., 2020). However, ERT exacerbated existing socio-economic challenges in the sector.

In South Africa, the Department of Higher Education and Training (DHET) has highlighted the importance of 'opening up' learning through the provision of strategically increased use of information and communication technologies (ICTs) in education as part of an open learning initiative. In the draft *Open Learning Policy Framework* (OLPF) *for Post-School Education and Training* (PSET), DHET conceives the open learning initiative as a way of:

> removing barriers to *access* created by various factors such as *geographic distance from educational campuses*, timetable scheduling that is incompatible with people's working lives or family responsibilities, unaffordable fees, *alienating pedagogic practices*, lack of *access to technology*, lack of physical educational infrastructure, and discrimination on the basis of gender, age, race, ethnicity, social class, language or disability. (DHET, 2017, p. 373, emphasis added)

This chapter thus explores how access to, and quality of, learning opportunities could be opened up and improved through the provision of technology infrastructure, and technology-enhanced learning practices, such as BL. Research conducted on BL in relation to HEI students' access and engagement is on an upward trajectory (Nash, 2014; Picciano, 2006), with BL demonstrating increasing influence on higher education, particularly with "carefully designed" pedagogical practices (Picciano, 2006). BL also holds the potential to contribute to removing many of the barriers to access faced by student cohorts in Technical and Vocational Education and Training (TVET) colleges (Richardson, 2012).

The extent to which TVET colleges have responded to DHET's call for 'open learning', and studies of best practice within this sector, have not been adequately documented. To this end, a case study was undertaken on BL at Northlink TVET College in Cape Town, South Africa. This chapter explores the extent to which BL initiatives at the college are enacting open learning principles and how the initiatives address key social justice concerns undeniably integral to open learning.

Prior to delving into the case study on Northlink College, it is critical to explore BL design and its potential to be explicitly undergirded by open learning principles as a means to achieving the ultimate goals of social justice: economically, culturally and politically. This will be followed by a description of the case study, methodology, findings, conclusion and recommendations.

Blended learning, open learning and social justice

According to DHET, BL is one of the learning and teaching (L&T) approaches that can be employed to 'opening' up learning. With the notion of open learning as having a social justice intent, it becomes critical to evaluate whether BL approaches, when adopted pedagogically and impacting learning design, are able to sustain the social justice ambitions inherent in open learning.

Blended learning in HEIs and the TVET sector

HEIs and TVET colleges are increasingly adopting BL as a mode of offering classes and courses (Garrison & Vaughan, 2007), which has become "an almost indispensable segment of the complex ensemble of higher education" (Bauk, 2015, p. 323). BL, also referred to as "hybrid learning" (Gecer & Dag, 2012), involves "integrating online with traditional face-to-face class activities in a planned, pedagogically valuable manner (Picciano, 2009, p. 10). The 'blend' of L&T fuses two historically distinct modes of delivery. According to Bath and Bourke:

> Blended learning is realised in teaching and learning environments where there is an effective integration of different modes of delivery, models of teaching and styles of learning as a result of adopting a strategic and systematic approach to the use of technology combined with the best features of face-to-face interaction. (2010, p. 1)

That is, BL is fundamentally constructed with fully online ICT-mediated activities on the one extreme and conventional classroom activities on the other, with a range of BL activities in between. In addition to this framing, DHET elaborates upon BL as being:

> The provision of structured learning opportunities using a combination of contact, resource-based, and/or distance education methodologies, with different levels of ICT support to suit different purposes, audiences, and contexts. (DHET, 2017, p. 362)

This more comprehensive framing of BL, through the extension of the conventionally constructed face-to-face domain to include resource-based and distance education methodologies, provides a wider scope for BL application. Indispensable to BL, especially for transforming TVET, is the context and approaches to 'blending', so as to "gain maximum advantage" from the modes of provision (Latchem, 2017, p. 31). For this study, BL is construed as integrating face-to-face classes with online resource-based learning and activities.

Implementation of blended learning in TVET colleges

While many studies have explored the importance of ICTs in education, particularly their potential to transform HEIs and TVET colleges, not much attention has been given to examples of best practice that are contextually relevant to the South African TVET sector (Balfour et al., 2015; Latchem, 2017). At the same time, a variety of financially related aspects, such as infrastructural, capacity and resourcing requirements often present themselves as challenges that dominate in developing countries' colleges in the TVET sector of Africa and particularly, South Africa (Athanase et al., 2015; Obwoge & Kwamboka, 2016). As a result, not many TVET colleges in South Africa have been in a position to fully explore ICTs in education (Isaacs, 2007; Mata, 2015) and by extension, to roll out BL opportunities as yet.

However, as a result of the lockdowns enforced in South Africa during 2020, and face-to-face teaching not being permitted in the more stringent periods, TVET colleges were forced to shift to online and emergency remote L&T[1]. As the lockdown restrictions were eased, but face-to-face teaching was still limited, some TVET colleges responded with combinations of online and face-to-face L&T, that is, possible BL approaches. DHET facilitated the shift to increased online L&T in the TVET sector by providing online and remote L&T support initiatives, inclusive of supporting colleges with their learning management systems (LMS), having college websites zero-rated (i.e., Internet Service Providers do not charge students for the usage of selected educational websites)[2], and aiding with multimodal ways of disseminating knowledge via TV and radio broadcasts (PMG, 2020). However, most colleges in the TVET sector still face substantial challenges in effectively employing ICT-mediated L&T approaches to provide quality learning experiences for students (Mboweni, 2020).

Pedagogical design implications for blended learning

According to Yasak and Alias (2015), the use of ICTs in TVET institutions, specifically in e-learning and BL initiatives should be aligned with improving student learning outcomes. For instance, in Drysdale et al.'s (2013) study, best practices and pedagogic value for BL and open and distance learning (ODL[3]) were foregrounded. Likewise, Balfour et al. (2015) posit that the introduction of ICTs necessitates the consideration and rise of "innovative" pedagogies and "alternative approaches" to L&T. Balfour et al. (2015, p. 4) cite Thorne (2003) who proposes that "the skill of being able to marry pedagogy to an appropriate blend of technology and learning is not simply the outcome of linking conventional approaches to the online environment". It requires critical consideration of all dimensions of the holistic L&T experience.

As described above, BL essentially draws on pedagogies that are primarily underpinned by two different modes of provision, namely, online learning, and face-to-face (conventional) learning. In order for BL to achieve improved outcomes, appropriate pedagogies that speak to the specific context of the L&T encounters, have to be selected (McGee & Reis, 2012), and all factors relevant to the students, courses, lecturers and institution should be considered (Bañados, 2013; Ozdamli, 2012; Precel et al., 2009). Furthermore, on the basis of their analysis of 205 doctoral dissertations and Masters theses in the domain of BL, Drysdale et al.

---

[1] According to Hodges et al. (2020), emergency remote teaching is a temporary shift of instructional delivery to an alternate delivery mode due to crisis circumstances. It involves the use of fully remote teaching solutions for instruction or education that would otherwise be delivered face-to-face or as blended or hybrid courses and that will return to that format once the crisis or emergency has abated (p. 6).

[2] https://www.vox.co.za/education-website-zero-rated

[3] As cited by DHET (2017, p. 363), "the use of the acronym 'ODL', implies erroneously that ALL distance programmes are based on open education principles. This policy framework does not support this term because of the ambiguity associated with its meaning." ODL is used here with specific reference to how some institutions may self-categorise themselves, and how the term is found in literature.

(2013) argued that institutional policy and adoption of BL could strengthen an educational institution's ability to improve their pedagogical practices.

A crucial area that surfaces as a result of foregrounding particular pedagogical approaches to effective BL implementation is the learning design of the course. BL should be "fully adaptable to the program or institutional needs and does not need to be complicated" (Drysdale et al., 2013, p. 93). While there are multiple approaches to learning design, sometimes referred to as instructional design[4] (particularly in reference to the online learning component of a BL iteration), it might be useful to consider a simplified list of key considerations for designing courses and learning encounters that include online learning activities, such as BL. Domingue (2016, pp. 372–377) outlines such key course considerations as including the:

- diversity of student demographics
- user (lecturers and students) familiarity with, and required support to use, the technological platform
- choice of the learning formats (synchronous and asynchronous) to best support student needs
- course structure and delivery
- course activities
- accommodations for students with English as an additional language as well as those with disabilities.

By engaging in a critical and deeper deliberation of these design considerations, a response should be found to the fundamental priorities of how BL could remove barriers to "access", forgo "alienating pedagogies" and be more inclusive (DHET, 2017, p. 373). Deliberations such as these may be more comprehensive when engaging with the notion of 'open learning'.

Open learning

In particular contexts, the term 'open learning' is used synonymously with 'open education' (see Bates, 2005), while in DHET's draft OLPF, 'open education' is part of a more comprehensive 'open learning' ambition. The philosophy of 'open education' has a long history and started with various open universities offering access to those who did not necessarily qualify for entry into undergraduate courses. In this context Bates (2005) emphasised open learning was associated with the removal of barriers to learning – specifically "no prior qualifications to study" (p. 5). He asserts that open learning must be "scalable as well as flexible", and that 'openness' has "particular implications for the use of technology" (Bates, 2005, p. 5).

On the contrary, in the South African context, 'open learning' is associated with PSET formal education, with institutions having stringent entry requirements. The DHET draft policy framework conceives 'open learning' as:

---

[4] Instructional design is defined as "the systematic process by which instructional materials are designed, developed, and delivered. The terms instructional design, instructional technology, learning experience design, educational technology, curriculum design, and instructional systems design (ISD), are often used interchangeably" (Instructional Design Central, 2017). https://www.instructionaldesigncentral.com/whatisinstructionaldesign

An educational approach which combines the principles of learner-centredness, lifelong learning, flexibility of learning provision, the removal of barriers to access learning, the recognition for credit of prior learning experience, the provision of learner support, the construction of learning programmes in the expectation that learners can succeed, and the maintenance of rigorous quality assurance over the design of learning materials and support systems. (DHET, 2017, p. 363)

According to DHET, as a principle-based concept, "open learning is fundamentally about access and success, with flexibility of provision contributing to expanded access, and quality of provision contributing to improved student success" (2017, p. 373). Flexibility of provision "allows learners more scope to determine where, when, what and how they will learn", whereas conditions for "a fair chance of learner success [include] contextually appropriate resources and sound pedagogical practices" (DHET, 2017, p. 373). That is, learning provision must be flexible and of quality.

With open learning principles serving as a set of possible characterising descriptors, flexibility can be achieved via a range of modes of provision, including BL (DHET, 2017). BL is a suitable mode for the realisation of open learning goals – provided there is access to ICT for all – due to its ambition to remove barriers to learning, and offering flexible and scalable learning provision. In the context of the 50 public South African TVETs offering campus-based education and training, BL is more suitable compared to other ICT-mediated modes of learning provision, such as distance learning[5] and fully online learning. In fact, DHET (2013, 2020) emphasises that there is no provision for distance learning in the TVET sector, and "the few colleges that make use of distance provision still use the traditional correspondence paper-based model, which does very little to support student success" (p. 20).

While ICTs have, undoubtedly, become increasingly available over the last several decades, there has been little attention to how ICTs support or hinder goals of educational diversity, inclusion, and social justice (Sull, 2013, as cited in Domingue, 2016, p. 370). In a similar light, a deeper evaluation of BL as a form of open learning necessitates exploring issues of social justice.

Social justice and open learning

With the ambition of widening access to quality education through deliberate and inclusive mechanisms, particularly in consideration to developing economies, open learning initiatives and institutions often find themselves duly aligned to social justice imperatives (Tait, 2013). Nancy Fraser, a social justice theorist and philosopher has written extensively about social justice, and views it as "parity of participation" (2005, p. 73), whereby all "relevant social actors" are in a position to participate and engage "in fair and open processes" (Fraser, 2005, p. 87). Fraser (2005) holds that social justice comprises three critical and interrelated dimensions: economic, cultural and political.

---

[5] In the South African context, distance education is conceptualised as "a mode of provision based primarily on a set of teaching and learning strategies (or educational methods) that can be used to overcome spatial and/or temporal separation between educators and students (DHET, 2014, p. 12). It has had a trajectory, starting off with paper-based resources and communication followed by other media, such as radio, telephone, audio cassettes, satellite television, video, interactive computer software including open source learning environments, collaborative networks on the World Wide Web and the inexhaustible learning resources of the Internet (DHET, 2012).

In terms of economic justice, Fraser argues that individuals can be excluded, or their participation inhibited, through inadequate resources, deemed to be "economic maldistribution" (2005). In an open learning context, in which L&T is done partially online, access to internet, availability of devices, and access to appropriate facilities and platforms for online components of BL are but some of the areas which would be categorised as economic concerns. Responses to economic maldistribution, to advance social justice imperatives, would take on "affirmative" (or "ameliorative" as termed by Hodgkinson-Williams and Trotter [2018]) forms of "economic redistribution" or "restructuring" (Fraser, 2005). These could include paying attention to student access to devices, internet connectivity, and learning platforms.

From a cultural perspective, Fraser asserts that participants may face "misrecognition" through "institutionalised hierarchies of cultural value that deny them the requisite standing" (2005, p. 73). Fraser (2005) contends that social justice calls for recognising the cultural backgrounds, histories and practices of the "social actors" in the institution. In applying this principle to open learning advanced through blended learning, students' 'cultural' backgrounds (such as languages, race, and gender) and knowledge and skills, are often not recognised. This form of misrecognition can be addressed through pedagogical and learning design approaches that pay attention to these above-mentioned cultural aspects.

The political dimension, according to Fraser (2005), explores who: (1) has a voice in decision-making; and (2) is included or excluded, which are categorised as political "representation" and "framing" respectively. Participants would face political inequality if they are excluded from decision-making processes, platforms or structures (misrepresentation), which ultimately result in social injustice being perpetuated. With respect to misframing, "the injustice arises when the community's boundaries are drawn in such a way as to wrongly exclude some people from the chance to participate *at all* in its authorized contests over justice" (Fraser, 2005, p. 76). In relation to open learning, political issues arise in terms of who decides on the pedagogical approaches and delivery modes of learning, among other concerns. From a BL perspective, political representation and reframing are addressed by including lecturer and student voice in the choice, design and sequencing of their BL content and activities.

Foregrounding social justice in blended learning approaches

Domingue (2016) asserts that lecturers must explore ways in which ICTs in education advance and not harm the goals of social justice. The guiding principles that Domingue developed for the offering of an online course for social justice education, are easily adaptable for a general BL course that seeks to foster and work towards social justice goals. These underscore the need to:

- Foster community and interpersonal relationships among students and the facilitator
- Create an inclusive learning environment that is adaptable to diverse learning styles and social identities
- Emphasise dialogue and solicit multiple voices and perspectives
- Facilitate the learning and model of dialogic, inclusive participation
- Provide course material that addresses contemporary social justice topics while also providing historical contexts for these legacies

- Promote experimental activities that provoke and involve question-posing, moving students beyond the "comfort zone" toward perspective-taking and new knowledge
- Provide for an exploration of social identities so that students can understand how these identities are situated within systems of power and privilege
- Provide opportunities for application of course material and experimentation of social action beyond the classroom context. (Domingue, 2016, p. 371)

Considering the principles and goals of open learning that have a firmly embedded social justice intent, and the framing of BL, this study adopted a critical, social justice lens in examining effective BL practices at the TVET college, illustrated in Figure 1.

Figure 1. Framework of the study

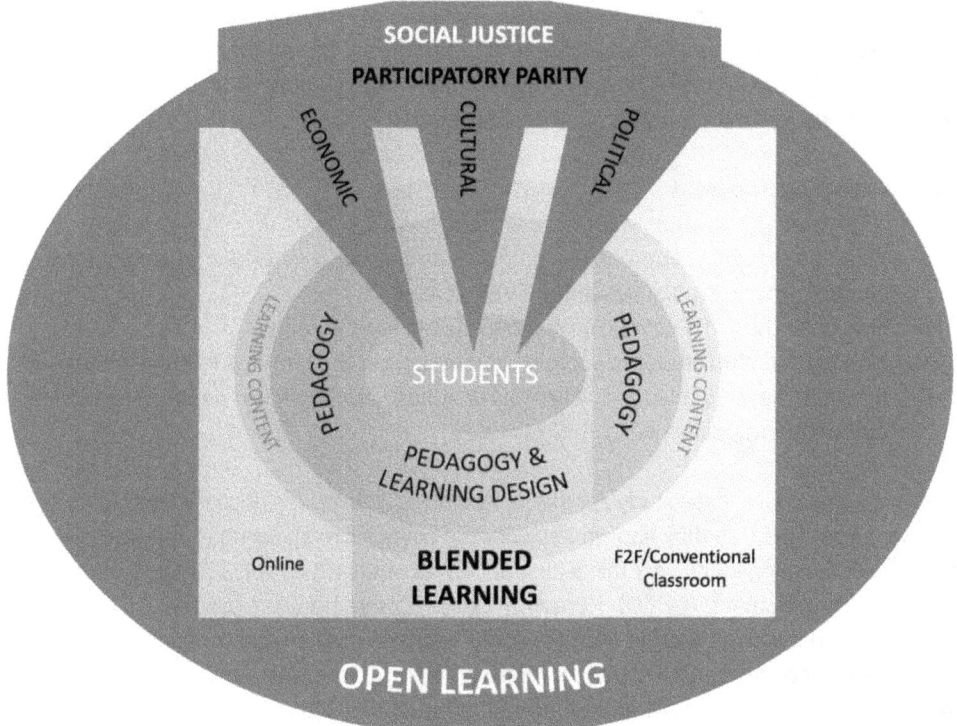

With blended learning having been explored as a means of providing open learning, the social justice underpinning of open learning with its economic, cultural and political dimensions served as the critical lens through which the blended learning encounters experienced by the students were examined.

In short, with emerging scholarship focusing on the pedagogic uses of technology, especially the potential of foregrounding BL best practices, this study sought to interrogate these areas in the context of open learning, examining the extent to which these could advance social justice aspirations.

The case

Research was undertaken at Northlink College in Cape Town, which is ranked as one of South Africa's top TVET colleges[6]. Northlink College has seven campuses and about 18 000 students, and its BL initiatives are broadly driven by its Education and Training Unit (ETU). As early as 2013 and 2015, Northlink College was part of the Laptop Initiative[7], and Innovative laptop e-book project[8], where the Microsoft Technology Associate (MTA) students as well as second year Tourism and ICT students, each received a laptop. With respect to the latter, the then HoD for Blended Learning pronounced that students would "be able to blend traditional teaching with 21st Century technology in a responsible and innovative way".

Research methodology

The objective of this study was to establish the ways in which BL is opening up learning opportunities for students at a TVET college in South Africa. The following main question was used to guide this study: *In what ways is blended learning opening up learning and enabling participatory parity for students at Northlink College?*

The subsidiary questions:

- What pedagogical approaches and/or learning designs underpin and inform the blended learning initiatives at the TVET college?
- How does the TVET college operationalise blended learning?
- How do staff and students perceive and engage in the blended learning initiatives?
- In what ways is blended learning enabling participatory parity, economically, culturally and politically?

Following a qualitative, case study approach, Northlink College was purposively chosen based on advice from DHET as they had worked with the college's main campus and were aware of this blended learning initiative. Ethical clearance was obtained from UCT's Centre for Higher Education Development (CHED) Research Ethics Committee, permission to access the college participants was received from the DHET research division and consent obtained from interviewees. Though the COOL project commenced in 2019, data was generated in 2020, under lockdown restrictions due to the outbreak of the COVID-19 pandemic. Hence, online data collection methods, such as Zoom and WhatsApp were used. We approached the Manager of the ETU who then recruited lecturers and students she had supported on blended learning. This was an effective snowball sampling approach (Cohen et al., 2007). Semi-structured interviews were conducted with the Manager, ETU and two lecturers, and a focus group was held with six students enrolled in different programmes based in four campuses. The focus group discussion took place synchronously in a Zoom meeting, and the same participants subsequently formed part of, and participated in, a WhatsApp group chat (their mobile numbers were confirmed during the synchronous session) asynchronously over the period of one week. The purpose of

---

[6] https://www.northlink.co.za/northlink-college-ranked-number-1-in-the-country/
[7] https://www.northlink.co.za/northlink-college-laptop-initiative-giving-students-the-edge/
[8] https://www.northlink.co.za/innovative-laptop-e-book-project/

this extension was to accommodate any student afterthoughts and the first author also used the opportunity to pose clarity-seeking questions that allowed for more detailed responses when compared to those of the synchronous discussion.

The recordings and chat were transcribed, and data was coded and analysed using Atlas.ti. An inductive approach was applied, where the research questions served as a framework for descriptive analysis and responses to these questions were grouped into emerging themes. The social justice-informed framework was deductively used to normatively gauge the extent to which the BL initiative was socially just.

Findings and discussion

The study's findings and discussion presented below, centre around the operationalisation and offering of BL. Since the practices were more likely to change to emergency remote teaching during the pandemic, the findings are grouped into two categories: before and during the pandemic and ERT.

Operationalising blended learning as a means to 'open' learning: Prioritising access and support

With a motto of "No student or staff member left behind" (ETU Manager), the study revealed that Northlink College employed a sound strategy in operationalising and employing BL on a college-wide basis. Based on information from the ETU manager, the blended and online learning of the college is broadly overseen and driven by the Education and Training unit. The Unit also focuses on providing professional development opportunities for staff and oversees the use and maintenance of their systems. The college has a Digital Learning Committee (DLC) that consists of management, campus, staff, lecturer and student representatives. The DLC focused on crafting the college's plans to increase awareness and use of ICTs in education. The DLC surveyed lecturing staff in 2019 to determine the types of technologies and approaches in use and audited the infrastructure and resources available to them. The survey results provided the committee with insights to refine the college's plans and focus on areas that needed urgent attention. The college consolidated its drive to promote BL approaches through including it in their teaching and learning policy.

Blended learning before the pandemic and ERT

According to the ETU Manager, the college utilised Moodle as their learning management system (LMS), supporting the online L&T needs of about 475 staff members and 18 000 students. The Education and Training unit produced video tutorials and online guides for students and staff, to familiarise them with accessing and navigating the LMS. The unit also aims to establish and enhance the quality of the online component. For instance, it prescribed minimum standards for Moodle course sites and digital material, and disseminated templates to academic staff to facilitate quality learning resource development. While the college has the LMS in place, lecturers were encouraged to use other technologies and platforms, in conjunction with Moodle, to accomplish the goals of BL.

The college established a "Moodle Framework", which is hierarchical in structure, to explicate accountability and lines of reporting to the Education and Training unit and college management. This framework served as a support mechanism that enabled academic staff to locate relevant colleagues that could assist them with various aspects of their online L&T needs. Each campus has a "Moodle Manager", viewed as a "Moodle Champion", to drive the use of ICTs in education and Moodle on the specific campus (ETU Manager). The Manager further shared that:

> The (Moodle) framework was important because staff didn't really know who they must go and speak to. ... Now you know exactly who to go to for help. And even if you went through the training, but you're still unsure, then that person would assist you. (ETU Manager)

One lecturer also shared that a community of practice was fostered through staff members using sessions in the scheduled staff meetings to share best practices with each other. This lecturer emphasised, "The open sharing of practices with other lecturers contributed to the online and BL culture fostered on a specific campus" (Lecturer 1).

The college also has an Open Learning Centre (OLC) on each of its campuses, which provides students with access to computers and the internet, and has staff available to support students' online learning needs. The OLCs are managed and run by the Student Support department of the college. The college also has Wi-Fi available to all students and staff on all of their campuses.

However, the Manager highlighted the discouraging culture developing on certain campuses and in specific Science, Technology, Engineering and Mathematics (STEM) disciplines as one of the challenges the college experienced in effectively deploying BL. BL was viewed to be methodically incompatible with the conventional disciplinary L&T approaches in STEM disciplines. Student participants from STEM qualifications confirmed that they experienced minimal online elements during lockdown, in comparison to student participants from other disciplines.

Blended learning and ERT during the pandemic

The COVID-19 pandemic resulted in heightened use of online L&T, and the college relied on WhatsApp for facilitating communication with students and distributing their initial learning materials. As a result, "WhatsApp will become a norm for communication, from the point of future course registration, as new students shift to learning via the LMS" (ETU Manager). The use of online and BL during the lockdowns also resulted in the DLC re-evaluating its function, and the Manager of the ETU acknowledged that they would have to shift to a more comprehensive support-oriented role going forward.

Overall, the approach of Northlink College in operationalising BL can be viewed as a means to 'opening' up learning. With BL recognised as one of the ways in which 'open learning' can occur (Balfour et al., 2015; DHET, 2017), Northlink's approach to providing a supportive network, albeit largely targeted at staff currently, fosters open learning principles such as flexibility of learning provision. To better gauge the extent to which the learning provision is socially just, it is useful to analyse the operationalisation via Fraser's (2005) dimensions of social justice.

From an economic perspective, the provision of campus-wide Wi-Fi, access to OLCs, a functional LMS, and using WhatsApp for student communication and material dissemination can all be viewed as ameliorative responses to economic injustices or resource maldistribution.

While Gon and Rawekar (2017) assert that WhatsApp is an effective means for fostering online learning practices, the greatest challenge cited by the student participants in the study, in relation to engaging in the BL, was obtaining data for engaging on WhatsApp as well as accessing the LMS and learning resources off-campus. A partial response to this was fully zero-rating the LMS, but the college experienced issues with students using certain mobile network providers, being able to access it on a zero-rated basis.

In another setback, online resources (such as videos) stored on external servers but linked to the college's LMS were not zero-rated and required data when accessed off-campus. One student also shared that not all students had personal devices and at the same time, were not in a position to remain on campus after lectures, to use the computers in the OLC, due to travel limitations (Student 1). Another student shared that some had a device, and even data, but network reception in their residential areas was poor, thus preventing them from fully engaging online (Student 4). A lack of access to the internet, which in turn serves as the greatest barrier to students effectively enjoying the richness of BL encounters was also noted elsewhere (Larbi-Apau et al., 2020; Songsangyos & Ruangthong, 2016). It is worth noting that there are over 100 public internet access sites (including libraries) in Cape Town[9], but students may either be unaware of them or live far away from them, which may relate to transport challenges as well. Also, libraries only allow users one-hour internet access per day and are closed at night and during lockdown when students are most likely to require internet connectivity for learning.

The second Northlink College priority is supporting lecturers to become "actors" (Fraser, 2005) or enactors of BL through building their capacity to use the LMS, and thereby, allowing lecturers to influence how students take up BL. Al-Busaidi's (2012) study on the link between a functional LMS and BL success emphasises that instructors play a significant role in students' take of an LMS and the BL approach more broadly. The provision of support to staff in terms of training and professional development, is a form of cultural recognition of lecturers' digital literacy and pedagogical skillset. Literature abounds on the importance of providing adequate staff and student training and support for successful BL initiatives. The college's approach illustrates an entanglement of economic and cultural responses which potentially enhance the implementation of BL.

However, the findings highlight the lack of BL uptake in the STEM programmes at the college, which illuminates a political misrepresentation of STEM students. While this may be traced to lecturer perceptions that STEM subjects cannot be effectively taught online (ETU Manager), studies show that additional pedagogical guidance may be needed to support STEM academics in their use of BL (Hains-Wesson & Tytler, 2015). Interestingly, Owston et al.'s (2020) study comparing performance and perceptions of STEM and non-STEM students in BL programmes found that STEM students performed significantly higher and had more positive perceptions than the non-STEM students.

It is worth noting that Northlink's approach to operationalising BL is significantly politically inclusive and representative, with respect to the lecturers. The establishment of a representative DLC, surveying of staff to determine their needs and obtain their input, formulation of 'Moodle Frameworks' for inclusion and support, and fostering of an agentive environment that lets lecturers drive their individual BL agendas (but from a basis of minimum

---

[9] https://www.capetown.gov.za/Explore%20and%20enjoy/Get-online/Public-Wi-Fi-zones/Public-Wi-Fi-across-the-city

Northlink quality standards) culminate in broad political representation. The inclusion of the BL approaches in the college's L&T policy and practices can be considered to be politically transformative. While all of these steps were taken by the college to foster an inclusive and supportive environment for staff, the college acknowledged that it is yet to share the same level of input and representation from students. As such, the absence of increased student input in the operationalisation of BL is politically misframing. At the time of conducting this study, the college was in the process of surveying students to obtain increased insights into their perceptions of online and BL, to further refine their future approaches. This activity would provide ameliorative relief to student representation in their continued BL initiatives.

In short, Northlink invests in BL, which focuses on widening flexibility of learning provision and providing lecturer professional development to enhance the quality L&T fundamental principles of open learning (DHET, 2017).

The blended learning encounters: Perceptions, pedagogical and learning design considerations, and student engagement

Staff and student perceptions of blended learning

Staff who participated in this study held overwhelmingly positive views of BL, citing it as a "miracle", "absolutely brilliant" (Lecturer 1) initiative that "is aligned with our times as we're moving forward ... at an extreme pace" (Lecturer 2). One lecturer further commented that BL holds the potential to reduce limitations imposed by the type of registration and facilitates the L&T project:

> With BL, you will not have any type of full time, distance nor part-time, but we'll just have a student who will have access to material on his or her time ... which makes teaching much easier. (Lecturer 2)

Student participants were divided in their views of BL. While most of them appreciated some form of online learning, the majority preferred the face-to-face mode, citing "the richness of social engagement that prevails in contact sessions" (Student 2).

Pedagogical considerations prior to the pandemic and ERT

With respect to pedagogical considerations, lecturers shared that they mainly used the online learning component for resource-based learning and resource sharing. The LMS was used as a repository of lecture slides, videos, and past question papers. One lecturer highlighted that quizzes were also released, via a different online platform, as a means of formative assessment (Lecturer 1). Another lecturer asserted that because of his developed proficiency in the Google Classroom platform, he actively used it for online L&T (Lecturer 2). Staff and students highlighted the value of using WhatsApp as a tool for online communication and engagement with each other. Lecturers also emphasised that they promoted 'cultural inclusion' in their BL approaches by drawing on examples from the students' immediate environments and South African contexts and considering how students can apply concepts outside of the lecture halls, and in future situations (Lecturer 1; Lecturer 2).

Students viewed their 'online learning' as mainly revision opportunities, consolidating what was taught in the face-to-face classes (Student 1). When the Manager of the Education and Training unit was asked if any collaborative learning was taking place online, she responded by highlighting that their initial priority was to get lecturers comfortable with using Moodle for resource-based learning (ETU Manager). The lecturers further acknowledged that additional training, in the form of pedagogical support, would be needed to improve the quality of their BL offerings.

Two lecturers highlighted that students were duly considered in the design of their BL offerings. One lecturer shared that the students' financial and cultural backgrounds were factored into how she structured the learning encounters, by considering the platforms she used and ways in which students were able to access online content, and the type of content included in her classes (Lecturer 2). Highlighting the importance of selecting content to which the students can relate, she stated:

> Our students tend to avoid things that are different, things that are unfamiliar... So, with my students, if I show them a video of a British person speaking and using British terminology, for example, they do not feel comfortable because it's almost that they feel a bit inferior because this person is sounding a little bit unfamiliar to them (Lecturer 2).

The lecturer reported that she drew on examples from South African communities, so that students were able to relate to the content. Both lecturers confirmed that relevant, locally-produced online resources (videos) that resonate with South African students are extremely limited, thus hindering adequate cultural relevance of their BL encounters. While the lecturers highlighted the cultural considerations made in the designing of BL encounters, the student participants never explicitly acknowledged that these resonated with their learning resources. Students and staff highlighted that the English language tended to pose a barrier to learning, and suggested that the language policy of the college accommodates multilingual practices (Lecturer 2; Student 3). The Manager of the Education and Training unit confirmed that the college had started to use other languages in specific programmes where student demographics and linguistic backgrounds called for another language of L&T to be considered.

The college also shared that a substantial hindrance to shifting to more online assessment, particularly summative assessment, which would impact the uptake of BL, is the DHET policy limitations that still mandate all assessment to be completed offline in hard-copy formats (ETU Manager).

Pedagogical considerations during the pandemic and ERT

The COVID-19 context forced the college to shift quite swiftly to more online offerings, with limited face-to-face engagement. When lockdown restrictions gradually eased, the students were permitted back on campuses. The hasty shift to ERT left some students feeling overwhelmed, more so because they had to "find their way" on their own (Student 4). This student shared that they were often inundated with a lot of resources being sent to them, usually via WhatsApp, but inadequate explanations or clarity providing them with the 'bigger picture' about what they were learning. They felt 'disconnected' from their lecturers during ERT and appreciated the face-to-face learning more, as they were able to pose questions to their lecturers directly if something was unclear, or engage with peers in their classes to translate and clarify concepts (Student 4).

However, one student confirmed that the approachable nature of their lecturer enabled them to pose questions online:

> We have an open relationship with our lecturers. So, if you don't understand something and you're uncomfortable to tell the lecturer in class, then you go to the teacher after the class and then she'll explain to you, or she'll have a video call with you, like she had with me, a Zoom video call and then she explained to me. Because I was in front and I was shy, and I didn't want to speak in front of the class, and then she helped me. And that's why I say I was comfortable talking to the lecturer (Student 5).

Generally, students felt that BL does present opportunities for rich learning experiences, however, this view was based on comparisons drawn with their university student peers that are successfully learning and engaging online. The participants, as TVET college students, felt that they are yet to experience BL in that manner. Another student shared:

> I feel like, with colleges, we have limited access, like, … at university, their classes are more online; whereas college, they don't even do Zoom meetings or Google meetings. It's just like, WhatsApp. Why can't colleges also be like that? (Student 2).

Students shared that they required additional support in terms of 'how to learn online' but emphasised that they were not prepared to forego face-to-face learning in its entirety.

In using Domingue's (2016) guidelines for learning design considerations and learning online for social justice, it can be argued that Northlink College largely advances pedagogical approaches to BL that fundamentally 'open' learning. The consideration of students' demographics and backgrounds, flexibility in the modes of delivery, open engagement between lecturers and students, attempts to foster an inclusive curriculum, and the dialogic nature of the learning encounter comprehensively have traces of social justice-framed BL encounters – which can be viewed as ameliorative means to 'opening' up learning – cultural recognition. Domingue (2016, p. 371) advocates that online learning for social justice must "create an inclusive learning environment that is adaptable to diverse learning styles and social identities", and "emphasise dialogue and solicit multiple voices and perspectives". The participants' responses suggest that Northlink College is on the trajectory of solidifying these features in their approach to BL.

The lecturers' considerations of students' cultural backgrounds in selecting resources for BL activities is commendable in its cultural recognition. The inclusion of relatable and contextually-appropriate learning content is also considered to be a trait of a "decolonised curricula," which complementarily seeks to foster socially just learning experiences (Lebeloane, 2017). However, this is contrasted with the sense of Anglocentric approaches that reinforce the hegemony of English, and linguistically excludes students with lesser English proficiencies, which is a form of cultural misrecognition. In addition to the limited multilingual learning opportunities, the lack of preparedness to learn online, or digital literacy for academic purposes, experienced by students is also a form of misrecognition. The pedagogical disconnect, whereby students might not experience the BL encounters in the ways they may have been designed by lecturers, similarly requires an evaluation of how this cultural injustice can be ameliorated or transformed. The cultural concerns embedded in the Northlink College's approach to BL lie in the pedagogic and learning design areas, which might have to be ameliorated through additional support, foregrounding and explicating the pedagogical approach and learning plan, and increasing multilingual practices. Foregrounding and discussing the pedagogical approaches and learning plans aligns with Pask's Conversation Theory (1976), considered as a method to enhancing BL encounters (Raban, 2018); and ties in with Domingue's (2016) recommendations for a more dialogic learning experience for socially just BL. Ortega (2017) argues that increasing multilingual practices in online engagement is definitively linked to social justice considerations. Therefore, increasing multilingual learning opportunities in BL encounters will undoubtedly advance the social justice intent of BL approach to opening up learning.

In terms of having a say in how or what they learn, the students shared that their lecturers often solicited their feedback and input on particular approaches or content, and the lecturers were generally receptive to recommendations (Student 6). From a political perspective, students' expressed freedom to engage with their lecturers, and provide input and feedback for the BL encounters resembles representation in the student-lecturer L&T relationship. This conforms to Domingue's (2016) notion of 'fostering a community' and 'interpersonal relationships' between students and lecturers, which is a hallmark characteristic of socially just BL. When social justice informs online and BL, "dialogue", "solicit(ing) multiple voices and perspectives", and "dialogic, inclusive participation" are vital (Domingue, 2016, p. 371).

Overarchingly, the BL encounters employed at Northlink College address some of the social justice concerns inherent to L&T, which encouragingly can be viewed as being on path of providing socially just open learning opportunities.

Conclusions and recommendations

This case study investigated the ways in which BL at Northlink College provides flexible learning opportunities for its students. The study used Fraser's (2005) trivalent lens of social justice to evaluate the extent to which the blended learning implementation at the college is socially just.

From an economic perspective, the study found that the college, within its limited capacities, amelioratively responds to economic injustices, through the provision of campus-wide Wi-Fi, a functional LMS, and increased access to computers and internet in their OLCs. However, for parity of participation (Fraser, 2005), every student needs to own a personal mobile device (tablet or laptop) suitable for learning and have reliable internet connectivity off campus. While there are public libraries and other internet sites in Cape Town, these have their own limitations. A transformative response would involve widening internet access in Cape Town and South Africa.

Culturally, the college and lecturers are making attempts to recognise their students through the contextualisation of learning resources and diversifying modes of learning provision, thereby increasing flexibility of learning. However, the study found that additional professional development for lecturers, the foregrounding of pedagogically sound practices, and increased student academic support by lecturers, are needed to mitigate cultural misrecognitions. The issue of anglocentric approaches and limited multilingual opportunities in BL encounters was also raised, highlighting the urgency for ameliorative and transformative action.

With respect to the political dimension of BL, the study found that the college followed fairly inclusive approaches in planning and operationalising it, with staff validating their representation, and college policies and procedures fostering best practice. Students also echoed the sentiment that they felt they had 'a seat at the table' when engaging with their lecturers concerning BL approaches and learning designs. However, at the national level, DHET policy needs to articulate clear guidelines on online continuous assessment.

Based on the findings of the study, it is recommended that: (1) the college provides students with additional training and support for the online learning component, as well as advance multilingual teaching and learning practices, which may aid in enhancing cultural recognition; (2) DHET collaborates with the Department of Communications with respect to the reduction of data costs for students, zero-rating of educational and institutional resource sites, and provision of nation-wide internet connectivity; and (3) DHET adapts its TVET assessment policy to complement the BL and open learning ambitions of the college and TVET sector, by allowing continuous assessments to be conducted completely online. Generally, with support from TVET college management and DHET, blended learning has the potential to enhance flexible learning provision and pedagogically inclusive education.

Acknowledgements

Many thanks to Colleen Cozett, the management, staff and students from Northlink College, whose inputs made the case study possible. Special thanks are due to reviewers Dr Shikha Raturi and Dr Nompilo Tshuma for their thoughtful, incisive feedback on the chapter, and Emeritus Associate Professor Cheryl Ann Hodgkinson-Williams for additional writing support. Thanks are also due to the Centre for Innovation in Learning and Teaching at the University of Cape Town, which hosted the COOL project, and the South African Department of Higher Education and Training for funding it.

References

Al-Busaidi, K. A. (2012). Learners' perspective on critical factors to LMS success in blended learning: An empirical investigation. *Communications of the Association for Information Systems*, 30(2). DOI: 10.17705/1CAIS.03002

Allen, I. E., & Seaman, J. (2014). *Opening the curriculum: Open educational resources in US higher education*. Babson Survey Research Group.

Athanase, N., Cangru, J., Hongbing, L., & Zhihua, C. (2008). Organizational e-learning strategies for technical and vocational education and training (TVET) in Sub-Sahara Africa. In 2008 International Conference on Computer Science and Software Engineering, 5, 267–270.

Balfour, R. J., Van der Walt, J. L., Spamer, E. J., & Tshivhase, A. C. (2015). Blended learning, and open and distance learning: Implications for best practice in higher education. *Progressio*, 37(1), 1–18.

Bañados, E. (2013). A blended-learning pedagogical model for teaching and learning EFL successfully through an online interactive multimedia environment. *CALICO Journal*, 23(3), 533–550.

Bates, A. W. (2005). *Technology, e-learning and distance education*. (2nd ed.). Routledge.

Bath, D., & Bourke, J. (2010). *Getting started with blended learning*. Griffith University, Australia: Institute of Higher Education.

Bauk, S. I. (2015). Assessing students' perception of e-learning in blended environment: An experimental study. *Procedia - Social and Behavioral Sciences*, 191(2015), 323–329.

Cohen, L., Manion, L., & Morrison, K. (2007). *Research methods in education*. Routledge.

DHET (Department of Higher Education and Training). (2012). Draft policy framework for the provision of distance education in South African universities. https://www.che.ac.za/publications/frameworks/dhet-draft-policy-framework-distance-education-south-african-universities

DHET. (2014). Policy for the provision of distance education in South African universities in the context of an integrated post-school system. https://www.saide.org.za/documents/Distance_education_policy.pdf

DHET. (2017). Call for comment on the Open Learning Policy Framework for Post-School Education and Training. *Government Gazette*, 40772. http://pmg-assets.s3-website-eu-west-1.amazonaws.com/170407openlearningframework-postschooleduc.pdf

DHET. (2020). Annual performance plan 2020/21.

Domingue, A. D. (2016). Online and blended pedagogy in social justice education. In M. Adams & L. A. Bell (Eds.), *Teaching for diversity and social justice* (3rd ed., pp. 369–396). Routledge.

Drysdale, J. S., Grahams, C. R., Spring, J. K., & Halverson, L. R. (2013). An analysis of research trends in dissertations and theses studying blended learning. *Internet and Higher Education*, 17(2013), 90–100.

Fraser, N. (2005). Reframing justice in a globalizing world. *New Left Review*, 36, 69–88. https://newleftreview.org/II/36/nancy-fraser-reframing-justice-in-a-globalizing-world

Fraser, N. (2009). *Scales of justice: Reimagining political space in a globalizing world* (vol. 31). Columbia University Press.

Gaebel, M., Kupriyanova, V., Morais, R., & Colucci, E. (2014). E-learning in European higher education institutions: Results of a mapping survey conducted in October–December 2013. European University Association. http://old.eua.eu/Libraries/publication/e-learning_survey

Garrison, D. R., & Vaughan, N. D. (2007). *Blended learning in higher education: Framework, principles, and guidelines*. Jossey-Bass.

Gecer, A., & Dag, F. (2012). A blended learning experience. *Educational Sciences: Theory and Practice*, 12(1), 438–442.

Godlewska, A., Beyer, W., Whetstone, S., Schaefli, L., Rose, J., Talan, B., & Forcione, M. (2019). Converting a large lecture class to an active blended learning class: Why, how, and what we learned. *Journal of Geography in Higher Education*, 43(1), 96–115. https://www.tandfonline.com/doi/full/10.1080/03098265.2019.1570090

Gon, S., & Rawekar, A. (2017). Effectivity of e-learning through Whatsapp as a teaching learning tool. *MVP Journal of Medical Sciences*, 4(1), 19–25. DOI: 10.18311/mvpjms/2017/v4i1/8454.

Graham, C. R. (2013). Emerging practice and research in blended learning. In M. G. Moore (Ed.), *Handbook of distance education* (3rd ed., pp. 333–350). Routledge. https://www.routledgehandbooks.com/doi/10.4324/9780203803738

Hodges, C. B., Moore, S., Lockee, B. B., Trust, T., & Bond, M. A. (2020). The difference between emergency remote teaching and online learning. http://hdl.handle.net/10919/104648

Hodgkinson-Williams, C. A., & Trotter, H. (2018). A social justice framework for understanding open educational resources and practices in the Global South. *Journal of Learning for Development*, 5(3), 204–224. http://www.jl4d.org/index.php/ejl4d/article/view/312

IDC (Instructional Design Central). (2017). What is instructional design? https://www.instructionaldesigncentral.com/whatisinstructionaldesign.

Isaacs, S. (2007). ICT in education in South Africa. *Survey of ICT and education in Africa: South Africa country report* (pp. 15–54). https://www.researchgate.net/profile/Shafika_Isaacs/publication/335015106_ICT_in_Education_in_South_Africa_Survey_of_ICT_in_Education_in_Africa_South_Africa_Country_Report/links/5d4a9d614585153e5941578a/ICT-in-Education-in-South-Africa-Survey-of-ICT-in-Education-in-Africa-South-Africa-Country-Report.pdf

Larbi-Apau, J., Sampong, K., & Kwofie, B. (2020). Barriers to online learning adoption in higher education. *University World News Africa Edition*. https://www.universityworldnews.com/post.php?story=20200506200743715

Latchem, C. (2017). ICTs, blended learning and TVET transformation. In C. Latchem (Ed.), *Using ICTs and blended learning in transforming TVET* (pp. 27–53). UNESCO and Commonwealth of Learning. https://unesdoc.unesco.org/ark:/48223/pf0000247495

Lebeloane, L. (2017). Decolonizing the school curriculum for equity and social justice in South Africa. *KOERS – Bulletin for Christian Scholarship*, 82(3). https://doi.org/10.19108/KOERS.82.3.2333

Marinoni, G., Van't Land, H., & Jensen, T. (2020). The impact of Covid-19 on higher education around the world. *IAU global survey report*. https://www.iau-aiu.net/IMG/pdf/iau_covid19_and_he_survey_report_final_may_2020.pdf

Mata, S. (2015). E-skills and employability: A Technical and Vocational Education and Training (TVET) curriculum perspective [Master's dissertation, University of the Western Cape]. http://hdl.handle.net/11394/5576

Mboweni, V. S. (2020). Remote teaching and learning at TVET colleges: A COVID-19 challenge. Webinar. https://www.saera.co.za/zoom/remote-teaching-and-learning-at-tvet-colleges-a-covid-19-challenge/

McGee, P., & Reis, A. (2012). Blended course design: A synthesis of best practices. *Journal of Asynchronous Learning Networks*, 16(4), 7–22.

Nash, J. M. (2014). Using blended learning to increase student engagement in a large undergraduate class. Presented at 43rd Conference of the Southern African Computer Lecturers' Association, Port Elizabeth, South Africa. https://www.researchgate.net/publication/263582922_Using_Blended_Learning_to_Increase_Student_Engagement_in_a_Large_Undergraduate_Class

Obwoge, M. E., & Kwamboka, O. S. (2016). E-learning in TVET: An opportunity for developing countries. *IRA International Journal of Education and Multidisciplinary Studies*, 3(3), 347–352.

Ortega, L. (2017). New CALL-SLA research interfaces for the 21st century: Towards equitable multilingualism. *CALICO Journal*, 34(3), 285–316. https://doi.org/10.1558/cj.33855

Owston, R., York, D. N., Malhotra, T., & Sitthiworachart, J. (2020). Blended learning in STEM and non-STEM courses: How do student performance and perceptions compare? *Online Learning*, 24(3), 203–221. https://doi.org/10.24059/olj.v24i3.2151

Pask, G. (1976). *Conversation Theory. Applications in education and epistemology*. Elsevier.

Patton, M. Q. (2002). *Qualitative evaluation and research methods* (3rd ed.). Sage.

Picciano, A. G. (2006). Blended learning: Implications for growth and access. *Journal of Asynchronous Learning Networks*, 10(3), 95–102.

Picciano, A. (2009). Blending with purpose: The multimodal model. *Journal of the Research Center for Educational Technology*, 5(1), 4–14.

PMG (Parliamentary Monitoring Group). (2020). COVID-19 Response: University & TVET plans for 2020 academic year; DSI work on COVID-19; with Minister. https://pmg.org.za/committee-meeting/30102/

Precel, K., Eshet-Alkalai, Y., & Alberton, Y. (2009). Pedagogical and design aspects of a blended learning course. *The International Review of Research in Open and Distributed Learning*, 10(2). https://doi.org/10.19173/irrodl.v10i2.618

Raban, M. (2018). The implementation of blended learning in an English communication course for first-year university engineering students – a case study [Master's dissertation, Stellenbosch University]. http://hdl.handle.net/10019.1/104955

Richardson, A. M. (2012). *Flexible and blended learning in TVET*. UNESCO 3rd World Congress on TVET, Shanghai, China. http://www.unesco.org/education/TVET2012/special-sessions/Al-Mead-Richardson.pdf

Songsangyos, P., & Ruangthong, P. (2016). The supported factors and its barriers to blended courses. Presented at the 18th International Conference on Industrial Engineering, 10–12 October 2016, Seoul, Korea.

Tait, A. (2013). Distance and e-Learning, social justice, and development: The relevance of capability approaches to the mission of open universities. *The International Review of Research in Open and Distance Learning*, 14(4), 1–18.

Thorne, K. (2003). *Blended learning: How to integrate online and traditional learning*. Kogan Page.

Yasak, Z., & Alisa, M. (2015). ICT integrations in TVET: Is it up to expectations? *Procedia: Social and Behavioral Sciences*, 204(2015), 88–97.

HOW TO CITE THIS CHAPTER

Raban, M., & Mayisela, T. (2022). Blended learning as a means of opening up learning at Northlink TVET College in South Africa: A social justice perspective. In T. Mayisela, S. C. Govender & C. A. Hodgkinson-Williams (Eds.), *Open learning as a means of advancing social justice: Cases in post-school education and training in South Africa* (pp. 86–105). African Minds. doi: 10.47622/9781928502425_4

This work is licensed under a Creative Commons Attribution 4.0 International (CC BY 4.0) licence.

5

Online learning at the Durban University of Technology during the COVID-19 pandemic

Insights on openness and parity of participation

Sinethemba Zungu & Sukaina Walji

SUMMARY Online learning can be seen as a way to broaden educational provision. The South African Department of Higher Education and Training is turning to open learning approaches (such as online learning) to provide cost-effective mass enrolment in post-school education. This study adopts a qualitative approach to explore how online learning may be opening up education at the Durban University of Technology (DUT). The chapter shares the experiences of three staff members and one student, gathered via online interviews and WhatsApp chat discussions undertaken during emergency remote teaching (ERT). Although online learning is a strategic objective at DUT, it was not yet at full-scale implementation before the COVID-19 pandemic struck. The national lockdown thus accelerated the institution's plans to take teaching and learning online. This research uses Nancy Fraser's (2005) conception of social justice as parity of participation to examine the extent to which online learning creates 'participatory parity' economically, culturally, and politically for students at the DUT's Steve Biko Campus. The data suggests that economic challenges need to be addressed at national levels, while issues of cultural inclusivity and student and staff representation in decision-making can be addressed at an institutional level. Significantly, this study contributes towards the limited empirical research that exists around examining the extent to which online learning and ERT responded to participatory parity of staff and students at South African higher education institutions.

Keywords: online learning, barriers to learning, open learning, social justice, TVET

Introduction

As a result of South Africa's history and racially biased policies of institutionalized forms of exclusion, there are extensive inequities in terms of access to quality higher education and training for certain population groups (Foko, 2015; Letseka & Pitsoe, 2012; Walton et al., 2015). In 2016, the World Economic Forum deemed South Africa to be the most unequal country in the world (Swinnerton et al., 2018). For many South Africans, access to post-school education is a ticket to escape individual and intergenerational poverty. Walker and Mathebula (2020, p. 1194) assert that higher education contributes to opening up social mobility pathways and a tertiary qualification has "the potential of breaking the links that bind together low-income, inequality, and unemployment". For ordinary South Africans, the notion of access to higher education means access to traditional, full-time, campus-based contact at a higher education institution (Letseka & Pitsoe, 2012). By its own admission, however, DHET acknowledges that the current traditional learning system for post-school education and training (PSET) does not have the capacity to provide for diverse and affordable access to education and lifelong learning (DHET, 2017a). Thus, the cost of PSET remains unattainably high for most.

Online education is proposed as a strategy for widening access to PSET (DHET, 2017a). DHET has encouraged all universities to "expand online and blended learning as a way to offer niche programmes, especially at postgraduate level, to those who are unable to attend full-time programmes, either due to their employment status or their geographical distance from a campus" (DHET, 2013, p. 51). This is inculcated through DHET's draft *Open Learning Policy Framework* (OLPF), which introduces key principles that underpin the idea of open learning as a way of promoting a socially just PSET sector.

DUT took the decision to use online learning as a strategy to respond to the challenge of introducing more innovative ways of teaching or to improve the quality of learning locally[1]. The institution-wide implementation of digital technologies at DUT in 2012 was introduced as a 'technology imperative' and marked a shift from the voluntary use of the institutionally provided learning management system (Mistri, 2016). It was hoped that innovative and digitally supported learning would resolve the dilemma of widening access despite the shortcomings of inadequate infrastructural capacity and insufficient resources (Mistri, 2016).

Against this background, this study seeks to investigate the ways and extent to which online learning, as a way of opening up learning, provides an environment for economic, cultural, and political justice to be achieved for students at DUT. This chapter begins by contextualizing the concepts of open learning and online learning.

The state of online learning in South Africa and at DUT

There are currently no fully online universities in South Africa (DHET, 2017b). Online learning has been partially on offer in South Africa over the last 10 years (in the form of expanded blended learning modalities and online short courses as per the 2014 *Policy for the Provision of Distance Education in South African Universities in the Context of an Integrated Post-School System*), less so in the formal credit-bearing sector, especially as prior to 2014 contact universities were not able to offer any online learning (DHET, 2017b).

---

[1] See https://www.dut.ac.za/elearning/

Historically, DUT comprised two institutions, namely the Technikon Natal, which was a whites-only institution, and the ML Sultan Technikon which was built mainly to offer technical education for Indian people (DUT, 2008). As a response to the end of the apartheid era and the need to transform the tertiary education environment to reflect the inclusionary ideals of the new democratic state, the ML Sultan and Technikon Natal merged to form the Durban Institute of Technology (DIT) in 2002 (DUT, 2008). DIT undertook further rebranding in 2006 to be named DUT, in line with a recommendation from the then Department of Education (DoE) which called for tertiary education institutions to position themselves "against global benchmarks" (DUT, 2008, p. 2) and provide for the development of skills required through offering a combination of academic and vocational qualifications in alignment with the universities of technology and national developmental needs of South Africa (DUT, 2008). E-learning was introduced at DUT as a "core teaching and learning practice" in 2013 in response to "the rapid development worldwide of digital technologies to enhance learning and teaching (web-resources, mobile devices, multimedia)" (DUT, 2013, as cited in Mistri, 2016, p. 79).

At the time of writing, the world is confronted by the COVID-19 pandemic, which is impacting every aspect of life and demanding rapid changes to the way things are done. The impact of COVID-19 has especially impacted higher education institutions after the government ordered all universities and TVET colleges to shut down in an effort to curb the spread of the coronavirus. PSET institutions in South Africa were required to rapidly switch to remote or online teaching and learning as an urgent measure to salvage the academic calendar.

Although online learning was a strategic objective at DUT, it was not yet at full-scale implementation when the COVID-19 pandemic struck. The pivot to online learning took the form of emergency remote teaching (ERT) rather than the planned e-learning that DUT had previously encouraged the use of the Learning Management System, initially Blackboard (Qwabe & Khumalo, 2020), and subsequently a local instance of Moodle, called the Think Learn Zone.[2] However, during the ERT the use of social media (WhatsApp) was a convenient and affordable method for lecturers and students to interact. Students with connectivity challenges, who could not access DUT learning platforms, could submit assessments via email.

Hlengwa (2021, p. 3433) found that some students at DUT were not ready for online learning due to numerous challenges including "lack of laptops, network challenges especially in rural areas, data shortages, household chores that took priority, space constraints, noise and lack of support at home". These challenges would have been present during ERT. The problems of financial support for students persisted during ERT. Despite DHET reporting that the National Student Financial Aid Scheme (NSFAS) allowances will continue being paid to students, there are still concerns that the current trajectory of digitized learning presents multiple socio-economic and cultural social injustices for disadvantaged university students (particularly students living in poor, rural environments) and students in the TVET sector (Mthethwa, 2020; Myende & Ndlovu, 2020; Shoba, 2020a; Whitelaw et al., 2020).

Moreover, the movement to online or virtual teaching and learning comes with major socio-economic implications. It requires the reskilling of both students and lecturers and

---

[2] A learning management system, Moodle, put in place by the DUT which consists of a virtual classroom where students are able to access course notes, submit assignments, receive announcements, communicate with their lecturers and classmates, and undertake assessments (see https://elearning.dut.ac.za/e-learning-dut/).

access to technological infrastructure, and resources including electricity, the internet, data, a desk and a chair, and a quiet space that will be conducive to learning (Myende & Ndlovu, 2020). Myende and Ndlovu (2020, p. 1) caution "against a one-size-fits-all approach that will result in further marginalisation and recommend that more inclusionary and innovative strategies be found to accommodate students residing in rural communities affected by social exclusion [who] may experience the digital divide".

Qwabe and Khumalo's study at DUT (2020, p. 12) concludes that "even though the majority of students are aware of e-learning and make use of it, some are still left in the dark and do not use this platform [Think Learn Zone] at all". The authors suggest that all faculties should consider conducting computer literacy training, and that lecturers should be urged to post notes and learning materials on the platform for students to access on a daily basis. The state has a constitutional obligation to make higher education (as a fundamental human right) available and accessible to everyone (Mthethwa, 2020), however, online learning threatens the realisation of this right, particularly in rural parts of KwaZulu-Natal (Myende & Ndlovu, 2020). According to DHET (2013), an important element in expanding access to education and training must be the expansion of opportunities for part-time study for those who are working. This implies an expansion of open and distance education and the establishment of more satellite premises where universities or colleges provide classes at places (including in rural areas) and times convenient to students (DHET, 2013, p. 8).

Conceptualising open learning and online learning

This research study explores how online learning, as a mode of student engagement (see section below), may contribute to open learning as a form of social justice. Before discussing the concept of online learning and the way in which it may contribute to opening up learning to students in a formal education context, we need to locate this discussion in relation to the broader concept of open education.

Open learning in relation to open education

Knox (2013) relates 'open learning' to the open education movement that favours the principle of equitable access and draws on the idea of openness in terms of access to educational material. 'Open education' can be described as a movement aimed at widening access to formal and informal education for all through the use of open educational resources and open educational practices. The philosophy of 'open education' has a long history and started with various open universities offering access to those who did not necessarily qualify for entry into undergraduate courses. However, the qualifier 'open' now refers to more than access, it includes the sharing of resources, such as open educational resources (OER), and engaging in open educational practices (OEP) including the development of open textbooks and some Massive Open Online Courses (MOOCs) with openly licensed resources (Hodgkinson-Williams, 2014). The open education movement has aspirations to provide free and legally shareable resources for all, whereas the concept of open learning is usually applied in a more restricted manner to students within a formal education context.

Open learning in the South African context

The foundation for a new education and training system in South Africa was established in the 1995 *White Paper on Education and Training*, which defined open learning as:

> an approach which combines the principles of learner centredness, lifelong learning, flexibility of learning provision, the removal of barriers to access learning, the recognition for credit of prior learning experience, the provision of learner support, the construction of learning programmes in the expectation that learners can succeed, and the maintenance of rigorous quality assurance over the design of learning materials and support systems. (DoE, 1995, p. 28)

Additionally, the 1995 *White Paper* called for the establishment of the National Open Learning Agency (NOLA), to promote open learning principles, networks, and research in the education sector. This was later supported by the 2013 *White Paper for Post-School Education and Training* which aspires to the development of a PSET system that is grounded in open learning principles (DHET, 2013). More recently, the draft *Open Learning Policy Framework* for PSET, released for public comment in 2017, reiterates the definition of open learning offered in the 1995 White paper on Education and Training.

DHET claims that their conception of open learning as an "all-encompassing approach", aimed at addressing the numerous student needs, is "a viable option to be considered and implemented in the PSET system" (2017b, p. 2). However, in both practice (as the cases in this book demonstrate) and research, the concept of open learning is variously interpreted and with particular emphasis. For example, Letseka and Pitsoe (2012), describe the concept of open learning as an educational approach designed to reach learners at their preferred locations (home or office setting) and to provide learning resources that will enable them to qualify and succeed without attending formal classes in person. Letseka and Pitsoe's definition conflates open learning, distance learning, and online learning, treating them as equivalent and interchangeable. A study conducted by Moore et al. (2011) discovered that there was inconsistent use of the terms distance learning, eLearning, and online learning. The scholars loosely define distance learning as learning that takes place "(between a learner and an instructor) over different times and/or places, using varying forms of instructional materials" (Moore et al., 2011). On the contrary, DHET (2017a) argues against the tendency to conflate open learning with distance and online learning. DHET points out that "although online learning can potentially accommodate different ways and styles of learning (making for greater accessibility) and enable the construction of a potentially richer learning environment, it simply does not equate to open learning" (2017a, p. 373; 2017b, p. 2).

In the context of this study, open learning is understood as a "principle-based concept and approach to learning which has the capacity to transform teaching, learning and access to education and training in quite radical ways" (DHET, 2017a, p. 373). Online learning is a *mode* of teaching and learning that may be used in open education, open learning, or closed, proprietary learning contexts, for either campus-based or offered at a distance. The next section links the concepts of open and online learning to widening access to learning for all.

Online learning in the context of expanded access to learning for all

DHET (2017a, p. 2) describes online learning "as a collection of learning methods made available through the internet" that can include various aspects (i.e. delivery of content, learning resources, interactive learning activities, formative and summative assessment, and the recording and analysis of achievement data). Sidler (2018, p. 1) further defines online learning as a mode of teaching and learning made up of a "collection of webinars, online-collaboration tools, software that supports individually-paced learning, learning management systems and instant messaging and social networking". Scholars now use different terms such as 'e-learning' and 'networked learning' (Sidler, 2018) or 'online learning' to refer to the use of information communication technology (ICT) to enable two-way engagement with lecturers and learners.

The Government of South Africa has endorsed the expansion of online learning (alongside distance learning) as a gateway to increased higher education opportunities. The 2013 *White Paper for Post-School Education and Training* encourages the PSET sector to expand online learning to offer niche programmes while acknowledging the need to expand equitable access to ICT resources (DHET, 2013, p. xvi). According to the *Position Paper on Online Courses and Programmes*, it is the responsibility of DHET to "ensure that online programmes and course offerings are adopted to support and advance teaching, learning and accountable assessment strategies, whilst embracing open learning principles as espoused by the 2013 *White Paper for PSET*" (DHET, 2017b, p. 3). DHET is also "responsible for creating an enabling environment for institutions to deliver quality online programmes through the development and implementation of relevant policies, strategies and appropriate funding mechanisms" (DHET, 2017b, p. 3).

DUT defines e-learning as the use of technology to support teaching and learning[3]. E-learning is recognised as the delivery of modules using online (virtual) classrooms located within the institutional learning management system (LMS) as part of mixed mode (blended) delivery (DUT, 2016). The use of technology is also intended to be instrumental in facilitating a pedagogical shift from the traditional mode of knowledge transmission to student-centered learning at the university (DUT, 2015). Given the national goals of social justice and socio-economic upliftment, the decision at the institutional management level (at DUT), to emphatically advocate for the use of educational technologies, could be interpreted to align with the national imperatives of widening access to higher education in South Africa, whilst also addressing the need to be part of the global knowledge economy and fit into the digitally-focused world (Mistri, 2016, p. 7). This chapter understands the concept of online learning as the use of technology for teaching and learning to open up education by widening access and providing flexibility to students in formal education institutions.

Online learning and social justice as 'parity of participation'

Although open learning and online learning share the goal of widening access and providing flexibility, the two concepts are not automatically wholly aligned in relation to a social justice imperative. Fraser describes social justice as the organisation of social arrangements that make it possible for everyone to participate equally in society (2005). The principle of parity

---

[3] See https://elearning.dut.ac.za/e-learning-dut/

of participation according to Nancy Fraser's theory lies in the idea of all adults of society having the ability and being in the position of interacting with each other as peers (Armstrong & Thompson, 2009). Fraser (2005) suggests three dimensions of social injustice: (1) economic maldistribution, (2) cultural misrecognition, and (3) political misrepresentation and mis-framing.

Economic maldistribution, redistribution, and restructuring

According to Fraser (2005), economic maldistribution indicates the uneven or unequal distribution of economic resources. In the South African context, the lack of necessary resources and technological infrastructure (power supply, equipment, connectivity and data) (DHET, 2017a) create conditions of economic maldistribution, limiting the full participation of disadvantaged individuals and institutions. Even though some individuals and institutions may have internet connectivity, data is costly[4]. Razzano et al. assert that:

> Paradoxically, as more people are connected, digital inequality is increasing. This is not only the case between those online and those offline (as is the case in a voice and basic text environment), but also between those who have the technical and financial resources to use the Internet optimally, and those who are 'barely' online. (2020, p. 4)

The SADC Parliamentary Forum Discussion Paper reports that a third of South Africans believe data to be "unaffordable" (Razzano et al., 2020, p. 12). Based on a *Research ICT Africa* policy brief, South Africa ranks 33 out of 46 Africa countries, with 1GB of data in South Africa costing more than five times as much as data in Africa's cheapest country, Egypt (based on Figure 2, Chinembiri, 2020, p. 3). In a country of deep inequality, despite increased pressure from the Competition Commission and after reductions, data prices "remain anti-poor" (Chinembiri, 2020, p. 5) resulting in substantial if not complete exclusion from online learning activities.

Additionally, the move towards online learning in formal learning environments creates the possibility of economic exploitation of vulnerable populations. *The State of ICT in South Africa* reports that 50% of the country's population was not connected to the internet (Gillwald et al., 2018). It is further reported that the limited digital uptake is reinforced by the extreme inequalities faced by the country's population, particularly income and educational inequalities. Evidence shows that the digital divide is deepening between people living in rural and urban areas. Hlengwa (2021, p. 3437) recorded that 55.2% out of a sample of 104 students at DUT reported challenges around a shortage of data and 44.8% lacked "quality gadgets".

To address the injustice of maldistribution, Fraser (2009) points to a more just distribution of resources and opportunities, however, these may only partially address maldistribution, but leave "intact much of the underlying political-economic structure" (Fraser, 1995, p. 84). For example, students may be given laptops as part of a National Student Financial Aid Scheme (NSFAS) bursary, but still, be unable to participate in online learning due to the high data costs. Transformative economic restructuring would make devices affordable through

---

[4] https://researchictafrica.net/publication/despite-reduction-in-mobile-data-tariffs-data-is-still-expensive-in-south-africa/

government funded procurement; create better quality and more widespread networks through obligatory co-operation between internet service providers (ISPs); and reduce data costs for all South Africans by capping the data charges levied by ISPs.

Cultural misrecognition, recognition, and re-acculturation

Online learning may unintentionally create an environment for cultural misrecognition where students from rural areas are confronted by cultural injustices that impede their ability to access quality higher education. Cultural misrecognition refers to cultural inequality and the devaluing of cultural histories, norms, gender, language, race or ethnic perspectives, practices and values (Fraser, 2005, 2009). For example, only about "40% of rural dwellers us[e] the internet" (with persistent gender disparities) versus 61% in the urban areas (Mothobi et al., 2018, pp. 1–2). Therefore, it is no surprise that "rural students ... enter the university with limited cultural capital in terms of digital literacy" (Myende & Ndlovu, 2020, p. 178).

Myende and Ndlovu (2020) suggest that negative rural realities may render a socially unjust environment for students living in poor rural communities where there may be a lack of "familial setup and space for learning" (p. 178). The authors further assert that "the rural ecosystem and the lived experiences of students in these areas are multi-faceted and ... ignore and misrecognize the circumstances faced by rural students" (Myende & Ndlovu, 2020, p. 177). Many black students living in poor rural communities face challenging family circumstances, strenuous home responsibilities, and are overall impacted upon by the history of educational exclusion and digital illiteracy that limits their ability to get support from home (Myende & Ndlovu, 2020).

In some contexts, digital literacy is conflated with language literacy. For example, scholars argue that due to the Western influence, much of the online learning is available in English only and thus at a global scale is "socio-culturally exclusionary for the millions of non-English speaking people, those with English as a second or third language, and those native English speakers in colonised places like India and parts of Africa for whom the American or English content and cultural perspective was not applicable to their local context" (Adam, 2019). In the context of South African PSET and through this study, it will be useful to establish how online education is implemented considering the diversified linguistic population composition. For example, providing learning materials in multiple languages could serve as an ameliorative response to recognition. A more transformative re-acculturative response would include engagement with other knowledge systems including those that draw on students' lived experiences.

Political misrepresentation, representation, and reframing

Fraser (2005, p. 76) differentiates between two levels of political misrepresentation, the first concerns "political decision rules [that] wrongly deny some of the included the chance to participate fully, as peers", and is what she calls "ordinary-political misrepresentation". The second level of misrepresentation is what Fraser calls "mis-framing" which "concerns the boundary-setting aspect of the political" and "arises when the community's boundaries are drawn in such a way as to wrongly exclude some people from the chance to participate at all in its authorized contests over justice" (Fraser, 2005, p. 76). For example, if students are not represented in the DUT Senate that discusses academic matters like online learning, that would be a case of "ordinary-political misrepresentation". An example of misframing would be that students are not part of the ISP's decision-making on data costs that affect them directly.

This raises the question of how the politics of recognition are addressed (for long-term sustainability) in implementing online learning considering the diverse nature of South African higher education. This will assist with understanding the extent to which lecturers and students are represented in the decision-making processes, for example taking decisions on the accessibility of, and the appropriateness of course content and pedagogy of online learning. Fraser (2005) terms an affirmative intervention as 'representation' which in this study could translate into students and lecturers being given an opportunity to provide feedback on specific online learning programmes, but not in the wider decision-making, where a top-down approach is followed and the management of the institution makes all major decisions. Transformative intervention to political mis-framing is what Fraser (2005) identifies as 're-framing', which recognises the rights of everyone to participate in the decision-making and have a voice. This may include lecturers and students having a say in firstly, the choice of the online learning platform and secondly, the choices in what is taught.

Using Nancy Fraser's concept of 'parity of participation', this study analyses how DUT endeavours to mitigate the economic, cultural and political injustices faced by students in the PSET sector in order to enhance students' access and participation in education through online learning as a form of open learning.

The DUT case study

DUT is a multi-campus university of technology located in KwaZulu-Natal (KZN), with two main campuses located in Durban and Pietermaritzburg serving approximately 33 000 students[5]. This study focuses on the Steve Biko campus located in Durban. A large population of these students come from the rural parts of KZN and many from poor backgrounds (Lecturer 2).

Research methodology

This research adopted a qualitative approach (Maxwell, 2008) to gain insight into the use of the online mode of learning at DUT as a way of opening up learning. Drawing on empirical data that was elicited from in-depth interviews with three staff members two lecturers and a staff member from the Centre for Excellence in Learning and Teaching (CELT) and one student.

Sites and participants

Based on the preliminary interview with the coordinator of academic development and e-learning at the CELT, the Steve Biko campus in Durban was purposefully and conveniently chosen as the research site. A total of three staff members were interviewed using Zoom, and one student, completing a one-year Advanced Diploma in Business and Information Management, was interviewed via WhatsApp and telephonic discussion. Staff respondents

---

[5] https://www.dut.ac.za/about-dut/

were recruited using a snowball sampling method (Cohen et al., 2007) and only one student volunteered in response to the digital poster that was sent out. The student was interviewed over multiple days, to accommodate a busy schedule.

Recruitment and data collection

An in-depth interview was conducted with the Coordinator, Academic Development Department, at CELT to elicit information on the capacity development initiative of DUT lecturers in preparation for online learning implementation. The coordinator then referred to us lecturers with whom she had worked. To identify students to participate in the study, a recruitment campaign was undertaken through the use of a digital poster. The digital poster was posted on DUT student WhatsApp groups, canvassing for participants (with data offered as participation required the use of WhatsApp). Only one student responded via a telephone call and later communicated via WhatsApp.

The interview instrument comprised a series of open-ended questions, with the purpose of eliciting as much information as possible from the interviewees as well as allowing them to interpret the questions as they wished in order to make it easier for them to relate their personal experiences and everyday work. Questions such as "What do you understand by the term open learning" and "How do you think it is applied at DUT", allowed participants to answer freely and share a personal opinion or account.

Ethics, validity and limitations

All research participants were provided with detailed information sheets and consent forms following UCT guidelines (UCT's Faculty of Humanities Guide to Research Ethics: Research with Human Participants[6], outlining the details of the COOL project and the objectives of this case study. Participation was completely voluntary, and participants were advised of their right to withdraw from participation at any point in the research. Respondents were assured anonymity and the protection of their identities.

To strengthen the reliability and validity of the research instrument, the questions were screened to ensure that they were easily understood by allowing fellow researchers to scrutinise them.

Empirical data was gathered during the COVID-19 pandemic, so there were a number of limitations to data collection including conducting all interviews online and having limited access to interviewees, especially students, due to the disrupted university schedule. In addition, there were challenges of finding a suitable time to engage interviewees, considering the pressures to completing the academic year that universities were confronted with and within the limited timeframe of the project. Furthermore, attempts at securing access to internal DUT documents were not successful and curbed intentions to triangulate data from different sources.

---

[6] http://www.humanities.uct.ac.za/sites/default/files/image_tool/images/2/HumFaculty%20Ethics%20Guidebook%20August%20I%202016%281%29.pdf

Insights and lessons from emergency remote teaching at DUT

As the number of participants was much smaller than anticipated, we have opted to report on the respondents' experiences with online learning at DUT as 'insights' rather than 'findings'. Broadly, this section analyses in what ways online learning encourages an inclusionary and more equitable teaching and learning environment for both students and lecturers in contrast to how ERT was implemented amidst the pandemic. It specifically highlights the conceptions of open learning, implementation of online learning and ERT, staff development and student support available to enhance readiness for online learning and ERT, and factors hindering and factors enabling ERT.

But, firstly, it is instructive to understand the respondents' conceptions of open learning and how they thought it applied to online learning or ERT.

Conceptions of open learning: Conflating online and open learning

When asked about their conception of open learning, the staff at DUT thought of online learning as a form of open learning, much like DHET (2017a) had intended. Although it was unclear whether they had attended any formal DHET training on open learning, the three staff members said that they conceived of open learning in terms of the principles of learner-centredness, the removal of barriers to access learning, and flexibility of learning provision. However, one lecturer clearly conflated open learning with online learning:

> For me, [open learning] is using different platforms for teaching and learning and assessing … so more like a blended learning approach but seeing that now due to COVID everything is online like I said when we are speaking online, we are not only speaking learning management systems [LMS] like Moodle we are using every platform that is available to communicate with students and to use those platforms for teaching and learning. (Lecturer 1)

The aforementioned lecturer noted the use of technology beyond the 'formal' online platforms such as LMS, but also having the ability to use even social media platforms (which may be considered informal for teaching and learning) that are not only popular with students but may also be cheaper and conveniently accessible from mobile phones. Another lecturer further associated open learning with the practices of collaboration beyond geographic limits:

> Open learning, it's learning that happens outside of a building of the university and, it's not restricted to a sort of curriculum of one particular institution … and I'm not saying that's how it's done. But it's just my understanding that if we talk of open learning, we are saying that let's open up you know … collaborations and working together … for example, bringing in someone from Joburg to do a session on intellectual property, which came from my conversations with students, as they were concerned with issues of copyright. So I said I'm going to get somebody [in the industry] who will talk to you. (Lecturer 2)

The CELT staff member's understanding of open learning is directly related to the application of open learning principles in the Kresge-funded Siyaphumelela[7] project which sees "student

---

[7] https://siyaphumelela.org.za/

success as a collective responsibility of all at the university". The staff member further underscores the response of DUT's 2030 Strategic document in which open learning is a "central" tenet as it "underlies everything that we should be doing in our work to improv[e] lives and livelihoods" (CELT staff member). Reflecting on the degree to which open learning has been adopted at DUT (in relation to DHET's 2017 Draft OLPF), the CELT staff member questioned whether "adequate systemic change processes" have been introduced at the institution and suggested that there is still "a lot of work to be done".

Furthermore, there was an acknowledgment of the growing understanding of the term 'open learning' and a perception that "DHET's definition may be too broad, [which] makes the concept vulnerable to misconceptions and misunderstandings" (CELT staff member). The interviewee recognises the application of open learning as "focusing on equity, making people aware of prejudices, or existing prejudices, looking at how do we remove access barriers, encouraging lifelong learning, because the world is changing constantly" (CELT staff member).

The CELT staff member highlighted the need for change in the institutional processes and systems to reflect principles or characteristics of open learning. To some degree, the lecturers' conceptions of open learning are also centred around similar principles as those of DHET, much broader than online learning. Sharing common principles of lifelong learning, and breaking geographic barriers to learning might imply that DUT's move to open learning might not be too difficult.

The Implementation of online learning and ERT at DUT

One of the strategic objectives of DUT is to adopt an integrated digital environment to optimise services for students. Pre-COVID-19, DUT had been endeavouring to incrementally introduce and implement online learning. At this time, lecturers were using a blended approach, and then during the pandemic, like many universities around the country, DUT went fully online during the national lockdown of universities in March 2020. When the national restrictions eased, students returned to campus and DUT reverted to a blended approach. The excerpt below reveals how a lecturer prefers to apply a blended approach to learning as an affirmative response that partially ameliorates students' needs and lecturers' preferences.

> I am able to offer both contact and online but as I said that with students, you find that a large population of the students actually prefer contact classes because they can see the teacher. But also, they don't have to buy data, you know, everything is in the classroom. Then you've got those who prefer online ... So, it is blended ... But overall, if I were to choose next year ... There are specific courses that I would choose for online. And then there are specific courses I would want to have in the classroom, but I prefer blended rather than pure online or pure contact. (Lecturer 2)

The above raises the need to provide flexibility to suit students and staff choices in the mode of learning and teaching. Additionally, Lecturer 2 highlights the economic benefits that accrue with traditional 'contact classes' for some students, referring to full-time students living in residence. The staff and student shared some positive aspects to the overall online experience during ERT, reporting that:

> What I like about it... I feel like it's well organized because now you no longer have the paperwork that we had, where you've got to print, distribute notes to students. Like for me, the online facilities are great. So, I just upload my content online and I'm able to teach online from the comfort of my home. (Lecturer 2)

> It's good for me because it gives me flexible time, I can [fulfil] my responsibilities ... I mean going to work and also house chores ... Cooking and cleaning. (Student)

This excerpt implies that the student (who is also fully employed), could easily transition to ERT, mainly due to the flexibility of time and fewer costs associated with printing assignments. The student did not report any challenges to adapting to using the online platforms, which may be credited to the staff development and student support initiatives that were already in place to bolster the movement towards online medium of teaching and learning. Although it is acknowledged that this is the view of one part-time student only and the perception may be different for other, full-time students. A much larger sample would be needed in determining the effectiveness of the staff and student development programmes.

Staff development and student support for online learning and ERT

DUT, through the CELT, has multiple services directed at capacitating staff and students in an effort towards ensuring readiness for online learning. With respect to staff, CELT offers professional development for teaching online. For instance, a staff developer shared that pre-COVID CELT used a wrapped MOOC approach — the use of a pre-existing MOOC as the primary source of course content and learning activities and supplemented by face-to-face interaction with an instructor to enhance the experience (see Bruff et al., 2013) — to prepare lecturers for online learning course design and teaching. CELT offered a wrapped MOOC where they encouraged staff to "arrive as a team" (at least three per session) and preferably from the same department as "change was easier" and helped "in creating a new norm". Unfortunately, this was not always possible, which created "hiccups" in the implementation of the wrapped MOOC project.

With COVID-19, CELT had to pivot towards supporting lecturers during the ERT phase. The CELT staff member reported how they guided lecturers on pedagogical aspects, such as discouraging "long synchronous sessions" that replicated the 40-minute lecture and instead have "shorter sessions" and asynchronous tasks that would enhance student-to-lecturer and student-to-student interaction. Additionally, CELT held bi-weekly support sessions for academics to assist staff members and for them to share tips and skills on how to use technology (e.g., MS Teams projects) optimally and generate more active learning during ERT.

However, the lecturers had mixed responses with respect to the support that was offered by CELT. On one hand, Lecturer 1 felt that support was always available:

> Well, our CELT department is available ... I would like to say 24 hours but it seems like that, because when you are working online you are working remotely your hours are not confined to office hours, so whenever I manage to call them on Teams or drop them a message I normally get feedback from an assistant from our CELT department with regards to whatever issues I may be having. (Lecturer 1)

This lecturer also acknowledged that the training was helpful in the transition to ERT and it facilitated their acquaintance with Moodle and Teams. On the other hand, the other lecturer pointed out the unsuitable timing of the training and also felt that it increased his workload and seemed complicated. He said:

> So there have been training offered on how to teach online, but I think it was at the wrong time, when we are trying to get students to do online work... *nathi* (we) we are still learning the space, but *bayawa-offerisha amaCourses* (they do offer training courses), and for me I think they were really complicated and they did not sell the trainings (sic) as something that's going to help us... for me those trainings were more like compulsory or they seemed like it would be more work for me. (Lecturer 2)

With respect to students, the CELT staff member shared an example of how the CELT sub-unit, Student Support, supports students (particularly first years) through initiatives such as the "the first-year student experience (FYSE) project, academic advising, and the technology for learning (TFL). In early February, the institution assigned "12 tutors... to various faculties to address all student queries regarding familiarity with the learning software or tech issues" (CELT staff member).

While DUT, through prior arrangements for online learning and the programmes put in place by the CELT department has put great efforts to ensure that staff and students are ready for the effective implementation of ERT, many challenges were experienced which created unjust conditions for some students.

Factors hindering the implementation of ERT

Multiple challenges hindered the implementation of ERT which included lack of devices, poor connectivity, and data.

Lack of devices

The issue of a lack of access to devices was not only confronted by students, but also a challenge faced by lecturers. A lecturer emphasised the lack of office equipment at home to enable lecturers to work from home.

> I would have expected them to make sure that we have facilities at home to teach online. And you won't believe this, they once suggested that we have the desktop moved from campus and be brought to our homes. And I just said no, you know, I'm going to have this big machine here. What if it could get lost or something? (Lecturer 2)

From the student's perspective, he advised that he did not have a laptop and before the national lockdown he depended on using the computers on campus. However, when universities were closed due to the national lockdown, as a temporary/mitigation measure to ensure he could still submit tasks and assignments online, the student needed to borrow his classmate's laptop. This was somewhat challenging as he [the student] would not often have sufficient time:

> *because bekwenzeka aqede seksondele i-due date so mina sek'mele ngiseyenze fast fast ukuze ngikwazi ukuthi ngiSub'mithe, ngingas'tholi is'khathi esi-enough* (I had to wait for the person … to finish writing so that I can also do my schoolwork using their laptop … they would only finish their work when the due date is close and then I'd have to do my work fast so I can submit on time, which is not enough time. (Student)

Although the student was able to navigate the lack of a device, he acknowledged the institution's efforts to provide data, but noted that the data provided [on a month-month basis] was inconsistent, highlighting that, at times, some individuals would not receive data for a month.

Poor connectivity

The CELT staff member reported that staff and students were struggling with connectivity:

> So, there were students and staff who were battling connectivity, who were battling issues regarding access to devices. And this was not limited to students only there was a staff member who was saying, I have my computer at my office, but not at home – huge access barriers. (CELT staff member)

This is supported by Lecturer 2 who raises the issues of poor connectivity in rural areas, highlighting that from his experience students living in the outskirts of the city (for example Nongoma) are excluded. Some students, even the NSFAS recipients, did not have access to technology and internet connectivity. One lecturer shared that although laptops were "eventually" delivered for NSFAS funded students, some of his students were left behind with work during the lockdown period due to poor internet reception from home. Lecturer 2 further highlighted that the frustration of poor connectivity affected students emotionally and psychologically and they could not access student counselling services. The impact of this frustration led to at least one student wanting to drop out. Lecturer 1 raised awareness about the possible return of students (after the national lockdown) who may have not had online access and the need to bridge the gap so that they will be on an equal footing with those who had access for this period.

In summary, the responses reveal that some students living in rural areas face the interrelated problems of a lack of access to devices and/or a lack of connectivity.

Cost of data

Drawing from their experience of moving lectures online during ERT, the lecturers explained that, in addition to the challenges around devices and connectivity, the unaffordability of data is a challenge for all students and not just for NSFAS funded students. "The difficulties are that all students have to attend lectures online, which is a problem because of data, etc. Not all students have access online" (Lecturer 1). The students wonder, "Am I going to get data? [Because] NSFAS hasn't paid us allowances" (Lecturer 2).

Lack of capacity to adequately support students and circuitous institutional processes

Another challenge highlighted by staff was the lack of capacity to adequately serve the student population. The staff reported multiple challenges with regard to a lack of human capital across the different departments within the institution (including student support).

> I think our biggest frustration is that we feel under-resourced. We have ideals to strive towards, but our staff-student ratio is quite inhibitive. So, how much can you do when you're already feeling so thinly spread. (CELT staff member)

Lecturer 2 revealed that one of his students was falling behind in her studies due in part to living in a rural part of Tongaat, a rural town about 40km outside Durban, with poor connectivity and little support at home and wanted to drop out. He intervened as best he could, within his remit, to assist the student by informing all her lecturers of her challenges requesting them to "make plans" for the student to be offered an opportunity to "catch up" (Lecturer 2). The below quote describes what mitigation steps the lecturer undertook in order to assist the student:

> Then, I was like, let me contact student counselling because right now the student wants to drop out and I think that is heavy on the student's mental health. So, student counselling is telling me that the student must be the one phoning them, then once the student has phoned them, they will email the student the forms, then she has to sign those and then send them back to them. And once she has signed, they will then book a session for her. (Lecturer 2)

Lecturer 2 above reveals how the student support processes unintentionally undermined the purpose and roles of student support services, and may have inadvertently further marginalised students who were already feeling excluded by the ERT. The principles around the processes of requiring the student to initiate contact may have unwittingly made the process of getting assistance an additional challenge for a student in need of support.

Provision of data for staff and students

DUT's positive efforts to rapidly supply staff and students with data they needed (within its means) encouraged a positive attitude and willingness from staff and students to engage in remote teaching and learning. Below the CELT staff member describes the role taken by the university to provide data to enable the shift to ERT in a time of uncertainty.

> So, the university did everything in its power and it was excruciating waiting for the service providers to say that, you know, these sites will be zero-rated, etc. That period was very difficult, fortunately, the university agreed to make data available while we waited for the Minister of Higher Education to explain or to give us details on how to deal with the situation. (CELT staff member)

While the staff and students embraced the sudden shift to ERT, they also identified many shortfalls and gaps that may assist the institution in the future planning and implementation of online learning.

Shortfalls and gaps revealed in the unexpected shift to ERT

The sudden unexpected shift to ERT came with shortfalls and highlighted some gaps in pedagogy and addressing student needs.

Unrealistic expectations of mobile phone use for learning

Some pedagogical difficulties were experienced by the lecturers and students, including different experiences of student engagement during online classes. One lecturer identified a lack of online engagement which may be due to an incomplete understanding or unrealistic expectations of how students can or should utilize their mobile phones to engage in learning activities online.

> A lot of our students access all of our teaching and learning via their mobile devices and their cell phones and sometimes they cannot really read or access documents through cell phones so it would be highly recommended if they are given, for example, a laptop with data. (Lecturer 1)

Lecturer 1 acknowledged the limitations of using mobile phones only to access teaching and learning online for students.

Unsatisfactory timetable scheduling

Lessons learned from the implementation of online learning during the COVID-19 period show that staff at DUT feel that students may feel overwhelmed with the intensity of online teaching and learning due to the concentration levels required. This would require timetable rescheduling to reduce the number of lectures per day to avoid overburdening the students. Speaking on behalf of the students, Lecturer 2 shared that "it can be overwhelming" if all of the lecturers schedule assignments for the same day:

> *ukuthi nathi singabi, nama-submissions* (for us not to make submission dates) and lectures at the same time... one lecture a day because [of] the attention span for online is different from the attention span required for physical space. So, you can't have students attend three sessions a day online. Where each session is like two hours or three hours... we've got to make sure that the students are not sort of overwhelmed with the teaching and learning. (Lecturer 2)

He suggests that a student survey be administered to assist in the development of an improved schedule, to obtain insights from students on "how [the institution] can best re-package or improve the [online] experience" (Lecturer 2).

Fixed times for teaching and support

As students may be using cheaper data provision at night (e.g., Night Surfer package) in an effort to decrease costs, staff are in turn placed in a position where they are compelled to work outside of 'traditional' working hours. The lecturers highlight that, in future if online learning is to be adopted, it may require the need for added flexibility and redefinition of work hours on the part of lecturers and administrative staff, especially IT staff, in their engagements with students.

Lecturer 2 goes on to highlight the tension between the availability of the technology, but the unavailability of the staff to support it: "MS Teams is there but *indlela esi-improva ngayo isek'theni* (the way for us to improve, lies in whether), students have access to the people who are working behind those screens". Furthermore, Lecturer 2 criticises a college that limits student engagement to between 9am–5pm and accuses them of "still functioning in the 2003 mentality of the institution". He suggested ways in which the institution can improve the experience of staff and students.

> So, one thing I think iDUT *inga- improva kyona* (that DUT can improve on), I guess is the personnel... So, the staff members, our students still can't get hold of some people online ... so *uma ngisekhaya* (if I'm at home), but *uma nginenkinga* (if I have a problem) with IT, I can't get the person, *uma nginenkinga ngeAdmin*, I can't get that person. *Uma nginenkinga* with something, I mean even with equipment, you know anything... I think we need to work on our support teams and systems. (Lecturer 2)

In other words, Lecturer 2, suggested that in order to improve teaching and learning in the online space, administrative staff and lecturers need to be more flexible in their working hours in order to accommodate students at hours suitable to them and to optimise the resources available to them. On the contrary, Lecturer 1 highlighted that while it is important to take advantage of the social media platforms such as WhatsApp to enhance accessibility to learning for students, she also reported on the need to put measures in place to preserve stipulated working hours and protect against lecturers feeling compelled to use their personal family time to attend to students.

> So, we had to put in some measures to say students please try stick to certain hours you know if you need to address any queries rather email the lecturers as opposed to sending them messages at 22:00 or 23:00 at night and asking questions normally when your phone pings you are more compelled to want to respond so we had to put on some measures in place, so it is working. (Lecturer 1)

Drawing from their experiences during ERT, both Lecturers 1 and 2, raise important issues that must be considered in the future implementation of online learning. For example, if students are provided data packages that include night surfer, what are the concomitant expectations of staff and lecturers with regards to work hours, and how can this change be realistically addressed by the institution?

Excessive workload hindering pedagogic change

Another aspect to be considered in the change of mode of teaching and learning is the pressure that academics and staff members face, which may make it more difficult to introduce change.

> But I think the other factor is that we feel so frustrated by the pressures of work that it's easier to fall back to familiar practices. Because introducing a new practice requires a lot of planning and effort and there's a chance that it may work, and it may not work. So, people need to be sort of [be] encouraged to move towards change in ... in small little fractions of change, little segments of change. (CELT staff member)

Pressures experienced by lecturers, excessive workload, and fatigue associated with extensive engagement in the online space are some of the challenges that have been observed by lecturers and staff during ERT. This recognition by the CELT department is useful in the continued responsive and thoughtful planning and implementation of programmes to support and encourage lecturers to adopt innovative teaching practices.

Implications for the students' voice during ERT

Pre-COVID-19, lecturers and students would be invited to town hall talks held by the Vice-Chancellor, which would be geared towards initialising strategy plans/discussions (CELT staff member). The CELT staff member notes that during the pandemic there were various challenges around the provision of support for students during ERT, and so highlights the importance of using a range of channels, including social media, to ensure that the student voice was still recognised: "The student voice is very, very important, and it is via SRC. The SRC Facebook site [is] where people are often expressing unhappiness, anger and frustration" (CELT staff member).

However, from a student perspective, the SRC channels that are available for students to raise their concerns, don't necessarily help and direct contact with the HOD is more responsive.

> If it's an academic problem I go to my HOD then if *kuyenye nkinga ngiya kwiSRC* (If it's an academic problem I go to my HOD then if it's another problem, I go to the SRC) ... Lena *yokuya kwiHOD*, I think *ibe-effective yona, because ngike ngkwazi ukuthi ngithole i-response e-right* (The option to go to the HOD, I think is effective, because I able to get the right response). But *le yokuya kwiSRC, sometimes iba-effective sometimes ingabi effective ... Sometimes ngike ngibabhalele, ngingaytholi iResponse* (But the option to go to the SRC, sometimes is effective and sometimes it's not effective ... Sometimes I would write to them, and not get a response) from them, or if it is effective, I'll report and get some response from them. (Student)

The student reports that talking to the HOD appears to be the most effective way to address a student's academic problem rather than relying on the SRC, which may be at times inconsistent. After raising concerns/opinions with the university, when asked if they are taken seriously, the below is noted by the students: "Yes, the university takes our concerns seriously. For example, if we want to change the test date or assignment due date they do change sometimes" (Student).

Moreover, students can influence, or rather have input into, how online learning takes place at DUT through responses to surveys and evaluations that are administered by the quality office (Lecturer 2). In addition, students can influence what is taught in the curriculum, as indicated by one of the lecturers who shares her/his strategy of how s/he is able to elicit constructive student input:

> So, what I do is to go back to my students who have been in the industry. So, after a year *besebenza* (of working) and have been in and out of the system. I always go back to them and run a sort of qualitative survey or rather ask them to reflect on what I taught them in third year ... Was it useful or did you not see any relevance *mase ufika* (when you get to) to industry? ... So that's how I get to revise my curriculum. (Lecturer 2)

Unfortunately, students may see themselves as subordinates and may be afraid to provide "an honest critique" (Lecturer 2) unless they are good academic achievers. However, the CELT staff member, speaking of the ERT during the national shutdown, shared that some students were concerned that learning online may be exclusionary or unjust, and discussed the need to mitigate this risk by exploring "low-tech" options.

> They've voiced their concern saying that online learning is leaving too many people behind. It's, I think, the institution was trying to find a way of balancing all of these things, wanting to do as much as possible without disadvantaging some. So again, I think that student voice was important in tempering the implementation – moderating our online learning initiative by using the low-tech options as with most universities. (CELT staff member)

The next section discusses the extent to which online learning, as a facet of open learning, leads to parity of participation for students politically, culturally, and economically at DUT.

Discussion

It is not yet entirely clear whether online learning at DUT is consciously understood to be a form of "open learning" as defined in the OLPF and is being deliberately implemented as such. However, the interpretation is that online learning, as a means of opening learning, is partially addressing economic, cultural, and political injustices at DUT in 'ameliorative' (Hodgkinson-Williams & Trotter, 2018) or 'affirmative' ways (Fraser, 2005).

Economically ameliorative responses

There were a number of ways in which online learning as a means of open learning at DUT addressed economic injustices experienced by students during the ERT. In an institution where approximately 50% of the student population rely on NSFAS funding, there was an awareness of the economic barriers encountered by many students (Interview 1). One of the major injustices was around the maldistribution of resources that enabled access to online teaching and learning. DUT provided staff and students with data and implemented an institutional directive for the use of cost-effective online platforms including the use of different forms of social media (i.e., WhatsApp groups) and the introduction of zero-rated websites for teaching and learning. Although these efforts somewhat address the issue of access (through laptops and data), there is still a larger national issue of a lack of ICT infrastructure within the rural parts of South Africa, limiting the opportunity for students from rural areas to access online learning opportunities. This shows that while the institution is able to take some economically redistributive measures, further economic restructuring is beyond the capacity of DUT alone and will require the intervention of DHET and the wider ICT sector.

Other institutions can learn valuable lessons from DUT including how it is using a blended approach to incrementally implement online learning across the institution. Understanding that online learning is part of a larger macro movement, the next section outlines recommendations based mainly on the insights from the implementation of ERT at DUT.

Culturally ameliorative responses

The majority of students who attend DUT are black students who are predominantly isiZulu home language speakers – even those who come from outside of KwaZulu-Natal understand isiZulu (Lecturer 2). However, the medium of teaching and learning is English and it is clear that the online space does not directly accommodate students whose mother tongue is not English. Although not all lecturers understand or speak isiZulu, some can do so on occasion. However, this irregular use of isiZulu barely ameliorates the language barrier. This can be challenging for students not fluent in English, because the online space may be isolating as students do not have the peer support that would normally be available during traditional in-person classes, where students are likely to informally translate for each other.

The responses reveal that DUT experienced multiple challenges in the process of implementing ERT as well as adopting deliberately planned online learning within the institution. The institution has employed a series of ameliorative responses to overcome some of the barriers to mitigate the challenges. For example, the staff development programme assisted the development of lecturers' digital literacy and online pedagogy during the COVID-19 pandemic.

Politically ameliorative responses

During the period of ERT, students were encouraged to raise their concerns through various online platforms such as the SRC Facebook group, WhatsApp groups, emails and/or course evaluations. These activities, mostly conducted online, display an ameliorative response or what Fraser refers to as representative justice.

Lecturer 2, deliberately tried to elicit the student voice by asking past students and current students' opinions on the curriculum to better suit their needs and expectations. Although this can be classified as strongly ameliorative, this exercise did not alter the underlying curriculum structures and re-frame the curriculum in a transformative way.

Conclusion

DHET (2017) and scholars such Letseka and Pitsoe (2012) pose online learning as a potential strategy for addressing the challenge of widening access and increasing participation for those who may have been educationally marginalised. DHET considers online learning as a form of open learning. The DUT staff members that were interviewed show a similar understanding of the concept of open learning and see online learning as a way of encouraging collaboration and flexibility in the provision of teaching and learning.

This study reveals that the institutional plan for adopting online learning enabled staff to more easily transition to ERT. Reciprocally some of the challenges experienced by staff and students engaged in the ERT have highlighted some of the interventions needed for the successful adoption of online learning at DUT. Economically DUT was able to provide funding for data bundles for staff and students, but more extensive economic provision of devices and connectivity is beyond the remit of an individual university and will require the coordinated intervention from the national government and the wider ICT sector.

Culturally, the affirmative reaction to host programmes to enhance the technical skills of staff and students made apparent DUT's responsiveness. Lastly, political inequalities, exacerbated by COVID-19, were partially ameliorated by encouraging students to address their concerns through various online platforms or in-person engagements (when lockdown rules were eased). The COVID-19 pandemic and responses to it deepened the experience of some of these inequalities, which under normal circumstances may not be as acutely experienced, but many activities highlighted in the move to ERT, can provide productive ways to envisage online learning as part of a broader open learning imperative (e.g., flexible provision of teaching and support, timetable rescheduling and restructuring of assessment). The form of online learning in ERT implemented at DUT at the time when this research was undertaken meant that students were away from their residences, and staff were working remotely, thus away from their regular WiFi connectivity and hence learning under inequitable conditions. Longer-term online or blended learning could increase the parity of participation of students and staff if deliberately planned and adequately resourced.

Acknowledgements

Many thanks to the staff and students from the Durban University of Technology Centre for Excellence in Learning and Teaching whose inputs made the case study possible. Special thanks are due to reviewers Andrew Deacon, Dr Johanna Funk and Dr Joshua Kim for their thoughtful, incisive feedback on the chapter, Emeritus Associate Professor Cheryl Ann Hodgkinson-Williams and Shanali Govender for additional writing support, and Dr Tabisa Mayisela for guiding the entire COOL project. Thanks are also due to the Centre for Innovation in Learning and Teaching at the University of Cape Town, which hosted the COOL project, and the South African Department of Higher Education and Training for funding it.

References

Adam, T. (2019). Digital neocolonialism and massive open online courses (MOOCs): Colonial pasts and neoliberal futures. *Learning, Media and Technology*, 44(3), 365–380.

Armstrong, C., & Thompson, S. (2009). Parity of participation and the politics of status. *European Journal of Political Theory*, 8(1), 109–122.

Bruff, D. O., Fisher, D. H., McEwen, K. E., & Smith, B. E. (2013). Wrapping a MOOC: Student perceptions of an experiment in blended learning. *Journal of Online Learning and Teaching*, 9(2), 187. https://jolt.merlot.org/vol9no2/bruff_0613.pdf

Chinembiri, T. (2020). Despite reduction in mobile data tariffs, data still expensive in South Africa (Policy Brief No. 2). Research ICT Africa. https://researchictafrica.net/publication/despite-reduction-in-mobile-data-tariffs-data-is-still-expensive-in-south-africa/

Cohen, L, Manion, L., & Morrison, K. (2007). *Research methods in education* (6th ed.). Routledge.

DHET (Department of Higher Education and Training). (2013). White paper for post-school education and training: Building an expanded, effective and integrated post-school system. *Government Gazette*, 37229. https://www.gov.za/documents/white-paper-post-school-education-and-training-building-expanded-effective-and-integrated

DHET. (2017a). Call for comment on the Open Learning Policy Framework for Post-School Education and Training. *Government Gazette*, 40772(335). http://pmg-assets.s3-website-eu-west-1.amazonaws.com/170407openlearningframework-postschooleduc.pdf

DHET. (2017b). Department of Higher Education and Training's position on online programme and course offerings. https://www.dhet.gov.za/Part%20C%20Policies/CROSS-CUTTING%20FOCUS%20AREAS/OPEN%20LEARNING/DHET%20position%20on%20online%20programme.pdf.

DoE (Department of Education). (1995). White paper on education and training. DoE. https://www.gov.za/sites/default/files/gcis_document/201409/16312gen1960.pdf.

DUT (Durban University of Technology). (2008). Heralding the centenary: 100 years of wisdom. DUT Division of Corporate Affairs. https://www.dut.ac.za/wp-content/uploads/menu/DUT_100.pdf.

DUT. (2015). DUT Strategic Plan 2015–2019: Towards relevance, responsiveness and resilience. https://www.dut.ac.za/wp-content/uploads/2016/09/DUT-strategic-plan-2015.pdf.

DUT. (2016). Durban University of Technology annual report 2016. https://www.dut.ac.za/wp-content/uploads/2012/06/DUT_AR2016_web.pdf.

Foko, B. (2015). Closing South Africa's high-skilled worker gap: Higher education challenges and pathways. *Africa Economic Brief*, 6(7), 1–19. https://www.afdb.org/en/documents/document/africa-economic-brief-closing-south-africas-high-skilled-worker-gap-higher-education-challenges-and-pathways-85617

Fraser, N. (1995). From redistribution to recognition? Dilemmas of justice in a 'postsocialist' age. *New Left Review*, 1/212, 68–93. https://newleftreview.org/issues/i212/articles/nancy-fraser-from-redistribution-to-recognition-dilemmas-of-justice-in-a-post-socialist-age

Fraser, N. (2005). Reframing justice in a globalizing world. *New Left Review*, 36, 69–88. https://newleftreview.org/II/36/nancy-fraser-reframing-justice-in-a-globalizing-world.

Fraser, N. (2009). *Scales of justice: Reimagining political space in a globalizing world* (vol. 31). Columbia University Press.

Gillwald, A., Mothobi, O., & Rademan, B. (2018). The state of ICT in South Africa. Policy paper no. 5; Series 5: After Access-Assessing Digital Inequality in Africa). Research ICT Africa. https://researchictafrica.net/wp/wp-content/uploads/2018/10/after-access-south-africa-state-of-ict-2017-south-africa-report_04.pdf

Harding, M., & Brodie, M. (2020). The challenges of remote online learning in higher education and the missing middle. *Daily Maverick*. https://www.dailymaverick.co.za/article/2020-06-08-the-challenges-of-remote-online-learning-in-higher-education-and-the-missing-middle/.

Hodgkinson-Williams, C. A. (2014). Degrees of ease: Adoption of OER, open textbooks and MOOCs in the global South. Presentation at OER Asia Symposium 2014. https://www.slideshare.net/ROER4D/hodgkinson-williams-2014-oer-asia

Hodgkinson-Williams, C. A., & Trotter, H. (2018). A social justice framework for understanding open educational resources and practices in the Global South. *Journal of Learning for Development*, 5(3), 204-224. https://files.eric.ed.gov/fulltext/EJ1197462.pdf

Knox, J. (2013). The limitations of access alone: Moving towards open processes in education technology. *Open Praxis*, 5(1), 21–29. https://www.learntechlib.org/p/130657/

Lambert, S. R. (2020). Do MOOCs contribute to student equity and social inclusion? A systematic review 2014–18. *Computers & Education*, 145, 103693. https://doi.org/10.1016/j.compedu.2019.103693

Letseka, M., & Pitsoe, V. (2012). Access to higher education through Open Distance Learning (ODL): Reflections on the University of South Africa (UNISA). In R. Dhunpath & R. Vithal (Eds.), *Alternative access to higher education: Underprepared students or underprepared institutions?* (pp. 219–234). Pearson. https://www.academia.edu/6074232/Access_to_Higher_Education_Through_Open_Distance_Learning_ODL_

Maxwell, J. A. (2008). Designing a qualitative study. In L. Bickman & D. J. Rog (Eds.), *The Sage handbook of applied social research methods* (2nd ed., pp. 214–253). Sage. https://dx.doi.org/10.4135/9781483348858

Mistri, G. U. (2016). A social realist analysis of participation in academic professional development for the integration of digital technologies in higher education [Doctoral dissertation, Rhodes University].

Moore, J. L., Dickson-Deane, C., & Galyen, K. (2011). e-Learning, online learning, and distance learning environments: Are they the same? *The Internet and Higher Education*, 14(2), 129–135. http://portfolio.kgalyen.com/pdf/moore2010_journal.pdf

Mothobi, O., & Gillwald, A. (2018). Lagging ICT adoption in SA reflects social and economic inequalities. Policy brief no. 2; Africa Mobile Pricing. Research ICT Africa. https://researchictafrica.net/wp/wp-content/uploads/2018/09/Policy-brief-No.2_South-africa.pdf

Mthethwa, A. (2020). Remote learning challenges delay resumption of universities. *Daily Maverick*. https://www.dailymaverick.co.za/article/2020-04-22-remote-learning-challenges-delay-resumption-of-universities/

Myende, P. E., & Ndlovu, N. (2020). COVID-19 and emergency online teaching and learning: A challenge of social justice for university rural students. *Alternation* 4, 167–187. http://alternation.ukzn.ac.za/Files/books/series/04/07-myende.pdf

Qwabe, B. P., & Khumalo, P. (2020). Students' perspective regarding the usefulness of e-learning in a South African university of technology. *International Journal of Entrepreneurship*, 24(2), 1–13. https://www.abacademies.org/articles/Students-Perspective-Regarding-Usefulness-of-E-Learning-in-A-South-African-University-of-Technology.pdf

Razzano, G., Gillwald, A., Aguera, P., Ahmed, S., Calandro, E., et al. (2020). SADC Parliamentary Forum discussion paper: The digital economy and society. Research ICT Africa. https://researchictafrica.net/wp/wp-content/uploads/2020/11/digital-economy-report_04.pdf

Shoba, S. (2020a). Are mobile network providers doing enough to keep South Africans connected? *Daily Maverick*. https://www.dailymaverick.co.za/article/2020-03-18-are-mobile-network-providers-doing-enough-to-keep-south-africans-connected/

Shoba, S. (2020b). As South Africa goes into lockdown, the higher education department prepares for online learning. *Daily Maverick*. https://www.dailymaverick.co.za/article/2020-03-24-as-south-africa-goes-into-lockdown-higher-education-department-prepares-for-online-learning/#gsc.tab=0

Shoba, S. (2020c). Universities gear up to save the academic year. *Daily Maverick*. https://www.dailymaverick.co.za/article/2020-04-17-universities-gear-up-to-save-the-academic-year/.

Shoba, S. (2020d). Government's plan to save the tertiary academic year. *Daily Maverick*. https://www.dailymaverick.co.za/article/2020-05-15-governments-plan-to-save-the-tertiary-academic-year/.

Sidler, V. (2018). Online learning – The future of education in South Africa. *My Broadband*. https://mybroadband.co.za/news/industrynews/265149-online-learning-the-future-of-education-in-south-africa.html

Swinnerton, B., Ivancheva, M., Coop, T., Perrotta, C., Morris, N. P., et al. (2018). The unbundled university: Researching emerging models in an unequal landscape. Preliminary findings from fieldwork in South Africa. In *Proceedings of the 11th International Conference on Networked Learning 2018* (pp. 218–226). Leeds. https://eprints.whiterose.ac.uk/131028/3/swinnerton_23%20final.pdf

Walker, M., & Mathebula, M. (2020). Low-income rural youth migrating to urban universities in South Africa: Opportunities and inequalities. *Compare: A Journal of Comparative and International Education, 50*(8), 1193–1209. https://www.tandfonline.com/doi/pdf/10.1080/03057925.2019.1587705?needAccess=true

Walton, E., Bowman, B., & Osman, R. (2015). Promoting access to higher education in an unequal society. *South African Journal of Higher Education,* 29(1), 262–269. https://journals.co.za/doi/pdf/10.10520/EJC172787

Whitelaw, E., Culligan, S., & Branson, N. (2020). Students will return on an unequal footing because of poor remote-learning access. *Daily Maverick.* https://www.dailymaverick.co.za/article/2020-09-27-students-will-return-on-an-unequal-footing-because-of-poor-remote-learning-access/

HOW TO CITE THIS CHAPTER

Zungu, S., & Walji, S. (2022). Online learning at the Durban University of Technology during the COVID-19 pandemic: Insights on openness and parity of participation. In T. Mayisela, S. C. Govender & C. A. Hodgkinson-Williams (Eds.), *Open learning as a means of advancing social justice: Cases in post-school education and training in South Africa* (pp. 106–130). African Minds. doi: 10.47622/9781928502425_5

This work is licensed under a Creative Commons Attribution 4.0 International (CC BY 4.0) licence.

6

Exploring the possibilities and constraints of online assessment to advance open learning in a South African TVET college

A social justice perspective

Cheng-Wen Huang & Tabisa Mayisela

SUMMARY South Africa's Department of Higher Education and Training (DHET) has put forward 'open learning' as an educational approach to addressing issues of access and success in the post-school education and training sector. This chapter investigates the possibilities and limitations of online assessment to advance DHET's open learning agenda in the technical and vocational education and training (TVET) sector. Adopting a social justice lens, this chapter explores how online assessment has the potential to encourage as well as constrain 'parity of participation' (Fraser, 1995) from an economic, cultural and political perspective. A small empirical study involving interviews with four staff members from Tshwane North TVET College's Open Learning Unit and four students is employed to illuminate the themes of social justice. The findings indicate that online assessment has the potential to aid economic justice by creating the conditions for working individuals to improve their qualifications whilst working, but lack of access to material resources, such as suitable technologies and data, can be a deterrent. Culturally, in relation to pedagogy, the findings illustrate the potential for online assessment to support learning by providing immediate feedback and creating opportunities for self-assessment, although academic integrity surfaces as a major concern. Politically, the findings indicate how a lack of national policy can hinder the successful operationalisation of online assessment at the course and institutional level. The chapter highlights the need to develop policies that correspond with the philosophies and practices of online assessment and open learning. It proposes that principles of open learning, combined with the affordances of online assessment, allows for an opportunity to explore different modes of assessments from the fit-for-purpose perspective.

Keywords: online assessment, continuous assessment, open learning, social justice, TVET

Introduction

South Africa's Department of Higher Education and Training (DHET) conceives of 'open learning' as an educational approach that is characterised by diverse modes of provision with specific principles related to access, pedagogy and success. The concept of open learning was first introduced in the 1995 *White Paper on Education and Training* and reiterated in the 2013 *White Paper for Post-School Education and Training* as a strategy to expand access and success in post-school education and training (PSET). In 2017, a draft plan was released to the public for comments in the *Open Learning Policy Framework for Post-School Education and Training*. Open learning foregrounds removing barriers to learning and is motivated by a concern for social justice. In order to operationalise the open learning vision, DHET identified the need to institutionalise the concept. As communicated in the draft policy framework, "the deployment of open learning approaches and related modalities in PSET institutions cannot be left to chance in the hope that it will happen. It is important for DHET and PSET institutions to share the same understanding of open learning and how it applies to teaching and learning" (DHET, 2017, p. 21).

This chapter explores the possibilities and limitations of online assessment to support DHET's open learning agenda in the technical and vocational education and training (TVET) context. The case entails a small empirical study involving interviews with four staff members and four students from Tshwane North TVET College's (TNC) Open Learning Unit.

Working from the premise that DHET's open learning agenda has a socially just intent, the chapter draws on Nancy Fraser's (1995, 2005) theory of social justice to investigate the possibilities and limitations of online assessment to enable parity of participation from an economic, cultural and political perspective. Fraser's term 'parity of participation' can be described as fair or equitable participation by all. The concept calls for arrangements of social structures that would enable all members of society to interact with one another as peers (Fraser, 2005). This chapter focuses on the online context as a mode of assessment delivery and how this mode of delivery can enable or constrain the parity of participation of students in a TVET college.

The chapter illustrates that while online assessment has the potential to advance DHET's open learning agenda, complex social issues, particularly in relation to digital access, can hinder the successful implementation and unintentionally widen disparities. The chapter posits that in order for online assessment to be successfully operationalised in the TVET context, it is crucial that policies are developed to correspond with the philosophies and practices of open learning and online assessment.

Understanding DHET's open learning agenda and the implications for TVET colleges

Traditionally, delivery modes in the PSET sector involve predominantly contact (face-to-face) or distance learning. Open learning is conceived as an education model that will complement the traditional models through diverse modes of provision, whereby "courses and programmes are mediated by a range of distance, resource-based and contact-based methods, with the blend of methods varying from context to context" (DHET, 2017, p. 363). Specifically, DHET (2017) defines open learning as:

> An educational approach which combines the principles of learner-centredness, lifelong learning, flexibility of learning provision, the removal of barriers to access learning, the recognition for credit of prior learning experience, the provision of learner support, the construction of learning programmes in the expectation that learner can succeed, and the maintenance of rigorous quality assurance over the design of learning materials and support systems. (p. 363)

In this sense, besides being an educational model that is characterised by diverse modes of provision, open learning also encompasses principles to guide access (flexibility of learning provision, removal of barriers, recognition of prior experience), pedagogy (learner-centredness and lifelong learning) and success (provision of learner support, construction of learning programmes in the expectation that learners can success, maintenance of quality assurance).

According to DHET (2017), open learning "is driven by a concern for social justice and therefore motivated by the need for redress, equity in access to opportunity, flexibility and choice, and by an equal concern for quality and real success in learning" (p. 412). Hence, the concept "is fundamentally about access and success, with flexibility of provision contributing to access, and quality of provision contributing to improved student success" (p. 373). From this perspective, the two guiding tenets of open learning are access and success. For DHET, access translates to increased enrolment. Two crucial strategies outlined as necessary to facilitate enrolment involve (1) removing barriers to access, and (2) providing flexibility of provision. Factors that are noted as barriers that need to be removed include:

> geographic distance from educational campuses, timetable scheduling that is incompatible with people's working lives or family responsibilities, unaffordable fees, alienating pedagogic practices, lack of access to technology, lack of physical educational infrastructure, and discrimination on the basis of gender, age, race, ethnicity, social class, language or disability. (DHET, 2017, p. 373)

It is important to highlight that although access and removal of barriers are emphasised, DHET (2017) recognises that "learning programmes and courses cannot for the most part be fully 'open' (p. 373). In other words, it is acknowledged that courses and programmes will have prerequisites that set up conditions for access.

In terms of flexibility of provision, DHET outlines three tactics. They involve providing learners more agency to determine the pace and where, when, what and how they will learn, as well as whether they wish to acquire certification at the end of a course; recognising prior experience and learning that are not necessarily academically oriented; and allowing for credit transfer between qualifications programmes so as to enable lifelong learning.

The second tenet of open learning, success, translates to (1) improved throughput rate, (2) success rate, and (3) employability. Quality of provision is seen as crucial in achieving success. Some components that are noted as necessary to attain quality include a learner-centred approach to pedagogy, provision of learner support, as well as construction of accessible programmes and courses and learning materials.

In operationalising the mechanisms for access and success, DHET emphasises the use of cost-effective modalities. In particular, information and communication technologies (ICTs) are identified as key tools to assist this process. Besides being a mere tool, integration of

ICTs into the curriculum is also seen as important in developing a locally relevant curriculum that speaks to workplace practices and fostering employable skills. As DHET (2017) puts it, "TVET colleges need to structure themselves around increasing the employability of their students by considering additional, technology-based means of education and training delivery" (p. 380).

For the 50 public TVET colleges, the open learning principles provide a conceptual framework to enact the 2013 White Paper directive to increase access and success cost-effectively. The White Paper mandates an expansion of 2.5 million headcount enrolments in the TVET sector by 2030. The 2019/2020 target is 1 238 000 enrolments, but only 673 490 enrolments were reported in 2019 (DHET, 2021). Shortfalls in enrolments have been attributed to constrained funding of programmes (including limited student funding), inadequate physical infrastructure and insufficient human resources (PMG, 2018). Poor throughput rate is also an issue (Dessus et al., 2019). Defined as "the rate at which a cohort successfully completes a qualification within the stipulated timeframe for that qualification", the throughput rate is reported at 9.2% for the cohort that enrolled in 2016 for NCV Level 2 and who completed with NCV Level 4 in 2018 (Khuluvhe & Mathibe, 2021, p. 3). This number is significantly behind the National Development Plan target of 75% throughput rate by 2030. In order to improve access, the White Paper states the need to increase diversity of provision; that is, "cater[ing] for a very wide variety of potential student needs, including mature adult learners who have to study and work at the same time, as well as younger people who may have dropped out of the schooling system due to financial, social, learning or other barriers" (DHET, 2013, p. 48). These students are seen as needing the provision of a diverse range of programmes and appropriate modes of delivery to cater for their life and work contexts. Online assessment, which is often used in blended and online learning contexts, has the potential to support DHET's open learning agenda by catering for student groups that require flexibility in time and place of assessment, as well as provide means to promote and support learning through feedback on assessment.

Online assessment: A brief review of the mechanics

In a widely cited definition, the Joint Information Systems Committee (JISC) defines online assessment or e-assessment as "the end-to-end electronic assessment processes where ICT is used for the presentation of assessment activity, and the recording of responses", which can serve diagnostic, formative or summative purposes (JISC, 2007, p. 6). Online assessment, as such, covers a range of activities from design, delivery, marking, reporting (feedback) and storing of records.

There are two particular forms that online assessment can take: selected-response and constructed-response. Selected-response, also referred to as objective assessments, involve quizzes such as completion (fill-in-the-blank), true-false, matching, multiple choice and hotspot (see Babo et al., 2020; Faridah et al., 2018; Jordan, 2013; Nicol, 2006; Van der Westhuizen, 2016). These types of assessment are known for measuring knowledge and comprehension, but are noted to be inadequate for measuring "students' abilities to create, organize, communicate, define problems, or conduct research" (Nilson, 2016, p. 283). As a result, they have been critiqued for encouraging rote memorisation and factual recall rather than higher-order thinking (Conole & Warburton, 2005; Scouller, 1998). In recent literature, however, there is increasing recognition that selected-response assessments can measure higher-order thinking. Scully (2017), for instance, demonstrates how multiple-choice items can be constructed to measure higher-order thinking through strategies such as manipulation of target verbs, item flipping, use of high quality distractors and tapping 'multiple neurons'. Scully (2017) argues that rather than being "incapable of measuring complex cognitive processes" it may be a "more accurate assertion" to say that multiple-choice items "measuring complex cognitive processes are simply rarely constructed" (p. 10). Likewise, Faridah et al. (2018) illustrate how higher-order thinking can be developed in the context of mathematics using a web-based quiz application – ThatQuiz.[1] The authors conclude that while developing higher-order thinking-based problems in the application was easy, a significant time was required as well as a strong internet connection.

A distinct advantage of selected-response assessments is that they can be set up to provide automated marking and feedback. Some benefits of automated marking include increased reliability in producing consistent results, saving time and human labour needed for marking (Jordan, 2013). In this way, selected-response assessments are particularly suitable for contexts with high student to staff ratio. The automation capability also renders it possible to provide immediate feedback and allow for multiple attempts. Selected-response assessments, as such, can function as mechanisms for revision and self-assessment (Nicol, 2006). Problems that have been raised with assessment practices in TVET colleges in South Africa include the lack of structured remedial intervention (Sebetlene, 2016) and regularity of feedback (Sephokgole & Makgato, 2019). Whitelock (2006) maintains that a delay in feedback may reduce its effectiveness and posits that e-assessment can encourage students to become more reflective learners through its capacity to provide immediate feedback.

It is worthwhile noting that while selected-response assessments do not require human labour to mark, the design and setting up of the assessment demand significant work. Nilson (2016) writes that "[i]nexperienced instructors may think that objective questions are easy to construct, but "unambiguous and discriminating ones take time and thought" (p. 283). Nilson notes that professional test writers are generally only able to construct eight or ten usable questions a day.

Constructed-response assessment, commonly referred to as 'assignments', is another form that online assessment can take. Taking constructed-response in the broad sense to refer to any assessment where the response requires construction, other than the traditional short-answers and essays, newer assessment methods such as e-portfolios (Pallitt et al., 2015), blogs, wikis (Issa, 2020), and forums (Jordan, 2013) can also be understood as forms of constructed-response assessment. Constructed-response assessments are appropriate for assessing application type of knowledge or "higher-order thinking that requires construction, as opposed to selection of an answer" (Nilson, 2016, p. 291). Being flexible in format, these types of assessments are suitable for extended problem solutions. However, in doing so, fewer questions can be asked in a testing period, which affects the breadth of content coverage (Bennett & Ward, 2012). In addition, as constructed-response assessments require human markers, their validity and fairness have also been questioned (Jordan, 2013). Hepplestone et al. (2011) highlight how technology can be used to encourage student engagement with feedback in constructed-response assessments from using 'Track Changes' and 'Comments' in *Microsoft Word*, to audio feedback, which provides possibilities of greater detail and depth in information offered.

---

[1] https://www.thatquiz.org/

Aside from assessing, online assessment also has the function of record-keeping. Online assessment administered through learning management systems (LMS) can store evidence of work, feedback and marks. Online publication of grades and feedback through a LMS not only allows flexibility in terms of the time and place in which students can choose to access their grades and feedback, but also makes it easy to track progress, and enable students to use the LMS as a learning hub, since grades and feedback are automatically stored alongside learning resources and activities (Parkin et al., 2012). By storing evidence of work, feedback and marks, the online assessment system builds up a set of assessment data. In recent research into e-assessment, there is growing interest in understanding how assessment data can be drawn into a learning analytics strategy (Chan et al., 2019; Ellis, 2013; Nouira et al., 2017; Van der Westhuizen, 2016).

The review of the mechanics suggests that online assessment has the potential to advance both the access and success aspects of the open learning agenda. In relation to access, online assessment has the potential to open up education to non-traditional students, such as working individuals, by offering flexibility in time and place of assessment taking. As JISC (2007) asserts, "Anytime, anywhere assessments benefit learners for whom a traditional assessment regime presents difficulties due to distance, disability, illness, or work commitments" (p. 7). In relation to success, online assessment can support quality of learning by providing efficient ways for revision and self-assessment. In addition, the capability of tracking progress and generating assessment analytics in online assessment allows for making timely decisions, such as taking appropriate interventions, if necessary. In this sense, assessment data can serve as valuable information in making evidence-based decisions.

Despite the potential, it is necessary to acknowledge that, when situated in the social milieu, online assessment can take on particular challenges. One major challenge pertains to digital access. Online modes of delivery, such as online assessments, can expose individual inequalities in physical access to appropriate technologies (e.g., a computer and Internet connection) and inequalities in technical skills or capabilities. These barriers are commonly referred to as first-level and second level digital divides respectively (Aissaoui, 2021; Van Dijk, 2020).

Another challenge is the concern with academic integrity. The pivot to online modes of delivery during the COVID-19 pandemic has brought this issue to the fore (Gamage et al., 2020; Nggondi et al., 2021; Reedy et al., 2021; Selwyn et al., 2021; Verhoef & Coetser, 2021). While some studies support the dominant view that cheating or academic dishonesty occurs more frequently in online classes than traditional face-to-face classes (Dendir & Maxwell, 2020; Kennedy et al., 2000), other studies indicate that online assessments are less (Peled et al., 2019) or no more vulnerable to cheating than face-to-face assessments (Reedy et al., 2021). Arguing that academic dishonesty is more prevalent in online assessments, Dendir and Maxwell (2020) put forward online proctoring as the best mitigating strategy. Conversely, observing that students are no more likely to cheat in the online context than in the face-to-face environment, Reedy et al. (2021) propose an integrated approach that combines the use of technology, along with assessment design, and developing a culture of integrity, as ways to promote academic integrity. Harton et al. (2019) highlight that beliefs that students are more likely to cheat in online assessments than face-to-face assessments can hinder institutions from developments in distance education as the beliefs may prompt reluctance from faculty to adopt teaching online and deter students from taking online courses due to the perception that they are less rigorous.

Lastly, given that many TVET institutions are under-resourced, costs for institutions are another challenge that deserves a mention. In implementing online assessment, institutions would need to bear the cost of purchasing, installing and maintaining an institutional LMS, as well as developing a sustainable programme of technical and pedagogic support, for both staff and students. While costs have been noted as a reason for the slow uptake of online assessment prior to the COVID-19 pandemic, it has also been argued that the long-term benefits outweigh the upfront costs (JISC, 2007).

Theoretical framework: Fraser's theory of social justice

The theoretical approach that underpins the entire COOL project is Nancy Fraser's theory of social justice. Fraser's advocacy for social justice begins with the notion of 'parity of participation'. According to Fraser (2005), "justice requires social arrangements that permit all to participate as peers in social life" (p. 73). The term 'parity of participation' describes this ideal of equal or fair participation for all in the social realm. Fraser (2005) posits that "overcoming injustice means dismantling institutionalized obstacles that prevent some people from participating on par with others, as full partners in social interaction" (p. 73). She identifies three specific kinds of impediments to parity of participation which correspond with three kinds of injustices: economic, cultural and political.

The economic dimension of injustice stems from the problem of class structure. Fraser (2005) states that "people can be impeded from full participation by economic structures that deny them resources they need in order to interact with others as peers; in that case they suffer from distribution injustice or maldistribution" (p. 73). In other words, when people suffer from an uneven distribution of resources, this is seen as an economic injustice arising from *maldistribution*. In relation to online assessment, an example of economic maldistribution would be lack of access to data, connectivity and devices due to high costs (first-level digital divide). A maldistribution of any of these resources could prevent some students from participating in the online space and thereby lead to a disparity between those who can afford to engage online and those who cannot.

The cultural dimension of injustice stems from the problem of status order. Fraser (2005) posits that "people can also be prevented from interacting on terms of parity by institutionalized hierarchies of cultural value that deny them the requisite standing; in that case they suffer from status inequality or misrecognition" (p. 73). In other words, when people are barred from social interactions due to values attributed to culture, this is understood as a cultural injustice stemming from a *misrecognition* of values. In relation to online assessment, the concern with academic integrity is evidently an issue related to value. Gamage et al. (2020) illustrate this well as they identify diverse cultural backgrounds as one cause for academic malpractice. They indicate that in Australia, many international students struggle with acknowledging and citing sources according to Western academic convention. Drawing on the work of Scollon (1995), the argument is made that, in the case of Chinese international students, their struggles stem from "longstanding adherence to Chinese cultural rhetorical conventions that may have shaped their writing behaviour" (Gamage et al., 2020, p. 17). Academic integrity is thus not a neutral concept, but one which is grounded in Western academic standards. In this way, academic integrity valorises Western values.

Lastly, the political dimension of injustice is concerned with obstacles arising from the political constitution of society. It involves "the state's jurisdiction and the decision rules by which it structures contestation" (Fraser, 2005, p. 75). According to Fraser (2005), "misrepresentation occurs when political boundaries and/or decision rules function to deny some people, wrongly, the possibility of participation on a par with others in social interaction — including, but not only, in political arenas" (p. 76). In other words, political injustice can occur when there is a *misrepresentation* of people within a community.

Fraser identifies two levels of misrepresentation that can occur: *ordinary-political misrepresentation* and *misframing*. In ordinary-political misrepresentation, injustice occurs when "political decision rules wrongly deny some of the included the chance to participate fully, as peers" (Fraser, 2005, p. 76). As such, the injustice is about the "terms of engagement in a given political community" (Hölscher & Bozalek, 2020, p. 12); how some members of a given community are given more voice or representative power than others as a result of political decisions. For example, misrepresentation can happen when students and/or lecturers are not given free and equal participation in decisions about assessment. As McArthur (2016) writes:

> This is exemplified in the way in which predetermined learning outcomes are presented as a transparent contract between students and teachers. This is misleading on a number of levels. Firstly, students rarely make any contribution to the formulation of these contracts/learning outcomes. Secondly, the same is true of many teachers, constrained from change by tortuous bureaucratic processes, and the implications of this are exacerbated by a system in which courses (often the large undergraduate ones) are passed between academics as though a burden of which everyone has to take their turn. (p. 970)

Misframing, on the other hand, is concerned with "the boundary-setting aspect of the political" (Fraser, 2005, p. 76). According to Fraser (2005), "[h]ere the injustice arises when the community's boundaries are drawn in such a way as to wrongly exclude some people from the chance to participate *at all* in its authorized contests over justice" (p. 76). That is to say, in misframing, the injustice is no longer about whose 'voice' is heard or represented within a community, but it is about who is included in the community or not. In other words, it elevates the problem to "a matter of scope" (Hölscher & Bozalek, 2020, p. 12). For instance, in the case of this study, when there is a lack of suitable online assessment policy and guidelines are instead drawn from the assessment policy intended for face-to-face assessment, this can be considered as an example of misframing. In such an instance, it is no longer about who gets to have a say in what goes in the policy, but rather that there is no policy to address the practice. Fraser (2005) asserts that "frame-setting is among the most consequential of political decisions" (p. 77).

It is important to highlight that while the three dimensions of injustice relating to class structure (economic), status-order (cultural) and the political constitution of society (political) are conceptually distinct from each other, they are at the same time "inextricably interwoven" (Fraser, 2005, p. 75). As Fraser (1995) states:

in the real world, of course, culture and political economy are always imbricated with one another; and virtually every struggle against injustice, when properly understood, implies demands for both redistribution and recognition. (p. 70)

Fraser (1995) argues, however, that "for heuristic purposes, analytical distinctions are indispensable" as "[o]nly by abstracting from the complexities of the real world can we devise a conceptual scheme that can illuminate it (p. 70).

The idea of imbrication is well exhibited through the issue of the digital divide which sees an interplay of economic, cultural and political dynamics in leading to barriers to digital access (Bornman, 2016; Czerniewicz et al., 2020; Hutchings & Sheppard, 2021; Van Dijk, 2020). At the most basic level, lack of physical or material resources (first-level divide) bars one from access to the digital realm. However, as various studies show, an individual's economic status is closely linked to one's social position in society. For instance, Bornman's (2016) study into the digital divide in South Africa highlights correlations between digital access and gender, population groups and educational levels. The study indicates that more males than females have access to ICTs; Whites use ICTs more than other population groups; and those with tertiary education make more use of ICTs than those with matric (Grade 12) qualifications. Similarly, Hutchings and Sheppard's (2021) study into the impact of digital and data poverty on Black, Asian and Minority Ethnic learners in the UK shows a disproportionate impact of digital poverty on ethnic minorities. Political dynamics can also work to unfairly exclude some from digital access. Lephaka (2021) illustrates this through the example of the Regulation of Interception of Communications and Provision of Communication-Related Information Act (RICA) in South Africa. The RICA Act mandates the registration of sim cards in order to access network services. The registration process, however, requires providing proof of residence. Lephaka (2021) points out that this may pose a challenge to people in informal settlements and rural areas. In this sense, a government policy can inadvertently lead to exclusion of certain members of society from participating in the digital realm.

As remedies of injustice, Fraser theorises two approaches: *affirmation* and *transformation*. According to Fraser (1995), affirmative remedies entail "correcting inequitable outcomes of social arrangements without disturbing the underlying framework that generates them", while transformative remedies entail "correcting inequitable outcomes precisely by restructuring the underlying framework" (p. 82). That is to say, in affirmative remedies, the injustice is addressed within the boundaries of the established norm. In this way, it *affirms* the established social arrangement, but makes improvements within the framework to address an injustice. In contrast, in transformative remedies, the established norm is disturbed or uprooted to address an injustice. The remedy, as such, *transforms* the social arrangement to respond to the injustice. According to Fraser (1995), "[t]he nub of the contrast is end-state outcomes versus the processes that produce them. It is *not* gradual versus apocalyptic change" (p. 82). In essence, the two remedies involve either working to find a solution within a given framework (*affirmative*) or changing/uprooting the framework entirely (*transformative*) to achieve an equitable outcome. By addressing the end-state outcomes, affirmative remedies only provide some respite from injustices. By addressing root causes, transformative remedies provide the conditions for restructuring. Importantly, they "reduce inequality without creating stigmatized classes of vulnerable people perceived as beneficiaries of special largesse" (Fraser, 2003, p. 77). Fraser (2003) asserts that transformative remedies are "preferable in principle", but acknowledges that they are "more difficult to effect in practice" (p. 78).

The site of study

The site of study is Tshwane North TVET College (TNC), a technical and vocational college that is located in the greater Tshwane metropolitan area of Gauteng. In response to DHET's call to increase access by enrolling more students, the college's Open Learning Unit was established in 2019. The Open Learning programme follows the Report 191 (NATED) curriculum, but is delivered online with minimum contact. Contact sessions conducted by lecturers are deemed voluntary. Besides being a response to DHET's call to enrol more students, the Open Learning programme also replaces the now defunct part-time programme. Due to this change, some students who were in the pipeline have shifted over to the Open Learning programme.

Students who enrol in the Open Learning programme are primarily working students and/or those who failed the full-time programme. Besides increasing access by enrolling more students, the Open Learning Unit also contributes to improving student success by offering an alternative route for students who no longer qualify for the full-time programme to complete their qualification. In 2020, there were 547 students enrolled in the Open Learning programme at TNC.

Prerequisites to enrol in the Open Learning programme include a Grade 12 qualification and proof of employment for working individuals. Students are also required to have access to the internet and a device, as well as to be computer literate.

Students enrolled in the open learning courses undertake the online assessment that forms part of the internal continuous assessment (ICASS). The ICASS is structured to "prepare students for external examinations through formal assessment activities that support teaching and learning" (DHET, 2020, p. 2). It has a strong formative orientation, providing students and lecturers the opportunity to use assessments to "evaluate learning progress and determine whether remedial interventions are needed" (DHET, 2020, p. 4). For the mini and final exams, assessments are written on campus alongside the full-time students.

Method

The site of study was purposely chosen by DHET at the inception of the project because of its perceived innovation in deploying online assessment and open learning. Though the COOL project commenced prior to the outbreak of the COVID-19 pandemic, the field work took place during the period of the pandemic in 2020. Confined by lockdown regulations, the scale of the study was reduced significantly. Only four staff members and four students from the Open Learning Unit were interviewed. To obtain a range of perspectives, the staff members interviewed included managers and lecturers. One-on-one interviews with staff members were conducted remotely through Zoom, while interviews with students were conducted through WhatsApp interactions. The interview questions were structured around understanding the practice of online assessment at the college in an endeavour towards ascertaining the possibilities and limitations of the practice to open learning from a social justice perspective. After the interview transcripts were member-checked by the research participants, the interviews were divided into units of analysis and placed into an Excel spreadsheet. Together with the COOL project team, a coding framework that comprises both inductive and deductive codes was developed and applied to the units of analysis. These codes were further grouped into themes related to open learning and the three dimensions of social justice.

Aside from the small data set, the study has two other key limitations: (1) interviewing students who are already in the programme, and (2) using WhatsApp as an interview method. Firstly, by interviewing existing students, this secures the views of those who already have access to learning and inadvertently excludes those who may have been barred from the programme for whatever reasons. Secondly, at the time of data collection, asynchronous WhatsApp interactions were deemed an appropriate method of engaging with the students, as it required less data and allowed flexibility in time when responding. In hindsight, however, this approach generated a less rich response. Reasons for this could be that momentum is lost through asynchronous exchanges and it is more difficult to build a rapport through text messages than face-to-face interactions.

Findings and discussion

Perceptions of open learning at TNC

As previously mentioned, the COOL project was commissioned by DHET with the aim of understanding how institutions are comprehending and implementing open learning. Staff members were thus specifically asked about their understanding of open learning. The excerpt below aptly captures what they said generally:

> Open learning concept, to me, it's *distance learning*, a concept that one can describe as a *learning environment*, within and also beyond a formal education system, which exercises *flexibility to choose from a variety of options in relation to time, in relation to place, instructional methods, modes of access* and other factors related to the learning process. (Staff member, emphasis added)

Firstly, staff members described open learning in relation to distance or online learning. They mentioned that the uptake of online learning is necessary, as it makes it possible for the institution to overcome infrastructure limitations, whilst responding to the mandate to enrol more students. Secondly, open learning was described as being able to offer flexibility in time, place, instructional methods and access. Flexibility in time and place was seen as an important condition for working students as they could take their assessments off-campus and at their convenience. Staff members described diverse approaches to course delivery, ranging from online, blended and face-to-face modes. They also cited the different educational materials used, highlighting the multimodal resources such as text, audio, image, video and hyperlinks afforded by the online context. Importantly, they highlighted that open learning provides an opportunity for working students to improve their qualifications and allows students who no longer qualify for the full-time programme to complete their qualification. There were also descriptions of open learning in relation to removing barriers, particularly in relation to time-scheduling (work) and geographical distance. Open learning was also mentioned in relation to student autonomy and the necessity for them to take responsibility for their learning.

The findings suggest that by and large, staff members' understanding of open learning aligns very closely with DHET's conception, with the exception of conflating open learning with distance learning. Within the *Open Learning Policy Framework,* DHET strongly asserts that open learning is not synonymous with distance education. DHET maintains there is need to separate the concepts as terms such as 'open distance learning' and 'Open and Distance Learning' (ODL) have:

> created a misperception that distance education is inherently 'open'. This is a challenge, not only because poor distance education practice can easily close opportunities of actual learning, but equally because it incorrectly assumes that only distance education strategies are open. (p. 372)

It is necessary to highlight that while staff members from the Open Learning Unit generally had a good understanding of what open learning entails, one reported that the concept is not well understood within the institution, outside of the unit. The staff member recounted that there is the perception that they are "lazy" and "paid for doing nothing" since few students are seen visiting the unit.

> I don't see it as a mode that is fully understood ... in terms of the staff, the perception is negative, because it is seen as people who are just lazing around. For example, if you are coming to work in the morning, and then you're just sitting there with your laptop, sometimes drinking coffee, [and] the rest of your colleagues are in the class, with 30 students ... The people think that because your class is virtual, it means that you are just lazing around. You are actually being paid for doing nothing.

The staff member conveyed, however, that this perception is changing, following the COVID-19 pandemic, as various lockdown regulations necessitated full-time staff to consider remote ways of teaching.

The possibilities and limitations of online assessment from an economic perspective

The case with TNC suggests that online assessment has the potential to offer some degree of economic redistribution by providing flexibility in place and time of assessment as the flexibility enables students to save time and costs associated with travelling.

> When we do an assessment, unlike face-to-face, if you are giving a test today, the student must come to campus today; whether the student has got money to travel or whether the student has got problems or whatever challenge, the student must come on that particular day to access the assessment. But with online, all the student needs are data and a gadget. So, it does help alleviate issues with equity, overcoming barriers of time and cost. (Staff member)

Importantly, the affordance of being able to take assessments "wherever" and "at whatever time" sets the conditions for working individuals to pursue a qualification whilst working, as the following excepts reveal:

> I'm working and I'm doing night shifts. I can do my studies at night at work. (Student)

> We had some of our students, who were posted at other places where they do not normally reside, but they were still able to write wherever they were to complete the assessment, because it's online ... I'm going to give you a classic example of a student who works for the SABC. That student was supposed to go and shoot in Durban on the same day we were writing a mini exam. The student was able to write the mini exam, online on site, for that period. Unlike, if you were supposed to come here, imagine if the student was to fly from Durban to come here, just to write a paper that was only going to take one hour, and then fly back. So, it helps, especially for those who are working. That they can be able to do the assessment wherever they are, at whatever time. (Staff member)

Online assessment, as such, can support diversity of provision, creating possibilities for non-traditional students to attain a qualification.

Despite these potentials, accessibility issues related to data, device, connectivity and electricity surfaced as significant challenges to online assessment. A staff member mentioned that while data for completing assessments online is not a substantial issue, as the assessments themselves do not consume a lot of data, it was noted that some students did not review learning materials upon which assessments are based because of high data costs. This suggests that the practice of online assessment needs to be viewed as functioning in an ecology of online learning. That is, rather than as a practice that is contained in and of itself, online assessment needs to be seen as intricately linked to online teaching and learning activities. To put it in another way, for students to engage meaningfully with assessment, it is essential for them to access learning materials needed to complete an assessment. The link between learning outcomes, assessment, and teaching and learning activities is commonly referred to as 'constructive alignment' (Biggs, 1999). The concern with data described here presents a physical manifestation of the link, as success within an assessment task may be hindered by lack of access to learning materials.

In relation to devices, two specific challenges are raised. Firstly, there is the challenge of students not owning a computing device. Students mentioned that they mitigate this challenge to some extent by visiting internet cafés, sharing a device with others at home, or using a smartphone. However, complications have been raised with some of these strategies. For instance, in relation to the smartphone, a staff member reported that certain assessments do not function optimally on the phone interface and incoming calls can boot out students while undertaking an assessment. Secondly, there is the issue with device and software compatibility. The LMS software is said to pose a challenge for students whose devices are outdated with respect to their operating systems and internet browsers.

In addition to data and device issues, there are challenges with connectivity and electricity. Both staff members and students described connectivity hurdles when network providers' systems are down and when there is loadshedding (i.e., rotating blackouts to reduce strain on electrical grid). Connectivity and electricity, as such, can be considered more of a political barrier rather than an economic barrier, since the issue here lies with poor infrastructure and maintenance rather than whether staff and students can afford the material access.

The findings suggest that despite the economic redistribution in relation to time and travelling costs, issues with technology access can inadvertently heighten economic mal-distribution and increase the so-called digital divide.

The possibilities and limitations of online assessment from a cultural perspective

In relation to culture, both staff members and students claimed that attributes such as race, religion and gender are less noticeable or problematic in the online environment than in face-to-face settings.

> Because you do [the assessment in] your own space, don't think [race, religion and gender] will be a problem. (Student)

> So far, I must say, I haven't experienced any. Why I say so, because if I look at the first time when they are coming to write, I could see that I was dealing with different groups, different cultural backgrounds, people coming from different places. And then, when I'm listening to the questions and trying to answer, I am confident to say that I haven't experienced any problems in that regard. (Lecturer)

On the surface, this may suggest that the online context may be able to offer some respite from cultural misrecognition. However, as will be discussed further, this claim needs to be more carefully examined.

In terms of pedagogy, online assessment is described as being effective for remedial intervention and self-assessment. Staff members remarked that remedial interventions are easier to manage, since quizzes can be set up to provide immediate constructive feedback. In long question answers, the copy and paste function renders it less demanding to provide feedback to a large number of students. In addition, they mentioned online assessment as being suitable for self-assessment as assessments can be set up to provide multiple attempts or configured in a way that a subsequential lesson will only be accessible when the student attains a satisfactory mark.

The lack of digital literacy skills, nevertheless, surfaces as a significant challenge for both lecturers and students. Brown et al. (2016) break down the concept of digital literacy into four dimensions: operational, situated, critical and access. The operational dimension is concerned with the ability to "make meaning using diverse media and modes of communication" and is "often thought of as skills and competencies (especially regarding computer literacy and information literacy)" (p. 13). The lecturers' and students' struggle with digital literacy is at this level of the operational. Lecturers are cited as needing training on setting up assessments and marking online. Students' inability to adequately operate technologies is said to affect confidence in engagement, their ability to provide a desired answer in an assessment and in assignment submissions.

> I'm not sure [because when] we wrote assignments that had a time limit, I wasn't sure if everything I typed was there [because] they were jumping to another row and I couldn't fix [it], we could only just type. (Student)

> I've seen this a couple of times, whereby students will complain, after giving them feedback, that they did have the answer. But, when you look at the answer, how they typed, it gives you a different thing from what they could have typed there. You can see that the learner is almost there, but because of the inability to instruct the laptop, or to give instructions or to write the answer, then it becomes a problem. (Staff member)

In response to the persistent problem of poor digital literacy, the unit is working on providing ongoing training for both students and lecturers. Other than onsite training, videos on 'how to' are being uploaded on the LMS platform. The unit's LMS manager plays an integral role in the training and support initiatives.

For staff members, academic integrity, particularly around validating the identity of the person performing the assessment, was also expressed as a matter of concern. As articulated below:

> At the moment, we don't have those facilities that are able to monitor if the learner is the learner who is actually writing or if somebody is writing on their behalf. That could be a challenge. That could give you false results or false evidence. At the end of the day, if a learner gets 80%, is it really the learner, or is it somebody else? (Staff member)

Staff members' perceptions of students' academic integrity, in this sense, echo the dominant view that academic dishonesty is more likely to happen in assessments online than face-to-face.

The findings focus attention on the different purposes which assessments can serve and that online assessment may be better for formative purposes than summative purposes. For formative purposes, online assessment holds potential to support the assessment-for-learning intention that underpins the ICASS by making it easier for revisions and self-assessment. The concerns with academic integrity, however, suggest that online assessments may not be best in achieving summative purposes. Given that open learning advocates diverse modes of provision, it may serve the educational community well to rethink assessment practices from the perspective of 'fit for purpose'. That is, it may be useful to consider what modes of assessments are best for achieving what purposes and allow for both online and face-to-face modes of assessment to cater for specific purposes.

It is not surprising that lack of digital literacy, at the operational level, emerges as a key obstacle to engagement in this space. What is surprising though is that lecturers self-report that they too require strengthening of their digital literacy skills. This hints at the scale of support and training that would be needed to implement online assessment.

As mentioned, while both staff and students reported no discrimination due to gender, race and religion, this need to be investigated further since research indicates that visible characteristics such as race and gender are still enacted virtually (Grasmuck et al., 2009; Huffaker & Calvert, 2005). Indeed a person's name, alone, can be telling of the person's race and gender and research into unconscious bias in education suggests that biases that "we are unaware of, and which happens outside of our control" occurs (Equality Challenge Unit, 2003, p. 1). Hence, if cultural characteristics are reflected online, there is a need to further investigate how biases, whether intentional or unintentional, can manifest through teaching and assessing online.

Political barriers in the implementation of online assessment

The case with TNC indicates that there are two political barriers that can manifest in the implementation of online assessment. First and foremost, there is the issue of a lack of policy for online assessment. Drawing on Ripley (2009), Allan (2020) outlines two approaches in the adoption of online summative assessments: migration and transformation. In migration, "technology is regarded primarily as an instrument: a vehicle to 'move traditional paper-based tests to screen versions' in order to generate 'administrative gains and service improvements'"; while in transformation, "technology is positioned as an essentially disruptive, almost revolutionary force: transformation 'sets out to redefine assessment and testing approaches in order to lead educational change'" (Allan, 2020, p. 2280). In other words, migration involves moving merely from paper to screen, affirming the existing assessment structures, while transformation involves remodeling the assessment for the online space. In the case with TNC, the approach can be described as migration, as staff members reported that the online assessment practice follows the Report 191 ICASS guideline, which was developed for paper-based assessment.

Two problems are cited with the migration approach. The first is with moderation. Lecturers are reportedly still required to print out hardcopies to share with moderators, despite the assessments being conducted online. Another problem concerns the number of questions that comprise a question paper. The ICASS guideline stipulates a particular format and a number of questions that need to be contained within an assessment. A lecturer argued, however, that there are fewer questions that can be answered in an hour-long online test compared to a paper-based test, as it takes longer to read and submit answers online due to the screen/electronic set up. Insufficient time to complete assessments was also a problem raised by students. This suggests that a lack of policy specific to the practice of online assessment can disadvantage students pedagogically. In this sense, a political injustice can give rise to a cultural injustice. In essence, the migration approach results in a political misframing, as a policy developed for a different practice is imposed upon a mismatching practice. The case with TNC underscores the shortcoming of conceiving online assessment as a form of open learning, but basing it on assessment policies developed for the traditional campus-based model of education.

The second political barrier relates to the cost of installing and maintaining an LMS, as well as training staff and students on its use. At TNC, the Open Learning unit began with a free version of the commercial platform, *Schoology*. Lecturers reported that the free version offers limited functionalities and there is a tendency of the system to crash during peak submissions. Given that the LMS is the fundamental structure upon which online assessment is built, conducting an institutional assessment to determine needs and various costs associated with LMS implementation is important, as migrating to a different platform could be cumbersome later on.

While the challenge with the LMS is seemingly an economic issue, it can be argued that the problem stems from the political decision to allow institutions the autonomy to choose their own LMS. This autonomy may not be cost-effective in the long run, as by giving institutions the option to choose their own platforms, this means that the institutions themselves will need to carry the burden of training their own staff. Given that the TVET curriculum is standard across all 50 colleges, a common LMS platform may be more advantageous, as coordinated training may help save costs and allow for sharing of knowledge and training materials across institutions.

Conclusion and recommendations

This chapter has explored the potentials and limitations of online assessment to support DHET's open learning agenda using the case of TNC. Economically, the chapter demonstrated that the flexibility in time and place of assessment afforded by online assessment provides the conditions for working individuals to improve their qualifications whilst working. Accessibility issues, however, pose a challenge to both students and lectures. The chapter has proposed that online assessment is part of an ecology of online learning, thus barriers that hinder online learning also hinder online assessment.

Culturally, in relation to pedagogy, the chapter detailed the potential of online assessment to foster an assessment-for-learning environment through automation capabilities that allow for immediate feedback and self-assessment, but, at the same time, it also outlined concerns with academic integrity. The chapter has situated this discussion within the context of purposes of assessment, suggesting that online assessment performs formative assessments better than summative assessments. As open learning promotes diverse modes of provision, the chapter has proposed that this provides an opportunity to rethink assessment practices from the perspective of 'fit for purpose'. Moreover, the chapter has hinted at the scale of training that would be needed to implement online assessment as both students and lecturer report issues with digital literacy. Finally, while both students and staff report no overt manifestation of cultural biases, this chapter has proposed the need to probe this further, since literature suggests that cultural characteristics and biases can be enacted online.

Politically, the chapter has highlighted how a lack of policy at the national level can place a burden on institutions and subsequently disadvantage students and lecturers. Furthermore, the chapter has suggested that giving institutions the autonomy to choose their own LMS may not be cost-effective in the long run. Instead, a common LMS may be more advantageous, as this presents the opportunity for a coordinated response and sharing of knowledge across TVET colleges.

Overall, the case at TNC demonstrates an affirmative response to DHET's open learning agenda as practices are set up to address immediate shortcomings or injustices stemming from the traditional education model. This is particularly evident with the lack of policy for online assessment. Arguably, at the institutional level, a response can only be ameliorative as TVET colleges lack the power to transform accessibility and policy issues. A transformative response would require actions at the national level, with policies and practices developed specifically for the open learning model.

Based on these findings, the following recommendations can be made. At the national level, the most urgent issue is for DHET to develop a policy for online assessment. The case with TNC has shown the need for a set of protocols that speak to the practice. The issue with accessibility is arguably more complex, but responses during the COVID-19 pandemic have shown possibilities in the form of provision of educational data bundles, zero-rating institutional websites and laptop distributions. The most sustainable of these responses is possibly the project of connecting TVET colleges to the South African National Research Network (SANReN). The SANReN network is said to offer high-speed connectivity for teachers, researchers and students (TENET, 2020a). Like the Eduroam project (see TENET, 2020b), which is seeing the international roaming network being installed in public libraries, the extension of the SANReN to public spaces holds possibilities of easing economic maldistribution and bridging the digital divide for TVET college students.

At the institutional level, colleges need to assess institution needs and consider the costs of installing and maintaining a LMS, as well as training staff and students in its use.

At the individual level, the sharing of knowledge among lecturers and making case studies available (see Chan et al., 2019) may assist in cultivating motivation and innovation in the use of online assessment.

This chapter has explored the possibilities and limitations of online assessment to advance DHET's open learning agenda from a social justice perspective. To examine whether online assessment can indeed enable social justice and advance DHET's open learning agenda, a comparison of grade profiles, attainment gaps and progression trend of open learning students to traditional full-time students could be conducted in future research.

Acknowledgements

Many thanks to the staff – Dr Pieter Geel, Cornelius Machaka, Henrietta Mongola, Jacob Kwakwa, Anita Nieuwoudt – and students from Tshwane North TVET College's Open Learning Unit, whose inputs made the case study possible. Special thanks are also due to reviewers Dr Jan McArthur and Dr Pauline Hanesworth for their thoughtful, incisive feedback on the chapter, Ncebakazi Lutuli for breaking the ground on this research study, and Emeritus Associate Professor Cheryl Ann Hodgkinson-Williams and Shanali Govender for valuable feedback. Thanks are also due to the Centre for Innovation in Learning and Teaching at the University of Cape Town, which hosted the COOL project, and the South African Department of Higher Education and Training for funding it.

References

Aissaoui, N. (2021). The digital divide: A literature review and some directions for future research in light of COVID-19. *Global Knowledge, Memory and Communication*. Online ahead-of-print.

Allan, S. (2020). Migration and transformation: A sociomaterial analysis of practitioners' experiences with online exams. *Research in Learning Technology*, 28.

Babo, R., Babo, L. V., Suhonen, J. T., & Tukiainen, M. (2020). E-Assessment with multiple-choice questions: A 5 year study of students' opinions and experience. *Journal of Information Technology Education: Innovations in Practice*, 19, 1–29.

Biggs, J. (1999). What the student does: teaching for enhanced learning. *Higher Education Research & Development*, 18(1), 57–75.

Bornman, E. (2016). Information society and digital divide in South Africa: results of longitudinal surveys. *Information, Communication & Society*, 19(2), 264–278.

Brown, C., Czerniewicz, L., Huang, C. W., & Mayisela, T. (2016). Curriculum for digital education leadership: A concept paper. Commonwealth of Learning.

Chan, S., Walsh, N., Roo, A., Power, K., Stokes, C., et al. (2019). Guidelines for developing and using e-assessments with vocational learners: Project overview. Ako Aotearoa.

Conole, G., & Warburton, B. (2005). A review of computer-assisted assessment. *ALT-J*, 13(1), 17–31.

Czerniewicz, L., Agherdien, N., Badenhorst, J., et al. (2020). A wake-up call: Equity, inequity and Covid-19 emergency remote teaching and learning. *Postdigital Science and Education*, 2, 946–967.

Dendir, S., & Maxwell, R. S. (2020). Cheating in online courses: Evidence from online proctoring. *Computers in Human Behavior Reports*, 2, 100033.

Dessus, et al. (2019). *South Africa economic update: Enrollments in tertiary education must rise*. World Bank. http://documents.worldbank.org/curated/en/173091547659025030/pdf/133785-revised-jan22.pdf

DHET (Department of Higher Education and Training). (2013). White paper for post-school education and training. *Government Gazette*, 37229. https://www.gov.za/documents/white-paper-post-school-education-and-training-building-expanded-effective-and-integrated

DHET. (2017). Call for comment on the Open Learning Policy Framework for Post-School Education and Training. *Government Gazette*, 335(40772). http://pmg-assets.s3-website-eu-west-1.amazonaws.com/170407openlearningframework-postschooleduc.pdf

DHET. (2020). TVET Curriculum Instruction. Internal Continuous Assessment (ICASS) Guidelines Report 191 Programmes.

Ellis, C. (2013). Broadening the scope and increasing the usefulness of learning analytics: The case for assessment analytics. *British Journal of Educational Technology*, 44(4), 662–664.

Equality Challenge Unit. (2003). *Unconscious bias and higher education. Unconscious bias in higher education: Literature review*. Advance HE (advance-he.ac.uk).

Faridah, R., Siswono, T. Y. E., & Rahaju, E. B. (2018, July). Developing higher order thinking skill (HOTS) mathematic problem using that quiz application. In *Mathematics, Informatics, Science, and Education International Conference (MISEIC 2018)*. Atlantis.

Fraser, N. (1995). From redistribution to recognition? Dilemmas of justice in a 'postsocialist' age. *New Left Review*, 1/212, 68–93. https://newleftreview.org/issues/i212/articles/nancy-fraser-from-redistribution-to-recognition-dilemmas-of-justice-in-a-post-socialist-age

Fraser, N. (2003). Social justice in the age of identity politics: Redistribution, recognition, and participation. In N. Fraser, A. Honneth & J. Golb (Eds.), *Redistribution or recognition? A political-philosophical exchange* (pp. 7–109). Verso.

Fraser, N. (2005). Reframing justice in a globalizing world. *New Left Review*, 36, 69–88.

Gamage, K. A., Silva, E. K. D., & Gunawardhana, N. (2020). Online delivery and assessment during COVID-19: Safeguarding academic integrity. *Education Sciences*, 10(11), 301.

Grasmuck, S., Martin, J., & Zhao, S. (2009). Ethno-racial identity displays on Facebook. *Journal of Computer-mediated Communication*, 15(1), 158–188.

Harton, H. C., Aladia, S., & Gordon, A. (2019). Faculty and student perceptions of cheating in online vs. traditional classes. *Online Journal of Distance Learning Administration*, 22(4), n4.

Hepplestone, S., Holden, G., Irwin, B., Parkin, H. J., & Thorpe, L. (2011). Using technology to encourage student engagement with feedback: A literature review. *Research in Learning Technology*, 19(2), 117–127.

Hölscher, D., & Bozalek, V. (2020). Nancy Fraser's work and its relevance in higher education. In V. Bozalek, D. Hölscher & M. Zembylas (Eds.), *Nancy Fraser and participatory parity: Reframing social justice in South African higher education* (pp. 3–19). Routledge.

Huffaker, D. A., & Calvert, S. L. (2005). Gender, identity, and language use in teenage blogs. *Journal of Computer-Mediated Communication*, 10(2), JCMC10211.

Hutchings, C., & Sheppard, M. (2021). Exploring the impact of digital and data poverty on BAME learners. JISC.

Internet World Stats (2021). Internet world penetration rates by geographic regions 2021. https://www.internetworldstats.com/stats.htm

Issa, T. (2020). e-Assessments via Wiki and blog tools: Students' perspective. In *Educational Networking* (pp. 235–268). Springer.

JISC (Joint Information Systems Committee). (2007). Effective practice with e-assessment: An overview of technologies, policies and practice in further and higher education. http://www.jisc.ac.uk/publications/

Jordan, S. (2013). E-assessment: Past, present and future. *New Directions in the Teaching of Physical Sciences*, 9(1), 87–106.

Kennedy, K., Nowak, S., Raghuraman, R., Thomas, J., & Davis, S. F. (2000). Academic dishonesty and distance learning: Student and faculty views. *College Student Journal*, 34(2).

Khuluvhe, M., & Mathibe, R. (2021). Fact Sheet: Throughput rate for TVET College Students (National Certificate Vocational for the period 2016 to 2018). DHET.

Lephaka, P. (2021). SA's internet freedom ranks high despite limitations. SABC. https://www.sabcnews.com/sabcnews/sas-limited-internet-freedom-despite-free-rating-on-paper/

McArthur, J. (2016). Assessment for social justice: the role of assessment in achieving social justice. *Assessment & Evaluation in Higher Education*, 41(7), 967–981.

Nicol, D. (2006, December 3). Increasing success in first year courses: Assessment re-design, self-regulation and learning technologies. In *Proceedings of the 23rd Annual Ascilite Conference*.

Nilson, L. B. (2016). *Teaching at its best: A research-based resource for college instructors*. John Wiley.

Nouira, A., Cheniti-Belcadhi, L., & Braham, R. (2017). An ontological model for assessment analytics. In *Proceedings of the 13th International Conference on Web Information Systems and Technologies (WEBIST 2017)* (pp. 243–251). SCITEPRESS.

Pallitt, N., Strydom, S., & Ivala, E. (2015) E-portfolios. In W. R. Kilfoil (Ed.), *Moving beyond the hype: A contextualised view of learning with technology in higher education* (pp. 32–36). Universities South Africa.

Parkin, H. J., Hepplestone, S., Holden, G., Irwin, B., & Thorpe, L. (2012). A role for technology in enhancing students' engagement with feedback. *Assessment & Evaluation in Higher Education*, 37(8), 963–973.

Peled, Y., Eshet, Y., Barczyk, C., & Grinautski, K. (2019). Predictors of Academic Dishonesty among undergraduate students in online and face-to-face courses. *Computers & Education*, 131, 49–59.

PMG (Parliamentary Monitoring Group). (2018). *Higher Education Committee Reports*. Committee Report on Higher Education and Training 2018/19 Budget. https://pmg.org.za/committee-meeting/26339/

Reedy, A., Pfitzner, D., Rook, L., & Ellis, L. (2021). Responding to the COVID-19 emergency: Student and academic staff perceptions of academic integrity in the transition to online exams at three Australian universities. *International Journal for Educational Integrity*, 17(1), 1–32.

Ripley, M. (2009). Transformational computer-based testing. In F. Scheuermann & J. Bjornsson (Eds.), *The transition to computer-based assessment* (pp. 92–98). European Commission Joint Research Centre.

Scollon, R. (1995). Plagiarism and ideology: Identity in intercultural discourse. *Language in Society*, 24(1), 1–28.

Scouller, K. (1998). The influence of assessment method on students' learning approaches: Multiple choice question examination versus assignment essay. *Higher Education*, 35(4), 453–472.

Scully, D. (2017). Constructing multiple-choice items to measure higher-order thinking. *Practical Assessment, Research, and Evaluation*, 22(4), 1–13.

Sebetlene, S. P. (2016). Management of the implementation of internal continuous assessment at Western College in Gauteng [Master's disseration, University of Witwatersrand].

Sephokgole, D., & Makgato, M. (2019). Student perception of lecturers' assessment practices at technical and vocational education and training (TVET) colleges in South Africa. *World Transactions on Engineering and Technology Education*, 17(3), 398–403.

StatsSA (Statistics South Africa). (2019). General household survey. http://www.statssa.gov.za/publications/P0318/P03182019.pdf

TENET South Africa. (2020a). Ending bandwidth poverty at TVET colleges. https://www.tenet.ac.za/news/ending-bandwidth-poverty-at-tvet-colleages

TENET South Africa. (2020b). Bridging the digital divide with eduroam. https://www.tenet.ac.za/news/bridging-the-digital-divide-with-eduroam

Van der Westhuizen, D. (2016). *Guidelines for online assessment for educators*. Commonwealth of Learning. http://oasis.col.org/handle/11599/2446

Verhoef, A. H., & Coetser, Y. M. (2021). Academic integrity of university students during emergency remote online assessment: An exploration of student voices. *Transformation in Higher Education*, 6, 12.

Whitelock, D. (2006). Electronic assessment: marking, monitoring and mediating learning. *International Journal of Learning Technology*, 2(2–3), 264–276.

HOW TO CITE THIS CHAPTER

Huang, C.-W., & Mayisela, T. (2022). Exploring the possibilities and constraints of online assessment to advance open learning in a South African TVET college: A social justice perspective. In T. Mayisela, S. C. Govender & C. A. Hodgkinson-Williams (Eds.), *Open learning as a means of advancing social justice: Cases in post-school education and training in South Africa* (pp. 131–151). African Minds. doi: 10.47622/9781928502425_6

This work is licensed under a Creative Commons Attribution 4.0 International (CC BY 4.0) licence.

7

Exploring how student support services address economic, cultural and political injustices

Insights from Elangeni TVET College, South Africa

Sinethemba Zungu & Cheryl Ann Hodgkinson-Williams

SUMMARY South Africa's legacy of unequal access to learning opportunities and the need to create a conducive technical and vocational education and training (TVET) sector for a diversified student population has exposed a need for comprehensive learner support. The introduction by the Department of Higher Education and Training in 2017 of the *Open Learning Policy Framework*, which has an explicit social justice ambition, has recognized the salience of student support systems (SSS) at TVET colleges. However, the extent to which the current TVET student support models are designed to encompass open learning practices and the extent to which they are indeed socially just is not yet known. This chapter examines how SSS (as a means of enacting open learning principles) endeavour to create a socially just environment for students to have access to (pre-entry), progress through (on-course), and success (at exit) in a TVET college. The chapter employs Nancy Fraser's (2005) theory of social justice, understood as 'parity of participation', to interrogate the extent to which SSS address the economic, cultural, and political injustices faced by students at Elangeni TVET College in KwaZulu-Natal. This case study adopted a qualitative approach and data was generated via three virtual interviews with the SSS staff and telephonic and WhatsApp discussions with two students. Findings indicate that the institutional structures and activities in place to support students respond affirmatively to the economic inequalities, political injustices, cultural and social diversity at Elangeni College. While the economic, political, and economic issues are interlinked, this research has highlighted that the economic injustices faced by students cannot be settled at an institutional level, but can only be resolved at a national level. Furthermore, the SSS staff have revealed a willingness to address cultural inequities, but some of these affirmative responses are limited by economic resources (underfunding of TVET colleges). This study contributes to an under-researched topic that has potential to strengthen the further development of the OLPF in concert with annual strategic plans for SSS at TVET colleges. Despite the limited sample size, the insights from the chapter illuminates the need for further research in the areas of open learning, student support and social justice.

Keywords: student support, open learning, social justice, TVET

Introduction

During the time of the fieldwork and writing of this chapter, the world was confronted by the COVID-19 pandemic, which forced many institutions in South Africa to adopt emergency remote teaching and online modes of operation to temporarily replace existing in-person tuition and supplement established distance education provision. This study focuses on Student Support Services (SSS) for campus-based programmes (which are currently being offered in some form of remote teaching) and distance education programmes. The need for SSS has been intensified during this period to reduce the difficulties experienced by campus-based students in the rapid shift to remote modes of learning. The pandemic further exacerbated the pre-existing thorny issue of access to learner support services for students enrolled in distance education programmes (Nonyongo & Ngengebule, 1998, p. xii). The most crucial challenge confronting Technical and Vocational Education and Training (TVET) colleges (formerly known as Further Education and Training [FET] colleges) has been:

> the shift in student population: multiple language groups in one classroom; intake of students with varying disabilities; different age groups and therefore different students' needs on one campus; higher levels of cognitive demand in new programmes; demands for adequate infrastructure and resources for teaching and learning; student protests and thus a wider range of academic support requirements, to name but a few of the consequences of the shift in the student population. (DHET, 2020, p. 3)

A qualitative study conducted by Moodley and Singh (2015), identified that students faced economic and socio-cultural challenges such as scarce funding and poor academic performance, because students cannot cope with English as the medium of instruction, and lack of career guidance and information prior to entering higher education in South Africa. Paterson (2016, p. viii) argues that South African TVET colleges "seem to embody a fundamental institutional enigma – despite multiple changes intended to improve the quality and efficiency of the colleges, they are still viewed as underperforming, perhaps even impervious to change efforts". This view is also supported by Jeffery (2015) who claims that regardless of the measures in place to encourage SSS in colleges, the number of students who are likely to graduate after entering TVET colleges in South Africa remains significantly low (Papier et al., 2018). One of the challenges is how colleges can better support their students to "achieve success in their studies and employability" (Paterson, 2016, p. xiv).

In February 2009, the then Department of Education developed the *Student Support Services Manual* (DoE, 2009) for the public TVET institutions. The intention of this SSS Manual is to provide guidelines to colleges on how to best support their students to achieve academic success (DoE, 2009). The more recent *TVET Colleges' 2020 Student Support Services Annual Plan* (DHET, 2020) specifies more detailed implementation plans to attain the same end. A further response from the Department of Higher Education and Training (DHET) has been to advance the principles of open learning through its draft *Open Learning Policy Framework* (OLPF) *for South African Post-School Education and Training* (PSET) (DHET, 2017). This policy has been developed in the context of DHET's commitment to implement open learning principles and approaches across the PSET system and as a response to the social, economic and transformative needs of the country (DHET, 2017). DHET expects PSET institutions to pay careful attention to the provision of adequate SSS as a way of enacting open learning principles (DHET, 2017).

The draft OLPF outlines the measures and steps to be taken to advance SSS in PSET institutions across the country with the view that probable growth of open technologies and open learning practices may open PSET to wider and more diverse groups of students (DHET, 2017). This suggests that SSS in PSET should be an all-encompassing, holistic system that must cater to the economic, cultural, and political needs of diverse groups of students. To understand what is meant by 'all-encompassing student support for open learning', the key concepts 'student support' and 'open learning' are defined in line with the main aim of the study which is to understand the extent to which SSS enacts open learning principles to enable socially just education for students in a TVET college.

Open learning

The OLPF defines open learning as:

> An educational approach which combines the principles of learner-centeredness, lifelong learning, the flexibility of learning provision, the removal of barriers to access learning, the recognition for credit for the prior learning experience, *the provision of learner support*, the construction of learning programmes in the expectation that learners can succeed, and the maintenance of rigorous quality assurance over the design of learning materials and support systems. (DHET, 2017, p. 363, emphasis added)

The open learning principle of providing student support acknowledges the diversity of learning contexts of students across South Africa, and its approach to education which seeks to reduce barriers to learning within those different contexts (DHET, 2017). Furthermore, OLPF espouses an approach of shared expertise, knowledge, and resources in order to increase access to diverse learning opportunities and services for students (DHET, 2017, p. 5). This broad definition of open learning also highlights an opportunity for lifelong learning, regardless of geographic and demographic barriers (e.g., socio-economic status, age, family commitments), in the name of opening up access to PSET.

Knox (2013, p. 21), writing from the UK, describes the 'open education' movement as "an agenda of institutional transformation, calling for unrestricted access to educational materials and the diminishing of geographic and economic barriers to participation". Similarly, Letseka and Pitsoe (2012) in a South African context, discuss the concept of 'open learning' as an educational approach that is designed to reach learners at their preferred locations (home or office setting) to enable access to learning resources that can support them to qualify and succeed without attending formal classes in person. Although both 'open education' and 'open learning' clearly share an ambition to remove barriers inhibiting students' access, progress, and success, the former refers to informal and nonformal education and the latter primarily to the formal. Following Letseka and Pitsoe (2012, p. 221) "open distance learning

(ODL) ... provides higher education opportunities to working adults who would otherwise not have the opportunity to acquire a higher education qualification at full-time contact institutions". Letseka and Pitsoe (2012) argue that it is undeniable that the concept of open learning is related to the idea of distance learning or open distance learning (ODL) due to the concepts representing approaches that emphasize opening access to education and training provision (including learning material), freeing learners from the constraints of time and place.

The concepts of student support and open learning highlight that the provision of learner support and equal access to opportunities for students are key objectives. The open learning approach and the integrated methods for providing student support infers a social justice intent. The next section briefly conceptualizes open learning in relation to providing a socially just learning environment in PSET through the provision of learner support. The next section outlines SSS in the South African context.

Student support services in South Africa

According to DHET, "support is crucial to ensure that students adapt to the demands of college life and that they can meet the demands of college programmes" (2013, p. 17). The idea of student support in PSET endeavours to address South Africa's historical context of unequal access to quality education and poor throughput rate (DHET, 2018). SSS can be understood as "specialized non-educational services (including all human and value-added resources that deliver support to individual students) [that are] needed to improve the effectiveness of teaching and learning" (Steyn & Wolhuter, 2008, in Maimane, 2016, p. 1681). Following a neoliberal view, Maimane (2016) relates the necessity for student support in TVET to the growth of the economy by highlighting that the effective coordination of SSS could contribute greatly to the success of students and the labour market. Balwanz and Ngcwangu (2016) caution that inadequate student support may lead to a mismatch between what is required by the labour markets and what is produced from colleges (this may result in an over-supply of skills to a certain section of the labour market and low supply of obligatory (technical) skills (Maimane, 2016). It is therefore crucial for institutions to offer various types of support programmes including, career guidance and counselling, to channel students towards acquiring skills that are demanded by the labour market (Maimane, 2016).

Needham (2019, p. 83) argues that "South Africa's adoption of economic and neo-liberal reforms has led to a range of privatisation approaches in public education and training systems that affect TVET provision". Drawing terms such as 'endogenous privatisation and exogenous privatisation' from Ball and Youdell (2007) to contextualise the effects of privatisation on the TVET sector, Needham (2019) shows the antagonistic relationship between education and training policy interventions and privatisation approaches adopted in South Africa and how this has affected the TVET sector's ability to contribute to employment and economic development. He argues that South Africa's recent policy developments and the country's neoliberal approach have created few synergies between public and private sectors, as a result, the TVET sector is unable to supply the critical skills required to stimulate economic growth (Needham, 2019).

However, Powell and McGrath (2014) challenge the neo-liberal underpinnings of policies that reinforce human resource development as the main priority in the TVET sector. Using the capability approach, they emphasise that the FET (now referred to as TVET) sector's policy has shifted, noting DHET's focus on the needs of the poor and a policy discourse that centralises the needs of the students and communities rather than solely meeting the needs of industry. In this context, the scholars argue against a 'one size fits all' post-school system, and advocate for awareness and sensitivity to the need to create institutions that respond to different contexts. Powell and McGrath (2014) further reflect on the TVET evaluation approach to support policy and institutional transformation which highlights learner support as one of the key performance dimensions in measures of institutional efficiency and effectiveness. This is determined by indicators such as (1) the implementation of academic support programmes; and (2) the implementation of learner support programmes (Powell & McGrath, 2014, p. 132).

Student support services in the South Africa policy context

South African policy documents emphasize that SSS is essential for TVETs and it is the responsibility of each college to formulate proposals and apply for funding to DHET for student support activities (DHET, 2013; Jeffery & Johnson, 2019). According to DHET, TVET "colleges are at different stages of development, due in part to their history of differential access to resources, and therefore require different levels of intervention and support to achieve optimal functionality" (2013, p. 12). DHET further explains that the aim is not to make all TVET colleges the same, rather that individual characteristics of each college will require a response appropriate to "their local environments, creating a diverse subsystem that serves a wide range of needs" (DHET, 2013, p. 12).

Defining student support

The OLPF uses the terms 'student support' and 'learner support' interchangeably. The OLPF defines student support partially as a *principle* that "addresses open learning approaches and distance education methodologies" (DHET, 2017, p. 393) clearly including traditional face-to-face and distance modes of teaching. The OLPF also describes student support as a *strategy* through which institutions can collaborate in "establishing or supporting learning support centres and mentoring learner centre personnel" (DHET, 2017, p. 391) as part of a broad ambition for PSET institutions to "create conditions for a fair chance of learner success through learner support, contextually appropriate resources and sound pedagogical practices" (DHET, 2017, p. 371).

In alignment with DHET's model for student support in higher education, Maimane (2016) suggests that education support services for students should form a part of the entire institutional system (institutionally planned and embedded) which includes all human, financial resources, adequate infrastructure (ICT and technology) and other aspects (including learning material). Essentially, student support services should "provide learners with the support required to learn effectively, make career decisions and manage personal crises through student counselling" (Powell & McGrath, 2014, p. 132).

There are numerous models for SSS (Jeffery & Johnson, 2019). Broadly speaking these SSS models can be either student-centred, suggesting that they can follow a bottom-up process where students are actively involved in the design of the support services model adopted at the institution or a top-down approach where the model for SSS is designed at a macro-level (by the management of the institution or even by DHET) and implemented at a micro-level by student support officers with little or no involvement of students. This key difference between models of student support determines the value of the support services offered to students by their institutions (Jeffery & Johnson, 2019). Writing about South African students, Needham and Papier (2011) argue that vocational education neglects students' perspectives and interpretations of support. This means that colleges lack student involvement in the designing and implementation of SSS. Similarly, Jeffery (2015) sees the lack of engagement with students' interpretations and perspectives in SSS in South Africa as a significant shortcoming. An institutionally focused approach to the design of SSS may lack student-centredness and poses the question whether the student support framework adequately addresses the challenges faced by students in TVET colleges.

Creating a conducive environment for SSS in post-school education and training

While the country has taken measurable steps towards improving access to higher learning, there still remains a group or category of previously disadvantaged individuals that necessitates SSS in the PSET sector (Letseka & Pitsoe, 2012). Previously disadvantaged students (PDS) are often the first-generation university students in their respective families, who have little access to social networks or people who have experiences of university study and would therefore require student support (Slonimsky & Shalem, 2006, cited in Letseka & Pitsoe, 2012).

Some colleges already offer various SSS, such as academic support, social support, assisting students to obtain bursaries and complete their programmes of study, and assistance with finding workplaces for the practical components of their programmes and jobs on completion of their studies (DHET, 2013, p. 17). Currently, the holistic provision of student support has not been implemented in all colleges in the country and the focus in most colleges has been primarily on bursary administration with varied successes (DHET, 2020). Student support programmes are often not a priority and the limited resources available to improve them (DHET, 2013) are often one of the barriers to providing SSS at colleges. The SSS framework outlined that there are "several barriers to the provision of SSS in TVET colleges ... there is a lack of human and physical resources to support the provision of SSS" (Munyaradzi & Addae, 2019, p. 263). Acknowledging the need for a dedicated SSS office to coordinate support programmes, especially for students who have not been equipped with a sufficient educational background to enable them to cope with the requirements of college studies, "DHET will provide ring-fenced funding for student support activities" (DHET, 2013, p. 17). However, this funding is still not sufficient for the implementation of effective SSS (Munyaradzi & Addae, 2019).

Seven years after the 2013 White Paper, DHET released a *TVET Colleges' 2020 Student Support Services Annual Plan*, which aims to map the successful implementation of holistic SSS at TVET colleges (DHET, 2020). The SSS 2020 Plan (DHET, 2020) does not mention open learning directly, however, it seeks to provide a roadmap to how TVET's can implement SSS through the "provision of learner support" (2017, p. 363). DHET places importance on building SSS in a holistic and student-centred approach that seeks to increase the chances of success and employability of students (2020, p. 3).

The SSS plan lays out a model centred around the different phases of student life within the institution, and this is set as the foundation of services "that should be provided by all colleges as a bare minimum" (DHET, 2020, p. 7). This model involves providing pre-entry support, on-course, and exit support, comprising the following activities and elements of college life, as per the SSS Plan (DHET, 2020, p. 7).

Figure 1: Student support services model (DHET, 2020, p. 7)

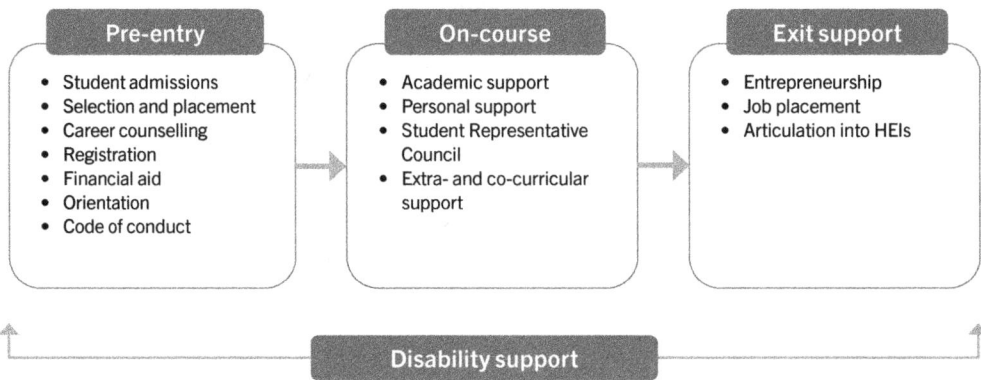

Figure 1 represents the benchmark for SSS and activities provided by TVET colleges. The 2009 SSS Manual and associated model show a linear model providing a 'checklist' of activities that must be undertaken by SSS departments at TVET colleges. This may seem to construe SSS to a mere 'tick box' exercise, whereas open learning principles espoused by the OLPF seem to be broader than that. DHET's OLPF prescribes that "comprehensive learner support" should cover four main elements, which are academic support, counselling support, administrative support, and technological support (DHET, 2017, p. 24).

Academic support

According to DHET (2017, p. 364), academic support "refers to a wide variety of instructional methods, educational services or educational resources provided to students in an effort to help them accelerate their learning progress, catch up with their peers, meet learning standards, or generally succeed in their learning endeavours". Jeffery and Johnson (2019) argue that DHET endorses a model of academic support that places the burden of responsibility on the institution for supporting struggling students. In some institutions, this includes the idea of students taking responsibility for their own academic performance through attending face-to-face tutorials and, remedial interventions for example, the colour-coded 'robot' method[1] for accessing academic performance. For this study, academic support will be understood as interventions or services made available by the institution to make learning easier and to increase academic achievement among students. Strengthening academic support is not only limited to making resources available but involves services that build upon student-lecturer relationships and develop interventions to build positive peer-to-peer relationships in order to encourage academic mindsets and culture.

---

[1] The robot (or traffic light) method is the idea that students monitor their own academic performance based on the notion of colour coding their academic performance. Green meaning 'good academic performance', yellow (meaning at risk) and red indicating the need to attend academic counselling or on academic probation.

Counselling support

Counselling support can be in "the form of career guidance, study skills and computer skills training and assistance for students facing crisis situations and adjustment issues" (DHET, 2017, p. 364). Jeffery and Johnson (2019) suggest that students are a product of their disadvantaged backgrounds and circumstances, therefore they require an institutional form of academic counselling. Student counselling offered to students includes aspects such as academic, therapeutic, and emotional support. Furthermore, counselling support entails taking care of students in terms of life, mentorship, and health counselling (for example, the HIV/AIDS support unit). For this project, counselling support is understood as support available to individual students on a personal level, including psychological support. "Psychological support is an essential part of the SSS structure and contributes in assisting the students to settle in the new environment through provision of counselling services which should cater for all students with their different backgrounds" (Munyaradzi & Addae, 2019, p. 263).

Administrative support

Administrative support serves as a point of contact and bridge between students and the institution. Administrative support entails "providing students with timely, accurate and accessible information to assist with all phases of the learning process" (DHET, 2017, p. 364). For example, this would require that students can easily access their student records (i.e. proof of registration, academic records). In this study, administrative support will include access to lecturers and general institutional processes such as assisting students with applications for National Student Financial Aid Scheme (NSFAS) and other available bursaries, orientation, as well as directing students to the correct personnel within the institution.

ICT/Technology support

According to DHET (2017, p. 364), technology support should be concerned with "providing students with access to technology, providing the necessary information relating to computer elements required to support course software, directions for using essential tools like email, chat and discussions for asynchronous and synchronous interaction with lecturers and tutors, and assignment drop boxes". For the purpose of this study, technological support is understood as the availability of professional technicians on campus to provide technical services for students in terms of devices and ensuring all students have access to the internet.

Considering the above definitions of open learning, it means that SSS in the PSET sector must be broad enough to support students from all backgrounds (economic, cultural, and political) and of all modes (on-campus, blended, and/or online) of education to adequately counter the current inequalities which characterise South Africa's population. In an effort to address some of the economic, cultural, and political injustices faced in the post-school education sector, DHET expects PSET institutions to pay particular attention to the provision of adequate student support by subscribing to open learning approaches and distance education methodologies (DHET, 2017, p. 393). We use Nancy Fraser's (2005) framework of social justice to show how socially just (economically, culturally, and politically) these services are from the perspective of the institution (represented by the SSS staff) and the students.

Theoretical framework: Social justice

Social justice is commonly defined as the fair and equitable distribution of power, resources and obligations in society to all people, regardless of ethnicity, demography and socio-economic status (Hage et al., 2011). The central ideologies underlying social justice include "values of inclusion, collaboration, cooperation, equal access and equal opportunity" (Hage et al., 2011, p. 2795). Similarly, Powell and McGrath (2014, citing Sen) highlight the capability approach, as a necessity in TVET, suggesting the development of the dignity of each person as an approach that would prioritise the needs of the people, espousing human rights, poverty alleviation and social justice.

While there are a number of approaches to the concept of social justice (e.g., Fraser, 2005; Nussbaum, 1992; Sen, 2009), this study will adopt Nancy Fraser's definition and interpretation of social justice. Fraser describes social justice as the outcome of social arrangements that make it possible for everyone to participate equally in society and a "process in which procedural standards are followed in fair and open processes of deliberation" (Fraser, 2005, p. 87). Fraser (2005) considers social justice as 'participatory parity' economically, culturally and politically. Participatory parity is enabled or constrained through these three mutually entwined dimensions (Fraser, 2005; Hölscher & Bozalek, 2020) that can be socially unjust through maldistribution, misrecognition and misrepresentation.

Fraser (2005) states that these outcomes and processes can be socially unjust through economic maldistribution, cultural misrecognition, and political misrepresentation and misframing. Economic maldistribution indicates the uneven or unequal distribution of economic resources. In the context of SSS, this suggests that students in TVET colleges face economic injustices, restricting them from accessing educational opportunities that would allow them to actively participate in academic and social activities due to poverty or financial distress. This obstacle, according to Fraser (2005) can be addressed through economic redistribution which is not a final solution to the problem, but a remedy which she refers to as 'affirmative' change. Economic redistribution in the SSS context could refer to financial support in the form of funding for tuition, accommodation and/or living expenses – especially for those who are not eligible for NSFAS funding. The more 'transformative' response to solving the problem of economic injustice would mean the complete restructuring of resource allocation in order to address the root causes of economic maldistribution (Hodgkinson-Williams & Trotter, 2018), which in this instance would be free TVET provision for all who are eager and eligible.

Second, cultural misrecognition refers to cultural inequality and the disregard of cultural histories, practices and values (Fraser, 2005). For example, Jeffery (2015) maintains that students in TVET colleges struggle to access support services even if that support is formally provided. There is a strong possibility that this barrier to participatory parity may be rooted in the misrecognition of the South African indigenous knowledge systems, as Western-oriented perspectives and languages, especially English, dominate the teaching and learning space particularly in higher education and training (Hodgkinson-Williams & Trotter, 2018). The remedy, or the 'affirmative' action, to cultural misrecognition would be the inclusion of South

African indigenous knowledge systems in the curriculum and use of local languages in SSS to facilitate easy communication. A transformative advance would be what Fraser refers to as 'deconstruction' or what Hodgkinson-Williams and Trotter (2018) term 're-acculturation'. Such a transformative action would require a radical change in cultural reconfiguration of the current higher education and training approach to teaching and learning (Hodgkinson-Williams & Trotter, 2018) as well administrative, academic and technical support as well as counselling.

Lastly, Fraser (2005) discusses social injustice in terms of political misrepresentation, referring to political misrepresentation or mis-framing. This social injustice expresses the presence of unequal power relations and non-representation. It exposes the fault lines between people who hold the power to take important decisions and those that do not hold the power over matters that impact them directly. In relation to student support, questions can be asked about who decides on which system or model should be adopted. An affirmative response to political misrepresentation, would be to present marginalised groups with a metaphoric 'seat at the table' and an opportunity to be represented. In other words, providing a platform for lecturers and students to convey their expectations of SSS, "focusing on building relationships between the providers and prospective users of support" (Jeffery, 2015, p. 49). "By expanding the capability of voice through the establishment of procedures for social choice and providing individuals with the abilities and space to meaningfully express their opinions" (Bonvin & Thelon, 2003, cited in Powell & McGrath, 2014, p. 141). Counteracting political misrepresentation on the transformative scale would include action towards a meaningful formal representation of the marginalised, the re-framing, and decentralisation of power. In this instance, a transformative response would be students acting as co-designers of the broader systems of student support with lecturers and support staff.

This research study uses Hodgkinson-Williams and Trotter's (2018) framework (Table 1), which builds from the work of Fraser (2005) of social justice as 'parity of participation'.

Table 1: Hodgkinson-Williams and Trotter's (2018) adaptation of Fraser's (2005) social justice framework

Injustice	Affirmative	Transformative
Economic maldistribution	Redistribution	Restructuring
Cultural misrecognition	Recognition	Re-acculturation
Political misrepresentation	Representation	Re-framing

Extracting from both the work of Fraser (2005) and Hodgkinson-Williams and Trotter (2018), this study applies Fraser's trivalent social justice lens to understand how SSS (as a practice of open learning), enables parity of participation for students at Elangeni College's Pinetown campus. The next section presents a background to the TVET sector in South Africa and provides the institutional context of Elangeni TVET college.

Setting the scene nationally and institutionally

There are 50 public TVET colleges with 252 registered campuses for the delivery of qualification and part qualifications in South Africa (DHET, 2017, p. 31). DHET (2017) recorded that student enrolment was sitting at a total of 688 028 in 2017 across the TVET sector. KwaZulu-Natal was one of the top three provinces which recorded the highest student enrolments in TVET colleges, enrolling 113 274 students (DHET, 2017, p. 35). The *White Paper for Post-School Education and Training* (PSET) envisions an enrolment target of 2.5 million students in the TVET sector by 2030. The 2018 statistics on PSET in South Africa (DHET, 2018) indicate that there are nine TVET colleges in the KwaZulu-Natal, with a total of 110 086 students enrolled in that year. This study focuses on one of these, namely Elangeni TVET College.

Institutional context: The case of Elangeni TVET College, Pinetown campus

Elangeni TVET college consists of eight campuses situated in and around Durban, KwaZulu-Natal. Namely, the Inanda campus, KwaDabeka campus, KwaMashu campus, Mpumalanga campus, Ndwedwe campus, Ntuzuma campus, Pinetown campus, and Qadi campus.

The institute offers tuition full-time, part-time, and distance education. Support services available to students include academic support, tutorials, bursary assistance, career guidance, counselling, and life skills programmes (Interviewee 1). Figure 2 is a depiction of Elangeni TVET College organogram, which helps us understand how the student support service is structured within the institution.

Figure 2 visualises the human resource distribution within the SSS department/unit. Based in the central office is the SSS manager, the student counsellor, academic support coordinator, two placement officers, a Student Development Officer (who deals with the Student Representative Council (SRC) and student activities) and recently introduced, a psychologist. One Student Liaison Officer (SLO) is located on each campus and functions as the contact personnel between the students on each campus and the SSS unit. The role of the SLO is vital in the structure of SSS at the college as the SLO (supported by campus management) manages and implements all the student support activities offered by the college within the campus, including liaising with the SRC and any other student bodies at campus level. The SLO reports to the central office on a weekly basis (Interview 3)[2].

There are approximately 1800 campus-based students (not including the distance learners) on the Pinetown Campus (Interview 3). The institution enrols students from around the country and from diverse backgrounds (Interview 2). Racially, most of the registered students are black, with a few coloured and Indian students and only two white students (Interview 3) in 2020. While the medium of teaching at the college is English, the peer-tutor and peer mentors' programme supports students who are not English mother tongue speakers.

Methodological approach

This research adopted a qualitative case study approach to understand the role of student support services in addressing injustices faced by students at the college. A qualitative approach and its component methods elicit more intricate details and insight about a setting and meaning for participants (Henning et al., 2004; Maxwell, 2008).

---

[2] As some of the information on institutional structure and functioning was not available on a publicly available site, details from the interviews were used to supplement the description of the college.

Figure 2: Organogram of the Student Support Services unit at Elangeni TVET College

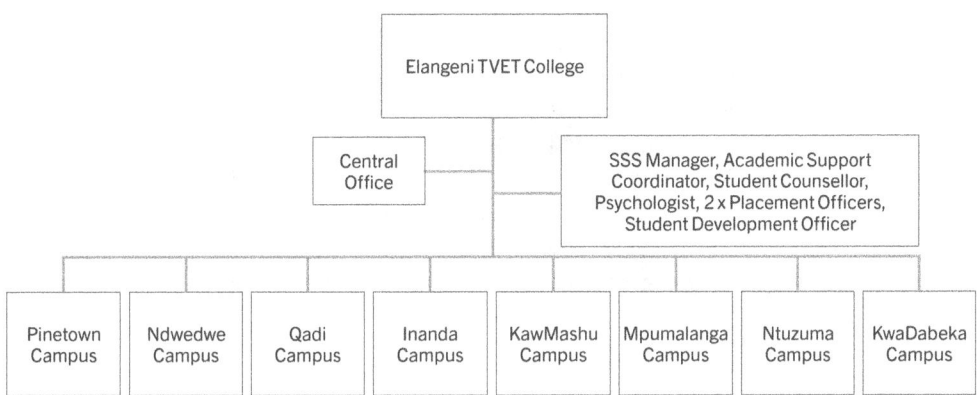

* Each campus has 1 Student Liaison Officer (SLO) on site

Limitations

Due to the COVID-19 restrictions (adhering to social distancing, observing travel restrictions, etc.) data was collected remotely using virtual methods such as WhatsApp chat and telephonic discussions. Ziegler and Mason (2020, p. 5) caution that "respondents may not be willing to discuss sensitive issues remotely, so enumerators may need to spend more time building rapport with target respondents over multiple data collection events" in order to elicit quality data. To do this, time had to be spent building rapport, especially with students, through regular telephonic communication to understand what challenges they were experiencing in the midst of dealing with the COVID-19 and the interrupted academic calendar.

Data collection and generation

The researcher engaged in primary (semi-structured interviews) and secondary (in the form of the Elangeni TVET College website) data generation and collection methods. A purposive sampling technique was used in selecting staff and students to participate in the study. Three staff members from the SSS unit were interviewed using video conferencing platform, Zoom, and two students were interviewed telephonically and/or using WhatsApp.

Sites and participants

Unfortunately, as a result of the COVID-19 interruption, Elangeni TVET College was busy with tests and final exams at the time this research was conducted so only two of the planned six students made themselves available for the interviews. Due to the national lockdown restrictions, students who did not have access to a smartphone were excluded from participation. The many conflicting priorities resulted in low participation rate and unfortunately no distance learners were interviewed. Only one part-time student enrolled in the N3 Business Management programme and one student who was unsure of whether she enrolled part-time or full-time, in the N2 Electrical Engineering National Accredited

Technical Education Diploma (NATED). The students and SSS staff who were interviewed were isiZulu home language speakers, although fluent in both isiZulu and English. For the comfort of the interviewees, the semi-structured interviews were bilingual. In terms of student accommodation, the college consists of one hostel on campus, which accommodates 70 students, exclusively for female students (Interviewee 3). Both students were in residence in this hostel prior to the strict lockdown period and so were at home at the time of the telephonic interviews. Challenges in trying to get hold of students telephonically included delayed responses on WhatsApp (therefore the interview had to be carried out over multiple days) and sometimes not be able to get hold of individuals as well as accommodating interruptions during the telephonic interview as the student was at home (divided attention with family).

Ethics and validity

To encourage participation and ensure confidentiality of the research participants, consent forms were shared with participants prior to the commencement of each interview. The consent form was made available in both the IsiZulu and English languages, to ensure interviewees have a clear understanding of their rights to participate and the purpose of the study. Furthermore, interview questions were shared with each interviewee prior to the discussion.

Analysis and findings

Challenges experienced by students and staff at Elangeni TVET College

Understaffing and under resourcing

On a national level, colleges operate differently and (based on the needs of the students with each unique locality) may have different portfolios within their SSS structures. According to Interviewee 2, the way SSS is structured at Elangeni College may be different from other colleges, however, there seems to be a national plan to align the SSS structures more similarly across the TVET sector. The greatest challenge that the SSS unit at Elangeni is faced with are the intertwined issues of understaffing and under resourcing as explained by Interviewee 2:

> While we are expected to provide a variety of services, there are not enough resources in terms of the staffing and in terms of infrastructure. You know *ama-offices ethu lapha ema-campusini* (our [students support service] offices at the campus level) are totally different you know, *uyabona eyasePinetown hlampe ayifani neyaseNdwedwe noma neyaseNtuzuma* (you see the offices maybe in Pinetown is not the same as the one in Ndwedwe or the one in Ntuzuma) …. But at the same time, we are expected to provide the same services … We shout, we shout, we talk and talk and talk … but no one listens to us … people know *ukuthike* (that) student support is one of the main functions but *ke sibonile koda ke*

ngesikhathi seCOVID uyabona nje ngeskhathi kuwama (we saw that during the times of COVID, during the period of) lockdown level three *kanje* (or so) level four[3] ...

The SLO plays a central role in the delivery and implementation of SSS on campus. A challenge in this regard is that the large number of students must go to the SLO office in search of support. This means that on the Pinetown campus the one SLO officer has an intensive workload to address the concerns of over 600 students. The excerpts from interviews with staff indicate that there is a possible mismatch between the job level and pay scale and the actual type and volume of work that is involved in the SLO position as explained by both staff members:

Ama-graduates, yezwa? (they are graduates, do you understand?) but ke *ngenxa yokuthi bangene la i-salary yakhona incane okusho ukuthi i-position* of a job *hlampe ifuna u-entry* level (because of the fact that they fill positions that pays small salaries that means the position of the job requires an entry level), which is level five *kanti bona* (but they) are well ahead *kulezozinto koda ngenxa* (of those things but because of the situation) and but *futhi* (also) the massive work, the volume of work *le ekufanele bayenze* (which they have to do) – which is expected to be done by them it's so massive. (Interviewee 2)

The SLO's are expected to provide the full range of SSS services, as Interviewee 3 bemoaned, "literally everything, we deal with everything!" However, during the busiest two to three months of the year, interns provide some assistance to the SLOs during to help with NSFAS applications (Interviewee 3).

Echoed by most of the respondents, are the economic constraints that are faced by the institution, which limits the college's ability to provide adequate infrastructure., These infrastructural deficits include the lack of a library, inadequate lecture rooms, insufficient desks, no laboratories, no computer room and unstable WiFi connectivity as Student 1 and 2 complain:

For me, it has to be about facilities, like there's no library access for students or a specific computer room where you can go through and research stuff or get books on what we're doing.... That's what I'm talking about ... like we don't even have proper WiFi. *Iyabheda iWiFi yala* (the WiFi here is bad). (Student 1)

I'm not being judgemental but ... at Elangeni, there's park-homes[4] and they use those as lecture room[s]. There are no labs at Elangeni College ... So, for students who do courses like engineering or courses that require experiments don't have those facilities. So, what's the use of trying to accommodate *wonke amaCourses kodwa izinto zokwenza ezinye azikho* (all courses but without the equipment and facilities)? ... The park homes are not big

---

[3] As a response to manage the COVID-19 virus and the gradual easing of lockdown, the South African government introduced a five-level COVID-19 alert system. Under level 4, it means extreme precautions were taken to limit community transmission and outbreaks. Therefore, institutions were still required to function remotely. See https://www.gov.za/covid-19/about/about-alert-system for further information.

[4] The term 'park-home' is used by the student to describe prefabricated mobile free-standing structures similar to temporary buildings like site offices. In this case they are used as classrooms.

enough to accommodate the classes. There's about 30 – 40 students per class and some people share desks *ngoba iskhala asikho* (because there's not enough space). (Student 2)

The next section highlights how student support is implemented at Elangeni TVET College in order to respond to the challenges that are faced by students.

Student support system employed at Elangeni TVET College

Elangeni TVET college adopts a SSS model which is prescribed in the 2020 SSS Plan as a bare minimum. According to the SSS staff, the programmes offered under each of these phrases includes:

- Entry support: orientation, pre-registration and career guidance.
- On-course support: academic support (includes peer tutors, peer-to-peer mentorship, winter school, book clubs, poetry and debates, study skills workshops, Fill-the-Gap programme), and extracurricular activities such as cultural and sport activities.
- Exit support: work readiness workshops, job and internship placement and articulation with post-school education.

As Interviewee 3 explains:

> We have entry support, on-course support and we have exit support. So *kwi-entry* (in entry) support. We would have [the] selection and placement test when they come in the beginning of the year or we would have pre-reg. But this year we haven't started because of COVID, but it usually about this time where we would have pre-registration where student would come in *senze ama-placement tests* (and do placement tests), career guidance and NSFAS applications so that would be the entry support *uma befika nje* (when they arrive on campus for the first time) that's what we assist them with.

Although due to the COVID-19 disruption, a number of the above-mentioned activities were unfortunately not implemented in 2020, or were implemented in new ways to adapt to the restrictions. As a result, this could have led to opaqueness of available college activities and support services that seems to have discouraged students from using them except for administrative purposes, as the two students explain:

> There's so much that Elangeni does not have that people think we have, but we don't. (Student 2)

> Elangeni just provides basic help. Like what they are doing, you basically can do it yourself with the student support. (Student 1)

Like the rest of the world, higher education institutions were caught off guard by COVID-19 and it has highlighted some areas of improvement for SSS. According to one interviewee, on-course support (academic) SSS is most often more reactive, as opposed to proactive, as it is intended to respond to the needs of the students. So, it seems that the way the SSS model is designed, the student support staff have to wait for teaching and learning to begin before implementing academic support programmes, as a staff member explains:

> First and foremost *kuthina kuba* (on our side it is) teaching and learning you know and then *bese kuza thinake* so *siyeke senze* (we come and usually make sure that) first teaching and learning must take place and then *thinake* (we) come in to provide the support in an event *hlampeke* (maybe) where there were gaps *kwi-teaching and learning* (in teaching and learning) teaching and learning *yabo* (you know) so during i-Covid that was a challenge *ngoba* (because) college like ours we wanted to make sure *ukuthi inganeke ziyazama ukuthi zenze* (that the students try to do) something *ngoba* (because) they were at home in terms of provision of teaching and learning more than to provide extra support *ngoba kuthina* (from our side) it's more of an extra support *uyabo* (you see) rather than *kushukuthi sadedela nje ukuthi kube* (that means we let the) teaching and learning first before *kuze enye i-support thina siye size ngamuva sithi* (we usually come after teaching and learning with support) there is teaching and learning took place where do you want support after the teaching and learning has taken place. (Interviewee 2)

So, when teaching and learning was interrupted by COVID-19, the staff were unsure how to respond except with mild affirmative administrative actions as their services are usually provided only after the teaching takes place. There seems to be a missed opportunity here as the pandemic probably placed all students in need of more extensive remote student support, despite some creative responses from a SSS staff member:

> As I've just mentioned … I've just printed those pamphlets to help them … and I've also posted on Facebook the information that may be able to assist them for those that can access the page but … *Sigh* … *Akusebenzeki* (It's difficult to work) … That's all I can say. (Interviewee 1)

There is also an absence of on-course technological support at the college which was accentuated by COVID-19. Among the challenges raised by the staff and students is the lack of resources such as computers/laptops and data particularly for students. Essentially, before COVID-19 there wasn't a pressing need for much technological support. This absence of technological support is also noted in the 2020 student support plan which is also silent on the need for technological support.

Challenges providing support to students living with disabilities

With regard to disability access which is a matter for all the phases of support (Pre-entry, On-course and Exit), two key issues that were revealed: (1) the lack of institutional capacity; and (2) the reluctance of students to disclose any conditions, disorders, impairments that may inhibit their studies and/or social life at the college (see Chapter 8, this volume). Students' reluctance to disclose disabilities upfront makes it more difficult for colleges to plan for facilities and services that they may need to provide.

> At registration students need to declare or disclose *ukuthi banayiphi* (what kind of) disability but *ke* (then) in most cases students fail to declare or disclose *ngoba besaba ukuthi ke*

> sizoba excluda yazibona lezozinto (because they are afraid that they will be excluded you see things like that), so *sinaleyo* (we have that) problem *ukuthi idisclosure* (that disclosure) is not as it supposed to be, *yah* (yes) but and when we accommodate people on disability *njengoba ngishilo* (like I said) we look at reasonable accommodation you know within our resources. (Interview 2)

According to Interviewee 2, it is difficult for student support at the college to make disability access a priority because of the limited resources available to accommodate the needs of the students with disabilities. The 2020 student support plan discusses students with disabilities as a priority area for student support with the expectation that there will be a "designated Inclusive Education unit, Disability Rights Unit (DRU), or allied health professionals/personnel within the SSS unit" (DHET, 2020, p. 8), but this is not the case at Elangeni college.

> No, I did not say that we are fully supporting, or we are fully providing them *sisashoda nje nathi koda* (we do not have enough – so there are still shortcomings but) we can improve … we can improve sisi (sister), but *okwamanje* (for now) you know for me, it's resources if we can get all the resources that we need then we can fully provide effective support to *ama-students wethu* (our students). (Interviewee 2)

Perceptions of open learning

SSS staff do not see open learning (OL) as part of student support. They see it as the responsibility of a different department, whose members have attended DHET training. In this case, the SSS staff believe that open learning is the responsibility of the Curriculum Unit. The first interviewee, who consulted the curriculum department prior to the interview, shows a better understanding of open learning, describing it as "an approach to learning that gives students visibility, a choice over what, where and what pace and where they learn" (Interviewee 1) which relates well to DHET's definition of OL. However, those who did not engage with the curriculum department, because they are unfamiliar with the OLPF reveal a different understanding and do not believe student support is a form of open learning.

> I would not agree with you entirely, *nathi nje* (we too) we also have a component you know, *ngoba thina okwethu* (because our task) is to provide extra support *yabo* (you see) but I wouldn't say open learning focuses on student support services, from your definition *yabo* (you see) … I don't think *ama* (the) colleges fall under the open learning *ngoba e-college lethu sinabo labantu abenza* (because at our college we do have students who are doing) distance learning, who only come for certain tutors *koda bazifundela bona* (but they are studying by themselves) but we assess them but *futhi* (and) they don't fall under student support *labo bantu* (those students) they fall into a different department. (Interviewee 2)

From the above excerpt, we can also identify that there is a misunderstanding of open learning. The SSS staff equate open learning with distance learning and perceive it to be associated merely with technological advancement and/or improvement as well as the availability of technological resources for the students. As Interviewee 3 explains, "I think it is very similar to *ukufunda* (studying) at UNISA, like getting all your work online, your assignment, your exams. It is basically doing all your work online just like UNISA does".

Interviewee 3 reveals partial familiarity with the term 'open learning' and the below excerpt explains how s/he came to know of the concept:

> I think it was introduced to us in 2017... Okay, I wasn't part of the group that went to training but I know of it. It is not implemented here at the college as of yet, but I think that will change especially with COVID and *ngiyazi amaStudents* (I know the students) would be getting laptops soon. I think *izosebenza* (it will work) right, not now our students don't even have laptops. (Interviewee 3)

Although some SSS staff may be partly familiar with the term open learning, they do not believe that it is applied at the college. This could stem from some misunderstanding of the concept of open learning but also from lack of information and being unaware of DHET's OLPF. More importantly, there is a lack of opportunity for SSS to engage with the concept of OL by not having attended the workshops and not having a report-back session at the college. This might have led to the staff not recognising OL as being applicable to the SSS unit:

> Maybe during the lockdown when we were doing the WhatsApp thing but *ukuthi* (the fact that) open learning is implemented here, no! Not yet, I think it is because we don't have resources mainly because our students come from a very poor background. *Ama* (the) resources like ... computers, some students do not even have smartphones, so we also have to consider the background of our students. (Interviewee 3)

> In my own opinion it doesn't apply to the college. (Interviewee 1)

The top-down approach that has been taken by DHET, of training a few staff members from the college in the hopes that a trickle-down effect will occur does not appear to be happening. The consequence is that information regarding open learning is not getting to the rest of the college staff as envisioned.

Expanding the institutional capability of voice by enabling spaces for students to express their opinions

Students have various platforms to address their concerns, namely through class representatives, or communication directly with the lecturer. Non-pedagogical concerns are addressed with the SLO, who depending on the nature of the concern brought by students, may refer them to the campus management team, a counsellor, or psychologist where necessary. Students also have recourse to the SRC which represents students in all governance structures within the college, including within the Council, Academic Board, Financial Aid Committee etc. The SSS staff reveal a clear understanding of the importance of the student voice and accurately distinguish between issues that can be raised at an institutional level and those that need to be directed at a national level (issues such as NSFAS allowances) and cannot be resolved within the college (as expressed in the excerpt from Interviewee 2):

Ukutelekake okusishaya eynganeni, ingane zethu zike zifike zifune kakhulu zifuna kakhulu, in most cases *zike zitelekele kakhulu i-bursary, 'awu i-bursary yami ayifikanga' uyabo, hlampe sekwabancono* of late *ngoba sekwafika legenge e-dealer noNSFAS* but still *zisateleka* and that becomes a challenge *kakhulukazi ema*-college, *ama* TVET *kade edominathe ngezitelekela kakhulu, zitelekelani? zitelekela* uNSFAS *uyezwa azitelekeli thina e-college zitelekela* NSFAS *koda ziteleka ema-college ethu*. (Interview 2)

Translation: We struggle with the student strikes, our students' demands are a lot at times. In most cases they go on strikes demanding bursaries things like 'I did not get my bursary', you see (maybe the situation has become better of late, because there are people who deal directly with NSFAS queries now, although they still go on strike and that becomes a challenge especially at the colleges ... Usually, it was the TVET that usually dominated the strikes. Why do they strike? they go on strike for NSFAS ... do you get that? They are not striking for college related issues, but they are striking for NSFAS related issues at the college [and or campus] level.

The students clearly understand the protocol and channels that are available for them to raise their concerns, which is through the SRC who will then escalate their concerns to management at a strategic level. Due to the national lockdown, remote channels for communications were established between students and the members of the SRC.

You can tell an SRC member or the president on WhatsApp, and they will forward your message to someone in management who may or may not respond on WhatsApp. If they respond, the SRC member will tell you, *kodwa mengamphendulanga* then *akamphendulanga* (if they don't respond then they don't respond). (Student 1)

Although they understand the limitations of the SRC to resolve their concerns, particularly when it comes to addressing the economic injustices:

Like you can talk to the SRC, but there's very little that the SRC can do, even in terms of getting the learning materials I have just counted. But they will take to management, *nakhona i-management* a plan to the head of budget, but *kohlezi kthiwa* budget budget... 'budget *isuke ingayvumeli lokho*' (there's no budget or that budget doesn't allow) ... I can raise my concerns, but will they be heard and addressed? It's pointless to have a platform where you can raise your issues and then they just sweep them under the carpet. Many issues have been raised in the past – some that I cannot recall, but they have never been taken seriously, so I think that's why many students don't even care anymore. (Student 1)

The majority of the concerns that are raised by students are directed towards addressing economic maldistribution. Because the colleges receive financial resources at a national level, it is beyond institutional control. Therefore, often management must escalate these concerns to DHET before they are able to respond to the SRC. This causes a delay in the turnaround time for students' issues to be addressed which often places management and staff on campuses on the backfoot when the students run out of patience and engage in strike action and demand to be addressed at town hall meetings. Furthermore, it also places students in a position where they do not trust the channels available to them to a point where they do not see a need to raise their concerns. This undermines the concept of political representation, making the channels less than an affirmative response to political misrepresentation and thereby discouraging students from voicing their concerns.

A staff member notes that there are evaluation forms in place for every activity that is offered to students to assist in the evaluation of the services offered by SSS. The feedback received from the evaluation forms are used to improve the SSS programmes to be offered the following year. This is also an affirmative response, because the improvements they can make to the services are also constricted by the limited resources available to the college.

Discussion

Politically partially affirmative responses

The Elangeni TVET college has good institutional protocols and structures in place to encourage student representation at the campus and institutional levels. Although we have termed most of the activities in place to address political misrepresentation as 'affirmative responses', in some cases the evidence challenges the Fraserian framework to suggest that activities can be 'less than affirmative' and instead re-inscribes the original injustice. For example, even though staff and students' descriptions of protocols and channels give the perception of being 'open' for students to engage the SRC and college management, the extent to which students are actually able to have their needs and concerns addressed is limited. The data from the student interviews highlights that student representation does not automatically equate to inclusive decision-making. As evidence from staff suggests, one of the barriers can be acknowledging that the lack of economic resources to address the concerns is not resolvable at an institutional level, but are decisions that need to be taken at a national level. As a result, students can feel frustrated and unmotivated, threatening their freedom to raise future concerns, thus sabotaging institutional efforts.

Economically partially affirmative responses

Reflecting upon ways in which student support (as a means of open learning) at the Elangeni TVET College addresses economic injustices faced by students, it is clear that some supportive activities – whether or not conceived of as 'open learning' or not – are taking place. These economic barriers are not always the overtly acknowledged needs for tuition, accommodation and transport, but can be very personal and intimate. For example, in relation to the needs of female students, Interviewee 3 reports that:

> We have a pad [feminine products] run, in the past we had a lady from Kotex that used to sponsor us with pads every year, she would come and ... dialog with all the female students. Okay that ended so what we decided to do in the staff room. I keep a big box and every month we buy pads, and we keep them in there for any student who may need them. Because they come to me and ask me for pads ... so we always have something on campus for them and trust me *ayaphela* (they get finished), but we all chip in for that. (Interview 3)

The challenge is sustaining this practical support once a company can no longer provide that sponsorship. Students still need and expect these supplies to be available, so the staff go the extra mile and continue providing pads even if it means they need to contribute from their own pockets. This highlights that TVET colleges cannot rely on additional funding from private sources as an affirmative solution and that a broader national plan for women is needed. Technically these needs should be met by living allowance funding for NSFAS-funded students, but not all students at TVET colleges are formally funded and so, at least at Elangeni TVET College, the staff themselves are bearing the burden.

Culturally partially affirmative response

The Elangeni TVET College (with external assistance from DHET and NSFAS) clearly currently makes affirmative efforts towards recognition, especially for the previously disadvantaged individuals. In terms of responding to cultural misrecognition, the responses are partially affirmative but not yet transformative.

The medium language for teaching and learning is English, but there are support activities for students who are not English mother tongue speakers which include peer to peer tutoring, extra lessons and the assistance of lecturers who are able to communicate in the vernacular. However, there are no support systems in place for older students who come from a background with minimal educational opportunities and currently no ways of supporting various cultural and or religious traditions (Interview 1).

Although the institution does have activities directed towards supporting female students such as the 'pad run' and additionally, activities directed towards addressing gender-based violence. The activities are directed more to merely recognize that the issues exist and create an awareness (where possible) around the challenges faced by the culturally marginalised, including the mentally challenged.

Students who experience mental health challenges are referred to the counsellor. More recently, there has been a psychologist added to the student support unit. Previously, there was only one counsellor to attend to all eight campuses, "So, the load is kind of lighter now with the psychologist" (Interview 3). In Fraser's terms, although the willingness of staff can be seen as culturally affirmative this cannot be enacted due to economic constraints they face. It may be the lack of personnel in the office to attend to the culturally vulnerable or the constrained budget that limits the SSS office to even plan towards achieving "re-acculturation" (Hodgkinson-Williams & Trotter, 2018).

The interviewed Elangeni College SSS staff are very aware of their human and financial resource restrictions and seem to work well within their limits and know how to reach out to other community services. For example, working hand in hand with the local public clinics (next to the campus), the SSS endeavour to ensure that students get access to healthcare needed if what is required is not available on campus. The SLO alerts the external public clinic and advises them of students that will be coming for assistance.

The SSS staff reveal an understanding of the limitations of the support provided by the college in relation to the students' needs and highlight that there may still be areas of improvement. The lack of resources is a big hurdle constraining Elangeni TVET College from providing SSS that can fully address the economic and cultural injustices experienced by students. The economic challenges are constraining the willingness to support students' culturally sensitive issues that are unfortunately reproducing the status quo.

These limitations highlight that there is no student support model that is a 'one size fits all' solution to TVET colleges. The broad definition and principles of open learning allow the institution more control in the design of the student support services that will respond to the particular needs of the students within their unique locality. Therefore, it is suggested that tailor-fitted student support models designed by the institution (working collaboratively with local students) have the potential to result in affirmative and hopefully transformative change. The SSS at Elangeni College does well to prioritise the most important services by students on campus, but they acknowledge that they are working within the limited resources available to them. The college endeavours to prioritise and improve upon the most frequently used services required or requested by students which means that certain services, for example support students with disabilities, is not high on the college's priority list.

Recommendations

The study makes multiple recommendations to DHET: firstly, to avail additional funding so that the college can expand the scope of SSS; secondly, to align the *Open Learning Policy Framework* with the SSS plan to make open learning practices implementable; and, thirdly, to extend training and advocacy on open learning. To enable the opening up of learning in order to improve the economic, cultural and political conditions for students, TVET colleges need to better understand the open learning principles espoused by DHET and then make funds available to encourage colleges by creating an enabling environment for OL to happen (i.e., students obtaining resources and/or services).

For example, Elangeni TVET College consists of eight campuses spread around eThekwini Municipality and Ilembe District. All campuses are strategically located in different geographic settings, covering the rural areas, township, and urban areas. This research has revealed that students in the different localities require different support services. And "given the potential of various (and rapid) growth of open technological advancement and the adoption of open learning practices to open up PSET to wider and more diverse groups of students" (DHET, 2017), SSS could play a vital role in enabling participatory parity. Furthermore, considering the current realities espoused by the COVID-19 pandemic, where emergency remote teaching and learning has had to take place in many post-school education institutions, student support was caught on the backfoot. In order to better prepare SSS in TVET colleges on how to support students who are learning remotely, it should be understood that student support must not be seen as operating in isolation from the wider social environment, but must work in assemblage with society and other public institutions such as municipal institutions available to embrace "free access/access to cost-effective value-added services (such as learning support, tutoring, and counselling and cost-effective registration and assessment opportunities)" (DHET, 2017, p. 5) and sharing of resources available to students from within their communities.

The study reiterates what has previously been suggested by Maimane (2016) that SSS should be systematically planned and not viewed as an independent programme. Therefore, it is recommended that this research be expanded, to better understand the influence of wider societal networks supported by open systems models applied in local government forecasting (Reitano, 2018). This could contribute to designing more effective student support services to better enable open learning in the sector and create a holistic educational approach for the realisation of socially just provision of learner support in local TVET contexts.

Conclusion

Participation in tertiary education has widened in South Africa and institutions are being pressured to cater to the student population more broadly to better address their economic strictures, cultural differences and political voice. As shown in the case study of Elangeni TVET college, Pinetown campus reveals that student support services are taking some affirmative steps politically to ensure that students have a platform to make their needs and concerns known. The college has put in place some partially ameliorate activities or actions to address the need for linguistic support in isiZulu, for counselling. Economically the interviewees reveal the need for much more funding to address infrastructural needs (e.g., lecture rooms, a library, a computer laboratory, desks and stable WiFi connectivity), as well as for personal care products for female students. The case study of Elangeni TVET college, Pinetown campus shows that the under-resourcing of SSS remains a challenge on the ground. Elangeni College is able to prioritise specific support services with the limited financial and human resources available to them, but acknowledge that they are falling short of their own ambitions as well as the minimum standards set by DHET.

Findings indicate that the SSS staff do not see student support services as part of open learning. The broad definition and principles of open learning could allow the college more control in the design of the student support services to be more responsive to the needs of the students within their unique locality. The three SSS staff members that were interviewed all see open learning as the responsibility of the Curriculum Unit within the college. This research set out to understand the ways and circumstances open learning practices (particularly the principle of learner support) is addressing economic, cultural, and political injustices faced at Elangeni TVET College. Acknowledging the limitations of the research in terms of sample size and at a time when SSS is constrained, the participants revealed that the politically affirmative responses to the challenges experienced by students is their availability of the SRC and student representation at management meetings, the 'open' channels to lecturers and SSS personnel.

However, it is noted that most of the student grievances are not at an institutional level, but at a national level, therefore the best the college can do is implement affirmative actions at the institutional level. Culturally, staff recognize the need and gap for culturally affirmative responses but are often hindered/limited by the lack of resources. Overall, evidence suggests that the student support services staff at the Elangeni TVET college play a supportive role for learners and lecturers at the institution. However, it is acknowledged that due to the limited sample size of the study, the findings cannot be used as a generalisation applicable to the entire TVET college sector, all generalizations made in this chapter are limited to the few insights of the five interviewees at the Elangeni TVET College Pinetown Campus.

Acknowledgements

Many thanks to the staff from Elangeni TVET College's Student Support Services Unit, whose inputs made the case study possible. Special thanks are due to reviewers David Jeffery and Dr Seamus Needham for their thoughtful, incisive feedback on the chapter, and Dr Tabisa Mayisela for guiding the entire COOL project. Thanks are also due to the Centre for Innovation in Learning and Teaching at the University of Cape Town, which hosted the COOL project, and the South African Department of Higher Education and Training for funding it.

References

Ball, S. J., & Youdell, D. (2007.) Hidden privatisation in public education. Preliminary Report delivered at the Education International 5th World Congress, Berlin, Germany, July 2007. https://pages.ei-ie.org/quadrennialreport/2007/upload/content_trsl_images/630/Hidden_privatisation-EN.pdf

Balwanz, D., & Ngcwangu, S. (2016). Seven problems with the scarce skills' discourse in South Africa. *South African Journal of Higher Education*, 30(2), 31-52. https://journals.co.za/doi/pdf/10.20853/30-2-608

DHET (Department of Higher Education and Training). (2013). White paper on post-school education and training: Building an expanded effective and integrated post-school system. https://www.justice.gov.za/commissions/FeesHET/docs/2013-WhitePaper-Post-SchoolEducationAndTraining.pdf

DHET. (2017). Call for comment on the Open Learning Policy Framework for Post-School Education and Training. *Government Gazette,* 40772(335). http://pmg-assets.s3-website-eu-west-1.amazonaws.com/170407openlearningframework-postschooleduc.pdf

DHET. (2018). Statistics on post-school education and training in South Africa: 2016. https://www.dhet.gov.za/DHET%20Statistics%20Publication/Statistics%20on%20Post-School%20Education%20and%20Training%20in%20South%20Africa%202016.pdf

DHET. (2020). Technical and vocational education and training colleges' 2020 Student Support Services Annual Plan. https://www.dhet.gov.za/SiteAssets/Technical%20and%20Vocational%20Education%20and%20Training%20Colleges%202020%20Student%20Support%20Services%20Annual%20Plan.pdf

DoE (Department of Education). (2009). Student support services manual: Further education and training colleges. https://www.saide.org.za/resources/Library/DoE%20-%20FET%20Student%20Support%20Services%20Manual.pdf

Fraser, N. (2005). Reframing justice in a globalizing world. *New Left Review*, 36, 69–88. https://newleftreview.org/II/36/nancy-fraser-reframing-justice-in-a-globalizing-world

Hage, S. M., Ring, E. E., & Lantz, M. M. (2011). Social justice theory. In R. J. R. Levesque (Ed.), *Encyclopaedia of adolescence* (pp. 2794–2801). Springer. https://www.researchgate.net/profile/Erin-Ayala/publication/310769309_Social_Justice_Theory/links/5836574508ae503ddbb3965a/Social-Justice-Theory.pdf

Henning, E., Van Rensburg, W., & Smit, B. (2004). *Finding your way in qualitative research*. Van Schaik.

Hodgkinson-Williams, C. A., & Trotter, H. (2018). A social justice framework for understanding open educational resources and practices in the Global South. *Journal of Learning for Development*, 5(3), 204–224. http://www.jl4d.org/index.php/ejl4d/article/view/312

Hölscher, D., & Bozalek, V. (2020). Nancy Fraser's work and its relevance to higher education. In V. Bozalek, D. Hölscher & M. Zembylas (Eds.), *Nancy Fraser and participatory parity: Reframing social justice in South African higher educa*tion (pp. 3–19). Routledge.

Jeffery, D. (2015). Academic support: How do students think about it? A study in a South African TVET College [Master's thesis, Nelson Mandela University].

Jeffery, D., & Johnson, D. (2019). Whose fault is failure? Contested perspectives of academic support in tertiary educational institutions in South Africa. *Research in Comparative and International Education*, 14(3), 376–393.

Knox, J. (2013). Five critiques of the open educational resources movement. *Teaching in Higher Education*, 18(8), 821–832. https://www.tandfonline.com/doi/abs/10.1080/13562517.2013.774354.

Letseka, M., & Pitsoe, V. (2012). Access to higher education through open distance learning (ODL): Reflections on the University of South Africa (UNISA). In R. Dhunpath & R. Vithal (Eds.), *Access to higher education: Under-prepared students or under-prepared institutions?* (pp. 219–234). Pearson. https://www.academia.edu/6074232/Access_to_Higher_Education_Through_Open_Distance_Learning_ODL_

Maimane, J. R. (2016). The impact of student support services on students enrolled for national certificate vocational in Motheo District, Free State, South Africa. *Universal Journal of Educational Research*, 4(7), 1680–1686. https://pdfs.semanticscholar.org/f23f/4581e977d55020562b7a9ac662b9a715e136.pdf

Maxwell, J. A. (2008). Designing a qualitative study. In L. Bickman & D. J. Rog (Eds.), *The Sage handbook of applied social research methods* (2nd ed., pp. 214–253). Sage. https://dx.doi.org/10.4135/9781483348858.n7

Moodley, P., & Singh, R. J. (2015). Addressing student dropout rates at South African universities. *Alternation*, 17, 91–115. https://openscholar.dut.ac.za/bitstream/10321/1648/1/Moodley_Alt_Special%20Edition_No17_2015.pdf

Munyaradzi, M., & Addae, D. (2019). Effectiveness of student psychological support services at a technical and vocational education and training college in South Africa. *Community College Journal of Research and Practice*, 43(4), 262–274. https://www.tandfonline.com/doi/pdf/10.1080/10668926.2018.1456379?casa_token=5IGlPIbq2DEAAAAA:2ohxxmYPz4n0OQdC7u5mkMlVyjjjkYVETqynb8TAZ6CPW-ywmCZkl7KRDH63EDwhaTs3SnLLZoLn

Needham, S. (2019). TVET policy in South Africa: Caught between neo-liberalism and privatisation? *Journal of Vocational, Adult and Continuing Education and Training*, 2(2), 82–101. https://jovacet.ac.za/index.php?journal=JOVACET&page=article&op=view&path%5B%5D=91&path%5B%5D=78

Needham, S., & Papier, J. (2011). *Practical matters: What young people think about vocational education in South Africa*. City and Guilds Centre for Skills Development.

Nonyongo, E. P., & Ngengebule, A. T. (1998). Introduction. In E. P. Nonyongo & A. T. Ngengebule (Eds.), *Learner support services: Case studies on DEASA member institutions* (pp. ix–xiv). Unisa Press. https://uir.unisa.ac.za/bitstream/handle/10500/19418/Nonyongo__EP__1868880486__Section1.pdf

Nussbaum, M. (1992). Human functioning and social justice. In defense of Aristotelian essentialism. *Political Theory*, 20(2): 202–246.

Papier, J., Powell, L., McBride, T., & Needham, S. (2018). Tracing the pathways of NATED programme graduates through TVET colleges and beyond. In M. Rogan (Ed.), *Post-school education and the labour market in South Africa* (pp. 165–183). HSRC Press. https://www.hsrcpress.ac.za/uploads/files/POST-SCHOOLING_CHP9.pdf

Paterson, A. (2016). Perspectives on programmes, projects and policies in the TVET colleges. In A. Kraak, A. Paterson & K. Boka (Eds.), *Change management in TVET colleges: Lessons learnt from the field of practice* (pp. vii – xxiii). African Minds & JET Services. http://www.africanminds.co.za/wp-content/uploads/2016/06/JET-TVET-text-and-cover-web-final-1.pdf

Powell, L., & McGrath, S. (2014). Exploring the value of the capability approach for vocational education and training evaluation: Reflections from South Africa. In G. Carbonnier, M. Carton & K. King (Eds.), *Education, Learning, Training* (pp. 126–148). Brill Nijhoff. https://library.oapen.org/bitstream/handle/20.500.12657/32180/613430.pdf?sequence=1#page=146

Sen, A. (2009). *The idea of justice*. Allen Lane.

Ziegler, J., & Mason, P. (2020). Adapting data collection and utilisation to a Covid-19 reality: Monitoring, evaluation, and learning approaches for adaptive management. Briefing note. https://www.odi.org/sites/odi.org.uk/files/resource-documents/odi-ml-mel4am-adaptingdatacollection-bn-sep20-final_3.pdf

HOW TO CITE THIS CHAPTER

Zungu, S., & Hodgkinson-Williams, C. A. (2022). Exploring how student support services address economic, cultural and political injustices: Insights from Elangeni TVET College, South Africa. In T. Mayisela, S. C. Govender & C. A. Hodgkinson-Williams (Eds.), *Open learning as a means of advancing social justice: Cases in post-school education and training in South Africa* (pp. 152–177). African Minds. doi: 10.47622/9781928502425_7

This work is licensed under a Creative Commons Attribution 4.0 International (CC BY 4.0) licence.

8

Staff insights on opening up learning to students with disabilities at Motheo TVET College, South Africa

A social justice perspective

Gertrude van Wyk & Cheryl Ann Hodgkinson-Williams

SUMMARY The extent to which open learning is being adopted by South African Technical and Vocational Education and Training (TVET) institutions in general and, more specifically, to support students with disabilities (SWDs) is not known. The aim of this study is to better understand the ways in which one 'disability-friendly' TVET college has opened up learning to students with mobility, visual, hearing, communication, intellectual, emotional and multiple limitations, impairments and/ or disabilities. Two senior managers and four staff members were interviewed in this qualitative study undertaken amid the COVID-19 pandemic. Fraser's (2005) conception of social justice as 'parity of participation' is used as a lens to untangle the economic, cultural and/or political injustices faced by SWDs as well as the staff who endeavour to support them. Several national government and institutional structural arrangements, institutional cultural conventions and individual activities have helped to ameliorate some economic and even transform some cultural injustices. However, more synergy and proactive interventions are required between policies and financial provision at national and municipal levels to ensure parity of participation of SWDs. These insights are applicable for implementation at the institution, in the TVET sector more broadly, for consideration by policymakers at the Department of Higher Education and Training, the National Student Financial Aid Scheme and Sector Education and Training Authorities as well as by employers seeking to increase access, progression and success of SWDs.

Keywords: disability access, students with disabilities, social justice, TVET

Introduction

Persons with disabilities (PWDs) unfortunately do not enjoy equitable access to Post-School Education and Training (PSET) in South Africa (Chiwandire & Vincent, 2019; Ndlovu, 2020) despite the efforts of national government[1], non-governmental organisations[2] and educational institutions[3]. Although much work has been done to better legislate for students with disabilities (SWDs) in particular (DHET, 2018), there is a weak research base on technical and vocational education and training (TVET) in developing contexts in general (Allais & Wedekind, 2020) and research on policy implementation concerning SWDs in TVET in South Africa in particular. This is also true for research on the implementation of the Department of Higher Education and Training's (DHET) draft *Open Learning Policy Framework* (OLPF) *for Post-School Education and Training* (DHET, 2017) which aspires to open up learning in the formal education sector, including for those with disabilities.

To date there has not been clarity on how the South African TVET colleges have responded to, or even operationalised, open learning principles and processes since the OLPF was published. Most pertinently for this study, there has not been any specific guidance or research on how institutions can support SWDs in relation to the inclusive principles, processes and practices detailed in the OLPF, which remain largely aspirational. This case study sets out to better understand the ways in which one institution, Motheo TVET College, which has been acknowledged for its inclusive activities[4], has opened up learning to students with diverse and multiple disabilities. It explores the ways in which these activities are providing SWDs with more socially just access to the college, support during, and planning for after the completion of, their studies.

Context: Disability inclusion in the TVET sector

The concept of '(dis)ability'

The definition of disability used in this chapter is linked to the social model of disability (see Leshota & Sefotho, 2020) in the *Strategic Policy Framework on Disability for the Post-School Education and Training System* which argues that:

> disability is caused by the way society is organised, rather than by a person's impairment or difference. It identifies systemic barriers, negative attitudes and exclusion by society (purposely or inadvertently) which means that society is the main contributory factor in disabling people. (DHET, 2018, p. 19)

---

[1] South Africa has a specific Ministry of Women, Youth and Persons with Disabilities; the Department of Social Development (DSD) published a *Policy on Disability* in 2009; Department of Higher Education and Training published the *Strategic Policy Framework on Disability for the Post School Education and Training System* in 2018.

[2] The DSD's list of national organisations of and for persons with disabilities http://www.women.gov.za/images/FACT-SHEET----National-Organisations-of-and-for-Persons-with-Disabilities.pdf

[3] An example of support for persons with disabilities for student (and staff) at the University of Cape Town http://www.students.uct.ac.za/students/support/disability-service

[4] https://www.news24.com/news24/SouthAfrica/Local/Express-News/principal-brings-change-20180703

Policy landscape on disability inclusion in South Africa

Although the commitment to the rights of PWDs has been enshrined in the Bill of Rights in the *Constitution of the Republic of South Africa (Act 108 of 1996)* (RSA, 1996), there was no formal policy that specifically provided guidance on the inclusion of PWDs in the PSET sector until the publication in 2018 of the *Strategic Policy Framework on Disability for the Post-School Education and Training System* (DHET, 2018). Moreover, as policy support of PWDs to access, progress and succeed in education is not entirely within DHET's remit, reference to other government policies also need to be taken into account, e.g., Department of Social Development's *Policy on Disability* (DSD, 2009) and its *White Paper on the Rights of Persons with Disabilities* (RSA, 2016); and the Department of Labour's *Employment Equity Act, 1998* (RSA, 1998) and its *Code of Good Practice on Employment of Persons with Disabilities* (DoL, 2015).

Participation of SWDs in the TVET sector

Given the challenges of who, according to various models (Pretorius et al., 2018), are considered to be SWDs, it is difficult to establish just how many people consider themselves, or are considered by others, to be experiencing some form of activity limitation, participation restriction, impairment and/or disability in the TVET sector. Nonetheless, participation of SWDs in the TVET sector in South Africa is considered to be low (Khuluvhe et al., 2021, p. 54). According to one estimate, the *Post-School Education and Training Monitor: Macro-indicator trends* (Khuluvhe et al., 2021, p. 54), 3,590 SWDs participated in TVET Colleges in South Africa in 2019. This represents 0.5% of the total enrolment of students (673 490) in the TVET sector in 2019. The writers of this report consider this to be "abysmally low" given that the "proportion of PWDs relative to the population aged 15-35 years is 6.4%" (Khuluvhe et al., 2021, p. 54). According to DHET's estimate, also for the TVET sector in 2019, there were:

> 2 537 students who reported [having] a disability, and the number of females with a disability was higher compared to males (1 468 and 1 069 respectively). Almost a third of students had a sight disability (32.8% or 832), followed by physical disability (15.9% or 403) and intellectual disability (11.2% or 284). Gender differences were more pronounced in the sight disability, where 266 more females reported to have this disability compared to males. (DHET, 2021, p. 35)

These differences in estimated numbers of SWDs may be due to different models of categorisation, but nevertheless highlight the necessity of obtaining the most accurate information possible about the number of SWDs so that DHET and colleges can adequately plan ahead financially and logistically.

Funding for SWDs in the TVET sector – individual and institutional

The National Student Financial Aid Scheme (NSFAS) provides financial aid to needy undergraduate students to help pay for the cost of their college education. One of the most important policy implementation guidelines for NSFAS relating to the funding of SWDs is the *Amended Rules and Guidelines for the Administration and Management of the DHET's Technical and Vocational Education and Training College Bursary Scheme* (DHET, 2020a). In short, these guidelines state that SWDs are allocated funds for tuition fees, travel, personal care and accommodation as would any other student awarded an allowance from NSFAS. An additional amount is made available to the TVET college for the "purchase of assistive devices and learning materials" for general, shared and individual access (DHET, 2020a, p. 17).

Open learning

Opening learning is at the heart of the implicit intention of widening education access to all, so inherently includes PWDs. As such it is closely aligned with the open education movement (Conole & Brown, 2018) that has in the past 20 years actively encouraged the opening up of education across the non-formal, informal and even the formal sectors. Open education is being enacted through the creation, adaptation and re-use of free and legally shareable open educational resources (OER) (d'Antoni, 2007), open content (Wiley, 2006), open textbooks (Feldstein et al., 2012) and Massive Open Online Courses (MOOCs) (Rambe & Moeti, 2017) which are all inherently underpinned by open educational practices (OEP) (Cronin & MacLaren, 2018).

Open learning is also associated with a slightly older concept implemented by open universities (e.g., Open University in the UK) where openness referred to the lack of barriers to entry to the formal university sector (Gourley & Lane, 2009). Initially this type of open learning was conducted at a distance, first as paper-based correspondence courses but later through online learning.

The OLPF's notion of open learning is, by contrast, a rather complex fusion of the older concept of open learning and the newer concept of open education. In the OLPF, DHET defines open learning as:

> an approach which combines the principles of *learner-centredness*, lifelong learning, flexibility of learning provision, *the removal of barriers to access learning*, the recognition for credit of prior learning experience, the *provision of learner support*, the *construction of learning programmes in the expectation that learners can succeed*, and the maintenance of rigorous quality assurance over the design of learning materials and systems. (DHET, 2017, p. 363, emphasis added)

Like the open universities, the OLPF aspires to operate within the ambit of formal education, and would still require tuition fees (or NSFAS subsidies), but lessen barriers to entry, enable flexible learning in terms of time and place, provide learning support, construct learning programmes in the expectation that learners can succeed, and maintain strict quality assurance of materials and systems. Added to this, the OLPF appropriates strategies from the open education movement and indicates that OER be used, wherever possible, and be curated on DHET's nascent National Open Learning System (NOLS). The OLPF also indicates that recognition for credit of prior learning experience should be provided for those successfully completing MOOCs and other online courses. The OLPF also subscribes to the open education tenet that OER can be cheaper than traditional educational resources and thus anticipates cost reductions for the TVET sector as a whole.

How these ambitions of the OLPF directly influence the provision of learning for SWDs at TVET colleges is the subject of this small study. The OLPF uses the term 'disability' only once on its own and once in relation to physical disability (DHET, 2017, p. 367), which could be interpreted as an oversight or, because the OLPF is cross-cutting and deems open learning as a strategy for all students, as a deliberate choice.

Challenges faced by SWDs in the PSET sector

A key challenge for SWDs is that they are "frequently assumed to share the same views, experiences, and priorities, regardless of gender, age, cultural background, sexual orientation, socio-economic status, religion, and other categories of difference" (Goethals et al., 2015, p. 75). This is a particular threat when "primacy is given to a 'disability' over other key elements, meaning that the interactions among all determinants are often neglected" (Goethals et al., 2015, p. 75) and the medical model terms are used exclusively.

From a more social-relational perspective (Reindal, 2007), a major challenge facing SWDs with degrees of physical or visual impairment is the inaccessibility of the built environment (Mvuyana, 2015) and access to resources originally designed for able-bodied students (Subrayen & Dhunpath, 2019). Drawing upon an implicit biopsychosocial view, research in a South African university context found that "visually impaired students often denied impairment and concealed their emotional pain" (Lourens, 2015, p. iii).

By contrast, the challenges for persons with hearing impairments are around the conceptions of what is construed as 'hearing loss', 'hearing impairment', 'hard of hearing' and 'deafness' which depend on the underlying discourses, communities, and associated identities therein. McIlroy and Storbeck's study of South African students concludes that "deaf identity is not a static concept but a complex ongoing quest for belonging, a quest that is bound up with the acceptance of being deaf while 'finding one's voice' in a hearing-dominant society" (2011, p. 494). Due to the "invisibility of hearing impairment, the assumed identity of the student with a hearing impairment is open to perpetual negotiation ('normal hearing' versus having a disability)" (Hindhede, 2011, as cited in Bell et al., 2016, p. 2). These challenges are compounded for students with dual sensory loss and there is scant research on their experiences in the TVET sector in South Africa.

Apart from having to navigate their way into buildings that are not necessarily purposefully designed for easy mobility access, the social model shows that students with mobility impairment also have to contend with organisational obstacles. For example, SWDs need to take a full course load, despite the energy and time costs of navigating physically challenging environments. They also need to contend with social stigma and a broad variety of other negative experiences, prejudice, and discrimination (Siwela, 2017).

With regards to persons with communication impairment, there is a challenge in conceptions of how it is defined and classified. An extract from the *Policy on Disability* illustrates how the term 'communication' is often conflated with those with hearing and/or sight impairments: "social integration of Deaf, Blind and Deaf-Blind People is still hampered by communication limitations between people with these disabilities and society they live in" (DSD, 2009, p. 12). By contrast, in DHET's report, 'communication' is defined as "talking, listening" (2021a, p. 35) and separates out students with 'hearing' and 'sight' disabilities.

In contrast to the foregoing discussion, students with intellectual challenges may not identify with, or be identified as, needing additional support as these are not always immediately discernible. In her Masters of Technology dissertation which investigates the experiences of students with learning disabilities at a TVET college, Fourie's findings on TVET students with dyslexia and attention deficit hyperactivity disorder (ADHD), in particular, reveal how students feel "lost", "isolated in the classroom" and that they lose "confidence in being able to catch up [with] work that was not understood" (2019, p. ii).

Students with psychosocial or psychiatric disabilities or emotional challenges (e.g., depression) are particularly vulnerable as they may not be willing to disclose their condition and therefore may not receive the necessary support from which they may benefit. Referring to postgraduate students at a South African university, Vergunst and Swartz (2021, p. 226) show how challenging it is for students to disclose "invisible disabilities, such as psychosocial disabilities, [as they] may be highly stigmatised".

Disability access implementation and practice

Although South Africa has a number of detailed policies related to planning for how PWDs in society should be supported (DoL, 2015; DSD, 2009; RSA, 2016), the actual implementation of these policies require attention as acknowledged by DHET (2018).

Accessibility of buildings, facilities, accommodation and transport

Before a TVET can begin offering courses to SWDs on campus, the physical environment needs to be optimally inclusive and compliant to universal design (Vincent & Chiwandire, 2017). This would mostly likely include accessible lecture rooms, workshops, computer laboratories and ablution facilities, with appropriate ramps, railings, lifts, signage, door widths and door handles as well as easy access to the library, administration offices, student cafeteria and sporting facilities. The inaccessibility of TVET college infrastructure is mentioned as a hindrance to students with physical impairments (Ntombela, 2020), as a pedagogic stumbling block for lecturers (Ngubane-Mokiwa & Khoza, 2016) and as a major concern of TVET management (Delubom et al., 2020). The *Report on the investigation of services offered to students with disabilities in Technical and Vocational Education and Training colleges*, explains that the "inaccessibility of the college infrastructure is attributed to the fact that the buildings were developed many years ago when issues of inclusivity were not upheld" (DHET, 2021b, p. 6).

Likewise, appropriately appointed student residences, or suitable accommodation close to the TVET college, would be necessary for SWDs to be able to physically attend a specific TVET college. If the latter, wheelchair friendly transport would also be necessary for those living off-campus. A recent study of the Majuba TVET College that investigated students' experience of private off-campus accommodation found that a "lack of facilities at private off-campus residences" (e.g., bathrooms and kitchens), amongst other factors, "also contributed to the participants' poor academic performance" (Mtshali, 2020, p. vi). Mtshali (2020) also reported that the type and cost of private accommodations is determined by each landlord and that this accommodation was some distance from the college and thus students incurred additional transport costs.

Technological infrastructure and assistive technologies

Although access to suitable technological infrastructure is important for students on-campus, the recent COVID-19 prompted pivot to emergency remote teaching in TVET colleges highlighted the unfavourable conditions for remote teaching for lecturers (Papier, 2021) and students. Prior to the pandemic, Mbanga and Mtembu (2020) reported the lack of technological infrastructure as one of the key challenges for lecturers at one TVET college. This was echoed in Khumalo's (2019) study that specifically identified the lack of resources for students with visual "disabilities".

Lack of lecturer professional development for teaching SWDs

An associated challenge is that in general TVET lecturers lack professional development in how to teach SWDs. In their study of two TVET colleges in South Africa, Ngubane-Mokiwa and Khoza (2016) reveal that lecturers reported a lack of specialised training on teaching SWDs, and how to integrate technology into the curriculum in general or how to support SWDs with assistive technologies in particular. In her more recent study on visual disability at a local TVET college, Khumalo (2019) revealed similar findings on the lack of lecturer professional development. Remarkably, both studies report that the lack of training did not deter all the lecturers and a small number experimented on their own with ways in which they could support students with a specific disability, most usually hearing and/or sight impairments (Khumalo, 2019; Ngubane-Mokiwa & Khoza, 2016). In addition, Khumalo's (2019) study identified the lack of support for lecturers from the institution and DHET as problematic.

Lack of student support and/or for Disability Support Units for SWDs

Some research has been undertaken on the importance of student support services for first time entrants in TVET colleges (Ngubane, 2018) and a study at a TVET college in KwaZulu-Natal (Munyaradzi & Addae, 2019) suggested that the provision of psychological support services was effective in improving student attendance, reducing student attrition and enhancing institutional reputation. However, this support does not necessarily extend to SWDs as was noted in a recent study of two public TVET colleges in KwaZulu-Natal (Munyaradzi et al., 2021).

Student support for SWDs is not restricted to a formal Disability Support Unit (DSU) that usually provides an inclusive educational environment for SWDs during pre-entry and entry, on-course and exit levels. However, the *Report on the investigation of services offered to students with disabilities in Technical and Vocational Education and Training colleges*, showed that through a survey of all 50 colleges, only 35 yielded responses and of these only 16[5] reported that DSUs or Disability Support Desks were in existence at the college. Although limited, these figures provide a sense of what is still needed institutionally in order to support students and staff with disabilities and/or how to best engage with those who do. A further distinct economic challenge is that TVET Colleges with DSUs do "not receive

---

[5] Ikhala, Port Elizabeth, Maluti, Tshwane North, Majuba, Umfolozi, Capricorn, Sekhukhune, Vhembe, Waterberg, Orbit, Northern Cape Rural, Boland, False Bay, Northlink and West Coast.

earmarked funding from government for their operations" (DHET, 2021b, p. 5) and "source funding or ring-fence funds from their own coffers" (DHET, 2020b, p. 37). The expectation is that individual colleges will need to attract funding from elsewhere in order to attain DHET's *Strategic Plan 2020-2025* indicator of success, establishing centres of specialisation in order to support SWDs (DHET, 2020b, p. 7).

Late payment of student funding

The predominant finding from prior studies is that all TVET students, and university students for that matter, struggle because of the late payment of allowances from NSFAS (Myataza, 2019; Webb, 2021).

Social justice

To assist us to better understand and hopefully explain ways in which Motheo TVET College has endeavoured to subscribe to open learning as a philosophy and to implement it to provide more socially just education, we draw upon the concept of 'social justice' and specifically the work of Nancy Fraser (2005, 2007) and her interpreters in South Africa (Leibowitz & Bozalek, 2016; Luckett & Shay, 2017).

Fraser (2005, p. 73) perceives social justice as "parity of participation", as both an outcome of a substantive principle of justice "where all the relevant social actors participate as peers in social life", and as a process in which actors engage in "fair and open processes of deliberation" (Fraser, 2005, p. 87). According to Fraser, there are three analytically distinct challenges to participatory parity, namely (1) economic injustice or maldistribution, (2) cultural injustice or misrecognition, and (3) political injustice or misrecognition. In seeking to better describe and explain how these types of injustice might be addressed, Fraser introduced the concepts of 'affirmative' and 'transformative' remedies to injustice. An affirmative response attends to the "inequitable outcomes of social arrangements in ways which make ameliorative changes" while a transformative response addresses the "root causes of the three dimensions through restructuring the generative framework which has given rise to impairment of participatory parity" (Leibowitz & Bozalek, 2016, p. 113). Where a response intentionally or unintentionally intensifies the original injustice, Fraser (2007) refers to this as being 'regressive'.

Economic dimension

In demonstrating how people may suffer distributive injustice or maldistribution, Fraser (2005, p. 73) maintains that, "people can be impeded from full participation by economic structures that deny them the resources they need in order to interact with others as peers". With regard to open learning, this suggests that SWDs may be impeded from full participation due to lack of access to geographically convenient campuses, inaccessible buildings, poorly equipped accommodation, lack of correctly designed ablution facilities, unaffordable tuition fees, the lack of special braille textbooks, or devices and software that can assist with transforming text into another mode to mediate for sensory deprived or physically challenged students. An example of an "ameliorative intervention" (Hodgkinson-Williams & Trotter, 2018, p. 207), toward open learning would include the availability of affordable full-time, part-time, and online tuition for SWDs and the use of OER including open textbooks in suitable modes that follow Universal Design for Learning (UDL) principles (Delubom et al., 2020). A transformative remedy in this regard would include restructuring of funding for the TVET sector, and include fully state-sponsored tuition, accommodation, transport and personal assistive devices, and fully supported placements by commerce and industry that are deliberately designed to accommodate those with various challenges, conditions, impairments and/or disabilities.

Cultural dimension

In addition, Fraser (2005, p. 73) asserts that culturally people can "be prevented from interacting on terms of parity by institutionalised hierarchies of cultural value that deny them the requisite standing". In this case SWDs can "suffer from status inequality or misrecognition" (Fraser, 2005, p. 73). An affirmative response would be acknowledging and making appropriate plans for SWDs and particularly those whose gender, race, ethnicity, language may exacerbate their existing disability. A fully transformative approach would involve what Hodgkinson-Williams and Trotter (2018) refer to as "re-acculturation" which is seen as a process of automatic inclusion of marginalised groups, the valuing varying cultural perspectives (e.g., epistemic, ethnic, religious) and the "reframing its curricula for a pluralist society" (Luckett & Shay, 2017, p. 3).

Political dimension

According to Fraser, the political dimension:

> tells us who is included in, and who excluded from, the circle of those entitled to a just distribution and reciprocal recognition ... sets the procedures for staging and resolving contests in both the economic and cultural dimensions ... (as to) how such claims are to be mooted and adjudicated. (Fraser, 2005, p. 75)

As such, this suggests the need for SWD representation in all facets and at all levels of the TVET educational processes and outcomes. An ameliorative response, for example, would be to have SWDs represented in the Students Representative Council at an institutional level, whereas national representation around SWD related matters would be transformative if the nominated students were accorded genuine power of decision-making.

Methodology

This case study adopted a qualitative approach using semi-structured interviews (Ayres, 2008) with two senior managers and four members of staff to ascertain in what ways Motheo TVET College is providing opportunities for access to, progress through and success of SWDs in order to mitigate the economic, cultural and political injustices they face. Unfortunately, due to COVID-19 students were not available to be interviewed which substantially limited the original intentions of the study.

Site selection and participant selection

Motheo College in Bloemfontein in the Free State was selected by DHET as a site to investigate given their recognised endeavour[6] to provide access to SWDs. The decision of whom to interview at the college was made by the principal. Author 1 interviewed the college principal, the head of academics, and two lecturers who teach SWDs.

Data generation methods, analysis and validity

Using a video-conference platform, Zoom, Author 1 interviewed the four members of staff at Motheo College using a semi-structured questionnaire. The conversation was recorded, subsequently transcribed and sent back to staff members to verify. Additional queries were clarified in email exchanges.

The textual data was analysed qualitatively using Excel according to two thematic analyses, firstly according to the opportunities for access, progression and success, and secondly, according to Fraser's (2005) social justice framework, to establish to what extent these interventions helped ameliorate and/or transform the economic, cultural and political injustice that they face. The categorisation of the thematic analysis was checked by the COOL mentor assigned to this study before the thematic synthesis was undertaken.

Ethics

To ensure that the research study was undertaken ethically, ethical clearance was first obtained from the Centre for Higher Education and Development at the University of Cape Town, then from the Division of Research in DHET, and lastly from Motheo College. Informed consent was granted by all the individuals interviewed.

Insights

Given that the number of participants was relatively small, and not representative of student perspectives because they could not be contacted during the COVID-19 lockdown, the authors have opted to provide 'insights' instead of the more usual 'findings'. These insights are grouped under key themes that were deductively drawn from policy documentation and prior literature, and inductively refined from the coding process. The insights are presented according to the ways in which the various practices at the institutional, municipal or national levels are mitigating some of the economic, cultural and political challenges faced by SWDs at Motheo College. But before delving more deeply into ways in which the college is endeavouring to provide SWDs with participatory parity, it is important to acknowledge the number and diversity of SWD admitted to the college.

During the interviews, the staff members explained that from 2014 the college opened its doors to students with *mobility challenges* (e.g., physical disabilities, cerebral palsy movement disorders, limb impairments) and *intellectual or learning challenges* (e.g.,

---

[6] Professional Marketing Research awarded Motheo College the Golden Arrow Award in 2014, and in 2015, 2016 and 2017 the Diamond Arrow Awards. Also, the European Society for Quality Research (ESQR) awarded the European Award for Best Practices 2018.

dyslexia, "slow learners"), in addition to the those with *sensory disabilities* (e.g., blind, partially sighted, deaf, deaf and blind) that they had been supporting previously. The staff elaborated that the college also accepts students with *psychiatric disorders* (referred to in the interview as "mental", "psychosocial" or "psychiatric" disorders) (e.g., bipolarism), *neurological disorders* (e.g., epilepsy, spinal cord injuries) and *genetic conditions* (e.g., albinism, dwarfism). The principal emphasised that, while some students at the college have suffered from a disability from birth, they also have students who have had accidents or suffer from a progressive disease.

At the time of interviewing in 2020 there were 291 differently abled students attending the college: 141 partially blind, 82 partially deaf, 21 deaf, 19 blind, 17 physically disabled, 5 dyslexic, 5 epileptic, 1 both deaf and blind. Interviewee 1 also pointed out that students can have complex combinations of conditions and disabilities (e.g., albinism tends to be accompanied by poor vision).

Mostly ameliorative economic responses

The first economic response is that NSFAS provides SWDs at Motheo TVET College with funding for tuition, accommodation, transport and personal care, but is ameliorative rather than transformative as the funding is inadequate to cover all the SWD's costs. As Motheo does not have student residences, all students live off-campus in privately provided accommodation and need to travel to campus each day. This is particularly expensive for SWDs as they either have to find (at premium prices set by landlords) or have existing accommodation specially adapted (usually bathrooms and kitchens) to suit their specific needs. During the COVID-19 lockdown in 2020 students were sent home, but were still required to pay rent or give up their rented accommodation and find a new abode when on-campus teaching was resumed. An associated economic challenge is that travel costs are high, as Interviewee 3 explains: "[SWDs] have to have a specialised transport. They can't just go to the street and point like anyone else, and it becomes more expensive" (Interviewee 3). Moreover, the staff explained that due to the poor maintenance of roads, pavements and traffic lights in the town, wheelchair-bound students and blind students are at great risk and often resort to paying for private transport to travel to the college. Like other NSFAS-funded students, they receive a transport allowance, currently R735 per month, but as Interviewee 3 explains, this "is like for a week for someone who is disabled". So, in short, staff members request specific funding to "cover their special costs for a certain time. If [NSFAS] are going to do the same as everyone else, it is going to be difficult" (Interviewee 3). An added complication is that NSFAS funding takes so long to get dispersed, resulting in students being economically vulnerable for many months, aggravating an already economically precarious group of SWDs.

A second economic mitigation strategy is that Motheo TVET College has established an Inclusive Learning Centre (ILC). In 2012, the college established what was then called the "Disability Unit", prompted by the close proximity of two special needs schools. This unit, now referred to as the ILC, is thoughtfully located on the ground floor with an extra wide door, and is staffed by two lecturers. However, Interviewee 2 was quick to point out that DHET does not make specific provision for posts in a DSU and that Motheo TVET College has appointed "additional staff members out of [their] current post provision", of which one is a braillist / editor. The braillist uses a dedicated braille printer which has the functionality "to print graphics and tables, not just texts" (Interviewee 1). Braille textbooks are printed by the college or purchased through services such as BlindSA at no cost to the students. In addition to specialised braille textbooks, test and examination scripts for severely visually impaired or blind students, one of the most important support services for partially deaf and deaf students provided at Motheo is sign language interpretation. The ILC employs sign language interpreters, but occasionally face challenges in matching signing dialects of sign language interpreters who sign in the Western Cape dialect and the students who are more familiar with the Free State dialect. So the provision of sign language interpretation can be confirmed as at least ameliorative in nature, but more specific staff procurement processes would be needed before this important service can be considered transformative. Of particular concern is that DHET does not provide special posts for the ILC nor pay for building and facility upgrades to ensure that the college is fully inclusive according to universal design principles. This disjunct between policy expectations and specific funding for capital and human resource funding is almost 'regressive' with respect to social justice as the situation is getting worse rather than improving marginally.

A third ameliorative economic remedy is the provision of funds from one of the Sector Education and Training Authorities (SETAs). If SWDs fail a course, like other students, they don't receive further funding from NSFAS to retake the course. Staff explain that given the challenges SWDs face with respect to academic work, there is the likelihood that some students will fail a course or two. If and when this eventuality arises, the college applies to a suitable SETA for funding to provide the SWDs with a second chance.

In contrast to the three ameliorative economic reponses, the final one is transformative as it gets to the root of the key economic injustice, namely that SWDs at the college cannot afford to purchase the assistive technologies they need. The college receives a Special Needs Education (SNE) budget from DHET to purchase the necessary assistive technology based on the needs of individual students. Interviewee 1 reported that staff members from the ILC consolidate these individual requests, obtain quotations, submit these requests, procure and allocate assistive technologies to the individual students. Interviewee 1 further explained that for SWDs to receive such devices they rely heavily on input from the students themselves, but are also guided by the medical certificates provided by their doctors as part of the application process and the team of medical practitioners and health professionals (e.g, an optometrist, a dentist) that come to the college during the registration process to undertake various tests and provide recommendations. Certain assistive devices (e.g., a laptop preloaded with JAWS screen-reading software) become the property of the individual so that they can be fully equipped for Work Integrated Learning (WIL) activities, and later for self-employment or formal employment.

Mostly transformative cultural environment

Perhaps the most striking impression of all the interviews is the galvanising role of strong leadership from the principal, and the evident passion and commitment from the other staff members. During the interview, one of the staff members referred to the principal as "an example of a transformational leader" (Interviewee 2). With respect to her personal engagement with those experiencing disabilities, the principal revealed: "During Disability Awareness Day, I participate in such activities. I ride on a wheelchair and try to have a feel of what it takes for a student to move from one point to another on a wheelchair." Staff interviewed at Motheo College also revealed an exceptional willingness to accept SWDs into the institution. This willingness even predates the establishment of a formal structure to manage services and specialist resources for SWDs. Staff explain that a successful initiative to support deaf students to complete a financial accounting course inspired what would become the present-day ILC. Staff members' willingness to support and walk alongside SWDs over-rode their lack of experience as they were committed to assisting those accepted to the college, as one of the staff members honestly reported about their acceptance of a dyslexic student:

> We did not have an idea what to do or what should we get, we learned as it goes and we didn't say no we're not gonna accept you. We will try, by all means, and see what it is that we can do… and the student passed. (Interviewee 3)

Motheo TVET College deliberately attracts SWDs, opening up access through marketing materials that include a short section on the requirements for SWDs, including a medical doctor's letter detailing the diagnosis, intensity and prognosis of the prospective student as well as the kind of assistance they would need. This is the first step in matching a SWD's educational aspirations with the courses that are suitable, given their specific disability. The staff provided an example of an incompatible course match, where a blind student wanted to study the Engineering Heavy Current specialism. Staff say that they endeavour to encourage SWDs to choose courses where they have a reasonable expectation of completing, as NSFAS does not provide funding to repeat a course that was previously failed. Interviewee 4 reports that: "Marketing and HR are the common ones that we recommend [blind] to do" and upholstery and carpentry for the deaf.

Another small, but transformative cultural change was the deliberate change in name from the "Disability Unit", which reflects a narrow medical model of students with disabilities, to a more socially inclusive name: Inclusive Learning Centre. The ILC provides a range of transformative services including sign language interpretation, scribing services. The ILC also arranges, where there are no lifts, for staff or students (referred to as "mobility instructors") to carry SWDs up and down a flight of stairs. The physical burden of carrying SWDs would seem to be a less than ideal practice and hopefully this could be remedied by the provision of lifts in strategic buildings.

Further small-scale, but potentially transformative cultural activities at Motheo TVET College include Casual Day and Disability Awareness Day. On Casual Day, the college celebrates with inclusive activities such as wheelchair races in which able staff (including the principal) participate, and blindfold games, where students are blindfolded and have to locate a particular place based on verbal instructions only. A sign language competition involves everyone learning how to sign their own name, the names of the various campuses and the towns or city in which they are located, thereby increasing the cultural awareness of sign language as means of communication[7]. The Disability Awareness Day is organised by

---

[7] South African Sport, Arts and Culture Minister, Nathi Mthethwa, said the "constitutional review committee had recommended that a section of the Constitution be amended to include South African Sign Language (SASL) as the 12th official South African language" https://www.iol.co.za/news/politics/process-to-make-sign-language-sas-12th-official-language-begins-b0b96b50-e3dc-4dec-966c-971ebdbb50c5

the Student Representative Council and celebrations arranged with Blind SA[8] and DeafSA in an endeavour to address "marginalisation and discrimination" (Interviewee 1) of PWDs.

This transformative work at the college around inclusivity has also attracted the attention of other South African institutions with visits from 16 other colleges reported in 2018 and 2019 alone as well as from the provisional Premier's office, DHET, and local and international partner organisation.[9]

In spite of this warm and welcoming cultural environment, staff report that students are not always willing to disclose their disabilities. SWDs are required to apply early as certain resources, for example braille textbooks can take about four weeks to prepare and if the students are undertaking a trimester course this means that by the time the textbook is ready, the student will be left with only a month before examinations. The pragmatic need to register early is not always understood or acknowledged by potential students who expect to be admitted in late January, and staff report that some students immediately report a declined response to the Public Protector. Staff report that they "normally get to know about their disability either if there is a situation where the student gets an epileptic attack or even when they start struggling with certain academic concepts" at which point students "would love to have some help" (Interviewee 1). However, staff report that it is "challenging to intervene in time particularly on the academic side especially if this is late in the year" and that there may be "many other students that we do not even know or [are] not aware of" (Interviewee 1). As we were not in the position to interview students at Motheo TVET College, we need to be cautious in over-generalising the transformative responses reported from the staff perspective to the student perspective. We are also not in a position to better understand why SWDs at Motheo chose not to divulge their particular challenge/s.

Interviewees reported that most of the lecturers are not specifically trained to teach SWDs or to use sign language and thus rely heavily on the sign language interpreters in class. The challenge is that there are not always sufficient sign language interpreters to sign simultaneously so ideally lecturers need to be trained in South African Sign Language. Pedagogically a few inclusive practices were mentioned by the interviewees, for instance in a Mathematics class, the lecturer was reported to use matchsticks to help blind students trace patterns of various diagrams. In response to another pedagogical line of inquiry the staff were asked if the college makes use of any OER or textbooks. Interviewees interpreted "open" as the availability of the ILC being 'open' at various times, not as OER, open textbooks or MOOCs. This is perhaps a missed opportunity to legally copy, edit, translate, record and/or convert educational materials with a Creative Commons[10] licence into braille amongst other affordances.

As an ameliorative strategy, Motheo TVET College initially used YouTube as a learning platform prior to the adoption of a learning management system. The Motheo TVET Learning Channel[11] is still in use, but is quite data intensive and many students, not only those living with disabilities, complain about the cost of data. By contrast, access to the open source learning management system, Moodle, has been zero-rated making it more accessible, but it is not

---

[8] https://nationalgovernment.co.za/units/view/75/blind-sa
[9] http://www.motheotvet.edu.za/partnership.html
[10] https://creativecommons.org/licenses/
[11] https://www.youtube.com/channel/UCAyirayT2p9vlN_T_vQSchA

yet available for all subjects. In addition, Facebook[12] is used primarily as a communication channel and for marketing. However, these platforms are not yet fully optimised for those with disabilities as videos don't yet have captions, or are unaccompanied by a sign language interpretation. Likewise, slide presentations with voice-overs may only include summary text on the slide, but no full notes or transcription of the explanations.

A transformative strategy used by the college is the implementation of test and examination concessions. Interviewee 1 explains that these concessions not only include extra time or the employment of scribes, but critically involves education of examiners in what to expect from a script from deaf students for example. Although a sticker is pasted on the script, the students' "horrible sentence construction" is distinctive as the deaf students write according to sign language "so a person who is marking their scripts, needs to understand it ... that you can't read 'I am going to town', you would read 'town going I'" (Interviewee 1). Not requiring students to "restructure" their grammar to align with the grammar of hearing examiners, is a powerful and transformative instance of recognition.

Like any other TVET students, SWDs need to fulfil the requirement of practical experience or work integrated learning (WIL) in an appropriate context. The college staff make sure that when they place SWDs that they first meet with the host employers, "to tell them about the kind of the students that [they] are sending to him (sic) and what support they must give to the student" (Interviewee 4). Moreover, the staff ensure that the student has the appropriate devices to work with in this context. For example, this may be a laptop preloaded with JAWS software, a combination that costs about R28 000 and would be too expensive for the student to buy or the WIL employer to provide. As interviewee 3 points out: "It's difficult for someone [an employer] to ... accept someone [a student] who is going to actually cost them more to hire".

College staff maintain their support for SWDs post their period of study as conveyed by Interviewee 4: "So when it comes to exit level we continue to give them the support that they need in order for them to ultimately sustain themselves in that way." SWDs are allowed to take their specific assistive devices with them so that they are immediately ready to engage in formal or self-employment. Former students approach staff for assistance or advice about structural, technical, social challenges they are facing. For example, a prior student contacted them to ask if it was possible to have the JAWS screen reader loaded onto the computer systems at police stations and hospitals. In this instance, the staff explained that they were not able to do this, but this raises important issues that need to be raised with other sections of government.

Mostly politically transformative

Motheo TVET College's commitment to inclusivity pre-dates the *Strategic Policy Framework on Disability for the Post-School Education and Training System* (DHET, 2018) by at least six years. The inclusive activities at the college strongly mirror this policy framework on disability, particularly in the cultural sphere where the practices of staff, as revealed in the interviews, display a profound commitment to the welfare of SWDs that is made possible by those in leadership positions making pro-SWD decisions at the institutional level. This impacts

---

[12] https://web.facebook.com/OfficialMotheoTVETCollege/

directly on the college's strategic planning, but also on the partnerships[13] that they have forged with international donor agencies, higher education institutions, public entities, state departments, schools, private business and industry. Engagement in these partnerships has enabled the college to gain some control over how they are able to realise some of their longstanding transformative aims and ambitions. However, these aims and ambitions can be partially thwarted by the dependence of this urban campus on municipal strategic planning for infrastructural development and maintenance. The interviewees complained about the poor maintenance of roads, pavements and traffic lights in the town, which were hazardous for wheelchair-bound students and blind students.

What is particularly interesting is that the institutional leadership does not hold all the power at the college as individually and as a collective, SWDs are very aware of their rights as Interviewee 3 remarked:

> If there is one person who knows their rights, it is a person with disabilities. They will come after January, but you know if you say it is full, and believe you me, you are going to get a call from a Public Protector or whoever saying you're denying them.

Although appealing to the Public Protector is not the first or most appropriate line of appeal in this instance – what Fraser (2005) would refer to as misframing – it is noteworthy that SWDs are confident to make their voices heard even before they are admitted to the college.

As expected, the college has a Students' Representative Council that has input at the institutional, regional and national level (Interviewee 4) and is therefore politically represented (Fraser, 2005). Input on policy issues is actively solicited from students. Interviewee 4 explains that students provide contributions to the student support service policy review session. Another example provided by Interviewee 3 provides further evidence of political representation of SWDs who attend the annual Motheo TVET College academic conference where they "represent others as well" on plans, projects and developments at the College[14]. To enable inclusivity at these meetings a sign language interpreter is used as a strategy not to segregate students according to those with hearing disabilities.

It was reassuring to be informed that one of the college staff is a member of the national Ministerial Task Team on Disability and can provide on-going advocacy for provision for SWDs by offering input from informed positions on disability issues pertaining to individual students, parents and guardians, staff members, TVET colleges, municipalities and DHET.

Conclusion

In summary, it was clear that the staff interviewed at Motheo TVET College did not understand open learning in the way it is laid out in the OLPF, but saw the existence of the ILC and its availability during various times as 'open learning'. While the infrastructural and organisational arrangements at Motheo TVET College seem to actively open up access to SWDs and ameliorate many of their challenges, there are some constraints that hinder optimal inclusivity, most of which are related to economic issues.

---

[13] http://www.motheotvet.edu.za/partnership.html

[14] https://web.facebook.com/story.php?story_fbid=4427974763925922&id=302995369757236&_rdc=1&_rdr

Economically the funding for SWDs may appear to open up education and represent an example of distributive justice, but because these students have higher costs of living, most particularly suitable accommodation and safe transport, they need to attract additional funding in order to be on a par with their nondisabled peers. Even though SWDs receive a NSFAS grant for specialised devices, a welcome ameliorative strategy, overall the present funding formula is insufficient to ensure their parity of participation in post-school education. One mitigating strategy is the financial support from the SETAs for students requiring a second chance to study.

Culturally Motheo College displays a commitment to inclusivity through the leadership of the principal, staff of the ILC and lecturers in honouring and respecting SWDs. The college deliberately attracts SWDs and opens up access through marketing materials, provides a range of services including sign language interpretation, scribing services, and provides various cultural activities, thereby ameliorating some of the cultural injustices that the students face. But further attention needs to be paid to more fully inclusive pedagogic strategies, including the development of sign-language capabilities of lecturers to work towards participatory parity of SWDs. An opportunity not yet taken up is the use of OER or open textbooks that can be legally copied, edited, translated and/or converted into braille. However, Motheo is undertaking the difficult cultural work and could respond even more justly given additional funding at the institutional level.

Politically there are a plethora of policies governing the plans for opening up and supporting those with disabilities to access the TVET sector, but the implementation of these is being undermined by insufficient funding to ensure participatory parity of these students. This is partially overcome through strategically forged partnerships with donor foundations and other non-DHET entities. However, the location of the campus in a town is complicated by the need for government action at the municipal level as urban campuses depend on the town infrastructure for physical access. Although SWDs have some opportunities to have their voices heard regarding the decisions that affect them, on-going advocacy is needed at the national, provincial, municipal levels for parity of participation to be possible.

In sum, Motheo TVET College is deliberately endeavouring to implement the *Strategic Policy Framework on Disability for the Post School Education and Training System* (DHET, 2018), but is hampered in realising their obvious passion by the lack of funds. Currently the *Open Learning Policy Framework* makes insufficient reference to open learning in relation to SWDs. As such the OLPF does not adequately guide institutions, lecturers, students, their parents and/or future employees about the specific opportunities for opening up learning to overcome or at least mitigate some of the social justice challenges faced by SWDs. Given that there is a global dearth of research on OER, open textbooks, MOOCs and their underlying open practices for PWDs (see Moon & Park, 2021), this would be a fruitful line of enquiry for further research.

Acknowledgements

Many thanks to the staff of Motheo TVET College – Principal Dipiloane Phutsisi, Susannie Odendaal, Adel Viljoen, Jacobeth Lethole, and Kagisho Selebano – whose inputs made the case study possible. Special thanks are due to reviewers Dr Marcia Lyner-Cleophas and Dr Desire Chiwandire for their thoughtful, incisive feedback on the chapter, Bianca Masuku for constructive engagement, and Dr Tabisa Mayisela for guiding the entire COOL project. The COOL project is hosted in the Centre for Innovation in Learning and Teaching at the University of Cape Town and is an initiative of the South African Department of Higher Education and Training.

References

Allais, S., & Wedekind, V. (2020). Targets, TVET and transformation. In A. Wulff (Ed.), *Grading Goal Four: Tensions, threats, and opportunities in the sustainable development goal on quality education* (pp. 322–338). Brill. https://doi.org/10.1163/9789004430365_015

Ayres, L. (2008). Semi-structured interview. In L. M. Given (Ed.), *The Sage encyclopedia of qualitative research methods* (pp. 811–812). Sage.

Bell, D., Carl, A., & Swart, E. (2016). Students with hearing impairment at a South African university: Self-identity and disclosure. *African Journal of Disability,* 5(1), a229. http://dx.doi.org/10.4102/ajod.v5i1.229

Chiwandire, D., & Vincent, L. (2019). Funding and inclusion in higher education institutions for students with disabilities. *African Journal of Disability,* 8, 1–12. https://ajod.org/index.php/ajod/article/view/336/965

Conole, G., & Brown, M. (2018). Reflecting on the impact of the open education movement. *Journal of Learning for Development,* 5(3), 187–203.

Cronin, C., & MacLaren, I. (2018). Conceptualising OEP: A review of theoretical and empirical literature in open educational practices. *Open Praxis,* 10(2), 127–143. https://search.informit.org/doi/abs/10.3316/INFORMIT.559671315718016

D'Antoni, S. (2007). Open educational resources and open content for higher education. *RUSC. Universities and Knowledge Society Journal,* 4(1). https://rusc.uoc.edu/rusc/ca/index.php/rusc/article/download/v4n1-dantoni/292-1209-1-PB.pdf

Delubom, N. E., Marongwe, N., & Buka, A. M. (2020). Managers' challenges on implementing inclusive education: Technical vocational education and training colleges. *Cypriot Journal of Educational Sciences,* 15(6), 1508–1518. https://www.un-pub.eu/ojs/index.php/cjes/article/view/5294

DHET. (2017). Call for comment on the Open Learning Policy Framework for Post-School Education and Training. *Government Gazette,* 40772(335). http://pmg-assets.s3-website-eu-west-1.amazonaws.com/170407openlearningframework-postschooleduc.pdf

DHET. (2018). Strategic policy framework on disability for the post-school education and training system. https://www.dhet.gov.za/SiteAssets/Gazettes/Approved%20Strategic%20Disability%20Policy%20Framework%20Layout220518.pdf

DHET. (2020a). Amended rules and guidelines for the administration and management of the DHET's technical and vocational education and training college bursary scheme for 2020. https://www.dhet.gov.za/SiteAssets/2020%20Bursary%20Rules%20and%20Guidelines.pdf

DHET. (2020b). Strategic plan 2020–2025. Department of Higher Education and Training. http://www.dhet.gov.za/SiteAssets/DHET%20Strategic%20Plan%202020.pdf

DHET. (2021a). Statistics on post-school education and training in South Africa. https://capebpo.org.za/wp-content/uploads/2021/04/Statistics-on-Post-School-Education-and-Training-in-South-Africa2019.pdf

DHET. (2021b). A report on the investigation of services offered to students with disabilities in technical and vocational education and training colleges. Chief Directorate: Programmes and Qualifications. https://www.dhet.gov.za/SiteAssets/A%20REPORT%20ON%20THE%20INVESTIGATION%20OF%20SERVICES%20OFFERED%20TO%20STUDENTS%20WITH%20DISABILITIES%20IN%20TVET%20COLLEGES.pdf

DoL (Department of Labour) (2015). Code of good practice on employment of persons with disabilities. https://www.saica.co.za/Portals/0/Technical/LegalAndGovernance/39383_gon1085%20Code%20for%20employing%20people%20with%20disabilities.pdf

DSD (Department of Social Development). (2009). Policy on disability. https://www.westerncape.gov.za/assets/departments/social-development/national_disability_policy.pdf

Feldstein, A., Martin, M., Hudson, A., Warren, K., Hilton, J., & Wiley, D. (2012). Open textbooks and increased student access and outcomes. *European Journal of Open, Distance and E-Learning*. https://scholars.fhsu.edu/cgi/viewcontent.cgi?article=1003&context=learning_tech_facpubs

Fourie, L. (2019). Experiences of adult learners with learning disabilities in cosmetology at a TVET college [Master's dissertation, University of Johannesburg]. http://hdl.handle.net/10210/296871

Fraser, N. (2005). Reframing justice in a globalizing world. *New Left Review*, 36, 69–88.

Fraser, N. (2007). Identity, exclusion, and critique: A response to four critics. *European Journal of Political Theory*, 6(3), 305–338.

Goethals, T., De Schauwer, E., & Van Hove, G. (2015). Weaving intersectionality into disability studies research: Inclusion, reflexivity and anti-essentialism. *DiGeSt. Journal of Diversity and Gender Studies*, 2(1–2), 75–94.

Gourley, B., & Lane, A. (2009). Re-invigorating openness at The Open University: The role of open educational resources. *Open Learning: The Journal of Open, Distance and e-Learning*, 24(1), 57-65.

Hodgkinson-Williams, C. A., & Trotter, H. (2018). A social justice framework for understanding open educational resources and practices in the Global South. *Journal of Learning for Development*, 5(3), 204–224.

Khuluvhe, M., Netshifhefhe, E., Ganyaupfu, E., & Negogogo, E.V. (2021). Post-school education and training monitor: Macro-indicator trends. DHET. https://www.dhet.gov.za/Planning%20Monitoring%20and%20Evaluation%20Coordination/Post-School%20Education%20and%20Training%20Monitor%20-%20Macro-Indicator%20Trends%20-%20March%202021.pdf

Khumalo, Z. P. (2019). Teaching students with visual 'disability': The experiences of technical and vocational education and training (TVET) lecturers [Master's dissertation, University of KwaZulu-Natal]. https://ukzn-dspace.ukzn.ac.za/handle/10413/17722

Leibowitz, B., & Bozalek, V. (2016). The scholarship of teaching and learning from a social justice perspective. *Teaching in Higher Education*, 21(2), 109–122.

Leshota, P. L., & Sefotho, M. M. (2020). Being differently abled: Disability through the lens of hierarchy of binaries and Bitso-lebe-ke-Seromo. *African Journal of Disability*, 9, 1–7. https://doi.org/10.4102/ajod.v9i0.643

Lourens, H. (2015). The lived experiences of higher education for students with a visual impairment: A phenomenological study at two universities in the Western Cape, South Africa. [Doctoral dissertation, Stellenbosch University]. http://hdl.handle.net/10019.1/96732

Luckett, K., & Shay, S. (2017). Reframing the curriculum: A transformative approach. *Critical Studies in Education*, 61(1), 50–65. https://www.tandfonline.com/doi/full/10.1080/17508487.2017.1356341

Mbanga, N., & Mtembu, V. N. (2020). Digital learning: Perceptions of lecturers at a technical vocational education and training college. *South African Journal of Higher Education*, 34(4), 155–173.

McIlroy, G., & Storbeck, C. (2011). Development of deaf identity: An ethnographic study. *The Journal of Deaf Studies and Deaf Education*, 16(4), 494–511. https://academic.oup.com/jdsde/article-abstract/16/4/494/551253

Moon, J., & Park, Y. (2021). A scoping review on open educational resources to support interactions of learners with disabilities. *The International Review of Research in Open and Distributed Learning*, 22(2), 314–341. https://doi.org/10.19173/irrodl.v22i1.5110

Mtshali, J. M. (2020). Technical and Vocational Education and Training (TVET) college students' experiences of the relationship between private off-campus residences and academic performance: a case of Majuba TVET College [Doctoral dissertation, University of KwaZulu-Natal]. https://ukzn-dspace.ukzn.ac.za/bitstream/handle/10413/19662/Mtshali_Josephine_Makhosazane_2020.pdf?sequence=1&isAllowed=y

Munyaradzi, M., & Addae, D. (2019). Effectiveness of student psychological support services at a technical and vocational education and training college in South Africa. *Community College Journal of Research and Practice*, 43(4), 262-274. https://doi.org/10.1080/10668926.2018.1456379

Munyaradzi, M., Arko-Achemfuor, A., & Quan-Baffour, K. (2021). An exploration of comprehensive student support systems in technical vocational education and training colleges for students with disability. *Community College Journal of Research and Practice*, 1-17. https://www.tandfonline.com/doi/full/10.1080/10668926.2021.1952914

Mvuyana, N. (2015). Understanding how people with acquired blindness experience and interact with higher education institutions: A proposed TVET college for Pietermaritzburg CBD [Doctoral dissertation, University of KwaZulu-Natal.]. https://ukzn-dspace.ukzn.ac.za/handle/10413/14332

Myataza, Y. S. (2019). Exploring factors influencing students' absenteeism at a TVET College in Nelson Mandela Bay District [Doctoral dissertation, University of South Africa]. https://uir.unisa.ac.za/handle/10500/26457

Ndlovu, S. (2020). Obstacles for students with disabilities in accessing higher education in South Africa: A decolonial perspective. In A. P. Ndofirepi & M. Musengi (Eds.), *Inclusion as Social Justice* (pp. 141–161). Brill. https://brill.com/view/title/58077?language=en

Ngubane, P. B. (2018). First time entrants' student support services in contributing to academic success in technical and vocational education and training colleges [Doctoral dissertation, University of Zululand]. http://uzspace.unizulu.ac.za/handle/10530/1836

Ngubane-Mokiwa, S., & Khoza, S. B. (2016). Lecturers' experiences of teaching STEM to students with disabilities. *Journal of Learning for Development*, 3(1), 37–50.

Ntombela, B. P. (2020). Exploring the experiences of students with physical impairments studying at a technical vocational education and training (TVET) college in KwaZulu-Natal [Master's dissertation, University of KwaZulu-Natal]. https://researchspace.ukzn.ac.za/handle/10413/19304

Papier, J. (2021). 21st Century competencies in Technical and Vocational Education and Training: Rhetoric and reality in the wake of a pandemic. *Journal of Education (University of KwaZulu-Natal)*, (84), 67–84.

Pretorius, A., Bell, D., & Healey, T. (2019). Access, equality and inclusion of disabled students within South African further and higher educational institutions. In T. Chataika (Ed.), *The Routledge handbook of disability in southern Africa* (pp. 153–168). Routledge.

Rambe, P., & Moeti, M. (2017). Disrupting and democratising higher education provision or entrenching academic elitism: Towards a model of MOOCs adoption at African universities. *Educational Technology Research and Development*, 65(3), 631–651.

Reindal, S. M. (2008). A social relational model of disability: A theoretical framework for special needs education? *European Journal of Special Needs Education*, 23(2), 135–146. https://doi.org/10.1080/08856250801947812

RSA. (Republic of South Africa). (1996). *Constitution of the Republic of South Africa*. https://www.gov.za/documents/constitution-republic-south-africa-1996

RSA. (1998). Employment Equity Act. *Government Gazette*, 19370(400). http://www.labour.gov.za/DocumentCenter/Acts/Employment%20Equity/Act%20-%20Employment%20Equity%201998.pdf

RSA. (2016). White paper on the rights of persons with disabilities. *Government Gazette*, 39792(230). https://www.gov.za/sites/default/files/gcis_document/201603/39792gon230.pdf

Siwela, S. (2017). An exploratory case study of the experiences of students with disabilities at a TVET college: Factors that facilitate or impede their access and success [Doctoral dissertation, University of KwaZulu-Natal].

Subrayen, R., & Dhunpath, R. (2019). A snapshot of the chalkboard writing experiences of Bachelor of Education students with visual disabilities in South Africa. *African Journal of Disability*, (8), 1–8. https://doi.org/10.4102/ajod.v8i0.523

Vergunst, R., & Swartz, L. (2021). "He doesn't understand that he's struggling with the way I felt": University students, psychosocial disability and disclosure in the Western Cape, South Africa. *Disability & Society*, 36(2), 226–239. DOI: 10.1080/09687599.2020.1730159

Vincent, L., & Chiwandire, D. (2017). Wheelchair users, access and exclusion in South African higher education. *African Journal of Disability*, 6(1), 1–9.

Webb, C. (2021). Liberating the family: Debt, education and racial capitalism in South Africa. *Environment and Planning D: Society and Space*, 39(1), 85–102.

Wiley, D. (2006). Open source, openness, and higher education. *Innovate: Journal of Online Education*, 3(1). https://www.learntechlib.org/p/104321/

HOW TO CITE THIS CHAPTER

Van Wyk, G., & Hodgkinson-Williams, C. A. (2022). Staff insights on opening up learning to students with disabilities at Motheo TVET College, South Africa: A social justice perspective. In T. Mayisela, S. C. Govender & C. A. Hodgkinson-Williams (Eds.), *Open learning as a means of advancing social justice: Cases in post-school education and training in South Africa* (pp. 178–198). African Minds. doi: 10.47622/9781928502425_8

This work is licensed under a Creative Commons Attribution 4.0 International (CC BY 4.0) licence.

9

Insights on OER adoption models to inform ways of opening up learning materials to address economic, cultural and political injustices in South African education

Anelisa Dabula, Glenda Cox & Cheryl Ann Hodgkinson-Williams

SUMMARY This chapter outlines current models of open educational resources (OER) adoption, in order to make recommendations to the Department of Higher Education and Training (DHET) around which model(s) could be introduced as a means of open learning in the local post-school education and training (PSET) sector in an attempt to respond to economic, cultural, and political injustices. Using the philosophical framework of social justice (Fraser, 2005), this desktop study explores the extent to which models of OER implementation respond to economic, cultural, and political injustices and could potentially provide more socially just access to educational resources in the technical and vocational education and training (TVET) and university sectors. The OER models are classified along the following lines: regional-geographic, the federal government, provincial, inter-institutional, institutional, intra-institutional, community, and commercial. Findings showcase examples of each of these and illustrate how an aggregated model which combines elements of a central model (for national funding), a provincial model (for funding to a managing institution for multi-institutional projects), an institutional model (for OER development with a social justice intent), and a peer-to-peer community model coul encourage peer engagement that might optimise the nascent National Open Learning System (NOLS) spearheaded by DHET. This aggregated model is recommended for DHET as it holistically considers economic challenges facing OER creation and use, endeavours to encourage curriculum transformation by addressing aspects of cultural misrecognition and, where possible, includes student voices to allow for some facets of political representation.

Keywords: open learning, open education, open educational resources, social justice, PSET

Introduction

Globally, post-schooling educational institutions are under pressure to provide a rising number of students with access to quality education in increasingly economically constrained environments (Hodgkinson-Williams, 2014) now aggravated by the COVID-19 pandemic (UNESCO, 2020a). A partial response to the issue of unequal access to education is the creation, use, adaptation, and sharing of open educational resources (OER) (OECD, 2007). The high cost of textbooks originally spearheaded the interest in OER in the United States and Canada after it was found that 94% of students in the US were being negatively affected by the high costs of textbooks and that almost 26% of students dropped out of courses (Jhangiani et al., 2018).

Students face unequal access to education and educational resources in South Africa, according to Bozalek et al. (2020) due to the rising tuition fees and the annual struggle of parents not being able to pay fees. Although poor students awarded a National Student Financial Aid Scheme (NSFAS) bursary receive funds for learning resources, students in the so-called 'missing middle', who are generally children of public servants, are often excluded from accessing expensive textbooks, which have been commodified into a private good that pursues making a profit at the expense of social justice (Bozalek et al., 2020).

The term open educational resources was conceived at the 2002 UNESCO Forum to describe the provision of openly licensed educational resources either in print or conveyed using information and communication technologies (ICTs), that are available for consultation, use, adaptation and dissemination by anyone (Butcher, 2010). According to the OECD (2007, p. 10), OER are "digitized materials offered freely and openly for educators, students and self-learners to legally use and reuse for teaching, learning and research". The alternative copyright mechanism, Creative Commons, serves the ideals of OER, making it easier for people to legally disseminate their work and share and build upon the work of others consistent with the rules of the specified open license (Okoro, 2013).

The use of OER were accentuated in the draft *Open Learning Policy Framework for South African Post-School Education and Training*[1] (DHET, 2017). According to DHET, open learning is fundamentally about expanding access to formal, non-formal, and informal learning with the flexibility of provision contributing to the accessibility, and hopefully quality, of post-school education and training (PSET) provision to contribute to improved student success (DHET, 2017). DHET's *Open Learning Policy Framework* (OLPF) aims to support the development and expansion of open learning principles and practices in the PSET sector, which intends to complement rather than replace traditional classroom/campus-based provision in TVET colleges (formerly Further Education and Training colleges) and universities (DHET, 2017).

The OLPF is "driven by a concern for social justice and therefore motivated by the need for redress, equity in access to opportunity, flexibility, and choice, and by an equal concern for quality and real success in learning" (DHET, 2017, p. 412). The policy framework advocates the establishment of a network of educational institutions and learning support centres to provide access to internet connectivity to learners and staff to enable them to create shared materials. The aim is to make available a wide range of learning opportunities

---

[1] The *Open Learning Policy Framework* was published on 7 April 2017, but has yet to be approved by the Minister of Higher Education and Training

to potential learners, closer to their homes and at times and dates suitable to their individual circumstances. The use of existing infrastructure is anticipated to enable the dissemination of well-researched, high-quality OER (DHET, 2017). The policy framework intends to:

> steer the sector towards making increasing use of cost-effective modalities conducive to open learning, in the interests of increased access (translating into increased enrolments) and increased success (translating into improved throughput, success rates, and employability), without sacrificing learning quality. (DHET, 2017, p. 386)

In support of this policy, DHET introduced a plan for the National Open Learning System (NOLS)[2], a platform established to share OER, with the hope of increasing access to learning opportunities for South Africans through "high quality, self-directed, interactive learning materials (online or offline) that enable learners to select and complete modules, including robust formative assessment" (DHET, 2017, p. 388).

The purpose of this study is to investigate what models of OER adoption are being implemented in international community colleges and universities, local higher education institutions (HEIs), and other independent organizations in order to distil possible models for OER implementation in South African Technical and Vocational Education and Training (TVET) colleges and universities.

PSET context in South Africa

The PSET sector in South Africa comprises 26 public and 131 private HEIs, 50 TVET colleges as well as nine Community Education and Training (CET) colleges and 287 private colleges (DHET, 2021, p. 6). Of the total PSET student enrolment of 2 279 925 in 2019, 1 074 912 were enrolled in public HEIs, 208 978 in private HEIs and 678 490 in TVET colleges. Of key importance is that in the public HEIs, 393 767 students received NSFAS bursaries of over R2.6 billion and in the TVET sector 346 270 students received over R5.1 billion (DHET, 2021, p. 92). These bursaries include funding for tuition fees, accommodation, travel and educational resources such as textbooks.

The OER production elements

In this chapter, the following terms are used to describe certain elements of the 'Open Education cycle' (Hodgkinson-Williams et al., 2017), namely: creation, use, adaptation, and dissemination. Creation describes the development or production of materials. Use is understood simply as the adoption of OER, without adaptation. The term 'adaptation' is used here to describe the process of editing, altering, or re-mixing existing work, including translation, inclusion of local content, and/or images. The adaptation of OER should also enable the expansion and diverse use of resources translated into local languages (Aesoph, 2016). Dissemination is the public sharing of OER on various public (e.g., OER Commons[3]) or institutional (e.g., OpenUCT[4]) repositories to expand their reach and possible use. How

---

[2] https://www.dhet.gov.za/SitePages/NOLS.aspx
[3] https://www.oercommons.org/
[4] https://open.uct.ac.za/

these different elements are funded provided a way of differentiating between different models in this study. Although OER are 'free' to the user, there is still a cost involved in their creation and/or adaptation. The funding of OER initiatives therefore involves various financial models to ensure their sustainability (Downes, 2007).

Empirical research has argued for OER efficiency, perceived value, and (importantly) cost reduction (Jung et al., 2017). However, research has shown that OER is still in the early stages of adoption and that wider acceptance requires increased recognisability of OER repositories, ensuring the quality of content, as well as the development of collaborative communities (Grimaldi et al., 2019). The lack of knowledge about OER and copyright mechanisms plays a major role in limiting OER use and calls for more diffusion of knowledge about OER (Hoosen & Butcher, 2019). Having said this, there are a number of national governments and HEIs that have implemented OER models or strategies and more are considering implementing OER in the near future (UNESCO, 2020b) to: (1) share knowledge; (2) reuse publicly available knowledge; (3) reduce the cost of knowledge creation; and (4) conduct good public relations (Hylen, 2006, as cited in Jung et al., 2017). This momentum has been driven by significant financial support from philanthropic foundations such as the Hewlett Foundation[5] and Andrew W. Mellon Foundation[6].

However, educational resources in the competitive, largely neoliberal world of higher education, are often considered key intellectual property, so access to these resources are most often restricted to privileged groups of institutions and/or students who can pay for them. By contrast, the OER movement specifically uses open licensing (for example Creative Commons[7]) to circumvent copyright constraints, but it requires significant investment and strategic planning (Jung et al., 2017). Financial support, incentives, and benefits are therefore at the forefront of educator and institutional interest as global use of OER evolves (Henderson & Ostashweski, 2018). Inherent in the creation, use, adaptation and dissemination are what open education practitioners and researchers describe open educational practices (OEP) (Cronin, 2017).

To provide a framework to better understand the social justness of the suggested OER models and their inherent OEP, these models are analysed using Fraser's (2005) social justice lens to map how, if at all, these models seek to redress economic, cultural, and political injustices and how these models can be adapted for the local PSET sector.

Social justice and OER

Nancy Fraser's (2005) social justice framework is used to assess and distil which models of OER implementation may respond to economic, cultural, and political injustices and could be, therefore, socially just options for OER implementation in the PSET sector.

Hodgkinson-Williams and Trotter (2018) used the social justice framework of Nancy Fraser (2005) to understand OER and their related practices in the Global South. This study will use a similar approach, using the theoretical framework to highlight models for OER adoption based on the principles of 'participatory parity' (Fraser, 2005).

---

[5] https://hewlett.org/strategy/open-education/
[6] https://mellon.org/programs/higher-learning/
[7] https://creativecommons.org/

According to Fraser, "social justice is both an outcome where all the relevant social actors participate as peers in social life and a process in which procedural standards are followed in a fair and open process of deliberation" (Fraser, 2005, p. 87). However, both these outcomes and processes can be socially unjust in three ways: (1) economically (maldistribution of resources); (2) culturally (misrecognition of culture); and (3) politically (misrepresentation or exclusion of voice). Fraser categorises affirmative approaches to injustices as those that do not go far enough, in that, while they may correct inequities created by social arrangements, they do not disturb the underlying social structures that generate these inequities (Bozalek et al., 2020). In order to do the latter, a transformative approach needs to be applied.

Economic maldistribution

Redistributive justice is the most long-standing principle of social justice and involves the allocation of material or human resources to those who by circumstance have less (Rawls, 1971, as cited in Fraser, 1995). People can be impeded from full participation by economic structures that deny them the resources they need in order to interact with others as peers (Hodgkinson-Williams & Trotter, 2018). In the context of this study, these economic injustices would equate to expensive textbooks and expensive data charges to access online materials. To respond to this economic injustice, or what Fraser refers to as maldistribution, institutions can prescribe open textbooks instead and zero-rate specific educational websites and platforms which include OER.

This economic redistribution is what Fraser refers to as a change where attention is paid to the inequitable outcomes by modest ameliorative adjustments that partially address maldistribution, but leave "intact much of the underlying political-economic structure" (Fraser, 1995, p. 84). Lambert (2018) cautions that even though OER are freely available (and thereby enacting economic redistributive justice), these free resources are not always licensed for adaptation (and, therefore, less able to be edited to respond to cultural injustices). On a more fundamental level, what is needed is economic restructuring through a "transformative" shift that addresses the root causes of maldistribution. This can be achieved, for example, by government agencies prioritising expenditure that supports the adoption and adaptation of OER.

Cultural misrecognition

Cultural misrecognition refers to the "inequality of status" Fraser (2005, p. 73). Fraser points out that "people can also be prevented from interacting in terms of participatory parity by institutionalized hierarchies of cultural value that deny them the requisite standing" (2005, p. 73). Students in the Global South may be deprived of participatory parity due to the current domination of Western-oriented epistemic perspectives (Hodgkinson-Williams & Trotter, 2018). Therefore, by countering cultural inequalities, or what Fraser refers to as "misrecognition", symbolic change would assist in valuing local languages and enabling various cultural interpretations of knowledge and ways of learning. However, this leaves intact the hegemonic knowledge structures, predominance of international languages and predominance of Global North cultural views. A truly "transformative approach would involve dismantling the power relations, social hierarchies, and cultural hegemonies that currently underpin the canons assumed norms and values of inherited curricula and setting up processes to reimagine more inclusive ways of participating in curriculum and pedagogic practices" (Luckett & Shay, 2017, p. 3). One of the ways in which cultural equality can be addressed is through the co-creation of OER with students (Gröblinger et al., 2018).

Political misrepresentation

Fraser (2005, p. 75) holds that political misrepresentation "tells us who is included in, and who [is] excluded from, the circle of those entitled to a just distribution and reciprocal recognition". According to Hodgkinson-Williams and Trotter (2018), OER creation allows educators to participate directly in knowledge production, thereby disrupting traditional power relations between publishers, knowledge producers in the Global North and knowledge producers in the Global South, consequently addressing political maldistribution in terms of voice and power. With respect to ownership of educational materials as stipulated by Hodgkinson-Williams and Trotter (2018), educators do not automatically possess copyright of teaching materials that they develop. National copyright laws typically state that any work produced during employment belongs to the employer (ROER4D, 2017). Moreover, in South Africa, universities can decide on their own intellectual property (IP) policies. For example, the Research on Open Educational Resources for Development (ROER4D) policy brief, *Spotlight on OER Policy in the Global South*, states that in relation to South Africa, "20 of the [then] 25 universities … have IP policies that align with the Copyright Act, vesting copyright over educators' works with the affiliate institution" (ROER4D, 2017, p. 4). However, universities can assign staff members' copyright over their works, including teaching and learning materials, so that they can, in turn, release these as OER if they so choose. One such arrangement is in place at the University of Cape Town, where the IP policy automatically assigns copyright to the authors of the work (ROER4D, 2017). Therefore, unless such IP policies state that educators have the right to decide whether to release teaching and learning materials, the more institutionally constrained IP policies actively reduce the opportunities that educators have to share their own materials publicly.

The inclusion of students' voice in the content, structure and/or language of their learning materials allows for conversations between educators and students and enables students to participate in decision-making that impacts their futures (Baker & Ippoliti, 2019). Although still not that common, there are examples of students assisting educators to create or adapt teaching and learning materials as OER (Baker & Ippoliti, 2019; Cox et al., 2020; Hodgkinson-Williams & Paskevicius, 2012; Zapata, 2020) or even create OER without the direct presence or support of educators (Paskevicius, 2011).

Research methods and selection

This chapter utilises a desktop review methodology, which includes a conceptual synthesis of models of OER funding, creation, use, adaptation, and dissemination that have been crafted or adopted by countries, states/provinces, or institutions that could usefully inform the PSET sector in South Africa. Journal articles, resources and websites on OER, implemented in formal education, non-governmental organisations (NGOs) and by commercial OER providers, were identified through Google Scholar searches and Google alerts. Keywords included 'open educational resources', 'open learning', 'higher education OER in Global North', and 'OER in Global South'. The term 'open content' was also used to locate information separately from and in combination with 'OER'. Authors sometimes use the terms 'open education' and 'open learning' interchangeably.

Models of OER

Different types of OER models were identified and it emerged that funding is a crucial component of OER creation and development and that without funding of some form, OER creation, use, adaptation, and dissemination is unlikely to be sustainable (Butcher & Hoosen, 2012). This echoes Downes' (2007) finding that the sustainability of OER depends on the consistent development and distribution of OER. Where Downes' seminal article in 2007 provided categories of OER by funding type only, this chapter includes funding as the fundamental element of an OER organisation and workflow model that disaggregates other elements such as creation, use, adaptation, and dissemination.

This study suggests the following seven categories of OER models: (1) regional-geographic; (2) central government; (3) provincial; (4) inter-institutional; (5) institutional; (6) community-based; and (7) commercial.

Regional geographic or linguistic model

Regional models are those where materials are authored by academics from a group of countries on the basis of geographic location (e.g., the Nordic network) or by common language on a continent (e.g., OER Africa for anglophone countries).

Nordic OER. In 2013, the European Union launched a large-scale initiative on "Opening up Education"; this was the beginning of the Nordic OER endeavour in promoting and utilizing OER in the Nordic countries, with a focus on creation (Ossiannilsson & Hoel, 2015). This cross-border Nordic OER initiative, financed until 2015 by the Nordic Council of Ministers, aimed to work for awareness, knowledge building, networking, and creating an arena for dissemination of OER and openness in education in Denmark, Faroe Islands, Finland, Iceland, Norway, and Sweden (Ossiannilsson & Hoel, 2015). This was a novel cross-border, cross-linguistic, and politically transcendent OER model that was initially funded for only one year (with a focus on advocacy and networking). It provides an illustration of a regional OER initiative, where there is "a tradition of cooperation, exchange of knowledge and solutions between the countries" (Ossiannilsson & Hoel, 2015, p. 1).

OER Africa. Launched in 2008, OER Africa[8] was established to help educators and the institutions in which they work to conceptualise, adapt, implement and use OER to improve both the content and practice of teaching and learning. OER Africa is involved in numerous projects supporting the adoption of OER in HEIs across anglophone Africa. These activities include OER advocacy; hosting a repository of OER developed by partner institutions as well as additional resources produced by other African institutions; supporting OER policy development and conducting research on OER[9]. This organisation has continued to benefit from funding from the William and Flora Hewlett Foundation from 2008 to date. This funder-supported model illustrates the value of cultivating a long-term relationship with a funder to optimise learning from one project to another.

---

[8] https://www.oerafrica.org/
[9] For OER Africa advocacy and research see: https://www.oerafrica.org/about-us/our-resources-and-publications

Central government model

United States of America's Federal Government. An example of a central government model is the US Federal Government's support for OER in post-secondary institutions. The first federal OER grants were made in 2010[10] and further grants of about $5 million each year for 2018–2020 were awarded for the Open Textbook Pilot program[11]. The conditions for the latter grants stipulate that applications should "demonstrate the greatest potential to achieve the highest level of savings for students through sustainable, expanded use of open textbooks in high-enrollment courses ... or in programs that prepare individuals for in-demand fields".[12]

Cox (2018) highlighted that former US President Barack Obama's administration supported open textbook development in the US, resulting in students saving over $1 billion (R13,8 billion) in the past five years. Clearly, for large economic benefits for students, large up-front grants from central governments would be needed for OER development.

Provincial government-financed and multi-institution model

British Columbia, Canada. An example of a provincial government-financed model is that of British Columbia (BC) in Canada, where the province has provided funding since 2012 to support innovation and collaboration for OER or low-cost textbook initiatives.[13]

The Zero Textbook Cost (ZTC) Program, also known as 'Zed Cred', is a provincial initiative where the funding for open or low-cost textbooks is managed by one institution, BCcampus[14], but are being created at individual institutions or via multi-institutional partnerships. Most uniquely the ZTC Program has groups of advisors from various BC institutions for the different disciplinary areas[15]. One of the key recommendations from the experience of the first university to launch Canada's ZTC Program, Kwantlen Polytechnic University (KPU), was the integration of the list of courses with open textbooks into the university's institutional course listing and scheduling (Jhangiani, 2020). KPU now has 800 courses that have zero textbook costs[16]. From 2018 to Spring 2021, KPU students saved over $5,9 million[17]. One of the other universities that also received an open education grant, Thompson Rivers University, has visually mapped an entire Certificate of General Studies based on OER[18] so that the students have a no- or low-cost option. These OER, either developed from scratch or

---

[10] https://obamawhitehouse.archives.gov/blog/2014/03/14/expanding-opportunity-through-open-educational-resources
[11] https://www.federalregister.gov/documents/2020/09/15/2020-20379/applications-for-new-awards-fund-for-the-improvement-of-postsecondary-education-open-textbooks-pilot
[12] https://www.federalregister.gov/documents/2020/09/15/2020-20379/applications-for-new-awards-fund-for-the-improvement-of-postsecondary-education-open-textbooks-pilot
[13] https://oerworldmap.org/
[14] https://bccampus.ca/bccampus-open-education-sustainability-grant/
[15] https://bccampus.ca/projects/open-education/zed-cred-z-degrees/ztc-business-programs/
[16] https://www.kpu.ca/open/ztc
[17] See KPU Zero Textbook Cost program dashboard at https://public.tableau.com/app/profile/rajiv.jhangiani/viz/KPUZeroTextbookCostprogramdashboard/KPUZTCdashboard
[18] https://oewg.trubox.ca/zed-cred/draft-pathway-certificate-of-gen-studies-1-1/

adapted from existing OER (e.g., OpenStax[19]) by the various universities, are curated in the BC Open Textbook Collection.[20]

Inter-institutional model

University of Pretoria–University of Cape Town. An example of an inter-institutional model is illustrated in the development of the *OER Term Bank*[21], which was a partnership between the University of Pretoria (UP) and the University of Cape Town (UCT). The *OER Term Bank* is a free multilingual glossary[22] that allows students and lecturers to check the meanings and definitions of words in other South African languages. This inter-institutional project was funded by a collaboration grant from DHET (Hoosen & Butcher, 2019).

Institutional model

University of Cape Town. In 2014, an Open Access policy was introduced at UCT that promotes the sharing of teaching materials (Cox, 2016). Lecturers are encouraged to share on a voluntary basis, as the institution wants to ensure that the developed content created is from an African perspective, curated by UCT, and shared locally and internationally. OpenUCT is an institutional repository that:

> makes available and digitally preserves the scholarly outputs produced at UCT, including theses and dissertations, journal articles, book chapters, technical and research reports, and open educational resources. (Open UCT, 2014, as cited in Cox, 2016, p. 55)

Academics at UCT have produced and shared teaching resources as OER since 2010 (Lesko, 2013). The most recent project, Digital Open Textbooks for Development (DOT4D)[23] (2018–2021), originally funded by Canada's International Development Research Centre (IDRC), aims to better understand the affordances of digital open textbook publishing for supporting openly licensed, localised content development approaches, curriculum transformation and cost alleviation both at UCT and at other South African HEIs (Cox et al., 2020). The DOT4D project allocated small grants to UCT academics to produce textbooks.

DOT4D's advocacy work, which built upon previous open education projects at UCT[24], resulted in an annual award by the Deputy Vice-Chancellor of Teaching and Learning for the open textbook(s) which best support the institution's transformation agenda[25]. The DOT4D project has used Nancy Fraser's (2005) trivalent lens to examine inequality (Cox et al., 2020). Open textbook authors are supported by DOT4D staff who can scaffold the development of OER, specifically with regard to copyright, editing, and publishing.

In 2020/2021 UCT, as well as other HEIs, partnered with Cell C, Telkom, Vodacom, and MTN to zero-rate access to certain educational websites. This kind of support was essential

---

[19] https://openstax.org/
[20] https://open.bccampus.ca/browse-our-collection/find-open-textbooks/
[21] http://oertb.tlterm.com/
[22] https://www.up.ac.za/african-languages/news/post_2728581-open-educational-resource-term-bank-pg2
[23] http://www.dot4d.uct.ac.za/
[24] http://www.cilt.uct.ac.za/cilt/open
[25] https://jime.open.ac.uk/articles/10.5334/jime.556/

to continue teaching and learning online during UCT's second term, especially while the practice of physical distancing continued in order to limit the spread of COVID-19 (ICTS, 2021).

Community-based model

Peer–2–Peer University. Peer–2–Peer University (P2PU)[26] was inspired by the 2007 Cape Town Open Education Declaration and has remained active in the field of open education ever since. P2PU hosts a platform where groups of people can share and participate in specially created or existing open courses freely available online. With a few exceptions, P2PU does not create or own this content – it is primarily a curated list. The open discussions are called 'learning circles', which are either online or in person. The learning circles are based on the principles of social learning, collaboration, and "education as a social good"[27]. This community has now extended to over 40 partnerships with libraries, educational institutions, community centres, and foundations. The P2PU is distributed internationally in over 50 countries with most of the uptake of the collaboration activities in their virtual community in the United States, Kenya, India, Poland, and South Africa.[28] All the materials on the P2PU site are OER and, as one of the grant-makers says, "P2PU neatly connects open educational resources to career pathways in an equitable and empowering way that few other organizations are even considering".[29] This initiative is funded by several huge foundations such as Erasmus+, Dollar General Literacy Foundation, Knight Foundation, Institute of Museum and Library Services, Open Society Foundation, and the Siegel Family Endowment.[30]

Commercial model

Lumen Learning. The company Lumen Learning[31] is an example of a sustainable business model where a private company curates and/or creates OER aligned with learning outcomes for general education courses on behalf of educational institutions. The result is a set of learning materials that faculty members and students can use to replace expensive textbooks. The content is free for students to access, but there is a cost for their services by the commissioning institution (a fee of $25 for each student per term[32]). Lumen Learning also integrates the course/s into the commissioning institution's learning management system (LMS).

In order for the OER models to be economically just, they need to include funding that will at least lower the creation, dissemination and purchase cost of textbooks and other resources (ameliorative remedy) or full support creation and dissemination cost to make them free to use (transformative action). Likewise in order for OER to be culturally inclusive they need to be developed and or adapted (e.g., translated) by a diverse range of epistemic

---

[26] https://www.p2pu.org/en/
[27] https://www.p2pu.org/en/about/
[28] https://www.p2pu.org/en/
[29] https://www.p2pu.org/en/
[30] https://www.p2pu.org/en/about/
[31] https://lumenlearning.com/
[32] https://lumenlearning.com/how/payment-options/

positions. The OER models described above are summarised in Table 1 in terms of their approaches to funding, creation, use, adaptation and dissemination.

Table 1: Summary of OER models in relation to funding, creation, use, adaptation and dissemination

Models	Funding	Creation	Use	Adaptation	Dissemination
Regional geographic or linguistic Model					
Nordic network	Regional government funding	Build networks to encourage the creation of OER. Develop position paper.	[Not in project scope]	[Not in project scope]	Facebook group for on-going or advocacy communication[33]
OER Africa	NGO funded by international donors	Commission and/or curate English OER from various institutions across Africa	No sign-in required	Adapt existing OER	OER hosted on website[34]
Central government Model					
USA Federal Government	Colleges and universities funded by USA government in a competitive bid	Create OER / open textbooks	Free sign-in with USA social security number	Adapt existing OER / open textbooks	Applications for awards on government website[35]
Provincial government-financed model with devolved management					
British Columbia	Funded by the Canadian Ministry of Advanced Education and Skills Training; managed by BCcampus	Create OER and/or low-cost textbooks from scratch	No sign-in required	Adapt existing OER (e.g., OpenStax)	Hosted on the B.C. Open Textbook Collection[36] website
Inter-institutional Model					
University of Pretoria – University of Cape Town	National government funding	Create OER from scratch	No sign-in required	No means by which to contribute or adapt	Available on a commercially hosted site
Institutional Model					
UCT	Donor funded	Create OER from scratch	No sign-in required	Adapt already existing OER	Hosted on the UCT site
Community Model					
Peer-to-Peer University	Multi-funder approach	Create the discussion space where OER are used	Free sign-in for learners	Use existing OER	Hosted on P2P website[37]
Commercial Model					
Lumen Learning	$25 member fee per term/course	Create OER from any number of institutions, individuals	Free sign-in for learners	Undertake at a cost to the commissioning institution	Integrated into commissioning institution's LMS

---

[33] https://www.facebook.com/groups/47334945518
[34] https://www.oerafrica.org/
[35] https://www2.ed.gov/programs/otp/awards.html
[36] https://open.bccampus.ca/browse-our-collection/find-open-textbooks/
[37] https://www.p2pu.org/en/

Discussion

This literature review demonstrated that there are a number of different models of OER adoption that can provide ideas for supporting the uptake of OER in the South African PSET sector. OER has the potential to address social injustice in the PSET sector and the models described above will be analysed using Fraser's (2005) trivalent theory of social justice.

OER models and responses to economic maldistribution

OER models used in North American universities are primarily focused on cost-savings as a way to help students succeed in tertiary education. Sustainable cost-saving models included here have been open textbook initiatives such as the central government model (e.g., USA) and provincial model (e.g., British Columbia, Canada). These central or provincial government OER funding initiatives can be considered as potentially economically transformative, as funding mechanisms for the production of educational materials are being addressed at a foundational level through the allocation of taxpayer funding. Although these central and provincial models are not yet at scale to completely transform the way students are supported with educational materials, they do provide useful models of national and provincial funding for DHET to consider, especially as the costs to the students in these models are considerably reduced, or not incurred at all.

While the commercial OER development company model (e.g., Lumen Learning) may illustrate a transformative response for students, the commissioning educational institution is still paying for the service (and perhaps even passing on these charges to the student – in which case it would be ameliorative). This commercial model provides educational resources at a lower cost in a commercially sustainable manner, but is not ideal in South Africa, as this model might be more accessible to historically advantaged institutions, whereas the South African emphasis would probably be on no-cost initiatives.

NOLS has the potential to be economically transformative, as it is envisaged as a repository where free teaching and learning materials can be disseminated to all South Africans. DHET, through collaboration with PSET institutions, intends to develop learning opportunities with high-quality open learning materials that are designed to be made available as OER on NOLS (DHET, 2017). Of course, the challenge of how these OER are developed and who bears the cost still remains.

OER models in response to cultural misrecognition

The model which has been identified as best addressing cultural misrecognition is the regional geographic model (e.g., Nordic network), which appears to be not only concerned with reducing costs but also with breaking barriers of OER access across the Nordic states by curating available OER on one platform where it can be stored and shared equitably. The Nordic network includes cross-cultural collaboration and the development, use, and reuse of OER in lesser-used languages and cultures. This model is ameliorative, in that it includes language translation. The cross-border collaboration takes this model further to a more transformative approach that recognises multiple cultures.

OER Africa ensures that OER material from across anglophone Africa, created by African contributors is curated on the website. Although this is an example of an ameliorative response culturally, a more multilingual initiative is required in order not to reinforce English as the only language of teaching and learning materials in South Africa. The DHET-funded inter-institutional model between the UP and UCT provides a potentially culturally transformative one as it includes a glossary of frequently used academic terms in 11 of the official South African languages.

In South Africa, cultural misrecognition from a colonial past and decades of apartheid lingers. Cox et al. (2020) highlighted that content underpinned by a Western view of the world is more prevalent in textbooks being used in classrooms in sub-Saharan Africa and these resources are written predominantly in English. The DOT4D project at UCT, an ameliorative institutional model, seeks to transform the curriculum with locally authored, contextually relevant textbooks that purposely seek to redress cultural (in)justice in South Africa (Cox et al., 2020).

OER models in response to political misrepresentation

A community-driven model (P2PU) ensures that OER from multiple repositories are used continuously, rather than merely being stored in repositories. Community-based models provide opportunities for the representation of marginalised voices through continuous engagement with peers about the educational materials. Since DHET hopes to use NOLS as an inclusive repository that "reflects open learning principles" (DHET, 2017, p. 409), it would be advised that NOLS incorporates aspects of the peer-to-peer model as a way to encourage institutional or cross-institutional engagement. Currently, NOLS is in its early stages of development and it needs to be marketed in order to optimise its everyday usage.

To address political misrepresentation in terms of voice and power, the DOT4D open textbook authors included students in their content creation, giving students a voice in resource development. The DOT4D project provided an example of an embryonic transformative open textbook development model where deliberation of what counts as knowledge, and how it can best be explained, is inclusive of student perspectives.

Aggregated model and recommendations

An ideal model of how OER projects can be funded, and the affordances of this model in terms of how materials can be funded, created, curated, used, adapted and enhanced through community engagement, is one which comprises an aggregate of elements of:

1. the USA central and Canada provincial government model (for funding);
2. the Canada provincial model (a way of employing an institution to manage multi-institutional projects);
3. the UCT and UP inter-institutional as well as the UCT institutional model (for OER creation with a social justice intent and small institutional grants);
4. an OER national repository (an extended linguistic model of what OER Africa currently provides for English materials at a regional level); and
5. a peer-to-peer community to supplement and enhance the use of OER.

DHET has already allocated national funding for the development of a national OER repository. The embryonic NOLS[38] developed by DHET has the ambition to offer "free digital content available specifically to TVET college students through the DHET website, institutional websites, and other sites, where students can find digital materials which will assist them in their learning and preparation for exams"[39]. NOLS can therefore serve as the lynchpin for curating OER and hosting peer-to-peer engagement that enables institutional and inter-institutional development of OER funded centrally and managed by an appointed institution or non-governmental organisation.

This collaborative, social justice-framed model is recommended as being suitable for uptake within the PSET sector. This model should also include resources to support lecturers in the form of copyright clearance, graphic design, editing, and publishing assistance, where needed, as well as small grants to develop materials.

The shortcoming of an institutional model (e.g., UCT) is that only UCT lecturers can add to the institutional repository. For a successful PSET model, all lecturers from any PSET institution should easily be able to add content to NOLS. The content in NOLS should be in various formats and easy to find and use. The commercial model has been deliberately excluded as it does not respond in a socially just manner.

Possible ways in which the aggregated OER model may address social injustices

A question that may be posed about the recommended aggregated OER model, is how it might address the economic, cultural, and political injustices faced by students.

Given the commodification of education and the high cost of educational materials to the students, this aggregated OER model seeks to place a large portion of the funding required on the shoulders of the national government. This is because the government, most particularly with respect to TVET colleges, is responsible through NSFAS for the purchase of key textbooks and resources and would benefit directly from the use of freely available OER and/or open textbooks.

The proposed aggregated OER model offers ways in which to counter the current misrecognition of students' language of choice, and more fundamentally, the value of knowledge systems other than the Western canon. The institutional OER model (e.g., DOT4D project) provides an example of how students can be included in deliberating what counts as valuable knowledge and in which language this could ideally be offered.

Moreover, students can be included as co-creators and/or evaluators of OER, thus increasing their ability to have their voices heard and expanding their decision-making power. Students may therefore have the opportunity to "disrupt dominant and singular hegemonic discourse about HE such as neoliberal views on students as consumers" (Bozalek & Hölscher, 2020, p. 6) and instead relate their academic texts more directly to their lived experience linguistically, epistemologically, and economically.

---

[38] http://nols.gov.za/
[39] https://www.dhet.gov.za/SitePages/NOLS.aspx

Conclusion

In this study, several OER models were considered and classified into the following: regional-geographic, central government, provincial government, inter-institutional, institutional, community, and commercial. The identified central government, provincial and the commercial models addressed key aspects of economic maldistribution by introducing OER and open textbooks to reduce the costs of learning materials for students, but not necessarily to the institution. The regional-geographic, inter-institutional, institutional, and community models provided examples of cultural recognition across countries, including recognition of different local languages and the valorisation of local knowledge systems. The regional geographic/linguistic model provided an example of advocacy for OER across national borders, while the institutional and community models illustrated how student voice can be acknowledged in OER creation and how a community of students can be rallied around the use of OER.

It is therefore suggested that an aggregated OER model, that adopts the ideal features of each of the above models, be adopted for the PSET sector in South Africa. Ideally, government policy should mandate the creation and/or use of OER and provide funding to support this process, for example, through OER small grants (see Chapter 10, this volume). In addition, institutional IP regulations need to be adjusted in order to give individual lecturers the right to publish and share their teaching materials. Once these policies are in motion, the next step could be a coordinated approach within and between PSET institutions to identify and collaboratively develop the most urgently needed teaching materials.

Acknowlegements

Special thanks are due to reviewers Professor Mpine Makoe, Dr Patricia Chikune, Dr Kerry de Hart and Professor James Glapa-Grossklag for their thoughtful, incisive feedback on the chapter, Michelle Willmers for constructive engagement, and Dr Tabisa Mayisela for guiding the entire COOL project. Thanks are also due to the Centre for Innovation in Learning and Teaching at the University of Cape Town, which hosted the COOL project, and the South African Department of Higher Education and Training for funding it.

References

Aesoph, L. M. (2016). *Adaptation guide*. BCcampus. https://opentextbc.ca/adaptopentextbook/

Baker, A., & Ippoliti, C. (2019). Student-driven OER: Championing the student voice in campus-wide efforts. In A. Wesolek, J. Lashley & A. Langley (Eds.), *OER: A field guide for academic librarians*. https://boisestate.pressbooks.pub/oer-field-guide/chapter/student-driven-oer-championing-the-student-voice-in-campus-wide-efforts/

Bozalek, V., Hölscher, D., & Zembylas, M. (Eds.). (2020). *Nancy Fraser and participatory parity: Reframing social justice in South African higher education*. Routledge.

Butcher, N. (2010). Open educational resources and higher education. OER Africa. https://www.oerafrica.org/FTPFolder/understanding/OER%20in%20HE%20concept%20paper.pdf

Butcher, N., & Hoosen, S. (2012). Exploring the business case for open educational resources. Commonwealth of Learning. http://oasis.col.org/bitstream/handle/11599/57/pub_OER_BusinessCase.pdf?sequence=1&isAllowed=y

Cox, G. (2016). Explaining the relation between culture, structure and agency in lecturers' contribution and non-contribution to open educational resources in higher educational institutions [Doctoral dissertation, University of Cape Town]. https://open.uct.ac.za/bitstream/handle/11427/20300/thesis_hum_2016_cox_glenda.pdf?sequence=1&isAllowed=y

Cox, G. (2018). Open access: How digital open textbooks could save students billions. University of Pretoria. https://www.up.ac.za/news/post_2736449-open-access-how-digital-open-textbooks-could-save-students-billions-

Cox, G., Masuku, B., & Willimers, M. (2020). Open textbooks and social justice: Open educational practices to address economic, cultural and political injustice at the University of Cape Town. *Journal of Interactive Media in Education*, 2020(1): 2, 1–10. https://doi.org/10.5334/jime.556

Cronin, C. (2017). Openness and praxis: Exploring the use of open educational practices in higher education. *International Review of Research in Open and Distance Learning*, 18(5), 15–34. http://www.irrodl.org/index.php/irrodl/article/view/3096/4263

DHET (Department of Higher Education and Training). (2017). Open learning policy framework for post-school education and training. *Government Gazette*. https://www.gov.za/documents/higher-education-act-open-learning-policy-framework-south-african-post-school-education

DHET. (2021). Statistics on post-school education and training in South Africa. https://capebpo.org.za/wp-content/uploads/2021/04/Statistics-on-Post-School-Education-and-Training-in-South-Africa2019.pdf

Downes, S. (2007). Models for sustainable open educational resources. *Interdisciplinary Journal of E-Learning and Learning Objects*, 3(1), 29–44. http://ijklo.org/Volume3/IJKLOv3p029-044Downes.pdf

Fraser, N. (1995). From redistribution to recognition? Dilemmas of justice in a 'postsocialist' age. *New Left Review*, 1/212, 68–93. https://newleftreview.org/issues/i212/articles/nancy-fraser-from-redistribution-to-recognition-dilemmas-of-justice-in-a-post-socialist-age

Fraser, N. (2005). Reframing justice in a globalizing world. *New Left Review*, 36, 69–88.

Grimaldi, P. J, Mallick D. B., Waters, A. E., & Baraniuk, R. G. (2019). Do open educational resources improve students' learning? Implications of the access hypothesis. *PLoS One*, 14(3), e0212508.

Gröblinger, O., Kopp, M., & Zimmermann, C. (2018). Students as active contributors in the creation of open educational resources. *INTED2018 Proceedings* (pp. 2260–2269). https://library.iated.org/view/GROBLINGER2018STU

Henderson, S., & Ostashewski, N. (2018). Barriers, incentives, and benefits of the open educational resources (OER) movement: An exploration into instructor perspectives. *First Monday*, 23(12). https://doi.org/10.5210/fm.v23i12.9172

Hodgkinson-Williams, C. (2014). Degrees of ease: Adoption of OER, open textbooks and MOOCs in the Global South. OER Asia Symposium 2014. https://open.uct.ac.za/handle/11427/1188

Hodgkinson-Williams, C., & Paskevicius, M. (2012). The role of post-graduate students in co-authoring open educational resources to promote social inclusion: A case study at the University of Cape Town. *Distance Education*, 33(2), 253–269.

Hodgkinson-Williams C., & Trotter, H. (2018). A social justice framework for understanding open educational resources and practices in the Global South. *Journal of Learning for Development*, 5(3): 204–224.

Hodgkinson-Williams, C., Arinto, P.B., Cartmill, T., & King, T. (2017). Factors influencing Open Educational Practices and OER in the Global South: Meta-synthesis of the ROER4D project. In C. Hodgkinson-Williams & P.B. Arinto (Eds.), *Adoption and impact of OER in the Global South* (pp. 27-67). African Minds, IDRC & ROER4D. https://doi.org/10.5281/zenodo.1037088

Hoosen, S., & Butcher, N. (2019). *Understanding the impact of OER: Achievements and challenges*. UNESCO Institute for Information Technologies in Education. https://www.oerafrica.org/system/files/13390/understandingtheimpactofoer2019-1.pdf?file=1&type=node&id=13390&force=1

Hylen, J., & Schuller, T. (2007). Giving knowledge for free. *OECD Observer*, 263, 21–22. https://oecdobserver.org/news/archivestory.php/aid/2348/Giving_knowledge_for_free.html

ICTS (Information and Communication Technology Services). (2021). Zero-rated mobile data access to specific UCT online resources. University of Cape Town. http://www.icts.uct.ac.za/Zero-rated-access-some-UCT-websites

Jhangiani, R. (2020). Kwantlen Polytechnic University. In S. Hare, J. Kirschner, & M. Reed (Eds.), *Marking open and affordable courses: Best practices and case studies*. Mavs Open Press. https://uta.pressbooks.pub/markingopenandaffordablecourses/

Jhangiani, R. S., Dastur, F. N., Le Grand, R., & Penner, K. (2018). As good or better than commercial textbooks: Students' perceptions and outcomes from using open digital and open print textbooks. *The Canadian Journal for the Scholarship of Teaching and Learning*, 9(1). https://ir.lib.uwo.ca/cjsotl_rcacea/vol9/iss1/5

Jung, E., Bauer, C., & Heaps, A. (2017). Strategic implementation of open educational resources in higher education institutions. *Educational Technology*, 78–84. https://www.jstor.org/stable/44430530

Lambert, S. R. (2018). Changing our (dis)course: A distinctive social justice aligned definition of open education. *Journal of Learning for Development*, 5(3). https://jl4d.org/index.php/ejl4d/article/view/290

Lesko, L. (2013). The use and production of OER & OCW in teaching in South African higher education institutions. (Case Study). *Open Praxis* 5(2), 103–121. https://pdfs.semanticscholar.org/1f25/14284bcf4f46848983570e9fb3402b6b9669.pdf

Luckett, K., & Shay, S. (2017). Reframing the curriculum: A transformative approach. *Critical Studies in Education*, 61(1), 50–65. https://www.tandfonline.com/doi/full/10.1080/17508487.2017.1356341

OECD (Organisation for Economic Co-operation and Development). (2007). *Giving knowledge for free: The emergence of open educational resources*. http://www.oecd.org/education/ceri/38654317.pdf

Okoro, H. C. (2013). Importance of creative commons licensing and the creative commons movement to open education resources initiatives in Nigeria. Nigerian Institute of Advanced Legal Studies (NIALS). http://oasis.col.org/bitstream/handle/11599/1826/2013_Chuma-Okoro_CreativeCommons.pdf

Ossiannilsson, E., & Hoel, T. (2015). OER in the Nordic countries the Nordic OER project. http://hoel.nu/files/oer14_Ossiannilsson_Hoel_OER_in_the%20_Nordic_countries_The%20NORDICOER%20Project.pdf

Paskevicius, M. (2011). Student perceptions of the reuse of digital educational materials: A case study of the social outreach group SHAWCO [Master's dissertation, University of Cape Town]. http://michaelpaskevicius.com/wp-content/uploads/2016/12/mpaskevicius_final_v7_edits.pdf

ROER4D (Research on Open Educational Resources for Development). (2017). *Spotlight on OER policy in the Global South: Case studies from the ROER4D project*. African Minds, IDRC & ROER4D. https://doi.org/10.5281/zenodo.844695

UNESCO (United Nations Educational, Scientific and Cultural Organization). (2020a). Global education meeting: Extraordinary session on education post-COVID-19. Background document. UNESCO. https://en.unesco.org/sites/default/files/gem2020-extraordinary-session-background-document-en.pdf

UNESCO. (2020b). OER dynamic coalition consultancy. UNESCO. https://en.unesco.org/themes/building-knowledge-societies/oer/dynamic-coalition

Zapata, G. (2020). Sprinting to the finish line: The benefits and challenges of book sprints in OER faculty-graduate student collaborations. *International Review of Research in Open and Distributed Learning*, 21(2), 1–17.

HOW TO CITE THIS CHAPTER

Dabula, A., Cox, G., & Hodgkinson-Williams, C. A. (2022). Insights on OER adoption models to inform ways of opening up learning materials to address economic, cultural and political injustices in South African education. In T. Mayisela, S. C. Govender & C. A. Hodgkinson-Williams (Eds.), *Open learning as a means of advancing social justice: Cases in post-school education and training in South Africa* (pp. 199–216). African Minds. doi: 10.47622/9781928502425_9

This work is licensed under a Creative Commons Attribution 4.0 International (CC BY 4.0) licence.

10

Advancing social justice through small grants for the development of open educational resources at the University of Cape Town and the Cape Peninsula University of Technology

Mahlatse Maake-Malatji & Glenda Cox

SUMMARY The Department of Higher Education and Training's (DHET) draft *Open Learning Policy Framework* (OLPF) *for Post-School Education and Training* (PSET) situates the creation and sharing of open educational resources (OER) at the heart of the open learning agenda. The OLFP suggests a range of diverse funding strategies to support the development of OER in the PSET sector. This study aims to explore the use of one funding strategy, namely small OER grants, at two higher education institutions in South Africa. This case study employs a qualitative research methodology, and interviews were conducted with a purposive sample of OER grant managers and grant recipients (lecturers and support staff) at the University of Cape Town and the Cape Peninsula University of Technology in order to highlight how these small-scale OER grants have supported the development of OER at their respective institutions. Moving from the premise that DHET's conception of open learning has a social justice intent, the study uses Nancy Fraser's (2005) theory of social justice, which includes the economic, cultural, and political dimensions of social justice, to appraise in what ways, if at all, these funding initiatives may be contributing to socially just education. This study found that economic support in the form of small grants alleviated OER development costs, although, in some instances, the funds did not cover the full costs of development. The creation of OER enabled a degree of cultural recognition of marginalized groups through the translation and production of locally contextualised resources. From the standpoint of political representation, most grant recipients collaborated with students and thus, to some extent, incorporated the student voice into the creation of resources. The study is important in that it provides recommendations on how DHET could provide relatively modest, targeted resourcing to support OER development projects so that these resources can be re-used by other institutions or as individual learners.

Keywords: open learning, open educational resources, small grants, social justice, university

Introduction

One of the key challenges facing higher education institutions is the increasing cost of teaching and learning resources. For example, in the United States, university textbook costs are calculated to have risen at more than triple the inflation rate since the late 1970s[1]. As a response, there is growing support for developing open educational resources (OER) initiatives worldwide (Brown et al., 2020; Hylén, 2006; Phillips, 2018). However, the time and expertise required to develop OER, including open textbooks, comes at a cost, so funding is essential. On a global scale, foundations such as the William and Flora Hewlett Foundation led the way in funding OER projects; however, funding for OER remains limited[1].

A fundamental approach to driving adoption of OER is providing lecturers funding to create, adopt or adapt open textbooks or resources. One of the ways in which this resourcing can be provided is in the form of small grants to enable the creation and/or adaptation of OER (Albro et al., 2020). Relatively small injections of funding can support the development of OER such as some of the examples discussed later in this chapter. Therefore, the promise of OER is the availability of free and legally shareable teaching and learning resources for all to retain, reuse, and even remix and redistribute. Stacey (2013) also claims that there is a growing awareness that governments can generate significant public benefits by supporting OER through incentive funding.

In South Africa, the government's *White Paper for Post-School Education and Training* (DHET, 2013) recognises the inequalities that exist in relation to access to learning opportunities. This *White Paper* recommended incorporating OER as one of the ways to build an expanded, effective, and integrated post-school system and mentions that assistance in the development of OER will be from the public and private organizations.

DHET's *Open Learning Policy Framework* (OLPF) *for Post-School Education and Training* (PSET) takes the idea of openness forward. It proposes a series of open learning principles, aimed at encouraging the current educational system to be open by increasing access to learning opportunities, improving the quality of the curriculum and learning experience, and improving student success. Open learning is defined in the OLPF as:

> an educational approach combining principles of learner-centeredness, lifelong learning, flexibility of learning provision, removal of barriers to access learning, recognition for credit of prior learning experience, provision of learner support, construction of learning programmes in the expectation that learners can succeed, and *maintenance of rigorous quality assurance over the design of learning materials* and support systems. (DHET, 2017, p. 363)

Amongst the priorities of DHET's OLPF is to identify and allocate sufficient resourcing to implement this framework. To this end, DHET commits to incorporating resourcing in the national funding allocation for institutions, as well as determining "funding norms and provid[ing] guidelines for funding open learning" (DHET, 2017, p. 410).

---

[1] https://opentextbc.ca/workinggroupguide/chapter/identify-funding-resources-support/

The chapter reports on the investigation of an aspect of open learning, namely the development of OER and specifically how two South African universities have used small grants to incentivise the creation of OER. OER grants are usually relatively small amounts of money that OER developers can use to employ a student, illustrator, graphic designer and/or a person skilled in editing to assist in the production process. As part of the Cases on Open Learning (COOL) project, the study hopes to inform policymakers, higher education management, and philanthropic agencies about the importance of relatively small grants for OER development.

Background of the study

In order to better understand the role of small grants in relation to social justice, we need to locate this practice within the open education landscape, internationally, regionally and locally.

Open educational resources

The open education movement has been seen as a "means of contributing to the challenge of expansion of scale and opportunity and lowering cost in particular in post-secondary education" (Tait, 2018, p. 111). Commencing in the late 1990s with initiatives such as the MIT OpenCourseWare project[2], which provided "free scholarly material" and the Connexions project at Rice University which in addition, released "software tools to help authors publish and collaborate" to assist lecturers to "build rapidly and share custom courses and learners explore the links among concepts, courses, and disciplines" (Atkins et al., 2007, p. 10).

In 2002, UNESCO coined the term "open educational resources" in order to assist the global community to optimise information sharing about what was then referred to as 'free scholarly material', 'open content', 'learning objects', 'open courseware', etc. (see Arinto et al., 2017). OER are teaching, learning, and research resources that have been released under an intellectual property license that permits them to be freely used, or re-purposed by anyone (Arinto et al., 2017). These resources may include videos, curriculum maps, course materials, textbooks, streaming videos, multimedia applications, podcasts, and any other materials that have been designed for use in teaching and learning. According to Bliss and Smith (2017), in order to be considered open, a resource should, at minimum, be freely available, and openly licensed for distribution and use. Additionally, resources may be licensed as open for adaptation, allowing users to 'remix' resources without cost.

The existence of OER is underpinned by practices that enable their creation and use. Hodgkinson-Williams et al. (2017) assert that open educational practices (OEP) that undergird OER include: individual or collaborative conceptualisation; creation, curation (retention), circulation (distribution) of OER through practices such as open pedagogies; crowdsourcing; and open peer review using open technologies so that they can be easily located to encourage copying (re-use 'as-is'), adaptation, re-curation and re-circulation. In other words, "for OER to exist, there must of necessity be prior OEP" (Hodgkinson-Williams

---

[2] The MIT OpenCourseWare project and the Connexions project were both funded by the William and Flora Hewlett Foundation.

et al., 2017, p. 31). Furthermore, the concepts of OEP and OER are intrinsically bound with a commitment to equity and social justice in education (Lambert, 2018).

In the South African context, the ambition to provide 'access to free education' to higher education institutions (HEIs) can be linked to ideas of OEP and OER. Free tuition for higher education should be supported by access to free accessible study material, created and made available by academics and other supporting bodies. In this regard, OER can act as a potential mechanism to address the inequality associated with a lack of access to study materials.

In South African HEIs, the cost of educational resources is one of the major hindrances to learning.[3] While the South African government provides financial aid to assist students from disadvantaged backgrounds, this funding does not cover all students' needs, particularly as textbooks become more expensive year by year (Nkosi, 2014). OER can potentially give every student access to course materials, as the cost of these materials is taken out of the equation.[4]

Although the creation and sharing of OER can potentially improve access to resources through reducing costs, such creation is time-consuming and a resource-intensive task (Whitfield & Robinson, 2012). In addition, as these materials are usually distributed via the internet, there will obviously be connectivity costs unless the Internet Service Provider has zero-rated the relevant OER sites. Unfortunately, OER approaches or initiatives still appear to be an 'add on' in education systems rather than being part of a mainstream approach to creating and adopting materials (Hoosen & Butcher, 2019). Thus, OER need integrated and sustainable business models and, most importantly, sustainable funding (Butcher & Hoosen, 2012; Stacey, 2010).

Funding OER

Funding for OER has taken a number of foci including, supporting the creation of OER, the reuse of OER, and the dissemination of OER via repositories and platforms. Historically, initial funding for OER has been offered by private donors, before being taken up in more permanent ways by institutions and governments. In this section, we look at the funding landscape in which the small grants initiatives are located.

Donor organisations have, in the past, and continue to provide funding for the conceptualisation, development and publication of OER (Brown & Adler, 2008). Key international supporters of OER have included the Hewlett (Bliss & Smith, 2017), Andrew W. Mellon, and Bill and Melinda Gates Foundations (Casserly & Smith, 2008). Historically, in Africa, funding for OER in English has been provided by international donors, through a small selection of institutions. For example, the Hewlett Foundation funded a consortium of institutions and an NGO for a cross regional project Africa Health OER Network (Hoosen & Omollo 2010). Another initiative that supported the development of OER was a project that brought together eight African countries to create the Teacher Education in Sub-Saharan Africa (TESSA[5]) project, supported by the Open University of the UK, and initially funded by

---

[3] https://www.oerafrica.org/content/creative-commons-and-access-knowledge

[4] https://canvas.instructure.com/courses/815700/pages/the-importance-of-open-education-resources.#:~:targetText=OER%20gives%20a%20wide%20variety

[5] https://www.tessafrica.net/supporters

the Alan and Nesta Ferguson Charitable Trust, supported by Open University alumni, and subsequently by the William and Flora Hewlett Foundation.

According to Hoosen and Butcher (2019), the adoption of OER in South Africa is increasing, supported by funding from international donors, administered by institutions and government agencies, but is not yet a mainstream practice (Mays, 2020). Government funding of OER in South Africa has, to date, two forms: the support for creation of OER, and support for the creation of a national repository. For example, DHET funded the development of a multilingual glossary of key academic terms for university education, called the OER Term Bank. Its development was undertaken by a partnership between the University of Pretoria and UCT (Butcher & Hoosen, 2019). DHET has also committed to develop and establish a National Open Learning System (NOLS), in South Africa "funded initially through the European Union Sectoral Support Programmes Budget. Funding has been secured for the implementation of the initial and second phases of the Open Learning initiative, up to 2025" (DHET, 2013, p. 411). However, the duration of such funding is limited, thus, looking forward, financial and other forms of support for OER must become part of mainstream practice (Hoosen & Butcher, 2019). Furthermore, the recent DHET commitment to NOLS is likely to limit the funding directly available to staff and students for the development of OER.

Small (or mini) grants for the creation and adaptation of OER

In their review of ways to incentivise the production and use of OER in HEIs, Annand and Jensen (2017) identify the provision of small grants as one strategy to enable and sustain OER creation and adaptation. These small or mini-grants (McGowan, 2020; Todorinova & Wilkinson, 2020) can be sourced from donors (Stacey, 2010) or crowdfunding initiatives awarded directly to institutions[6] and then re-granted to academics or senior students[7]. According to the University of Kansas Libraries, the goal of small grants is to encourage instructor experimentation and innovation in finding new, better, and less costly ways to deliver learning materials to their students through OER (Bardoloi, 2016). As far back as 2011, the University of Massachusetts Amherst Libraries established their Open Education Initiative (OEI), which includes crowdfunding, to provide small grants to "instructors who wish to flip their classes from expensive textbooks to OER"[8]. Also initiated in the library, the University of Wyoming provides grants, but of various amounts to cover costs for faculty depending upon the effort required to adopt, adapt, or create an OER text for a particular course (Smith et al., 2021).

In Canada, British Columbia provided funding to BCcampus to manage OER grants for other institutions in the province. These institutions regranted funds in the form of small grants to academics and/or senior students. In 2016, Kwantlen Polytechnic University (KPU) received funding from BCcampus to offer and manage an OER small grant programme (up to $2,000 per team) to support teaching staff to adapt or create OER[9]. Subsequently some of the funding for these small grants has been taken over by some institutions involved with BCcampus. For example, the British Columbia Institute of Technology (BCIT), now provides

---

[6] https://bccampus.ca/open-education-sustainability-grant-for-institutions/
[7] http://www.dot4d.uct.ac.za/
[8] https://minutefund.umass.edu/project/21870
[9] https://teachonline.ca/tools-trends/implementation-open-educational-resources-kwantlen-polytechnic-university-vancouver-british-columbia

small grants (up to $5,000) to support the development of OER (e.g., test banks, case studies, slide presentations), or the redesign of a course to incorporate OER and OEP[10].

This study investigates the role of small or mini OER grants to support the development of OER at the University of Cape Town (UCT)[11] and the Cape Peninsula University of Technology (CPUT)[12]. These institutions will be used as case studies to better understand the role of OER grants as a way of opening up educational materials in higher education institutions. The study will consider the challenges and opportunities experienced by the grant recipients in developing OER using these small grants.

Social justice and OER grants

In this study, Fraser's (2005) social justice theoretical framework is used to explain how OER grants support the development of OER in order to contribute to socially just education. Social justice is a philosophical construct that requires the organisation of 'social arrangements' that make it possible for everyone to participate equally (Fraser 2008, 2009). In this regard, social justice is construed as *'participatory parity'* along three dimensions: economic, cultural, and political (Fraser, 2005). Fraser emphasises that all three dimensions are intermeshed and that there can be "no redistribution or recognition without representation" (2005, p. 76). Responses to these injustices may, according to Fraser, be described as affirmative or transformative — "affirmative strategies seek to make ameliorative changes in unjust outcomes while transformative strategies seek to address the underlying causes of these unjust outcomes" (Leibowitz & Bozalek, 2016, as cited in De Kadt, 2019, p. 4).

Economic dimension

'Free' OER would assist in addressing economic injustice — what Fraser refers to as *maldistribution* — where there is a lack of *"just distribution of resources and goods"* (Fraser, 1998, p. 1) to the recipients or re-users of OER. These OER re-users, editors, curators and re-distributors can be other academics, students and self-learners — all of whom experience personal benefits as a result of access to OER. However, as the creation process bears a cost, as mentioned earlier, the actual creators of OER may experience an inherent economic injustice if the time that they spend creating OER is not adequately recompensed. There are examples of OER created with no additional grants or funding (Cox, 2016). If academics are developing these materials during the course of their preparation for their existing courses and can claim this as part of their teaching time, then an economic injustice will not have been perpetrated. However, if these academics or students develop OER in their own time and thus incur personal costs, then maldistribution of time and resources may be at play. This maldistribution of time and resources though, may not be perceived as economic injustice by the OER creators as they may willingly and altruistically give up some of their time and effort for the greater good of education. The challenge is how this altruism, especially in updating OER, can be maintained over time and whether this is truly economically just.

---

[10] https://commons.bcit.ca/library/2019/01/17/open-education-grants-at-bcit-apply-now-2/

[11] The University of Cape Town (UCT) is a public research university located in Cape Town in the Western Cape province of South Africa. UCT was founded in 1829 as the South African College making it the oldest higher education institute in South Africa.

[12] The Cape Peninsula University of Technology is the only university of technology in the Western Cape.

Research on OER in South African institutions of higher education has generally been focused on ways in which institutions may support the creation, production and adoption of OER (Chikuni et al., 2019; Cox & Trotter, 2017, 2019; Hoosen & Butcher, 2019), without carefully considering the economic implications. Where OER initiatives have been undertaken at an institution-wide level, they have usually received significant funding (Abelson et al., 2012), but this still requires attention to be paid to the longer-term sustainability of such initiatives. DHET has shown that it is willing to fund cross-institutional OER development activities such as the OER Term Bank, which is an encouraging development (Hoosen & Butcher, 2019).

In order to sustain and expand OER development, government and public funding should be in place, if possible, from an early stage to set solid foundations (Stacey 2010). In a blog written in 2013 by McGill, the sustainability of OER is held to be:

> closely linked to the business model or approach that an individual, group or institution adopts to release, manage and support OER. It is not just about sustaining existing OER but about embedding processes and transforming practices to support ongoing OER production and release.[13]

Hoosen and Butcher assert that where there is no clear, allocated funding, "OER initiatives are not sustainable" (2019, p. 12).

Cultural dimension

The study also highlights cultural dimensions of social justice, which function through misrecognition of cultural value and identity. The lack of recognition of various cultural differences results in what Fraser refers to as 'cultural misrecognition' (2005). Recognition is possible where valorisation of group differences is associated with mainstream multiculturalism (Fraser & Honneth, 2003). Cultural misrecognition denies equality on the basis of a range of aspects, including the languages in which OER are written and the epistemic assumptions of what counts as valuable knowledge worth sharing.

Rets calls attention to the fact that "most OERs are offered in English, and their language level creates a barrier to many potential learners who are non-native English readers" and accentuates that this does "not suit the inclusive rhetoric of OERs" (2021, p. ii). Although English has been highly instrumental in disseminating knowledge through OER, it is not understood by the vast majority of the world's population (McGreal, 2017). It is important to recognise various languages because language plays a pivotal role in using and adopting OER worldwide (Karakaya & Karakaya, 2020). Fortunately, the open licensing provisions of OER can include translation and thus provide the opportunity to those who understand English well enough to render the original into the language of choice.

However, translating OER is not just a matter of what Rets refers to as "linguistic accessibility" (2021, p. ii), but is also a matter of epistemology, in other words, whose perspective knowledge is being privileged in the translation. Hodgkinson-Williams and Trotter note the challenges associated with translating resources explaining that:

---

[13] https://openeducationalresources.pbworks.com/w/page/26789871/Sustainability

> While translation may change the linguistic interface through which students engage with this knowledge, it may not do much to alter the underlying frames of reference upon which that knowledge is built. In contexts where the translation of foreign language OER might contribute to a broader erosion of locally derived ways of knowing, this otherwise pedagogically practical form of OEP might also inadvertently reinforce or deepen prevailing cultural inequalities. (2018, p. 214)

Hence the challenge is to develop OER locally to include context-specific case studies and perspectives. This can affirm local epistemologies, thereby addressing what Fraser terms 'cultural misrecognition'. For a more transformative response Fraser posits: "What requires recognition is not group-specific identity but rather the status of group members as full partners in social interaction" (Fraser, 2001, p. 113).

Currently, OER tends to privilege Western cultures in which the relevance of non-English materials is limited (OECD, 2007). As most OER producers and projects are located in English-speaking countries in the developed world, this widens up inequalities by exacerbating the cultural and epistemic injustices in the world (Arinto et al., 2017; Cox et al., 2020).

OER inherently reveals cultural dimensions in that they give users "an insight into culture-specific methods and approaches to teaching and learning" (Albright, 2005). There is a potential wealth of multicultural and multilingual educational resources in Africa, waiting for proper structures and resources to transform them into OER (OECD, 2007). However, the resources, time and skills required to localize and translate OER created in English for adaptation and reuse into other languages are underestimated and underappreciated.[14]

Political dimension

Fraser's political dimension directs our attention to issues of ordinary (or first order) political representation, and second-order or "frame-setting" (Fraser, 2009, p. 15) in relation to questions of justice.

Representation and misrepresentation

Hodgkinson-Williams and Trotter interpret the issues of *political representation*, in relation to OER in the following way:

> Who has the right to decide on what counts as worthwhile knowledge, who decides on school and university curricula and who publishes and disseminates textbooks, journals, etc.? (2018, p. 5)

The application for, allocation and, subsequent, provision of mini-grants can raise the issue of 'political misrepresentation', asking who can apply for a mini grant, how funds are allocated and for what activities, and how such processes are monitored and evaluated. As mini-grants are awarded in support of the creation and adaptation of OER, the question of representations encourages us to widen who is supported in creation and adaptation processes. Cox et al. (2020) note that open textbook authors at UCT involve students in

---

[14] https://oloer.opened.ca/

content development processes to shift power dynamics and build confidence in students' ability to contribute.

Framing and misframing

Hölscher et al. (2020) describe framing decisions as focusing on "admission criteria and procedures concerning the award or denial of membership" (2020, p. 12). Thus, "framing issues are issues of scope and pertain to the question of who does and who does not count as subject of justice" (Hölscher, 2014, p. 24). Interpreted in this way, Fraser's notion of "frame-setting" (2005, p. 80) offers mini-grant processes a democratising perspective on the offering, allocation and monitoring of mini-grants – asking not only who is included or excluded in a process, but also to whom prospective and eventual grantholders may appeal in instances of exclusion.

Student input to OER, as creators or co-creators (Baker & Ippoliti, 2018), and as users are often not explicitly supported in grant briefs and eligibility criteria. However, the DOT4D project, based at UCT, specifically foregrounded support for the "inclusion of marginalised and student voices" in their call for proposals.[15] Such choices deliberately expand the criteria for eligibility for grants to include students, and to prioritise staff working with students to create a more inclusive framing.

Research methodology

In order to investigate how OER grants supported the development of OER, two universities, namely UCT and CPUT, were purposively selected, as they publicly advertised OER grants on their websites at the time the research project commenced[16]. The main research question is: *How have Open Educational Resources grants supported the development of OER in order to contribute to more socially just higher education?*

The study adopted a broadly qualitative approach, using in-depth interviews to ascertain the impact of small institutional grants to support the development of OER. In order to prepare for the interviews, publicly available information on the respective institutions' websites were consulted.

The interviews consisted of eight participants, three grant recipients and one OER manager from each institution. Participants were chosen based on a purposive method of sampling in order to build up an understanding of OER grant funding for creation and adaptation from 'knowledgeable people' (Cohen et al., 2017). All grant recipients were academics, except one support staff member (a courseware developer) at CPUT. Grant recipients in both institutions were from various disciplines, including Construction Economics and Management, Health Sciences, Environmental and Geographical Science, Industrial and Systems Engineering, Civil Engineering and Surveying, and the Centre for Innovative Educational Technology (CIET). Due to the COVID-19 pandemic, the interviews were conducted online via Zoom for an hour and more.

---

[15] DOT4D http://www.dot4d.uct.ac.za/news/uct-launches-call-digital-open-textbook-development-proposals

[16] Subsequently the North West University has also advertised OER grants: https://education.nwu.ac.za/UNESCO-chair-OER-Fellows

Two sets of standardised questions were prepared beforehand and shared with the grant recipients and OER managers in both institutions. Both institutions granted ethical clearance before we identified participants and conducted the interviews. Written consent from all participants was received before the interviews.

Interviews with recipients and managers at the two institutions enabled us to understand a wide range of issues in relation to these roles and compare their different contexts and approaches. OER grant recipients were interviewed because of their experience in the development of OER. OER grant managers were interviewed to provide a clear understanding of the scope and administration of these OER grants. Grant recipients were interviewed to ascertain the process of developing OER, as well as challenges and successes experienced while developing OER.

Interviews were transcribed by the first author and moved into *MS Excel* and coded deductively (Fereday & Muir-Cochrane, 2006) using the social justice framework and other key concepts that emerged during the literature review and inductively from the new categories that emerged from the specific responses to the research questions. With assistance from the assigned mentor and the principal lead, the author organized the codes into different themes to manage and organize the collected data. The data was reduced accordingly to assist in answering the relevant questions posed to the interviewees.

Contextualising the cases

Although both UCT and CPUT offer mini-grants for OER, the differences between the trajectories of development of these funding mechanisms, coupled with different socio-economic positions, offer a useful opportunity to explore the impacts of mini-grants in their contexts.

University of Cape Town

UCT has been engaged in the scholarship of open education since 2007. In that year, two UCT researchers contributed to the formulation of the Cape Town Open Education Declaration (CTOED), which aims to "accelerate efforts to promote open resources, technology and teaching practices in education"[17]. At the time, the Centre for Educational Technology (currently known as Centre for Innovation in Learning and Teaching) received its first grant from the Shuttleworth Foundation to explore the potential of open scholarship, which included OER. The Shuttleworth Foundation funded a follow-up project called OER UCT from 2008 to 2009. This initiative provided a support structure to academics engaged in OER production, particularly related to content licensing and curation.[18] The project was instrumental in surfacing a nascent network of 'open champions' and highlighting the authentic desire of academics at UCT to share their work products in teaching and research

---

[17] https://www.capetowndeclaration.org/
[18] http://www.cilt.uct.ac.za/cilt/oer-uct

contexts.[19] OER UCT subsequently developed a Drupal-based OER referatory[20] for UCT to provide a place for UCT academics to share OER.[21]

In 2013, funded by Canada's International Development Research Centre, the Research on Open Educational Resources for Development (ROER4D) project was initiated and lasted for five years.[22] This project contributed to a Global South research perspective on how OER can help to improve access, enhance quality and reduce the cost of education in the Global South.[23]

UCT funded one internal OER project, namely the Vice-Chancellor's OER Adaptation Project, which started from 2013 to 2016 (King, 2017). The purpose of this project was to fund students to assist lecturers to convert traditional teaching materials in the Humanities, Commerce, Science, and Engineering and the Built Environment Faculties to OER and grow the UCT open content collection.[24] According to Cox and Claassen (2016) these small grants of up to R10 000 supported academics in creating or adapting OER.

The UCT Open Access Policy adopted by the Council in June 2014, and updated in 2020, provides the basis for the university to preserve the scholarly work of UCT scholars and to make this scholarship discoverable, visible and freely available online to anyone who seeks it.[25] However, there are noticeably no funding provisions stipulated in the policy for creating OER per se, even though ad hoc OER grants are issued from time to time.

Another such ad hoc grant, the UCT Teaching Innovation Grant, was made available in 2018 to individuals or teams who were engaged in developing departmental, programme or faculty level innovations of curricula or courses which aimed at improving student learning, including the design of digital materials for blended or online learning as well as OER.[26] The same call was made in 2020 to improve learning, focusing on curricula and materials for emergency remote teaching and exploring the use of OERs.[27]

A nascent cultural shift occured when the UCT Open Textbook Award was instituted in 2020 "to incentivise innovation in teaching and learning, recognise the efforts of open textbook authors, and promote the creation and reuse of open educational resources".[28]

---

[19] http://www.cilt.uct.ac.za/cilt/oer-uct

[20] A referatory points to various content on online repositories.

[21] See http://www.cilt.uct.ac.za/cilt/projects/past-projects. The OER referatory, UCT Open Content, was superseded by the OpenUCT repository which was made available to share OER as well as pre-prints and student theses and dissertations (http://open.uct.ac.za/).

[22] The project was initiated from 2013 to 2018. The ROER4D project sought to build on and contribute to the body of research on how OER can help to improve access, enhance quality and reduce the cost of education in the Global South (http://www.cilt.uct.ac.za/cilt/roer4d). Other funders included the UK's Department for International Development (DFID) and the Open Society Foundations (OFS).

[23] http://www.cilt.uct.ac.za/cilt/special-projects#roer4d

[24] http://www.cilt.uct.ac.za/cilt/VCs-oer

[25] http://www.uct.ac.za/sites/default/files/image_tool/images/328/about/policies/Policy_Open_Access_2020.pdf

[26] https://www.news.uct.ac.za/images/userfiles/files/media/email/TGA2-Teaching-Innovation-Grants-application-form-2018.pdf. The same call was made in 2019.

[27] https://www.news.uct.ac.za/article/-2020-07-27-call-for-applications-uct-teaching-innovation-grant

[28] http://www.cilt.uct.ac.za/cilt/open/otaward

The Cape Peninsula University of Technology (CPUT)

At CPUT, the institution has an Open Access policy, but it does not stipulate any funding provision for OER development, although this has become a practice. CPUT has also received several grants to support such initiatives within the institution. In April 2010, a workshop on OER in Teaching and Learning was conducted to introduce participants to the concept of OER and highlight some of the benefits and challenges of creating or using OER.[29] In collaboration with UCT, the Educational Technology Unit presented a workshop focusing on the design and use of OER in 2016.[30]

In 2018, CIET offered funding to the value of R10 000 to lecturers interested in developing OER at CPUT.[31] Funding was provided by DHET through the University Capacity Development Grant (UCDG). An additional project, *Exploring OER practices at CPUT*, funded by the Teaching Development Grant, explored current perceptions and practices around OER by staff and students at CPUT.[32] During the first phase of this project, data was collected through a survey instrument and the second phase involved supporting academics interested in developing OER for their teaching.[33]

The information above was gleaned from existing articles and websites. However, it is not clear how many grants were provided, how many were successfully implemented and in what ways the creation and dissemination of OER at these institutions had any discernible influence on ameliorating economic, cultural and political injustices as a means to facilitate student access and success. In this case study, OER grant managers and grant recipients were interviewed to answer these questions.

Findings

The findings presented here are based on the interviews of both grant recipients and OER grant managers from CPUT and UCT. The approaches of the two institutions will be described, including details of how the various grants were administered. The actual OER developed from each institution will be described, and the accessibility of these resources will be outlined. Grant recipients were involved in different kinds of collaboration in the OER development process. Two main forms of collaboration occurred: grant recipients worked with students and, in some cases, external experts. This section will end with a discussion about the challenges experienced by grant recipients during the production process.

There was consensus across all grant recipients and OER grant managers in both institutions that there is a need to create more contextually relevant OER. Both OER grant managers also suggested that this development must be encouraged at an institutional level. In addition, lockdown conditions in 2020 due to the COVID-19 pandemic (at the time of the interviews) pivoted institutions towards emergency remote teaching, which has been

---

[29] https://www.cput.ac.za/about/facts/174-news/institutional-memos/5913-open-educational-resources-in-teaching-and-learning. This workshop was facilitated by Associate Professor Cheryl Hodgkinson-Williams from the University of Cape Town. In addition, the workshop provided participants with hands-on activities to find existing OER through international portals and run through the steps of re-purposing an existing OER or developing a new OER.

[30] http://www.cput.ac.za/blogs/oer/2016/06/15/open-educational-resources-pilot-kicks-off-with/

[31] http://www.cput.ac.za/blogs/oer/2018/06/07/2018-oer-projects-call-for-participation/

[32] http://www.cput.ac.za/services/ciet/projects

[33] http://www.cput.ac.za/services/ciet/projects

regarded as a motivator for lecturers to look for OER and identify content that would be suitable and accessible to their students. With respect to the grants, UCT invited applications from all staff and recommended that they consider initiating collaborations with students or other academics.

Some of the conditions attached to the grants at UCT included: educators could either create resources from scratch or adapt existing resources; thus, they had to "argue for the fact that this was something that hadn't been invented anywhere"; "the money should be spent on students or someone to assist to develop materials" (UCT Grant Manager), and the resources developed were required to be uploaded to the institutional repository. The UCT Grant Manager further reported that OER grant applicants had to demonstrate that there was an educational gap or a need and describe how the OER was related to their courses. UCT ran a project, Digital Open Textbooks for Development (2018–2021), which included grants for the development of digital open textbooks in which curriculum transformation, collaboration and inclusion of students were criteria for selection (UCT Grant Manager).

CPUT's grant conditions stipulated that the grant applicants were required to provide a detailed description of the project, including: "the educational value to be added by the planned resource; how the resource will be sustained in the future; and how the recipient intended to use the grant" (CPUT Grant Manager). Like UCT, these OER had to be shared on the institutional repository. OER creators at CPUT were further encouraged to reuse materials developed in the institution "and to contextualize them for their students" (CPUT Grant Manager) and stipulated that the OER represent local content.

Institutional grants systems

The data from the interviews revealed that funding for small grants originated from various sources, including private organisations, the institutions themselves and the government. The OER grant manager at UCT explained their sources of funding which included the: "Mellon Fund from 2011 to 2014 ... We also had additional funds from the Vice-Chancellors' fund ... I administered 89 grants with a total value of R860 000" (UCT Grant Manager). At CPUT, the OER Grant Manager revealed that funding was received from "the University Capacity Development Grant – a teaching and learning support grant from the Department of Higher Education and Training and as part of that we have run the OER project three times ... in 2016, 2017, and 2019" and "each year we have [had] about R100,000 that we can distribute among participants"

In both institutions, grant recipients received R10 000 each, except one recipient at UCT, who received R7 500. One grant recipient in each institution received an OER grant more than once. Grant recipients from both universities acknowledged the privilege of receiving a grant to enhance this kind of work. A grant recipient at UCT noted that the resources would not have been created without the grant. Similarly, two grant recipients at CPUT noted: "I wouldn't have done it without the grant ... I wouldn't have produced it in the first place ... I wouldn't have had the better ones, in different languages" (CPUT Lecturer 5) and "if it hadn't been for that cash injection, I would have never started" (CPUT Lecturer 6).

Two grant recipients (one from each university) noted that the grant motivated them to create OER and the grant manager from UCT further elaborated that with the grant in place, grant recipients made time to develop the resources. However, one grant recipient was still developing the OER at the time of the interview, but she felt accountable to complete the project as required. Some of the grant recipients highlighted that the grants were sufficient to support the creation of resources, and one grant in each institution was not taken up.

OER development

The grant recipients' purposes for developing OER included providing cost-free resources, translating existing resources from English to IsiXhosa and Afrikaans, and creating locally contextualised resources. The development of OER was also motivated by their need to support students in their learning challenges and/or to fill teaching gaps. The OER produced at both institutions included glossaries (with voice-over-text), images, videos, and screencasts.

Lecturers were strongly motivated to develop or adapt OER to address the economic inequality that impedes access for many students. As one UCT lecturer remarked: "the importance of access to knowledge and information is to create a knowledgeable civil society, but not everybody has money, the littlest, to spend on a textbook or in accessing this information. So, the inequality in the society is there" (UCT Lecturer 3). There is, therefore, a need to create more OER in Africa because of poverty and the resultant lack of access to information of which:

> is very important if we want to create a knowledgeable society … without knowledge, there is no way human beings can think of the imaginative, creative … if people don't think, if they don't have the information, how are they going to provide solutions to some of the challenges they are facing. (UCT Lecturer 3)

Translation into local languages (IsiXhosa and Afrikaans in the Cape Town context) appeared to be one of the key drivers for developing OER. A lecturer emphasised that

> a lot of the stuff is developed in the North and needs a Southern perspective or interpretation to make them more accessible to students [and] unless we start very consciously, purposefully bringing other South African languages into the teaching and learning space, it's never going to change. It's always going to stay English. (UCT Lecturer 1)

Recognition of local languages was viewed as a means of enhancing learning for students whose home language is not English. One grant recipient from CPUT adapted various resources in which academic concepts were translated. The reason behind this is to enable students to understand these concepts in IsiXhosa and Afrikaans. Similarly, one grant recipient at UCT, who was still in the process of developing the OER, noted that there were existing OER in English that she aimed to translate into other local languages. This lecturer was concerned that not much had been done, although "we talk so much about the need to shift our focus of English as the dominant language" (UCT Lecturer 1).

Another grant recipient at CPUT produced a glossary of 100 words, which were selected in consultation with students. This grant recipient explained that language was a barrier to students learning academic concepts, especially for the first time. The glossary was originally available in English and was translated into IsiXhosa and Afrikaans. Additionally, three voice-over artists were hired to produce voice-overs for the translated content.

One grant recipient at CPUT developed screencasts using screencasting software called Screencast-o-Matic[34] to teach basic statistics. The screencasts were developed for students and "anyone seeking an introduction on data and the different main character logistics" (CPUT Lecturer 5). These screencasts were created in English and subsequently translated into IsiXhosa and Afrikaans. In addition, these screencasts have also been made available as narrated PowerPoint presentations and are available on YouTube.

With respect to the localisation of content, resources such as videos and images were developed to disseminate local knowledge. Hence, the OER manager at UCT noted that OER creators were "focused on finding materials and creating materials that were locally relevant" (UCT Grant Manager). In terms of disciplinary relevance, one grant recipient in the Science faculty at UCT developed science-related, academic writing resources to address this existing gap. The academic related that most of the academic writing resources that students in the sciences used had been written by academics from the Humanities (UCT Lecturer 1).

Furthermore, in relation to the Global North-Global South knowledge production and consumption debate, two academics from UCT felt that knowledge produced in the Global North is sometimes less accessible for students in the Global South (UCT Lecturers 1 & 3). One of them said, "a lot of the stuff is developed in the north and needs a Southern perspective or interpretation to make them more accessible to students" (UCT Lecturer 1).

One grant holder at UCT adapted existing resources by redrawing images. The developed resource was focused on technologies used in construction. This resource "describes the different components of the building and construction processes" (UCT Lecturer 3). All resources developed are still in use as they include the fundamentals of the construction profession and make use of local examples. This example has been used in teaching and enabled the grant recipient to tell the story of technologies used in construction from an African perspective, preserving local practices and indigenous knowledge by providing a "platform to be able to tell this story, which may not have been told, because it's not available in regular textbooks". This also provided lecturers with additional "flexibility which you wouldn't have if you were using mainly westernized textbooks" (UCT Lecturer 3). Hence, OER could make teaching easier because "everything that we do with each OER ... there is something that I can use to teach further" (CPUT Lecturer 5).

In response to the teaching and learning challenge of a lack of available resources on 'vulnerability to environmental change'[35], internationally, a grant recipient from UCT adapted resources used in her course and made them openly available. This resource made use of local examples, one of which focused on a story written about a sangoma in Mpumalanga and the other on climate adaptation used by Rooibos farmers, providing local examples of the global issue of vulnerability to climate change.

One grant recipient at CPUT adapted, using an iPad and stylus, existing OER into videos to support students who were failing one area in civil engineering. The grant recipient noted that "I'm doing what I can to support the students that are standing in front of me" (CPUT Lecturer 5). The resources are shared and used on YouTube to be available to other people who are not students in this course.

---

[34] Screencast-O-Matic is a free online screen capture tool. This tool records a designated area of your screen as well as audio and webcam input. One can use this tool to record narrated presentations or demonstrations and produce the recordings as videos for your courses.

[35] http://open.uct.ac.za/handle/11427/6658

Benefits of OER

Highlighting one aspect of accessibility, namely cost, one grant holder noted that "The good thing about the OER is the accessibility. I think that is a great element of it [as we have] been paying a lot of money to learn things" (CPUT Courseware Developer). These materials are available online and can be downloadable from the institutional repository or external websites such as YouTube. Access to these materials is for anyone. However, students need an internet connection to access these materials. On-campus they have a free internet connection and can easily access the materials, but that is not always the case where they live.

The development of OER also comes with benefits and/or recognition. Except for one grant recipient, all other recipients noted that developing OER made them more visible in their spaces (institutions) and beyond. One grant recipient at UCT noted that requests for supervision and collaboration had increased. In addition, one grant recipient at CPUT contended that there was an increased demand for the developed glossaries[36] and another grant recipient noted that requests to make the developed resource available on other platforms such as YouTube were made by students. With this being done, the grant recipient received feedback and comments from subscribers and non-subscribers in relation to the resources shared.

One grant recipient at UCT received requests from other institutions of higher learning to distribute the developed resources. In addition, one grant recipient at CPUT was nominated as one of the top 10 finalists for the international E-Learning award, and another got contacts for projects. Furthermore, one grant recipient at UCT received an award from the Open Education Global Consortium.

Collaboration

The grant recipients in this study collaborated with students and external parties to develop OER. According to the UCT Grant Manager, collaboration with students and other collaborators is crucial as it "gives power to different people instead of keeping the power locked away".

Grant recipients and student collaboration

Collaboration with students in the development of OER was possible in both institutions. At UCT, only one of the three grant recipients worked with students to develop the OER. In this case, students also helped "in adding material, providing reviews or insights and distribution of the materials for other lecturers to use" (UCT Lecturer 3). Accordingly, collaboration with students is posited as seminal in that "most of the OER could have not been created without the support of students" (UCT Lecturer 3). Another grant recipient at UCT noted that the need for the inclusion of students in the process of translating OER to other local languages has emerged.

All grant recipients at CPUT worked with students to produce OER. In one case, the grant recipient noted that students were acknowledged and given attribution for their

---

[36] https://mlg.cput.ac.za/

contribution. Students were included in the production of OER in different ways. One grant recipient conducted and facilitated a workshop in which students were invited to participate in adapting existing resources. These students were allocated marks for participation, and most importantly, they were aware that their contribution would benefit their learning process. Students also narrated voice-overs for glossaries, translated resources to other local languages and made multilingual screencasts. Therefore, this creates a sense of equal participation, empowering students to "know that they are doing this for more than just them and on the other hand using it" (CPUT Lecturer 5).

External collaborative support

The development of some OER required collaboration with multiple stakeholders, including specialist expertise. Requests for collaboration were extended to other external parties for technical support, and resource production processes and content experts. The OER manager at CPUT noted that, in some cases, support was required from professional interpreters to assist in translating concepts. Voice-over artists and sound engineers were hired to assist in producing the resources, and, in one case, the grant was also used for technical resources such as software. The CPUT Courseware Developer noted that the process of producing OER involves a host of stakeholders. For example,

> The lecturers are there to confirm whether the translated content fits the context of the subjects. We also involve outside language specialists and field specialists ... This process is within the verification of the translated content. In the last process, we worked with voice-over artists from outside and students themselves, in that they've narrated the voice-overs of the glossaries. (CPUT Courseware Developer)

This is a multi-stakeholder collaboration for various reasons, including the fact that the quality of the produced content is vital.

Challenges for OER development and dissemination

Grant recipients in both institutions highlighted various challenges impacting the production process, including time, insufficient funds, difficulty recruiting external stakeholders, and fear of losing intellectual property (IP).

Both OER grant managers at UCT and CPUT noted that some OER developers ran out of time to complete their projects. The CPUT grant manager noted that "For most of the time we're happy that they even complete them ... because most of the time, they don't manage to complete" (CPUT Grant Manager). This manager further expressed that the "amount of bureaucratic resources and time that's needed ... to complete this project is not always worth the amount of funding" (CPUT Grant Manager). A UCT grant recipient disclosed that substantial resource development time was spent on redrawing images taken from other resources (as the standards of the resources change over time) and seeking permission to use copyright images from other resources.

Challenges also emerged in terms of recruiting external experts. A grant recipient at CPUT posited that she experienced human resource challenges as there were insufficient specialists in her projects, and it was difficult to recruit voice-over artists. She noted that, although students could translate the content from English to other local languages, language specialists were needed to verify the translated content. Reflecting on the difficulty in recruiting voice-over artists, one grant recipient at CPUT noted that the use of external parties requires much time and consequently resources "before you actually pay for the actual work" (CPUT Courseware Developer). The difficulty in recruiting external experts inhibited the development of OER, as the lecturers had to spend time finding the experts, and the grant was insufficient to pay the ideal experts.

Highlighting the cost of collaborating with students, a grant recipient at CPUT, who worked with 60 students in a three-hour workshop to develop multilingual videos, noted that paying the students would not have been possible with the grant received. As a way of encouraging student participation, she used the funds to buy them food.

Another barrier to creating OER emerged as some academics resist sharing content under a Creative Commons license as they feel they are giving up their intellectual property. In addition, the grant manager at CPUT noted:

> OER is not yet fully embraced. A lot of people still feel they want to keep their copyright that's intellectual property. They develop content that's quite niche... and they don't want to share necessarily under open education resources. I don't think all lecturers are necessarily open to OER. (CPUT Grant Manager)

Fears of loss of intellectual property are, however, misconceptions as a Creative Commons license protects the author's copyright as OER can require attribution.

Discussion

The findings revealed that small grants can be leveraged in many ways to enable the development of OER, whether creating from scratch or adapting existing resources. These developed resources play a role in addressing the dimensions of social justice (Fraser, 2005) by amelioratively redressing economic maldistribution, especially for students, recognising cultural diversity — especially linguistic accessibility, and representing the voice of the students. However, the findings also highlight various challenges impacting the production of OER.

Economic redistribution

In relation to the economic dimension of social justice, the availability of resources that would otherwise not have been available to students is a means of resource redistribution. Although these OER are free for students, the creation, dissemination and curation of OER does require funding. The grants enabled the development of OER, for, without such funding, many of these OER would not have been created or adapted. Grant recipients were driven by the desire to save costs for students and make materials accessible, and in some cases, they continued to work on these OER even after the funds were exhausted. Thus, the provision of the mini-grant was only partially ameliorative for the grant recipients, as some still needed to supplement OER development in their own time. However, the development of OER is certainly ameliorative for the students who are able to access the materials freely, at least on campus. As there are relatively few OER at present, the grant system has not yet supported sufficient OER development for students to see an economic benefit at a course level, let alone a programme or qualification level.

There is a need for further support of OER initiatives, driven by the institutions themselves with government's funding. For instance, UCT has received support from the institutional fund to develop OER (the Vice-Chancellor's OER Adaptation Project) and CPUT has received some UCDG funding. However, to support the development of high-quality OER by including various developers with different expertise – an objective noted in the OLPF – there needs to be an ongoing financial commitment from DHET for OER coordination and development. A transformative approach would include supporting institutional and cross-institutional collaborations in developing and adapting OER through DHET funding. The findings suggest that academics from both institutions are eager to translate existing resources from English to IsiXhosa and Afrikaans, but this needs coordination across institutions, so that OER, such as multilingual glossaries, are developed collaboratively and possibly in additional languages to optimise development expenses.

Cultural misrecognition and recognition

In this study, the findings show that the development and dissemination of OER can address issues of cultural misrecognition, such as the paucity of resources in local languages, and paucity of the physical and verbal representation of designated groups, and associated markers of identity such as accent or idiom from academic resources.

Firstly, cultural misrecognition was addressed in part through the development of OER that made use of local content and adaptation of content developed in the Global North to make it relevant to a Global South context. For example, all of the 11 projects, currently funded by the DOT4D mini-grants programme, sought to create local content, or to adapt international content for local contexts through the inclusion of local examples. Apart from the multilingual glossary, the three OER grant recipients at CPUT did not describe the inclusion of local content.

Secondly, cultural misrecognition was further addressed by the explicit focus on the use of historically marginalised and, in the context of academic spaces, under-represented South African languages in OER development. The grant recipients translated resources from English to IsiXhosa and Afrikaans, two widely spoken languages in the Western Cape. These resources made learning easier in that students had the opportunity to encounter new concepts in their home languages. Hodgkinson-Williams et al. (2017) have described the usefulness of the adaptation of OER through translation and how it enables student comprehension of translated content. However, the OER initiatives described in this study are ameliorative rather than transformative, as there were students whose languages were still not recognised, and for whom academic English as a register remains unfamiliar.

Furthermore, Hodgkinson-Williams and Trotter (2018) posit that the translation of OER is not a sufficient act of redress as, in most instances, the resources tend to be derived from non-local cultural contexts and knowledge traditions. A transformative means to developing OER that addresses cultural misrecognition would showcase local knowledge and perspectives. Hopefully, institutions and DHET will support these initiatives to narrow the Global North-Global South knowledge production and dissemination gap by embracing epistemic diversity.

Moreover, a nascent change in academics' mindsets was noted, but further awareness and adoption of open licensing is still needed before they are acculturated into sharing OER as a matter of course, rather than as an exception.

Political representation

Political misrepresentation occurs when there is a denial of participation in social interactions – the right to participation and influence, including decision-making processes (Fraser 2005). In order to fully address this injustice specifically in HE, marginalized groups should be included in the authoring, selection and procurement of teaching and learning materials. All grant recipients at CPUT included students in the development of OER. However, only one grant recipient at UCT included students.

The findings in this study show that, although the projects were not explicitly based on social justice and curriculum transformation, students and other external parties were involved in the development of OER to some extent. The findings indicate that collaboration with other parties for the development of OER is crucial. There are examples of collaboration with marginalized groups and experts in specific fields. Inclusion of students in either creation, editing, or giving feedback on the resources has been noted to redress the lack of student voice.

Conclusions and recommendations

The findings of this study point to examples of how participatory parity can be advanced through the careful consideration of economic, cultural and political injustices. The study has highlighted the role of OER grants to support OER developers to address social injustices.

This research also highlighted the importance of collaborative authorship models with colleagues, experts and students. Students' involvement can potentially empower them to grow as co-developers of content. The involvement of students in the development of OER can assist in evaluating the effectiveness of the resources. Thus, students can have a voice by contributing to teaching and learning through the development of OER. However, this study points to a key area for further study; the student perspective is not adequately represented here. The impact on students' learning experiences through a range of investigative approaches including surveys, focus groups and/or interviews, is a recommendation for future work. Institutional recognition should be given to OER developers through staff appraisal and promotions. The study showed that some nascent recognition of OER developers, where some received international awards and increased their online platform subscribers. Others received new requests for supervision of students.

Furthermore, government and private external funding can support OER production across more or all institutions in South Africa, not just these two included here. For instance, a shared database of multilingual glossaries could help leverage the time and funding resource constraints and reduce the duplication of effort among institutions, while on the other hand, having institutional collaborations could enhance scalability.

Although these resources are freely shared on either institutional repositories or other external websites, high connectivity cost is still a challenge. There is a need for zero-rated websites to enable access to these OER. Accordingly, the concern should be on how funding can be reserved and how we can increase access to these resources.

In conclusion, to address the possible injustices accompanying the development of OER, the developers must be encouraged to include students, consider developing localised content, and make provision for the translation of the content. In so doing, through careful consideration of parity of participation, funding of OER through mini-grants can respond to the need for socially just education.

Acknowledgements

Many thanks to the OER grant managers and grantees at UCT and CPUT, whose inputs made the case study possible. Thank you specifically to the members of CILT and CIET for sharing their experiences with us. Special thanks are due to reviewers Professor Cheryl Foxcroft, Lily Todorova and Maggie Albro for their thoughtful, incisive feedback on the chapter, Emeritus Associate Professor Cheryl Ann Hodgkinson-Williams for editorial feedback, and Dr Tabisa Mayisela for additional writing support and guiding the entire COOL project. Thanks are also due to the Centre for Innovation in Learning and Teaching at the University of Cape Town, which hosted the COOL project, and the South African Department of Higher Education and Training for funding it.

References

Abelson, H., Miyagawa, S., & Yue, D. (2012). MIT's ongoing commitment to Open Courseware. *MIT Faculty Newsletter*, 24(4). http://web.mit.edu/fnl/volume/244/abelson%20et%20al.html

Albright, P. (2005). Final forum report, UNESCO International Institute for Educational Planning, Internet Discussion Forum on Open Educational Resources. https://hewlett.org/wp-content/uploads/2016/08/IIEP_OER.pdf

Albro, M., Dobbs, A., & Foreman, M. (2020). Incentivizing OER adoption with course development mini-grants. *Journal of New Librarianship*, 4(2), 449–475. https://doi.org/10.21173/newlibs/8/1

Annand, D., & Jensen, T. (2017). Incentivizing the production and use of open educational resources in higher education institutions. *International Review of Research in Open and Distributed Learning*, 18(4), 1–15. http://www.irrodl.org/index.php/irrodl/article/view/3009/4226

Arinto, P. B., Hodgkinson-Williams, C., King, T., Cartmill, T., & Willmers, M. (2017). Research on open educational resources for development in the Global South: Project landscape. In C. Hodgkinson-Williams & P. B. Arinto (Eds.), *Adoption and impact of OER in the Global South* (pp. 3–26). African Minds & IDRC. http://www.africanminds.co.za/adoption-and-impact-of-oer-in-the-global-south/

Atkins, D. E., Brown, J. S., & Hammond, A. L. (2007). *A review of the open educational resources (OER) movement: Achievements, challenges, and new opportunities.* https://hewlett.org/wp-content/uploads/2016/08/ReviewoftheOERMovement.pdf

Baker, A., & Ippoliti, C. (2018). Student-driven OER: Championing the student voice in campus-wide efforts In A. Wesolek, J. Lashley & A. Langley (Eds.), *OER: A field guide for academic librarians*. https://boisestate.pressbooks.pub/oer-field-guide/chapter/student-driven-oer-championing-the-student-voice-in-campus-wide-efforts/

Bardoloi, Y. (2016). Why are university textbooks so expensive? https://www.scmp.com/yp/discover/lifestyle/features/article/3059094/why-are-university-textbooks-so-expensive

Bliss, T. J., & Smith, M. (2017). A brief history of open educational resources. In: R. S. Jhangiani & R. Biswas-Diener (Eds.) *Open: The philosophy and practices that are revolutionizing education and science* (pp. 9–27). Ubiquity Press. https://doi.org/10.5334/bbc.b

Brown J. S., & Adler, R. P. (2008). Open education, the long tail, and learning 2.0. *Educause Review*, 43(1), 16–20. https://er.educause.edu/articles/2008/1/minds-on-fire-open-education-the-long-tail-and-learning-20

Brown, M., McCormack, M., Reeves, J., Brook, D. C., Grajek S., Alexander, A., et al. (2020). *2020 Educause horizon report* (Teaching and learning ed.). EDUCAUSE. https://library.educause.edu/resources/2020/3/2020-educause-horizon-report-teaching-and-learning-edition

Butcher, N., & Hoosen, S. (2012). Exploring the business case for open educational resources. Commonwealth of Learning (COL). http://oasis.col.org/bitstream/handle/11599/57/pub_OER_BusinessCase.pdf?sequence=1&isAllowed=y

Chikuni, P. R., Cox, G., & Czerniewicz, L. (2019). Exploring the Institutional OER policy landscape in South Africa: Dominant discourses and assumptions. *International Journal of Education and Development using Information and Communication Technology (IJEDICT)*, 15(4), 165–179. https://files.eric.ed.gov/fulltext/EJ1239627.pdf

Cohen, L., Manion, L., & Morrison, K. (2007). *Research methods in education* (6th ed.). Routledge.

Cox, G., & Claassen J. (2016). In open education @ UCT: Becoming an open educator. https://vula.uct.ac.za/x/qcwOgs

Cox, G., & Trotter, C. (2017). An OER framework, heuristic and lens: Tools for understanding lecturers' adoption of OER. https://open.uct.ac.za/bitstream/item/28124/King_OER_2017.pdf?sequence=1

Cox, G., & Trotter, H. (2019). Factors shaping lecturers' adoption of OER at three South African universities. University of Cape Town. In C. Hodgkinson-Williams & P. B. Arinto (Eds.), *Adoption and impact of OER in the Global South* (pp. 3–26). African Minds, IDRC. https://zenodo.org/record/1094852#.YNySQugzY2w

Cox, G., Masuku, B., & Willmers, M. (2020). Open textbooks and social justice: Open educational practices to address economic, cultural and political injustice at the University of Cape Town. *Journal of Interactive Media in Education*, 1(2), 1–10. https://jime.open.ac.uk/articles/10.5334/jime.556/

DHET (Department of Higher Education and Training). (2013). White paper for post-school education and training: Building an expanded, effective and integrated post-school system. *Government Gazette*, 37229. https://www.gov.za/documents/white-paper-post-school-education-and-training-building-expanded-effective-and-integrated

DHET. (2017). Call for comment on the Open Learning Policy Framework for Post-School Education and Training. *Government Gazette*, 40772(335). http://pmg-assets.s3-website-eu-west-1.amazonaws.com/170407openlearningframework-postschooleduc.pdf

Fereday, J., & Muir-Cochrane, E. (2006). Demonstrating rigor using thematic analysis: A hybrid approach of inductive and deductive coding and theme development. *International Journal of Qualitative Methods*, 5(1). https://journals.sagepub.com/doi/10.1177/160940690600500107

Fraser, N. (1998). Social justice in the age of identity politics: Redistribution, recognition, participation. Discussion paper / Wissenschaftszentrum Berlin für Sozialforschung, Forschungsschwerpunkt Arbeitsmarkt und Beschäftigung, Abteilung Organisation und Beschäftigung (pp. 98–108). Wissenschaftszentrum Berlin für Sozialforschung. https://nbn-resolving.org/urn:nbn:de:0168-ssoar-126247

Fraser, N. (2001). Recognition without ethics. *Theory, Culture and Society*, 18(2–3), 21–42.

Fraser, N. (2005). Reframing justice in a globalizing world. *New Left Review*, 36, 69–88.

Fraser, N. (2008). Reframing justice in a globalizing world. In K. Olson (Ed.). *Adding insult to injury: Nancy Fraser debates her critics* (pp. 273–291). Verso.

Fraser, N. (2009). *Scales of justice: Reimagining political space in a globalizing world*. Columbia University Press.

Fraser, N., & Honneth, A. (2003). *Redistribution or recognition? A political-philosophical exchange*. Verso.

Hodgkinson-Williams, C., Arinto, P. B., Cartmill, T., & King, T. (2017). Factors influencing open educational practices and OER in the Global South: Meta-synthesis of the ROER4D project. In C. Hodgkinson-Williams & P. B. Arinto (Eds.), *Adoption and impact of OER in the Global South* (pp. 27–67). African Minds & IDRC. https://doi.org/10.5281/zenodo.1037088

Hodgkinson-Williams, C., & Trotter, H. (2018). A social justice framework for understanding open educational resources and practices in the Global South. *Journal of Learning for Development*, 5(3): 204–224. https://jl4d.org/index.php/ejl4d/article/view/312

Hölscher, D. (2014). Considering Nancy Fraser's notion of social justice for social work: Reflections on misframing and the lives of refugees in South Africa. *Ethics and Social Welfare*, 8(1), 20–38.

Hoosen, S., & Butcher, N. (2019). Understanding the impact of OER: Achievements and challenges. OER Africa, UNESCO Institute for Information Technologies in Education. https://iite.unesco.org/publications/understanding-the-impact-of-oer-achievements-and-challenges/

Hoosen, S., & Omollo, K. L. (2010). The African Health OER Network: Advancing health education in Africa through open educational resources. *African Journal of Health Professions Education*, 2(2), 21–22.

Hylén, J. (2006). *Open educational resources: Opportunities and challenges*. Centre for Educational Research and Innovation, OECD. https://www.oecd.org/education/ceri/37351085.pdf

Karakaya, K., & Karakaya, O. (2020). Framing the role of English in OER from a social justice perspective: A critical lens on the (dis)empowerment of non-English speaking communities. *Asian Journal of Distance Education*, 15(2), 175–190. http://asianjde.org/ojs/index.php/AsianJDE/article/view/508/328

King, T. (2017). Postgraduate students as OER capacitators. *Open Praxis*, 9(2), 223–234. https://www.learntechlib.org/p/181417/

Lambert, S. R. (2018). Changing our (dis)course: A distinctive social justice aligned definition of open education. *Journal of Learning for Development*, 5(3), 225–244. https://jl4d.org/index.php/ejl4d/article/view/290

Mays, T. J. (2017). Utilising open educational resources in support of curriculum transformation at Africa Nazarene University: A participatory action research approach [Doctoral thesis, University of South Africa]. http://uir.unisa.ac.za/bitstream/handle/10500/22619/thesis_mays_tj.pdf

McGowan, V. (2020). Institution initiatives and support related to faculty development of open educational resources and alternative textbooks. *Open Learning: The Journal of Open, Distance and e-Learning*, 35(1), 24–45, DOI: 10.1080/02680513.2018.1562328

McGreal, R. (2017). Special report on the role of open educational resources in supporting the Sustainable Development Goal 4: Quality education challenges and opportunities. *International Review of Research in Open and Distributed Learning*, 18(7), 292–305. https://doi.org/10.19173/irrodl.v18i7.3541

Nkosi, B. (2014). Students hurt by pricey textbooks. *Mail & Guardian*. https://mg.co.za/article/2014-10-03-students-hurt-by-pricey-textbooks/

OECD (Organisation for Economic Co-operation and Development). (2007). *Giving knowledge for free: The emergence of open educational resources*. Centre for Educational Research and Innovation, OECD. https://www.oecd.org/education/ceri/givingknowledgeforfreetheemergenceofopeneducationalresources.htm

Phillips, A. (2018). Open resources in an age of contingency. *Inside Higher Ed*. https://www.insidehighered.com/digital-learning/views/2018/01/31/oer-movement-poses-risks-time-and-resource-starved-contingent

Rets, I. (2021). Linguistic accessibility of open educational resources: Text simplification as an aid to non-native readers of English [Doctoral dissertation, The Open University]. http://oro.open.ac.uk/75140/

Smith, M. S., & Casserly, C. M. (2006). The promise of open educational resources. *Change: The Magazine of Higher Learning*, 38(5), 8–17. https://www.learntechlib.org/p/100448/

Smith, S. M., Hutchens, C., & Kvenild, C. (2021). WY Open: A grassroots open educational resource initiative. In B. Buljung & E. Bongiovanni (Eds.), *The scholarly communications cookbook* (pp. 82–89). Association of College and Research Libraries. https://scholarworks.boisestate.edu/cgi/viewcontent.cgi?article=1162&context=lib_facpubs

Stacey, P. (2013). Government support for open educational resources: Policy, funding, and strategies. *The International Review of Research in Open and Distributed Learning*, 14(2), 67–80. https://doi.org/10.19173/irrodl.v14i2.1537

Stacey, P. (2010). Foundation funded OER vs. tax payer funded OER – A tale of two mandates. In *Open ED 2010 Proceedings*. Barcelona: UOC, OU, BYU. http://openaccess.uoc.edu/webapps/o2/bitstream/10609/5241/6/Stacey_editat.pdf

Tait, A. W. (2018). Education for development: From distance to open education. *Journal of Learning for Development*, 5(2), 101–115. http://www.jl4d.org/index.php/ejl4d/article/view/294

Todorinova, L., & Wilkinson, Z. T. (2020). Incentivizing faculty for open educational resources (OER) adoption and open textbook authoring. *The Journal of Academic Librarianship*, 46(6). https://doi.org/10.1016/j.acalib.2020.102220

Whitfield, S., & Robinson, Z. (2012). Open educational resources: The challenges of 'usability' and copyright clearance, *Planet*, 25(1), 51–54. DOI: 10.11120/plan.2012.00250051

HOW TO CITE THIS CHAPTER

Maake-Malatji, M., & Cox, G. (2022). Advancing social justice through small grants for the development of open educational resources at the University of Cape Town and the Cape Peninsula University of Technology. In T. Mayisela, S. C. Govender & C. A. Hodgkinson-Williams (Eds.), *Open learning as a means of advancing social justice: Cases in post-school education and training in South Africa* (pp. 217–240). African Minds. doi: 10.47622/9781928502425_10

This work is licensed under a Creative Commons Attribution 4.0 International (CC BY 4.0) licence.

11

"Understanding the TVET game"

A case study on maximising available opportunities for open educational practices within the broader TVET field in South Africa

Sara Black

SUMMARY This case study examines the management practices of False Bay College (FBC), a TVET college deemed 'successful' by the Department of Higher Education and Training (DHET), asking what local practices support this success. However, rather than seeking a-contextualised 'best practice' to transfer to other colleges, the case study takes a relational Bourdieusian approach as a language of description, analysing decision-making in relation to the broader contours of power and structure. In doing so, I seek to locate 'strategy' back into a dynamic conversation with context. Bourdieu's framework offers a rich conceptual apparatus for considering not just False Bay, but the state of relations in the broader TVET field and how vocational education is positioned against both basic education and broader political economic forces. In considering the 'logic of practice' underpinning FBC's institutional organising and decision-making, the chapter asks how these broader practices support both 'open learning' as a policy imperative from DHET, as well as broader social justice concerns (cf. Nancy Fraser's approach, the overarching framework for the Cases of Open Learning, of which this study is one). The case study's findings suggest that institutional arrangements and activities are not specific to open learning, but are generic features of leadership and decision-making practice that strategise within the prevailing TVET field and its policy and resource constraints. That these practices are historically and contextually specific suggests that there is no 'silver bullet' to learn from FBC that would transfer to other TVET colleges without significant change in the broader educational field in South Africa.

Keywords: institutional leadership, policy enactment, Bourdieu, open learning, TVET

Introduction

What distinguishes 'successful' education institutions from 'unsuccessful' ones has vexed policymakers since modern schooling was made more widely available from the mid-20th century. Increasingly constrained resource environments now make identifying 'key policy levers for success' a wicked problem, and strategies to capacitate ground-level institutions need nuanced understanding of causal relations and contexts to understand 'mechanisms' of success and how to encourage them. This case study explores a particular TVET college deemed 'successful', namely False Bay College (FBC). In particular, it asks how *enabling conditions* are created within the institution for open learning practices. How this college makes decisions at the local level may identify key levers for policymakers and other institutions to learn from, with the caveat that "the bricolage of local circumstance will shape how colleges respond to each new intervention." (Paterson, 2016, p. 1). What any college does strategically at a local level is always influenced by historical and contemporary relations at a broader scale: *meaningful* opportunities for change (Christie, 2008; Shalem, 2003) are hence shaped by context and differ from institution to institution. The chapter therefore seeks to offer a description of both the possibilities *and limits* of institutional 'agency' at FBC, particularly as these are exercised towards open learning and social justice.

To relate local strategizing to broader context, the chapter deploys the conceptual framework of Pierre Bourdieu, utilizing his focus on fields of practice and the shared beliefs (doxa) that orient said practices towards specific (valorised) ends. TVET management and leadership in South Africa is thinly researched, particularly with sociological approaches that locate institutional organisation and decision-making in broader historical and socioeconomic context. The chapter thus offers an original contribution to the literature regarding critical sociological studies of education leadership, management and administration (ELMA) in TVET colleges in South Africa.

The chapter begins with a brief sketch of the context of post-apartheid TVET in South Africa, including some of the local policy trends that shape contemporary education fields that TVET managers and leaders must navigate. Key concepts from Bourdieu's framework are then summarised, followed by a brief description of the methodology deployed for this particular case study. Finally, the findings are described and analysed using the concepts from Bourdieu's toolbox, foregrounding what aspects of FBC's general practice support open learning, as well as the limits of transferring blindly between FBC's approach and the different contexts other TVET colleges must contend with.

Context

The idea of universal 'best practice' in education institutions is one that deserves healthy scepticism, especially in a context as deeply marred by multi-faceted inequality like South Africa. In addition to broader contours of difference along lines of location, language, race and class, TVET colleges in South Africa occupy a plural and contradictory role in the education landscape which their institutional leaders must navigate. TVETs are simultaneously institutions of post-school education for adults (some of whom are working and/or shouldering responsibilities towards dependents) while also serving as 'alternative high schools' for students who were alienated by mainstream secondary schooling. Aspirant to be considered on par with their university counterparts, TVETs are still governed by policy frameworks that look remarkably similar to those of high schools: they have councils similar to school governing bodies, centralised and standardized curriculum and assessment, and educators who are governed by the school-oriented Employment of Educators Act, who are subject to the same performance appraisal system as school teachers, and for whom the standards for being 'qualified' (DHET, 2013) echo similarities with those used to adjudicate qualified teacher status in basic education institutions (DHET, 2018). That is, while being formally identified as a 'critical' part of the post-secondary education system (DHET, 2013), TVET college *policy* looks remarkably similar to that of high schools. These colleges – and their leaders – thus sit astride multiple contradictory lines of fracture in the system both in policy and everyday activity.

Managing and leading under neoliberal conditions

What it means to manage and lead an education institution has changed significantly over the last 35-40 years (Anderson et al., 2013; Ball, 2018; Courtney, 2015; Heystek, 2007; Niesche & Thomson, 2017; Thomson, 2017, 2014, 2011; Thrupp, 2003). As explored later, the 'logics' shaping the field of education at large, and its more specific sub-fields – including TVET – have increasingly aligned with those of business, markets, financialization, audit-culture and competition. Emerging from international isolation in the mid-1990s, South Africa's newly installed democratic policymakers were caught up in the apogee of neoliberal thinking (Christie, 2008), with PSET institutional mergers and restructuring in the early 2000s reflecting that orthodoxy's emphasis on efficiency and rationalisation. The decentralisation of TVET college management to councils while centralising curriculum and standardising assessment also bear hallmarks of neoliberal 'technologies of management' (Ball, 2008). For TVETs in particular (previously referred to as Further Education and Training, or FET, colleges), mergers created challenges of legitimacy for new leadership, with those who had once been principals of colleges in their own right now being folded under the aegis of a new principal. Newly installed leaders and managers had to guide multi-campus, geographically distributed and culturally heterogeneous institutions. These institutions were assembled from differentially developed colleges, with roots in racially segregated, apartheid-era departments, each with their concomitant degree of development and (under-) investment (Wedekind, 2016). Thus South African TVET leaders not only contend with contemporary neoliberal conditions of management and administration, but do so bearing deeply differentiated historical burdens across the sector. FBC is not exempt from these conditions, and any narrative that offers description of the college's practices must necessarily do so in conversation with these broader historicized concerns.

Research questions

Such complex factors make identifying transferable drivers of 'success' a fraught process. In addition, the original mandate of the case – namely to study the 'counter-culture' of the college as it relates to open educational practices (OEP) and open learning – proved too broad for a small case study. Rather, the case focused on trying to identify *enabling conditions* at the college that supported adopting OEP (including historical conditions), and the local systems and beliefs (see *doxa* below) that inclined the college to do so.

The following key questions were thus devised to explore what FBC does well, but still locate their success in context:

1. What conditions at False Bay College support and enable the adoption of open educational practices?
    a. How are these conditions produced and reproduced?
    b. How are these conditions, and the practices they undergird, related to concerns of social justice, defined as parity of participation in economic, cultural and political terms?

These questions attempt to put the present in conversation with the past, as well as leadership decisions and activities in dynamic tension with systems and meaning-making, to portray the college's work in descriptive rather than normative brushstrokes, and by doing so describing the logic of FBC's local practices in situ. While this short case cannot describe every aspect of FBC's conditions of operation, it attempts to sketch the key features salient to these questions.

Conceptual framework

Connecting institutional 'culture' to everyday practices and broader policy frameworks requires a relational language of description: one that can locate decisions and approaches in the context of systems, history and discourses. To achieve this, this chapter deploys the conceptual apparatus of Pierre Bourdieu (1968, 1974, 1986, 1990, 2000) to relate institutional-level activities and beliefs to the broader landscape in which FBC operates. In particular, Bourdieu's concept of practical reason is useful. 'Practical' reason suggests that what is 'logical to do' is not the practice of cold rationality towards fixed ends, but a strategic navigation of prevailing power valences, including meanings and affordances (what he distinguishes as the difference between 'the practice of logic' and the 'logic of practice' (Bourdieu, 1990). It is FBC's logic of practice, and how this relates to its own local conditions, as well as those in the broader TVET sector, which are of interest.

By considering the *field* of TVET education in SA, its 'doxa' (i.e. prevailing beliefs and logics), and its 'illusio' (i.e., what stakes and signals represent 'success'), novel understandings of the college's past and present decision-making can be produced that offer both insights as to its relative success, as well as which aspects of FBC's approaches might (not) transfer to other colleges.

Field

The concept of field is the most salient for this study. A 'field' is an internally coherent social realm of activities, meanings and systems which need not be physically co-located, but rather delimits a terrain of practices within which there is a shared understanding. Fields can also be 'nested' or embedded within each other. In the case of TVET colleges, vocational education sits within the broader field of 'education' at large, which in turn is constituted by – and (singularly) constructive of – the broadest field of socio-economic and political power. Education, for Bourdieu, is the field of practice that reproduces power relations in society by concealing economic and cultural advantage as merit (see Bourdieu, 1967, 1974, 1984/1990, 1990, 1998; Bourdieu & Passeron, 1977).

Fields are characterised by *illusio* (the stakes for which people engage in that practice) and *doxa* (the shared, tacit beliefs about how to obtain said stakes). A strong component of the TVET field's *illusio* is offering industry-aligned/labour-market compatible skillsets that result in employment after qualifying. This particular focus distinguishes the vocational education field from its academic counterpart (which valorises the pursuit of knowledge, however esoteric, over employability). TVET *doxa* that ties to this *illusio* might include the necessity of workplace learning for such skills to be acquired, or the framing of a particular mix of knowledges in terms of theory, practical and work integrated learning (WIL). The doxa of a field is not about the truth value of shared beliefs, but rather the 'rules of the game' as constructed by the field (a distinction that becomes clearer when considered as the root of the concepts ortho*doxy* and hetero*doxy*). In education, common *doxa* includes the idea that one should 'stay in school', that 'working hard produces results' and that the system is meritocratic (empirical evidence troubles whether these are indeed steadfast truths). Rather, doxic ideals offer descriptions of 'how to play the game of schooling' (Grenfell & James, 1998) and illusio the prize for which one plays.

Forms of capital

The resources deployable in a field are said to be forms of capital (Bourdieu, 1986, 1990). Beyond the (now) universal money-form, Bourdieu reasoned that multiple resources take on contingent value and exchangeability within different fields of practice. In particular cultural capital (knowledge, certain forms of language, dress, cultural representations such as music, literature, and art) are particularly salient in the domain of education. Institutional ratification of the acquisition of cultural capital — normally in the form of a recognised certificate — is considered symbolic capital, tradeable for opportunities or economic currency at a later stage.

Unlike more traditional academic education where this exchangeability is disavowed (albeit omnipresent), vocational education is explicit about instrumentalist skills acquisition towards future economic capital: in this sense, vocational education could be described as less obscurantist than its academic counterpart. However, the differential social status between vocational and academic forms of learning could be described in terms of what Bourdieu calls *misrecognition*. For Bourdieu, misrecognition sustains relations of power by portraying arbitrary elite practices as normatively superior, primarily by establishing hegemony *through doxa*.

How cultural capital bestowed by vocational institutions relates to that of basic education, the labour market and academic forms locates the relation of the TVET field to other education fields. How FBC understands what constitutes 'capital' in the TVET field is illustrative in this study.

Habitus

Habitus is the hardest of Bourdieu's concepts to operationalize. But it is habitus — the embodied, pre-cognitive dispositions that orient players towards the 'game' of TVET —

which is both produced by, and productive of, the field (Bourdieu, 1990, 2000). While the individual habitus of TVET lecturers was not the focus (see "Methodology"), the 'habits and dynamism' of decision makers — their sense of 'how to go about doing things' — are lifted out to illustrate how FBC decision-makers intuitively (or explicitly) understand the logic of practice and how this sustains their strategizing in accordance with the prevailing logics of the TVET field. Ironically, the best description of habitus as a non-cognitive, un-represented sense of practical logic was not from Bourdieu:

> To speak of the subject now is to speak of duration, custom, habit, and anticipation. Anticipation is habit, and habit is anticipation: these two determinations — the thrust of the past and the élan toward the future ... are the two aspects of the same fundamental dynamism. ... Habit is the constitutive root of the subject, and the subject, at root, is the synthesis of time — the synthesis of the present and the past in light of the future. (Deleuze, 1991, pp. 92–93)

That is, habitus is the *feel for the game* (Bourdieu, 1990), a tacit sense of how things 'should' be done to obtain certain aims, but premised on a practical, embodied sense of action, rather than a rational calculation of probability. Field and habitus are mutually co-constructive, although neither determines the other.

The TVET field and its relation to other fields

Considering vocational education as a field of practice in Bourdieusian terms is instructive for this case and for understanding TVETs in general. Figure 1 attempts to visually describe how vocational education, and TVET colleges as institutions, sit in a field of practice that adopts logics from — and must articulate with — multiple other fields. Individual institutions will each have their own 'field' at the local level, taking up the practices of their broader field and interpreting these into local variants depending on context, history, available forms of capital and historical orientations of institutional culture. Internal to a specific field, such as TVET, different institutions will relate to each other according to the logic of the broader field e.g., inter-institutional relations might be cooperative, competitive or indifferent.

What Figure 1 attempts to describe is the multiple forces under which vocational education institutions operate. As stated by Papier (2011) and Chappell (1999), TVET colleges must look 'both ways' and take cognisance of industry movements, standards and trends in ways that universities and schools need not (yet). FBC, as well as other TVET colleges, must juggle multiple issues including (1) the quality and form of the basic education their students bring to their vocational studies; (2) the changing demands of industry for whom they are attempting to prepare students; (3) the policy imperatives of the Higher Education field that they must satisfy (i.e., DHET policy mandates); and (4) constant comparison with university education (cf. Bathmaker et al., 2018); as well as (5) the broader field of South African and global social relations, wherein factors such as race, class, language, geography, gender, religion and sexuality all shape life opportunities and experiences.

Figure 1: Vocational education's relations to other fields that shape its goals, logics and practices

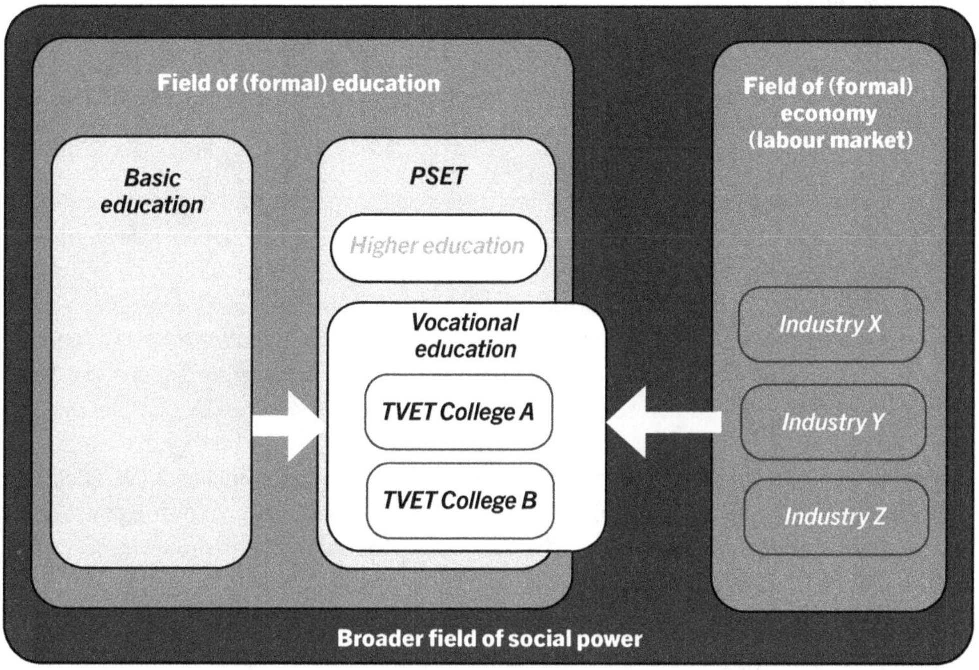
Field of (formal) education
Basic education
PSET
Higher education
Vocational education
TVET College A
TVET College B
Field of (formal) economy (labour market)
Industry X
Industry Y
Industry Z
Broader field of social power

Relating Bourdieu's field theory to open learning and social justice

The concepts of field, capital and doxa place ideas such as 'open learning' and 'social justice' into an historicized and contextualised frame. Education has been under increasing pressure from economic forces since the 1970s (Ball, 2012; Rizvi & Lingard, 2010) and is still widely viewed as a policy lever that can right social wrongs by producing improved access to opportunities for human capital development (a theory of change that has been critiqued: see Vally & Motala, 2014). What doxa invites us to notice is that 'open learning' and OEP, as espoused by DHET (2017), will be subject to the broader contours of logic and practice in the field of education, and that OEP might conform with a field's doxa (i.e., be affirmative) or disrupt prevailing logics (i.e., be transformative) (cf. Fraser, 2005). Noticing how fields relate to each other (as in Figure 1) also helps us to theorise the reach and influence of local or regional changes, and contextualize social justice in relation to its framing (Fraser, 2009).

Vocational education, in particular, is hoped to offer increased economic parity of participation (Fraser, 1995) for students marginalised by more traditional forms of education. But as Akoojee (2016) and Allais (2020) both point out, this is unlikely while education continues to subscribe to the dominant doxa of the prevailing political economy, especially in light of South Africa's particular industrial profile. Akoojee (2016) suggests that the narrow 'employable skills' illusio of the TVET field threatens its capacity to offer social justice to its attendees, given the rapidly changing broader field of skills and labour relations; he states that TVET must:

redefine its traditional relationship with the economy. This does not mean that the interest of the economy is subverted, but that the role of the formal economy becomes a subset of wider societal perspectives. It requires the interest of people to come first, with the notion of *communities* and *responsiveness* replacing the economy as the primary category of responsiveness. Thus the much-touted perspective within TVET discourse that it was *demand driven* needs reconsideration. (Akoojee, 2016, p. 5)

Such a perspective – that the economy meets the needs of people, rather than vice versa – would require a substantial shift in the doxa and illusio of the broader field of power, making the endgame of social arrangements not profit or growth, but human flourishing and social justice. As illustrated in Figure 1, current prevailing structures and discourses place TVET institutions on the receiving end of forces emanating from basic education, higher education and broader economic arrangements. These contradictions place limitations on TVET institutions' freedom to pursue social justice in their practice, whether by open learning or other means.

Bourdieusian analyses of leadership, management and decision-making in TVET colleges was not found in the extant literature. The next section locates this chapter against other research, attempting to synthesise existing ELMA field theory literature drawn from schools and vocational education studies.

Bourdieu and education leadership and management

Very little is written about management and leadership in TVET colleges in South Africa, with no discernible studies evident that use a field theoretic or Bourdieusian framework. In the South African case, the similarity in governance structures between TVETs and schools offers some useful parallels between the ELMA literature in basic education and some of the potential issues in TVETs.

Naidoo (2004) is the closest to *this* chapter's focus on the relations of the post-school field in South Africa. Her study examined the field of universities in SA in the transition period from 1985–1990 at the end of apartheid, outlining the structure of the field of higher education at the time and how institutions replicated their relative positions of (dis)advantage *in relation to each other* (i.e., that 'success' is a relative measure, not an absolute one).

However, while the apartheid regime made explicit the project of stratification and race-based exclusion, the post-apartheid government espouses a *doxa* of 'freedom' and meritocracy. Bourdieu points out exactly this capacity of education institutions to quietly replicate social inequality under the guise of meritocracy, suggesting that his theory of power is more applicable to post-apartheid South Africa than the apartheid era (Muller/Black, 2017).

In literature from further afield, Thomson and Niesche (2017) ask the pertinent question, "freedom to what ends?", foregrounding that superficial 'autonomy' for education leaders and administrators is increasingly folded into market logics and new managerialist approaches[37]. Although analysing more 'developed' contexts in Australia and the UK, they observe that the 'logic of reform' in both locations purports to offer principals increasing autonomy, but that

---

[37] This question echoes David Harvey's (2018) analysis of Marx: "freedom to work for wages or starve – that is not freedom."

this obscures the effects of market forces on decision makers, framing this as a 'globalized education reform logic at work' through institutions such as the OECD, World Bank and others (Gunter [2017] refers to this as the Transnational Leadership Package). Given South Africa's shared colonial history and policy borrowing from both the UK and Australia, there is some validity to considering the implications of this research in the South African TVET case; increased local institutional governance has not necessarily offered colleges the freedom to prioritize their students' wellbeing or academic development without constraint. In particular, Thomson and Niesche note that a critical part of this 'globalized education reform logic' formulates that:

> Local leadership is (seen as) key to improvement, as local leaders know and can cater for local variations in ways in which central and regional managers cannot. This is achieved *both through competition for position, and also the development of strategic alliances and confederations with other local leaders.* (Thomson & Niesche, 2017, p. 6, emphasis added)

As discussed in the analysis later, this formulation of local leadership in *both* competition *and* strategic cooperation describes well the situation of FBC in the TVET field.

The education field is generally understood as in a subservient position to a number of other fields, including the economy and the political field. Doxa from outside the education field has steadily gained in influence on education practices, with neoclassical economic doxa (including human capital formation, entrepreneurialism, the benefits of competition, the inevitability of globalisation) framed as the most effective modus operandi in all spheres (Addison, 2009; Lingard & Rawolle, 2013; Lingard et al., 2015; Thomson, 2005). Managers and leaders of education institutions increasingly require marketing knowledge and 'entrepreneurial dispositions' (Courtney, 2015) to navigate the fields in which they work. Education leaders simultaneously look 'out' towards other institutions, and are brought into competition with each other for resources (including students) as neoliberal logics deepen the penetration of new managerialism into public services. As Bathmaker (2015) notes, applying Bourdieusian lenses to twenty-first century education institutions has stretched his original work to consider how increasing globalization has imbricated once semi-autonomous fields of practice into tighter and tighter constellations of power where what happens outside the field of vocational or higher education increasingly shapes what happens within (what some have called 'heteronomy' (see Bathmaker, 2015; Deer, 2003). Policies and 'ideals' in education leadership and management increasingly define 'success' in terms of test scores, rather than holistic student development and their relation to broader society (Crow et. al., 2016; Lumby & English, 2009), even as

> educational leadership literature is also largely mute on the ways public schools – and teachers and leaders within them – become both scapegoat and solution for problems of growing social inequality which are largely beyond their control. (Anderson et al., 2013, p. 44).

These forces, their contradictions and the ever-tightening enmeshment of education logics with those of other fields will shape practices in South African TVET colleges like FBC.

Methodology

Understanding an entire institution's practices in depth requires extended ethnographic approaches which were not possible for this case, not only due to time restrictions for the project but also as fieldwork was interrupted by the 2020 COVID-19 pandemic. The analysis offered here, then, is far from comprehensive or complete. Rather, it lightly sketches key aspects of FBC's leadership and management practices that support open learning approaches and offers one explanatory possibility for their efficacy.

Three sets of data were laid side by side to gain insights on the conditions of practice at the college, how these relate to the doxa of the broader field at large, and where they align with — or are in tension with — open learning and social justice principles. These included: desktop and historical research on FBC in particular, and TVET in South Africa in general; an in-depth exploratory interview with the academic leaders of the college; and a survey of False Bay College lecturers from across multiple campuses on how they perceived college decision-making, as well as management's priorities and values within the institution.

Operationalising Bourdieu's conceptual apparatus is summarized in his interview with Loic Wacquant as follows:

1. analyse the position of the field(s) vis-à-vis the field of power,
2. map out the objective structures of relations between the positions occupied by the agents or institutions who compete for the legitimate forms of specific authority of which this field is a site, and
3. analyse the habitus of agents, the different systems of dispositions they have acquired by internalising a determinate type of social and economic condition, and which find in a definite trajectory within the field ... a more or less favourable opportunity to become actualized. (Bourdieu & Wacquant, 1992, pp. 104–105)

To this list, I would introduce a fourth element often discussed in Bourdieu's primary texts (e.g., 1990, 2000) but often stated as absent from his method by his critics (and certainly absent in the quote above):

- analyse how the habitus of agents — and their differentiated actualization — reproduce, reform or resist the prevailing objective structures of relations in the field and the outcomes of the tensions produced by the latter[38].

Each of these steps maps onto the data sources described in Table 1.

---

[38] For an excellent discussion of 'mismatch' between habitus and field, in Bourdieusian terms, see Strand and Lizardo (2017) on resolution of hysteresis towards change — or lack thereof.

Table 1: Relating data sources to method

	Step	Data source
1	analyse the position of the field(s) vis-à-vis the field of power	Relations between the field of vocational education and the field of power have been sketched lightly in the preceding "Conceptual Framework", and will be elaborated more in the findings.
2	map out the objective structures of relations between the positions occupied by the agents or institutions who compete for the legitimate forms of specific authority	To map the 'structures of relations' between False Bay College and other institutions, as well as DHET, included data obtained through: • desktop research exploring FBC's website for their espoused ethos (doxa), foci and past results and accolades (symbolic capital) • broader research on the TVET field which included college statistics and historical records on college mergers and other shifts in the field, particularly as they related to FBC • exploratory questions in interviews with academic leadership of the college also explored these relations • lecturers' perspectives on how FBC 'competes for legitimate forms of specific authority'.
3	analyse the habitus of agents, the different systems of dispositions they have acquired by internalising a determinate type of social and economic condition	'systems of dispositions' were explored through the interviews with college academic leadership but also through surveying lecturers (n=36) for their perspectives on leadership competencies, priorities and values. By cross-referencing lecturers' sense of how decisions are made in and for the college with those of decision makers themselves, subtle differences in the internal field of the college itself could be brought into view that describe the contradictions and trade offs that leaders at FBC must make.
4	analyse how the habitus of agents – and their differentiated actualisation – reproduce, reform or resist the prevailing objective structures of relations in the field	While not a lot of evidence of 'habitus' was available, what evidence of habitus amongst FBC leaders was evident from the interview was considered in how this relates to field of TVET to lift out any 'ontological complicity' (Bourdieu, 1990) or mismatch evident.

This approach sought to ground any local/institution-specific findings in a broader view of the TVET field in South Africa. According to Thomson (2017), a Bourdieusian approach to studying education institution leadership requires:

> always starting from the macro—the wider society, the field of power. This beginning point stands in contrast to ELMA research which often starts with a position, either a particular kind of school—successful, failing or coasting for example—or with a particular person—the headteacher, the bursar, the head of department. *This is particularly the case when the doxa of governing suggests that process does not matter as long as designated outcomes are met.* (Thomson, 2017, p. 49, emphasis added)

Thomson's observations above are particularly salient for the original mandate of this case, namely that of a 'successful' TVET institution considered outside of context and relations. But I suggest that the approach of locating practices within macro field arrangements is more compatible with a concern for social justice (as per this edited volume), since it notices that what constitutes normative judgments on leadership or management practices is social, contingent and necessarily dependent on the prevailing contours of social *power* at play in a given moment. School *effectiveness* approaches that prioritize outcomes over processes set up the individual (leader or institution) as the unit of analysis, ignoring the 'doxa of governing' which may very well be one that reproduces or entrenches social *injustice*.

A good sense of the game: How FBC navigates the TVET field

That FBC manages to navigate the complex work of a TVET institution with relative success is the premise that precipitated this case study. Rather, what is of interest here is an understanding of *how* the college does so, what 'generative structures' (Bourdieu, 1990, 2000) enable said 'successful navigation', and whether these are (not) replicable at other colleges.

Descriptively, the college decision makers demonstrate an understanding that some practices matter more than others in sustaining the college and carving out relative autonomy from external overt interference, and it is this stability and (relative) autonomy that enables the college to dabble with change strategically, including open learning.

The characteristics of interest that emerged from the data gathered include: institutional stability; pre-emptive anticipation of policy changes by leadership and management; strategic allocation of roles and resources to enact college policies (within given limitations); clean financial audits[39] that ensure sufficient freedom to internally redirect funds where desired/required (e.g., internally fungible academic support funds); robust appointment processes oriented to pedagogy; focusing on key lynchpins in students' academic success, such as literacy; inter-campus and intra-department information sharing; early, targeted remedial academic interventions; leveraging social capital where economic would not suffice/be adequate (e.g., memoranda of understanding with other colleges to allow FBC distance learners to write exams at a different TVET college rather than travelling to Cape Town); a blend of 'invite' and 'instruct' when organising staff activities so as to create a sense of inclusion in decision-making; and a keen awareness of the necessity of material provision (esp. infrastructure) for the successful production of sustained rhythms of teaching and learning.

Some aspects of the college are notably aligned with the broader education field in South Africa. The college still engages with relatively top-down decision-making, using rigid structures to do so (a phenomenon that came through in interviews with both leadership and lecturers). Such a decision-making approach is not normatively problematic in and of itself — it can function very well. Rather, given the top-down nature of DHET towards colleges, structuring a local college field in a counter-vailing manner would be difficult to sustain. Leading education institutions under neoliberal conditions involves simultaneously 'looking outwards and inwards' (Lumby, 2003), and hence de-centralised control at the level of the institution might make navigating the broader field almost impossible.

Also in keeping with the broader field of education and power is FBC's focus on key performance indicators. Figure 2 shows where there are alignments and discrepancies in priorities for 'success' between what lecturers believe matters most, and what lecturers believe matters most to the FBC's leadership/management structures.

---

[39] The over-arching field of power, and public service provision, is one beholden to the doxa of *accounting*, more broadly valorised in the discourse of *accountability*. This is a doxa in which financial governance as adjudicated by accounting measures is supreme over other outcomes — see Biesta (2004) for a discussion of accountability vs. responsibility in education institutions.

Figure 2: Lecturers' opinions of what matters most compared to their impressions of management priorities (n=36)

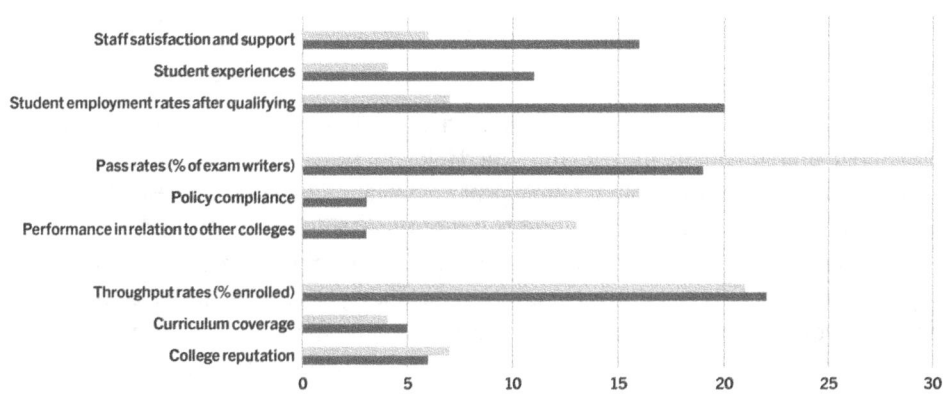

- Lecturers' opinions about what matters most to leadership
- Lecturers' opinions about what matters most

Lecturers' rating of aspects of TVET success were compared to their sense of management's priorities. Three factors converged as common: throughput rates (rated as relatively important by both groups), along with curriculum coverage and college reputation (not as highly prioritised).

But the other six factors showed significant divergence in prioritization: many lecturers thought 'staff satisfaction and support', 'student experience' and 'student employment after qualifying' are important to be considered a 'successful college', but felt that FBC management did not prioritise these. Conversely, lecturers felt that management were far more interested in 'exam pass rates', 'policy compliance' and 'performance in relation to other colleges' but did not rate these factors as important to a college's success.

Once again, the purpose of this comparison is not a normative judgement as to whose priorities are 'better'. Rather, these divergences suggest how the field of TVET education is structured, and how management responds to this field. Outward performance indicators in a neoliberalized system include competitive advantage (see later for a discussion on FBC's strategic 'compete and/or cooperate' disposition with other colleges), exam results (DHET's primary indicator of success) and policy compliance; that FBC is considered a 'successful' college by DHET is likely due to management's (tacit or explicit) knowledge that these indicators *matter* in the current arrangement of the field. As per Thomson's observation above, "process does not matter as long as designated outcomes are met" (Thomson, 2017, p. 48).

This suitability of top-down structures and focusing on key performance indicators is encapsulated by one lecturer's comment when asked "what works or doesn't work at False Bay College":

> I think the college is doing relatively well compared to other colleges in terms of structure and stability. The system of governance is a hybrid with merits and demerits. In terms of policy enforcement and compliance it is highly effective. However, it has its own short comings as some people are very sceptical and suspicious of a controlled environment.

> However, it is effective when you have clear targets and goals that you want to achieve as an organisation. All in one go, I think False Bay TVET College is one of the best run institutions with capable leadership and sound management of finances and resources. (Lecturer 7)

This quote summarizes FBC's relation to the field of TVET: it works *given the conditions at play*, although one should not mistake this functioning for some normative ideal.

Claiming what Bourdieu termed 'ontological complicity' between False Bay College as an institution and the prevailing doxa and illusio of the TVET field in South Africa is bold, given the limited data available and the meagre evidence this case can present within word limitations. The following three extracts from a lengthy discussion with FBC academic managers (backed up with lecturers' anonymized comments) illustrate the basis of this claim and how a Bourdieusian analysis applies to support such an observation.

On institutional stability and anticipating change

Two of the claims this case makes regarding the conditions FBC produces to support specific practices include institutional stability coupled with an ability to anticipate coming changes. A change in executive leadership at the college was discussed as follows:

> To come back to your... the question, of being proactive, rather than reactive... with [the previous executive], I think he's a visionary leader, he's very sharp at picking up changes and trends. He would go to meetings and someone would be mentioning something, and *snaps fingers* he would pick it up and bring it back and say, "I hear these rumours, we must act on it". But I don't think that that has stopped... [the current executive] is still attending the same forums and meetings, and gets the same communications, and is also ahead of what is coming down. (Interview with FBC management)

It is this ability to anticipate, yet treat anticipation as 'common-sensical', that Bourdieu reasons is indicative of synergy between habitus and field:

> In short, being the product of a particular class of objective regularities, the *habitus* tends to generate all the 'reasonable', 'common-sense' behaviours (and only these) which are possible within the limits of these regularities, and which are likely to be positively sanctioned because they are objectively adjusted to the logic characteristic of a particular field, whose objective future they anticipate. At the same time, 'without violence, art or argument', it tends to exclude all 'extravagances' ('not for the likes of us'), that is, all the behaviours that would be negatively sanctioned because they are incompatible with the objective conditions. (Bourdieu, 1990, pp. 55–56)

This sense of 'keeping an eye on what's coming' but also knowing what to leave and what to prepare for, is indicative of the fit between FBC and the field of TVET.

On strategic risk-taking

FBC decision-makers see (measured) risk-taking as a part of sustaining distinction and managing/anticipating change:

> Sometimes it's like that, we jump first and then we think afterwards, 'what did we do?'. But then, where angels fear to tread, that is where False Bay college goes so whether it's out of 'you wanna be first' or you're stupid (enough) to do it, but every time that we've done that, we've seen that *we took the lead* on inclusive education, the lead on blended learning, the lead on distance learning, and um, ya, and that also assists the sector. (Interview with FBC management, emphasis added)

This quote illustrates the confidence (both in subjective sense of self, and objective estimate of the probability of success) that FBC can deploy to reproduce its field location. Decision makers simultaneously have the affective confidence to take measured, considered risks towards change (agency), as well as the stability and foundations to do so (structures) and an appreciation of the logic of the game at play (discourse/doxa/meaning). So while a risk is taken, it is not an improbable one – the 'calculations of success' are reasonable given both prior successes and prevailing arrangements. In this way, success begets success. And it is the gap between 'probable' vs. 'certain' that shapes the difference between *strategy* and *rule* (Bourdieu, 1990, p. 99) – it is because FBC is making a probabilistic decision that includes risk that their gambit appears 'innovative'; in the words of Bourdieu, '*ars inveniendi* is an *ars combinatoria*' (the art of invention is the art of combination) (Bourdieu, 1990, p. 100). FBC decision makers are skilled and experienced at rallying existing forms of capital into combinations that pre-empt and even leverage exigent change:

> We carefully assess the risk. You know, if it's, if it's going to be something that's going to be to the detriment, you know, we won't take unnecessary risk. But we are prepared to, to maybe sort of forge ahead and take calculated risks. Let's put it that way. (Interview with FBC management)

This statement is indicative of FBC decision-making habitus – a balance between risk and calculation that is attuned with the reasonable probabilities of success premised on past successes and a knowledge of the game. The concept of 'calculated risks' is at the heart of habitus that is 'ontologically complicit' with field (Bourdieu, 1990):

> the sense of the probable outcome that is given by practical mastery of the specific regularities that constitute the economy of a field is the basis of 'sensible' practices, linked intelligibly to the conditions of their enactment, and also among themselves, and therefore immediately filled with sense and rationality for every individual who has the feel for the game (hence the effect of consensual validation which is the basis of collective belief in the game and its fetishes). Because native membership in a field implies a feel for the game in the sense of a capacity for practical anticipation of the 'upcoming' future contained in the present, everything that takes place in it seems sensible: full of sense and objectively directed in a judicious direction. (Bourdieu, 1990, p. 66)

But while FBC is far from passive in the efforts to prepare for, and take advantage of, opportunities (i.e. habitus is active, not inert), decision-makers at other colleges with *different* habitus attuned to the *different* objective regularities of an alternative field position (e.g., colleges who experience frequent student protest action, or infrastructural break down, or are under financial audit) might be equally active but have far less to show for it. Practical sense involves combining sense-of-the-game and forms of capital strategically, and colleges without one of these (or both) might expend energy and resources, yet not reap the rewards FBC does, due to their inability to practice 'the art of combination' in accordance with the prevailing doxa of the TVET field.

On recognising what constitutes capital in this field

A third example of FBC leadership being 'attuned' to the field, the logic at play and the stakes of the game, includes focusing on what constitutes cultural capital in this field. TVET colleges, being wedged as they are between GET grades in basic education and industry standards for vocational qualifications, are reliant on the prior learning their students bring to college programmes. This prior learning is highly variable due to the non-standardized end-of-phase assessment at the end of Grade 9 (Daily Maverick, 2019) and so to ensure throughput and pass rates, TVET colleges need to be very careful about their admissions (if they can afford to be) while not enrolling too few students as to financially compromise the institution. FBC leadership understands this tension, and leveraged an opportunity to provide 'promising' applicants some extra support through a DHET pilot support initiative known as the 'PLP' programme. The PLP programme offers extra funding to colleges for 'shoring up' first year college students' prior knowledge in science, mathematics, language and Life Orientation, i.e., economic capital for colleges to assist newcomer students to improve (insufficient) cultural capital for college success.

But even then, FBC leadership also demonstrates a 'sense of the game' in being shrewd and strategic about the use of this programme: "It's just to close those gaps. *So it's the student who hasn't quite met the entry requirements, but who shows potential. It's not the student who's really not gonna make it*" (interview with FBC management, emphasis added).

Realising that the programme is *supplementary* and not a remedy/redress for significant loss of learning, FBC targeted students they knew would maximise the success of the programme without drawing excessively on college resources. That is, on being offered an *opportunity*, leadership had a sufficiently tuned *habitus* to the field, and a sense of the *capital to be gained and to be invested* in the correct amounts, at the correct moment. Again, however, having sufficient 'promising' candidates is as much a function of the applicant pool FBC enjoys, which is likely to have a different profile of prior cultural capital as compared to TVET colleges in rural and/or poorer areas where students bring larger GET learning backlogs. That is, FBC's success in this regard is a dialectic function of strategy/choice *and* historical/geographical advantage. Neither alone is sufficient.

How prevailing conditions support open learning

Returning to the focus of this case requires relating how these conditions support open learning practices at FBC. What the data suggests is that the conditions that support such practices are not specific to open learning – these are the foundational conditions that support institutional balance between stability and change, and undergird decision makers' ability to adopt new ideas, strategies and technologies in their everyday work. That is, such conditions support 'open learning' as a relatively new policy idea in the DHET field, but would also support any other practices that policymakers might introduce. For example, if the change required was that colleges integrate more with industry partners, or 'decolonise' their practices, these conditions would equally support these types of imperatives. What enables FBC to engage with open learning practices is not specific to open learning per se. Rather, it is the mutually productive and supportive relation between the habitus of decision makers at FBC, the doxa and structure of the TVET field, and the college's historical advantage and momentum, that enables FBC to 'play the game' effectively, including the open learning game. That open learning is in keeping with prevailing ideas about institutional management and *illusio* makes this synergy possible, but also condemns open learning initiatives to always be affirmative/ameliorative in nature (Fraser, 2009; Hodgkinson-Williams & Trotter, 2018) given the necessity of articulating with broader fields of practice and power.

How field relations constrain FBC's practices

Despite this fine attuning to what the TVET field demands, the overall relation of TVET to other education fields and the broader field of power places a limit on what FBC can achieve without broader social reform. TVET colleges are still, broadly, seen as less prestigious compared to their university counterparts, and academically 'strong' students will continue in the main to select university education over vocational qualifications.

The policy structure of TVET also produces a contradictory identity, treating these institutions in a similar manner as high schools (see earlier discussion), while performatively changing surface indicators (e.g., calling TVET educators 'lecturers' not teachers). In the words of one lecturer at FBC:

> The TVET sector at False Bay has become cumbersome, especially if we are inclusive as well. We therefore seem to compare ourselves to tertiary institutions and have the strain of trying to meet those criteria in our outcomes. This can create an identity crisis and confused execution of our curricula. (Lecturer 28)

As the management at FBC noted in their interview, TVET colleges do not enjoy curriculum or assessment autonomy like universities do, and this places limitations on what the college can influence. In addition, TVET institutions exhibit qualities similar to those of broader neoliberal reforms in education, such as 'customer-orientation' and financialised logics premised on enrolment and throughput. Such limitations raise questions regarding individual TVET institutions' *reach* (Jacklin, 2004) for implementing social justice for their staff and students without broader field reform.

It is also interesting to consider whether a field characterised by top-down decision-making structures and key performance indicators could be supportive of social justice concerns, given that such practices might crowd out other aspects of internal college organisation, such as democratic consultation or inclusion, or student articulation from college into the workplace. The next section explores the normative ideal of social justice that frames the broader COOL project in relation to the description offered of the TVET field.

Barriers to participation: Enacting social justice at FBC

While FBC is located in a relatively economically advantaged area of the country and in a province that enjoys historical investment and development without the burden of apartheid-era homeland territories, socioeconomic conditions in the Western Cape exhibit the extreme inequality that hallmarks South Africa as a country. Urban spaces in the Cape Town metropole enjoy amongst some of the most expensive and prestigious properties in the world, but rural areas in the Cape Winelands have amongst some of the highest unemployment rates and adult illiteracy rates in the country (Land & Lyster, 2019), and suffer the highest incidence of Foetal-Alcohol Syndrome in the world (Rendall-Mkosi et al., 2008).

Economic barriers

FBC's students, drawn primarily from the Western Cape, experience a heterogenous mix of economic barriers to participation. By lecturers' reckoning, students at FBC experience significant challenges regarding transport, financial dependents, unsupportive home environments for learning and studying, and lack of access to digital means (incl. lack of data, lack of internet connectivity and inadequate access to digital devices appropriate to learning). The latter became particularly acute when the college had to move all learning online during the COVID-19 pandemic. While some students experience food and housing insecurity, or debt and health issues, these were perceived to be fewer than those experiencing the other concerns. That is, FBC's students are not the most economically well off, or the most destitute. As with most students in TVET colleges nationally, the majority of FBC's students receive National Student Financial Aid Scheme (NSFAS) funding — FBC management estimated 90% of FBC students come from households with income lower than R350 000 per annum, a threshold below which 82% of South Africans overall are estimated to live[40]. NSFAS funding offers living allowances and pays fees, but prohibits repetition of failed courses on the bursary, and so financial support for students who need to repeat is limited.

FBC's clean financial audits and liquidity mean the college has sufficient economic capital to bridge the gap between the start of the academic year and late or delayed payments from NSFAS (management interview); this exhibits how FBC's conditions enable affirmative responses to economic exclusion and allow the college to weather short-term challenges in a way that a college with less financial liquidity and reserves might struggle. But the college is not in a position to offer transformative economic remedies for either repeating students or those who fall outside of NSFAS criteria (e.g., the 'missing middle', or students who are not South African citizens), given the structure of the field in which it must engage.

Cultural barriers

Cultural impediments to participation at the college were not perceived as particularly significant by lecturers. Digital literacy was perceived to be the biggest concern, followed by 'routines and habits that are strange and unfamiliar' (indicating a potential mismatch

---

[40] According to the SALDRU income comparison tool, 82% of South Africans live in households under this threshold (based on a household of five people) (SALDRU, 2019).

between students' *habitus* and the prevailing practices at the college), gaps in prior learning from school and challenges with English as the medium of instruction.

The tensions in cultural 'barriers' to participation, however, did not only occur at the level of individual students in their relation to the college, but rather in the contradictions the college has to negotiate between students' cultural resources (including prior educational attainment), the cultural capital recognised by the TVET field and that recognised by broader fields of industry for which FBC must prepare students. The issue of curriculum autonomy arose on multiple occasions, as exemplified in the following extract from the interview with management:

> Some of our syllabi are outdated. Telegrams and telexes! And faxes! Faxes even. Who sends a telegram? I mean, I don't think I've seen a telegram in years. Um, you know, the generation that we're teaching now, they don't know about dial up telephones. This generation was born when the internet was there, when CDs were there. They don't know about turning over an LP and listening to the other side, you know? So it's about what do we teach that is relevant?... We're also a little bit hamstrung by the outdated syllabi that we deal with, but you know, we always, I always say to people "bring into your curriculum what is going to add value". We also send lecturers out on lecturer-workplace exposure. Um, so we're going to send twenty odd this year for about five days. I mean, and then I ask them to reflect, "what did you see in industry that you can bring back into the practices in your classroom? How's that going to affect your pedagogy? How's that going to affect your examples that you share with students?" you know? So I think it's about relevance. (Interview with FBC management)

Rather than considering individual students, then, it is more productive to think about the relations between fields and the tensions these relations produce between competing and contradictory *doxa*. FBC, as an institution, strategizes around these, but will be limited to simultaneously trying to meet industry requirements, DHET requirements and filling gaps in students prior learning. Broader transformational remedies to cultural alienation (such as translanguaging or decolonising curriculum) will not find fertile ground at individual colleges amidst such tensions.

Political barriers

Political participation for students at FBC is still relatively traditional in the form of an SRC which is periodically consulted (an instance of affirmative, not transformative, justice). Lecturers' sense of inclusion, based on the lecturer survey for this case study, varied greatly, and trended according to campus location, indicating that lecturers' sense of voice and inclusion depended on middle management at the campus level. Almost all lecturers surveyed indicated that paperwork and administration contributed significantly to their workload, but acknowledged this was a function of the broader TVET field as set by DHET policy, not the local field as set by management. That is, lecturers felt disempowered by the nature of the TVET field at large, which focused on exam results and performative accountability, even when this interfered with teaching and learning and/or prioritising students. Decision-making participation for both students and lecturers, then, was strongly regulated by the top-down decision-making structures described earlier and the limits of the game which FBC must play.

Issues of the frame (meta-concerns of justice)

A prevailing theme throughout discussions with both management and lecturers at the college was that of needing to sustain strong boundaries between those 'inside' the college and those beyond – this particularly manifested in discussions about admissions criteria for students and hiring practices for lecturers. Again, such an observation is not normative regarding the college, but indicative of the nature of the field and the reach of the college to influence what it can while strongly defending the frame of who the college supports and works with. The dominant field of power, globally, nationally and locally, is one of strong frames, with concepts of 'registration', 'citizenship', 'enrolment' hallmarking ingroup/outgroup dynamics and 'legitimacy of participation' at every level.

However, focusing on *students'* experiences of barriers to participation (of any kind) at FBC raises concerns of framing that excludes, by definition, those prevented from participating by not being included at the college. For instance, at a staff workshop for inclusive education, FBC management had to explain how admission criteria are enforced during student registration, primarily along lines of prior academic attainment. This same strong framing is evident in how the college works with the *FET College Student Support policy framework* (DoE, 2009):

> So it's entry support, on-course support, and exit support. And it categorises the kinds of support at each of those levels. And our, um, plan, our student-support development services which falls under my part... so it's academics, it's student support, it's inclusion ... how do we support students on entry? How do we support them on course? And what is the exit support? And the WIL office has some of that exit support. (Interview with FBC management)

As discussed later, the loosening or tightening of college boundaries is strategically deployed when FBC selectively cooperates or competes with other colleges; what this section is attempting to foreground is that the TVET field that prioritises financial and policy-compliance aspects of college management and leadership are not always conducive conditions for transformative social justice or student-centred practices. Such contradictions are also echoed in the *Open Learning Policy Framework* (DHET, 2017) through tensions between access, success and cost effectiveness (see Black, 2022), and these contradictions play out in the everyday activities of colleges.

Finally, a significant challenge to education institutions overall, as sites of social change, are the decades of empirical evidence that suggest that such institutions *tacitly sanction pre-existing social relations of inequality*. English (2012) notes that policy "statement(s) about social justice do(es) not address the real cause of social injustice or the school's role in legitimising it" (p. 164). This trend of education to tacitly legitimize pre-existing inequality by disguising economic and cultural advantage as merit was at the core of Bourdieu's concern regarding education and social reproduction (Bourdieu, 1990, 2000; Bourdieu & Passeron, 1977). Such observations cannot be ignored if transformative social justice is a genuine priority.

Can others play too? The limitations of the current field arrangement for transferring FBC's practices to other TVET colleges

One of the primary motivations to show-casing FBC's relative success in this case study was to foreground transferable practices for other colleges. Understanding the relations of the prevailing TVET field adds further insight into how context shapes such practices, which might transfer, and which might not. Three examples arose from discussions regarding how FBC relates laterally to other colleges: conference organising, policy-sharing and inter-college committees in the Western Cape region.

False Bay bears a self-adopted mantle of 'leading' in the TVET space through hosting international conferences on 'innovative' ideas:

> A: through that conference, *we've also sort of set the trend*, um, in terms of including technology in your classroom, best practices in the classroom. We had a lot of topics... first we focused on the lecturer, the enabling classroom, and all of those things. And through that we've actually assisted a lot of the other colleges to also start to implement blended learning at their colleges and get on board, and those types of things. So it became *the* event of the year for other colleges to visit, to learn and to take back ideas."
>
> B: And it wasn't only South African institutions. So we had, um, people from the UK, Norway...
>
> A: Norway, the Netherlands, King William University I think it was?
>
> B: yes
>
> A: ya, speakers from America, from France, and everywhere.
> (Interview with FBC management, emphasis added)

Such efforts indicate FBC management's tacit understanding that economic capital can build social and symbolic capital, signalling a field position not only to other colleges but also to DHET. That FBC can rally the necessary resources to host such events (which are time-consuming and expensive) where other colleges would probably struggle is indicative of FBC's dominance in the South African TVET landscape. Again, this is not a normative judgement on the college – any college able and aware of the nature of the 'game' before them would do the same. Rather, such events raise the question of the field doxa and illusio, since if *all* colleges engaged in such practices, it is questionable whether these conferences would signal the same type of capital.

The second example of inter-college relations is in FBC's strategic deployment of cooperation with other colleges. Horizontal field relations are not just brute competition red-in-tooth-and-claw; social capital and cooperation serve colleges' interests too, so long as they do not subvert the autonomy of individual institutions. FBC understands that cooperation is best achieved with other institutions *that have something to exchange,* i.e., are geographically collocated, or can share infrastructural assets with FBC (see the prior example of memoranda of understanding regarding distance students and writing exams).

But collaboration was less enthusiastic for assisting multiple colleges that are perceived to be 'take but no give'. Again, this is *not* an indictment on FBC but rather illustrative of the social relations of the field in which the college must operate – selective collaboration suggests (historical) social capital matters for strategic decision-making:

Interviewer:	What do you think gets in the way of the other TVET colleges doing what you do? What do you think is impeding them from doing what you do?
A:	Maybe its… maybe, you know, what, what we do, every time that we start with an initiative, we would put people in place to drive the initiative, so I think that might be it? That they would want to do something, but they haven't' got the right people there to do it. They would dwindle it down to the lecturer in the classroom, or the programme head that needs to take on an additional responsibility and then it just doesn't… follow through.
	Yeah, I think also… I'm just thinking here with my distance learning cap on… you know, the experiences that I've had since we started with distance learning. We did it very well thought out. We had a lot of meetings around "how are we going to do this?" and which courses to choose, and "how are we going to offer it", whatever… *and then, now that we are doing it, I've found – especially last year – colleges knocking on my door and saying, "we want to come and benchmark on you and what you're doing" and they will come and sit in my office and we will chat and ask questions. And eventually obviously there's the question, "can you share your policy with us? can you share your documents with us?"*
	So it's, it's where I say the vision and *to put the right people in place, to roll out these things*, it's as if there's sort of this thinking, "ok, False Bay College is already doing this and doing it well – *so we're going to visit them, we are going to get from them, they can share with us and we're just going to implement"*…
Interviewer:	Yes. Mm, but policy doesn't transfer that way does it?
B:	No! Cos you've got to have the structures and there…
A:	You've got to have the structures… so I found with many of those, they didn't grow through the ranks…
B:	They come there and they just want to take our policy and think they can walk off to their college and implement it where they don't even have connectivity, where they don't even have a Learning Management System, they haven't got a… *and it's a totally different context*! (Interview with FBC management, emphasis added)

FBC management expressed reluctance to share internal policy documents with other colleges. The above extract indicates a (most likely accurate) diagnosis that such policies will not find fertile ground in the absence of structures and resources. It also indicates a selectivity on FBC's part regarding give-and-take with colleges who are not perceived as being able to offer anything in return. Interpreting this as just tight-fisted-ness elides a deeper, more descriptive possibility: that colleges cannot afford to be un-strategically charitable given the resource scarcity within not only the TVET sector, but the broader public sector at large. That is; indiscriminate charity is an unsustainable practice for any college, dominant or otherwise.

FBC collaborates where it is strategic to do so, and appreciates its own historical advantages that enable success:

Interviewer: Why do you think this region is stronger?

Respondent: I think it has a bit of a historical issue. So before, when we were a provincial competency, we were under the WCED [Western Cape Education Department]. And there was a very strong support structure ... so when we moved over to a national competency, many of those people came over ...

So I think that the Western Cape had a regional office before any other province had a regional office. And because of that, we collaborated as the six colleges. On assessment. On common exam timetables. And we had focus groups. And we shared assessments. And we had the asset system where we could upload assessments and colleges were writing common assessments. And that was something that wasn't happening in other provinces. And I think that has been our growth point. (Interview with FBC management)

The college clearly sees itself as a pioneer in the sector: "if it has to be us then it will be us – there's gotta almost be someone who goes and does the groundwork and be the forerunner and then others will obviously follow" (Interview with FBC management). While this willingness to lead and pioneer clearly indicates confidence and a sense of agency at FBC, it is questionable whether the broader field is structured in such a way that 'others will obviously follow' – action occurs in dialogue with circumstances, and many colleges do not enjoy FBC's circumstances. Such a sense of 'self innovation' is also in keeping with the hegemonic neoliberal ideal of 'striving individualism' which backgrounds its own zero-sum nature: if everyone is an 'innovator', then no one is. This is not to say that FBC explicitly leverages comparative advantage to the detriment of other colleges; rather it foregrounds the wicked problem of *the broader field of social relations that rewards and valorises zero-sum comparative approaches to thinking about success*. FBC is simply playing the game set before it, and not even necessarily consciously so:

Each field mirrors the social space in having its own autonomous and heronomous (sic) poles, its own dominant and dominated agents and institutions, its mechanisms for reproduction and its struggles for usurpation and exclusion. Thus, many of the strategies function as `double plays' (Bourdieu, 1996, p. 271) in the sense that *although these field-specific strategies are not expressly conceived as such nor the product of conspiracy among the dominants in the various fields, they are objectively organized in such a way that they contribute to both the accumulation of field specific capital and to the reproduction of the structure of `social space'*. (Naidoo, 2004, pp. 459-460, emphasis added)

Changing the field: The role of DHET

Transference and sharing of practices that support open learning and social justice would require a different illusio and doxa in the broader field of TVET. FBC indicated an awareness of the prevailing policy zeitgeist of mandates without support:

> with respect to the DHET: they say 'lets open access'... *but the systems are not in place.* So we've had to put our own systems in place: we've had to be very innovative in terms of how we do things, and how we think about doing things in terms of distance learning... it's been a bit of a struggle. (Interview with FBC management, emphasis added)

This insight indicates the broader top-down structure of the TVET field, one that bears the hallmarks of neoliberal responsibility at the bottom and accountability at the top. Colleges must mobilise internal resources and systems to meet policy demands, yet cannot rely on provision of the requisite *enabling conditions* from the broader field. For those colleges that have less historical and contextual advantage than FBC, it is questionable whether such enabling conditions as described in this case are realisable without changes in the broader field.

Conclusion

This case study has sought to understand the enabling conditions at a college deemed 'successful' in the TVET arena in South Africa, and how these conditions relate not only to institutional level decision-making, but broader relations of meaning-making and structure. Such conditions have been identified as supporting open learning practices, but what the data suggests from this study is that this support is not specific – these are the enabling conditions that allow an institution to navigate change in an increasingly precarious world.

What has also emanated from this study is that the relations between the TVET field that FBC must navigate, and broader relations of power in education and at large, constrain the college's ability to pursue social justice in transformative ways. Such relations are also, currently, antagonistic to blind transference of 'good practice' from the dominant college in the field (FBC) and other colleges that occupy different field positions. In other words, "We need to get away from formulae and the search for elusive 'best practices' and rely on deeper economic analysis to identify binding constraints" (World Bank, 2005, as cited in Akoojee, 2016, p. 3).

This reflection, albeit a full 180 from the World Bank, is salient – rather than seeking to transfer 'best practice' a-contextually from FBC to other TVETs. The lessons to be learnt from this case study are in how FBC identified its local binding constraints and strategized to overcome them *with its given context and resources.*

Given the 'waves of change' (Paterson, 2016) that TVET colleges have been subjected to over the last two decades, this case study of FBC affirms a return to what might be termed 'bread and butter basics' in order for institutional conditions to support growth, autonomy and change, including mandates regarding open learning and social justice. Rather than focusing on individual institutions to producing 'enabling conditions' locally, questions must be asked regarding the broader TVET space and how enabling conditions can be set at this scale for all colleges to pursue 'best practice' in response to their local conditions and challenges.

Acknowledgements

Many thanks to the current and former management staff – Karin Hendricks, Carol Dwyer, Melanie Vermaak, Marian Theron, Cassie Kruger – and educators and students from False Bay College, whose inputs made the case study possible. Special thanks are due to reviewers Dr Bruce Kloot and Professor Pam Christie for their thoughtful, incisive feedback on the chapter, Emeritus Associate Professor Cheryl Hodgkinson-Williams for mentoring the case study, Shanali Govender for her critical reading of the chapter, and Dr Tabisa Mayisela for guiding the entire COOL project. Thanks are also due to the Centre for Innovation in Learning and Teaching at the University of Cape Town, which hosted the COOL project, and the South African Department of Higher Education and Training for funding it.

References

Addison, B. (2009). A feel for the game – a Bourdieuian analysis of principal leadership: A study of Queensland secondary school principals. *Journal of Educational Administration and History*, 41(4), 327–341.

Akoojee, S. (2016). Developmental TVET rhetoric-in-action: the White Paper for post-school education and training in South Africa. *International Journal for Research in Vocational Education and Training*, 3(1), 1–15.

Allais, S. (2020). Skills for industrialisation in sub-Saharan African countries: why is systemic reform of technical and vocational systems so persistently unsuccessful? *Journal of Vocational Education & Training*, 1–19.

Anderson, G. L., Mungal, A., Pini, M. Scott, J., & Thomson, P. (2013). Policy, equity, and diversity in global context: educational leadership after the welfare state. In L. C. Tillman & J. J. Scheurich (Eds.), *Handbook of research on educational leadership for equity and diversity* (pp. 43–61). Routledge.

Ball, S. J. (2018). Commercialising education: profiting from reform! *Journal of Education Policy*, 33(5), 587–589.

Ball, S. J. (2012). *Global education Inc.: New policy networks and the neo-liberal imaginary*. Routledge.

Ball, S. J. (2008). New philanthropy, new networks and new governance in education. *Political Studies*, 56(4), 747–765.

Bathmaker, A.-M. (2015). Thinking with Bourdieu: Thinking after Bourdieu. Using 'field' to consider in/equalities in the changing field of English higher education. *Cambridge Journal of Education*, 45(1), 61–80.

Bathmaker, A.-M., Graf, L., Orr, K., Powell, J., Webb, S., & Wheelahan, L. (2018). Higher level vocational education: The route to high skills and productivity as well as greater equity? An international comparative analysis. In C. Nägele & B. E. Stalder (Eds.), *Trends in vocational education and training research. Proceedings of the European Conference on Educational Research (ECER), Vocational Education and Training Network (VETNET)* (pp. 53–60). https://doi.org/10.5281/zenodo.1319628

Black, S. (2022). Marx's ghost in the shell: Troubling techno-solutionist utopias in post-secondary education and training policy imaginaries. In S. Vally & E. Motala (Eds.) [untitled book compilation – NRF chair in Community Adult and Worker Education].

Bourdieu, P. (1967). Systems of education and systems of thought. *International Social Science Journal*, 19(3), 338–352.

Bourdieu, P. (1974). The school as a conservative force: Scholastic and cultural inequalities. In J. Eggleston (Ed.), *Contemporary research in the sociology of education* (pp. 32–46). Methuen.

Bourdieu, P. (1984 & 1990). *Homo academicus*. Polity.

Bourdieu, P. (1986). The forms of capital. In J. Richardson (Ed.), *Handbook of theory and research for the sociology of education* (pp. 241–258). Greenwood.

Bourdieu, P. (1990). *The logic of practice* (R. Nice, Trans.). Stanford University Press.

Bourdieu, P. (1996) *The state nobility*. Polity.

Bourdieu, P. (1998). *Practical reason: On the theory of action.* Stanford University Press.

Bourdieu, P. (2000). *Pascalian meditations* (R. Nice, Trans.). Stanford University Press.

Bourdieu, P., & Passeron, J-C. (1977/1990). *Reproduction in education, society and culture* (R. Nice, Trans.). Sage.

Bourdieu, P., & Wacquant, L. (1992). *An invitation to reflexive sociology*. Polity.

Chappell, C. (1999). Issues of teacher identity in a restructuring VET system. Working paper, UTS Research Centre for Vocational Education and Training.

Christie, P. (2008). *Opening the doors of learning*. Heinemann.

Courtney, S. (2015). Corporatised leadership in English schools. *Journal of Educational Administration and History*, 47(3), 214–231.

Crow, G., Day, C., & Møller, J. (2016). Framing research on school principals' identities. *International Journal of Leadership in Education,* 265–277. DOI: 10.1080/13603124.2015.1123299

Daily Maverick. (2019). Grade 9 exit certificate would give learners an imminent sense of possibility. https://www.dailymaverick.co.za/article/2019-10-16-grade-9-exit-certificate-would-give-learners-an-imminent-sense-of-possibility/

Deer, C. (2003). Bourdieu on higher education: The meaning of the growing integration of educational systems and self-reflective practice. *British Journal of Sociology of Education*, 24(2), 195–206.

Deleuze, G. (1991). *Empiricism and subjectivity: An essay on Hume's theory of human nature*. Columbia University Press.

DHET (Department of Higher Education and Training). (2013a). White paper for post-school education and training: Building an expanded, effective and integrated post-school system. *Government Gazette*, 37229. https://www.gov.za/documents/white-paper-post-school-education-and-training-building-expanded-effective-and-integrated

DHET. (2017). Open learning policy framework for post-school education and training (draft). *Government Gazette*, 40772(335). http://pmg-assets.s3-website-eu-west-1.amazonaws.com/170407openlearningframework-postschooleduc.pdf

DoE (Department of Education) (2009). Student support services manual for further education and training colleges. http://www.saide.org.za/resources/Library/DoE%20-%20FET%20Student%20Support%20Services%20Manual.pdf

English, F. W. (2012). Bourdieu's misrecognition: why educational leadership standards will not reform schools or leadership. *Journal of Educational Administration and History*, 44(2), 155–170. DOI: 10.1080/00220620.2012.658763.

Fraser, N. (1995). From redistribution to recognition? Dilemmas of justice in a 'postsocialist' age. *New Left Review*, 1/212, 68–93. https://newleftreview.org/issues/i212/articles/nancy-fraser-from-redistribution-to-recognition-dilemmas-of-justice-in-a-post-socialist-age

Fraser, N. (2009). *Scales of justice: Reimagining political space in a globalizing world*. Columbia University Press.

Grenfell, M., & James, D. (1998). *Bourdieu and education: Acts of practical theory*. Falmer.

Harvey, D. (2018). Reading Marx's *Capital* Volume 1 with David Harvey [Video]. The People's Forum NYC. https://www.youtube.com/watch?v=cpW1Q9sgUB0

Heystek, J. (2007). Reflecting on principals as managers or moulded leaders in a managerialistic school system. *South African Journal of Education,* 27(3), 491–505.

Hodgkinson-Williams, C. A., & Trotter, H. (2018). A social justice framework for understanding open educational resources and practices in the Global South. *Journal of Learning for Development*, 5(3), 204–224.

Jacklin, H. (2004). Repetition and difference: A rhythm analysis of pedagogic practice [Doctoral thesis, University of the Witwatersrand].

Lyster, R., &, Land, S. (2019). Proposals for Community College Pilot Project roll-out in each province in South Africa. *Technical report on community colleges.* Durban University of Technology.

Lingard, B., Sellar, S., & Baroutsis, A. (2015). Researching the habitus of global policy actors in education. *Cambridge Journal of Education*, 45(1), 25–42.

Lumby, J. (2003). Managing external relations in South African schools. *Management in Education,* 17, 24–28.

Lumby, J., & English, F. (2009). From simplicism to complexity in leadership identity and preparation: Exploring the lineage and dark secrets. *International Journal of Leadership in Education*, 12(2), 95–114.

Maxwell, J. (1992). Understanding and validity in qualitative research. *Harvard Educational Review*, 62(3), 279–301.

McGrath, S. A., Badroodien, A., Kraak, A., & Unwin, L. (Eds.). (2004). *Shifting understandings of skills in South Africa: Overcoming the historical imprint of a low regime*. HSRC Press.

Muller/Black, S. (2017). Bourdieu on the barricades: Understanding the symbolic violence of education institutions in 21st century post-apartheid South Africa. *IFAA student and youth social theory reader 'reimagining education'*. https://ifaacapetown.files.wordpress.com/2015/02/the-ifaa-student-and-youth-social-theory-reader-reimagining-education-june.pdf

Naidoo, R. (2004). Fields and institutional strategy: Bourdieu on the relationship between higher education, inequality and society. *British Journal of Sociology of Education*, 25(4), 457–471.

Niesche, R., & Thomson, P. (2017). Freedom to what ends? School autonomy in neoliberal times. *The Wiley international handbook of educational leadership* (pp. 193–206). Wiley-Blackwell.

Papier, J. (2011). Vocational teacher identity: spanning the divide between the academy and the workplace. *Southern African Review of Education,* 17, 101–119.

Paterson, A. (2016). Introduction. In A. Kraak, A. Paterson & K. Boka (Eds.), *Change management in TVET colleges: Lessons learnt from the field* (pp. vii–xxiii). JET Education Services.

Rawolle, S., & Lingard, B. (2013). Bourdieu and educational research. In M. Murphy (Ed.), *Social theory and education research: Understanding Foucault, Habermas, Bourdieu and Derrida* (pp. 117–137). Routledge.

Rendall-Mkosi, K., London, L., Adnams, C., Morojele, N., McLoughin, J-A., & Goldstone, C. (2008). *Fetal Alcohol Spectrum Disorder in South Africa: Situational and gap analysis*. UNICEF. https://www.unicef.org/southafrica/media/2441/file/ZAF-fetal-alcohol-spectrum-disorder-South-Africa-2008.pdf

Rizvi, F., & Lingard, B. (2009). *Globalizing education policy*. Routledge.

SALDRU (South African Labour & Development Research Unit). (2019). Income comparison tool. SALDRU, University of Cape Town. https://www.saldru.uct.ac.za/incomecomparison-tool/

Shalem, Y. (2003). Do we have a theory of change? Calling change models to account. *Perspectives in Education*, 21(1), 29–49.

Strand, M., & Lizardo, O. (2017). The hysteresis effect: Theorizing mismatch in action. *Journal for the Theory of Social Behaviour*, 47(2), 164–194.

Thomson, P. (2005). Bringing Bourdieu to policy sociology: Codification, misrecognition and exchange value in the UK context. *Journal of Education Policy*, 20(6), 741–758.

Thomson, P. (2010). Headteacher autonomy: A sketch of a Bourdieuian field analysis of position and practice. *Critical Studies in Education*, 51(1), 5–20.

Thomson, P. (2011). Creative leadership: A new category or more of the same? *Journal of Educational Administration and History*, 43(3), 249–272.

Thomson, P. (2014). 'Scaling up' educational change: Some musings on misrecognition and doxic challenges. *Critical Studies in Education*, 55(2), 87–103.

Thomson, P. (2017). *Educational leadership and Pierre Bourdieu*. Routledge.

Thrupp, M. (2003). The school leadership literature in managerialist times: Exploring the problem of textual apologism. *School Leadership & Management*, 23(2), 149–172.

Vally, S., & Motala, E. (2014) *Education, economy and society*. Unisa Press.

Wedekind, V. (2016). Introduction. *SAQA Bulletin,* 15(1), 1–29.

HOW TO CITE THIS CHAPTER

Black, S. (2022). "Understanding the TVET game": A case study on maximising available opportunities for open educational practices within the broader TVET field in South Africa. In T. Mayisela, S. C. Govender & C. A. Hodgkinson-Williams (Eds.), *Open learning as a means of advancing social justice: Cases in post-school education and training in South Africa* (pp. 241–268). African Minds. doi: 10.47622/9781928502425_11

This work is licensed under a Creative Commons Attribution 4.0 International (CC BY 4.0) licence.

12

Enabling open learning and participatory parity through increased e-learning

The case of leadership at Gert Sibande TVET College, South Africa

Mukhtar Raban & Tabisa Mayisela

SUMMARY At the core of challenges besetting most South African Technical and Vocational Education and Training (TVET) colleges are poor leadership and management which lead to inadequate guidance and support for open learning, in general, and, more specifically, technologically innovative practices such as e-learning. E-learning contributed to improving learning flexibility for financially precarious students at Gert Sibande TVET College (GSC), who were unable to commute daily. Flexible modes of learning provision tie in with the South African Department of Higher Education and Training's (DHET) open learning principles. A small-scale qualitative study was undertaken to investigate leadership approaches and practices in its promotion of open learning via the prioritisation of e-learning at GSC, identified by DHET as a forerunner of e-learning. In-depth interviews with senior management and college lecturers were conducted online. Due to the social justice intent foregrounded in DHET's draft *Open Learning Policy Framework*, Nancy Fraser's social justice framework was used to determine the extent to which the leadership processes and practices enabled socially just environments for increased e-learning initiatives. The study found that visionary and socially just leadership practices contributed to increasing e-learning implementation at the college, although certain economic, cultural and political injustices in terms of effectively enabling e-learning still prevailed. This study holds the potential to further influence the social justice imperatives of leadership of e-learning at the institution, as well as contribute to leadership for open learning initiatives in South Africa and abroad.

Keywords: visionary leadership, distributed leadership, open learning, e-learning, TVET

Introduction

Accelerated developments in technology-enhanced learning (TEL) in many parts of the world have resulted in a rise in e-learning offerings (Gaebel et al., 2014; Kanuka, 2008). While the COVID-19 pandemic undoubtedly resulted in a rapid rise of online learning and teaching, preceding this period, the global education sector already experienced an annual increase of 15.4% in e-learning offerings (Alqahtani & Rajkhan, 2020).

The *White Paper for Post-School Education and Training* calls for institutions to widen flexible access to learning by varying their modes of provision to include e-learning and blended learning, and becoming more open, accessible and inclusive (DHET, 2013). DHET (2017), via the draft *Open Learning Policy Framework* (OLPF) *for PSET*, further intensifies the call for increased open learning opportunities that can be facilitated via e-learning. While DHET does not deem open learning an all-encompassing solution to the many and varied challenges facing Technical and Vocational Education and Training (TVET) colleges and the PSET sector at large, it is encouraging institutions to embrace open learning principles as a means to widen access, improve quality of provision and enhance success. Writing from a South African TVET position, Balkrishen (2015) suggests that college leadership plays a significant role in how these principles are interpreted, taken up and enacted in institutions.

In response to the DHET call, the TVET college sector is steadily attempting to increase its exploration and deployment of e-learning. However, poor leadership and management in the sector results in insufficient support for these innovative practices (Badenhorst & Radile, 2018). Educational leadership researchers assert that effective college leadership is central to the maintenance and support of high-quality education, particularly with respect to curriculum-related innovations, such as e-learning, and student achievement and success (Balkrishen, 2015; Balkrishen & Mestry, 2016; Leithwood et al., 2010).

Despite the literature on educational leadership in the TVET sector, there are limited empirical studies (see, for example, chapter 11 in this volume) that specifically explore college leadership's responses to advancing open learning in the South African context. Through a small-scale qualitative approach, this study explores educational leadership for promoting open learning at one South African college, Gert Sibande TVET College (GSC) in Mpumalanga. The study investigates the extent to which GSC leadership processes and practices have fostered open learning and, in so doing, increased parity of participation through its e-learning offerings.

Prior to delving into the study, we explore the literature on open learning, educational leadership and social justice. Thereafter, the methodology, deduced insights, conclusion and recommendations are provided.

Open learning, educational leadership and social justice

This study is located at the intersection of open learning and its principles, and e-learning, exploring how educational leadership in the TVET sector is advancing open learning principles through e-learning, and to what extent these support the social justice imperatives of open learning.

Open learning

The United Nations Educational, Scientific and Cultural Organization (UNESCO) views 'open learning' as:

> an approach to education that seeks to remove all unnecessary barriers to learning, while aiming to provide students with a reasonable chance of success in an education and training system centred on their specific needs and located in multiple arenas of learning. (2015, p. 6)

Similarly, DHET's draft OLPF emphasises the importance of removing barriers to learning and, drawing heavily on the UNESCO definition, describes 'open learning' as:

> An educational approach which combines the principles of learner-centredness, lifelong learning, flexibility of learning provision, the removal of barriers to access learning, the recognition for credit of prior learning experience, the provision of learner support, the construction of learning programmes in the expectation that learners can succeed, and the maintenance of rigorous quality assurance over the design of learning materials and support systems. (DHET, 2017, p. 363)

For the purpose of this study, the ways in which college leadership responds to the global and national calls for removing barriers to learning, particularly through e-learning, is critical to advancing the open learning agenda in the TVET sector.

Opening up learning via e-learning

DHET (2017) has identified open learning as a potential response to students' 'geographic isolation from campuses or learning centres within reasonable proximity', and recommends e-learning – also referred to as 'technology-enhanced learning' (p. 362) – as a potential mode of learning provision. E-learning offers "a growing range of innovative and effective teaching and learning methods (increasing learners' chances of success)" (DHET, 2017, p. 368).

Sana and Adhikary (2017) define e-learning as computer-enhanced learning that "deals with both the technologies and associated methodologies in learning using networked and/or multimedia technologies" (p. 507). The OLPF describes how e-learning uses information and communication technology (ICT) to facilitate access to programmes or courses:

> It involves the use of electronic devices (for example computers and mobile devices) to provide, access or interact with learning materials, interact with peers and lecturers, participate in discussions and do assessments. e-Learning can take place online, offline, or in a combination thereof. (DHET, 2017, p. 362)

It is worth noting that e-learning is merely a vehicle of flexible provision among others, such as distance education, resource-based learning, online learning and blended learning, and "none of [these] should be equated with open learning, [as] open learning has no conceptual value as a synonym for any of them" (DHET, 2017, p. 372). Furthermore, if one conflates e-learning with open learning, when e-learning excludes some students due to lack of access to devices and reliable internet connectivity, the ideological stance of open learning is weakened.

According to Sana and Adhikary (2017), e-learning is one of the four categories of a myriad of ICT-mediated teaching and learning provisions, as illustrated in Figure 1.

Figure 1: Categories of ICT-Mediated Teaching and Learning

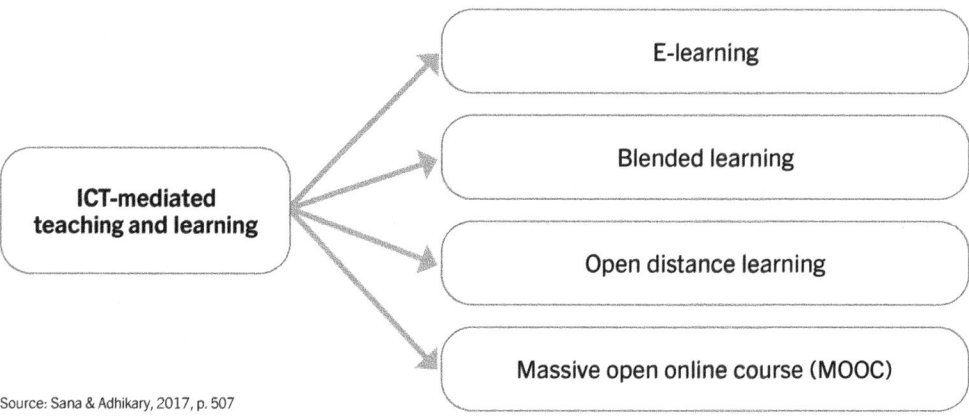

Source: Sana & Adhikary, 2017, p. 507

In this study, the terms e-learning and blended learning — an education program (formal or informal) that combines online digital media with traditional classroom methods — are used interchangeably.

The use of e-learning in the TVET sector is recognised as a crucial "resource to be drawn on to maximise learning opportunities in developing economies" (Obwoge & Kwamboka, 2016, p. 348). However, TVET colleges face multiple constraining factors, such as lecturer attitude and reluctance to change, and lack of adequate funding to develop ICT infrastructure, train and support staff in implementing ICTs (Obwoge & Kwamboka, 2016, p. 348). This implies that college leadership has to develop clear, strategic e-learning priorities that stem from a vision seeking to impart the principles of open learning. Vision-driven leadership, in its deeper and more critical interpretation and exploration of open learning, should explore considerations of social justice, given what Robertson and Frick (2018) describe as the transformative role of TVET colleges in South African society.

Educational leadership in the South African TVET sector

TVET colleges have "historically played a key part in UNESCO's mandate for education" (Tikly, 2013, p. 3) – which is underpinned by the notion of sustainable development. According to Tikly (2013, p. 15), "sustainable development has been linked with the concept of lifelong learning, which is perceived as a means to promote sustainable economies and livelihoods". It is in this context that the TVET sector has been mandated with a transformative role, including "the conception of education to address the skills gap created by basic education"

(Tikly, 2013, p. 15) and equipping youth with skills that make them employable. Similarly, DHET highlights that lifelong learning, a principle of open learning, has the potential to "widen participation, promote equity and social mobility, and improve the quality of life of our people" (2017, p. 380). TVET colleges in South Africa are expected to play this transformative role in the vocational education landscape (DHET, 2013), however they need visionary and effective leadership to navigate the current and future demands of TVET learning and teaching, such as the curriculum and modes of learning provision (Badenhorst & Radile, 2018).

Robertson and Frick (2018, p. 72) cite Callan et al. (2007) as defining leadership in vocational education institutions as being:

> the capacity at both the individual and institutional levels to identify and define organisational goals and desired outcomes, to develop strategic plans to achieve these goals and deliver the outcomes, and to guide the organisation and motivate people to reach these goals.

The ability for TVET college leadership to strategically develop a shared vision and goals and guide the institution towards the accomplishment thereof is arguably at the very centre of transforming a college's performance and achievement of greater success. Educational leadership is one of the most influential factors that impacts on college student achievement (Leithwood et al., 2010). In addition, Terblanche and Bitzer (2018) advocate for strong and effective leadership in TVET colleges to lead to significant change, particularly in the area of curriculum reform.

A crucial area of inquiry for TVET colleges is determining what constitutes effective leadership, as "not enough is known about exactly what makes an individual effective as a leader and what, in turn, may make them ineffective" (Balkrishen & Mestry, 2016, p. 29). There is a scarcity of empirical studies that focus on educational leadership in the South African TVET sector, which is particularly disconcerting given the crucial role TVET colleges have to play. Literature reveals that two key approaches to leadership, particularly suited for the TVET sector, are distributed and visionary leadership.

Distributed leadership

Singh et al. (2007) argue that a college culture that supports shared decision-making processes is more important than an individual's (the principal) cognitive abilities or technical expertise. Research shows that:

> Leadership works best when it is shared (distributed) in educational contexts, and leadership is more likely to succeed if the leader brings other people along into the same vision, enabling them to work together and trust one another. (Badenhorst & Radile, 2018, p. 5)

It is in this context that Chagi (2020) recommends that leadership in South African TVET colleges shift away from the dated, heroic models of leadership that centred around individual leaders and their personality traits, towards post-heroic models that share leadership and decision-making powers in the institution. Leadership of educational institutions should be constructed from the basis of being a "shared, reciprocal influence process" (Yukl, 2010, p. 46), distributed among and enacted by different people in the institution. Sharing or distributing leadership decentralises it from a single individual and draws other staff into a shared vision. As Badenhorst and Radile (2018, p. 5) aptly state:

> If the distributed instructional leadership model is premised on the expansive involvement of staff in decision-making and forward planning, then the redefined principal's role will be chiefly concerned with creating the conditions for others to lead rather than leading from the front.

This leadership model results in the sharing of decision-making and power that could lead to the college principal or chief executive officer (CEO) not holding exclusive authority at times. Furthermore, Robertson's study (2015, p. 31) of a curriculum for TVET college leadership development in South Africa positioned the 'distributed' leadership model as an integral inclusion in the "'tool kit' of skills and knowledge" needed by college leaders to respond effectively to the complexities of the TVET sector. The above suggests that college leadership must advance the institution through a shared and contemporary vision, responsive to modern-day contexts and be realistically future-oriented.

Visionary leadership

Having an idealistic, yet accomplishable vision is integral to any contemporary institutional advancement. A vision can be "an inspiring declaration of a compelling dream, accompanied by a clear scenario of how it will be accomplished" (Whitaker & Moses, 1994, as cited in Lashway, 1997), or as Sergiovanni (1994, as cited in Lashway, 1997) argues, an "educational platform" that creates a "community of mind" that ultimately establishes behavioural norms in the organisation. Leaders who articulate and strive towards accomplishing dynamic visions are commonly referred to as 'visionaries', or exemplars for 'visionary leadership' (Guskey, 2003; Nanus, 1992).

Westley and Mintzberg (1989, p. 17) highlight that leadership vision, or the process of 'visioning' entails three essential stages: (1) envisioning the future state of the organisation; (2) effectively articulating and communicating the vision to the 'followers', and (3) empowering those who follow to enact the vision, illustrated in Figure 2.

Figure 2: Visionary leadership process (adapted from Westley & Mintzberg, 1989)

These stages provide a fundamental framework against which 'visionary leadership' may be evaluated.

UNESCO's International Centre for Technical and Vocational Education and Training (UNEVOC) argues that TVET leaders "need to have a clear vision to trigger and lead change". By the same token, Chagi (2020) and Robertson (2015) assert that effective leadership in the South African TVET sector requires college leaders to demonstrate visionary behaviours.

Another leadership approach that surfaces in the literature, which is related to the two approaches, and particularly distributed leadership, is *open leadership*. Open leadership is described as the ability of a leader to "have the confidence and humility to give up the need to be in control while inspiring commitment from people to accomplish goals (Li, 2010, p. 14). This approach foregrounds traits of transparency, open sharing of information, participation and inclusion of employees in decision-making (Alexander, 2018; Li, 2010; Mozilla, n.d.), implying that "employees should be empowered to make decisions on behalf of the organizations within broad, transparent, and strategic boundaries set by upper management" (Philpot, 2013, p. 86). According to Philpot (2013):

> Translated to IT adoption and use, this means that employees should be entrusted to lead themselves and their teams of collaborators to select which technology applications work best under which circumstances, how content should be structured and managed, and what tool implementations or experimentations should be pursued in an attempt to boost … learning. (p. 87)

With the conceptualisation of open learning still at its infancy, and e-learning practices potentially emerging in the South African TVET context, open leadership is not a suitable approach at the moment. Hence, for the purpose of this study, the authors draw on the strengths of both distributed and visionary leadership as well as principles of social justice in educational leadership.

Tait (2013) asserts that e-learning often has explicit links to social justice, while DHET's 'open learning' concept, as it currently stands, has an explicit social justice intent. This suggests the need for space to explore the kind of leadership that is required to make open learning and e-learning flourish in TVET colleges.

Social justice, educational leadership and leadership for open learning

One social justice theorist, Nancy Fraser, has written extensively on social justice issues, but only to a limited extent on how it could be drawn into educational contexts. Fraser conceives of social justice as "parity of participation" (2005, p. 73), as both an outcome where "all the relevant social actors … participate as peers in social life" and a process in which procedural standards are followed "in fair and open processes of deliberation" (Fraser, 2005, p. 87). However, these outcomes and processes can be socially unjust in three ways, which Fraser terms: (1) economic maldistribution; (2) cultural misrecognition; and (3) political misrepresentation and misframing. Although, maldistribution, misrecognition and misrepresentation can be mitigated through ameliorative measures, transformative responses which address the root causes of injustice would be more ideal (Hodgkinson-Williams & Trotter, 2018).

Social justice in educational leadership

Blackmoore (2009) draws on Fraser (2005) to describe socially-just educational leadership as leadership that is aware of, and sensitive to, issues of class, culture, race, religion and gender. It is in this context that Pazey and Cole (2013, p. 179) emphasise that educational leaders have to develop "equity consciousness" "equity consciousness", which is an "understand[ing] that all [students] can achieve academic success, regardless of race, social class, gender, sexual orientation, learning difference, culture, language, religion, and so forth". This heightened awareness and "degree of reflexivity" (Blackmoore, 2009, p. 4) is intended to trigger a culture change in the educational institution, which subsequently leads to a shared and common awareness of these issues, thereby framing how the college (in the context of this case study) approaches the teaching and learning agenda.

Social justice from an educational leadership perspective requires leaders to become more reflexive about their leadership roles, with a heightened awareness of their "own positions within the relations of ruling" (Blackmore, 2009, p. 4). According to Blackmore (2009, p. 4), this then becomes central to their leadership for social justice, as they learn not to "impart agency to others", but create "the conditions that provide students, parents and teachers with a sense of being able to change things and make choices". That is, socially-just leaders are described as creating and enabling environments that are inclusive and, by virtue of the environment, lead to all sharing in a sense of agency and choice-making (Blackmoore, 2009).

The leadership task of contributing towards enabling participatory parity (Fraser, 2005) for all students and staff can be too weighty for an individual, and models of distributed and visionary leadership might have to be explored. Socially just leadership for open learning at a TVET college would lean towards distributed and visionary leadership models, coupled with a heightened equity consciousness, and steer away from heroic charismatic leadership. Bogotch's (2002, p. 8) study of social justice in educational leadership confirms that, "heroic individuals often have a single-mindedness to pursue their own vision tenaciously and apart from others who may not share their particular vision", which would vehemently oppose the foundational nature of socially just open learning. Thus, along the lines of socially just educational leadership, TVET colleges could ideally give practical expression to open learning principles through distributed and visionary leadership – the specific leadership processes and practices serve as the focus of inquiry in this study.

Social justice in leadership for open learning

This section uses Fraser's three dimensions to explore how educational leaders could lead open learning in the context of this study.

Economic maldistribution, redistribution and restructuring. With respect to economic injustice or maldistribution, Fraser explains that "people can be impeded from full participation by economic structures that deny them the resources they need in order to interact with others as peers" (2005, p. 73). In relation to open learning, distributive injustice or maldistribution of resources may impede full participation of students in the PSET sector in South Africa. As mentioned earlier, in this particular case, there is lack of access to geographically convenient campuses, as well as limited financial resources for students, internet connectivity on/off-campus, and devices to facilitate e-learning. These types of hurdles need to be addressed through economic redistribution or economic restructuring.

Cultural misrecognition, recognition and re-acculturation. In relation to cultural inequality, or "misrecognition", Fraser points out that "people can also be prevented from interacting in terms of [participatory] parity by institutionalised hierarchies of cultural value that deny them the requisite standing" (2005, p. 73). More simply phrased, Fraser "seeks justice that is inclusive and egalitarian in terms of ... recognising cultural histories and practices of diverse groups in the institutional formations within which they are subjected" (Zipin, 2017, p. 68).

In terms of open learning, TVET college students may be deprived of participatory parity due to lack of cultural recognition of marginalised groups. For instance, the prevalence of Western-oriented epistemic perspectives in educational resources such as textbooks may be culturally inappropriate or alienating. In the context of this case study, assuming that digital literacy and digital equity prevail among all students could be culturally misrecognising them.

Ameliorative and transformative responses to cultural misrecognition in e-learning and other open learning opportunities, might mean that college leadership explores how the college addresses specific areas in which cultural recognition and re-acculturation could be achieved.

Political misframing, representation and reframing. In terms of political inequality, or "misframing", Fraser explains that this "tells us who is included in, and who is excluded from, the circle of those entitled to a just distribution and reciprocal recognition" (2005, p. 75). Simply stated, political misframing surfaces "asymmetries of political power" (Fraser, 2009, p. 103) between those who have the power to decide on behalf of others. "Misframing" is to wrongly exclude those who deserve to be subjects of justice (Fraser, 2005, p. 76). "Misrepresentation" encompasses systemic denial of parties participating in decision-making processes (Fraser, 2005).

In relation to open learning, political questions can be asked about who decides on the programmes offered and modes of delivery, who decides on online resources, who decides on the type and scope of student support, and who decides on the quality of the programmes.

Contributing factors to and processes followed by TVET college leadership in reaching or influencing decisions such as these play a seminal role in the political representation and reframing dimension of social justice. The challenges are broadly about who has the right to take leadership in a TVET college and ways in which input is received and acknowledged (an ameliorative response) to how responsibility is shared (a more transformative response).

In sum, educational leaders must acknowledge that "technological innovation is perhaps the single most compelling factor that is driving them toward new organisational structures and new pedagogical models" (Beaudoin, 2002, p. 134). In the same light, educational leaders must embrace their positions as social change agents, using their roles to lead for social justice and equity (Brown, 2004).

The case study

The empirical site of study was the Gert Sibande TVET College (GSC) in Mpumalanga, South Africa. GSC has six campuses spread throughout the province and has an established Open Learning Unit that serves the entire college. What aided the college tremendously, in terms of the open learning initiative, was the historic prioritisation of e-learning, whereby the preceding leadership ensured that e-learning was firmly embedded into the college's trajectory. The former college principals established e-learning as part of technological innovation, and with subsequent changes of leadership, the college continued to prioritise the institutional development of e-learning.

Methodology

The study was located within the interpretive paradigm so that meaning and human phenomena could be studied in social contexts (Babbie, 2007). This small-scale qualitative study set out to determine what leadership approaches and practices are necessary for enabling ICT-mediated, open learning opportunities at a TVET college in South Africa, and how these are aligned to the social justice underpinnings of open learning.

The following questions were used to guide this study:

- What are effective leadership approaches and practices enabling ICT-mediated open learning at Gert Sibande College?
- In what ways are these enabling participatory parity economically, culturally and politically?

The study used purposive, convenience sampling (Cohen et al., 2007). DHET, who has been working with GSC on this initiative, identified the college as a potential 'leader' in the TVET sector for expanding e-learning offerings. Ethical clearance was obtained from the University of Cape Town's Centre for Higher Education Development (CHED) Research Ethics Committee, and permission to access the college participants was received from the DHET research division. Informed consent was obtained from interviewees.

The first author interviewed the College Principal, Assistant Director: Office of the Principal, Assistant Director: Open Learning, and two lecturers who use e-learning approaches. These lecturers were identified by the Assistant Director: Open Learning (as part of her role is to support lecturers), and their data was used to triangulate the leadership's responses. Due to the tight timeframe for data collection, it was impossible to either find more lecturers or invite student participants. Interviews were held with these participants and codes and/or pseudonyms were used to present their responses (Table 1) in the next section.

Table 1: Data collection

Data collection tool/method	Participant(s)	Codes/ Pseudonyms
Interview couplet	College Principal and Assistant Director: Office of the Principal	IC1-P and IC1-AD
Interview	Assistant Director: Open Learning	I-M
Interview couplet	Two lecturers who use e-learning approaches	IC2-L1 and IC2-L2

Data collection took place online via virtual video conferencing, to adhere to safety precautions during the COVID-19 pandemic, and in accordance with the lockdown regulations in South Africa. Recordings from the interviews were transcribed and then analysed thematically using Atlas.ti. An inductive approach was applied, where the research questions served as a framework for descriptive analysis and responses to these questions were grouped into emerging themes. The social justice framing was deductively used to normatively gauge the extent to which the college leadership processes and practices were socially just.

Insights into leadership for enabling open learning and participatory parity in TVET colleges

The study focused on the leadership approaches and practices employed at the college that relate to the enabling and advancing of e-learning, as a possible vehicle for promoting open learning. The study found that the college leadership formulated and employed numerous strategies to advance e-learning that were enacted in multiple stages as described below.

Contextual analysis and environmental scanning

A critical step that the college leadership followed to adequately inform the formulation of a vision and corresponding strategies to enact the vision for advancing e-learning was conducting a holistic analysis of the college's multiple contexts.

The college principal drew on global trends and contrasted those with the direct context of the college:

> As I travelled the world and I saw other countries' models, I started to think of my own, because those are developed nations, so, you cannot exactly duplicate their models, but you can take what you can, and bring that learning home. (IC1-P)

What was of great significance to the principal, while developing a vision, was recognising challenges in the immediate situational context of the college:

> I had to do my own environmental scanning and saw the doom and gloom that covers our villages, and looking at it, and I saw the frustrations of students having to receive a stipend of R3000 and go stay in Johannesburg, drop out because they cannot afford to stay 18 months there, and having to look at all of that. And then it began to grow into ideas. (IC1-P)

The college principal recognised that e-learning and authentic learning opportunities must be provided at, and by, the college campuses in Mpumalanga, to prevent students from having to incur additional expenses to tuition when seeking quality learning opportunities in other provinces. She highlighted that students often dropped out of their studies due to the inability to cope financially. The college acknowledged the financial challenges facing many of their students, with the principal stating, "we are very much aware about the needs and the poverty levels in our communities", and that "we cannot ignore the social economy of our people. People are really poor" (IC1-P). It is clear that the financial circumstances of their students are at the core of e-learning planning, as the college principal commented, "There are students that are really, really poor from our communities. And when we speak (about) online ... we need to put those students at the centre" (IC1-P).

The college leadership also consulted with various staff and student representatives, particularly those serving on various committees, such as the Student Representative

Council to establish the educational needs of all parties, so that the scope of opportunities for advancing e-learning could be determined.

Developing a vision

The college had already established the e-learning unit in 2008, which was subsequently renamed as the Open Learning Unit under the current leadership – this was a way of "aligning to DHET nomenclature" (I-M). The Assistant Director: Open Learning remarked:

> I can honestly say that all three principals (the two former principals and the current one), they have a very strong vision, ... of moving forward, moving with technology. And then they have been taking that step, of taking innovation and technology as a value for the college. They adopted it as a value for the college. (I-M)

This excerpt demonstrates how technological innovations and e-learning have been embraced in the college's value system.

A 'culture of innovation' was mentioned by the College Principal and Assistant Director: Open Learning and a lecturer as being vital in leading and advancing e-learning, and the principal acknowledged that it contributed to effective leadership at the college by remarking, "the innovative nature in the college assists me a lot in my leadership" (IC1-P).

Visionary leadership was cited as critical and possibly a prerequisite for advancing e-learning at the college, as the Assistant Director: Open Learning shared, "I want to mention visionary leaders, and that is, I think [a] requirement that a college needs to have. So, in our case, we had visionary leaders" (I-M). The college principal shared aspects of their vision for the college, "my vision is to see the college fully online in terms of teaching and learning ...and your distance learning running fully online ... and your repeaters getting the attention they deserve" (IC1-P). That is, the principal envisaged that e-learning could serve as an 'equaliser' of access and quality education for students, particularly those who are distance learners or repeaters of subjects.[1] The principal also highlighted that staff should be adequately trained and supported to teach using e-learning: "my other vision for staff is for everybody to become competent in terms of the use of technology" (IC1-P). A functional and appropriate learning management system (LMS) was also included as an integral component of the vision for the college, with the principal adding: "my open learning vision for the college is to have an online platform that is actually able to carry the capacity of the students that are currently enrolled" (IC1-P).

The principal's vision for e-learning and open learning (as being transformative) was not geographically limited to the Mpumalanga sites of the college, but extended to the entire African continent, highlighting how exchanges and resource-sharing could occur:

> We can reach the African continent. You know, your Zimbabwean students and your Malawian students can enroll for college programmes, wherever they are using the open learning system, where we can exchange[;] the transformation in Africa can actually happen very fast. ... we can be able to share the resources with each other. (IC1-P)

---

[1] If a student who is funded by **NSFAS** fails a subject, they repeat that subject at their own cost (see Chapter 3, this volume).

However, the college leadership also shared that limited finances and budgetary allocations for advancing e-learning was a highly significant factor that affected the extent to which e-learning could be rolled out at the college.

Articulating and communicating the vision

The college principal indicated that the self-conviction of one's ideas and aspirations is vital in having a vision realised; sharing that, "if you have a conviction of your own vision, others will have to join in" (IC1-P). She added that:

> I just desire that the entire team can catch it and be able to run with it and make it happen for the people of this place, because, you know, every city was once a rural place and somebody had a vision to see it transform. So that is my dream as well, to see my village here transform into another Cape Town. (IC1-P)

These quotes illuminate how passionate the college principal is about her vision. The college leadership views the uptake and enactment of the vision by staff as pivotal to improving the educational and socio-economic conditions of the communities they serve, with an aspiration of transforming the smaller towns into larger, metropolitan cities.

Consultation with staff and general communication was highlighted as being critical for this approach. The college principal emphasised that, "consultation, communication and getting the buy-in of different stakeholders within the institution, I think, is very important" (IC1-P). The strategies and plans for advancing e-learning were shared with staff, with a particular priority of obtaining 'buy-in' from all. Consultation and communication with various stakeholders, such as the council in establishing and enacting a vision was also cited on numerous occasions by the leadership, as crucial to the success of enabling and advancing e-learning at the college:

> Once you have a vision, you need to ... consult with other people because they are able to show you things that you never thought of. They can affect your vision or hinder it from happening. And you also communicate to the funders and communicate to your council. (IC1-P)

The two lecturers also hinted at the importance of communication about the strategies and deployment of e-learning although they acknowledged that they may have missed some of the leadership communication. One lecturer shared: "the communication, the way it's done, or the procedure, somewhere, or somehow, it gets lost" (IC2-L2).

Alongside the above, the establishment of a vision and development of strategies and plans for advancing e-learning took place, following required protocol for acceptance by the college's council:

> So it started ... to be documented bit by bit ..., I had to get the council approval, because with us, before it can be documented, it must be presented and accepted... phase by phase, with its action plan, and the council will look at it, if it's doable in terms of the finances as well. And in terms of the capacity as well and when they approve it, then you can document it. So, it is documented for 2021 strategic planning . (IC1-P)

The above excerpts demonstrate the subtle political nuances leading to the college leadership's incorporation of a vision into their strategic plan and subsequently enacting it. There is also a sense of distributed leadership among these key stakeholders.

Enacting the vision

Critical to enactment of the vision for advancing e-learning at the college, was the establishment of an enabling environment. The college's Assistant Director for Open Learning acknowledged that, "that vision of leaders, I think, played a very, very big role in … the enabling environment for open learning" (I-M). However, enactment of the vision proved to be of the most challenging for the college leadership as many staff members were hesitant to adapt to changes in teaching and learning. The College principal shared that a challenge they faced was that staff were " not buying into the vision, especially of a new thing [as] they think of failure more than thinking of it happening … they don't want the status quo to be challenged" (IC1-P). However, the college leadership was driven to obtain stakeholder buy-in across the institution and were adamant that the lecturers would adapt to change at some point.

With respect to creating an enabling environment, the college prioritised the revamping of its online systems and LMS, in response to the teaching and learning needs of staff and students. The college leadership provided laptops to lecturers and facilitated internet access for them as a means of equipping them with resources for teaching online (IC1-AD). The leadership reported that the renewed approach to e-learning on a revamped LMS, with additional functionality was first piloted on a small scale by rolling it out in one of their campuses. This was done to evaluate how the LMS and e-learning approach was being received by campus staff and students, before refining the approach and rolling it out in other campuses. At this stage, wi-fi access was made available to all staff and students at all of their campuses.

During the lockdown, as a way of 'opening' up access to learning opportunities, the college delivered their teaching and learning via multiple platforms, including broadcasting recorded lectures on TV and radio, releasing podcasts online, and using WhatsApp for material dissemination. However, two leadership members cited the lack of data for staff to work remotely, particularly during the lockdown, as a significant challenge. Lecturers highlighted that the limited operational hours of computer labs impeded students' access to e-learning activities, especially students who did not have access to personal devices when off-campus.

Empowering lecturers on the implementation of e-learning

The college leadership prioritised training and supporting of lecturers; the Open Learning Unit offered training and professional development opportunities to staff. According to the Assistant Director: Open Learning, this was also recognised as a means of promoting and fostering e-learning. The principal confirmed this:

> Our curriculum team; they develop intervention strategies to support, because sometimes, it's not because people don't want to use the systems that we have, it's because they are not confident. … So, therefore, you give them more support. (IC1-P)

The above illustrates that pedagogical training is important for the implementation of e-learning at the college.

Challenges with supporting the implementation of e-learning at the college

The data reveals that the college leadership tried its level best to ensure that the essential structural requirements were in place for e-learning to proliferate. However, a few concerns were raised in relation to using e-learning.

With respect to students, the college principal highlighted that not having access to the financial background information of their students prevented them from adequately evaluating whether a student was able to afford a device, ultimately inhibiting the advancement of e-learning. It was also noted that students studying via a distance or part-time model were not eligible to receive the National Student Financial Aid Scheme (NSFAS) funding, and as such, would encounter difficulty in wholly funding their online open learning in the future, if and when it is offered in such a manner.

The college leadership acknowledged that the uptake of e-learning by staff was slower than anticipated, which they felt could be attributed to the fact that using e-learning and blended learning approaches was optional and not mandatory. The Assistant Director: Open Learning highlighted that, "there's no incentive in it, and it is just a free choice: I go online, I don't go online. There's nothing that forces them to do it" (I-M). This sentiment was echoed by the lecturers who confirmed that the lack of compulsion hinders the uptake and use of e-learning by many of their colleagues.

Furthermore, the Assistant Director: Open Learning hinted at a lacklustre attitude from some staff towards adopting e-learning approaches, while the lecturers who participated in the study shared that they sometimes felt that the training was inadequate to harness best practices of e-learning or did not match their training need: "With devices, must come the training that we need" (IC2-L1). The lecturer went on to say:

> My suggestion is that if we can practice more, or be engaged or be trained on that [using e-learning], so that we can be comfortable and confident to practice that … [and] implement it in [the] classrooms. (IC2-L1)

The above challenges were stunting the rate at which the college shifted to more ICT-mediated learning practices.

The college leadership shared that it noted some areas continued to present challenges, and the college had scheduled change management processes and workshops to facilitate mind shifts and general adjustments to the college culture.

Discussion

This small-scale study provides an intriguing narrative of how the college leadership approached ICT-mediated learning, specifically e-learning, which is offered under their banner of 'open learning'. Particular areas of the critical analysis surfaced, which are discussed below.

A socially just leadership model for open learning and advancing ICT-mediated learning at a TVET college

In analysing the approaches and leadership practices employed by the college leadership to advance ICT-mediated learning, the study found some alignment to the model of distributed leadership, in terms of sharing of the vision, ownership and decision-making, as well as to the fundamental components of Westley and Mintzberg's (1989) model of visionary leadership, namely, "Vision – Communication – Empowerment". As part of the leadership's advancement of e-learning at the college, the leadership conducted a contextual analysis to elicit the challenges that could be addressed through e-learning, as well as consulted with staff and student representatives to determine their needs in relation to e-learning. This process is crucial in a social justice approach to leadership, as Blackmoore (2009) emphasises that addressing issues of student difference and inequalities is key to improving student learning opportunities. The data informs us that the college leadership is committed to communicating throughout the stages and this helps them understand the student and lecturer needs, as well as create a conducive environment for the enactment of its vision. Therefore, in further development of Westley and Mintzberg's (1989) model, the data reveals that the college engaged in contextual analysis and environmental scanning; had envisioning and vision enactment as separate stages; and communication happened throughout the stages.

Figure 3 provides an overview of the various stages followed by the college leadership, with key activities, events and strategies included in each stage.

Figure 3: Approach and strategy for advancing e-learning at Gert Sibande TVET College

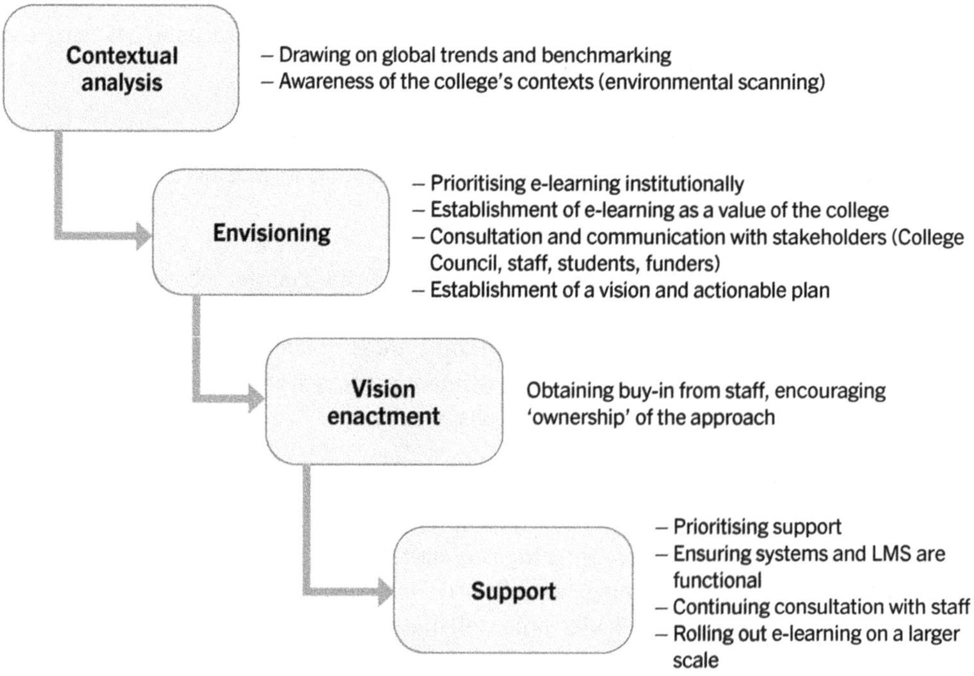

Contextual analysis
- Drawing on global trends and benchmarking
- Awareness of the college's contexts (environmental scanning)

Envisioning
- Prioritising e-learning institutionally
- Establishment of e-learning as a value of the college
- Consultation and communication with stakeholders (College Council, staff, students, funders)
- Establishment of a vision and actionable plan

Vision enactment
Obtaining buy-in from staff, encouraging 'ownership' of the approach

Support
- Prioritising support
- Ensuring systems and LMS are functional
- Continuing consultation with staff
- Rolling out e-learning on a larger scale

In Westley and Mintzberg's (1989) model, communication of the vision and related strategies, and empowerment of all parties are critical for the effective enactment of a vision. In the case of GSC, while the leadership reportedly prioritised these areas of their approach, the lecturers that participated in the study seemed to miss some communications of the vision and/or strategy. There might be political misframing at the college as some of the lecturers who are involved in e-learning have not been in the leadership communication loop, where they could both receive communication from the leadership and have a voice in the decisions made in relation to e-learning implementation at the college. The same applies to educational leadership underpinned by social justice; clear and increased communication of the vision for open learning would have to prevail for fully, effective implementation of e-learning at the college. However, the lecturers' expectations of leadership communication about strategies for the deployment of e-learning reflects some tension between visionary and distributed leadership, as Badenhorst and Radile (2018, p. 5), writing from a distributed leadership perspective, argue that subsequent to the communication of the vision, "the principal's role [becomes] chiefly concerned with creating the conditions for others to lead".

The main insight related to the political dimension of social justice lies in the extent to which staff felt included as part of the college vision. Consultation and communication with various stakeholders within the institution and externally, is a strategic way of working towards a shared vision. The college has mechanisms for staff and student representation on higher committees and forums, and these are arguably politically representational from an institutional perspective; these may need to be strengthened. Focusing on enhancing communication with all staff and stakeholders allows for inclusivity and representation, thereby advancing the goals of social justice (Huffman, 2014; Vu, 2015).

Economically, resource redistribution of a functional LMS, laptops and data to staff, and providing learning materials for their students on multiple platforms and media was done with relative success at the college. However, for students, the use of multiple platforms and media during lockdown was only ameliorative, as this was underpinned by an assumption that all students had reliable access to TV sets and smartphones (with data). It is quite clear that for some students, lack of these resources impeded their participation in e-learning activities. The college may need to consider ways of providing students with personal mobile devices and data so they can access their activities from anywhere and at anytime. Further research could also be conducted with students to establish how they coped with these challenges during lockdown.

Related to the aforementioned is a high-level economic injustice, whereby students are inadequately financed for e-learning. Hence, a transformative measure that would be required for students to study online with TVET colleges would be for policies to change at the DHET level and for NSFAS to finance such studies. Van den Berg's (2021) study of exploring open distance learning at a South African higher education institution with a view to addressing social justice highlights that inequitable and inadequate access to digital technologies and applicable support exacerbate injustices. Through economically redistributive and transformative measures, the college's students would be able to obtain increased access to flexible e-learning opportunities equitably, thereby fulfilling a fundamental tenet of social justice (Fraser, 2005) and open learning.

From a cultural perspective, staff, students and the surrounding communities were recognised in the envisioning of the college, as well as the open learning initiative. Staff's digital literacy was additionally recognised in the provision of basic platform-using training, and prioritisation of their confidence in using ICT-mediated learning practices from a strategy standpoint. The most notable cultural misrecognition that lecturers shared was the lack of pedagogical training provided by the college. The college leadership had implemented support mechanisms, but the training was either inadequate to harness best practices of e-learning, or did not match the lecturers' pedagogical training needs. Mahlangu (2018) argues that insufficient technical support and training, coupled with inappropriate educational modelling, is one of the most significant challenges facing the higher education e-learning initiatives. Related to the issue of investing in pedagogical training or professional development for ICT-mediated learning is the opt-in approach adopted at the college. Possibly, more visibility of, and pedagogical training and support from, the Open Learning Unit would help those lecturers who opt in to effectively implement e-learning. In the long run, this could increase lecturer uptake of e-learning.

The above discussion suggests that economic redistribution, in terms of providing lecturers with technological resources, is insufficient on its own for enabling e-learning at the college. The college must equally address cultural misrecognition and political misrepresentation of lecturers. That is, with these enabling conditions being in place, lecturers would have a sense of agency and decision-making for their e-learning implementation. Furthermore, with the above in order, the college leadership's aspiration of resource-sharing and increased collaboration in Africa (open educational practices[2]) would fall into place more easily.

Leading open learning initiatives would necessitate an awareness of the social justice underpinnings and intent of open learning itself, which then ultimately guides the subsequent implementation and operationalisation of teaching and learning; in other words, how the ICT-mediated learning opportunities are rolled out. Further, a focus on social justice is core to visionary leadership in the contemporary South African context (ie visionary leadership may look different at another time and place) and the focus on the socially just, drives a distributed model of leadership, implying that the ideas of visionary and distributed leadership may have to be sewn together.

Conclusions and recommendations

This chapter reports on leadership approaches and practices employed by a South African TVET college in advancing ICT-mediated learning and teaching as a vehicle for promoting open learning. The study found that the leadership approaches and strategies in practice at GSC resembled elements of distributed and visionary leadership models. The study further highlighted how leadership underpinned by social justice principles aligns to leadership for open learning. As part of GSC's vision enactment and following of strategies to advance e-learning at the college, plans were executed and certain infrastructural accommodations were made. However, leadership for advancing e-learning, as a vehicle for promoting open learning, requires particular ameliorative and transformative responses for a more enhanced progression towards social justice.

The study illuminates that, while participatory parity can be traced in certain areas of the leadership's strategies, communication and pedagogical support for lecturers may need to be improved. These contributed to political misframing and cultural misrecognition of lecturers. However, with the aforementioned noted, the leadership model in practice

---

[2] https://www.capetowndeclaration.org/read-the-declaration

(Figure 3) is structured and has the full potential to engender and enable socially just open learning at a TVET college. Another impactful challenge for e-learning implementation at the college highlighted by this study, is a lack of NSFAS funding for e-learning and distance students.

The most significant conclusion is that the alignment of a college leadership's vision for open learning with how open learning is defined is vital for holistic, socially just educational leadership. With respect to enhancing the effectiveness of the leadership approaches for advancing open learning at the college, it is recommended that the college leadership revisits the ways in which it expands staff involvement in "decision-making and forward planning" (Badenhorst & Radile, 2018). It would also be advantageous for the Open Learning Unit at the college to explore how staff could be additionally trained and supported from pedagogical perspectives. Recommendations for transformative action are for policy changes to be made by the NSFAS and DHET. NSFAS should consider adjusting the eligibility criteria and include students who may opt to study online with TVET colleges.

For future studies, it is recommended that additional contextualised research is undertaken to further explore appropriate leadership strategies for South African TVET colleges seeking to advance open learning, to add to the body of literature in this field.

Acknowledgements

Many thanks to the staff at Gert Sibande TVET College whose inputs made the case study possible. Special thanks are due to reviewers Dr Clive Smith and Dr Jo Badenhorst for their thoughtful, incisive feedback on the chapter, and Emeritus Associate Professor Cheryl Ann Hodgkinson-Williams and Shanali Govender for additional writing support. Thanks are also due to the Centre for Innovation in Learning and Teaching at the University of Cape Town, which hosted the COOL project, and the South African Department of Higher Education and Training for funding it.

References

Alexander, D. (2018, December 4). What is open leadership? *Opensource.com.* https://opensource.com/open-organization/18/12/what-is-open-leadership

Alqahtani, A. Y., & Rajkhan, A. A. (2020). E-learning critical success factors during the COVID-19 pandemic: A comprehensive analysis of e-learning managerial perspectives. *Education Sciences*, 10(216), 1–16. http://dx.doi.org/10.3390/educsci10090216

Babbie, E. (2007). *The practice of social research* (11th ed.). Thomson/Wadsworth.

Badenhorst, J. W., & Radile, R. S. (2018). Poor performance at TVET colleges: Conceptualising a distributed instructional leadership approach as a solution. *Africa Education Review*, 15(3), 91–112. https://doi.org/10.1080/18146627.2017.1352452

Balkrishen, P. (2015). The leadership role of campus managers to improve student achievement in further education and training colleges in Mpumalanga [Master's thesis, University of Johannesburg]. http://hdl.handle.net/10210/63944

Balkrishen, P., & Mestry, R. (2016). The leadership role of campus managers to improve student achievement in colleges. *South African Journal of Higher Education*, 30(5), 28–47. https://www.journals.ac.za/index.php/sajhe/article/view/571

Beaudoin, M. F. (2002). Distance education leadership: An essential role for the new century. *The Journal of Leadership Studies*, 8(3), 131–144.

Blackmore, J. (2009). Leadership for social justice: A transnational dialogue. *Journal of Research on Leadership Education*, 4(1), 1–10.

Bogotch, I. E. (2002). Educational leadership and social justice: Practice into theory. *Journal of School Leadership*, 12(2), 138–156.

Brown, K. M. (2004). Leadership for social justice and equity: Weaving a transformative framework and pedagogy. *Educational Administration Quarterly*, 40(1), 77–108.

Bryman, A. (2007). *Effective leadership in higher education: Summary of findings.* Leadership Foundation for Higher Education.

Callan, V., Mitchell, J., Clayton, B., & Smith, L. (2007). *Approaches for sustaining and building management and leadership capability in VET providers.* NCVER.

Chagi, N. (2020). A critical investigation of leadership in a technical, vocational education and training college in the Eastern Cape [Master's dissertation, Rhodes University]. http://hdl.handle.net/10962/140045

Cohen, L., Manion, L., & Morrison, K. (2007). *Research methods in education* (6th ed.). Routledge.

DHET (Department of Higher Education and Training). (2013). White paper for post-school education and training: Building an expanded, effective and integrated post-school system. *Government Gazette*, 37229. https://www.gov.za/documents/white-paper-post-school-education-and-training-building-expanded-effective-and-integrated

DHET (2017). Call for comment on the Open Learning Policy Framework for Post-School Education and Training. *Government Gazette,* 40772. http://pmg-assets.s3-website-eu-west-1.amazonaws.com/170407openlearningframework-postschooleduc.pdf

Fong, B. C. (2008). Open for what? A case study of institutional leadership and transformation. In T. Iiyoshi & M. S. V. Kumar (Eds.), *Opening up education: The collective advancement of education through open technology, open content, and open education* (pp. 401–416). MIT Press.

Fraser, N. (2005). Reframing justice in a globalizing world. *New Left Review*, 36, 69–88. https://newleftreview.org/II/36/nancy-fraser-reframing-justice-in-a-globalizing-world

Fraser, N. (2009). *Scales of justice: Reimagining political space in a globalizing world.* Columbia University Press.

Gaebel, M., Kupriyanova, V., Morais, R., & Colucci, E. (2014). E-learning in European higher education institutions: Results of a mapping survey conducted in October-December 2013. European University Association. http://old.eua.eu/Libraries/publication/e-learning_survey

Guskey, T. R. (2003). Analyzing lists of the characteristics of effective professional development to promote visionary leadership. *NASSP Bulletin*, 87(637), 4–20.

Hallinger, P., & Lee, M. (2013). Exploring principal capacity to lead reform of teaching and learning quality in Thailand. *International Journal of Educational Development*, 33(2013), 305–315.

Hodgkinson-Williams, C. A., & Trotter, H. (2018). A social justice framework for understanding open educational resources and practices in the Global South. *Journal of Learning for Development*, 5(3), 204–224.

Huffman, T. (2014). Imagining social justice within a communicative framework. *Journal of Social Justice*, 4, 1–14.

Kanuka, H. (2008). Understanding e-learning technologies-in-practice through philosophies-in-practice. In T. Anderson (Ed.), *The theory and practice of online learning* (pp. 91–118). AU Press.

Lashway, L. (1997). Visionary leadership. *ERIC Digest*, 110. https://files.eric.ed.gov/fulltext/ED402643.pdf

Leithwood, K., Louis, K. S., Wahlstrom, K. L., & Anderson, S. E. (2010). Investigating the links to improved student learning: Final report of research findings. University of Minnesota Press.

Li, C. (2010). *Open leadership: How social technology can transform the way you lead.* John Wiley.

Mahlangu, V. P. (2018). The good, the bad, and the ugly of distance learning in higher education. *Trends in E-learning*, 17–29. DOI: 10.5772/intechopen.75702

Mitgang, L. (2012). *The making of the principal: Five lessons in leadership training.* The Wallace Foundation.

Mozilla. (n.d.). Open leadership framework. https://mozilla.github.io/open-leadership-framework/framework/

Nanus, B. (1992). *Visionary leadership: Creating a compelling sense of direction for your organization.* Jossey-Bass.

Obwoge, M. E., & Kwamboka, O. S. (2016). E-learning in TVET: An opportunity for developing countries. *IRA International Journal of Education and Multidisciplinary Studies*, 3(3), 347–352. http://dx.doi.org/10.21013/jems.v3.n3.p8

Pazey, B. L., & Cole, H. A. (2012). The role of special education training in the development of socially just leaders: Building an equity consciousness in educational leadership programs. *Educational Administration Quarterly*, 49(2), 243–272. https://doi.org/10.1177/0013161X12463934

Philpot, E. L. (2013). Social media adoption and use among information technology professionals and implications for leadership [Doctoral dissertation, University of Phoenix].

Robertson, C. (2015). Leadership development for technical and vocational education and training college leaders in South Africa: A post-graduate curriculum framework. [Doctoral dissertation, Stellenbosch University].

Robertson, C., & Frick, L. (2018). Conflicting priorities: The dichotomous roles of leadership and management at TVET colleges. *Journal of Vocational, Adult and Continuing Education and Training*, 1(1), 71–87.

Sana, S., & Adhikary, C. (2017). ICT mediated teaching learning in higher educational enterprise. *International Journal for Science and Advance Research in Technology*, 3(8), 506–511. https://www.academia.edu/35314341/ICT_Mediated_Teaching_Learning_In_Higher_Educational_Enterprise?auto=download

Sergiovanni, T. J. (1994). *Building community in schools*. Jossey-Bass.

Singh, P., Manser, P., & Mestry, R. (2007). Importance of emotional intelligence in conceptualizing collegial leadership in education. *South African Journal of Education*, 27(3), 541–563.

Tait, A. (2013). Distance and e-learning, social justice, and development: The relevance of capability approaches to the mission of open universities. *The International Review of Research in Open and Distance Learning*, 14(4), 1–18.

Terblanche, T., & Bitzer, E. (2018). Leading curriculum change in South African technical and vocational education and training colleges. *Journal of Vocational, Adult and Continuing Education and Training*, 1(1), 104. https://doi.org/10.14426/jovacet.v1i1.16

Tikly, L. (2013). Reconceptualizing TVET and development: A human capability and social justice approach. In UNESCO-UNEVOC (Ed.), *Revisiting global trends in TVET: Reflections on theory and practice*. UNESCO-UNEVOC International Centre for Technical and Vocational Education and Training. http://www.unevoc.unesco.org/fileadmin/up/2013_epub_revisiting_global_trends_in_tvet_chapter1.pdf

UNESCO (United Nations Educational, Scientific and Cultural Organization). (2015). *A basic guide to open educational resources (OER)*. UNESCO.

Van den Berg G. (2021). The role of open distance learning in addressing social justice: A South African case study. In W. Pearson Jr., & V. Reddy (Eds.), *Social justice and education in the 21st century: Research from South Africa and the United States* (pp. 331–345). Springer. https://doi.org/10.1007/978-3-030-65417-7_17

Vu, S. T. (2015). Social justice education: Using communication activism pedagogy to help university cultural centers increase campus diversity & inclusivity [Bachelor's thesis, California Polytechnic State University, San Luis Obispo]. https://digitalcommons.calpoly.edu/joursp/103

Westley, F., & Mintzberg, H. (1989). Visionary leadership and strategic management. *Strategic Management Journal*, 10(S1), 17–32.

Whitaker, K. S., & Moses, M. C. (1994). *The restructuring handbook: A guide to school revitalization*. Allyn and Bacon.

Yukl, G. (2010). An evaluative essay on current conceptions of effective leadership. *European Journal of Work and Organisational Psychology*, 8(1), 33–48.

Zipin, L. (2017). Pursuing a problematic-based curriculum approach for the sake of social justice. *Journal of Education*, (69), 67–92. http://www.scielo.org.za/scielo.php?script=sci_arttext&pid=S2520-98682017000200004

HOW TO CITE THIS CHAPTER

Raban, M., & Mayisela, T. (2022). Enabling open learning and participatory parity through increased e-learning: The case of leadership at Gert Sibande TVET College, South Africa. In T. Mayisela, S. C. Govender & C. A. Hodgkinson-Williams (Eds.), *Open learning as a means of advancing social justice: Cases in post-school education and training in South Africa* (pp. 269–290). African Minds. doi: 10.47622/9781928502425_12

This work is licensed under a Creative Commons Attribution 4.0 International (CC BY 4.0) licence.

13

Access, quality and success

Working towards social justice through open initiatives at the University of the Free State

Thasmai Dhurumraj & Shanali C. Govender

SUMMARY Education in the South African context is widely promoted as a tool for achieving equity through increasing the life opportunities for those involved. The promotion of open learning as a strategy for shaping the post-school education and training sector (PSET) seeks to address the historical suffocation of the educational dreams and opportunities of black people, and contemporary poverty, lack of services and limited access to opportunities. The broad ambitions of open learning – improving access, quality and success – find expression in multiple ways in the diverse and complex PSET sector, with institutions taking different paths towards different kinds of 'openness'. This research explores stories of openness at the University of the Free State (UFS), through tracing the history of five initiatives that seek to open up learning. We adopted an interpretivist case study approach, collecting a variety of data, including four semi-structured interviews, institutional reports, and public-facing documentation. Underpinned by Fraser's social justice framework, we ask in what ways, and to what extent, initiatives supporting access, quality and success respond to historical and contemporary social injustices, and what conditions enabled and constrained their scope and success. Through our interpretation of the data, it emerged that understandings of 'open' in this context are shifting and contingent, and are strongly shaped by conceptualisations of, and contextual readiness for, open learning. Many initiatives established in support of 'opening up' education may be described as ameliorative responses to inequalities. However, activities such as the reimagining of marginalisation and pedagogy in the PSET context and the increasing recognition of the importance of leadership and governance, are working towards addressing economic, cultural and political injustices, creating more enabling conditions for transformative shifts towards opening up education.

Keywords: academic professional development, open learning, access, social justice, university

Introduction

The South African government has for many years advocated the promotion of "equity of access and fair chances for success to all who are seeking to realise their potential through higher education" (Essop, 2020, p. 9). However, questions have been frequently posed about the sufficiency of access for social equity in South Africa (Machingambi, 2011; Machingambi & Wadesango, 2012). As a response, the Department of Higher Education and Training (DHET) proposed that open learning principles would expand access to education and training opportunities and offer diversified provision across the Post-School Education and Training (PSET) sector (DHET, 2013). To this end, DHET released its draft *Open Learning Policy Framework for PSET* in 2017. However, to date there is little research on the adoption of these open learning principles in the PSET sector.

The Cases on Open Learning (COOL) project, of which this case is one, was commissioned by DHET to explore different aspects of open learning in the PSET sector, which according to their definition includes the

> principles of learner-centredness, lifelong learning, *flexibility of learning provision*, the *removal of barriers to access learning*, the recognition for credit of prior learning experience, the *provision of learner support*, the *construction of learning programmes in the expectation that learners can succeed*, and the maintenance of rigorous quality assurance over the design of learning materials and support systems. (DHET, 2017, p. 363, emphasis added)

This paper seeks to explore how 'open learning' finds expression in the context of the University of the Free State (UFS), through telling their stories of movements towards open learning and highlighting the milestones that mark shifting engagements with key aspects of openness, including equity of access, quality and success. The story of 'open' at UFS is further viewed through Nancy Fraser's dimensions of social justice – economic, cultural and political – and her notions of parity of participation and affirmative or transformative responses to inequality.

Open learning in South Africa

Key South African policy documents in the PSET sector (DHET, 2013), together with the draft *Open Learning Policy Framework* (OLPF) (DHET, 2017), make explicit reference to 'open learning', 'open content', 'open educational resources' (OER), and 'open (and) distance learning' (ODL). While these concepts are widely used and well-defined in the scholarly literature, their use in the local context sometimes differs in significant ways from those used more widely in the global literature.

Conceptions of open learning in South Africa have been influenced by international instances of open learning, most specifically in the United Kingdom (see Introduction, this volume). Definitions of open learning in the 1970s and 1980s, linked to the establishment of national distance teaching institutions such as the Open University (OU) in the UK, emphasised the minimising of constraints on formal opportunities for learning (Caliskan, 2012). For example, Paine describes open learning as:

both a process which focuses on access to educational opportunities and a philosophy which makes learning more client and student centred. It is learning which allows the learner to choose how to learn, when to learn, where to learn and what to learn as far as possible within the resource constraints of any education and training provision. (1989, as cited in Fraser & Dean, 1997, p. xi).

According to Wheeler, open learning focuses on creating opportunities for access, flexibility of location and mode, pacing and even content (2010, p. 105). In many ways, understandings of open learning in the South African context owe more to these definitions of open learning than they do to the open education movement that emerged in the early 2000s (Atkins et al., 2007). The earlier definitions of open learning referred primarily to providing entry to formal higher education institutions for those who would not usually have been admitted, whereas the latter open education movement endeavoured to provide access to legally shareable (and sometimes editable) open educational resources, freely available open textbooks, free open online courses and/or communities to anyone who wanted to study irrespective of their backgrounds, socio-economic status, race, gender, prior learning, country of origin, etc.

In the context of the strategic vision for opening up education combined with pressure to provide cost-effective and flexible access to PSET, the then Department of Education (DoE) proposed open learning as one of a number of strategies to improve access to flexible, affordable and quality ongoing education and training (DoE, 1995).

DHET's conceptualisation of open learning is developed in a number of documents, including the *White Paper for Post-school Education and Training* (DoE, 1995), the 2013 *White Paper for Post-school Education and Training* (DHET, 2013), and the draft *Open Learning Policy Framework for Post-School Education and Training* (DHET, 2017). The role of open learning as an 'ideal' or principled, learner-centred, transformative approach (DHET, 2017), is understood by DHET in relation to three pillars, namely issues of:

- *access*, including flexible provision of learning, supporting lifelong learning, the removal of barriers to access learning, and the recognition of prior learning experience as a route to access,
- *quality*, including the maintenance of rigorous quality assurance over the design of learning materials and support systems, and
- *success*, including the provision of learner support, the construction of learning programmes in the expectation that learners can succeed, the recognition of prior learning experiences for credit. (DHET, 2013, 2017)

The term open learning is often used inconsistently, collapsed into open education, or used "interchangeably to refer to e-learning, flexible learning, and distance learning" (Caliskan, 2012, p. 143) or even distance education (Zawacki-Richter et al., 2020). Although DHET, in the local context, cautions against the co-location and sometimes conflation of open learning with terms such as 'distance education', 'resource-based learning', and 'e-learning or technology-enhanced learning' (DHET, 2017, p. 6), the provision of distance education in South Africa nonetheless makes reference to open learning. The *Policy for the Provision of Distance Education in South African Universities,* in the context of an integrated post-school system, describes open learning as "making provision to support a wider range of student choices regarding access, curriculum, pacing, sequencing, learning modes and methods, assessment and articulation" (DHET, 2014, p. 20).

A social justice perspective on open learning

Post-1994 South African educational legislation has consistently articulated the value of an inclusive education and training sector, in line with the *Universal Declaration of Human Rights* (1948) and *Freedom Charter* (1955). Focusing particularly on redressing issues of access and opportunity, DHET in its *White Paper for PSET* asserts that:

> Education has long been recognised as providing a route out of poverty for individuals, and as a way of promoting equality of opportunity. The achievement of greater social justice is closely dependent on equitable access by all sections of the population to quality education. (DHET, 2013, p. 5)

In particular, the PSET sector is simultaneously tasked with addressing the demand for a skilled and economically relevant labour force while playing "a vital role in relation to a person's health, quality of life, self-esteem, and the ability of citizens to be actively engaged and empowered" (DHET, 2013, p. 3).

However, both basic and post-secondary education are plagued by deeply rooted historical inequalities which produced grossly differentially resourced and positioned educational sectors along racialised lines. These historical inequalities are exacerbated by multiple contemporary challenges, including poor economic growth, fragmented infrastructure development, and political and social disunity. Given the persistent inequalities of opportunities and outcomes in the field of education, a concern with social justice should be a key focus, not only in educational interventions, but also in educational research. Accordingly, initiatives that seek to 'open up' education must be explored through a social justice lens.

Fraser's social justice lens

While recognising that, in the formal education context, "learning programmes and courses cannot for the most part be fully 'open'" (DHET, 2017, p. 373), open learning, as published by DHET in the OLPF, has a social justice imperative:

> democratising the education system, overcoming unfair discrimination, expanding access to education and training opportunities, and improving the quality of education, training and research. (DHET, 2013, p. 1)

Nancy Fraser's conception of social justice (2005) offers a generative framework for exploring the extent to which the five selected UFS open learning initiatives are iterating towards socially just education. In so doing, we are following in the path of local authors (Hodgkinson-Williams & Trotter, 2018; Hölscher & Bozalek, 2020; Leibowitz & Bozalek, 2016) who have also used Fraser's three-dimensional, multi-level theory of social justice to explore educational initiatives in South Africa through a social justice lens.

Among the "tools for expanding and deepening relations of justice as well as resisting encroaching injustices" (Hölscher & Bozalek, 2020, p. 8), Fraser offers the notion of parity of participation which has been a core element since her earlier work (1996, 2005). Fraser asserts that justice "requires social arrangements that permit all to participate as peers in social life" (Fraser, 2011, p. 455). Fraser locates injustices, not at the level of the individual, but at the level of structures, that create classes and categories of persons who are marginalised economically, culturally and/or politically, and therefore excluded from participation.

In addition to improving participatory parity through addressing the intersection of distribution (economics), recognition (culture) and representation (politics), Fraser offers two categories of response to injustice: affirmative, sometimes referred to as ameliorative (Hodgkinson-Williams & Trotter, 2018), or transformative shifts. Affirmative (or ameliorative) responses to the inequitable social outcomes leave "intact much of the underlying political-economic structure" (Fraser, 1995, p. 84). In line with the view of social justice as conditions that permit parity of participation, at its most transformative, "overcoming injustice means dismantling institutionalized obstacles that prevent some people from participating on a par with others, as full partners in social interaction" (Fraser, 2005, p. 73).

Economic injustices and responses

Injustice in the economic dimension produces structures that maintain the maldistribution of material resources and (re-)produce classes of person who are less likely to be able to participate fully in the context as a result of limited access to material resources such as food, transport, housing, electricity, health care, data, devices, and funding (Hodgkinson-Williams & Trotter, 2018; Leibowitz & Bozalek, 2016). To counter this economic maldistribution, "the distribution of material resources must be such as to ensure participants' equal capacity for social interaction" (Fraser, 2011, p. 455). This can take the form of modest affirmative responses where the actions ameliorate or alleviate the conditions to a certain extent – what Fraser (2005) refers to as "redistribution". If the response is more radical, and gets to "the root of the matter" (Zipin, 2017, p. 68), then Fraser would refer to this as "restructuring" (Fraser 2005).

Cultural injustices and responses

Injustices in the cultural dimension concern the misallocation of recognition, producing categories of persons who are not recognised as equal, who experience "a status differentiation, rooted in the status order of society" (Fraser, 2007, p. 26). Leibowitz and Bozalek suggest that "forms of status inequality include: degrading students' prior knowledges, colonisation of settler groups where the values and attributes of certain other groups are backgrounded and rendered invisible in the curriculum" (2016, p. 111). To counteract this cultural misrecognition, social justice is contingent on the existence of a status order that "express[es] equal respect for all participants and ensure[s] equal opportunity for achieving social esteem" (Fraser, 2011, p. 455). An ameliorative form of cultural recognition would, for instance, acknowledge the value of knowledge systems other than the Western-centric canon, but not necessarily change the structure of the curriculum to accommodate these viewpoints. By contrast:

> A transformative approach would involve dismantling the ... social hierarchies and cultural hegemonies that currently underpin the canons, the assumed norms and values of inherited curricula and setting up processes to reimagine more inclusive ways of participating in curriculum and pedagogic practices. (Luckett & Shay, 2017, p. 52)

Political injustices and responses

Expanding on her initially two-dimensional model, Fraser argues that it is a condition of justice that "the political constitution of society must be such as to accord roughly equal political voice to all social actors" (2011, p. 455). Acknowledging that in the contemporary context both the subject of justice and the boundaries of political space are "objects of struggle", Fraser invokes the notion of framing to challenge us to consider the risks of misframing, including a kind of political death to those who are excluded from a political space. In drawing such frames, we make decisions about who is represented in the space. While Fraser's theory operates at a broad social level, Garraway (2017, p. 113), applying this to a higher education classroom, interprets Fraser's question to be "who is permitted or has the right to make claims of maldistribution or misrecognition". Leibowitz and Bozalek (2016) offer the powerful example of framing challenges at institutional or even individual levels as opposed to sectoral concerns, resulting in the misplacement of responsibility.

Although Fraser offers the analytically distinct dimensions as a tool for exploring the nature of parity of participation in a space, she also notes that some categories of difference can function in multiple dimensions. For example, Fraser discusses this most clearly in relation to gender, arguing that the displacement of concerns related to redistribution with concerns related to recognition produce "a truncated economism for a truncated culturalism", demanding instead a "broader, richer paradigm that could encompass both redistribution and recognition" (Fraser, 2007, p. 25). While in this study, we will represent these dimensions as "analytically discrete" (De Kadt, 2020, p. 875), we will, as Fraser insists, also view them as "inextricably interwoven" (2005, p. 75).

Methodology

For the purposes of this study, we adopted a case study method (Flyvbjerg, 2011), taking as our case the concept of openness and its trajectory in a single institution. Case studies provide an opportunity to understand principles or ideas in real-world situations (Cohen et al., 2017), tending to allow for the 'fuzzy realities' of context — through acknowledging these as:

> unique and dynamic ... case studies investigate and report the real-life, complex, dynamic and unfolding interactions of events, human relationships and other factors in a unique instance. (Cohen et al., 2017, p. 376)

Our case study adopted an interpretivist position and utilised a qualitative approach. We collected a variety of data, including interviews with four key participants, institutional reports, and publicly-facing documentation such as policy documents, annual reports and handbooks (UFS, 2008, 2011, 2014, 2017, 2020).

Interviews, interviewees and ethical concerns

Gaining access to interviewees posed a number of challenges. Given the size of the PSET sector in SA, and the scholarly and community-oriented text arising from the project, anonymity was impossible to guarantee. We have not, thus, identified the specific roles of the individuals who agree to be identified. Additionally, the commissioned nature of this research created potential for a tense relationship between researchers and participants, and researchers and the commissioning body. Unlike independent researchers who are perceived to be studying a phenomenon for its own sake, to some extent the COOL project team was viewed as doing research on behalf of DHET. This had the potential to heighten existing concerns about being interviewed, in light of perceived risk to individual and institutional reputation. Finally, this research was conducted in 2020, during the COVID-19 pandemic at a time when many staff were already experiencing great stress.

Ultimately, our primary goal was to do no harm while pursuing our scholarly interests. Ethical clearance and permissions were obtained from the UFS. In addition to the institutional requirements for ethical clearance, which are primarily procedural, we adopted a strongly relational orientation (Ellis, 2007). Participants were identified based on their role at UFS and referrals during interviews. Interviewees were purposively (Cohen et al., 2017) chosen for their insights into particular projects and structures within the institution and subsequently recommended other colleagues within the institution, in a snowballing effect (Cohen et al., 2017). Due to the exploratory nature of the research and the relatively limited access to interviewees and the institution, we opted for a semi-structured interview process, which allowed staff to direct the flow of the conversation. Interviewees were offered primarily open questions to encourage the telling of stories about open and openness at UFS. These extensive interviews were subsequently transcribed and analysed using thematic analysis and coding. The first phase of analysis used the key concepts of access, quality and success, adopted from the OLPF, to analyse the data, before turning to Fraser's dimensions of social justice to understand the extent to which access, quality and success initiatives could be seen to be 'opening up' learning.

Our commitment to treating our interviewees fairly affected not only the obvious issues of confidentiality and anonymity, but also the kinds of questions we were willing to ask our participants, and the kinds of analysis we were willing to undertake in relation to the data. Weighing up who was protected by our discretion and who was harmed has not been a simple process. Furthermore, although we have adopted a social justice approach, which is fundamentally concerned with matters of power, we were, at least in part, inspired by the work of Appreciative Inquiry theorists (see for example, Jones & Masika, 2021) who work with narrative and a focus on the positive to generate change, while being open to the 'shadow' of experiences.

Towards the shape of open at UFS

This exploration of 'open' was undertaken at UFS, which was suggested by DHET as a site for research. UFS serves approximately 41 675 students, on three main campuses: Bloemfontein campus, historically the site of the University of the Orange Free State; the Qwaqwa Campus in the eastern Free State, formerly a branch of the University of the North; and the Campus of Open Learning, historically part of Vista University. The Campus of Open Learning is the current home of various programmes focused on opening up learning, focusing on school leavers, and working professionals such as teachers and nurses, while offering a range of short learning programmes in other fields.

The story of open learning at UFS is rooted in the context of formal education. For the purposes of this study, we describe five initiatives that interviewees raised as 'opening up' learning at UFS: the University Access Programme (UAP), the Advanced Certificates in Teaching (ACTs), the Grade R Teaching Diploma, the Advanced Diploma in TVET teaching, and the establishment of the Campus of Open Learning. Borrowing from the policy framework provided by DHET and adopted by UFS, we will identify actions that interviewees saw as addressing issues of access, quality and success at UFS. The extent to which these initiatives could be described as addressing inequality, and thus, socially just, follows later in the section entitled "From access, quality and success to social justice".

University Access Programme (UAP)

Access through UAP

Although the University Access Programme (UAP) has its roots in the academic support programmes of the 1990s, unlike extended degree programmes, UAP does not target students who have gained entry to the institution on the basis of their matric results, but rather seeks to create an opportunity for students who have failed to "perform themselves into higher education" (UFS, 2017, p. 1). Access to UAP is limited to students who meet the following requirements: A National Senior Certificate (NSC) or National Certificate: Vocational (NCV) Level 4, with an admission point (AP) of either 18 for Higher Certificates, or 20 for UAP study options, four subjects on Level 3 (40%–49%), and Language of instruction on Level 3 (40%) (UFS, 2020). One of our interviewees described UAP as:

> a programme for Grade 12 learners that passed Grade 12 but did not do well and want to go to university. The programme is a Grade 12 programme that gives learners who didn't make it, the opportunity to get it – allowing access. Poorer communities have limited access to extra lessons and technology that more economically stable families would have. (Participant 1)

In the absence of this programme, such students would not have a route of access into the university. While the programme has historically attracted students from South Africa and a number of southern African countries, more recently participants have come from as far afield as Nigeria and Mali (Participant 1).

UAP developed out of a series of access interventions in the early 1990s. The Need for Education and Elevation (NEED) Programme, launched in 1991, began as a bridging intervention for 'at risk' students. It quickly rebranded as the Career Preparation Programme, and was offered in collaboration with, at the time, eight colleges in the Free State, the Northern Cape and Western Cape (Rabie, 2008). By 1994, it offered courses in Human and Social Sciences (HSS), Natural and Agricultural Sciences (NAS) and Economic and Management Sciences (EMS) (Hay & Marais, 2004). UAP currently offers three Higher Certificate (HC) programmes in EMS (Commerce), in Economic and Management Sciences (Administration) and in Humanities at several UFS and TVET college sites. Historically, a broader range of programmes including one targeting the natural sciences, one focused on engineering, and another with a health care orientation, were offered, but these have subsequently fallen away.

Participant 2 was eager to point out that the curricula of the certificate courses were also focused on remediating the inequalities of the schooling sector, responding to specific inequalities such as a lack of access to ICTs for education:

> We can't fully just use a learning management system because the type of student there has, basically, never touched a computer. And for us to expect them to now learn online whilst they've never touched a computer, it's a bit of a high ask. We have to increase [their] digital literacy first before we get to that stage. You can't plunge people into the pool of learning online if it's always been blackboards, paper, and pen, kind of thing. (Participant 2)

The curricula for these programmes combine substantive, university accredited first-year courses with a General Language Course, an Academic Literacy Course, a Computer Practice course, a discipline-oriented Mathematical Literacy course, and a Basic Skills & Competencies for Lifelong Learning course (Participant 1 & Participant 2).

Quality through UAP

These programmes are characterised by a blended approach, incorporating "a variety of delivery styles and accommodat[ing] different student and organisational needs to achieve the most effective learning outcomes" (UFS, 2008). There is a strong emphasis on small group learning which the lecturers believed would create "a culture of learning" (Participant 1) and scaffolding or what they referred to as "nurturing" (Participant 2) towards more independent learning. A focus on group work supports the development of a shared culture of collaborative learning (Participant 1). Three of our interviewees referred directly to the success of the pedagogical strategy adopted by the programme. One emphasized that "Access with success" was at the heart of the UAP offering, emphasising that "these students end up performing better than, uh, the mainstream students" (Participant 2). Participant 1 similarly claimed that:

> they say that the South Campus (Campus of Open Learning) students stand out because once they get to, uh, Bloem Campus, they're able to question and they debate, you know? It gives them some confidence to say, 'I shouldn't take what my lecturer is saying at face value. I can always challenge and question if I don't understand'.

Two participants made explicit mention of "resource-based learning" supplemented with extensive small-group tutorials (Participant 1 & Participant 2). Resource-based learning surfaces in the literature as response to massification and diversifications of education in the South African context, paired with limited funding (Holtzhausen, 1999). While the term 'resource-based learning' is used in varying ways in the literature, Holtzhausen provides a detailed definition of resource-based learning that includes, inter alia, shifts in the conceptualisation of the role of the lecturer, the student, and materials, that adopts a broad understanding of resources, and that leans on "open-learning and distance education principles" (1999, p. 32).

While the UFS Annual Report notes that "the needs of students differ, equity in education is likely to require unequal resources and services applied to different students to obtain expected outcome" (UFS, 2017, p. 109), the reality of funding is often shaped by national and international forces. The UAP has, over time, moved from relying primarily on self-funded student fees (Rabie, 2008) or small-scale bursary schemes to the majority of students being funded by the National Student Financial Aid Scheme (NSFAS) (Participant 1). However, government funding to institutions for student completion remains limited as Participant 3 highlighted about the UAP programme: "50%. You get funded 50%". Furthermore, funding is distributed unequally based on various formulae, such that social science and humanities programmes receive less funding, and STEM subjects attract a greater percentage of government funding. This unequal funding is perceived to create "cash cows", and is seen as part of the "neoliberalist paradigm of the university" (Participant 3).

In addition to shifts in access to fee-funding, the UAP has over the last three decades moved to support students' social and material needs, in order to improve the quality of their learning experience. The initial programme at UAP predated the building of the residences, and worked around a schedule that ended by 5 p.m., "because students had to go home". As, over time, UAP students came to be accommodated in the residences at Main campus, students would:

> commute between the two campuses. We had a bus service which we contracted by outside people that ran between the two campuses. But it took time. Now, we have our own residences. Even though some of the students still stay at the Bloemfontein Campus. But, you know, at least it helps a lot with accommodation. (Participant 1)

Success through UAP

The UAP Annual Report of 2017 reflects mixed results across the three certificates with the Commerce track of Economic and Management Science experiencing a better student pass rate, 73%, followed by Humanities 63%, and the Administrative track of EMS at 49% (UFS, 2018). The report also disaggregates the data on the basis of institution and campus, which provides a snapshot of the extent of the variation in pass rates.

In addition to tracking progression through the programme, UAP also tracks the progression of its students if they remain at UFS, but cannot do so if they change institutions. Students successfully completing the UAP may continue to study at UFS or, from 2017, may exit with a Higher Certificate qualification, which can be used as an alternative entry qualification to mainstream higher education nationally (UFS, 2018). The recent longitudinal report undertaken notes enrollments up to 2017: of the 1013 students registered for UAP, 660 successfully passed the programme. Data for Table 1 is provided in the UAP Annual Report of 2017, showing the qualifications completed by students exiting the UAP to date.

Table 1: Longitudinal report: UAP programme

Qualification	Number
Undergraduate Degrees	4 659
MBCHB	9
Honours	391
Masters	45
PhD	3

Although uptake of these students into mainstream higher education courses is harder to track as students may apply to different institutions, Hay and Marais report that students, after successfully completing UAP, gain access to a wide range of institutions including "Rhodes University, the University of Port Elizabeth (under certain conditions), the University of the Western Cape, the University of Stellenbosch, the Vaal Triangle Campus of the University of North West, and the University of Pretoria" (2004, p. 63).

In these ways UFS endeavoured to 'open up' learning by "remov[ing] barriers to access learning", and "construct[ing] learning programmes in the expectation that students [could] succeed", as stipulated in the OLPF (DHET, 2017, p. 363)

Advanced Certificates in Teaching (ACTs)

Emerging from the decades of apartheid and colonial history, the new democratic South African government faced the substantial challenge of restructuring the national education system, built at that point entirely, from Grade 1 to educator training, on race-based policies. The racially-ordered underpinnings of the system pervaded every aspect of educational life, from curricula to funding, and functioned to ensure that one's opportunities and life path were almost entirely determined by race. Since as early as the 1980s there were shifts to mandate higher qualifications for educators (Adams, 2004). Nonetheless, by the early 1990s, the under-qualification of educators, especially black people, women, and those living in rural areas, coupled with the wide-spread teacher shortages in black schools, posed a substantial threat to the development of an equitable and suitable education system. The Advanced Certificates in Teaching were developed as part of a national initiative to enable teachers to upgrade their existing qualifications to align with the requirements of the *Norms and Standards for Educators* policy (DoE, 2000).

Access through ACTs

The Advanced Certificates in Education (ACTs) are offered through the School of Open Learning and provide a lower entry point to tertiary qualification than that required for an undergraduate degree. As explained by Participant 4:

> It's not your, I hate the word 'mainstream', but it's not your mainstream student that needs opportunities like this. It's your student that's not got the mainstream opportunity, whether it's electronic or not, virtual or not, that we need to cater for.

Providing lower entry point qualifications is a contentious decision in many institutions, as these attract relatively poor funding, and do not have an obviously positive impact on the research output of universities (Participant 3).

Our participants' claims align with other research conducted at Rhodes University (Schäfer & Wilmot, 2012) which suggests three substantial needs: access to an initial higher education qualification, strengthening pedagogy, and reskilling educators for new disciplines and curricula. Furthermore, as Participant 2 reminded us,

> this qualification also needs to... [provide] ... access to your Bachelor of Education and foundation phase or any of the Bachelor of Education qualifications, if those teachers wish to ... continue. (Participant 2)

UFS developed a series of ACTs to address the multiple intersecting needs of in-service teachers. Chief among these is the need for a recognisable qualification to ensure continued employment for in-service teachers who, holding a teaching diploma, are not qualified to teach under the current dispensation (Participant 2).

Undertaking the ACTs has financial implications for students. The students who undertake this course of study are poorly paid and, unfortunately, are often the responsible breadwinners in their families. But successfully completing the course impacts positively on their earnings. The Department of Basic Education (DBE) funds students to complete an ACT as long as they are progressing satisfactorily. However, as Participant 2 notes, "numbers have been on the decline because clientele is dependent on bursaries" and in the face of other pressures funders make strategic decisions about how many students to support. While the institution has been unable to waive or reduce fee costs, close relations with the provincial DBE secures some bursaries, and offering the courses in block release or distance mode reduces the costs for educators who would otherwise potentially miss work, or need to travel and find accommodation close to campus.

Quality through ACTs

The higher certificate programmes consist of ten courses which students can undertake consecutively, starting four times a year. Although advanced certificates are generally constructed nationally as two-year, part-time programmes, in a contact format, UFS offers the ACTs in distance or mixed mode format in parallel. The mixed mode takes the form of materials, either paper-based or online, with a limited number of face-to-face workshops at a number of satellite locations.

Despite the technological constraints of the contexts in which students undertake the programme, including poor ICT infrastructure and the limited digital literacies of the students themselves, the programme works to develop students' digital literacies and equip them for study through online learning.

In addition to the option to learn online, the distance mode of learning, underpinned by a commitment to resource-based learning and supplemented by periodic face-to-face workshops at satellite locations, is a key step in enabling students to access the programme. As one of our participants shared: We drove weekends to Queenstown and Aliwal North and then the students from Sterkspruit and those regions could come and they could attend over weekends. We offered it in a distance education mode, so they had resource-based study material that they could work through and they had assignments and so on and then they would come and engage … Same in Aliwal North. Same in Kimberley where there wasn't a university [at the time]. Same in Ladybrand, which is close to the Lesotho border, so the Lesotho students would come there. (Participant 4)

Reflecting a change in the practice, Participant 2 confirms that the current focus is to "enhance the study material" in order to support students in remote areas.

Success through ACTs

In the past, ACTs have been successful in reaching students through their use of limited satellite workshops in remote areas. As Participant 4 points out:

There were so many students that we had to repeat the workshops. There were like 70, 80 students in a workshop and we would repeat it, so in total it was 160 to 200 just in Queenstown. We worked our butts off, but the students made progress. And, yes, it's quite true that they don't have access to the library and all those [sic] and it was in the days where electronic versions of everything wasn't [sic] so available.

In the contemporary context, there has been a shift to online modes for providing additional teaching and enhancing success. However, such modes require access to technical infrastructure, digital literacies and conducive learning environments that are not equitably distributed in society.

In this fashion, UFS endeavoured 'open up' learning by offering "flexible provision for learning" and additional teaching as part of the setting up of learning programmes in the expectation of success as aspired to in the OLPF (DHET, 2017, p. 363).

Grade R Teaching Diploma

Access through Grade R Teaching Diploma

In the same way that the ACTs responded to a need in the broader educational context, the newly accredited Diploma in Teaching Grade R (Reception year) in 2020 – and in future the RR (Pre-reception year: 4–5 year olds) and RRR (3–4 year olds) – responds to shifts in the location of pre-school education. The relocation of "creche or early-childhood development (ECD)" from the Department of Social Development to the DBE, prompted a change in requirements for those teaching in that category, creating a category of educator in need of further education. As Participant 2 explained:

> You've got lots of, even, learners who are from matric, then they just went to ... cousin John's creche ... and cousin John just gives them a few instructions and tells them what to do. Because they are kids, they believe anyone can teach kids. There is a lot of emphasis on their care, but not... the development part. So, they would take care of the child, but not the development of the child, which we see as two different elements in ECD.

Unlike the ACTs which typically attracted older educators seeking to reskill and remain employable, the Grade R Teaching Diploma attracts younger students, entering the workforce with limited access to educational opportunities, either as a result of poor schooling histories, or limited funding.

Unfortunately, at this point, students enrolling in the programme are not eligible for NSFAS funding. However, as Participant 2 noted:

> That one is not funded. That one is self-funded. So, we're funding it ourselves in its development. And we are hoping that the returns will come when the learners are now funded. Because already the Free State Department of Education has a policy, a Grade R Teaching funding policy, which means that they are serious about taking their targeted students through the program.

UFS has seen, in the past, a shift towards access programmes attracting funding.

Quality through Grade R Teaching Diploma

The Grade R Teaching Diploma may be taken over three or four years, face-to-face or at a distance. By the end of the qualification, they are qualified Grade R teachers who also have access to Bachelor of Education in Foundation phase. Participant 2 made clear that the programme allows for recognition of prior learning, enabling students to leverage their experience to enter the programme, and to accelerate their progression through portfolio submissions for access to university studies.

Success through Grade R Teaching Diploma

The Grade R Teaching Diploma programme is relatively new, and thus there is little data on the extent to which this programme will address issues of success for students.

In the Grade R Teaching Diploma UFS endeavoured to open up education by reducing the financial barriers and allowing students to leverage their prior knowledge and experience for entry, through a recognition of prior learning process, to further university studies.

Centralised curricula: Advanced Diploma in TVET teaching

As with basic education, shifting demands of the sector, including massification, the integration of previously racially segregated institutions, the elimination of job reservation, and the weakening route of the master-apprentice relationship (Gamble, 2013), led to increased demand for the development a skilled body of educators capable of navigating the complex requirements of vocational education. A sectoral report based on 2015 data established that, of the 6 775 lecturers surveyed (out of a possible total of 7 043 participants), 11.9%

were neither academically nor professionally qualified; 29.2% were academically qualified but professionally unqualified; 33.4% were academically and professionally qualified for the schooling sector; and only 10.4% were considered as academically and professionally qualified for the TVET sector (DHET, 2016).

A relatively new project in the UFS open learning initiative is the development of an Advanced Diploma in TVET teaching. Tasked by DHET to support the further professional education of TVET lecturers, along with 14 other institutions, UFS's School of Open Learning partnered with the South African Institute for Distance Education to develop a centralised curriculum. The curriculum will be hosted on the National Open Learning System (NOLS)[1] and will enable institutions who wish to run such programmes access to a suite of OER to support the implementation and teaching of the programme. As Adendorff and Van Wyk explain:

> A segment of this system will be used to host formal professional qualification programmes for TVET lecturers which may be used either in their entirety by universities that choose this option, or as selections of component modules which universities may choose to insert into programmes of their own construction, and possibly adapt (the modules will all be hosted as open education resources licensed for re-use and adaptation. (2016, p. 3)

Institutions would need to obtain accreditation for offering the Diploma, but could then develop versions of the programme with their own "institutional flavour" (Participant 2). The development of this centralised curriculum aims to reduce development costs and time, allowing institutions to offer qualifications more quickly to TVET lecturers wishing to undertake formal professional development.

In this way UFS is iterating towards the open vision of the OLPF by sharing curricula and, when ready, curating these on NOLS as OER. This initiative draws on the open education movement with an intention to share beyond a single institution. At this point, it is not entirely clear if these materials will be open to all or retained by the formal institutions offering the Advanced Diploma in TVET teaching.

Establishing the School of Open Learning (South Campus)

The bringing together of a number of innovative initiatives at the School of Open Learning, on what was previously the Vista campus, and is now known as the South Campus, was a critical step in moving towards what UFS sees as opening up learning. These initiatives included access programmes, the short learning programmes in both face-to-face and online modes, the Ideas Lab, the Internet Broadcasting Project, and a number of collaborative projects with schools across the province.

Linking those innovations under the banner of open learning and on a physical campus created the material conditions that enabled substantial growth in relation to staffing, space for students, and partnerships. For example, when the School of Open Learning was initially established in 2011 (UFS, 2011), it employed about 20 staff members. In its current incarnation, it employs over 120 full-time staff members and 600 part-time staff members (Participant 3). As has been previously discussed, locating the access programme and,

---

[1] http://nols.gov.za/

more recently, the residential spaces for these programmes on the South Campus created supportive transitional residential spaces for students entering UFS from backgrounds that are fundamentally different from the traditional university space (Participant 1).

The additional physical space provided an opportunity for the building of a state-of-the-art studio, the Ideas Lab. This led to the development of a partnership with a Texas educational institution to support online learning design development within the School of Open Learning. The building of the studio strengthened the development of capacity in online learning design or e-learning, impacting not only on fully online courses, but also on the increasingly popular blended learning offerings within the institution.

Also hosted on the South Campus is the Internet Broadcast Project (IBP), a partnership between the Free State Department of Education and the ICTISE (ICT Innovation in School Education). Since 2011, the project has provided curriculum support, in a range of subjects, to 80 000 high school students and educators (Participant 3; UFS, 2014).

The establishment of the School of Open Learning as a structure within the institution, and the concomitant creation of the South Campus as the home of the School of Open Learning, created an opportunity for leadership within the School of Open Learning to be elevated within the institution. The principal of the School of Open Learning, and of the South campus, "became a part of top management in terms of being a part of the rectorate" (Participant 3). This positioning brought issues linked to open education, including issues of distance education and access to academically or historically excluded students, into mainstream conversations about the shape of the university. Combined with the positive support of two generations of senior management, this has resulted in open learning activities attracting centralised funding for staffing from the institution.

Open learning initiatives at UFS: A summary

As Adendorff and Van Wyk argue, open learning is "focused on removing barriers to learning" (2016, p. 4), including the time required to travel to or from sites of learning, being unavailable to employers, the cost of study, and so on. UFS has in place a number of initiatives – the University Access Programme, Advanced Certificates in Teaching, Grade R Teaching Diploma, Centralised curricula: Advanced Diploma in TVET teaching, the School of Open Learning at the South Campus – that seek to remove barriers to learning, improve flexibility of learning provision, and provide learner support, as outlined in the OLPF. These programmes paid attention to a range of individuals, from potential students seeking access to higher education (UAP and ACTs) to students seeking to study in programmes not historically offered in the higher education context. Although the initiatives undertaken by UFS are well aligned with activities suggested in the OLPF, these activities are often not grounded in conceptual understandings of the inequalities that they seek to address. Reviewing these activities through Fraser's social justice lens allows us to better understand the complexities of intersecting inequalities.

Discussion: From access, quality and success to social justice

Having described the shape of a selection of interventions working towards 'opening up' learning at UFS, we begin to consider in what ways, and to what extent, these interventions respond to historical and contemporary social injustices, along economic, cultural and political dimensions. Equal access to and equal likelihood of success in educational endeavours sits at the nexus of Fraser's three dimensions of social justice.

Access as social justice

Viewed through a social justice lens, the development of academic access programmes as an instance of opening up learning can be seen as an attempt to strengthen participatory parity. At UFS, the commitment to offering alternative access routes to higher education through certificate programmes for students who did not obtain the required marks in their final school examinations is complemented by the provision of diplomas as routes to accessing higher education for working professionals, particularly in under-respected fields such as teaching and nursing. Such initiatives, while clearly aligned with the OLPF, are at best ameliorative efforts, leaving the structures that determine access largely untouched, at least in the short to medium term.

Access to higher education is also an economic issue, as increasing demands for fee-free education clearly indicate. As this rising demand is not matched by governments' or parents' ability to fund all those who would like to attend, access to higher education is likely to remain a cause of annual conflict and rising uncertainty. Additionally, access to higher education is currently also determined on the basis of matriculation results and national benchmarking tests. Both of these are strongly impacted on by economic inequalities such as the resourcing of schools, staffing ratios in different schools and materials access. As the UAP programmes do not all attract NSFAS funding, while some barriers to participation are addressed, economic barriers remain a constraint. Initiatives to sources additional funding to subsidise the costs of programmes before they become fundable through NSFAS, while a commendable ameliorative strategy, do not challenge the notion of higher education as a private good, to be funded primarily by the individual, with limited state support for redress purposes.

While the development of academic development programmes seek to ease students' transitions into learning in higher education institutions, using a Fraserian lens, these programmes are an ameliorative response to complex economic and cultural inequalities. Such programmes might, in other terms, be described as assimilationist, as their focus is seldom on changing the structures of power and value in the institution, so much as strengthening students' capacity to navigate those structural inequalities underpinned by a certain set of cultural norms. Access programmes can also respond to issues of framing, most often offering ameliorative responses to the question "who belongs?". The expanded routes of access offered by UFS remain unequivocally an improvement on conventional routes of access, enabling participation in spaces from which certain categories of student would historically remain entirely excluded. However, the recent discontinuation of the programmes offering access to the powerful professional fields of science and engineering is an unfortunate consequence of limited government funding for such programmes.

Given the historical bar to access that excluded black students from historically white and well-resourced institutions, access programmes that seek not just to include black faces and bodies, but that also seek to include those whose life chances are limited by poor school conditions, are doing two kinds of work – redressing issues of racial exclusion, and redressing issues of exclusion on the basis of class, which in the South African context are lamentably and painfully entwined.

Quality as social justice

Since the late 1980s and early 1990s, access, in terms of massification and diversifying access to PSET institutions, has been a point of attention institutionally and nationally. Noting, however, that it would be "wasteful and negligent to permit quality to lag while access expands" (DHET, 2020), quality is also a key focus in DHET's *Strategic Plan 2020–2025*. In a discussion of macro trends, the PSET Monitor acknowledges that both definitions and indicators of quality are challenging to spell out in ways that distinguish them from issues of success. Both documents offer some examples of markers of quality, including quality of teaching and learning, the qualifications of staff, their publication record, reducing student to staff ratios, and enrollment in STEM subjects (DHET, 2019, 2020).

Issues of gender, access to hegemonically valued languages and accents, consumption of valued (often synonymous with Western, literature and media) knowledge, and ease of participation in culturally western, or urban, or modern activities can ease students' pathways through schooling, and into PSET. Various open initiatives at UFS work to impact on quality, including particular pedagogic approaches in access programmes, modes of teaching in professional development courses for basic education and PSET educators, and the provision of accommodation as part of creating conducive learning conditions. While such ameliorative interventions can soften participants' experiences of the barriers to parity of participation posed by a range of economic, cultural and political injustices, the fundamentally hierarchical and unequal construction of economic, cultural (specifically epistemological and linguistic) and political structures, continue to produce barriers to parity of participation in learning environments.

Success as social justice

In the local context, however, success in the Matric exams is strongly related to the economic, social and political contexts of high schools. Schools in areas which experience social ills, or political unrest, are often less able to adequately prepare students. Active interventions on the part of higher educational institutions such as the access programme at UFS are a key ameliorative step towards social justice. However, success during schooling is also strongly shaped by conceptualisations of the ideal in the schooling and PSET sector, in effect by what Fraser would call the cultural dimension of social justice.

Instead of success being defined as simply the acquisition of a qualification, it can usefully be thought of in connection to life opportunities and possibilities after post-secondary education. With success in higher education degrees being strongly linked to employability in the South African context, students' desire for access to higher education is likely to continue to increase. Needham claims that university graduates are likely to "earn up to four times more than matriculants" (2021, p. 44), but that this is not comparable to TVET graduates where "barely more than half of graduates were employed or in paid, work-based learning programmes 18 months after graduation" (2021, p. 46). Despite international trends suggesting an overproduction of graduates and a saturated market, data from Stats SA suggest that individuals with higher education qualifications are substantially less likely to fall into poverty (Stats SA, 2017), thus we can anticipate the continued value of university qualifications and particularly alternative paths to opening up access such as those undertaken at UFS, even as current university curricula are deliberated to better represent local knowledges, languages and cultural norms. Due to the recency of the development of the Advanced Diploma in TVET teaching there is at present insufficient evidence of the development and uptake of centralised curriculum to make an informed judgement about the value of this initiative for the institutions offering this qualification or for the TVET lecturers it intends to serve.

Conclusion

Opening up learning, or 'open learning', in the context of UFS, has deep historical connections with access programmes, designed at the time to enable access for students of colour to the historically white, Afrikaans institution. These connections continue to powerfully shape mainstream open learning initiatives, although they are by no means the sole factors shaping access interventions at UFS today. Concerns with openness in relation to quality of educational experience produce activities such as residential support and the creation of learning communities among students, focusing not only on improving access, but also on improving student outcomes.

The conceptualisations of open learning at UFS reproduce much of the language and orientation of the *Open Learning Policy Framework* (DHET, 2017), drawing on a lineage of DoE and DHET texts, including the 1995 *White Paper* (DoE, 1995) and work done by the Working Group on Distance Education and Open Learning (WGDEOL, 2002, p. 19). UFS's policy on *Open, Blended, and Engaged Learning* articulates a commitment to a flexible, student-centred, learning-centred approach to teaching and learning, using blended and engaged learning through computer- and mobile-supported (UFS, 2008). While in the OLPF, DHET cautions against equating open learning with distance education and online learning, it is clear that there are historical connections between the imperatives of distance education initiatives and open learning, and contemporary connections that link the affordances of online learning with the imperatives of open learning.

In this chapter, we have discussed Fraser's dimensions of inequality separately, following De Kadt's (2020, p. 4) description of these as "analytically discrete", through examining initiatives for a range of open moves, and framing these as responses to maldistribution, misrecognition, misrepresentation and misframing. However, we hope to have shown how no dimension of inequality exists in isolation from, and unsupported by, inequalities along other dimensional axes in particular contexts. As Fraser (2007, p. 25) notes, resolving complex social inequalities requires "a broader, richer paradigm" that addresses the multiple dimensions along which exclusion can be enacted. Indeed, in some instances where responses are only ameliorative in nature, while issues of locus of control may play a role, considering the other dimensions of inequality may also shift the initiative towards transformative effects.

Reporting on the key 'open learning' activities of UFS through a Fraserian lens that considers parity of participation in relation to the three dimensions of social justice, frames many of the open learning initiatives as ameliorative, as opposed to transformative. While this may be the case, such an interpretation is worth understanding in light of the complexity of the systems at work. The PSET sector does not exist in isolation from historical moments and the broader national and even global context. Economic issues at national and at global levels shape funding. Conversations at a global level powerfully influence our fundamental understanding of what constitutes higher education studies. While it is tempting to demand transformative responses, and while we might never take our eyes off what constitutes a radically reshaping of a just society, such responses are not always immediately in the power of institutions, programmes or individuals to provide. In such cases, ameliorative steps provide very necessary groundwork for more substantial changes to follow.

Acknowledgements

Many thanks to staff from the University of the Free State whose generous interviews made this chapter possible. Special thanks are due to reviewers Professor Jako Olivier, Professor Martin Weller and Dr Rob Farrow for their thoughtful, incisive feedback on the chapter, and Emeritus Associate Professor Cheryl Ann Hodgkinson-Williams for valuable feedback, and Dr Tabisa Mayisela for guiding the entire COOL project. Thanks are also due to the Centre for Innovation in Learning and Teaching at the University of Cape Town, which hosted the COOL project, and the South African Department of Higher Education and Training for funding it.

References

Adams, N. D. (2004). A conceptual analysis of teacher education in South Africa in relation to the norms and standards for educators [Doctoral dissertation, University of Stellenbosch]. https://scholar.sun.ac.za/handle/10019.1/16031

Adendorff, M., & Van Wyk, C. (2016). Offering TVET college lecturers increased access to professional qualification programmes through a national open learning system in South Africa. http://dspace.col.org/bitstream/handle/11599/2572/PDF

Atkins, D. E., Brown, J. S., & Hammond, A. L. (2007). A review of the open educational resources (OER) movement: Achievements, challenges, and new opportunities. Report to The William and Flora Hewlett Foundation. http://hewlett.org/wp-content/uploads/2016/08/ReviewoftheOERMovement.pdf

Beukes, J. A. G. (2018, July). The need for the development of formal qualifications for TVET Lecturers. In Proceedings of International Academic Conferences (No. 6508641). International Institute of Social and Economic Sciences. https://ideas.repec.org/p/sek/iacpro/6508641.html

Caliskan, H. (2012). Open learning. In N.M. Seel (Ed.), *Encyclopedia of the sciences of learning* (2516–2518). Springer. https://www.researchgate.net/publication/271201894_Open_Learning

Cohen, L., Manion, L., & Morrison, K. (2017). *Research methods in education* (8th ed.). Routledge.

De Kadt, E. (2020). Promoting social justice in teaching and learning in higher education through professional development. *Teaching in Higher Education*, 25(7), 872–887. https://doi.org/10.1080/13562517.2019.1617685

DHET (Department of Higher Education and Training). (2011). The minimum requirements for teacher education qualifications (MRTEQ). Government Printer. https://www.dhet.gov.za/Teacher%20Education/National%20Qualifications%20Framework%20Act%2067_2008%20Revised%20Policy%20for%20Teacher%20Education%20Quilifications.pdf

DHET. (2013). White paper for post-school education and training: Building an expanded, effective and integrated post-school system. *Government Gazette*, 37229. https://www.gov.za/documents/white-paper-post-school-education-and-training-building-expanded-effective-and-integrated

DHET. (2016). Qualification profile of lecturers employed in public technical and vocational education and training colleges in South Africa. http://www.dhet.gov.za/Outcome/DHET%202014%20TVET%20Lecturer%20Qualifications%20Profile%20Report.pdf

DHET. (2017). Call for comment on the Open Learning Policy Framework for Post-School Education and Training. *Government Gazette,* 335(40772). http://pmg-assets.s3-website-eu-west-1.amazonaws.com/170407openlearningframework-postschooleduc.pdf

DHET. (2019). Post-School education and training monitor: Macro-indicator trends. Government Printer. https://www.dhet.gov.za/SiteAssets/Post-School%20Education%20and%20Training%20Monitor%20Report_March%202019.pdf

DHET. (2020). Strategic plan 2020–2025. Government Printer. https://www.dhet.gov.za/SiteAssets/DHET%20Strategic%20Plan%202020.pdf

DoE (Department of Education). (2000). Norms and standards for educators. Government Printer. https://www.gov.za/sites/default/files/gcis_document/201409/20844.pdf

Ellis, C. (2007). Telling secrets, revealing lives: Relational ethics in research with intimate others. *Qualitative Inquiry,* 13(1), 3–29. https://doi.org/10.1177/1077800406294947

Essop, A. (2020). The changing size and shape of the higher education system in South Africa, 2005–2017. http://heltasa.org.za/wp-content/uploads/2020/08/Size-and-Shape-of-the-HE-System-2005-2017.pdf

Flyvbjerg, B. (2011). Case study. In N. K. Denzin & Y. S. Lincoln (Eds.), *The Sage handbook of qualitative research* (4th ed., pp. 301–316). Sage.

Fraser, N. (1995) From redistribution to recognition? Dilemmas of justice in a 'post-socialist' age. *New Left Review,* July–August, 212, 68–93.

Fraser, N. (1996). Social justice in the age of identity politics: Redistribution, recognition, and participation. *World Bank Economic Review,* 16(3), 345–373.

Fraser, N. (2005). Reframing justice in a globalizing world. *New Left Review,* 36, 69–88.

Fraser, N. (2007). Feminist politics in the age of recognition: A two-dimensional approach to gender justice. *Studies in Social Justice,* 1(1), 23–35. https://doi.org/10.26522/ssj.v1i1.979

Fraser, N. (2011). Social exclusion, global poverty, and scales of (in) justice: Rethinking law and poverty in a globalizing world. *Stellenbosch Law Review,* 22(3), 452–462. https://hdl.handle.net/10520/EJC54809

Fraser, S., & Deane, E. (1997). Why open learning? *Australian Universities' Review,* 40(1), 25–31. https://files.eric.ed.gov/fulltext/EJ557068.pdf

Gamble, J. (2013). Why improved formal teaching and learning are important in technical and vocational education and training (TVET). *Revisiting global trends in TVET: Reflections on theory and practice.* https://unevoc.unesco.org/fileadmin/up/2013_epub_revisiting_global_trends_in_tvet_chapter6.pdf

Garraway, J. W. (2017). Participatory parity and epistemological access in the extended curriculum programmes. *Education as Change,* 21(2), 109–125. http://dx.doi.org/10.17159/1947-9417/2017/2008

Hay, H. R., & Marais, F. (2004). Bridging programmes: Gain, pain or all in vain. *South African Journal of Higher Education,* 18(2), 59–75. https://journals.co.za/doi/pdf/10.10520/EJC37080

Hodgkinson-Williams, C. A., & Trotter, H. (2018). A social justice framework for understanding open educational resources and practices in the global south. *Journal of Learning for Development,* 5(3), 204–224. https://jl4d.org/index.php/ejl4d/article/view/312

Hölscher, D., & Bozalek, V. (2020). Nancy Fraser's work and its relevance to higher education. In V. Bozalek, D. Hölscher, & M. Zembylas (Eds.), *Nancy Fraser and participatory parity: Reframing social justice in South African higher education* (pp. 3–19). Routledge. https://doi.org/10.4324/9780429055355

Holtzhausen, S. M. (1999). Change in higher education: The psychological experience of facilitators and co-ordinators in a resource-based learning course [Doctoral dissertation, University of the Free State]. http://scholar.ufs.ac.za:8080/xmlui/handle/11660/2818

Jones, J., & Masika, R. (2020). Appreciative inquiry as a developmental research approach for higher education pedagogy: Space for the shadow. *Higher Education Research & Development,* 1–14. https://doi.org/10.1080/07294360.2020.1750571

Leibowitz, B., & Bozalek, V. (2016). The scholarship of teaching and learning from a social justice perspective. *Teaching in Higher Education*, 21(2), 109–122. https://doi.org/10.1080/13562517.2015.1115971

Luckett, K., & Shay, S. (2017). Reframing the curriculum: A transformative approach. *Critical Studies in Education*, 61(1), 50–65. https://www.tandfonline.com/doi/full/10.1080/17508487.2017.1356341

Machingambi, S. (2011). Is access to higher education a sufficient condition for social equity in South Africa? A critical analysis. *Journal of Social Sciences*, 28(1), 13–20.

Machingambi, S., & Wadesango, N. (2012). The problem of access, quality and equity in South African higher education and strategies for revitalisation. *Journal of Social Sciences*, 30(3), 283–291.

Needham, S. (2021). No higher education or good jobs without 'normal' university matric pass. *New Agenda: South African Journal of Social and Economic Policy*, 2021(80), 44–48.

Rabie, N. E. (2008). Access to higher education: The case of the career preparation programme at the University of the Free State [Doctoral dissertation, University of the Western Cape]. https://etd.uwc.ac.za/bitstream/handle/11394/2772/Rabie_MED_2008.pdf?sequence=1

Schäfer, M., & Wilmot, D. (2012). Teacher education in post-apartheid South Africa: Navigating a way through competing state and global imperatives for change. *Prospects*, 42(1), 41–54. https://doi.org/10.1007/s11125-012-9220-3

Stats SA (Statistics South Africa). (2017). Poverty trends in South Africa: An examination of absolute poverty between 2006 and 2015. Statistics South Africa. http://www.statssa.gov.za/publications/Report-03-10-06/Report-03-10-062015.pdf

UFS (University of the Free State). (2008). Open, blended, and engaged learning at the University of the Free State. https://www.ufs.ac.za/docs/default-source/all-documents/open-blended-and-engaged-learning-121-eng.pdf

UFS. (2011). School of Open Learning opens access to education. *UFS Online*. https://www.ufs.ac.za/templates/news-archive/campus-news/2019/february/worldmothertongueday-celebrating-your-native-langue-mother-tongue?NewsItemID=2174

UFS. (2014). University of the Free State. https://www.uv.ac.za/docs/default-source/all-documents/2014_varsity_profile.pdf?sfvrsn=0

UFS. (2017). Annual report 2017 to the Department of Higher Education and Training. https://www.ufs.ac.za/docs/default-source/all-documents/annual-report-2017.pdf?sfvrsn=e5388d21_0

UFS. (2020). University Access Programme. https://www.ufs.ac.za/docs/librariesprovider44/virtual-open-day-documents/south-campus/brochure-uap/university-access-programmes.pdf

WGDEOL (Working Group on Distance Education and Open Learning). (2002). Distance education and open learning in sub-Saharan Africa. A literature survey on policy and practice. Association for the Development of Education in Africa (ADEA). http://oasis.col.org/bitstream/handle/11599/183/02DEinSSA_LiteratureSurvey.pdf?sequence=1&isAllowed=y

Wheeler, S. (2010). Open content, open learning 2.0: Using wikis and blogs in higher education. In U.-D. Ehlers & D. Schneckenberg (Eds.), *Changing cultures in higher education: Moving ahead to future learning* (pp. 103–114). Springer. https://doi.org/10.1007/978-3-642-03582-1_9

Zawacki-Richter, O., et al. (2020). Elements of open education: An invitation to future research. *International Review of Research in Open and Distributed Learning*, 21(3), 319–334. https://doi.org/10.19173/irrodl.v21i3.4659

Zipin, L. (2017). Pursuing a problematic-based curriculum approach for the sake of social justice. *Journal of Education*, 69, 67–92. http://www.scielo.org.za/pdf/jed/n69/04.pdf

HOW TO CITE THIS CHAPTER

Dhurumraj, T., & Govender, S. C. (2022). Access, quality and success: Working towards social justice through open initiatives at the University of the Free State. In T. Mayisela, S. C. Govender & C. A. Hodgkinson-Williams (Eds.), *Open learning as a means of advancing social justice: Cases in post-school education and training in South Africa* (pp. 291–313). African Minds. doi: 10.47622/9781928502425_13

This work is licensed under a Creative Commons Attribution 4.0 International (CC BY 4.0) licence.

14

"Who do you think they are?" Troubling how mental conceptions of TVET lecturers shape lecturer support interventions

The case of the Lecturer Support System in South Africa

Sara Black

SUMMARY Underpinning any intervention to develop, support or capacitate lecturers in the TVET system sits a tacit idea of who TVET lecturers are, as well as an 'ideal imagined TVET lecturer' towards which change initiatives strive. This case study examines one lecturer development intervention, the Lecturer Support System (LSS): how it has changed since it was first established, and how it relates to other intended interventions (e.g., the National Open Learning System). It does this through the lens of the 'imagined ideal TVET lecturer', i.e., who decision-makers wish lecturers to be. Interviews with key stakeholders within DHET were held to explore their perspectives and motivations for what they felt the LSS was and is (or isn't) able to achieve, in terms of lecturer development. Deploying the theoretical work of Foucault, the case explores discourses about how to change TVET lecturers' practices, and what these discourses suggest about how TVET lecturers are imagined by those designing development interventions. By contrasting the different policy 'ideas' about who TVET lecturers 'should' become underpinning each of these past, present and future interventions, the case offers policymakers tools to consider how to learn from past decisions, as well as a novel framing for how different TVET lecturer support interventions relate and complement each other. Any effective continued professional development programmes, whether credentialled or informal, must reckon with this 'imagined ideal' (Jacklin, 2018) and how it relates to the realities and pluralities of lecturers' own subjectivities and experiences. How change interventions relate to present and future lecturer subjectivities raises some complex questions about core themes in the Cases of Open Learning (COOL) project of which this study forms a part; in particular whether 'open learning' is always the path to improved teaching and learning. The question of subjectivities also challenges a Fraserian framework of social justice as used in the COOL project, asking who subjects of justice are and how their sense of self might inhibit engagement with justice-oriented initiatives.

***

Keywords: continuing professional development, subjectivity, ideal subject of justice, open learning, TVET

Introduction

'Open learning' (see Introduction, this volume) is often portrayed as a priori and intrinsically good, rather than as one of many contingent approaches to addressing complex education concerns (Almeida, 2017; Farrow, 2016). This chapter describes one such complex concern, namely the systematic development and support of in-service Technical Vocational Education and Training (TVET) lecturers in South Africa. The case explores a national intervention for TVET lecturer continuing professional development (CPD), and its evolution from a system conceived broadly in line with open learning ideals (the TVET 'Community of Practice' [CoP] system), to its current form, the Lecturer Support System (LSS). In doing so, the case raises tensions and potential contradictions between ideals of open learning and ideals of social justice. Further theoretical avenues are also suggested for exploring the relationship between human subjectivity and Fraser's (1995, 2009) conception of social justice, foregrounding that 'parity of participation', as Fraser's key characteristic of justice, assumes an inclination to participate as a subject of justice.

The LSS case study, as commissioned by the Department of Higher Education and Training (DHET), seemed to arise from a tension between different theories of change amongst stakeholders regarding how best to support TVET lecturers in their work. Some espoused open learning systems as an avenue to utilise, while others felt a more tightly scaffolded, closed system was appropriate for prevailing conditions in the sector. This chapter does not seek to make a normative judgment regarding which theory of change is 'correct' or 'better', but rather suggests an analysis that might offer existing decision makers, future scholars and policymakers interested in system-wide educator support, some tools and insights for understanding the issues involved in such interventions.

The theoretical approach adopted here posits that the *imagined TVET lecturer* in the minds of both policymakers and intervention designers is key to understanding how interventions are designed and to what ends. In particular, the approach taken explores *lecturer subjectivity* as: a) plural and b) potentially contradictory. Vocational lecturers are simultaneously professional tradespeople/artisans, pedagogues/educators *and* employees of the state in public institutions. These three aspects of who lecturers are overlap, contradict, or enforce each other differently across historical and contemporary contours of power, shaping TVET lecturers' sense of self and how they approach their work and their professional development. I argue that failing to engage with this complexity when interpreting lecturers' decisions and actions, or designing support interventions, offers some explanatory power when considering weak or partial uptake of CPD opportunities amongst TVET lecturers.

The chapter begins by locating the case in the broader context of TVET lecturer development conditions in South Africa. Key questions that guided this research are then offered, along with a set of theoretical tools drawn from the work of Foucault (1980, 1991, 1997) which were used to produce and interrogate interview data. The case was primarily conducted through an interpretive approach, conducting a number of interviews, three of which are drawn upon in this chapter, to understand the perspectives and theories of change amongst key decision makers and policymakers in DHET about how to best design lecturer support systems and interventions. After reflecting on the strengths and limitations of such an approach, evidence and discussion is offered regarding the LSS as a CPD intervention for TVET lecturers, its relation to 'open learning' as an ideal, and to 'social justice' in Fraserian terms in TVET education in South Africa. Finally, an analytic sketch summarising the key concerns of the case is offered, suggesting avenues for future research.

Context: TVET lecturer support and development

TVET colleges remain beset with many of the challenges and historical burdens of South Africa's education systems as a whole (McGrath et. al., 2004; Wedekind, 2016a, 2016b). However, the sector bears a disproportionate expectation regarding its role in alleviating the 'triple cocktail' of poverty, inequality and unemployment (DHET, 2013a; NPC, 2013). Industrial development – and the development of artisans and occupational workers – has become a primary lever of policymakers seeking to remedy these socio-economic ills.

Such expectations stand in contrast to past and present efforts to capacitate the sector for such a purpose: specialist formal initial vocational teacher education (IVTE) qualifications for TVET lecturers remain embryonic and intermittent in provision (Papier 2010, 2011); CPD efforts struggle to confront enormous disparities in both industry experience as well as pedagogic training amongst existing lecturers (Van der Bijl & Oosthuizen, 2019); and institutional factors are still differentiated along historical lines of location, language and race, even as contemporary policy concerns restrict resourcing and prioritise universities in the post-school education and training (PSET) sector. Multiple attempts at sector reform over the last 18 years, including mergers and curriculum overhaul, have seismically shifted both the staff and student profiles of TVET colleges (Adendorff & Van Wyk, 2016; Papier, 2011; Wedekind, 2016b). A survey conducted by DHET in 2014 suggested that 15% of lecturers were both academically *and* professionally qualified, while 34.5% had school-teaching qualifications, 38.6% were academically qualified to teach in TVET but not professionally qualified, and 12% were not qualified professionally or pedagogically (DHET, 2014) (with caveats to this: see Wedekind, 2016b). Moreover, TVET lecturer development opportunities have been piecemeal, and lecturers reported scant development opportunities (Manyau, 2015), depending on informal learning and coaching by peers and supervisors to develop skills (Van der Bijl, 2015). Much research remains to be done regarding TVET lecturer development in South Africa (Papier, 2011; Wedekind, 2016a), particularly on the relation between lecturer development and the TVET sector as a whole.

Against this backdrop, the predecessor to the Lecturer Support System, the 'CoP', was first conceptualised in 2013 as a philanthropically funded intervention in TVET lecturer CPD, a product of partnership between DHET and the government of the Netherlands (Koch, 2019). Parallel interventions were being attempted in IVTE through higher education institutions (HEIs) (e.g., the Vocational Educator Orientation Programme, or VEOP – see DHET, 2013), as well as others focused on work-integrated learning (e.g., see Chapter 15 of this volume; the Lecturer Workplace Exposure programme funded through the Swiss South

Africa Cooperation Initiative [Van der Bijl & Taylor, 2016]; and the ETDP SETA-SSACI WIL for Lecturers Project [Van der Bijl & Taylor, 2018]). But the original CoP was meant to support and assist *in-service* TVET lecturers through creating a digital commons of learning and teaching support materials (LTSM) online. When uptake was not as anticipated, the CoP was overhauled and a new system – the LSS – was developed to respond to lecturers' in-service needs.

Originally the mandate for this case study on the LSS was framed in the negative, enquiring as to 'what went wrong' with the original system that precipitated the change in design and approach. Subsequent investigation suggested, however, that this framing elided key aspects of the system's adaptation. The focus for this chapter, thus, is *describing* the rationale(s) for this change and the assumptions/ideals on which it was based, rather than a normative appraisal of the existing system. Also of interest for the case is how the new system articulates with principles of open learning, and how this articulation relates to questions of social justice. These foci are condensed into the following research questions:

How are TVET lecturers 'imagined' (that is, mentally envisaged with all concomitant assumptions) by different decision makers involved in TVET lecturer CPD?

- How does this imagining (pedagogic, professional and political) relate to the design of a CPD intervention (the LSS) for lecturers past, present and anticipated?
- How do decision makers in the TVET sector understand the relation between power and lecturer performativity?
- How does this imagining relate to open learning?
- How does this imagining relate to social justice?

Intrinsic to the primary question is how decision makers understand the 'gap' between who they think TVET lecturers *are* and who they think TVET lecturers *should be* (i.e. their *imagined ideal* TVET lecturer), as well as theories of change on how this gap can be bridged. By describing how these two imaginaries relate, questions are thrown up about lecturers' assumed subjectivities, how they are discursively constituted in policy documents and decision-making corridors, and how power is exercised through CPD towards sector reform. The case attempts to foreground hidden assumptions, commonalities, and contradictions on the part of those driving interventions which may assist in future efforts to meaningfully support TVET lecturers.

Imagining TVET lecturers: Real and ideal

Although the primary lens used for the case studies in this volume is the work of Nancy Fraser (1995, 2005, 2009), her normative conceptual framework does not offer a language of description for mental conceptions. This particular case hence uses the work of Michel Foucault (1980, 1991, 1997) as a *descriptive* theoretical language to consider the role of discourse in meaning-making and 'constituting the objects of which it speaks', particularly in education policy (Ball, 1993, 2015). In particular, the concepts of *performativity* and *subjectivity* are useful, along with his formulation of *power* as relational, being both oppressive and productive. After outlining the concepts used in this case, some remarks are offered regarding the relation of these ideas to open learning, as well as to Fraser's normative framework of social justice.

Foucault: Power, discourse, subjectivity and performativity

The concept of the *ideal TVET lecturer* is drawn from the work of Jacklin (2018) and Silbert (2012) to analyse how systems and policies attempt to construct particular subjects through discourse. But rather than analysing policies (Silbert, 2012) or rituals (Silbert & Jacklin, 2015), this case focuses on the imagined TVET lecturer as expressed through different stakeholders' interpretations of lecturers' (non-)engagement with CPD opportunities, as well as how stakeholders' understandings relate to an imagined, but perhaps uninterrogated, 'ideal'.

Power

Underpinning most of Foucault's work is the concept of power, as it is played out not only through violence and repression, but subtly through representations and discourse. Power, for Foucault, is not totalising (Mills, 2003) but productive. He writes:

> [P]ower would be a fragile thing if its only function were to repress, if it worked only through the mode of censorship, exclusion, blockage and repression … exercising itself only in a negative way. If, on the contrary, power is strong this is because, as we are beginning to realise, it produces effects at the level of desire – and also at the level of knowledge. (Foucault, 1980, p. 58)

Power also acts at the level of the micro, in everyday action and language use, as a state of *relations* rather than a thing one 'has' or 'claims' (Foucault, 1980, p. 58). It is 'capillary' (Foucault, 1977), reaching into everyday life and dialectically producing subjects and representations, as it is performed or resisted. For Foucault, one of the core 'technologies' or mechanisms of power is that of discourse.

Discourse

Foucault expands the linguistic concept of discourse beyond interconnected text to consider how language affects power relations in the world. Through discourse, he attempts to examine how our ability to make meaning, delineate ideas, define, and categorize concepts – or not as the case may be – affects what we think *is* in the world, and hence how we interact with the world:

> Discourse is the production of knowledge through meaning. But … since all social practices entail meaning, and meanings shape and influence what we do – our conduct – all practices have a discursive aspect. (Hall, 1992, p. 291)

Critically, discourse often operates at the level of the assumed. In doing so, unwittingly, we reinforce discursive framings of the world by acting out particular norms and assumptions:

we do not speak discourse, but it speaks us. It is in this manner that discourse conveys and produces power. But in noticing and interrupting dominant representations, new meanings can be developed, and assumptions can be questioned. This has significant implications for social change and for interrupting prevailing social asymmetries to produce more just and equitable social relations.

Subjectivity

How we dynamically (re)constitute ourselves as malleable subjects, under tacit or explicit social forces, has been a focus of interest for multiple postmodern and poststructuralist thinkers (cf. Foucault, 1977, 1980, 1991; also Hall, 1992, 2001). While often used interchangeably with the term 'identity', the concept of the subject foregrounds socially produced (and contested) ideas of who we are, rather than essentialist traits. Subjectification, as a function of discourse, is not purely externally imposed but internally regulated as the subject self-curates and self-censors, producing themselves in accordance with the social norms they believe apply to them; this is what Foucault termed 'technologies of the self':

> the practices by which individuals *act upon themselves*, and form themselves as subjects. These strategies constitute ways in which individuals' understanding of themselves in terms of *what is expected of them* is internalised. (Silbert, 2012, p. 19)

Lecturers' externally- or self-constituted subjectivity is alluded to in the TVET lecturer literature, particularly regarding their sense of self as *educators* being in tension with their sense of self as *artisans/professionals* in their trade. What is less explicitly considered is TVET lecturers' sense of self as *citizen/public servant*. In this chapter, I refer to these three different subjectivities as *pedagogic, professional* and *political* respectively, the last encompassing both a lecturer's broader relationship to the imagined South African community (spaced, 'raced', gendered and classed) as well as to the state as their employer setting their working conditions through enacting public policy.

Performativity

Performativity refers to representing the *self* in accordance with a discursive ideal desired or assumed by the other. When our sense of self does not comply with social expectations, we pretend or 'perform' to meet these expectations in order to avoid normative judgment. Foucault's formulation of power is tangled up in performativity, through tacitly attempting to conform to some desired 'ideal', but also as individuals vacuously feign compliance without authenticity (i.e. resist that discursive ideal). In South African education (including TVET colleges), the Integrated Quality Management System (IQMS) is an example of this power struggle between educators and management, wherein ideals for 'being a good educator' are constructed discursively through a system of appraisal, and these credentials can be 'met' without necessarily changing beliefs, attitudes, or practices in the classroom. Regimes of 'accountability' in education tend to encourage performativity in this manner (Ball, 2003).

The ideal subject of open learning

The concept of 'open learning' is variously understood in different international contexts (see Introduction, this volume), but is understood in South African policy to be:

> An educational approach which combines the principles of learner-centredness, lifelong learning, flexibility of learning provision, the removal of barriers to access learning, the recognition for credit of prior learning experience, the provision of learner support, the construction of learning programmes in the expectation that learners can succeed, and the maintenance of rigorous quality assurance over the design of learning materials and support systems. (DHET, 2017, p. 363)

Of relevance in this chapter is the assumed subject of open learning – especially how pedagogues are discursively constructed in the *Open Learning Policy Framework* (DHET, 2017) – requires careful scrutiny. Who is the ideal subject of open learning? What qualities are they assumed to possess? Oliver (2015) and Knox (2013) both raise this question, highlighting that tacit expectations are made in much of the literature on open learning about who learners and teachers are, and how they engage with open learning practices. As explored later, the 'ideal subject of open learning' as it relates to SA TVET lecturers is problematized by the change from the CoP to the LSS, with implications for future open learning and open education initiatives in the sector.

The ideal subject of social justice

Social justice, according to American political philosopher Nancy Fraser (2005), comprises 'parity of participation' which "requires social arrangements that permit all to participate as peers in social life" (2005, p. 73). Fraser identifies three analytically distinct, but practically overlapping, dimensions that can influence parity of participation, namely, the economic, the cultural and the political.

But discursive constructions of the self-as-subject are also significant for Fraserian (1995, 2009) conceptions of social justice. While Fraser identifies structural barriers to justice (particularly economic maldistribution, political misrepresentation and issues of the political frame), as well as cultural misrecognition (her axis of justice more closely related to representation), she assumes throughout that those subject to *in*justice will contest said injustices and strive for parity of participation along these axes. However, what discourse and subjectification problematize is the idea of subjects of injustice: (a) recognising the discrimination to which they are subject; and (b) staking a claim for justice. That is, Fraser's concept of parity of participation is premised on a sense of self that wishes to participate. If discourse speaks to us, this raises thorny challenges regarding the role of the subject in justice processes and struggle. Fraser's assumed 'ideal subject of social justice' may not bear out empirically.

The following diagram attempts to lay out the problematic of this chapter using the concepts outlined here.

Figure 1: Sketching relations between how TVET lecturers are imagined in relation to a discursive ideal

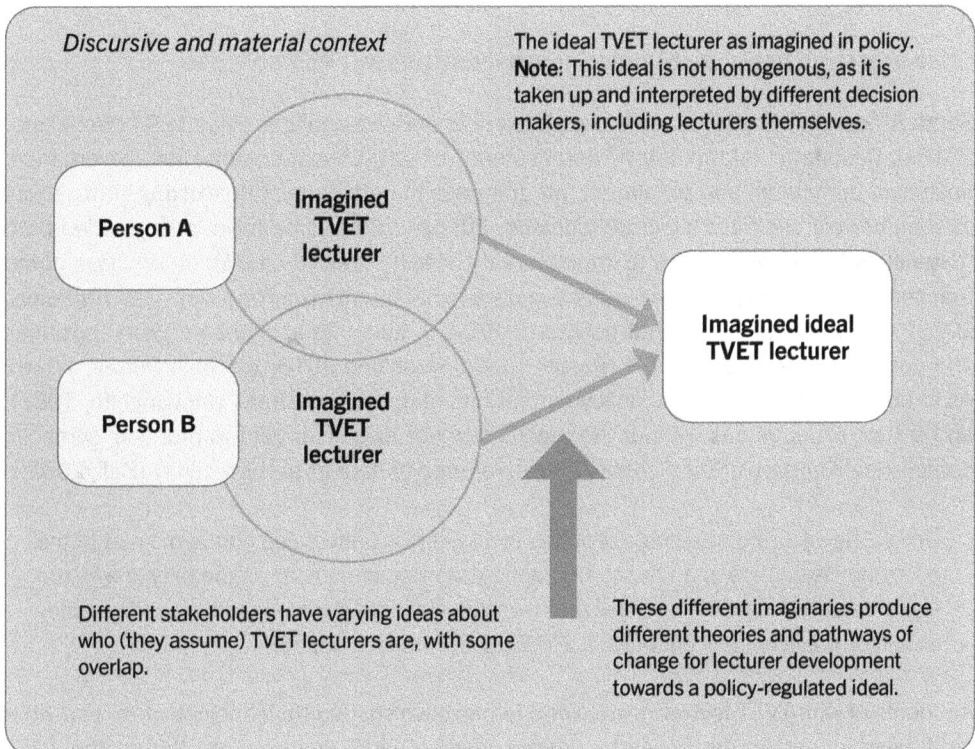

Figure 1 attempts to relate different accounts of TVET lecturers' current subjectivities, and how CPD interventions are built around differences of how lecturers are perceived compared to a discursive 'ideal' forming the target of interventions. Both conceptions of who lecturers *are* and who they *should be* are discursive, albeit the ideal more explicitly: how decisionmakers constitute who they think TVET lecturers are is a product of their own subjective worldview. The imposition of these imaginings, and actions premised on them, all constitute attempts to exert power – often through shaping discourse – which may be accepted, reinterpreted or resisted. That is, lecturers' own subjectivities – and how these relate to policymakers' understanding of them – necessarily mediates efforts at change.

The role of subjectivity on vocational lecturer/teacher development

While less established than its schooling counterpart, there is a growing international literature exploring the commonalities and differences between the training and support of vocational lecturers (teachers) and those in mainstream schooling, including studies from South Africa. This brief literature review starts with a short consideration of challenges with change in the TVET sector in South Africa, followed by a summary of who TVET lecturers are expected to be (both internationally and locally), and a brief description of the thin literature on who TVET lecturers *are*.

Challenges with change: Mandating what matters in TVET colleges

South African TVET colleges have been subject to massive changes since 1994 (Wedekind, 2016a). Despite a "reform storm" across issues of institutional organisation, governance, financing, curriculum and enrolment, programmes to both capacitate existing staff as well as train newcomers have lagged (Wedekind, 2016a). While some have foregrounded both material and cultural 'barriers to implementation' (e.g., Sooklal, 2005), others have noted that conditions on the ground are not conducive for lecturers to perform well (e.g., Buthelezi, 2018), and still others note that policies that fail to take into account lecturers' positions and conditions are questionable (Papier, 2011; Wedekind 2016; Wedekind et al., 2016). As in other education sectors, policy cannot 'mandate what matters' (McLaughlin, 1987), and setting expectations without the means to meet these is bound to produce 'symbolic compliance' (Jansen, 2002; Sooklal, 2005), referred to here as performativity (Ball, 2003):

> Unless the agency of the range of actors in a system is understood and forms part of the policy process, there is a chance that good policies can founder *as the people who are expected to implement them make their own sense of what the policies mean and how they should be implemented.* (Wedekind, 2016a, p. 2, emphasis added)

Accounts of who TVET lecturers are, what forces have shaped their subjectivities, and what tacit assumptions inform policy formations of *ideal TVET* lecturers are thin in the TVET literature.

Split subjectivity: Vocational teachers/lecturers astride two worlds

Barnett (2006) summarises a common theme in both international and local literature on TVET lecturer subjectivities in saying that they must "look both ways" i.e. towards their pedagogical practice as teachers/lecturers *and* towards their industry and practical knowledge of their discipline. This duality of competing demands is echoed across international literature, cf. Vähäsantanen and Hämäläinen (2019) in Finland; Grollmann (2008) in Germany; Broad (2015) in England; Farnsworth and Higham (2012) in Canada; Brennan Kemmis and Green (2013) in Australia; and Andersson and Köpsén (2019) in Sweden. Several of these studies explore the limitations imposed by resourcing and structural conditions on reconciling these forces (e.g., Andersson & Köpsén, 2019; Broad, 2015), while others highlight that such challenges generate tensions between vocational educators and their more academic counterparts (cf. Brennan Kemmis & Green, 2013). Vähäsantanen and Hämäläinen (2019) note that TVET lecturers' relations between workplace and sense of self affects their commitment to their job and their emotional experiences of their work, an issue echoed by Wedekind et. al. (2016) and Papier (2010, 2011) in the South African case. As with the UK (Broad, 2015), South African TVET lecturers have increasingly experienced work intensification as they take on more diverse student groups, adapt to curricula changes and produce larger volumes of paperwork in the name of accountability (Wedekind 2016b; Wedekind et al., 2016), a phenomenon Ball describes as 'the terror of performativity' (2003).

Three publications stand out in the South African case that consider TVET lecturers' sense of self as important for improvement of teaching and learning in the sector. The first is Wedekind et al.'s 2016 *SAQA Bulletin*, a comprehensive description of reform in the sector, along with the challenges created by rapid top-down reform in what they term 'fragile institutions'. The others are Papier (2010, 2011) who, like this study, takes subjectivity (referred to by Papier as 'identity') as a fluid, socially malleable construct both productive of and produced by everyday life. Both texts foreground that ignoring TVET lecturers' sense of self when attempting changes in classroom practice risks intervention failure.

Wedekind (2016a) offers evidence for the presence – and tension – between pedagogic and 'professional' (i.e. artisanal) subjectivities amongst South African TVET lecturers, stating that technical artisans who do not see themselves as teachers struggle with this role, and may leave TVETs altogether if they find these dimensions irreconcilable, leading to an outflow of expertise from colleges. He foregrounds that relatively little rich data is available about lecturers' trajectories, motivations, values and attitudes, how they came to TVET teaching and how they see their future in the sector (2016b).

Papier (2010) offers a succinct synopsis of vocational teacher development policy and practice in South Africa, particularly foregrounding the antagonistic forces and logics which vocational education institutions (and educators) must juggle. She also notices policy borrowing (cf. Ball, 2017; Mukhopadhyay & Sriprakash, 2011; Rizvi & Lingard, 2010) is rife in the sector from European vocational sectors, although she suggests that, overall, such transfer has at least productively expanded discussions on vocational education. Papier's consideration of TVET lecturer 'identity' is close to this study's:

> *The production of meaning is a necessary condition for the functioning of all social practices*, hence 'an individual's identification with shared social meanings constitutes identity formation and can be seen as a process of reality construction through which social actors interpret particular events, actions or situations ... including those practices conducted at work' (Chappell, 1999, p. 4). *This view of identity is not static or reified; rather it holds that identities are formed at particular moments and in specific spaces, and result from both personal and social influences*. (Papier, 2011, p. 105, emphasis added)

Included in these social influences are the effects of what has been termed 'new vocationalism' (riffing off the term 'new managerialism' in education leadership literature). 'New vocationalism' is a shorthand for neoliberal inclinations towards 'efficiency', 'accountability' and labour-market responsiveness, and, according to Papier:

> dissolves the discursive boundaries between the organisation of work and the organisation of education, where the workplace is increasingly regarded as a site of learning and the education institution as a site of workplace preparation. *Vocational teachers are consequently required to span these two spheres and embrace a dual identity that combines liberal education and economic enterprise, placing them in a state of tension between 'industry expert' and 'expert educator' identities, even though they are dislocated from both traditional sites – the industrial workplace and the traditional school.*

Vocational teachers in South Africa thus find themselves subject to contradictory, complex and confusing demands as they struggle to construct an identity aligned to images espoused in policy. (Papier, 2011, p. 106, emphasis added)

Papier's concern above is the object of enquiry in this case study, particularly as DHET simultaneously asks TVET lecturers to reconcile these contradictory forces in their work. However, Papier's primary interest is in the *actual* subjectivities of TVET lecturers, whereas this case study focuses on how DHET *imagines* lecturers, not only in policy (DHET, 2013a, 2013b, 2017) but in theories of how TVET lecturers change.

Reform fatigue, eroded confidence and resistance amongst TVET lecturers

In the South African case, both Papier (2008, 2011) and Wedekind et al. (2016) provide evidence that rapid, top-down change in curriculum and enrolment has had a detrimental effect on TVET lecturers' sense of professional self. Wedekind et al. (2016) identify three contributing factors:

1. the introduction of the National Certificate (Vocational) (NC[V]), which brought not only new subjects and new organizational constraints, but also created divisions between 'technical' or 'vocational' and 'core' subject lecturers in school-equivalent mathematics, language and Life Orientation (LO);
2. the new students that the NC(V) brought into colleges, functioning now as an alternative 'technical matric' rather than as a skills development institution for in-service professionals; and
3. how lecturers perceived different factors at work that shaped their sense of self.

Training on the new curriculum was piecemeal and expected to 'cascade' from two or three 'workshopped' lecturers who would then pass on what they knew to their colleagues on returning to campus. New assessment structures such as 'Internal Continuous Assessment' (ICASS) presented challenges to existing staff unfamiliar with the system, and general frustration at lack of preparation or consultation has led to disengagement and/or passive non-compliance in certain circumstances (Wedekind et al., 2016).

Kelchtermans (2005, p. 2) notes that "sense-making determines teachers' eventual reactions to reforms", reactions which may include passive resistance or 'non-implementation' (McLaughlin, 1997) when reform ambitions are considered too lofty or far-removed for the material and organisational context. A Foucauldian approach suggests that non-implementation is a form of power-as-action/relation, producing a type of disposition in which non-take-up or symbolic cap-doffing to policy requirements, as described by Wedekind et. al. (2016) and others, are the last line of defence for those on the receiving end of contradictory and relentless top-down pressure to do the impossible. That is: by setting an unrealistic ideal, policy may ironically contribute to producing a different type of resistant subject, a mistrustful 'street-level bureaucrat' (McLaughlin, 1987) sedimented into a defensive disposition by reform fatigue.

The strong emphasis on NQF-aligned/-articulated TVET lecturer training

Compounding lecturers' sense of self is the *Policy on Professional Qualifications for Lecturers in Technical and Vocational Education and Training* (DHET, 2013b), a relatively new set of regulations outlining the ideal knowledge mix and competencies for the 'ideal' TVET lecturer in the minds of policymakers, and a standard which many lecturers have not attained (Papier, 2010; Van der Bijl & Oosthuizen, 2019). Without glossing over the real concerns regarding lecturers' (lack of) training and workplace (in)experience (see Van der Bijl & Oosthuizen, 2019; Van der Bijl & Taylor, 2016, 2018), Wedekind et al. (2016) point out that the phenomenon of 'unqualified lecturers' is as much a function of the goalpost for 'being qualified' moving as it is of lecturers' actual training and skills. That is: the promulgation of this policy widened the gap between who TVET lecturers are and the imagined ideal TVET lecturer, with as yet unexplored implications for lecturers' sense of self when declared 'unqualified'. Adendorff and Van Wyk (2016) suggest recognition of prior learning (RPL) as an open learning principle that might articulate experienced but officially unqualified lecturers into NQF-aligned learning structures, but the emphasis in all of the examined literature is on formal learning as the primary driver of TVET lecturer development, with little to no consideration of non-formal learning as a vehicle for change in the sector. The LSS system examined in this case study is an example of organised and structured non-formal learning, and offers a subtly different theory of change than those present in the literature. The next section outlines how this case study unfolded, and how analysis was conducted on the data produced.

Methodology and validity of findings

Investigating the LSS was somewhat circuitous, as the initial framing was relatively loose and constituted as a process of discovery. Given the changes in the LSS occurred some time prior to the case study (several years), observing change in action was not possible, and documentation on the old system was also limited. This necessitated an interpretative study, where the understandings of the various stakeholders and actors is the object of inquiry. While attempts were made to contact lecturers who might have been party to both the older CoP and the new LSS, these efforts were unsuccessful. The sources of data were hence limited.

The data produced for this study involved long interviews with key stakeholders within DHET, three of which are drawn upon for this chapter, exploring their perspectives and motivations for what they felt the system was and is (or isn't) able to achieve regarding TVET lecturer CPD. While preliminary questions were drafted to shape conversation, these often proved inaccurate as discussion unfolded. However, the concept of lecturer subjectivity proved a robust approach. Interviews were thus guided with the primary interests in mind, namely how stakeholders involved in decisions about the LSS and TVET lecturer CPD in general, understand lecturers and their work, and how these understandings relate to the concepts of open learning and social justice over-arching the broader project.

All interviews were transcribed in full and analysed thematically for *subjectivity* of different types, *performativity, power,* open learning ideas and principles, and discussions of inequity or parity of participation in economic, cultural and political terms. Much of what was said in the interviews cannot be shared for ethical reasons, nor would sharing this data contribute to the purpose of this chapter. Rather, the thematic analysis of differing interpretations by decision makers sought points of contradiction, convergence and divergence, as well as various perspectives on the system, with a view that this might offer productive avenues of future development and understanding for both DHET and others interested in TVET lecturer development. These interpretations are treated as valid in-and-of themselves, insofar as people's perspectives on the world are *of* the world, and play a part in shaping the world.

Studying people's perspectives on the system qualitatively through in-depth interviews necessarily means that descriptive validity is not of concern to this case, nor are the findings here generalisable (cf. Maxwell, 1992). Since the case is not normative, no attempt is made at evaluating the LSS, or the perspectives of those involved. For interpretive validity, all transcribed interviews were returned to interviewees for verification and correction. A focus on discourse was considered theoretically valid for a case study focused on interpretations, since Foucault's work examines meaning-making and its relation to action, reaction and power, and how these relate to the constitution of the self.

Findings and discussion

What works: From CoP to LSS

The current LSS has changed significantly from the previous CoP system. The CoP was intended as a pilot with five TVET colleges (selected across multiple provinces by a development partner and DHET), to build a resource portal for colleges for developing and sharing materials, with the intention of recognising and drawing on internal expertise in the sector. This was seen as preferable to transnationally importing systems and materials from more established TVET sectors, a move which risked replicating colonial relations and excluding local competence.

When initially approached, colleges suggested that an online repository where they could upload materials would suit their needs. However, it became apparent that this approach was not producing the desired engagement: not much content was uploaded and the lecturers made very limited use of the system, mostly when prompted and largely for social rather than professional purposes. Motivations for not sharing resources included both reticence to admit subject knowledge gaps or uncertainties, but also a sense that curriculum competence is a relative advantage in a challenging sector ('knowledge is power' – Respondent B), an advantage not to be yielded. To paraphrase multiple respondents in this study, developing a sharing culture takes time and effort and cannot be assumed, and may even encounter antagonistic practices regarding competition and maximisation of resources.

Colleges' response to the CoP catalysed a rethink of the system between 2013 and 2014. By combining student assessment data and qualitative feedback from lecturers, it was established that lecturers wanted curriculum-aligned materials, particularly related to the (then relatively new) NC(V), that they 'could use tomorrow' (Respondent B). Areas of curriculum weakness evidenced by assessment data were cross-referenced with insider knowledge of colleges to select three initial curriculum areas as foci: automotive, fitting and turning, and life orientation (LO). After these initial three, multiple other subjects and skills were targeted.

Uptake remained a risk factor for the new materials (referred to as 'LSS Packages' in the new system), as merely 'delivering' these to the colleges was not assumed to guarantee lecturer adoption and use. Qualitative investigation suggested that college academic support structures were heterogeneous in their activities, and lecturers' engagement in CPD events organised at the college level varied widely. The LSS thus developed roles, processes and systems over and above the digital LTSM to facilitate engagement: the deputy principal academic at each TVET college was designated as the LSS Manager, accountable to DHET for LSS implementation; LSS activities were included in college council agendas; and several LSS facilitators were appointed at each of the 50 colleges to facilitate access to LSS packages made available by DHET.

Finally, the third aspect of the revamped system was to prioritize whole sector reach: rather than five pilot colleges, the new system sought to offer a facility accessible to all colleges. This necessarily meant that data-intensive and synchronous online formats were unviable, given that — at the time — more than half of colleges struggled with reliable internet connectivity (Respondent A). Materials designed for asynchronous use meant that LSS facilitators at the college level could schedule package download at quieter hours (e.g., late at night and on weekends) when bandwidth was less strained. The packages could then be facilitated at times convenient to the college yet in compliance with deadlines defined by DHET.

The new system pivoted around 'packages' for curriculum areas which colleges could download and use to offer development opportunities to their lecturers. This was part of a structured process where colleges would acknowledge the availability of a new package, manage lecturer registration prior to release, and then access and 'run' the package with their staff at a coordinated event before the materials were then made available for use across all campuses. In this way, the system designers sought to generate a 'pull' factor into package uptake and engagement.

At the time of this publication, the LSS attempts to offer curriculum support to lecturers within the colleges with limited material footprint. Rather than a cascade model of 'training' wherein a subset of lecturers annually attends centralised once-off workshops and then passes this knowledge on when they return to campus, the LSS system prompts local organising of curriculum update opportunities where all lecturers attend. Packages offered are not NQF-aligned or credit bearing (although there is a desire to offer South African Council for Educators CPD points as recognition for participation), and thus LSS activities are not conceived as rivals to, or replacements for, formal qualification processes such as those outlined for the National Open Learning System (NOLS) (Adendorff & Van Wyk, 2016). Rather, the LSS is a complementary, needs-responsive effort to rapidly organise college-level, curriculum-aligned, *non-formal* education to reach all lecturers and support them on a low budget.

While the redesign has borne more fruit than its predecessor, this is not to say the new LSS is without challenges. Securing sustainability has been challenging, especially in light of various confounding factors including but not limited to college closures due to political unrest, staff turnover or the COVID-19 pandemic. While efforts are made to keep packages responsive to needs, implementing a routine whole sector 'lecturer needs survey' has been difficult across all 50 colleges, and further research is required to establish classroom uptake of training and whether the LSS has translated into improved teaching and learning for students. Structural barriers present in other education sectors also affect TVET colleges, where over-full schedules and large classes impede 'meaningful opportunities for change' for educators (see Muller/Black, 2020; Shalem, 2003). The preliminary phase of the LSS has involved a more 'centralised dissemination' model for knowledge flow into the sector;

however, aspects of the original CoP that enabled lecturer dialogue and engagement remain in the current site design, with the view that as lecturers grow in confidence in their subject knowledge, material production and sharing can slowly be developed into peer-to-peer or college-based mentoring relations.

Currently, the LSS remains a 'closed' system exclusively for public TVET lecturers. This is to construct both a sense of being prioritized ("this is for us" – Respondent B) in a sector accustomed to being marginalised, but also to create spaces in which lecturers can become more confident in admitting their challenges and needs for development without excessive scrutiny. That 'closedness' might increase engagement raises questions as to whether principles of 'openness' are always aligned with effective reform or social justice.

The imagined TVET lecturer

Throughout all interviews, how respondents imagined TVET lecturers and their relation to their work was complex and at times contradictory. Inconsistencies, however, were often the result of attempting to discuss a heterogeneous sector in uniform terms. Some of the prevailing inconsistencies included framings that cast lecturers as agentic ("I have met many lecturers in South Africa who really want to make a difference" – Respondent C), but also passive; or lecturers simultaneously needing to be 'managed', but are also capable of autonomous decision-making. At different times, they were viewed as both professional artisans who are uninterested in pedagogy *and* inexperienced pedagogues with little to no workplace experience. In reality, these different subjectivities are all likely to be present in the 10 000+ lecturers in the system, casting doubt on any one-size-fits-all interventions for the sector.

This section attempts to describe some of these axes of differentiation in order to wrestle with the challenges of a sector-wide theory of change across such plurality.

Professional

Two primary axes differentiated imagined TVET lecturers' disciplinary/vocational knowledge when considered as practitioners or professionals in their field: curriculum and age (taken to be a proxy for mode of training, including work-place experience). Younger lecturers – especially those trained in universities – were seen as inadequately prepared for industry-based subjects ("when I asked him to show me his hands I could see he has never changed an oil filter" – Respondent A), while older lecturers trained under the previous dispensation were considered very experienced practically, but unable to convey this information ("they know by the smell of it that this has got the right amount of cement, but they don't know how much they put in" – Respondent A). This distinction mattered more for imagining lecturers whose subjects were industry-specific and technical and who taught on the National Accredited Technical Education Diploma (NATED) or technical NC(V) subjects. For those teaching 'core' NC(V) subjects such as mathematics, LO, language, etc., their curriculum area more closely align to those of high schools, and hence these lecturers may not have to "look both ways" (Papier, 2011). With the replacement of paid apprenticeships by 'learnerships', and industry experience *not* being a prerequisite for TVET lecturing, younger lecturers of technical subjects – especially in hard-to-staff rural colleges – were considered to be lacking industry insider knowledge.

Lecturers' salaries also cannot compete with those of experienced artisans and specialists from the private sector, making enticing those *with* industry experience back to the colleges to teach very difficult. Lecturers were thus – legitimately – understood as driven by material concerns (an understandable motivation given the economic precarity of the majority of South Africans, especially those from marginalised groups).

Pedagogic

Interviewees also offered a varied picture of lecturers as pedagogues, from those who have come through more traditional pathways of initial teacher education (ITE) with the commensurate standards but lacking vocational pedagogic knowledge, to those who teach vocational subjects who are perceived as: (a) being more interested in the industry work than the teaching; and (b) often perceived as academically inferior and disinterested in 'book learning'. Some of these distinctions are historical, based on prior vocational pathways available for lecturers through the racially stratified and under-developed apartheid-era manpower and skills centres. However, contemporary differences continue through (self-affirming) power relations between academic and vocational tracks in lower levels of education; those who have specialised in vocational subjects will have often chosen to do so through being alienated by, or struggling with, academic learning and hence have pursued (under-funded, often less prioritised) alternatives which did not focus on academic concerns and practices.

Such a conception of self-in-relation-to being a teacher/pedagogue is illustrated by the following description from a respondent in this study when describing why lecturers do not use available video materials:

> [The lecturer] doesn't want to deal with the stress of receiving questions on a video that he doesn't understand what he is talking about. He doesn't want to deal with the stress of technology where the video might get stuck sometimes. He doesn't want to deal with the stress of those students not listening to the video because he was never taught how to use videos in his classroom. As a result, (he) avoids the stress about it, he parks the materials. (Respondent B)

Although risking a potentially deficit framing, this insight into the imagined TVET lecturer suggests an appreciation for the *affective* experience of lecturers when presented with materials and modes of pedagogy that they find alienating. That is: there is a recognition of the emotional experience lecturers may have (and the subsequent avoidance behaviours) when *asked to be someone they (believe they) are not*.

However, again, plurality is evident: the following extract from the same respondent reflects an appreciation for the pedagogic expertise – and autonomy – within the sector:

> What we did was we just developed the templates and everything. We said, "Guys, here's the old curriculum, here's the new curriculum, please look at what is needed, what can be removed, and once you have done the template, consult anyone in the industry that you know that can guide you, guidance in terms of the latest developments." And they've done that. And we took it to Umalusi and to QCTO [Quality Council for Trades and Occupations].

> Curriculum approved! And ... now they are evaluating the books. So what I'm saying is that not all is bad. We've got good pockets of success. But it's few. So if we use those, if we use those that are good to capacity-develop others, we'll go far. (Respondent B)

Here we can begin to see that the imagined TVET lecturer is not homogenous, and that some lecturers adhere more closely to the 'imagined ideal' than others.

All the respondents for the study recognised that the diversity of pedagogical experience and approaches in the sector was a challenge, and most converged on the 'imagined ideal' as an expert pedagogue *and* experienced industry professional, a person able to marry these two (at times contradictory) worlds and make professional decisions to further the learning of their students (navigating what Papier termed the discourse of 'new vocationalism'). However, this vision of an autonomous, self-driven professional sits in tension with the third subjectivity examined in this study, that of the public employee working in a top-down bureaucracy.

Political

The imagined lecturer as an employee of a public institution and a citizen bearing the burden of South Africa's history interacts with the other two imaginations in important ways. While the previous two focused on lecturers' relation to knowledge and classroom practice, this aspect of who lecturers are imagined to be describes how they navigate both lateral relations with peers, as well as vertical relations with management at the local and higher levels.

The college mergers of 2002 put very different TVET lecturers side by side (Respondent A). Wedekind (2016a) argues that very little has been done subsequently to build a sense of a cohesion amongst staff in the colleges. Respondent B echoed this challenge with peer-to-peer inter- and intra-college support, especially across historical, economic and cultural contours of (dis)advantage. When asked if 'communities of practice' across such power differentials could be possible, Respondent B suggested that colleges in similar conditions were far more likely to learn from each other, since context strongly shaped who works at colleges, who their students are, and how they solve problems, and hence a meaningful, reciprocal connection was more likely.

In addition to challenges of peer-led support across vastly different contexts, imagined vertical relations with DHET were also muddled in the data. Respondents seemed to simultaneously see lecturers as autonomous professionals who needed to 'take charge' of their work, but also should be compliant with centralised authority and follow instructions. Such contradictions are well theorised in basic education both in South Africa as well as elsewhere as a form of re/decentralisation that heralds a neoliberal zeitgeist (Sayed, 1997; Tikly, 2003), and there is no reason to believe the TVET sector has escaped this policy trend. TVET curriculum and assessment is highly centralised, even while college governance is more devolved (Wedekind, 2016b). Wedekind (2016a) notes that the lack of resistance to the college mergers in 2002 is indicative of the top-down contours of authority in the TVET sector, noting that "staff members in Colleges to whom the researchers spoke at the time reported that they did not feel that they had a say and did not really expect to have a say" (p. 11). Such contradictory messages to lecturers about their responsibilities and constraints may well be eroding efforts at developing their professional and pedagogic sense of self.

From an LSS perspective, the imagined lecturer is someone who needs careful scaffolding and specific, detailed instruction, and there appears to be an empirical basis for this. However, such framing risks reproducing a dependent subjectivity entrenched over decades of top-down control and now reluctant to engage in any other way. How this mode of engagement will incrementally shift towards more creativity and autonomy from lecturers remains to be seen.

However, the imagined ideal lecturer engaging with the NOLS is considered to participate through "'making the Open Learning road by walking it together', encouraging collaboration and participation rather than top-down, distributive strategies" (Adendorff & van Wyk, 2016, p. 8). Such an appeal to collegiality and voluntary participation seems to ignore prevailing forces that encourage a passive policy subjectivity through the top-down imposition of tightly constrained curricula and external assessment, a narrow focus on examination results as an indicator of success, and only NQF-aligned recognition of lecturers' abilities and skills. This imagined ideal lecturer is simultaneously 'professional' and 'accountable' while not being trusted to make contextually informed judgment (Biesta, 2004).

Differing theories of change and problems of performativity and resistance

The 'different theories of change' at play in TVET lecturer development might be visualised as shown in Figure 2.

Figure 2: How differing imaginaries shape CPD intervention design

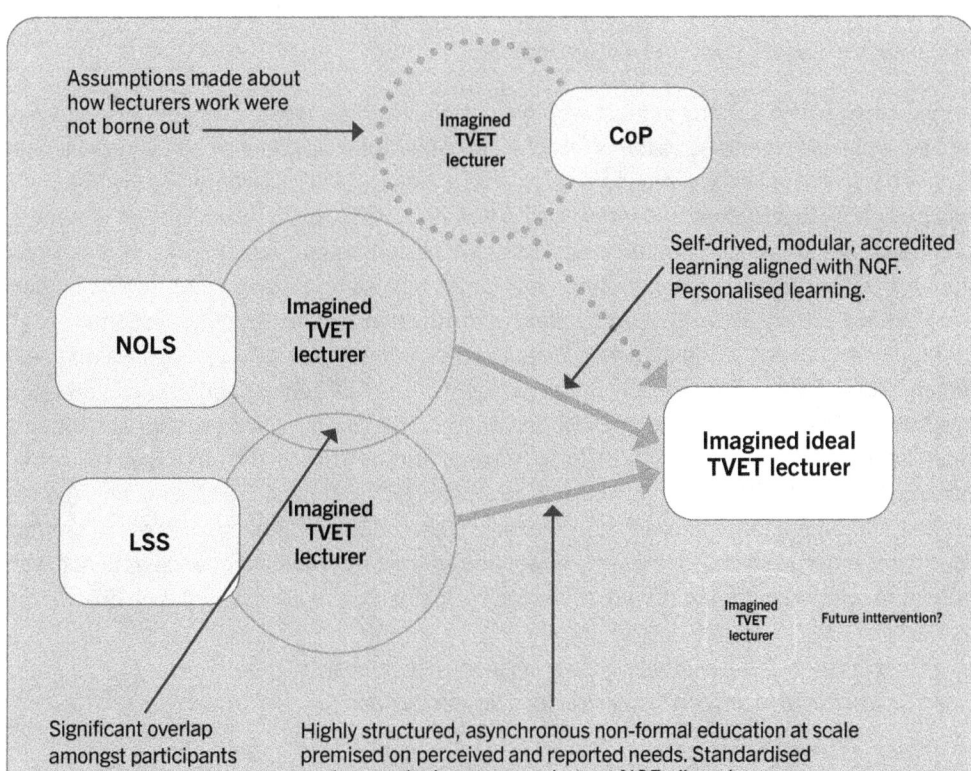

The two theories of change (the NOLS and the LSS) in Figure 2 might be seen as more complementary than competitive, given their overlapping imagined ideals and complementary approaches of non-formal and formal education. Given the heterogeneity already described, it is possible that a multi-faceted approach might be necessary, with more responsive, rapid non-formal education in the LSS providing more immediate support and the NOLS offering longer-term opportunities for accredited further study once lecturers reach certain thresholds of competence, confidence and digital literacy. While differentiated treatment is politically difficult given South Africa's past, centralised one-size-fits-all theories of change across such heterogeneity encourage performativity. Those unable to meet the ideals of a reform may well offer vacuous compliance with policy mandates without meaningful change.

Performativity in general is a 'wicked' policy problem (given how blunt an instrument policy *is* – Ball, 1993, 2015) and while lecturers should be fairly compensated for all their work (including CPD), artificial incentivisation is known to produce distorted behaviours. None of the theories of change examined in this study had entirely comprehensive responses to the performativity problem, recognising that their 'policy technologies' (Ball, 2003) to shift priorities and shape discourse in the colleges is limited.

Material constraints were also a common theme in discussions of barriers to lecturer development efforts, although different solutions were offered as to how to address this (e.g., low-cost, low-tech LSS packages vs. openly licensed LTSM). The inter-relation between discursive and material concerns in colleges is beyond the scope of this case study; however, *that there is a relation between the two* should be held in view when considering how lecturers are conceived or conceive of themselves and their work.

The imagined ideal subject of open learning

An imagined self-governing subject who has internalised the ideals of those setting policy and direction is clear in the vision of DHET for TVET lecturer development in particular, and for open learning in general, envisioning "open learning in PSET develop[ing] a life of its own and begin[ing] to sustain itself" (Adendorff & Van Wyk, 2016, p. 7). Whether such directions and ideals are 'good' or not is not what is being foregrounded: rather, what is of interest here is the desired subject in long-term imaginations of open learning in the sector, namely autonomous activity with distributed uptake and little need for extrinsic motivation.

Many open education imaginaries assume such autonomous, engaged, active and self-driven subjects who can participate in activities such as OER, online courses, etc. and who see these as rightfully theirs to attempt and access. But this is an assumption which bears more interrogation (cf. Knox, 2013). In the case of the CoP, the 'build it and they will come' approach was greeted with a startling non-response. Lecturer subjectivities not only did not see the offered platform as one that would yield personal or professional benefits to them; it is possible that such a practice was so far outside the realm of their experience as to not even appear to offer the affordances it did.[1] Assuming that lecturers are inclined (and able) to:

- accurately self-identify their own development needs;
- participate in asynchronous learning opportunities;

---

[1] One respondent echoed a grey literature finding that lecturers used Facebook, but could not use a browser to surf the internet. See Mirani (2015).

- fit these into their overfull schedules;
- engage in literacy practices in English with confidence, and to do so via digital means;
- engage in pedagogical practices far removed from their own experience both as teachers and as students; and
- trust the integrity and legitimacy of materials that they perceive as 'developed by anyone' rather than by a hegemonic pedagogic authority...

... seems a far reach for a sector as strongly shaped by inequality as South Africa's.

The relation between the affordances of open educational practices and the subjectivities (and hence imaginations) of those who are expected to engage with such practices is an important, ongoing question for proponents of conventional definitions of 'open'. As explored by Farrow (2016), the removal of inhibitions to freedoms, both positive and negative, as a condition for opening is insufficient. This case suggests that the ideal subject of open learning must at minimum *recognise* such freedoms as a prerequisite for engagement.

The imagined ideal subject of social justice

Similarly as described above for open educational practices, Fraser's theory of social justice necessarily makes assumptions about the actor as a subject of justice, recognising both positive and negative freedoms against which they might make justice claims. What the LSS case suggests is that barriers to social justice may not only be structural in the form of economic maldistribution, cultural misrecognition or political misrepresentation at the level of the collective, but may also be psycho-social in the form of internalised ideals, subjectivities and at the level of the individual. Interventions towards social justice that fail to acknowledge the internalised imaginations of different actors, and how they have been shaped by the systems and discourses under which they have lived and learned, may find themselves frustrated at a lack of uptake when opportunities are presented to those who never had access before. That is, any social justice intervention, on whatever axes, that fails to ignite the imaginations of those it propounds to act on behalf of, almost seems destined to fail. Social justice, at whatever scale, cannot be done *to* or *for* but must emerge as a project *with* and *by* those who suffer marginalisation and injustice. Efforts to establish parity of participation must enable subjects of justice to reimagine themselves *as participants*.

Conclusion

This case has examined change in an existing intervention towards TVET lecturer support in South Africa. The problematic of understanding this intervention and its history, and how it relates to other theories of change in the sector, was framed as a descriptive task by examining the imagined TVET lecturer underpinning said theories of change and how this imagination might relate to an ideal in the minds of intervention designers and policymakers.

What has emerged is that while different theories of change share multiple commonalities regarding the imagined TVET lecturer and the ideal towards which development should occur, there is an underlying challenge about meaningful reform across such a heterogeneous population of lecturers with significant material constraints, as well as a paucity of research on how lecturers understand their own subjectivities. By exploring assumed TVET lecturer subjectivities in pedagogic, professional and political terms, the case sought to draw attention to contradictions in how TVET lecturers are imagined that might inhibit present and future efforts at change. That the sector has been subject to a flurry of policy change – what might be termed a 'reform storm' – further blunts the already limited reach of policy as an instrument of change amongst a sector mistrustful of further policy mandates.

Amongst the wicked issues to be addressed is lecturer performativity, for which respondents in this case had limited remedy. But another that cannot be ignored is a perennial problem in teacher education, namely the assumption that lecturer development necessarily improves pedagogic practice, which in turn improves teaching and learning outcomes for students. Given how exogenous socio-economic factors affect student access and success in education institutions, the efficacy of lecturer development may have limited results. However, addressing shortcomings amongst TVET lecturers is certainly a necessary, if insufficient, prerequisite to improved quality of TVET provision, and thus for seeking social justice in the sector.

What this case has attempted to suggest is that sophisticated empirical work and theorising regarding who TVET lecturers *are* is necessary prior to any normative intervention:

> [T[hese institutions are still relatively new and fragile and are in some instances based on historically weak predecessors. When forced to confront conflicting questions about what they are for, such institutions have relatively weak resources on which to draw. Understanding these institutions *and the people in them* is critical for understanding the entire sector. (Wedekind, 2016b, p. 32, emphasis added)

By considering how TVET lecturers are imagined amongst decision makers, this case attempts to offer conceptual tools regarding how lecturers are (not) considered, what assumptions are being made, and how tacit ideals shape theories of change, including assumptions regarding open learning and social justice.

Acknowldgements

Many thanks to the staff at the Department of Higher Education and Training whose inputs made the study possible. Special thanks are due to reviewers Professor Joy Papier and Dr Patti Silbert for their thoughtful, incisive feedback on the chapter, Emeritus Associate Professor Cheryl Ann Hodgkinson-Williams and Shanali Govender for mentoring the case study, and Dr Tabisa Mayisela for guiding the entire COOL project. Thanks are also due to the Centre for Innovation in Learning and Teaching at the University of Cape Town, which hosted the COOL project, and the South African Department of Higher Education and Training for funding it.

References

Adendorff, M., & Van Wyk, C. (2016). Offering TVET college lecturers increased access to professional qualification programmes through a national open learning system in South Africa. 8th Pan-Commonwealth Forum on Open Learning (PCF8), 27–30 November 2016. http://oasis.col.org

Almeida, N. (2017). Open education resources and rhetorical paradox in the neoliberal univers(ity). *Journal of Critical Library and Information Studies,* 1(1). DOI: 10.24242/jclis.v1i1.16

Andersson, P., & Köpsén, S. (2019). VET teachers between school and working life: boundary processes enabling continuing professional development. *Journal of Education and Work,* 32 (6–7), 537–551. DOI: 10.1080/13639080.2019.1673888.

Ball, S. J. (1993). What is policy? Texts, trajectories and toolboxes. *The Australian Journal of Education Studies,* 13(2), 10–17.

Ball, S. J. (2003). The teacher's soul and the terrors of performativity. *Journal of Education Policy,* 18(2), 215–228.

Ball, S. J. (2015). What is policy? 21 years later: Reflections on the possibilities of policy research. *Discourse: Studies in the Cultural Politics of Education,* 36(3), 306–313.

Ball, S. J. (2017). Labouring to relate: Neoliberalism, embodied policy, and network dynamics. *Peabody Journal of Education,* 92(1), 29–41.

Barnett, M. (2006) Vocational knowledge and vocational pedagogy. In M. Young & J. Gamble (Eds.), *Knowledge, curriculum and qualifications for South African further education* (pp. 143–157). HSRC Press.

Biesta, G. J. (2004). Education, accountability, and the ethical demand: Can the democratic potential of accountability be regained? *Educational Theory,* 54(3), 233–250.

Brennan Kemmis, R., & Green, A. (2013). Vocational education and training teachers' conceptions of their pedagogy. *International Journal of Training Research,* 11(2), 101–121. https://doi.org/10.5172/ijtr.2013.11.2.101

Broad, J. H. (2015). So many worlds, so much to do: Identifying barriers to engagement with continued professional development for teachers in the further education and training sector. *London Review of Education,* 13(1), 16–30.

Buthelezi, Z. (2018). Lecturer experiences of TVET College challenges in the post-apartheid era: a case of unintended consequences of educational reform in South Africa. *Journal of Vocational Education & Training,* 70(3), 364–383.

DHET (Department of Higher Education and Training). (2013a). White paper for post-school education and training: Building an expanded, effective and integrated post-school system. *Government Gazette,* 37229. https://www.gov.za/documents/white-paper-post-school-education-and-training-building-expanded-effective-and-integrated

DHET. (2013b). Policy on professional qualifications for lecturers in technical and vocational education and training. *Government Gazette,* 36554.

DHET. (2014). Qualifications profile of lecturers employed in public technical and vocational education and training colleges in South Africa. Report from the Chief Directorate: Teaching and Learning Development. https://www.dhet.gov.za/Teacher%20Education%20Reports/DHET%20%20Qualification%20Profile%20of%20Lecturers%20Employed%20in%20Public%20Technical%20and%20Vocational%20Education%20and%202015.pdf

DHET. (2017). Open learning policy framework for post-school education and training (draft). *Government Gazette,* 40772(335). http://pmg-assets.s3-website-eu-west-1.amazonaws.com/170407openlearningframework-postschooleduc.pdf

Farnsworth, V., & Higham, J. (2012). Teachers who teach their practice: the modulation of hybridised professional teacher identities in work-related educational programmes in Canada. *Journal of Education and Work,* 25(4), 473–505.

Farrow, R. (2016). Constellations of openness. In M. Deimann & P. Michael (Eds.), *The philosophy of open learning: Peer learning and the intellectual commons.* Peter Lang. http://oro.open.ac.uk/50799/

Foucault, M. (1980). *Power/knowledge: Selected interviews and other writings 1972–1977* (C. Gordon, Ed.). Pantheon.

Foucault, M. (1991). Governmentality. In G. Burchell, C. Gordon & P. Miller (Eds.), *The Foucault effect: Studies in governmentality.* University of Chicago Press.

Foucault, M. (1997). *Discipline and punish: The birth of the prison.* Vintage/Random House.

Fraser, N. (1995). From redistribution to recognition? Dilemmas of justice in a 'postsocialist' age. *New Left Review,* 1/212, 68–93.

Fraser, N. (2005). Reframing justice in a globalizing world. *New Left Review*, 36, 69–88.
Fraser, N. (2009). *Scales of justice: Reimagining political space in a globalizing world*. Columbia University Press.
Grollmann, P. (2008). The quality of vocational teachers: Teacher education, institutional roles and professional reality. *European Educational Research Journal*, 7(4), 535–547. DOI: 10.2304/eerj.2008.7.4.535.
Hall, S. (1992). The question of cultural identity. In S. Hall, D. Held & T. McGrew (Eds.), *Modernity and its Futures*. Polity and The Open University Press.
Hall, S. (2001). Foucault: Power, Knowledge, and discourse. In M. Wetherell (Ed.), *Discourse theory and practice: A reader* (pp. 72–81). Sage.
Jacklin, H. (2018). The imagined subject of schooling in the logic of policy. *Journal of Educational Administration and History*, 50(4), 256–269.
Jansen, J. D. (2002). Political symbolism as policy craft: Explaining non-reform in South African education after apartheid. *Journal of Education Policy*, 17(2), 199–215.
Kelchtermans, G. (2005). Emotions, teacher identity and change. *Journal of Teaching and Teacher Education*, 21(8), 995–1006. https://doi.org/10.1016/j.tate.2005.06.009
Knox, J. (2013). The limitations of access alone: Moving towards open processes in education technology. *Open Praxis*, 5(1), 21–29.
Koch, F. (2019). Institutionalizing the Lecturer Support System. Internal report for the Department of Higher Education and Training. June 2019.
Manyau, T. (2015). Assessing skills development management for lecturers in technical vocational education and training colleges in North-West province. North West University.
Maxwell, J. (1992). Understanding and validity in qualitative research. *Harvard Educational Review*, 62(3), 279–301.
McGrath, S. A., Badroodien, A., Kraak, A., & Unwin, L. (Eds.). (2004). *Shifting understandings of skills in South Africa: Overcoming the historical imprint of a low regime*. HSRC Press.
McLaughlin, M. W. (1987). Learning from experience: Lessons from policy implementation. *Educational Evaluation and Policy Analysis*, 9(2), 171–178.
McLaughlin, M. (1997). Implementation as mutual adaptation: Change in classroom organization. In D. Flinders & S. Thornton (Eds.), *Curriculum studies reader*. Routledge.
Mills, S. (2003). *Michel Foucault*. Routledge.
Mirani, L. (2015). Millions of Facebook users have no idea they're using the internet. *Quartz*. https://qz.com/333313/milliions-of-facebook-users-have-no-idea-theyre-using-the-internet/
Mukhopadhyay, R., & Sriprakash, A. (2011). Global frameworks, local contingencies: Policy translations and education development in India. *Compare*, 41(3), 311–326. https://doi.org/10.1080/03057925.2010.534668
Muller (Black), S. (2020). The tyranny of timespace: Examining the timetable of schooling activities as the interface between policy and everyday rhythms [Doctoral dissertation, University of Cape Town]. http://hdl.handle.net/11427/32292
NPC (National Planning Commission) (2013). National development plan 2030. https://www.gov.za/documents/national-development-plan-2030-our-future-make-it-work
Oliver, M. (2015). From openness to permeability: Reframing open education in terms of positive liberty in the enactment of academic practices. *Learning, Media and Technology*. DOI: 10.1080/17439884.2015.1029940
Papier, J. (2008) Report on the training of FET college lecturers in South Africa, England and other international contexts. EAP project, UWC.
Papier, J. (2010). From policy to curriculum in South African vocational teacher education: A comparative perspective. *Journal of Vocational Education and Training*, 62(2), 153–162.
Papier, J. (2011). Vocational teacher identity: spanning the divide between the academy and the workplace. *Southern African Review of Education*, 17, 101–119.
Rizvi, F., & Lingard, B. (2010). *Globalizing education policy*. Routledge.
Sayed, Y. (1997). Understanding educational decentralization in post-apartheid South Africa. *Journal of Negro Education*, 354–365.

Shalem, Y. (2003). Do we have a theory of change? Calling change models to account. *Perspectives in Education*, 21(1), 29–49. https://hdl.handle.net/10520/EJC87182

Silbert, P. (2012). The imagined learner in neoliberal times: Constructions of the South African learning subject in education policy discourse and school practice [Doctoral dissertation, University of Cape Town].

Silbert, P., & Jacklin, H. (2015). 'Assembling' the ideal learner: The school assembly as regulatory ritual. *Review of Education, Pedagogy, and Cultural Studies*, 37(4), 326–344.

Sooklal, S. (2005). The Structural and Cultural Constraints on Policy Implementation: A case study of FET colleges in South Africa [Doctoral thesis, University of Pretoria].

Tikly, L. (2003). Governmentality and the study of education policy in South Africa. *Journal of Education Policy*, 18(2), 161–174.

Vähäsantanen, K., & Hämäläinen, R. (2019). Professional identity in relation to vocational teachers' work: an identity-centred approach to professional development. *Learning: Research and Practice*, 5(1), 48–66. DOI: 10.1080/23735082.2018.1487573.

Van der Bijl, A. (2015). Mentoring and the development of educators in South African technical and vocational education [Master's thesis, Stellenbosch University].

Van der Bijl, A., & Oosthuizen, L. J. (2019). Deficiencies in technical and vocational education and training lecturer involvement qualifications and its implications in the development of work related skills. *South African Journal of Higher Eeducation*, 33(3). DOI: 10.20853/33-3-2886.

Van der Bijl, A., & Taylor, V. (2016). Nature and Dynamics of Industry-Based Workplace Learning for South African TVET Lecturers. *Industry and Higher Education*, 30(2), 98–108. DOI: 10.5367/ihe.2016.0297.

Van der Bijl, A., & Taylor, V. (2018). Work-integrated learning for TVET lecturers: articulating industry and college practices. *Journal of Vocational, Adult and Continuing Education and Training*, 1(1), 126–145.

Wedekind, V. (2016a). Introduction. *SAQA Bulletin* 15(1), 1–29.

Wedekind, V. (2016b). Literature on Technical Vocational Education and Training (TVET) College lecturers: a review. *SAQA Bulletin*, 15(1), 31–59.

Wedekind, V., Watson, A., & Buthelezi, Z. (2016). Lecturers in distress: fractured professional identity amongst TVET college staff in South Africa. *SAQA Bulletin*, 15(1), 117–142.

HOW TO CITE THIS CHAPTER

Black, S. (2022). "Who do you think they are?" Troubling how mental conceptions of TVET lecturers shape lecturer support interventions: The case of the Lecturer Support System in South Africa. In T. Mayisela, S. C. Govender & C. A. Hodgkinson-Williams (Eds.), *Open learning as a means of advancing social justice: Cases in post-school education and training in South Africa* (pp. 314–337). African Minds. doi: 10.47622/9781928502425_14

This work is licensed under a Creative Commons Attribution 4.0 International (CC BY 4.0) licence.

15

Opening up TVET lecturer professional learning and development through work integrated learning in South Africa

A social justice perspective

Shanali Govender & Thasmai Dhurumraj

SUMMARY Providing professional learning and development opportunities for lecturers is necessary for enabling 'open learning', as promoted by the Department of Higher Education and Training (DHET). In the Technical and Vocational Education and Training (TVET) sector, there are desperate shortages of suitably qualified and experienced lecturers. This shortage is a multifaceted problem, with some staff lacking formal qualifications, some lacking vocational experience, and others lacking professional educator training for the TVET context. This chapter explores how approaches to professional learning and development, particularly work integrated learning (WIL) opportunities for TVET staff, coordinated by DHET through collaborative linkages with industry, drew on and/or contributed to open learning. The study used a range of secondary sources of information, supplemented with five semi-structured interviews and a structured email-based questionnaire. Open learning has a strong social justice intention. Thus, we adopted Fraser's three-dimensional conceptualisation of social justice to illuminate the extent to which these interventions sought to create conditions of participatory parity, and in so doing address economic, cultural and political injustices experienced by lecturers. The study identifies a number of instances of injustice, including the direct and indirect costs of WIL, the extent to which misrecognition excludes marginalised individuals from WIL, and the extent to which governance structures entrench inequalities. Furthermore, we suggest how the design of these interventions might take these barriers to parity of participation into consideration in future designs. Critically, we suggest that locating WIL in formal learning opportunities, and reviewing merit awards systems might lead to greater uptake and, in the long run, improved teaching and learning.

Keywords: TVET lecturers, professional development, work integrated learning, open learning, social justice

Introduction

There is a paucity of research on TVET college lecturers and their professional development in particular, with much of the existing research "remaining grey", produced by various national institutes[1], a handful of centres in universities[2], governments and international development agencies (Wedekind, 2016a, p. 42). Research points to a limited focus on the professional learning and development of staff in Technical and Vocational Education and Training (TVET) colleges (Msibi, 2015; Ngubane-Mokiwa & Khoza, 2016), with Jephcote and Salisbury referring to TVET lecturers as the "shadowy figures" (2009, p. 967). Similarly, Wedekind asserts that colleges remain something of a "black box", urging researchers to better understand "who the College lecturers are and what motivates them, and crucially, how they see themselves as educators and specialists" (2016a, p. 39). However, there have been emerging bodies of research on shifting professional identities (Batholmeus & Pop, 2019; Buthelezi, 2016; Van der Bijl & Taylor, 2016), staff satisfaction and engagement (Mmako, 2015) and high workloads (Buthelezi, 2016; Jeremiah & Martin, 2019; Jonker, 2016) that seek to uncover how TVET staff view their lived experience in the TVET sector.

This chapter explores whether, and in what ways, work integrated learning (WIL), as a form of professional learning and development for staff, supports the Department of Higher Education and Training's (DHET's) open learning approach while addressing issues of social justice. This is a small empirical study, drawing on pre-existing quantitative data, reports on initiatives from DHET and industry and non-governmental organisations, and subsequent qualitative interviews to better understand the contribution of WIL to opening up education and addressing inequalities in the local context.

We start by outlining the problem of professional learning and development of TVET lecturers, and subsequently how WIL supports the capacity building of TVET staff. We establish the widespread inequalities that characterise the broader context which frames this particular challenge, and, thus, argue for the use of Nancy Fraser's social justice framework. This offers a way to understand how approaches to professional learning and development and particularly WIL opportunities for TVET staff, coordinated by DHET through collaborative linkages with industry, responded to inequalities and drew on and/or contributed to open learning and lecturer parity of participation. We briefly sketch the research design of this study before sharing our findings and relating these to Fraser's key concept of participatory parity, and economic, cultural and political injustices experienced by lecturers.

---

[1] Such as the Joint Education Trust (JET), the FET Institute (FETI), the Eastern Cape Consortium for Socio-Economic Cooperation (ECCSEC), the SAQA-UKZN Partnership Research, and the Human Sciences Research Council (HSRC) (Wedekind, 2016a).

[2] Including an FET unit at the University of the Western Cape (UWC); the University of Witwatersrand Education Policy Unit; and the Centre for Integrated Post-School Education and Training (CIPSET) at the Nelson Mandela Metropolitan University NMMU) (Wedekind, 2016a).

The professional learning and development of TVET lecturers: Framing the problem

For almost a decade, DHET has identified the employment of appropriately qualified lecturers as key to enhancing the quality of education offered in the TVET sector (DHET 2013a). The state of flux and uncertainty in the sector for the last two decades have negatively impacted on the retention of existing staff (Wedekind et al., 2016). More recently, the Heher Fees Commission again pointed to a shortage of suitable lecturing staff in the TVET sector (Heher Commission, 2017, p. 332). This shortage is attributed to a number of factors, including a lack of experience, a lack of suitable qualifications, limited industry experience and "a lack of professionalism" (Olowoyo et al., 2020; Verster, 2011). In the absence of suitable appointees, colleges are "forced" to appoint "top-performing students" on graduation (Beukes, 2018, p. 7; DHET, 2017). Alternatively, colleges hire retired industry professionals (DHET, 2017; Van der Bijl, 2021).

Although the *White Paper for Post-School Education and Training* (PSET) (DHET, 2013a), "hint[ed] at the current shortcomings experienced in respect of lecturing staff" (Beukes, 2018, p. 53), it was the *Qualification Profile of Lecturers Employed in Public Technical and Vocational Education and Training Colleges in South Africa* reports of 2014, 2015 and 2016 (DHET, 2015), that fully exposed the extent of the staffing qualification challenge facing TVET colleges (summarised in Table 1 below). This was reiterated in the *Draft National Plan for PSET* (DHET, 2017).

Table 1: Summary of Qualification Profile of Lecturers Employed in Public Technical and Vocational Education and Training Colleges in South Africa reports (DHET 2014, 2015, 2016)

Categorisation of staff	2014	2015	2016
Unqualified lecturers	683	809	1726
Academically qualified but professionally unqualified	2202	1975	3037
Academically qualified and professionally qualified, but for the schooling sector	1973	2262	2774
Academically and professionally qualified as a college lecturer	854	703	400
Undefined	n/a	1026	438
Total	5712	6775	8375

The qualifications for TVET college lecturers were established in the *Policy on Professional Qualifications for Lecturers in Technical and Vocational Education and Training* (DHET, 2013b). This policy mirrors, but does not fully align with, the *Policy on the Minimum Requirements for Teacher Education Qualifications* (DBE, 2011) and, subsequently, with the *Policy on Minimum Requirements for Programmes Leading to Qualifications for Educators and Lecturers in Adult and Community Education and Training* (RSA, 2014). Although these policies are "intended to produce professionally qualified lecturers" for secondary schools, TVET and community education and training (CET) colleges, they were not universally well received in the TVET and CET sectors (Van der Bijl & Taylor, 2020, p. 23). Furthermore, TVET colleges sometimes hire staff from secondary and community education backgrounds, resulting in staff bodies that are qualified in different ways.

The *Policy on Professional Qualifications for Lecturers in Technical and Vocational Education and Training* (DHET, 2013b) emphasised the importance of pedagogy, didactics, and workplace experience. Similarly, Van der Bijl and Oosthuisen note that "ideally TVET college lecturers should have an academic qualification, teaching qualification, and workplace qualification and experience" (2019, p. 219). In alignment with this, the Qualification Profile reports categorised staff as "Unqualified lecturers", "Academically qualified but professionally unqualified", "Academically qualified and professionally qualified, but for the schooling sector" and "Academically and professionally qualified as a college lecturer". Thus, some TVET lecturers require opportunities for learning that strengthen their formal qualifications, others require opportunities for professional learning in the workplace, and another group may well require both.

Moreover, the lack of education and training opportunities to gain additional qualifications limits the pools of qualified staff, often resulting in the recruitment of unqualified and under-qualified staff (Wedekind et al., 2016), leading to what Blom refers to as "a weak training base" (2016, p. 49). The complexity of this situation is exacerbated by the fact that South Africa "does not have a convention of vocational teacher education policy, or of industry placements for vocational teachers" (Van der Bijl, 2021, p. 14).

Unfortunately, reports after 2016 are not publicly available and the recent TVET Sub-sector report for the 2019/2020 Sector Skills Plan laments the fact that "the available TVET lecturer data … says nothing about the specialisation that the lecturer has in their prior qualification and whether [this] is appropriate for what they currently teach" (ETDP SETA, 2021, p. 19). The consequence is that "there is almost no way of knowing what areas of teaching specialisation universities should focus on, or which avenues of industry specific qualifications other than universities (sic) need further development" (ETDP SETA, 2021, p. 19).

Furthermore, while the practice of WIL for learners seems to be gaining ground, the *Research Report on Work Integrated Learning at South African TVET Colleges and Workplaces* reports that 78% of workplaces have "little or no understanding or knowledge of WIL for lecturers" (ETDP SETA, 2021, p. 32).

It is widely acknowledged that DHET faces a complex challenge with regard to the professional development of lecturers (see Chapter 14, this volume). The importance of WIL (also known as workplace-based learning [WPBL] – see Van Staden, 2015) for lecturer development cannot be overemphasised because it affects the quality, relevance and credibility of lecturers' teaching.

Professional development through work integrated learning

Defining WIL

The practice of linking formal, in-class education with learning at commercial, retail, professional and industrial sites is well established. Students in a wide variety of professional and vocational fields experience some degree of exposure to the workplace during their formal education – through, for example, apprenticeships for mechanics, teaching practicals for teachers, and clinical placements for medical professionals. A number of terms, including work integrated learning (WIL), workplace-based learning (WPBL), and workplace-based exposure/ experience (WBE)[3], have been used to describe this practice.

In the South African context, WIL was defined by the Council on Higher Education as "an umbrella term to describe curricular, pedagogic and assessment practices, across a range of academic disciplines that integrate formal learning and workplace concerns" (2011, p. 4) — a definition that has persisted to date (ETDP SETA, 2021). Van Rensburg describes WPBL as "any period of work experience undertaken by students in a real work environment that forms a credit-bearing component of a higher education qualification" (2008, p. 224), and Scholtz (2020) claims that WPBL can be used synonymously with WIL. WBE emphasises short periods of exposure to workplaces, with students working alongside employees to understand formal learning in relation to work contexts (JET, 2015; SSACI, 2015).

These terms have emerged at slightly different points in time, and can signal subtly different approaches to this practice. For example, Atkinson (2016) points in the Australian context to a shift from the term "work-based learning" to "work integrated learning" to learning that largely occurs in authentic work contexts in which the learner tends to be employed to learning that occurs in the integration of work and learning contexts. However, their concurrent use persists and they tend also to be used with varying degrees of specificity.

Furthermore, in the context of staff development in the TVET colleges sector, all three terms have been used[4]. For the purposes of this paper, to maintain alignment with the terminology currently used by DHET, we will be talking about work integrated learning. However, it must be noted that given the non-formal, voluntary, unaccredited nature of the professional learning discussed in this paper, there are definite overlaps with the idea of work-based exposure, which signals a less integrated approach to learning in work contexts.

The need for WIL for TVET lecturers

Papier (2011) points out that, unlike general education teachers,

> Vocational teachers are ... required to span these two spheres (work and education) and embrace a dual identity that combines liberal education and economic enterprise, placing them in a state of tension between 'industry expert' and 'expert educator' identities, even though they are dislocated from both traditional sites — the industrial workplace and the traditional school. (p. 106)

However, Wedekind suggests that the identities of TVET lecturers tend to be "centre[d] primarily on their subject disciplines or professions" (2016b, p. 22). While many definitions of WIL take a student-oriented, formal education position, Scholtz (2020) offers an interesting perspective by considering the lecturers' experience of WIL: "WIL is the vehicle to integrate theory with practice by incorporating pedagogic practices such as work placements, problem-based learning, project-based learning, service learning and simulated learning" (p. 26).

---

[3] Furthermore, these terms are variously hyphenated. For the purposes of this chapter, we will not be hyphenating these terms, unless quoting a source that does so.

[4] For example, for work integrated learning see Van der Bijl & Taylor (2020); for workplace-based learning see Blom (2019); and for work-based exposure see Nduna (2017).

Given the paucity of TVET lecturers with both disciplinary and professional experience, opportunities to engage in WIL have the potential to enhance TVET lecturer identities, bringing existing disciplinary identities into conversation with professional identities (Van der Bijl, 2021).

A number of empirical studies report on the need for WIL for TVET college lecturers. For example, participants in Manyau's (2015) research, assessing the skills development management process for TVET lecturers in the North West province, specifically pointed to the need for WIL. Similarly, Adendorff and Van Wyk (2016) point to the lack of WBE for both TVET college graduates and secondary school educators who became TVET college lecturers, and allude to the potential of open learning initiatives as a possible response to this gap.

Benefits of WIL

Apart from helping lecturers to keep up-to-date with developments in industry in order to help them better prepare the students for the realities of the workplace, the value of WIL can assist lecturers in ensuring that the curriculum offered at TVET colleges is adjusted timeously to keep pace with the workplace needs and demands (Wedekind, 2016a). There may also be mutual benefits for both the industry and TVET lecturers if the latter could be directly involved in workplace skills training, and given opportunities to provide feedback on it. In addition, lecturers may be much better informed about the specific opportunities in industry and thus in a better position to ensure that students are placed at relevant workplaces and that their progress is monitored throughout (ETDP SETA, 2021).

Despite the potential benefits for TVET lecturers' practices and their students' experiences, not all WIL opportunities are widely or enthusiastically taken up by TVET staff. For example, Oosthuizen and Van der Bijl (2019) reported that many TVET staff opted to keep current with knowledge and practices in industry through informal practices such as reading, or through achieving additional qualifications, which had a more likely impact on their career prospects, as opposed to seeking out or enrolling in WIL opportunities.

Offering WIL through CPD activities

One of the ways in which TVET lecturers can improve their professional skills is by undertaking work integrated learning in partnership with local and/or international industries. WIL for lecturers has typically been approached from a continuous professional development (CPD) perspective.[5] Ideally, staff, colleges and DHET should work in partnership to seek out opportunities to partner with industry and other organisations to create opportunities for WIL for staff. However, this is not reported to be the case. Mgijima reports that staff were:

> offered in-service training (INSET) courses regardless of their relevance to their needs. This one-size-fits-all approach has been a source of great dissatisfaction to the lecturers themselves as well as a great disappointment to the policy-makers as it yields no real benefits in terms of improving lecturer competence. (2014, p. 365)

---

[5] Chetram (2017, p. 15) defines CPD as: "refers to any expert growth events lecturers have interaction in, with the intention to upgrading their education and skills that will allow them to be concerned about methods and styles to the education of youths with an aim of enhancing the value of education".

Similarly, in a different institutional context, Chetram asserts that existing CPD programmes do not meet lecturers' needs, and "colleges are not managing the continuous professional development of lectures. It is left upon the lecturers themselves to manage their professional development" (2017, p. vii). Both these studies point to a breakdown in the capacity of colleges to initiate, develop and maintain relationships with industry and commerce that support opportunities for WIL for lecturers.

In the face of the inability of colleges to secure WIL opportunities for lecturers, DHET has initiated a handful of programmes, supported at a national level. Some of these programmes will be discussed later in this chapter. Sporadic in-service training programmes for lecturers are undertaken by various NGOs, such as the Swiss-South African Collaboration Initiative (SSACI) and the National Business Initiative (NBI), with funding from business, donors and international aid agencies. In general, this has meant that TVET lecturers have been on the receiving end of "fragmented" in-service training and development and on-going curriculum change (DHET, 2017b, p. 6).

Offering WIL through formal educational activities

Unfortunately, until recently, WIL has not been a standard part of TVET teacher training (Papier, 2017). While TVET lecturer programmes consistently include from 18 to 40 weeks of practical experience in teaching settings, as is the norm for most educational qualifications, WIL in industry or commercial settings is neither mandated in the same way, nor does it receive the same attention (Batholmeus & Pop, 2021; Van der Bijl & Taylor, 2018). Given the CPD difficulties outlined above, high quality initial lecturer development, including elements of WIL, must become the norm. Thus, formal TVET lecturer educational qualifications, from basic degrees through advanced diplomas and other postgraduate qualifications, must assist established and "trainee lecturers ... to understand that their professional community includes the education and industry community in their subject field and they need to be given the capacity to build relationships and work with industry" (Van der Bijl & Taylor, 2018, p. 142).

Increasingly, despite the historical emphasis on WIL as part of a continuous development perspective, WIL has been incorporated into most initial educator training qualifications and postgraduate educator training qualifications. However, managing such programmes of study requires the development of complex relationships between multiple stakeholders: the higher education institutions (HEIs) offering the qualifications, the TVET colleges at which graduates will practice, and the industries in which graduates are, ideally, professionals and experts. DHET has overseen a project to create formal qualifications for TVET lecturers through a number of HEIs in order to support the ongoing professionalisation of TVET lecturers.

Challenges with WIL research

Despite the increased interest in researching TVET colleges, the quality of empirical research on the educational profile of lecturers remains poor for a number of reasons, inter alia, the quantitative analysis of data can be problematic. Although Gamede and Uleanya report that 97% of their participants had "suitable academic qualifications", describing this as a "great improvement" (2019, p. 7), there are some challenges in reading this data. If read alongside the criteria for suitability laid out in the *Policy on Professional Qualifications for Lecturers in Technical and Vocational Education and Training* (DHET, 2013b) and referred to in the report on the *Qualification Profile of Lecturers Employed in Public Technical and Vocational Education and Training Colleges* in South Africa (DHET, 2015), their conclusion could be questioned. These findings are contrasted with those of Zinn et al. who claim that only "one in five vocational lecturers in South Africa" (2019, p. 174) currently can fulfil the minimum requirements for TVET lecturers' basic qualifications.

Additionally, research on the ongoing professional learning and development of lecturers is often grounded in human capital theory (Moodie et al., 2019) only. For example, based on focus group interviews with teaching staff and management at a TVET college in Mpumalanga, Ndlovu's (2019) recommendations focus on the creation of policies and programmes that improve attendance and engagement, awards, quality assurance, and buy-in from staff. There is unfortunately little attempt to understand the positions taken up by staff in unjust conditions.

WIL must, however, be understood in the context of the broader national picture, including the particular context of the TVET college's themselves, and national PSET plans.

Context for the study

In the current South African context, unemployment is rife and, together with the challenges of poverty and inequality (Akoojee, 2016), makes for a very unequal society. Education, and particularly TVET education, is promoted as the solution to what Rittel and Webber term a "wicked problem" (1973). For example, DHET asserts that "Education has long been recognised as providing a route out of poverty for individuals, and as a way of promoting equality of opportunity" (2013, p. 5). Similarly, a UNESCO report claimed:

> Since education is the key to effective development strategies, technical and vocational educational and training (TVET) must be the master key that can alleviate poverty, promote peace, conserve the environment, improve the quality of life for all and help achieve sustainable development. (Marope et al., 2015, p. 13)

While similar perspectives are upheld by many researchers (Gamede & Uleanya, 2019; Poh & Smythe, 2014; Poonam, 2013), there are voices that seek to convey the complexities of the relationship between economic development and education (Allais et al., 2019; Ngcwangu, 2015).

Despite the framing of the TVET sector as a potentially powerful driver of economic growth and a historically "unprecedented focus on the public TVET sector" (Blom, 2016), the sector struggles with a number of historical challenges. Immediately post-apartheid, the 153 "ethnically defined" TVET colleges were rapidly, and with minimal consultation, merged into 50 Further Education and Training (FET) colleges (Wedekind, 2016b, pp. 10–11; 2016c, pp. 93–96), causing substantial stress for lecturers at the time (Wedekind & Buthelezi, 2016). A hotly contested turf war between the then Ministries of Education and Labour for control of the colleges resulted in staff insecurity and attrition (Cosser et al., 2011) and a further declining apprenticeship system (Blom, 2016), the scars of which remain today.

More recently, TVETs have faced additional challenges, linked to shifts in the structure of TVET and the role of TVET colleges in the PSET. These challenges can be clustered around curricula, institutional context, and students and their experiences. The rapid changes to curricula to respond to demands for a larger TVET sector were often carried out with little consultation, and little consideration for varied contexts (Buthelezi, 2016; Paterson, 2016; Terblanche, 2017; Wedekind, 2016b). At an institutional level, issues of leadership (Badenhorst & Radile, 2018; Motaung, 2020; Sithole, 2019), the massification and mixed ability classrooms (Buthelezi, 2016; Ngoveni, 2018; Singh & Shawa, 2021) and, increasingly, material shortages such as workshops, textbooks, protective equipment, etc. (Buthelezi, 2016; Gamede & Uleanya, 2019; Ngwato, 2020), have made lecturers jobs more challenging. Furthermore, the type of students in TVET classrooms (Buthelezi, 2016; Nthako, 2020), their poor post-study employment prospects (Buthelezi, 2016; Mabunda & Frick, 2020; Masoabi & Alexander, 2021) and increasing financial pressure on students, coupled with reduced funding in real terms (Matsolo et al., 2018; Singh & Shawa, 2021; Yende, 2021), result in students in TVET classrooms struggling to focus on their studies. These contemporary challenges create difficult teaching contexts for lecturers, and at the same time, difficult contexts for their professional learning and development.

Open learning

Open learning is part of DHET's response to the context and challenge it faces. DHET has, in a number of documents since the mid-1990s (DoE, 1995; DHET, 2013, 2017), referred to "open learning", defining it in the *White Paper for Post-school Education and Training*, as:

> an approach which combines the principles of learner centredness, lifelong learning, flexibility of learning provision, the removal of barriers to access learning, the recognition for credit of prior learning experience, the provision of learner support, the construction of learning programmes in the expectation that learners can succeed, and the maintenance of rigorous quality assurance over the design of learning materials and support systems. (DHET, 2013, p. 48)

Although this definition has its roots as early as the *White Paper on Education and Training* (1995), it is most recently affirmed in the *Open Learning Policy Framework* (OLPF) (DHET, 2017). DHET has built its conceptualisation of open learning around four issues – access, flexibility, quality and success – and develops initiatives to improve performance in relation to these issues. Access is addressed through, for example, recognition of prior learning experience. Flexibility is provided through the provision of tuition and peer engagement through various modes of learning (i.e. face-to-face, blended and online learning) and either synchronously or asynchronously. Quality is supported by, for example, the development of learning materials. Success is addressed through, for example, offering work integrated learning opportunities for students (DHET, 2013, 2017). However, in the conclusion of the OLPF, DHET is at pains to assert that "open learning focuses directly on making access to learning a primary goal", with little comment on issues of flexibility, quality or success (DHET, 2017, p. 412).

Unfortunately, the term 'open learning' as used in this study has the potential to be slightly confusing. In the first instance, it is used consistently in DHET policy documents to refer to widening access, improving quality and strengthening markers of success. In the second instance, it is linked, in DHET's policy documents, to a cluster of opens – open education, open educational practices, and open educational resources — which have strong social justice imperatives and have clearly defined meanings, different from that espoused in the DHET documentation. Thirdly, it is sometimes used imprecisely, in various local studies, in relation to online, distance, or resource-based learning.

The OLPF makes explicit reference to OER, advocating for the creation of "high quality, shared teaching and learning resources" and the use of these to reduce costs where possible (DHET, 2017, p. 386). Additionally, as a part of the Capacity Building of TVET College Lecturers through Open Learning programme, a national open learning management system will be established, acting as a repository for re-useable and adaptable OER, for student learning and staff development (Adendorff & Van Wyk, 2016). However, the notion of OER is strongly connected to ideas of open education and open educational practices which have strong social justice imperatives, but which are not referred to in DHET's PSET policies.

DHET has actively advised against using terms such as 'distance education', 'resource-based learning', and 'e-learning or technology-enhanced learning' synonymously with open learning (2017, p. 372). However, the frequent co-location of such terminology in official documentation, and the slippage in empirical literature in the local context, leads to a collapsing and/or conflation of concepts and associated debates that causes some confusion.[6]

'Open learning', referring to the removal of barriers, as used by DHET is stretched to accommodate, not just students, but also staff, specifically TVET lecturers. Adendorff and Van Wyk take up the idea of removal of barriers to consider the professional learning and development of TVET staff, acknowledging that many TVET lecturers are, due to staffing constraints and operational requirements: (1) unable to take off time to study; (2) may work and live in rural and semi-rural areas at a distance from universities; (3) may be incapable of affording university fees on their salaries; (4) may lack the qualifications for university access; and (5) will almost certainly have experienced encounters with pedagogic practices that were inaccessible and alienating (2016, p. 4).

The value of a social justice perspective on WIL

While there is an ongoing and heightened urgency, both globally and locally, to address the inequities of our social, economic and political reality (Hölscher & Bozalek, 2020), this urgency is itself not always equally distributed (Moodie et al., 2019). As DHET pointed out, the attention of policymakers and South African society in general is focused on the resistant and persistent challenges of unemployment, poverty and inequality (DHET, 2013). In both the higher education and TVET contexts, social justice perspectives have often been brought to bear on the experiences of students and the creation of curricula (Hlatshwayo & Fomunyam, 2019; Leibowitz & Bozalek, 2015; Luckett & Shay, 2017; Winberg & Winberg, 2017; and in this edited volume). By comparison, the professional development and learning, in formal or informal modes, of lecturers in PSET contexts, is examined far less often through this lens, leading to:

---

[6] See Letseka et al. (2018) for slippage between "open" and "distance" learning, and Francken (2020) for interchangeable use of "open" and "online" learning.

a lack of clarity around what kinds of international, national and institutional policies, curricula, scholarly and pedagogical practices may be required to advance just social arrangements and just ways of relating and access so that students and academics feel that they belong and can participate on an equal footing in this sector. (Hölscher & Bozalek, 2020, p. 5)

Similarly, Daniels challenges the contemporary focus on "promoting efficiency and accountability in education", at the expense of "practices promoting social justice at TVET colleges" (2018, p. iv).

Thus, in this paper, we draw on Fraser's social justice framework to explore whether and in what ways professional learning and development, in the context of open learning, addresses issues of social justice. In the next section, we briefly review Fraser's concept of parity of participation, dimensions of injustice, and outline what might constitute an ameliorative or transformative response to injustice. Further, we consider whether adopting this three-dimensional approach to social justice can prevent the creation of new hurdles, and address pre-existing institutionalised obstacles to full participation in professional development and learning opportunities for TVET lecturers.

Towards parity of participation

A key concept in Fraser's (1996) conceptualisation of social justice is the notion of participatory parity or parity of participation. Fraser links justice and participatory parity, asserting "justice requires social arrangements that permit all (adult) members of society to interact with one another as peers" (1996, p. 30). Initially, she defined 'interact(ing) with one another as peers' to include legal equity, material equity and cultural equity (1996); later, she reduced the emphasis on legal equity in favour of incorporating the axis of political equity (2005). Subsequently, Fraser has insisted that parity "is a qualitative condition, the condition of being a peer, of being on a par with others, of interacting with them on an equal footing" (2007, p. 28), expressed along multiple dimensions of injustice. In the context of this study, the notion of parity of participation encourages us to consider what conditions need to be in place to allow TVET staff to "interact with one another as peers", and what conditions might be in place that prevent them from doing so, in relation to their professional development and learning.

Illuminating economic injustice

Economic injustices occur as the result of distributive injustice or maldistribution of resources in society (Fraser, 1995). Full participation in the social life of any group can be limited by access to material resources creating "inequality in income and property ownership; in access to paid work, education, health care and leisure time; but also more starkly in caloric intake and exposure to environmental toxicity" (Fraser, 1995, p. 68).

Fraser argues that such maldistribution is produced by "social arrangements that institutionalise deprivation, exploitation, and gross disparities in wealth, income, and leisure time" (Fraser, 2007, p. 27). Remedies for maldistribution typically include redistributing income through, for example, taxation, and setting quotas on categories of labour such as affirmative action.

In the context of South Africa, wracked by extreme and increasing inequality (Hundenborn et al., 2019), interventions, which seek to support open learning either directly for students, or indirectly through supporting staff, must consider economic justice. In the context of this study, this might point us to thinking about how considerations of economic equity in relation to professional development and learning opportunities would allow participants to participate as peers. Questions raised by considering economic injustices might include:

- What does it cost staff directly to participate in such opportunities?
- What does it cost staff indirectly to participate in such opportunities?
- What is the opportunity cost for staff should they participate in such opportunities?
- Who might be included or excluded as a result of maldistribution of resources?

Illuminating cultural injustice

Fraser describes the "struggle for recognition" as "the paradigmatic form of political conflict in the late twentieth century" with claims about nationality, ethnicity, 'race', gender, and sexuality (inter alia), superseding the class conflicts of earlier in the century (Fraser, 1995, p. 68). She describes a culturally just context as characterised by equal respect for all participants and equal opportunities for categories of participants to achieve social esteem (Fraser, 2007, 2011). Fraser's (2000, p. 113) particular use of 'status' draws her ideas about recognition, strongly away from recognition as an "intersubjective, affective relation" between individuals, moving it instead towards a macro perspective. Thus, a culturally unjust society is predicated on 'misrecognition' and grounded in:

> institutionalized value patterns that systematically depreciate some categories of people and the qualities associated with them. Precluded, therefore, are institutionalized value patterns that deny some people the status of full partners in interaction – whether by burdening them with excessive ascribed "difference" or by failing to acknowledge their distinctiveness. (Fraser, 2007, p. 27)

Attempts to address issues of cultural injustice have addressed questions of who might be valued in spaces, leading to gender, race or caste quotas in various contexts. However, according to Hölscher and Bozalek, such attempts have tended to "prioritis[e] an individualised, interpersonal reading of misrecognition over an understanding of misrecognition as a status subordination, that is, a structural, macro-level concern" (2020, p. 11).

In the South African context, historically, belonging to particular racial, ethnic or linguistic groups has limited the possibility of students (Calitz, 2018) and staff to participate as peers in academic contexts. Luckett and Shay's interpretation of Fraser, in light of the local education context, argues that her:

> status-based approach to recognition is particularly pertinent to social analysis in a country such as South Africa, where institutionalised racism, founded on essentialist colonial notions of 'race', set up a social hierarchy that justified the capitalist exploitation of black labour and in turn led to the low socio-economic status and poverty of all black people, reinforcing the devaluing and destruction and of their cultures. (2017, p. 6)

Considering issues of cultural inequality in relation to WIL for lecturers might lead us to enquire how a particular category of difference is valued or devalued in the context of professional development and learning opportunities:

- How does misrecognition in relation to gender produce obstacles to participatory parity?
- How does misrecognition in relation to linguistic background produce obstacles to participatory parity?
- How does misrecognition in relation to age produce obstacles to participatory parity?
- How does misrecognition in relation to urban or rural locations produce obstacles to participatory parity?

Illuminating political injustice

By 2009, Fraser's bivalent theory of social justice (which includes the economic and cultural dimensions) had moved towards a trivalent theory (which includes the political dimension). She describes the political dimension as:

> furnish[ing] the stage on which struggles over distribution and recognition are played out. Establishing criteria of social belonging, and thus determining who counts as a member, the political dimension of justice specifies the reach of those other dimensions: it tells us who is included in, and who excluded from, the circle of those entitled to a just distribution and reciprocal recognition. (2009, p. 17)

This dimension focuses on membership and procedure (Fraser, 2009) at three levels. The first is the 'ordinary political' concept of representation or, conversely, misrepresentation. Examples of ordinary political claims, or instances of misrepresentation, include:

> Demands for gender quotas on electoral lists, multicultural rights, indigenous self-government, and provincial autonomy, on the one hand, to demands for campaign finance reform, redistricting, proportional representation, and cumulative voting, on the other. (Fraser, 2010, p. 285)

The second offers the concept of 'misframing', and "concerns the prior establishment of who counts as a member in the first place" (Fraser, 2010, p. 286), and in a corollary, who is not a member. The third is the 'meta-political (mis)representation', which can fruitfully allow us to think about where injustices, and consequently, appeals for justice might be located, for example, "as being located in individual higher education institutions rather than the education system as a whole" (Hölscher & Bozalek, 2020, p. 13).

In the local context, and considering Fraser's understanding of political inequality in relation to WIL, we might ask questions such as:

- Are all staff represented in the WIL initiatives across dimensions of difference such as socio-economic status, gender, language, race and location?
- Are considerations of WIL appropriately "framed" – who is considered to be a "member" in the configurations that offer WIL initiatives, and who is not? To what

extent are TVET lecturers considered to be decision-making members of these configurations?
- Finally, Fraser's notion of 'meta-political (mis)representation' encourages us to look at where initiatives are located – at local, provincial, national and international levels.

Approaches to addressing overlapping dimensions of inequality

While Fraser offers these three dimensions as "analytically discrete" (De Kadt, 2020, p. 875) tools for understanding and responding to inequalities, she urges us to see the economic and cultural dimensions as "usually interimbricated so as to reinforce one another dialectically" (Fraser, 1995, p. 72). North proposed a circular, three sphere interpretation of Fraser's model where issues of economic, cultural and political injustice, "overlap and remain in tension with each other" (2006, p. 509).

Coupled with the dimensions of inequality discussed above, Fraser also offers a useful distinction for categorising initiatives that respond to injustices. While affirmative, sometimes called ameliorative (Hodgkinson-Williams & Trotter, 2018), interventions leave "intact much of the underlying political-economic structure" (Fraser, 1995, p. 84), transformative interventions seek to act on injustices by "dismantling institutionalised obstacles that prevent some people from participating on a par with others, as full partners in social interaction" (Fraser, 2009, p. 16). Luckett and Shay describe affirmative approaches as working "within a given framing or 'grammar' – it accepts the social structures and institutions that have framed the social practices that need changing" (2017, p. 2).

Effectively, affirmative or ameliorative interventions seek to strengthen parity of participation by creating categories of persons who require additional support in relation to an area of injustice, while transformative interventions target the structures that produce the inequality. Thus, transformative approaches "interrogate the frames themselves" such that "new democratic spaces will open up where the voices of the affected can be heard and from where a rethinking of 'how' more just social practices can be implemented will be worked out" (Luckett & Shay, 2017, p. 2).

This study draws on Fraser to understand the design of WIL interventions in relation to participatory parity, and affirmative or transformative approaches to Fraser's imbricating dimensions of economic, cultural and political inequality.

Methodology

The study sought to explore whether and in what ways TVET lecturers' professional learning and development supports DHET's open learning approach while addressing issues of social justice. The nature of the intended study is exploratory and descriptive and so we have opted for a qualitative research design employing a case study method. The case study method affords us a productive way to study a "particularity and complexity of a single case, coming to understand its activity within important circumstances" (Stake, 1995, p. xi). Moreover,

> Case studies accept that there are many variables operating in a single case, and, hence, to catch the implications of these variables usually requires more than one tool for data collection and many sources of evidence. Case studies can blend numerical and qualitative data. (Cohen et al., 2018, p. 376)

This case study makes use of pre-existing, publicly available data such as websites, reports and specially arranged private in-depth interviews or direct email questionnaires to explore key stakeholders' understanding of what shapes the college lecturers' uptake of WIL and more broadly the contribution of WIL to opening up education in the local context more fully.

Data collection and generation methods

Various secondary sources of information were identified as useful to understanding the practices and roles of WIL in the TVET context. These sources included:

- Materials released by the Swiss-South African Cooperation Initiative (SSACI) on their website https://www.ssaci.org.za/
- Reports generated by DHET, including critically, the Qualification Profile of Lecturers Employed in Public TVET Reports (DHET, 2014, 2015, 2016), and the Monitoring and Evaluation Performance Report (DHET, 2020)
- Reports generated by the Education, Training and Development Practices – Sector Education and Training Authority (ETDP SETA, 2018a, 2018b, 2021).

While this data provided a useful framing of the extent of WIL opportunities for staff, its predominantly quantitative nature limited the insights we could draw from this about the extent to which these initiatives contributed to open learning, and in so doing to social justice.

In order to more fully understand the extent to which WIL opportunities for staff could be seen as 'open learning', and addressing injustices in the system, we conducted in-depth interviews with four key DHET staff. Participants from DHET were purposefully (Cohen et al., 2018) selected due to the role they played in the processes involved in establishing collaborative partnerships with industry. Additionally, we interviewed the principal and deputy principal from a TVET college, and received completed email questionnaires from two administrative staff who supported lecturers in gaining WIL placements.

Due to the COVID-19 pandemic, data collection was confined to remote means, resulting in live interviews with six participants. An open, unstructured conversational approach in the interviews with participants yielded productive conversations which were recorded, and subsequently, professionally transcribed.

Data analysis and synthesis

Following a denaturalised approach (Davidson, 2009), in presenting the data from the interviews, we have taken the liberty of removing filler and repeated words, stutters, and grammatical errors from extracts quoted, and translated everything to English when possible. Omissions are indicated by ellipses. The email questionnaire sent, at the principal's suggestion to two staff members responsible for supporting WIL, unfortunately yielded rather constrained responses.

Once data had been collected, it was analysed using a two-step thematic process. Initially the data was examined for how WIL is conceived as a mechanism for TVET lecturer professional development, and then, examined, using Fraser's three-dimensional social justice framework, for the extent to which the initiatives could be described as responding to economic, cultural and political injustices, in ameliorative or transformative ways. Given the relatively small scope of the study, and the mixed access to qualitative data analysis software by the researchers, we opted not to code using proprietary software. Instead, the authors read and re-read, and annotated the interviews manually, and our analysis was reviewed by a reader within the COOL research group.

Considerations of ethics and quality

In our approach to this research, we sought to consider issues of harm and benefit, grounded in a relationally oriented perspective. Ethical clearance for this study was obtained through the University of Cape Town for the entire project, and through DHET, for access to DHET and TVET staff. It was important to us that the participants in our study incurred no harm as a result of being willing to participate in this research. Thus, although direct quotes from interviewees have been included, interviewees are simply referred to as Interviewee 1, 2, etc. Identifying markers such as positions have been removed, and potentially identifying details have been deliberately obscured. Information on named organisations such as SSACI, GIZ and Woolworths was drawn from publicly available reporting. Protection and storage of interview data was aligned with the COOL project requirement, and uploaded to a secure repository and transcribed by a data transcription company that has a track record of undertaking confidential transcriptions.

The trustworthiness of contemporary qualitative, naturalistic research often draws on concepts such as 'credibility', 'reliability', 'transferability', and 'confirmability' (Chowdhury, 2015; Stenfors et al., 2020). Credibility requires that we question the plausibility of our findings. The participation of key role-players in the national WIL programme for TVET staff, and exploration of the three larger WIL programmes strengthens the plausibility of this study. However, credibility is weakened by limited access to internal reports for these WIL programmes. Transferability, or the applicability of these findings in other contexts (Kyngäs et al., 2020) is a key criterion for this study. The value of this research lies not only in evaluating sampled WIL programmes through a social justice lens, but in so doing, to validate this lens as a useful design tool for future interventions.

Insights into WIL for TVET lecturers in the South African context

In trying to understand the contribution of work integrated learning to opening up education and addressing inequalities that impacted on lecturers' professional learning and development, we addressed the following questions:

- How did interviewees describe the need for WIL for Professional Learning and Development for TVET lecturers?
- Who took what roles in finding workplace-based placements for TVET lecturers??
- What structures exist to support WIL for TVET lecturers?
- How do collaborative linkages, with international and local partners, impact on WIL for TVET lecturers?
- What experiences did interviewees have of WIL opportunities for TVET lecturers?

Need for WIL for professional learning and development of TVET lecturers

It is widely acknowledged, as discussed earlier, that DHET faces a complex challenge with regard to the professional development of lecturers. In response to this widely held belief, from 2018, DHET established a target for placing 20% of staff in WIL opportunities, however, finding placements for this many staff proved to be challenging (Interviewee 2). As interviewee 2 noted, "Now that was a huge toll ... So it's not really possible." Similarly, Interviewee 1 pointed to a 30% target, but did not specify the time frame, noting that this was a "big ask". In the recently published, *Teaching and Learning Plan 2021 for Technical and Vocational Education and Training (TVET) Colleges*, DHET affirms the following target for lecturers: "10% of lecturers placed in WPBL/WBE (NB: target of 30% annually by 2022)" (DHET, 2021, p. 22). These varying targets (10-30%) unfortunately seem to result in some confusion and make evaluation of WIL over time quite complicated.

As many TVET lecturers have been employed directly from graduation or from school teaching positions, practical skills in relation to professional roles in industry, commerce or retail are often in short supply. Interviewee 2 described WIL learning for staff as playing "a very critical role", emphasising the importance of lecturers "doing the practical training", while continuing to teach. Examination of reports on one of the longest-standing linkages with SSACI, however, pointed to the focus often being on supporting students' WIL experience, and skilling lecturers in the support of this, with only minor attention being paid to the technical skill of the lecturers themselves. For example, much of the SSACI focus in terms of lecturing staff has been in relation to supporting staff to manage the following activities in relation to WIL:

> (a) integrate lessons learned at the workplace back into college curricula, (b) manage legal liabilities (including the provision of personal protective equipment and preventing injuries to students and damage to equipment), and (c) monitor and assess learners' performance during their WBE periods. (SSACI, 2017)

From 2019, a project, under the ambit of GIZ, was run by the Inter-Company Training Center in Eastern Bavaria (Überbetriebliches Bildungszentrum in Ostbayern [ÜBZO]). The project adopted a blended model, comprising of a kick-off meeting, an eight-week e-learning modules and online tutoring block, a week-long intensive training block, another online learning block, followed by a week-long intensive training block, a period of implementation in the TVET colleges, followed by coaching and experience exchange.

In the interviews with DHET staff, it became abundantly clear that WIL provides much more than technical skills that could be acquired through other modes of learning. For example, Interviewee 1 described being invited to join a practical examination in a hospitality course in a poorly resourced, rural college. In addition to fairly basic amenities with which to work, students lacked an appreciation of common practices in the hospitality industry such as serving beverages on a tray or placing a napkin for a client. Interviewee 1 explained that the lack of experience of lecturers in broader work contexts had implications both for what they taught and how they assessed their students.

> They don't know what they don't know. So, they teach the students for instance what they know. Now, their perception, their framework is the students did so well, I'm giving them

nine out of ten, for instance. Now you come into another province and ... and they give the student eight out of ten because their framework is bigger. What happens is the one with nine out of ten ends up in industry with actually no framework of what he or she must be doing. (Interviewee 1)

Given the disparities in access to experiences in the South African context, exposing lecturers and students to experiences outside of their personal framework of experience is critical to better prepare students from a wide diversity of backgrounds for the workplace.

Roles in finding workplace-based placements

Whose responsibility it was to secure workplace-based opportunities for staff was addressed by a number of interviewees. Interviewee 2 pointed out that in a notable case, where a college seemed to be particularly successful, partners from business and industry sought them out to offer workplace-based opportunities:

> They are saying to me, now it is business and industries coming to them, it's not them going more to them, to industries and businesses, because of the attitudes that they've changed, because of the work that the outside world is seeing that they are doing. And I can tell you, that college is ... It's moving. (Interviewee 2)

Furthermore, Interviewee 2 named a number of colleges that fared well in finding workplace-based opportunities for lecturers, attributing them having a "very good and very strong manager who could assist them to place more lecturers." Interviewee 3 addressed the issue of finding workplace learning opportunities for staff and student simultaneously, noting:

> The thing is, though, that ... if our colleges were to succeed, and we have to get the work placement thing right, ... *they're* [verbal emphasis] going to have to do this. *They* are going to have to understand who are the companies in my area ... While it has been difficult, I think it's essential.... Our colleges have to become more, uh, company focused in the end. (Interviewee 3)

Interviewee 2, however, pointed to the need for centralised involvement in creating opportunities for workplace-based placements. S/he also explained that having DHET representation in industry forums was critical to building relationships and initiating WIL projects. This needed to be paired with having "someone in a senior position monitoring what the colleges are doing with these clients" (Interviewee 1) in order to ensure the value and sustainability of projects.

Structures supporting WIL for lecturers

Interviewees made mention of various structures, existing, proposed and or now defunct that were seen as necessary in supporting WIL for lecturers, such as the South African Institute for Vocational, Education and Training (SAIVCET), WIL Forums, and WIL Reporting and Placement Offices.

A key provincial structure that was mentioned as potentially supporting WIL for lecturers (and students) is the WIL Forum. Interviewee 2 referred to this when describing how projects are developed: "I open it up, present it to the WIL Forum and then the WIL Forum is taking it into colleges." These WIL Forums are structured to enable dialogue between DHET, colleges, TVET college lecturers and industry:

> What we did in the Western and Northern Cape, and it's also now rolling out into the other provinces, we have forums. And one of our forums is the Work Integrated Learning Forum where we discuss things like placement and why do lecturers not want to go into industry and why do industry struggle with students? Why don't they want some of the TVET students? (Interviewee 2)

No mention was made of such forums in other provinces, and a search of DHET sites and materials did not yield further mention of WIL forums in other contexts.

WIL Reporting and Placement Offices, where they exist, play a key role in enabling reporting and monitoring on WIL learning. Interviewee 1 emphasised the extent to which centralising reporting on WIL, while new, could have a substantial impact on encouraging the uptake of WIL activities for lecturers.

> You see, there was always lecturer placement, but there was never a thing that the strat (strategic) plans had to make provision for all the colleges that lecturers must be placed … It's the mandate of the minister – lecturer placement, student placement, career guidance. And they focus now much more because the principals will sit with the regional managers and their regional managers will say, why did you not do this, this and that? And you did not meet the target. So, it goes down then to your WIL people at colleges, etc. (Interviewee 1)

Interviewee 1 also made explicit mention of provincial WIL placement offices, which were unfortunately not available in all provinces.

An additional critical structure to support the uptake, monitoring and evaluation of WIL for lecturers may be SAIVCET. Envisaged as a coordinating structure, SAIVCET has "been long in the making" (Interviewee 4) with responsibilities related to, inter alia, curriculum development, industry partnerships, promoting the dual-system apprenticeship programme, the Centres of Specialisation Programme, and crucially, lecturer development. Despite being first mentioned in policy in 2013, at the time of interviewing, Interviewee 4 indicated that "it's never been 'activated' as a piece of legislation … one of the difficulties is to introduce yet another entity". However, Interviewee 4 noted: "we're doing quite a bit of work on lecturer development – professionalisation of lecturers and continuous professional development."

Collaborative linkages with international organisations

In interviews with DHET representatives, a number of partnerships between DHET or the SETAs and international agencies or organisations were discussed as routes to offering professional learning and development for TVET lecturers through WIL.

Swiss South African Collaborative Initiative (SSACI) partnership with DHET

As WIL is a critical aspect of lecturer development, DHET partnered with the Swiss South African Collaborative Initiative (SAACI), to create opportunities for TVET lecturer development.

> SSACI really did assist TVET colleges and TVET college lecturers to prepare them for placements, teach them about the elements of WIL. What is required, what should be expected, how they should integrate within the industry space, and how to do it basically. (Interviewee 2)

Such initiatives have been adopted to address the reports of poor effectiveness of the TVET colleges in terms of lecturer effectiveness and poor responsiveness to the needs of students (DHET, 2012b).

The SSACI project began in early 2014 and "successfully placed hundreds of lecturers in industry for short periods of time; in the process developing skills and improving alignment between practices in education and industry" (Van der Bijl, 2020, p. 17).

There are detailed reports on the successes and challenges of the SSACI project (see Smith, 2016). The SSACI project with DHET reached lecturers from about 28 colleges (Interviewee 2).

> So from there, because SSACI's programme came to an end there, ... then SSACI proceeded with other TVET colleges. But because we could not endorse SSACI as the only organisation that could assist colleges with WIL, we then did not endorse it. (Interviewee 2)

While some TVET colleges proceeded with further WIL for lecturers with the SSACI, others decided to create their own linkages, consequently preventing standardisation across all TVET colleges.

> We have a strategy target which requires us to one, assist colleges to get into partnerships, signing protocols with industry for work integrated learning and work-based exposure and workplace-based learning for students as well. (Interviewee 2)

However, as SSACI was not endorsed by DHET, the formal project ended in 2017, with SSACI continuing to work with individuals and colleges on an ad hoc basis. This remains one of multiple projects supporting WIL for lecturers in the South African landscape.

Deutsche Gesellschaft für Internationale Zusammenarbeit (GIZ) with DHET

Another current partnership with the German based organisation, GIZ, caters for lecturer capacity building. This programme began in 2020, with a total of 40 participants in areas such as electrical and plumbing services. This program is based on a blended mode for the training of lecturers, thus lecturers have the opportunity to relate the theory gained over this program to practice when they are placed in work integrated learning posts. The present project has partnered with SAR Technologies based in Pretoria. Lecturers participating in this programme have an opportunity to be placed at SAR Technologies, allowing lecturers to develop both scientific knowledge and practical skills. As Interviewee 2 pointed out:

> According to the science, you don't install like this, this is what you must do, and so on. And one gap we have discovered from this practical WIL kind of a project, is that some of our lecturers are lacking in knowledge about the South African National Standards. (Interviewee 2)

Such WIL opportunities allow for the identification of knowledge gaps that impact on lecturers' teaching practice. Consequently, these programs can then address those knowledge gaps moving forward. In doing so, the likelihood of misconceptions being carried over to students is reduced.

This blended learning approach in teaching and learning for lecturers is aligned with the dual system apprenticeship programmes that are being employed in countries such as Switzerland and Germany. The curricula for such programmes are designed around four pillars namely:

1. curriculum and material development,
2. lecturer development or CPD,
3. partnerships (with the intent of supporting the curriculum development), and
4. skills planning (how is the TVET college geared to meet the skills demand).

In order for TVET lecturers to join the GIZ programme, they need to respond to the DHET invitation sent to all colleges and complete the online application. Interviewee 2 explained that the rationale behind the use of an online application is attributed to the fact that lecturer commitment and motivation is required. At present CPD points are awarded to lecturers that engage in professional development programmes. Interviewee 2, however, asserts that the rewarding of points without concomitant financial and status rewards, is unlikely to sufficiently incentivise staff. Interviewee 2 links the need for multiple reward structures to histories of devaluing of TVET lecturers, highlighting the need to ensure that financial rewards were paired with socially significant rewards.

It is interesting to note that, under the then Department of Education (DoE), TVET colleges were previously referred to as Further Education and Training Colleges and lecturers were pegged at a much lower salary scale. Although post-2011, attempts were made by DHET to bring salaries on par across the TVET sector[7], the misperception that TVET lecturers are paid more in other countries than in South Africa still persists.

British Council partnership with the merSETA

Interviewee 2 briefly made mention of the British Council partnership with the Manufacturing, Engineering and Related Services Sector Education and Training Authority (merSETA) which sought to connect "selected TVET colleges with United Kingdom colleges in terms of curriculum development, management capacity building and TVET lecturer development"

---

[7] Minister Education, Blade Nzimande, https://pmg.org.za/committee-question/9539/

(merSETA, 2021, p. 56). This was offered as another example of the kinds of collaborative linkages that have been pursued to support WIL.

Germany's KfW Development Bank with DHET

In a more recent partnership, the German Embassy announced the signing of an agreement between Germany's KfW Development Bank and DHET in September 2020 to establish an in-service skills development centre for TVET lecturers at Ekurhuleni East College (Embassy of the Federal Republic of Germany, 2020). As a part of this agreement, DHET will receive a grant of €8.25 million[8]. Accessible to TVET college lecturers from across South Africa, the centre will provide vocational training in the fields of electrical and mechanical engineering.

Collaborative linkages with local business and industry

According to Interviewee 1, a number of collaborative linkages with local businesses, organisations and industry have been developed. For illustrative purposes, we discuss one in this paper. In some instances, these linkages are driven by DHET staff, and in others are initiated by TVET colleges or business and industry.

Woolworths partnership with the W&RSETA

DHET has nurtured a number of long-standing linkages with local retailers that support WIL for lecturers. A good example of this is the Inside Retail Programme[9], a five-day, work-based placement offering with Woolworths that typically runs during the mid-year vacation. Having run since 2013, the Inside Retail Programme annually supports 30 participants from a wide range of colleges[10]. As Interviewee 1 explained:

> Woolworths is not just wholesale and retail. It's accounting, it's marketing. ... But to get [lecturers] there is a massive story and you can only do 30 at a time. Woolworths are sponsoring this ... it's millions. You must see the things they get. They go to supply chains, they go to factories. And Woolworths give state of the art food and all kinds of things. They [Woolworths] don't pay them. They say they're doing them a favour. But I said when we started speaking about this and we have to report on strat plans, etc., I said these people need to get money. Even if you have a travel allowance, but they need to feel worthy ... proud of this. (Interviewee 1)

This project is linked to the Wholesale and Retail Sector Education and Training Authority (W&RSETA), but unlike the formal offerings through the SETAs, it does not offer a qualification or a stipend to staff. In addition to established projects such as the Inside Retail programme, the W&RSETA facilitates connecting individual lecturers from specific colleges to companies

---

[8] Notes taken from https://www.youtube.com/watch?v=wFrtfn8J21w
[9] https://www.woolworths.co.za/images/elasticera/New_Site/Corporate/lecturer_guide_online.pdf
[10] For example, in 2018, attendees included lecturers from the College of Cape Town, False Bay College, Northlink College, Boland College, and South Cape College plus the Cape Peninsula University of Technology (CPUT), Mthashana College. West Coast College. Buffalo City College, Esayidi College, and Gert Sibande College.

offering workplace experience or exposure via an application process on their website[11]. Hosting companies are compensated at a rate of R1000 per lecturer per day, and provided with a list of required activities, linked to the specific subjects taught. Hosting companies will sign-off on lecturers' logbooks, report on attendance and conduct of lecturers, and make suggestions about improvement areas[12].

Collaborative linkages with higher education institutions

WIL opportunities can be offered to staff through structured, formal qualifications. As early as 2013, DHET established key qualifications for TVET staff in the *Policy on Professional Qualifications for Lecturers in Technical and Vocational Education and Training* (DHET, 2013b). In this document, DHET established professional qualifications for TVET lecturers, including a Diploma, a Bachelor of Education, and an Advanced Diploma in Technical and Vocational Teaching. At the same time, post-professional qualifications, including an Advanced Certificate, an Advanced Diploma, and a Postgraduate Diploma in Technical and Vocational Teaching were established. This laid the groundwork for a DHET project funded by the European Union, for 14 universities nationally to offer these qualifications. This policy reiterated the importance of a work-based component asserting that

> A strong workplace component must be built into lecturer qualification programmes for programmes that prepare lecturers to teach the practical or workshop-based components of programmes, in order that lecturers are able to prepare learners for the demands and requirements of the workplace. (DHET, 2013b, p. 12)

It further defined workplace as encompassing both the educational workspace, essentially requiring teaching practicums, similar to those undertaken in teacher education; and workplaces in industry, service, commerce and retail, supporting the development of the professional identity of educators.

Since then, as part of the Teaching and Learning Development Capacity Improvement Programme (TLDCIP) funded by the EU and co-ordinated by DHET, a number of institutions (Sethusha, 2020) have designed, received accreditation for (2018 to date), developed and rolled out professional and post-professional qualifications for TVET lecturers. In certain instances, TVET employees have already registered and completed these qualifications. For example, Nelson Mandela University formed partnerships with eight local TVET colleges, resulting in "486 students both part-time and full-time, 187 graduating soon with 21 cum laude"[13], and Tshwane University of Technology's Advanced Diploma in Technical and Vocational Teaching was accredited in 2019, and rolled out in 2020, graduating 56 students from four colleges.[14]

---

[11] https://www.wrseta.org.za/

[12] An example of the detail on the contracts for Expression of Interest can be found here: https://www.wrseta.org.za/downloads/Epression%20of%20interest%20-%2029%20July.pdf

[13] https://www.wrseta.org.za/downloads/Epression%20of%20interest%20-%2029%20July.pdf

[14] https://www.wrseta.org.za/downloads/Epression%20of%20interest%20-%2029%20July.pdf

Reported experiences of WIL

In addition to reflecting on the range of projects supporting WIL as a form of professional learning and development, participants in this study commented on the experiences participants had of these WIL learning opportunities. Interviewees commented on the perceived quality of staff engagement with WIL opportunities, and on the economic and cultural obstacles related to staff attendance at these opportunities.

Interviewees also raised the nature and quality of the staff engagements during WIL. This is expressed clearly by Interviewee 2 who said:

> They were very clear to say, for instance, the issue of placing lecturers just for observation of, or exposure, it's not enough. It's actually wasting industry's time, because lecturers come in for a day or two, they are like visitors. Somebody has to take his time away from production and walk them around and so on. It's not really productive ... They would like to see lecturers getting immersed so that they then have a clear understanding of what it means to be in an industry and how industry conducts business. And really learn the practical side, which I agree with. (Interviewee 2)

Placement of staff during weekend and non-contact times was difficult, as staff saw this as imposing on their private time. Interviewee 1 explained:

> Now the government says you need to go and do some in-service training and they don't want to because there's no remuneration. They don't see it as an extra because they're tired. So, we have big problems regarding that. (Interviewee 1)

Similarly, Interviewee 2 noted:

> Some lecturers would agree to go to industries on Saturdays, and businesses of course. Either on Saturdays or they would do during their college closure periods. But colleges reported that most of the lecturers are reluctant, because lecturers were looking at having to be remunerated for that. (Interviewee 2)

Unlike lecturers enrolled in formal qualifications who are eligible for bursaries through the SETAs, lecturers undertaking workplace-based learning do so at their own cost. In some cases, industry partners may provide some remuneration, or provide accommodation and/or meals but this is by no means mandated.

Interviews noted that no financial provision was made to support the financial implications and cost factors involved in getting to these WIL sites, even when these necessitated travelling distances, which has specific implications for rurall campuses. For example, Interviewee 2 noted:

> And can you imagine the prestige of going to present a paper internationally or even within Africa or even within the country and all the costs are paid for you? Travelling, accommodation and everything, overnight allowances and everything. Look, that will inspire our lecturers. (Interviewee 2)

Interviewee 2 went on to contextualize this statement in light of the historical inequalities and contemporary fall in status experienced by lecturing staff.

A social justice perspective on WIL for lecturers

In the next section, we take two steps using Fraser's social justice framework. First, we ask how the WIL initiatives proposed by DHET aspire to participatory parity and, in so doing, address economic, cultural and political injustices experienced by staff in ameliorative or transformative ways. Second, we describe the stubborn economic, cultural and political injustices that continue to prevent TVET college staff from participating fully in formal or work integrated professional learning and development.

Addressing economic injustice

As Adendorff and Van Wyk report (2016), the economic burden of professional learning and development is often carried directly by individual staff. Based on a recent range of advertisements, lecturer salaries (PL1) range from just over R211 000 to around R345 297 per year; senior lecturer salaries (PL2) salaries appear to range from R347 703–R411 147[15]. These salaries are roughly equivalent to the salaries of high school teachers[16]. In the context of South Africa's rate of unemployment, however, such staff may seem comparatively well paid, particularly in the case of those working at colleges in rural or historically economically under-developed homelands. In these cases, stably employed TVET lecturers may have relatively a large network of dependents, and be subject to "black tax"[17] (Mashiloane, 2019).

Professional learning and development, in both formal and work integrated learning forms, incurs travel and living costs. Travel to and from sites of formal study, usually at universities and universities of technology, incur a cost that staff carry in a direct and personal capacity. Similarly, travel to and from sites of vocational learning, usually at national companies, located at industrial sites close to urban areas, also often incur a cost that staff carry in a personal capacity. In instances where DHET or TVET colleges are able to recompense staff with a living stipend and travel allowances, interviewees report more positive attitudes to and greater uptake of training. Thus, provision of such stipends is likely to have an ameliorative effect on economic demands. Ideally, staff should be able to access such training without incurring these costs; making such opportunities more widely available such that travel costs are substantially reduced or even eliminated would be a transformative act.

Interviewees also pointed to the indirect costs and opportunity costs of professional learning and development, in both formal and work integrated learning forms. Indirect costs refer to the costs that a TVET lecture might incur in order to be available to participate in professional learning and development activities such as finding and compensating a

---

[15] These ranges were built using the vacancies on the following sites https://www.westcoastcollege.co.za/vacancies-positions-7417-7617/, https://tnc.edu.za/archives/vacancies.php, https://www.cct.edu.za/index.php/en/vacancies/academic-positions, https://edupstairs.org/wp-content/uploads/2021/01/25JANUARY2021-Adverts.pdf

[16] https://pmg.org.za/committee-question/9539/

[17] Black tax is used in the South African context to refer to the financial contribution in the form of remittances made by employed, increasingly financially independent black people to their less financially secure families. This is slightly different from how it is used in the United States. For more on this, see Mangoma & Wilson-Prangley (2019).

baby-sitter, or acquiring suitable equipment and clothing for vocational work. Opportunity costs refer to income that is foregone. It is common practice for TVET lecturers to have additional jobs, colloquially referred to as 'side hustles', which supplement their salary. This is particularly true for those who work in vocational roles, as opposed to general education posts. Participating in work integrated learning reduces TVET lecturers' opportunities to engage in paid work after hours, on weekends, or during the holidays. One ameliorative approach to the opportunity cost of participating in work integrated, professional learning and development include the payment of a stipend for attendance. This stipend should at least cover the potential income lost. However, funding such a stipend can incur costs for the state at a time when there are increasing pressures to reduce budgets. An alternative ameliorative approach is to link work integrated learning to formal professional learning and development qualifications, allowing participants to claim formal credits for work integrated learning, against their formal assessment.

Fraser's theory of social justice also raises the question of who might be included or excluded from specific activities as a result of maldistribution of resources. In the South African context, maldistribution of resources is still strongly linked to dimensions of identity, such as race, linguistic background, gender and geographical location, pointing us in the direction of Fraser's claim that economic and cultural dimensions of inequality often work to entrench inequalities and exclusions. While both the higher education and community college sectors report on staffing, in the annual Statistics on Post-School Education and Training in South Africa (see for example, DHET, 2016, 2017, 2018), the TVET college sector does not report on staffing in this document, making evidence-based research very difficult.

Addressing cultural injustice

If we consider who takes responsibility for identifying opportunities for workplace-based placement for lecturers through the dimension of cultural injustice, the complexity of the issue comes into focus. As Mgijima (2014) and Chetram (2017) suggest, much responsibility for workplace-based placement for lecturers is currently deemed to be an individual responsibility or the responsibility of the college in question. However, valuing colleges that are successful in placing their staff as 'inspiring' (Interviewee 2) runs the risk of misrecognising participants, and creating unjust hierarchies of value, premised on factors outside of participants' control. Moves towards strong centralised support for identifying opportunities for workplace-based placement can address inequalities related to misrecognising not just participants but also institutions and contexts, as Interviewee 1 noted: "with some colleges, if you say for instance a name, the industry will jump. If it's another college, they say no".

The WIL initiatives supporting professional learning and development initiated by DHET are premised on the recognition that not all TVET staff have the same cultural capital to draw on in their professional practice. Due to staffing shortages, many staff who have been educated within the TVET system are hired immediately after graduation. These staff have not had an opportunity to develop vocational knowledge in the field. In designing CPD WIL opportunities for staff, misrecognition of participants can lead to activities and programmes which inadvertently prevent parity of participation. Interviewees referred to staff feedback which suggests that this is a concern. Interviewees, reflecting on the design of programmes indicated that programmes that deliberately prepared all participants to participate in workspaces were well received. For example, by making explicit workplace expectations that might not be equally understood, activities and programmes allow all participants, regardless of, for example, gender or linguistic background, to have a better chance at participating fully in, and gaining the most from, the training.

In some cases, issues of misrecognition intersect with economic standing to amplify inequalities and exclusions. For example, not all staff are able to participate equally in WIL opportunities on grounds of gender. In many ways, South Africa remains a fairly conservative country with household responsibilities and childcare remaining largely the province of women (Erse et al., 2021; Hatch & Posel, 2018). This is particularly the case in rural households. In cases where female lecturers from more rural colleges are required to travel to industrial or commercial centres for WIL, they must identify someone able to take care of children or elderly family members. This may incur a direct cost, for example, for a nanny or carer to stay an additional day, or a social obligation to a relative may be in place. In either case, it remains easier for male lecturers in, or close to, urban centres to access WIL opportunities, than their rural, female counterparts.

Addressing political injustice

Wedekind reports the prevalence of a "top-down culture of management and governance in the Colleges and the largely disempowered role of staff" (2016b, p. 11). Such a culture may well be associated with instances of political injustice, including a lack of consultation with staff about the nature of and need for professional development and learning opportunities. However, interviews with DHET representatives working on professional learning and development for staff through WIL suggest that DHET sees its role as brokering and supporting relationships between TVET colleges and the private sector. At first glance this seems like an enabling position, creating conditions for staff in TVET colleges to take greater ownership of professional development and learning opportunities, and creating the possibility of greater diversity in linkages and collaborations. In Fraser's terms, one might claim that enabling colleges to seek out opportunities for professional learning and development for staff through WIL, effectively freeing them from 'endorsed' national programmes, has an ameliorative effect on an issue of political injustice.

However, given the complex network of economic and cultural inequalities within which TVET colleges are located, such 'freedom' may unwittingly entrench existing inequalities. For example, in cases where colleges are located at a distance from industrial hubs, access to opportunities for professional learning and development though WIL are likely to be limited. Access to these opportunities is further likely to be limited to those individuals who are able to step away from home and other responsibilities, in line with local distributions of labour and formulations of identity.

The establishment of structures that enable democratic conversation between various stakeholders in the process is critical in addressing issues of political inequality. The WIL forums, for example, provide in specific provinces key opportunities for all stakeholders to provide direct feedback about their WIL experience to college management, DHET and industry partners. Such forums have the potential to open up "who counts as a member", and who can be "included in, and who excluded from, the circle of those entitled to a just distribution and reciprocal recognition" (Fraser, 2009, p. 17).

Obstacles to designing WIL activities and programmes (intersecting dimensions)

While Fraser's social justice framework and the notion of parity of participation are very useful as a tool for thinking about the design of WIL activities and programmes, there were issues raised in interviews that did not fit neatly into the separate dimensions of the framework. In some cases, these issues seemed to sit at the intersections of dimensions of inequality, such as at the intersection of economic maldistribution and cultural misrecognition, and are thus resistant to interventions that seek to address these separately.

Enabling the successful offering of WIL opportunities by commerce and industry requires addressing the capacity of lecturers to be useful in the WIL placements. While social justice is often applied as a concern with the experiences of the most vulnerable in a particular claim, attention must be given as to how to create genuinely, mutually beneficial relationships. In the case of WIL, this might mean developing long term rather than short term relationships between individual lecturers and specific worksites. This would allow a lecturer to visit perhaps fairly briefly, but, over time, to develop relationships at, and an understanding of, a particular worksite that would remediate their 'visitor' status. Potentially, developing stronger collaboration through more localised curricula between TVET colleges and worksites might similarly address the role of lecturer as 'visitor' in the workplace. This more agential activity overlaps with the more 'political' voice of the lecturer and the prevailing culture of the particular worksites in commerce and industry.

Another obstacle that does not fit discretely into a specific dimension of Fraser's framework is the effect of culture on the uptake of WIL opportunities, highlighting the extent to which these dimensions are entwined, what Fraser refers to as "imbricated". Interviewees comments about the culture of institutions can be seen as responding to economic, cultural and political practices that support the persistence of cultures such as those that underpin Interviewee 2's comment, when they say, "But obviously, we know, given the economics of our country and the lifestyles that people live, people always look out to say, what is in there for me? What comes to me? Is there any cash benefit that is coming to me?"

Interviewee 2's comment highlights how lecturers choices sit at the intersection of Fraser's dimensions: economic (lecturers can earn more running their own businesses), the political (have the agency to decide over what suits them best – i.e., they are not 'forced' into WIL) and the prevailing culture of not routinely taking up opportunities for WIL.

The value of a social justice lens is that it assists in illuminating the economic, cultural and political injustices separately and together and thereby aids us to consider the interactions and entwinements in any intervention, such as WIL as a form of professional development, and alerts us to the possible entanglements that may undermine the best made plans from DHET, industry or the TVET colleges.

Limitations of this research and avenues for future study

Access to staff for this study was limited by the COVID-19 pandemic, resulting in a chapter that, in many ways, offers as many questions as empirically supported answers. However, there is substantial opportunity here for further study that engages directly with the staff designing and implementing professional learning and development opportunities, both in its formal modes and through work integrated learning, and for research that engages directly with staff taking up these learning opportunities. The other substantial limitation of the study was related to access to statistics and documentation. The reporting practices around professional development for lecturers at TVET colleges have been in flux over the last 10 years, and the TVET college sector is not publicly reported on by the national government, in the same way as the remainder of the higher education sector. Making data on staffing, including equity reporting, in the TVET sector, publicly available would substantially assist further studies in this area.

Conclusion and recommendations

A social justice perspective on professional learning and development of TVET lecturers, as with any other staff, points in two directions: (1) responding to the injustices faced by the staff themselves as experiencing participatory parity in the roles as participants and in their work context as lecturers; and (2) through the design of the programmes, on enabling staff to create and advocate for learning conditions that approach participatory parity for students. Many of the design decisions and implementation choices that shape the professional learning and development of staff through WIL are ameliorative. They seek to respond to economic, cultural and, to a lesser but significant degree, political injustices that inhibit TVET lecturers from participating fully in learning experiences.

Considering this issue through Fraser's interest in political inequality points to fruitful ground for further change in the sector. This could include more open and consistent reporting practices, and the creation, and strengthening of structures, such as SAIVCET, the Work Integrated Learning Forum and the WIL Reporting and Placement Offices, would be a productive step in supporting WIL for lecturers. Additionally, a systematic framework would make evaluating interventions more rigorous, by providing a shared framework for understanding value creation.

Although DHET's 'open learning' approach to education has an implicit social justice imperative, adopting a more systematic framework for social justice in the PSET sector that encompassed a wider range of stakeholders, particularly through explicitly including staff, would strengthen the possibility of interventions to create more socially just professional learning opportunities.

Acknowledgements

Many thanks to the WIL experts whose inputs made this chapter possible, as well as staff from Ekurhuleni West TVET College. Special thanks are due to reviewers Dr Henri Jacobs and Dr Cookie Govender for their thoughtful, incisive feedback on the chapter, Emeritus Associate Professor Cheryl Ann Hodgkinson-Williams for valuable feedback, and Dr Tabisa Mayisela for guiding the entire COOL project. Thanks are also due to the Centre for Innovation in Learning and Teaching at the University of Cape Town, which hosted the COOL project, and the South African Department of Higher Education and Training for funding it.

References

Adendorff, M., & Van Wyk, C. (2016). Offering TVET college lecturers increased access to professional qualification programmes through a national open learning system in South Africa. http://dspace.col.org/bitstream/handle/11599/2572/PDF?sequence=1&isAllowed=y

Akoojee, S. (2016). Developmental TVET rhetoric in-action: The White Paper for Post-School Education and Training in South Africa. *International Journal for Research in Vocational Education and Training*, 3(1), 1–15.

Allais, S., Cooper, A., & Shalem, Y. (2019). Rupturing or reinforcing inequality? The role of education in South Africa today. *Transformation: Critical Perspectives on Southern Africa*, 101(1), 105–126. https://muse.jhu.edu/article/745637/pdf

Atkinson, G. (2016). Work-based learning and work-integrated learning: Fostering engagement with employers. National Centre for Vocational Education Research, Adelaide. https://files.eric.ed.gov/fulltext/ED568154.pdf

Badenhorst, J. W., & Radile, R. S. (2018). Poor performance at TVET colleges: Conceptualising a distributed instructional leadership approach as a solution. *Africa Education Review*, 15(3), 91–112.

Batholmeus, P., & Pop, C. (2019). Enablers of work-integrated learning in technical vocational education and training teacher education. *International Journal of Work-Integrated Learning*, 20(2), 147–159.

Beukes, J. A. G. (2018). The need for the development of formal qualifications for TVET lecturers. In *Proceedings of International Academic Conferences* (No. 6508641). International Institute of Social and Economic Sciences.

Blom, R. (2016). Throwing good money after bad: Barriers in South African vocational teachers experience in becoming competent educators. In A. Kraak, A. Paterson & K. Bok (Eds.), *Change management in TVET colleges: Lessons learned from the field of practice* (pp. 47–63). African Minds.

Blom, R. (2019). Politics or pedagogy? The emergence of workplace-based learning in South Africa. In J. Talbot (Ed.), *Global perspectives on work-based learning initiatives* (pp. 26–56). IGI Global. DOI: 10.4018/978-1-5225-6977-0.ch002

Buthelezi, Z. (2018). Lecturer experiences of TVET college challenges in the post-apartheid era: A case of unintended consequences of educational reform in South Africa. *Journal of Vocational Education & Training*, 70(3), 364–383. https://doi.org/10.1080/13636820.2018.1437062

Calitz, T. (2018). Recognition as reparation: A participatory approach to (mis)recognition and decolonisation in South African higher education. *Educational Research for Social Change*, 7(SPE), 46–59. http://www.scielo.org.za/pdf/ersc/v7nspe/05.pdf

CHE (Council on Higher Education). (2011). Work-integrated learning: Good practice guide. *Higher Education Monitor*, 12. http://www.che.ac.za/sites/default/files/publications/Higher_Education_Monitor_12.pdf

Chetram, R. (2017). The management of continuous professional development at a TVET college in KwaZulu-Natal [Master's dissertation, University of South Africa]. https://core.ac.uk/download/pdf/158576844.pdf

Chowdhury, I. A. (2015). Issue of quality in qualitative research: An overview. *Innovative Issues and Approaches in Social Sciences*, 8(1), 142–162. https://citeseerx.ist.psu.edu/viewdoc/download?doi=10.1.1.681.6965&rep=rep1&type=pdf#page=142

Cohen, L., Manion, L., & Morrison, K. (2018). *Research methods in education* (8th ed.). Routledge.

Cosser, M., Netshitangani, T., Twalo, T., Rogers, S., Mokgatle, G., Mncwango, B., et al. (2011). *Further education and training colleges in South Africa at a glance in 2010*. HSRC Press.

Davidson, C. (2009). Transcription: Imperatives for qualitative research. *International Journal of Qualitative Methods*, 8(2), 35–52. https://journals.sagepub.com/doi/pdf/10.1177/160940690900800206

De Kadt, E. (2020). Promoting social justice in teaching and learning in higher education through professional development. *Teaching in Higher Education*, 25(7), 872–887. https://doi.org/10.1080/13562517.2019.1617685

DHET (Department of Higher Education and Training). (2011). The minimum requirements for teacher education qualifications (MRTEQ). Government Printer. https://www.dhet.gov.za/Teacher%20Education/National%20Qualifications%20Framework%20Act%2067_2008%20Revised%20Policy%20for%20Teacher%20Education%20Quilifications.pdf

DHET. (2013a). White paper for post-school education and training: Building an expanded, effective and integrated post-school system. *Government Gazette*, 37229. https://www.gov.za/documents/white-paper-post-school-education-and-training-building-expanded-effective-and-integrated

DHET. (2013b). Policy on professional qualifications for lecturers in technical and vocational education and training. Government Printers. https://www.dhet.gov.za/Gazette/Policy%20on%20professional%20qualifications%20for%20lecturers%20in%20technical%20and%20vocational%20education%20and%20training.pdf

DHET. (2014). Qualification profile of lecturers employed in public technical and vocational education and training colleges in South Africa in 2014. https://www.dhet.gov.za/Teacher%20Education%20Reports/DHET%20%20Qualification%20Profile%20of%20Lecturers%20Employed%20in%20Public%20Technical%20and%20Vocational%20Education%20and%20Training%202014.pdf

DHET. (2015). Qualification profile of lecturers employed in public technical and vocational education and training colleges in South Africa in 2015. https://www.dhet.gov.za/Teacher%20Education%20Reports/DHET%20%20Qualification%20Profile%20of%20Lecturers%20Employed%20in%20Public%20Technical%20and%20Vocational%20Education%20and%202015.pdf

DHET. (2015a). Policy framework for workplace-based learning in an integrated and differentiated South African post-school education and training system. https://www.dhet.gov.za/Gazette/Policy%20Framework%20on%20Differentiation%20in%20the%20South%20African%20Post%20School%20System.pdf

DHET. (2016). Qualification profile of lecturers employed in public technical and vocational education and training colleges in South Africa. http://www.dhet.gov.za/Outcome/DHET%202014%20TVET%20Lecturer%20Qualifications%20Profile%20Report.pdf

DHET. (2017). Call for comment on the Open Learning Policy Framework for Post-School Education and Training. *Government Gazette*, 335(40772). http://pmg-assets.s3-website-eu-west-1.amazonaws.com/170407openlearningframework-postschooleduc.pdf

DHET. (2019). Post-school education and training monitor: Macro-indicator trends. Government Printers. https://www.dhet.gov.za/SiteAssets/Post-School%20Education%20and%20Training%20Monitor%20Report_March%202019.pdf

DHET. (2020). Strategic Plan 2020–2025. Government Printers. https://www.dhet.gov.za/SiteAssets/DHET%20Strategic%20Plan%202020.pdf

DoE. (Department of Education). (2000). Norms and standards for educators. Government Printers. https://www.gov.za/sites/default/files/gcis_document/201409/20844.pdf

Embassy of the Federal Republic of Germany. (2020). South Africa and Germany to establish the first national TVET lecturer development centre. https://cisp.cachefly.net/assets/articles/attachments/83239_prgermanembassy01082020.pdf

Erzse, A., Goldstein, S., Tugendhaft, A., Norris, S. A., Barker, M., Hofman, K. J., & INPreP group. (2021). The roles of men and women in maternal and child nutrition in urban South Africa: A qualitative secondary analysis. *Maternal & Child Nutrition*, 17(3), e13161.

ETDP SETA (Education, Training and Development Practices Sector Education and Training Authority). (2018a). Report on work integrated learning (WIL) and recognition of prior learning (RPL) in technical and vocational education and training colleges. https://www.etdpseta.org.za/education/sites/default/files/2020-06/Report%20on%20WIL%20and%20RPL%20in%20TVET%20Colleges.pdf

ETDP SETA. (2018b). TVET sub-sector report for the 2019/2020 Sector Skills Plan. https://www.etdpseta.org.za/education/sites/default/files/2020-06/TVET%20Sub-sector%20Report%20for%20the%202019-20%20Sector%20Skills%20Plan.pdf

ETDP SETA. (2021). Research report on work integrated learning at South African TVET colleges and workplaces. https://www.etdpseta.org.za/education/sites/default/files/2021-03/Work%20Intergrated%20Learning%20at%20South%20African%20TVET%20Colleges%20and%20Workplaces%202021.pdf

Franken, E. J. (2020). The implementation of open learning in the South African TVET college sector [Doctoral dissertation, University of Pretoria]. https://repository.up.ac.za/bitstream/handle/2263/80438/Franken_Implementation_2020.pdf?sequence=1

Fraser, N. (1995). From redistribution to recognition? Dilemmas of justice in a 'postsocialist' age. *New Left Review*, 1/212, 68–93.

Fraser, N. (1996). Social justice in the age of identity politics: Redistribution, recognition, and participation. *World Bank Economic Review*, 16(3), 345–373.

Fraser, N. (2000). Rethinking recognition. *New Left Review*, 3, 107–120.

Fraser, N. (2005). Reframing justice in a globalizing world. *New Left Review*, 36, 69–88.

Fraser, N. (2007). Feminist politics in the age of recognition: A two-dimensional approach to gender justice. *Studies in Social Justice*, 1(1), 23–35. DOI: https://doi.org/10.26522/ssj.v1i1.979

Fraser, N. (2009). *Scales of justice: Reimagining political space in a globalizing world*. Columbia University Press.

Fraser, N. (2010). Who counts? Dilemmas of justice in a post-Westphalian world. *Antipode*, 41, 281–297.

Fraser, N. (2011). Social exclusion, global poverty, and scales of (in)justice: Rethinking law and poverty in a globalizing world. *Stellenbosch Law Review*, 22(3), 452–462. https://hdl.handle.net/10520/EJC54809

Gamede, B. T., & Uleanya, C. (2019). Factors impacting entrepreneurship education in TVET colleges: A case of South Africa. *Journal of Entrepreneurship Education*, 22(3), 1–12.

Hatch, M., & Posel, D. (2018). Who cares for children? A quantitative study of childcare in South Africa. *Development Southern Africa*, 35(2), 267–282.

Heher Commission. (2017). Report of the Commission of Enquiry into Higher Education and Training to the President of the Republic of South Africa. http://www.thepresidency.gov.za/sites/default/files/Commission%20of%20Inquiry%20into%20Higher%20Education%20Report.pdf

Hlatshwayo, M. N., & Fomunyam, K. G. (2019). Theorising the #MustFall student movements in contemporary South African higher education: A social justice perspective. *Journal of Student Affairs in Africa*, 7(1), 61–80.

Hodgkinson-Williams, C. A., & Trotter, H. (2018). A social justice framework for understanding open educational resources and practices in the Global South. *Journal of Learning for Development*, 5(3), 204-224. https://jl4d.org/index.php/ejl4d/article/view/312

Hölscher, D., & Bozalek, V. (2020). Nancy Fraser's work and its relevance to higher education. In V. Bozalek, D. Hölscher & M. Zembylas (Eds.), *Nancy Fraser and participatory parity: Reframing social justice in South African higher education* (pp. 3–19). Routledge. https://doi.org/10.4324/9780429055355

Hundenborn, J., Woolard, I., & Jellema, J. (2019). The effect of top incomes on inequality in South Africa. *International Tax and Public Finance*, 26(5), 1018–1047.

Jeremiah, A., & Martin, J. (2019). Prognosticating job satisfaction and morale determinants of public Technical Vocational Education and Training (TVET) educators. *Problems and Perspectives in Management*, 17(3), 350–361.

JET. (2015). JET Bulletin: Improving students' performance in TVET colleges. https://www.jet.org.za/resources/bulletin-august-2015/download

Jonker, L. C. (2016). Stress in a college workplace and its relationship with certain correlates and predictive variables [Doctoral dissertation, Stellenbosch University].

Kraak, A., & Paterson, A. (Eds.) (2016). *Change management in TVET Colleges: Lessons learnt from the field of practice*. African Minds. http://www.africanminds.co.za/wp-content/uploads/2016/06/JET-TVET-text-and-cover-web-final-1.pdf

Kuehn, M. (2019). The South African technical and vocational education and training system from a German perspective. *Balkan Region Conference on Engineering and Business Education*, 3(1), 226–234. https://www.sciendo.com/article/10.2478/cplbu-2020-0026

Kyngäs, H., Kääriäinen, M., & Elo, S. (2020). The trustworthiness of content analysis. In H. Kyngäs, K. Mikkonen, &. M. Kääriäinen (Eds.), *The application of content analysis in nursing science research* (pp. 41–48). Springer. http://dl1.tarjomac.ir/nursing-ebooks/TPC202203.pdf#page=45

Leibowitz, B., & Bozalek, V. (2015). Foundation provision-a social justice perspective. *South African Journal of Higher Education*, 29(1), 8–25.

Letseka, M., Letseka, M. M., & Pitsoe, V. (2018). The challenges of e-Learning in South Africa. *Trends in E-learning*, 121–138. https://www.jovacet.ac.za/index.php?journal=JOVACET&page=article&op=view&path%5B%5D=122

Mabunda, N. O., & Frick, L. (2020). Factors that influence the employability of National Certificate (Vocational) graduates: The case of a rural TVET college in the Eastern Cape province, South Africa. *Journal of Vocational, Adult and Continuing Education and Training*, 3(1), 89–108. https://journals.co.za/doi/pdf/10.14426/jovacet.v3i1.127

Mangoma, A., & Wilson-Prangley, A. (2019). Black tax: Understanding the financial transfers of the emerging black middle class. *Development Southern Africa*, 36(4), 443–460.

Manyau, T. (2015). Assessing skills development management for lecturers in technical vocational education and training colleges in North West Province [Doctoral dissertation, North-West University]. https://repository.nwu.ac.za/bitstream/handle/10394/20690/Manyau_T.pdf?sequence=1

Marope, P., Chakroun, B., & Holmes, K. (2015). Unleashing the potential: Transforming technical and vocational education and training. UNESCO. http://www.ibe.unesco.org/sites/default/files/resources/unleashing-potential-2015_eng.pdf

Mashiloane, T. M. (2019). Stories of experience: Lecturers' pathways of learning to teach in technical and vocational education and training (TVET) colleges [Doctoral dissertation, University of KwaZulu-Natal].

Masoabi, C. S., & Alexander, G. (2021). Possible merger, entrepreneurship education in TVET engineering studies: A case for South Africa. *Journal of Entrepreneurship Education*, 24(2), 1–20.

Matsolo, M. J., Ningpuanyeh, W. C., & Susuman, A. S. (2018). Factors affecting the enrolment rate of students in higher education institutions in the Gauteng Province, South Africa. *Journal of Asian and African Studies*, 53(1), 64–80.

merSETA. (Manufacturing, Engineering and Related Services Sector Education and Training Authority). (2021). Final Sector Skills Plan update 2021/2022. https://www.merseta.org.za/wp-content/uploads/2021/04/Sector-Skills-Plan-2021-22.pdf

Mesuwini, J., Thaba-Nkadimene, K. L., & Kgomotlokoa, L. (2021). Nature of TVET lecturer learning during work integrated learning: A South African perspective. *Journal of Technical Education and Training*, 13(4), 106–117. https://penerbit.uthm.edu.my/ojs/index.php/JTET/article/download/9301/4744

Mmako, M. M. (2015). Employee engagement: Evidence from TVET colleges in South Africa. In *Proceedings of the 28th Annual Conference of the Southern African Institute of Management Scientists*. http://www.up.ac.za/media/shared/643/ZP_Files/2016/Papers/hrl5_full.zp9

Moodie, G., Wheelahan, L., & Lavigne, E. (2019). Technical and vocational education and training as a framework for social justice: Analysis and evidence from world case studies. Ontario Institute for Studies in Education, Toronto. https://issuu.com/educationinternational/docs/2019_eiresearch_tvet

Motaung, M. R. (2020). Improving the management of the professional development of lecturers at a selected technical and vocational education and training (TVET) college [Doctoral dissertation, University of South Africa].

Msibi, A. N. (2015). An exploration of the identities of qualified artisans employed as Technical Vocational Education and Training College lecturers [Doctoral dissertation, University of KwaZulu-Natal]. https://ukzn-dspace.ukzn.ac.za/bitstream/handle/10413/13462/Msibi_Alice_Ntombikayise_2015.pdf

Nduna, N. J. (2017). Current work-integrated learning practice in South African technical and vocational education and training colleges: A concern for student employability. In *Refereed Proceedings of the 20th WACE World Conference on Cooperative and Work-Integrated Education, 2017, Chiang Mai, Thailand.*

Ngcwangu, S. (2015). The ideological underpinnings of World Bank TVET policy: Implications of the influence of human capital theory on South African TVET policy. *Education as Change*, 19(3), 24–45.

Ngoveni, M. A. 2018. Factors linked to poor performance for NC(V) Level 2 mathematics students [Doctoral dissertation, University of Pretoria].

Ngubane-Mokiwa, S., & Khoza, S. B. (2016). Lecturers' experiences of teaching STEM to students with disabilities. *Journal of Learning for Development*, 3(1), 37-50. https://jl4d.org/index.php/ejl4d/article/download/125/121

Ngwato, S. E. (2020). Factors which contribute to poor academic achievement in TVET colleges: A case study [Doctoral dissertation, University of South Africa]. https://core.ac.uk/download/pdf/334609814.pdf

North, C. E. (2006). More than words? Delving into the substantive meaning(s) of 'social justice' in education. *Review of Educational Research*, 76(4), 507–535. https://journals.sagepub.com/doi/pdf/10.3102/00346543076004507

Nthako, M. D. (2020). Factors contributing to low completion rates of National Certificate Vocational (NCV) students at a TVET college in the Northwest Province [Doctoral dissertation, University of South Africa].

Olowoyo, M. M., Ramaila, S., & Mavuru, L. (2020). Levels of readiness and preparedness of selected South African TVET colleges in meeting the requirements of the hospitality industry. *International Journal of Learning, Teaching and Educational Research*, 19(11), 53–70.

Oosthuizen, L., & Van der Bijl, A. (2019). Maintenance of industry skills and knowledge by vocational lecturers at South African technical and vocational education and training colleges. In *2nd International Conference on Tourism Research* (p. 208). http://digitalknowledge.cput.ac.za/handle/11189/6984

Papier, J. (2011). Vocational teacher identity: Spanning the divide between the academy and the workplace. *Southern African Review of Education*, 17, 101–119.

Papier, J. (2017). A comparative study of TVET in 5 African Countries with a specific focus on TVET Teacher Education. *Vocational Education and Training in Sub-Saharan Africa*, 41.

Paterson, A. (2016). Introduction: Perspectives on programmes, projects and policies in the TVET Colleges. In A. Kraak, A. Paterson & K. Bok (Eds.), *Change Management in TVET Colleges: Lessons learnt from the field of practice* (pp. vii–xxiii). African Minds. http://www.africanminds.co.za/wp-content/uploads/2016/06/JET-TVET-text-and-cover-web-final-1.pdf

Poh, N., & Smythe, I. (2014). To what extend can we predict students' performance? A case study in colleges in South Africa. In *2014 IEEE Symposium on Computational Intelligence and Data Mining (CIDM)* (pp. 416–421). IEEE.

Rittel, H. W., & Webber, M. M. (1973). Dilemmas in a general theory of planning. *Policy Sciences*, 4(2), 155–169.

RSA (Republic of South Africa). (2015). Policy on minimum requirements for programmes leading to qualifications for educators and lecturers in adult and community education and training. Government Printer. https://www.dhet.gov.za/Teacher%20Education/Policy%20on%20minimum%20requirements%20for%20programmes%20leading%20to%20qualification.pdf

RSA. (2020). Performance agreement between the President of the Republic of South Africa and the Minister of Higher Education, Science and Innovation (Period of agreement June 2019 to April 2024). https://www.gov.za/sites/default/files/The/PA-higher-education-nzimande.pdf

Scholtz, D. (2020). Assessing workplace-based learning. *International Journal of Work-Integrated Learning*, 21(1), 25–35. https://files.eric.ed.gov/fulltext/EJ1241256.pdf

Setusha, S. (2020). Progress on lecturer development towards professionalisation within the TVET sector. Presentation delivered to South African Public Colleges Organisation. https://sacpo.co.za/wpcontent/uploads/2021/01/PROGRESS-ON-LECTURER-DEVELOPMENT-TOWARDS-PROFESSIONALISATIONWITHIN-THE-TVET-SECTOR.pptx

Singh, V., & Shawa, L. B. (2021) Lecturers' experiences of massification at a Technical and Vocational Education and Training College in South Africa and the development agenda: A social identity theory. *African Journal of Development Studies*, 11(3), 121–145. https://journals.co.za/doi/full/10.31920/2634-3649/2021/v11n3a6

Sithole, M. D. (2019). Enhancing management structure at the TVET colleges: A case study of uMgungundlovu TVET College [Doctoral dissertation, University of KwaZulu-Natal]. https://researchspace.ukzn.ac.za/xmlui/handle/10413/19054

Smith, J. (2016). ETDP SETA/SSACI WIL for lecturers in public TVET colleges project: Formative evaluation – Final May 2016. https://www.ssaci.org.za/images/Formative_Evaluation_report_WIL_Project.pdf

Spaull, N. (2015). Schooling in South Africa: How low-quality education becomes a poverty trap. *South African Child Gauge*, 12(1), 34–41.

SSACI (Swiss South African Cooperation Initiative). (2017). The Workplace-based Experience Programme. https://unevoc.unesco.org/home/Promising+Practices+in+TVET/lang=en/id=6087

Stats SA (Statistics South Africa). (2017). Poverty trends in South Africa: An examination of absolute poverty between 2006 and 2015. Statistics South Africa. http://www.statssa.gov.za/publications/Report-03-10-06/Report-03-10-062015.pdf

Stenfors, T., Kajamaa, A., & Bennett, D. (2020). How to assess the quality of qualitative research. *The Clinical Teacher*, 17(6), 596–599. https://onlinelibrary.wiley.com/doi/pdfdirect/10.1111/tct.13242

Terblanche, T. E. D. P. (2017). Technical and vocational education and training (TVET) colleges in South Africa: A framework for leading curriculum change [Doctoral dissertation, Stellenbosch University].

Van der Bijl, A. J. (2020). Implications of TVET and ACET policy frameworks for teaching practice. *Proceedings of the Seventh Annual Teaching Practice / Didactics Symposium*.

Van der Bijl, A. J. (2021). Integrating the world of work into initial TVET teacher education in South Africa. *Journal of Education and Research*, 11(1), 13–28.

Van der Bijl, A., & Oosthuizen, L. J. (2019). Deficiencies in technical and vocational education and training lecturer involvement qualifications and its implications in the development of work related skills. *South African Journal of Higher Education*, 33(3), 205–221.

Van der Bijl, A., & Taylor, V. (2016). Nature and dynamics of industry-based workplace learning for South African TVET lecturers. *Industry and Higher Education*, 30(2), 98–108.

Van der Bijl, A., & Taylor, V. (2020). Developing a WIL curriculum for post-school lecturer qualifications. *Journal of Vocational, Adult and Continuing Education and Training*, 3(1), 22–42.

Van Rensburg, E. (2008). Evaluating work-based learning: insights from an illuminative evaluation study of work-based learning in a vocational qualification. *Industry and Higher Education*, 22(4), 223–232. https://journals.sagepub.com/doi/pdf/10.5367/000000008785201739

Van Staden, E. L. (2015). A work place-based learning (WPBL) policy: The national perspective. http://www.saair-web.co.za/wp-content/uploads/2015/08/06-EvS-WBL-for-PSET.pdf

Wedekind, V. (2016a). Literature on technical and vocational education and training (TVET) college lecturers: A review. *SAQA Bulletin*, 15(1), 31–59.

Wedekind, V. (2016b). Technical and vocational education and training (TVET) reform in South Africa: Implications for college lecturers, context, background. *SAQA Bulletin*, 15(1), 1–29.

Wedekind, V. (2016c). Chaos or coherence? Technical and vocational education and training (TVET) college governance in post-apartheid South Africa. *SAQA Bulletin*, 15(1), 85–116.

Wedekind, V., Watson, A., & Buthelezi, Z. (2016). Lecturers in distress fractured professional identity amongst TVET college staff in South Africa. *SAQA Bulletin*, 15(1), 117–142.

Winberg, S., & Winberg, C. (2017, April). Using a social justice approach to decolonize an engineering curriculum. In *2017 IEEE Global Engineering Education Conference (EDUCON)* (pp. 248–254). IEEE.

Yende, S. J. (2021). Funding opportunities and challenges: A case of South African institutions of higher learning. *Journal of Public Administration*, 56(1), 70–79.

Zinn, B., Raisch, K., & Reimann, J. (2019). Analysing training needs of TVET teachers in South Africa. An empirical study. *International Journal for Research in Vocational Education and Training*, 6(2), 174–197. DOI: 10.13152/IJRVET.6.2.4

HOW TO CITE THIS CHAPTER

Govender, S. C., & Dhurumraj, T. (2022). Opening up TVET lecturer professional learning and development through work integrated learning in South Africa: A social justice perspective. In T. Mayisela, S. C. Govender & C. A. Hodgkinson-Williams (Eds.), *Open learning as a means of advancing social justice: Cases in post-school education and training in South Africa* (pp. 338–373). African Minds. doi: 10.47622/9781928502425_15

This work is licensed under a Creative Commons Attribution 4.0 International (CC BY 4.0) licence.

16

The potential for microcredentials as a form of open learning to contribute to a social justice agenda in South African higher education

Barbara Jones

SUMMARY This study explores how microcredentials could be directed towards social justice ends in South African (SA) Higher Education (HE). The Department of Higher Education and Training (DHET) draft *Open Learning Policy Framework* (OLPF) is premised on understanding open learning as a social justice imperative, identifying digital badges and microcredentials as strategically significant in open learning. Microcredential activities in SA HE are still nascent, so academic staff from only one SA university, who were actively experimenting with digital badges and microcredentials, were able to be interviewed. Interviews with selected local and international informants involved in researching and/or working with microcredentials in HE were also conducted, to investigate other practices and approaches in this field that could advance social justice in SA HE. The social justice framework of Nancy Fraser, which theorises 'parity of participation' in the dimensions of economic, cultural and political injustice, provided the analytical lens with which to interrogate the qualitative data. The findings indicate that microcredentials can remedy systemic inequities for both staff and students in the university studied. More broadly, microcredentials can afford the recognition of alternative epistemologies and cultural practices, and linking microcredentials to qualifications frameworks can allow for increased mobility of workers who can access an 'ecosystem' of work and educational opportunities, and potentially improve their lives. However, a coherent, integrated national post-school education and training (PSET) policy environment, explicitly based on social justice principles, is urgently needed to facilitate and guide further microcredential development so that it may help remedy inequities in SA HE.

Keywords: microcredentials, badges, accreditation, open learning, social justice

Introduction

This study investigates the ways in which microcredentials could contribute to social justice in South African higher education (HE). The Department of Higher Education and Training (DHET) is investigating new models of educational delivery and of acknowledging and accrediting learning, framed by open learning principles, and has identified microcredentials and digital badges as a possible social justice strategy in this endeavour. The guiding research question was: How could microcredentials contribute towards social justice in HE in South Africa (SA)?

The nature and purpose of higher education institutions (HEIs) is changing worldwide, with 'unbundling' of curricula and services, the use of technologies in massification of education, and marketisation of courses. At the same time, continuing reductions in government funding for the sector and escalating fees make attaining a qualification increasingly unaffordable (Swartz et al., 2019). South African HE is no different, but is additionally challenged by deep inequities in the education system that does not prepare school leavers adequately for post-secondary education (Keevy et al., 2020). Furthermore, despite efforts to transform the HE sector to become more equitable, it nevertheless "continues to be characterised by low participation and high attrition rates" (Baijnath, 2018, p. 1), with access and success being strongly associated with socio-economic demographics and significantly lower success rates for black students (Swartz et al., 2019). Indeed, Keevy et al. (2020) denounce the post-school education and training (PSET) regulatory framework and qualifications system as exclusionary; replicating and perpetuating the socially unjust "bimodal education system" which is "good for 20%, poor for 80%" (p. 8).

It is being acknowledged internationally that one way in which PSET can become more equitable and enable access to affordable learning opportunities is through the awarding of credits – microcredentials – for partial or full completion of courses that can count towards a formally accredited qualification (Oliver, 2019). Microcredentials are identified in Europe as a way of upskilling/reskilling professionals, of making higher education more open and inclusive through supporting lifelong learning, and of increasing flexibility and permeability between education sectors and pathways (Finochietti & Lockoff, 2021). They can provide alternative solutions to preparing for the world of work (Chakroun & Keevy, 2018; Keevy & Chakroun, 2019; Keevy et al., 2020), and are important components of transparent, agile credentialing systems that can be a "key lever" for reducing unemployment (Keevy et al., 2020, p. 3).

The DHET draft *Open Learning Policy Framework* (OLPF) is premised on understanding open learning as a social justice imperative, aimed at "redress, equity in access to opportunity, flexibility and choice, and by an equal concern for quality and real success in learning" (DHET, 2017, p. 44). It advocates open learning approaches that recognise prior learning, that facilitate articulation where gaps exist, and that take account of non-formal learning represented by digital badges. In particular, the OLPF notes the social justice potential of microcredentials and digital badges in expanding access to employment and to lifelong learning pathways.

Microcredentials

In contrast to macrocredentials, which traditionally certify the achievement of a full qualification in a formal education system, microcredentials allow for the recognition of smaller units of learning. The definition of microcredentials adopted in this study is that they are a digital form of recognition and *"certification of assessed learning* [emphasis added] *that is additional, alternate, complementary to or a component part of a formal qualification"* (Oliver, 2019, p. 19). This definition locates microcredentials partially in the realm of non-formal learning, particularly for recognition of vocational competencies [*competency-based* alternative digital credentials [ADCs]), but also as credits towards a formal qualification (*learning-achievement* ADCs) (ICDE, 2019, p. 24).

The dominant microcredential terrain

Commonly, microcredentials are online offerings that have a work-related or professional value and are verified by a recognised, reputable issuing authority such as an educational institution or industry body (Rossiter & Tynan, 2019). Microcredentials can fill specific gaps between HE programmes and the skills sought by companies; can increase the efficiency of HE systems through more targeted, alternative training programmes; and can promote innovation in HE (Kato et al., 2020). The 2020 Educause Horizon Report proposes that microcredentials are a growth point in HE, and that HEIs will need to rethink their qualification pathways for "a changing student demographic and employment landscape" through more flexible and online models that incorporate microcredentials (Brown et al., 2020, p. 11).

Microcredential provision is frequently through collaborative partnerships between HEIs, business and not-for-profit organisations, such as where global online learning platforms (e.g., edX, Coursera, Udacity and FutureLearn) host university credit-bearing courses and Massive Open Online Courses (MOOCs). Many large companies offer their own internal training courses and certification, while others (e.g., Google, Amazon, Microsoft and IBM) make these available to the general public (Kato et al., 2020, pp. 18–19).

Initial scepticism of microcredentials and digital badges, related to the standard of the achievement that they represent, has largely shifted, due in part to the 2015 Groningen Declaration[1] and the technological, developmental support provided through Mozilla's Open Badges Infrastructure (OBI) (Elkordy, 2012). The OBI is an open source badging ecosystem that provides a standard technical specification for anyone to develop open digital badges and tools across the web, and for multiple open badges from different issuers to be collected by learners into a digital backpack that can be shared digitally for employment, education or lifelong learning.[2]

Three possible models of integrating microcredentials into a formal qualification have been identified by Kato et al. (2020): an embedded model, a Recognition of Prior Learning (RPL) model and a modular model, all of which could play a part in remedying social injustices. In the embedded model, a microcredential, offered by another institution as

---

[1] http://groningendeclaration.org/201703/waves.html. The Groningen Declaration was signed in 2015 by the U.S. and European countries in recognition of the necessity for professionals to carry credentials accepted by multiple countries, and addresses validity, credibility and reliability of these credentials (Lemoine & Richardson, 2015).

[2] https://openbadges.org/Issue

a MOOC or as an OER, is included as a component of the programme. In the RPL model, microcredentials provide alternative entry mechanisms to formal learning programmes, or credit pathways within a qualification. The modular model enables learners to undertake a range of short courses offered on different learning platforms (e.g., EdX, Coursera) and stack them up towards achieving a qualification, for instance, a MicroMasters from EdX or Master Track certificates from Coursera (Kato et al., 2020, pp. 17–18). Gallagher (2018a) speaks of three HEIs in the United States which are experimenting with 'rebundling' and integrating formal and non-formal learning and microcredentials for learners to devise their own coherent learning pathways.

Microcredential offerings are increasingly stackable in online HE offerings, across multiple learning pathways, from small units to partial degrees such as MicroMasters, or all the way up to a full degree (Pickard, 2018). These stackable credentials can be a welcome alternative pathway towards a degree, ameliorating inequities relating to cost, flexibility and admissions criteria.

Interface of microcredentials with macrocredentials

Morgan (2020) emphasises that well developed RPL and credit accumulation and transfer (CAT) systems, and the collaboration of industry, professional bodies and HEIs in the design of microcredentials, is key to the portability and recognition of microcredentials. But for microcredentials to articulate with both HE qualifications systems and the vocationally oriented workplace, they need to become standardised and quality assured by educationally recognised agencies. Furthermore, a well-developed taxonomy of credentials that frames the relationship between credentials and articulation possibilities, is essential (Rossiter & Tynan, 2019). Chakroun and Keevy (2018) point out that the interface between macrocredentials and microcredentials is where the biggest challenges and opportunities lie for education systems.

National qualifications frameworks around the world are starting to interface with emerging microcredentials in various ways. For example, globally, OECD[3] governments are exploring ways to integrate microcredentials into their qualifications systems, as well as to fund these alternative mechanisms and processes (Kato et al., 2020).

All European Union (EU) countries have aligned their qualifications systems with a common European Qualifications Framework (EQF), and this is linked to the Europass Digital Credentials Infrastructure (EDCI) which is being developed to facilitate recognition, transfer and portability of qualifications and other learning achievements across Europe.[4] When fully operational, the new Europass will include an e-portfolio of the user's skills and work experience, opportunities for work and study in different EU countries, and a digital credential infrastructure for issuing a range of macro and microcredentials.

The New Zealand Qualifications Authority (NZQA) is leading the way in establishing specific criteria for recognising training schemes that are not registered on the New Zealand Qualifications Framework (NZQF) which will facilitate articulation possibilities and assure the quality of microcredentials. In addition to considering the credentials offered by NZ HEIs, the NZQA also "evaluates the content of these credentials offered by HEIs outside of New

---

[3] Organisation for Economic Co-operation and Development (OECD)
[4] https://europa.eu/europass/en

Zealand and New Zealand organisations that are not HEIs, and issues statements presenting the credit value and level of such learning activities against the NZQF" (Kato et al., 2020, p. 30).

Canada has a national degrees framework, but not a national vocational qualifications framework (Contact North, 2020). However, since 2017, eCampus Ontario has been driving the development of microcredentials and of principles and processes for the recognition of microcredentials that are geared towards local employment as well as provide pathways into post-secondary education and training.[5]

Criticism of the microcredential terrain

Despite this encouraging progress, the rise of microcredentials has been criticised by some as an "outgrowth of the neoliberal learning economy", where education is viewed as a profitable commodity (Ralston, 2020, p. 2) for continuous upskilling in the "learn-to-earn" economy (p. 14). Ralston argues further that microcredentials privilege technical skills and competencies over educating the whole person, thereby neither liberating "learners' potentialities" nor developing lifelong learning dispositions of critical intellectual enquiry (p. 14).

On a more cautious note, Chakroun and Keevy (2018) warn that stacking a combination of microcredentials towards a macrocredential (qualification) may not be conceptually sound nor "lead to coherent qualifications" that are formally recognised (p. 29) or portable beyond the institution or organisation offering it. Another concern is that, although individual microcredentials may seem affordable, in the end the cost of a stacked qualification may exceed that of a traditional, credit-bearing HE qualification (Morgan, 2020).

Gallagher (2018a) argues that online, "(a)lternative credentialing, when pitched as a social progress program that replaces degrees, has the profoundly undemocratic potential of creating a second-class educational tier" (p. 1) that does not live up to the claims of a route into better jobs, social equality or mobility (ibid), and where academic rigour and educational quality have been questioned (Gallagher, 2018b). Similarly, Ralston (2020) warns, not only can microcredentials perpetuate the capitalist status quo, but also they can threaten "to exacerbate class divisions" (p. 15) and reinforce social injustices, rather than redress them.

Open recognition of learning

In contrast to these critiques, the open recognition movement espouses a radically different view of microcredentials: that competence is holistic and embodied in a person as a set of practices — values, knowledge, skills and attitudes — associated with the community of practice in which it is embedded (Ravet, 2020). This facilitates the recognition of new practices as they emerge, through the awarding of open badge awards, as developed by a community of practitioners, that can then be endorsed by a post-school institution.

The Bologna Open Recognition Declaration (BORD) (ORA, 2016) espouses a "universal open architecture for the recognition of lifelong and life-wide learning achievements", whether formal, informal or non-formal. Such an open, socially inclusive system could reset the parameters for employability, enhance mobility and foster personal agency. But to be effective, this requires national and institutional open recognition policies that honour and

---

[5] https://www.ecampusontario.ca/micro-certifications/

connect all forms of learning, that guarantee flexible, accessible and multiple developmental pathways that include "socially excluded and disenfranchised groups" (ORA, 2016). This indicates the kind of regulatory frameworks which would be needed to steer microcredentials to transformative ends.

Social justice in higher education

The DHET draft OLPF emphasises promoting social justice through equitable access to quality post-school education for all sectors of the population, but particularly young people, which will enable a route out of poverty and "economic, social and cultural development for society as a whole" (DHET, 2017, p. 371). OER and open educational practices[6], in particular, can contribute to social justice by improving preparedness for HE, by widening access and reducing costs for learners, and improving retention and success rates through participatory pedagogies (Bajnath, 2018, pp. 91–92).

Fraser defines social justice as "parity of participation" which, by virtue of it being both an outcome and a process, has an "inherent reflexivity" (Fraser, 2005, p. 87). Social justice is attained as an outcome when "all the relevant social actors ... participate as peers in social life" and as a process when the social norms are legitimated by all concerned "in fair and open processes of deliberation, in which all can participate as peers" (Fraser, 2005, p. 87). Fraser postulates three dimensions of social justice – economic, cultural and political – each of which can be interrogated at multiple levels (Fraser, 2005, p. 87). These outcomes and processes can be socially unjust in three ways, which Fraser terms: (1) economic maldistribution, (2) cultural misrecognition and (3) political misrepresentation, with remedies ranging from what Fraser terms "affirmative" to "transformative" responses. An affirmative response merely alleviates the injustice – what Hodgkinson-Williams and Trotter refer to as an "ameliorative intervention" (2018, p. 207) – whereas a transformative response addresses the *root* of the injustice and is aimed at "correcting inequitable outcomes precisely by restructuring the underlying generative framework" (Fraser, 1995, p. 82). In practice, responses to social inequities may range from slightly ameliorative to fully transformative actions, rather than as binary analytical categories.

Economic maldistribution, distribution and restructuring

Fraser explains that economic maldistribution occurs when economic structures impede people from full participation by denying them "the resources they need in order to interact with others as peers" (2005, p. 73). In this study, an ameliorative response would be to have educational institutions and/or employers recognise badges obtained for non-formal courses for purposes of access to HE programmes, employment and/or promotion, or to assist educators and employers "better match individuals with non-traditional experiences to relevant opportunities"[7]. A transformative response would aim to allow students to choose courses to suit their financial situation, and have these microcredentials articulate to further qualifications or employment. RPL practices could also be considered as transformative.

---

[6] Open educational practices (OEP) can be understood as "a broad descriptor of practices that include the creation, use, and reuse of OER as well as open pedagogies and open sharing of teaching practices" (Cronin, 2017) that give effect to the open education philosophy.

[7] https://openbadges.org/Issue

Cultural misrecognition, recognition and re-acculturation

Cultural "misrecognition" occurs when people are prevented from equal participation by "hierarchies of cultural value that deny them the requisite standing" (Fraser, 2005, p. 73). An ameliorative response in this study could be for HEIs and employers to formally recognise digital badges or microcredentials that represent alternative forms and perspectives of knowledge, for credit/exemption or employment/promotion respectively. By contrast, the restructuring of a National Qualifications Framework would guarantee flexible, accessible and multiple developmental pathways for all learners as a way of transforming geographic, racial, gender and disability exclusion — what Hodgkinson-Williams and Trotter (2018) refer to as "re-acculturation" (p. 207).

Political misframing, representation and reframing

Fraser proposes that the third dimension of social injustice, political inequality, can be understood as encompassing two categories of injustice: ordinary-political misrepresentation and misframing. Political representation refers to who is included in political decision-making (Fraser, 2009, p. 103), whereas political framing or "misframing", "tells us who is included in, and who is excluded from the circle of those entitled to a just distribution and reciprocal recognition" (Fraser, 2005, p. 75).

International, national and institutional open recognition policies, that undergird the mechanisms for the implementation of microcredentials, would transform and reframe how all forms of formal and non-formal learning are honoured and how they articulate, worldwide.

Research methodology

This study investigates how microcredentials could contribute towards parity of participation in HE in SA. A preliminary scoping of microcredential practices in SA HE for this study in 2020 revealed very little activity. One private university was offering a modular microcredential alternative to its full qualifications, and two public universities were experimenting with digital badges, but no public reporting or research on these activities could be ascertained. The private university did not respond to our research requests, therefore the public university that was most active in experimenting with microcredentials, and willing to participate in the study, was chosen as the main research site. Because of the limited data on microcredential practices in HE in SA, informants who were involved in the field beyond SA were invited to participate in the study, for their perspectives on the topic.

Study examples

North-West University (NWU), South Africa, formed the main site for this study as it had been experimenting with digital badges, OER and ways of collaborating with other universities for some years. Two academic staff, who were key in actively promoting digital badges and OER at NWU, were interviewed: Prof. Jako Olivier and Dr Marieta Jansen van Vuuren. In addition, one local and three international informants involved in researching and/or working with microcredentials were interviewed. The interviewees all agreed to be identified as listed in Table 1.

Table 1: List of interviewees

Interviewee	Relevance to the study
Dr Marieta Jansen van Vuuren	Senior Academic Developer/Teaching and Learning Domain Liaison at NWU
Prof. Jako Olivier	UNESCO Chair on Multimodal Learning and OER; Prof in Multimodal Learning at NWU
Mike Adendorff (SA)	Retired Project Manager: Open Learning at DHET
Dr Wayne Mackintosh (New Zealand)	Director of the OER Foundation and coordinator of the establishment of the OER University (OERu)
Dr Tannis Morgan (Canada)	Advisor for learning and teaching and researcher for open education at BCcampus, Canada
Deborah Arnold (France)	National and international projects coordinator at AUNEGe, the French digital university for economics and management

Methodological approach

Marieta J. van Vuuren was interviewed individually as well as jointly with Jako Olivier; Tannis Morgan and Deborah Arnold were interviewed jointly; Wayne Mackintosh and Mike Adendorff were interviewed individually.

A descriptive qualitative research approach was taken, and vignettes compiled of the differing practices and perspectives of how digital badges and microcredentials were and could be used towards a social justice agenda.

Data generation

COVID-19 limitations during 2020 meant that all interviews had to take place online. This allowed for greater flexibility in setting up meeting times and allowed interviews to be conducted across the different international time zones. All interviews were recorded, transcribed and member checked by interviewees.

Data analysis

Data were disaggregated and coded in Excel spreadsheets, using descriptive codes that emerged from the literature and analytical codes that were derived from Fraser's social justice framework. This enabled an understanding of how the practices described were or could be contributing to social justice in HE.

Ethical considerations

Ethical protocols were followed for UCT (for the overall project) and NWU (the specific site), which gave consent for the data collection and to be identified in the study. Consent for participation in the study and for permission for the findings to be published, was obtained from all interviewees. All interviewees elected to be identified and their real names are used.

Findings

Informants from New Zealand, Canada, France and SA provided examples and insights into how microcredentials were serving a social justice agenda in their different contexts, which suggest how they could contribute to redressing inequities in the SA HE system.

Perspectives on microcredentials from Canada

Tannis Morgan reported that, at eCampus Ontario, a multi-stakeholder working group had been collaborating in designing a number of microcredential pilot projects that align HE more closely to industry in the province. She recounted that the most successful projects "were the ones that were co-designed, where they actually designed the recognition part of it, the assessment" together with the local Indigenous communities.

Using Hodgkinson-Williams and Trotter's (2018) terms, this example illustrates a means of "re-acculturation" (p. 207), whereby the voices and interests of all stakeholders, including marginalised Indigenous groups, were considered and incorporated. It is also politically transformative in the way that those previously excluded from educational decision-making were being included.

However, Morgan expressed concern at the "hype" around microcredentials, and that "there's a sort of reductionist skills approach that's emerging but at the same time, there's this sort of gold rush", while her research has shown little evidence of microcredentials leading to better jobs or educational opportunities. Instead, she advocated for a non-instrumentalist approach, where microcredentials are intentionally designed within a social justice framework that takes all three dimensions proposed by Fraser (2005) into account, so as to ensure inequities are not reproduced.

This example illustrates that, if microcredentials are to serve participatory parity, then the forms of governance and engagement are the most important issues.

Perspectives on microcredentials from France

The European Credit Clearing House for Opening up Education (ECCHOE)[8], a project which Deborah Arnold was coordinating, analyses credentials and microcredentials up to a diploma level, and her focus was on the information these credentials should contain to describe the learning opportunity in a meaningful way. She explained that ECCHOE is linked to the new Europass[9], a "European-wide ecosystem" of skills, competencies, qualifications and microcredentials, linked to learning and employment opportunities. The Europass is framed by the overarching European Qualifications Framework (EQF), but is "driven by the Directorate General for Employment and not the Directorate for Education", hence its emphasis on employment. This has caused tensions for academics trying to "squeeze" their programmes "into something which has been designed primarily with employment in mind", but it is nevertheless aimed at ameliorating many of the economic inequalities for workers in the EU. Besides, by "restructuring the underlying generative framework" (Fraser, 1995, p.

---

[8] Moves are afoot to rebrand it more accurately as the European Credential Clearing House for Opening up Education

[9] https://europa.eu/europass/en

82) of formal, non-formal and informal learning recognition, it is essentially a transformative response to economic inequalities.

Arnold also spoke of the open recognition movement in France, which contends that "fragmenting" people into skills, represented by credentials and badges, erases individual agency, and that the whole person should be recognised as a chef, a teacher, etc. "It's unpacking the whole system of recognition. …You are not your diploma, you are a person who has a wide variety of skills, abilities and experience." Communities of practice – not an external authority – bestow the recognition, thus making open recognition "hyper-local" and essentially "decolonising microcredentials". This disruptive approach could be truly culturally, economically and politically transformative but, as Morgan cautioned, in Canada at least, the "permissive hyper-local" open recognition approach may deter academics, reversing the strides that have been made in getting them to participate in the open education space and in "de-siloing" HE.

Arnold described an example of a regional digital badging initiative for enhancing the employability of migrants and young people for the local job market. Using an existing "soft skills" framework, "people from employment agencies, …from primary and secondary education, from higher education, from professional vocational education" came together as a community of practitioners to design badges for their regional context. Arnold reflected this was "sustainable on a regional level, because they knew who they were doing it for, and they were doing it together." This example of recognition (Fraser, 2005), shows not only how the cultural capital of all stakeholders was drawn upon, but also how the badges were designed explicitly to recognise the "soft skills", the cultural capital that these marginalised groupings already possessed.

This also illustrates how cultural and economic injustices are so often intertwined, as are the socially just remedies. In this case, although the employment system was not being transformed in any fundamental way, the intention instead was to open up opportunities for employment and thus the redistribution of economic resources, through transforming the mechanisms by which these people's capabilities could be recognised for the job market.

A perspective from New Zealand

The NZQF

The informant, Wayne Mackintosh, explained that the integration of microcredentials into the NZQF began only in 2019, so it was too early to pronounce on its success, but that:

> where I think the New Zealand Qualifications Authority (NZQA) has been particularly strong, is providing an authorised channel for learning that doesn't quite fit within traditional formal qualifications, you know, something that has not quite been picked up by the formal education sector yet, and that there is a framework that can validate that learning. So in part what the NZQA has done is not only in terms of providing opportunities for tertiary state-funded institutions to offer microcredentials, they've also got a system whereby international providers or open online learning internationally can get a statement of equivalence within the NZQA. (W Mackintosh)

In Fraser's terms, a transformative response changes structures and systems. Therefore, restructuring the NZQF in this way is economically transformative, opening up accredited training opportunities geared to vocational employment, and via flexible, accessible and more affordable learning pathways, towards recognised qualifications. Moreover, it may well become culturally transformative through restructuring the systems that give rise to misrecognition of differing cultural perspectives.

The OERu

Based in New Zealand, Mackintosh is the director of the OER Foundation and is coordinating the establishment of the OERu, an international innovation partnership which aims to widen access to more affordable education for all. The OERu as a global online HEI, he explained, aims "to provide more affordable and sustainable pathways for learners who have been excluded from the formal education system… to achieve formal academic credit towards university recognised qualifications". There are even two full university qualifications in the offing that are "a working model of transnational credit transfer" comprised entirely of a selection of OER modules from different universities worldwide. OERu modules are offered free by their international partner HEIs, following "the best current understanding of how you teach for learning independently, online". Access is open to all but, in order to be awarded credits for the modules, learners need to complete the assessments, which are charged on a cost recovery basis only, and are therefore very affordable. Mackintosh explained that the assessments are the same for both OERu participants and students enrolled at the respective HEI, "so there is equivalence and parity", and that they can be completed for RPL purposes, as an alternative to costly and time-consuming RPL portfolio assessments.

In Fraser's terms, the OERu appears as a deliberately economically transformative initiative, providing a model of the most affordable, accessible and flexible way for learners to earn a qualification of international standing. However, the online delivery modality of OERu modules may not allow participatory parity to those most marginalised if they do not have access to the required technological infrastructure or if they cannot afford the assessment fees; thereby perpetuating economic inequalities. Also, the authority for designing the OERu courses and their assessment remains with the traditional universities, which may not consider issues of cultural misrecognition or political misframing.

Perspectives on microcredentials from South Africa

Policy

Despite DHET's interest in microcredentials at a national policy level for redressing education and training inequalities, former DHET open learning manager, Mike Adendorff, emphasised that moves towards recognising and implementing microcredentials in HE are being hampered by tardiness in finalising a national open learning policy. He also warned that other policies and regulations are at odds with the draft OLPF, including DHET and National Student Financial Aid Scheme (NSFAS) funding policies. These policies will need to be aligned before implementation of microcredentials can be scaled up.

Adendorff asserted that a new generation of qualification frameworks is needed, where online learning and credentialing, credit transfer and advanced standing RPL are recognised.

He argued that offering a greater selection of courses through microcredentials from SA universities could facilitate transdisciplinary learning and encourage the decolonising of the curriculum (both issues of increasing importance in HE in SA and globally) while ensuring that the academic integrity of the qualifications is maintained.

North-West University

The awarding of digital badges was pioneered at NWU some years ago, when Marieta Jansen van Vuuren experimented with giving badges to lecturers for satisfactorily completing certain continuous professional development (CPD) workshops and courses. This act of cultural recognition – explicitly valuing other epistemologies in the institution – proved to be highly motivational, with lecturers competing to fill their badge books. However, because this was such a new concept at the time, there were challenges in obtaining institutional buy-in and building a sustainable model across all campuses, and eventually the practice was discontinued.

Nevertheless, Van Vuuren reported that some lecturers saw the potential of these badges in their own teaching. For example, badges were awarded to Law students instead of marks for certain learning activities – e.g., awards of 'judge', 'magistrate', 'clerk', depending on their level of mastery of the activity – which proved to be highly motivational. Jako Olivier gave an example of an OER that had been "adapted and localised" from an OERu module and integrated as an activity into a Business course curriculum, linked to a badge award. He suggested that this example could be modelled "to embed" OER in other modules and courses in future.

Olivier conjectured that, although there was some reluctance "to embrace the idea of microcredentials", once the NWU OER policy was in place it was expected that attitudes to OER and microcredentials would change. To grow participation in the open learning movement, OER and microcredentials would need to work synergistically. He proposed that the adoption of an OER policy and the thoughtful, more widespread use of microcredentials and OER that allow for credit transfer and mobility, could transform the economic model of HE to the benefit of both students and HEIs, especially if implemented on a large scale.

Following internal structural changes at NWU, renewed opportunities for micro-credentialing had emerged and two projects were being envisioned by Van Vuuren for 2021 going forward. The first was a three-year pilot to award digital badges for lecturer CPD via an open source digital badging platform. Should this be successful, ways of gaining institutional recognition for digital badges – as proxies for competencies – in performance appraisals and promotion, would be explored so that these could be integrated into career trajectories.

Van Vuuren mentioned that a benefit of awarding digital badges for CPD was that, because the courses had to be carefully designed to meet the learning outcomes recognised by the badges, the quality of teaching and learning in the courses had improved.

The second project envisioned was the development of a portfolio platform with an integrated digital badge function. Initially, it was intended that the platform would issue digital badges to students who satisfactorily complete their training as mentors, tutors and supplemental instructors. But should it gain support, it could also issue badges for components of formally assessed student learning, such as for work-integrated learning, as well as for extra-curricular projects, student exchange projects, service learning, graduate attributes and so on. In time, the portfolio platform could serve to showcase holistic competencies and achievements for both staff and students, to enable them to develop their academic, professional and personal profiles. Van Vuuren insisted that, even if it was not possible to finalise the portfolio system in 2021, the digital badging pilot for students would go ahead, "with the intention to actually roll it out on a bigger scale." This shift towards the cultural recognition of non-formal knowledge affirms the importance of the holistic personal development of students – an often neglected or 'misrecognised' aspect of HE. Integrating digital badges into a portfolio platform for staff and students can go even further in providing a system that foregrounds the validity of all forms of learning, challenging hegemonic forms of recognition in HE – a potentially culturally transformative initiative.

Olivier described the extensive possibilities for the development of intra-institutional micro-credentials, especially for small units of learning within certain courses such as Communication. He suggested that these could also be shared between universities to reduce duplication of learning and teaching and facilitate credit transfer: "We've had students come in, in the middle of a degree, and then we either have to get them to do additional modules unnecessarily or let them do an oral exam ... And that's really unfortunate." This use of microcredentials for credit would ameliorate the financial burden on students who might otherwise have to repeat these units, and the associated financial and human resources burden on the university.

Olivier also reported that two CPD short courses, which would normally be accessible only through the university short courses office, were being finalised for offering by the OERu. This would allow learners to be assessed and certificated by NWU for no cost, as these costs would be covered by the OERu Trust, although the development costs of the courses would be borne by NWU. Restructuring the financial model of CPD in this manner can eliminate not only economic barriers for potential participants but also, as an open access offering, circumvent the limitation on the number of participants – a constraint for contact courses – and admit participants regardless of educational background or geographic location.

Olivier mentioned conversations with colleagues from other universities where "we started comparing what we're doing, and we started to move a little bit closer in terms of content between the different universities, allowing for some variation. ... So I think in that sense microcredentialing can definitely be of value." Indeed, NWU has been instrumental in formulating a proposal to DHET for developing standards, guidelines and policies towards implementing microcredentials in HE in SA.

Significant funding as well as support from the accrediting authorities will be required to take the microcredentialing initiative further, but it has the potential to change the architecture of post-school education in SA, and radically transform some of the root causes of economic, cultural and political inequities in HE.

Discussion

The OLPF promotes open learning as a way of addressing inequities in the PSET system, and envisages microcredentials as one of the components of this reimagined system, with the potential to facilitate access to work opportunities and to education for those who have been excluded.

The vignettes of the Europass and the NZQF show that linking microcredentials to qualifications frameworks gives them currency and transferability, not only affirming the value of a person's learning, and hence affording some degree of cultural recognition, but also giving it both an economic value in the job market and educational credit value. This allows for increased mobility of workers who can access an 'ecosystem' of work and educational opportunities, and potentially improve their lives.

Being oriented to the world of work, there are concerns that microcredentials have emerged to serve the neo-liberal agendas of global economies and industry, where they can wittingly or unwittingly perpetuate or even exacerbate social inequalities. Furthermore, there is an intrinsic tension between the purpose of universities as "places that create citizens with humane perspectives and critical stances serving the public interest" (Czerniewicz, 2018, p. 20) and more narrowly focused, functionalist microcredentials. However, as the eCampus Ontario example shows, collaborative design of microcredentials can enable economic, cultural and political injustices to be remedied. Furthermore, as Adendorff pointed out, universities can find ways to draw on microcredentials in their curricula, especially OER microcredentials, whilst retaining their academic focus on disciplinary knowledge and critical scholarship. This could allow for both the recognition of other forms of knowledge, a culturally affirmative response, and also for restructuring the economic model of HE to redress some of the economic inequalities for students, and for reducing the costs to universities.

The open recognition movement stresses the recognition of practices owned by the practitioners themselves, rather than the disembodied competencies represented by decontextualised credentials, and the conferring of such recognition by the communities of practitioners rather than by an external credentialing authority. This approach validates all forms of learning, challenging the 'gatekeepers' of knowledge and knowledge production in HE and of industry-oriented microcredentials and is aimed at transforming both cultural and political inequities. Digital badges in this model would signify holistic competencies.

The vignette of microcredential and digital badging practices at NWU illustrates how they can remedy social injustices for both staff and students. Digital badges awarded for CPD courses could be acknowledged in performance evaluations and promotion decisions, thus ameliorating economic and cultural inequities for staff. For students, the formal recognition of microcredentials and digital badges by the university can facilitate their mobility through transferability of credits, reducing the cost of education to both learners and the institution. When digital badges are awarded for non-academic achievement, the recognition afforded can contribute to a holistic profile of learning that acknowledges the entire person and not merely their grades. The development of a portfolio platform that integrates academic achievement and digital badges, could shift the understanding of microcredentials and encourage their use more widely to rectify social injustices.

Conclusion

Traditional credentials, issued by schools, colleges and universities, have historically legitimised only certain types of learning and favoured certain types of learners, subjects, and assessments, resulting in a considerable amount of learning that has not been recognised. HEIs, in particular, have the authority to decide not only what is valued, taught, and assessed, but also how, which means that it is a potentially highly exclusionary system. Microcredentials and open badges allow the redistribution of some of that authority and responsibility within the public domain, enabling the recognition of other forms of knowledge and knowing, which is ostensibly a more just and inclusive system. This is extended even further in the open recognition movement.

That said, microcredentials that are set up to serve the neo-liberal employment agenda can reinforce and even exacerbate social injustices. Yet, as the vignettes and informant observations here indicate, microcredentials may be adopted in ways that could make them a valuable tool in addressing some of the social injustices in HE today, and in so doing, ameliorate or even transform economic, cultural and political inequalities in the system.

However, an integrated national policy environment for PSET that is explicitly framed by social justice concerns needs to be in place to guide the process of developing and implementing a system for recognising microcredentials and OER in HE. This can assist in changing HEI attitudes towards these practices, be used to leverage support for rolling out the use of such initiatives and encourage the more widespread use of microcredentials and OER in the pursuance of social justice.

Acknowledgements

Many thanks to Professor Jako Olivier and Dr Marieta Jansen van Vuuren from North-West University, whose inputs made the case study possible, as well as to Dr Wayne Mackintosh, Dr Tannis Morgan, Deborah Arnold and Mike Adendorff. Special thanks are due to reviewers Dr Nicola Pallitt, Dr James Keevy and Professor Beverley Oliver for their thoughtful, incisive feedback on the chapter, Ncebakazi Lutuli for breaking the ground on this research study, Professor Laura Czerniewicz for her critical reading of this work, Ntobeko Mbuyisa for his patient support throughout, Emeritus Associate Professor Cheryl Ann Hodgkinson-Williams for mentoring the case study, Shanali Govender for her helpful suggestions and Dr Tabisa Mayisela for guiding the entire COOL project. Thanks are also due to the Centre for Innovation in Learning and Teaching at the University of Cape Town, which hosted the COOL project, and the South African Department of Higher Education and Training for funding it.

References

Baijnath, N. (2018). Learning for development in the context of South Africa: Considerations for open education resources in improving higher education outcomes. *Journal of Learning for Development,* 5(2), 87–100.

Brown, M., McCormack, M., Reeves, J., Brook, D.C., Grajek, S., et al. (2020). *2020 Educause horizon report* (Teaching and learning ed.). EDUCAUSE. https://www.learntechlib.org/p/215670/

Chakroun, B., & Keevy, J. (2018). *Digital credentialling: Implications for the recognition of learning across borders.* UNESCO Education Sector.

Contact North. (2020, November). Microcredentials and the skills agenda. https://teachonline.ca/sites/default/files/tools-trends/downloads/micro-credentials_and_the_skills_agenda.pdf

Cronin, C. (2017). Openness and praxis: Exploring the use of open educational practices in higher education. *International Review of Research in Open and Distributed Learning,* 18(5). http://www.irrodl.org/index.php/irrodl/article/view/3096/4301

Czerniewicz, L. (2018). Unbundling and rebundling higher education in an age of inequality. *Educause Review,* 10–24 https://er.educause.edu/articles/2018/10/unbundling-and-rebundling-higher-education-in-an-age-of-inequality

DHET (Department of Higher Education and Training). (2017). Open learning policy framework for post-school education and training. *Government Gazette,* 40772.

Elkordy, A. (2012). *The future is now: Unpacking digital badging and microcredentialing for K-20 educators.* http://ncpeapublications.blogspot.com/2012/10/the-future-is-now- unpacking-digital.html

Finochietti, C., & Lockoff, J. (2021). The promise of micro-credentials? The road to recognition. *University World News.* https://www.universityworldnews.com/post.php?story=20210224114309588

Fraser, N. (1995). From redistribution to recognition? Dilemmas of justice in a 'postsocialist' age. *New Left Review*, 1/212, 68–93.

Fraser, N. (2005). Reframing justice in a globalizing world. *New Left Review*, 36, 69–88.

Fraser, N. (2009). Feminism, capitalism and the cunning of history. *New Left Review,* 56, 97–117.

Gallagher, C. W. (2018a). Colleges re-bound? *Inside Higher Ed.* https://www.insidehighered.com/views/2018/06/13/alternative-credentials-create-social-and-economic-inequities-and-shouldnt-be-seen

Gallagher, C. W. (2018b). Educational credentials come of age: A survey on the use and value of educational credentials in hiring. Centre for the Future of Higher Education and Talent Strategy. https://www.northeastern.edu/cfhets/wp-content/uploads/2018/12/Educational_Credentials_Come_of_Age_2018.pdf#_ga=2.222542232.2017494023.1558311521-1516438236.1558311521

Hodgkinson-Williams, C. A., & Trotter, H. (2018). A social justice framework for understanding open educational resources and practices in the Global South. *Journal of Learning for Development*, 5(3), 204–224. https://jl4d.org/index.php/ejl4d/article/view/312/339

ICDE (International Council for Open and Distance Education). (2019). Report of the ICDE working group on the present and future of alternative digital credentials (ADCs). https://www.icde.org/knowledge-hub/2019/4/10/the-present-and-future-of-alternative-digital-credentials

Kato, S., Galán-Muros, V., & Weko, T. (2020). The emergence of alternative credentials. *OECD Education Working Papers,* 216. https://dx.doi.org/10.1787/b741f39e-en

Keevy, J., & Chakroun, B. (2019). Beyond qualifications as we know them today: Digital credentials and interoperability. In European Centre for the Development of Vocational Training (Cedefop), European Training Foundation (ETF), United Nations Educational, Scientific and Cultural Organization (UNESCO) and the UNESCO Institute for Lifelong Learning (UIL) (Eds.), *Global inventory of regional and national qualifications frameworks* (vol. 1): *Thematic chapters* (pp. 26–34). ETF. https://www.etf.europa.eu/sites/default/files/2019-05/03%20P221543_Volume%20I%20-%20PROOF%202_IC%20-%20080519%20-%20x%20copies.pdf

Keevy, J., Hazell, E., & Matlala, L. (2020). Towards an agile credentialing schema in South Africa: Recommendations. https://www.academia.edu/43449293/Towards_an_Agile_Credentialing_Schema_in_South_Africa

Lemoine, P. A., & Richardson, M. D. (2015). Microcredentials, nano degrees, and digital badges: New credentials for global higher education. *International Journal of Technology and Educational Marketing*, 5(1), 36–49.

Mackintosh, W. (2020). International credit transfer for OERu micro-courses now an option for global learners. *OER Foundation.* https://oerfoundation.org/2020/06/10/international-credit-transfer-for-oeru-micro-courses-now-an-option-for-global-learners/

Morgan, T. (2020). Alternative credential stacking. *Explorations in the Ed Tech World.* https://homonym.ca/published/alternative-credential-stacking/

Oliver, B. O. (2019). Making microcredentials work for learners, employers and providers. Deakin University. http://wordpress-ms.deakin.edu.au/dteach/wp-content/uploads/sites/103/2019/08/Making-micro-credentials-work-Oliver-Deakin-2019-full-report.pdf

ORA (Open Recognition Alliance). (2016). The Bologna open recognition declaration. https://www.openrecognition.org/bord/

Pickard, L. (2018). Analysis of 450 MOOC-based microcredentials reveals many options but little consistency. https://www.classcentral.com/report/moocs-microcredentials-analysis-2018/

Ralston, S. J. (2020). Higher education's microcredentialing craze: A postdigital-Deweyan critique. *Postdigital Science and Education*, 3, 83–101. https://doi.org/10.1007/s42438-020-00121-8

Ravet, S. (2020). Competency badges: The tail wagging the dog? *Learning Futures.* https://www.learningfutures.eu/2020/03/competency-badges-the-tail-wagging-the-dog/

Rossiter, D., & Tynan, B. (2019). *Designing and implementing micro-credentials: A guide for practitioners.* Commonwealth of Learning. http://oasis.col.org/bitstream/handle/11599/3279/2019_KS_MicroCredentials.pdf

Swartz, R., Ivancheva, M., Czerniewicz, L., & Morris, N. P. (2019). Between a rock and a hard place: Dilemmas regarding the purpose of public universities in South Africa. *Higher Education, 77,* 567–583.

Vallim, S., & Motala, E. (2017). Education, training and work under neoliberalism in South Africa: Toward alternatives. *Education as Change,* 21(3), 1–20.

Zipin, L. (2017). Pursuing a problematic-based curriculum approach for the sake of social justice. *Journal of Education,* 69, 67–92. http://www.scielo.org.za/scielo.php?script=sci_arttext&pid=S2520-98682017000200004

HOW TO CITE THIS CHAPTER

Jones, B. (2022). The potential for microcredentials as a form of open learning to contribute to a social justice agenda in South African higher education. In T. Mayisela, S. C. Govender & C. A. Hodgkinson-Williams (Eds.), *Open learning as a means of advancing social justice: Cases in post-school education and training in South Africa* (pp. 374–390). African Minds. doi: 10.47622/9781928502425_16

This work is licensed under a Creative Commons Attribution 4.0 International (CC BY 4.0) licence.

About the authors and the COOL team

SARA BLACK was a COOL researcher. She now works as a Lecturer in Education at King's College London. She has worked in public education for 14 years as a teacher, analyst and researcher. In 2019 she submitted her PhD which examines how key policies in the basic education sector reproduce existing inequalities in high schools. She has also worked in teacher development, heading up the Newly Qualified Teachers Project at the University of Cape Town for its first two years, as well as working with Community Colleges while completing a postdoctoral fellowship at the Centre for Education Rights and Transformation at the University of Johannesburg. Her research interests include critical sociology of EdTech, the politics of space and time as they play out in institutional forms, the privatisation of public education, education leadership and change, philosophy, and critical policy analysis.

TESS CARTMILL was the COOL interim project manager. After many years in Information Systems in the corporate world, she decided to change direction and completed a Master's degree (Information and Communication Technologies in Education). As part of the degree, she did a minor dissertation on the use of Open Educational Resources (OER). Thereafter she became the Project Manager for the Research on Open Educational Resources for Development (ROER4D) project in the Global South. When that project ended, she worked in various research projects as project manager or in data analysis.

GLENDA COX was a COOL mentor. Holding a PhD in Education from the University of Cape Town (UCT), she is a senior lecturer in the Centre for Innovation in Learning and Teaching (CILT) at UCT where her portfolio includes Curriculum projects, Teaching with Technology innovation grants, Open Educational Resources (OER) and Staff Development. She holds the UNESCO Chair in Open Education and Social Justice (2021–2024), has an NRF C rating, and is recognised as an established researcher in the field of Open Education. She is currently the Principal Investigator in the Digital Open Textbooks for Development (DOT4D) initiative. Her current research includes analysing the role of open textbooks for social justice. Glenda is passionate about the role of Open Education in the changing world of higher education.

LAURA CZERNIEWICZ was a COOL mentor. She is a professor at the Centre for Innovation in Learning and Teaching (CILT) at the University of Cape Town, where she was also its founding director. She has worked for decades in many roles in education including academic, researcher, strategist, advocate, teacher, teacher-trainer and educational publisher. Threaded through all her work has been a focus on equity and digital inequality.

These have permeated her research interests which focus on the changing nature of higher education in a post-digital society and new forms of teaching and learning provision. She plays a key strategic and scholarly role in the areas of blended/online learning as well as in open education institutionally, nationally and internationally.

ANELISA DABULA was a COOL researcher. She holds a Bachelor's of Social Sciences in Geography and Environmental Management and a Master's in Population Studies from the University of KwaZulu-Natal (UKZN). Her MA research explored father-child relationships through the perspectives of young fathers. Her background is in developmental economics, migration, fertility, sexual and reproductive health and rights, gender equality, educational development and adolescent health. She has worked as a research assistant for Maurice Webb Research Relations as well as an academic mentor, advisor, tutor and team leader for Academic Monitoring Support at UKZN. She is now working on a PhD in Geography and Environmental Management with a focus on human geography.

THASMAI DHURUMRAJ was a COOL researcher. She completed her PhD in Education, specialising in Curriculum Studies, focusing her dissertation on teachers' experiences with the Physical Sciences curriculum. She currently serves as a lecturer in science education at the University of Johannesburg. Her research areas include social injustices, teacher education and curriculum development in the field of science. She also serves as an external curriculum advisor for the South African Quality Assurance Body, Umalusi, and the International Open University in Gambia.

SHANALI C. GOVENDER was a COOL mentor and editorial team leader. She is a lecturer within the Staff Development unit at the Centre for Innovation in Learning and Teaching (CILT) at the University of Cape Town (UCT). Although Shanali's teaching experience began in secondary education, a return to higher education to pursue her own studies prompted a shift to an interest in the higher education landscape. She has worked at three South African higher education institutions and has strong interests in the scholarship of learning and teaching. At CILT, she supports part-time and non-permanent teaching staff. She teaches on the Postgraduate diploma in educational technologies, co-convening the Online Learning Design module. She has designed several online staff development short courses, and teaches on Core Concepts in Learning and Teaching, and An Online Introduction to Assessment. While continuing to work in the field of staff development, she is working towards her PhD at UCT, exploring the experiences of non-permanent staff who teach in higher education.

SUSAN GREDLEY was a COOL researcher. She holds a Masters in Adult Education from the University of Cape Town (UCT) and is a PhD candidate at the University of the Western Cape (UWC). Her doctoral research explores socially just pedagogies in higher education through the lens of participatory parity. She has worked as a lecturer and course convenor at UCT and UWC. She now works at the Cornerstone Institute as lecturer and coordinator of the BA Alternative Education programme. Her teaching and learning experiences continue to reinforce her passion for exploring feminist, socially just, authentic and innovative ways of teaching and learning.

CHERYL ANN HODGKINSON-WILLIAMS was the first principal investigator of the COOL project until her retirement in 2020 and then continued as a COOL mentor and editorial team leader. She holds a Masters and PhD in computer-assisted learning. She taught in the secondary school sector before designing and developing technology enabled learning programmes for the school and training sectors. She then taught, researched and supervised in the areas of Information and Communication Technology in Education, Online Learning Design, Qualitative Research Design and Open Education for the next 26 years, first at the University of Pretoria, then at Rhodes University in Grahamstown and finally at the University of Cape Town (UCT). She was the Principal Investigator of the IDRC-funded Research on Open Educational Resources for Development (ROER4D) project which investigated the adoption and impact of the use of OER in 21 countries in the Global South. She was an advisor on the Digital Open Textbooks for Development (DOT4D) project and a UNESCO Chair of Open Education and Social Justice at UCT. She is still active as a consulting researcher and online learning advisor and continues to be an Open Education and Social Justice advocate.

CHENG-WEN HUANG was a COOL researcher. She is a senior lecturer based in the Academic Staff Development team at the Centre for Innovation in Learning and Teaching at the University of Cape Town (UCT). She holds a PhD in Education from UCT. Her current work includes the University Capacity Development Grant project, Enabling Student Success Through Transformed Programmes of Assessment, and sub-projects of the Learning Platforms Update Project on assessment and course evaluations. She has previously worked on the Commonwealth Digital Education Leadership in Training in Action (2016) project. Cheng-Wen has a research background in multimodal social semiotics, argumentation, academic literacies, digital literacies, open learning, assessment and social justice.

BARBARA JONES was a COOL researcher. She has a Master's degree in Education (Curriculum Development) from the University of Cape Town, and a strong background and continuing interest in adult education, driven by ongoing social justice concerns. She has considerable and varied experience as a freelance higher education researcher, most notably on projects investigating Recognition of Prior Learning practices in higher education institutions and on flexible and blended learning and teaching in higher education. Access to and success in higher education has also been a focus of several research projects in which she has collaborated. In the last few years she has been working as a Curriculum Development Specialist, first at the Cape Peninsula University of Technology and presently at the University of the Western Cape.

THOMAS KING was the COOL project curator. He holds a Master's degree in Education from the University of Cape Town (UCT), focusing on the creation and adaptation of Open Educational Resources. Previously, he has worked as a Data Curation Officer in the Digital Library Services unit in UCT Libraries, the Project Curator for the Research on Open Educational Resources for Development programme, the student coordinator for the Vice Chancellor's Open Educational Resources Adaptation project and as a Research Assistant for the Scholarly Communication in Africa Programme. He is currently working as a Learning Designer based in the Centre for Innovation in Learning and Teaching (CILT), assisting

UCT lecturers interested in adopting blended learning approaches or taking parts of their teaching online. His primary research interests revolve around Open Educational Resources and Open Data, particularly in the fields of qualitative de-identification and management.

MAHLATSE INNOCENT MAAKE-MALATJI was a COOL researcher. She holds a Bachelor of Laws (LLB) from the University of Limpopo and a Professional Master's (Labour Law) from the University of Cape Town (UCT). She has worked as a student assistant, lecturer, coordinator and research assistant at UCT for a Dispute Resolution Course at Law@work (an initiative with the Commission for Conciliation, Mediation and Arbitration). She has also served as a research clerk for the Democratic Governance and Rights Unit (DGRU) at UCT. In addition, she has also worked as a coordinator at Student Housing and Residence Life (SHRL) at UCT. She now works as a Law Researcher at the Supreme Court of Appeal (SCA), Bloemfontein. She is passionate about research, education, law and development. She has served in various positions for student support services in institutions of higher learning and community development programmes.

TABISA MAYISELA was the COOL project's principal investigator and a mentor for three case studies. She holds a PhD in Education from the University of Cape Town (UCT). Tabisa has worked as an Information Systems lecturer and e-Learning Specialist/Instructional designer at Walter Sisulu University. In 2014, she joined UCT's Centre for Innovation in Learning and Teaching (CILT) as a Digital Literacy Coordinator and then joined the staff development cluster as a lecturer in 2017. She is currently a senior lecturer, coordinator of the Staff Development cluster and Deputy Director of CILT. As part of her staff development work, she works with academics on the integration of educational technologies and digital literacies into course curricula. Related to her expertise in digital literacy, where she is an advocate for the social practice perspective, she, together with two CILT colleagues developed a Commonwealth Digital Education Leadership Training in Action (C-DELTA) concept document, as commissioned by the Commonwealth of Learning (COL) in 2016. Tabisa also convenes and co-teaches courses in the Postgraduate Diploma in Education, in both the Higher Education Studies and Educational Technologies streams, as well as supervises Master's students and a PhD on the integration of educational technologies and digital literacies into course curricula, humanisation of the curriculum and academic staff (professional) development.

NTOBEKO MBUYISA was the COOL project manager. He holds a Bachelor of Science and Postgraduate Diploma in Finance, Banking and Investment Management. He is currently completing a Master's degree in Commerce. He is the Manager for Academic Staff and Professional Development in the Centre for Higher Education Development at the University of Cape Town. He previously worked as a Research Manager at the University of KwaZulu-Natal. He is passionate about working in Higher Education to support, enhance, deepen and transform teaching and learning, academic staff and professional development.

JANICE MCMILLAN was a COOL mentor. She is an Associate Professor who joined the University of Cape Town (UCT) in 1994, first in the Department of Adult Education, and since

2000, in the Centre for Higher Education Development. From 2010–mid-2019, she was the Director of the UCT Global Citizenship: Leading for Social Justice programme (GCP), and from 2010–2014, she was also the service-learning coordinator for Stanford University's Bing overseas study programme in Cape Town. Within UCT she is a member of several university and faculty committees including the Senate University Social Responsiveness Committee. Janice was also on the Board of SHAWCO, a large student volunteer organization from 2006-2015. Janice completed her PhD in Sociology at UCT in 2008, focusing on service learning as a form of boundary work in higher education. Although organisationally still located in the academic staff development cluster in the Centre for Innovation in Learning and Teaching, since 2017 Janice has been seconded to work at the institutional level as SR coordinator reporting to the Deputy Vice Chancellor Professor for social responsiveness (SR). Since late 2020, Janice is also involved in work on 'decentring whiteness' as a contribution towards UCT's dismantling institutional racism strategy.

MUKHTAR RABAN was a COOL researcher. He is a lecturer in the Faculty of Humanities at Nelson Mandela University. After teaching in English as a Second Language (ESL) programmes in colleges in the Middle East, he joined the university's Linguistics and Applied Linguistics department. He currently lectures in professional English communication and language learning and teaching modules. He was awarded the university's "Excellent Teacher of the Year" in 2015. His research interests include technology-enhanced language learning, digital humanities, open learning and critical humanising pedagogies. He is currently completing a PhD in education with a focus on critical digital language pedagogies.

HENRY TROTTER was the COOL scoping researcher, editor and publishing manager. He holds a BA in English from California Polytechnic State University, San Luis Obispo and Masters degrees in African Studies and History from Yale University. Over the past decade, he has worked with the Centre for Innovation in Learning and Teaching (CILT) at the University of Cape Town (UCT) as a researcher, research capacity development officer and/or editorial manager for a number of projects, including the Scholarly Communication in Africa Programme (SCAP) and the Research on Open Educational Resources for Development (ROER4D) project. With a keen interest in African history, culture, and higher education, Henry is the author of *Cape Town: A Place Between* (2020), the lead author of *Seeking Impact and Visibility: Scholarly Communication in Southern Africa* (2014) and the author of *Sugar Girls & Seamen: A Journey into the World of Dockside Prostitution in South Africa* (2008).

GERTRUDE VAN WYK was a COOL researcher. She holds a Master's degree in Education with a focus on Gifted Education from the Central University of Technology (CUT) in the Free State of South Africa. She has more than two decades of teaching experience and has worked as an elementary school teacher and a part-time lecturer in Teacher Education at CUT. She is currently a doctoral student in the Educational Leadership program, with a focus on Education of Diverse Learners (as well as Gifted Education) at Western Kentucky University in the United States. She is passionate about meeting the educational needs of the unidentified and underrepresented 'gifted' children in South Africa's rural primary schools.

SUKAINA WALJI was a COOL mentor. She has a Masters in Online and Distance Education from the Open University UK, and a BA in History from Oxford University. She is the Director of the Centre for Innovation in Learning and Teaching (CILT) at the University of Cape Town (UCT) and oversees operational functions for the department including supporting the growth and development of CILT's capacity to design and develop blended and online courses. She provides strategic advice for university senior leadership for digitally enabled education, participates in university level committees and initiatives, and is Chair of the Online Education sub-committee. In her previous role as Coordinator of CILT's Curriculum and Course Design team she oversaw the work of the Digital Media unit and the Learning Design team. Her research interests include learning design, MOOCs, Unbundled Higher Education and assessment practices.

SINETHEMBA NOMALUNGELO ZUNGU was a COOL researcher. She holds a Master's degree in Housing and a Bachelor's degree in Community Development from the University of KwaZulu-Natal (UKZN). She has worked in higher education as a Research Coordinator for the Department of Science and Innovation-funded Municipal Innovation Maturity Index project. She has also worked as a Local Economic Development Research and Support intern at the Department of Economic Development, Tourism and Environmental Affairs. She has further experience working in the NGO/non-profit sector with Harambee Youth Employment Accelerator in KZN. Sinethemba is passionate about land reform, inclusive policy development, innovation and social justice. In the future, she hopes to attain her PhD to sharpen her expertise and to grow within academia.

www.ingramcontent.com/pod-product-compliance
Lightning Source LLC
Chambersburg PA
CBHW080353030426
42334CB00024B/2865